THE
BOSS'S
ENCYCLOPEDIA

The Boss's Encyclopedia

BY THE EDITORS AND EXPERTS OF BOARDROOM® REPORTS

BOARDROOM® BOOKS

330 West 42nd Street, New York, New York 10036

Fifth Printing

Library of Congress Cataloging in Publication Data

The boss's encyclopedia.

    1. Industrial management—Addresses, essays,
lectures. 2. Business—Addresses, essays, lectures.
I. Boardroom reports. II. Title.
HD31.B624   1983   658   83-2498
ISBN 0-932648-39-8

Printed in the United States of America

CONTENTS

4. COMMUNICATING YOUR IDEAS   85

Writing   85

Talking and Listening   87

Public Speaking   91

Running Effective Meetings   95

PART II
FINANCIAL MANAGEMENT   99

5. FINANCIAL ANALYSIS AND CONTROL   101

Financial Analysis   101

Budgets   102

Paying Bills   104

Credit   105

PART III
MARKETING AND SALES MANAGEMENT

175

PART IV
ADMINISTRATION AND OFFICE
MANAGEMENT   273

PART V
OPERATIONS
MANAGEMENT   341

PART VI
PERSONNEL ADMINISTRATION
AND LABOR RELATIONS
385

PART VII
PERSONAL BUSINESS   467

PART I

Effective Management Techniques

1 MANAGING PEOPLE

MANAGERIAL SKILLS

What makes an effective manager?

There is no such thing as one single effective executive personality. Those effective executives vary widely in temperament, operating style, abilities, knowledge, and interests. What they do have in common are certain practices. The key ones:

1. Know where their time goes. In any organization, executives have little control over their time. The trick is to systematically manage whatever time can be brought under their own control.

2. Focus on results.

3. Build on strengths. Capitalize on their own and those of their superiors, colleagues and subordinates.

4. Concentrate on the few major areas where superior performance will produce outstanding results. They set priorities, follow them.

5. Make decisions based on dissenting opinions. To judge, alternatives from which to choose are important. Dissent brings these out.

Source: Peter F. Drucker, *The Effective Executive,* Harper & Row, New York.

Leadership skills

Management-training courses help executives sharpen existing skills and may encourage them to acquire others. But training rarely gives them the type of inherent interpersonal skills needed to manage a dynamic company successfully.

Some of the most critical managerial talents:

• Ability to use their power and personality to change their own style when necessary and to influence others.

• Courage to make a decision when risk is present.

• Capability to motivate others by knowing when to exert their power and when to avoid the use of it.

• Endurance. Training courses can teach executives time-management techniques, but the techniques can't keep them alert during a 12-hour day.

• Objectivity. It's virtually impossible to teach managers to avoid their own biases when evaluating others.

• Optimism.

Source: George E. Manners, Jr., of Rensselaer Polytechnic Institute, and Joseph A. Steger, director of human resources, Colt Industries, Inc., quoted in *Inside R&D,* Fort Lee, N.J.

Acting like a leader

Acting like a leader means behaving in ways to make employees feel secure and to give them a sense of harmony. A leader should be able to:

- Handle social occasions well.
- Use stress constructively.
- Be smooth and unruffled in tense situations.
- Rally group to a common goal.
- Feel comfortable when faced with diverse points of view.

A nonleader sees diversity as a threat and emphasizes the differences among people. This type of behavior disrupts the group's solidarity.

Source: Marsha Sinetar, Ph.D., psychologist, head, Sinetar and Associates, El Segundo, Calif.

Improving leadership abilities

- Make decisions that support independent employee behavior within organizational limits.

- Take time each day to think about general business and social trends. Then look for ways the company can benefit from them.

- Learn more about individual subordinates to better match their jobs to their goals and abilities.

- Review your recent decisions. If too many were risk-free, it could be a danger sign.

- Note the dimensions of recent changes. If all were minor, it might be a sign of reluctance to change.

- Evaluate all your current duties to see whether delegating some of them to subordinates might help develop their abilities.

Source: Donald B. Miller, *Working with People,* CBI Publishing, Boston.

Key skills for managers

- Interest in improving the way things are done.
- Continuing desire to initiate.
- Confidence in abilities and goals.
- Ability to develop, counsel and help others improve.
- Concern with the impact managerial actions have on the activities of others.
- Capacity to get others to follow the manager's lead.
- Knowledge of how to inspire teamwork.
- Capability of influencing others to form alliances or teams.
- Faith in others.
- Skill in oral and written communication.
- Tendency to put business needs before personal needs.
- Spontaneity of expression.
- Objectivity in a dispute.
- Knowledge of own strengths and weaknesses.
- Adaptability to change.
- Mental stamina to put in long hours.
- Logical thought.
- Ability to use information to create new, meaningful concepts.

Source: *International Management,* New York.

How to operate at the highest skill level

No one should perform a task that can be performed just as well by someone who is paid less.

Managers should identify their own highest skills. Concentrate time and effort on using those skills. Delegate as many of the other jobs as possible. This presumes that the subordinate is capable of being trained. Also, that the delegating executive is willing to teach him. Be explicit about what's wanted.

Delegation is not abdication. The delegated work is still part of the manager's job. Stay off the subordinate's back. But do review performance regularly to make sure that problems are being resolved and work is moving forward toward objectives.

Source: *The Practical Manager's Guide to Excellence in Management,* AMACOM, New York.

Recognizing management styles

When managers know their own style and how others react to it, they are more likely to get the responses they desire.

Basic categories:

• Intuitive. Executives who use this style take a longe-range view, seek out relationships among disparate elements, and believe disorder is often the rule. They are creative, imaginative, able to understand long-range problems. But they tend to fantasize and be impractical, give the appearance of being out of touch, aloof, and impersonal.

• Intellectual. These managers avoid emotionalism, rely on empiricism, are prudent, and have orderly work habits. But they tend to be skeptical and generate little enthusiasm in others. Their style can be a stabilizing force, guarding against unpromising risks. But they are often indecisive, often very cautious, too serious.

• Sensory. Managers with a sensory style work on a wide variety of jobs at one time, give close attention to detail, are often abrupt and too busy to be neat. They are pragmatic, results-oriented, and rarely misled, but are unable to see long range, tend to nitpick, are impatient, lack trust in others, and often run behind schedule.

• Feeling. These executives are people-oriented and sensitive to the needs of others. They can anticipate the impact of changes on employees, are friendly, stimulating, and usually considered warm. They are spontaneous, persuasive, loyal, and have the ability to draw out the feelings of others. But they tend to manipulate people, be impulsive, and stir up conflicts unintentionally.

Intuitive managers usually get poor results when they approach sensory types for long, abstract discussions of problems. Feeling managers run into problems when they ask thinkers about who might be hurt by planned changes.

Source: *Iron Age,* Radnor, Pa.

Timing: a neglected management skill

The pressure on managers to deliver the right answer to a company problem often blinds them to an equally important management task: timing the solution so that it has the best chance of being fully accepted.

Simply telling another person what should be done, without assessing whether the time is right, frequently results in an idea wasted, a sale lost, or a useful relationship unnecessarily soured.

Good timing is just as important as the quality of an idea to: persuade an employee, colleague, or customer to accept a new position; negotiate a contract settlement or other dispute; or influence a favorable group decision at a meeting.

The basic rules are:

Allow time for a warm-up. Anyone is more responsive, more readily influenced, after a conversational warm-up has thawed the atmosphere. A period of easy give-and-take gives participants time to adjust to each others' styles.

To warm up the target person or group find neutral subjects to kick around to draw each person out. Find common ground on small issues so when the time comes for agreement or cooperation on real issues, the reaction will be positive.

Sense when the right time is near. A signal—the other party begins to speak easily and with some amination. It means the stage is set for responsive interaction.

Larger meetings need warm-up time, too. During the first half-hour, members need to establish their credentials or argue about agenda, but once this nonproductive muddling is over, the group is ready for constructive problem-solving. The time is right when the group is receptive to solutions, when there is a consensus on the definition of the problem and the relevant issues.

When timing is right, grab the opportunity. Agreement on minor matters is self-perpetuating as larger, more important issues come up. Ideas that would have been rejected earlier are now accepted.

The best moment is at hand when everybody is desperate for the one bright idea that will resolve the quarreling and solve the problem that has been defined. Offer the idea now.

Timing strategy to settle a dispute. Here, it's not so much warm-up as heat-up that must precede receptivity to an imaginative compromise.

How it works. Two department heads first need to wrangle over who lost an order. Representatives of labor and management clear the air by exchanging accusations and expressing pent-up resentments over extraneous issues, not just the one now on the table. Model: Any trained mediator waits for this venting of feelings and buildup of frustrations before exercising influence.

The best (often the only) time to recommend an innovative solution comes when desperation peaks. Both sides know they have a problem. And both know they can't settle it without third-party help.

To be a management hero deliver a solution where mutual goals are not being met and where all parties already recognize that there is a gap between expectations and performance.

Timing is essentially patience. To exert influence on an organization, take the time to hear all the relevant power centers. Key executives will be insulted by the bright manager who is too eager to offer ideas when all those affected have been consulted. But these same executives can become powerful allies if part of their thinking is incorporated into a solution offered at the right time.

An exhaustive procedure that demands both time and patience does not come easily to managers. The best managers are by nature and training time-conscious. Their training and instinct to solve problems propel them to rush to tell others what to do as soon as they identify an answer. Resist that temptation.

Source: Dr. Leonard R. Sayles, professor of management, Columbia University Graduate School of Business.

Managers' roadblocks to creativity

• Assuming that creative means new. Instead, borrow and modify the ideas of others.

• Relying too heavily on experts or self-styled creative types, who often are blinded by traditional approaches.

• Believing that only a few gifted people can be creative. Many rank-and-file employees come up with workable ideas.

• Confusing creativity with emotional instability. What is needed instead is the ability to let the mind wander without fear of losing control.

• Failing to promote ideas voluntarily. Not pointing out achievements to superiors (a common failing of fired executives).

• Waiting for inspiration. Concentration and fact-finding are the most solid bases for innovation.

• Getting bogged down in technology. Look for solutions. Then try to accomplish them with existing ways of doing things.

Source: M. LeBoeuf, *Imagineering: How to Profit from Your Creative Powers,* McGraw-Hill, New York.

How to delegate successfully

Managers are constantly being pushed to delegate more responsibility. To build the skill of delegating:

• Delegate all types of jobs, not just difficult or boring ones.

• Be patient. People who take on jobs need time to learn.

• Assign work gradually. Do not expect a subordinate to assume all responsibility for the job overnight.

• Try to delegate in advance. Avoid dropping a problem in a subordinate's lap.

• Assign an entire job, not parts, whenever possible. It reduces confusion and errors.

• Communicate specific results you expect from the job.

• Discuss the project before delegating it.

• Once the job is delegated, leave the person alone to do it.

Source: Jack D. Ferner, *Successful Time Management,* John Wiley & Sons, New York.

Steps to take in delegating

Delegating authority is among the most difficult functions for some managers. To make it easier:

• Analyze the functions you perform. Realistically determine which ones you can let someone else do without loss of efficiency.

• Ask staff members, either at a meeting or in private, if they would like to take on particular functions.

• Examine the credentials of the people working for you. Look for individuals who fit specific activities.

• If there isn't anybody on your staff who can handle the task now, find those who can be trained for it.

The subtle fear of delegating

Managers who don't delegate are often restrained by fear and lack of confidence.

Fear is based on:

• Loss of control. Need to know all the answers lest the boss ask questions.

• One-upmanship. Subordinates may do a better job.

• Loss of esteem. Subordinates may be credited for doing a better job.

• Loss of authority. Responsibilities cut back and given to subordinates.

• Excess work. Delegating away easy tasks and leaving only the difficult ones.

Lack of confidence is based on:

• Distrust. Belief that subordinates lack skills, knowledge, or experience.

• Apathy. Subordinates actually shy away from doing job.

Some managers feel positive in not delegating, believing they can do the task better and faster. Besides, they enjoy the operations end of the job.

To change tactics and start delegating. Do it one step at a time, building subordinates' and boss' confidence. Here are six openings. (The first three are risk-resistant.)

1. "Check this out and give me the particulars. I'll decide."

2. "I'll review your analysis and recommendation."

3. "Decide and let me know your decision. But wait for my go-ahead."

4. "Decide, then notify me of your decision. Then implement it if I don't get back to you (in specified time)."

5. "Decide and take action, but let me know what you did."

6. "Decide and take action without checking back with me."

But before making the decision to delegate, make sure that subordinates have access to all information needed to do the job and are granted authority to achieve task.

Source: *Sales Manager's Bulletin,* National Sales Development Institute, Waterford, Conn.

How to know what's really going on

The trouble with much of the information chief executives get is that it is secondhand. It is filtered first through various reporting levels.

To get a firsthand feel for how things are going, spend an unannounced day with a company salesperson, going along on the normal rounds. Listen and ask questions of everyone you meet: customers, non-customers and distributors. If it is necessary, go on the rounds incognito.

Prearranged visits have their place, but they are not an effective way to find out about problems. More likely, the plant will be cleaned up and problems will be swept under the rug instead of dealt with.

Better yet, use less conspicuous people as surrogate eyes and ears, someone from the personnel department, for example. Debrief them upon their return for their impressions.

One roadblock to communications is a manager who doesn't want to be the one to tell the boss the bad news. No manager does. Top management must do everything to encourage honest reporting from the company's middle managers.

Use a positive approach: "Tell me all the bad things first. I'll find out the good things in my own way."

Never jump on the manager who reveals a serious problem. Positively don't do it during a meeting or when anyone else is present. Hold off even if the manager is the one responsible for the problem. Instead, take the person to task afterward.

Watch older executives. They have a tendency to be too gentlemanly or thin-skinned at company meetings. The more aggressive young managers may grate sensitive egos. But they keep an organization vital. A company that faces up to tough questions is more likely to keep its competitive edge.

Outside consultants can be useful for dredging up ideas and comments that were for one reason or another blocked from reaching top management through regular channels. A frustrated middle manager may confide in a consultant even though most employees would not dare to go over an immediate manager's head.

Hold planning sessions at least biannually to review painstakingly both the company's strengths and weaknesses. For optimum results, take key people away for an informal two- or three-day retreat. Some of the most successful companies review and revise plans on a monthly or even weekly basis.

Directors' meetings can provide additional opportunities for sensitive listening. Pay special attention to the thoughtful questions raised by outside directors who use their own business experience to probe for potential trouble spots or opportunities. By questioning the validity of a capital project, for example, a director might stir up valuable discussion about alternatives. Outside directors can pick up clues to problems that managers would rather not discuss, for example: What's the turnover in this division? Why is market share slipping for this product?

Source: Robert W. Lear, former chief executive of the F&M Schaefer Brewing Co. and executive in residence, Columbia University Graduate School of Business.

The executive's spy network

Apart from conventional sources of information, effective managers should consider tapping employees in the company who are naturally good sources.

Develop sources of information below the executive ranks. Well-placed secretaries and maintenance personnel have access to inside information. High-level employees may have too much at stake in their jobs to be unbiased sources.

Never pay information sources with money. Instead, compensate them with friendship, a well-timed family gift, personal concern.

Use multiple sources. By using employees with overlapping knowledge, a manager can double-check the information and reliability of sources.

Stress the need for early information. Give large rewards for it.

Encourage subordinates to air their grievances directly to you. Listen to what one manager has to say about others.

Listen to trade gossip about the company.

When evaluating information, look for the worst possible news. Listening to gossip and office informants can help the company anticipate a problem, but not if the executives are only looking for a rosy view to confirm their own actions.

When it's wrong to be right

Managers' obsession with being right brings about rigidity of thinking. That stifles creativity, discourages risk taking, polarizes people over issues, and leads to the recycling of old ideas.

Highly intelligent executives with large egos and top positions to protect are usually the most effective at stifling new ideas of others. The more intelligent the executive, the more capable the person is of defending a position, regardless of its merits.

Criticism is another way of bolstering the need to be right and screening out new ideas. Workers quickly decide that silence is the safest position when the boss agressively pushes an idea. And the most timid workers even allow highly critical (and threatening) managers to preempt ideas and solutions that they actually originate.

Top management must support the right to be wrong to encourage the flow of fresh ideas and new approaches to the business. Some techniques that work at meetings:

• A rule that two positive points must be presented about an idea before one negative comment is made should be implemented. This puts the focus on positive aspects of an idea, promoting open-mindedness.

• Once an idea is presented, others at the meeting must make a positive comment, a negative comment, and add an interesting point to the idea. The goal is to provide creative spark to the discussion.

• Everyone at the meeting agrees to spend a few minutes considering another participant's idea, regardless of how radical or far-out it may seem.

Remember that thinking ability is not an inherited trait. Thinking is as much a learned skill as riding a bicycle. And the best thinkers are not always the most intelligent. Intelligent people are often caught between their need to be right and their egos.

Source: Eric M. Bienstock, Ph.D., managing director, The Edward de Bono School of Thinking, New York.

Giving and taking orders

Good managers expect subordinates to disagree sometimes. They don't want a yes response to every instruction. The best managers provide more ideas and projects than their subordinates can possibly accomplish. They want their staff members to use their knowledge and judgment in deciding priorities. Effective managers expect to be told when an instruction is faulty or can't be followed. They should be told by the employee who is closest to the situation when the realities contradict the boss' assumptions.

Well-managed companies encourage managers and subordinates to balance out these initiatives.

Managers should want to know about legitimate objections and barriers. They should provide a responsive ear to ideas and warnings the subordinates feel are important. But when time is critical, or when a broad view should prevail, the manager still can insist on going ahead.

Sensible subordinates must be able to blend the desire to be heard with the willingness to defer. Managers evaluate their employees on their ability to stand up and disagree. Also important is the employees' willingness to accept orders after their objections have been heard.

When order-giving generates a power struggle, the relationship has broken down badly.

How to push for change

To improve the likelihood that a recommendation for a change will be accepted:
- Demonstrate a thorough knowledge of the status quo, including essential figures.
- Make the claims for improvement absolutely accurate. Quantify them whenever possible. Do not play down the real costs of change.
- Investigate the less obvious effects a change in one area or department could have in other areas, in order to head off a quick rejection because of the side effects.
- Find someone to play devil's advocate and test the validity of the proposal before presenting it.
- Bring copies of supporting data to the proposal meeting.

Source: *Purchasing,* Boston.

Preparing for a crisis

If managers cannot actually plan for crises, they can at least prepare for them. Keys:
- Be alert. The best way to handle a crisis is to anticipate it.
- Stay flexible. Make a commitment to change prices, vendors, suppliers, and business practices swiftly, if necessary. Make provisions ahead of time for doing so.
- Know the options. Options must be developed before a crisis interrupts a business routine or threatens survival. The business' basics should be reviewed in terms of the options available.
- Establish clear communications. Good internal and external communications reduce panic, ease tension, and make quick changes possible.
- Recognize a crisis. It may create opportunities as well as problems. Management's goal in any crisis should be to play up any advantages, rather than be content simply to survive.

Source: Walter Johnson, president of Quadrant Marketing Counselors, Ltd., New York.

How to save face while encouraging criticism

While most managers agree that dissent and discussion are vital, many bristle when their own ideas are challenged or criticized. How to be open and avoid ego damage:
- Ask for specific ways to strengthen or improve an idea rather than for a general opinion.
- Meet in individual sessions rather than a group. Opposition is easier in private.
- Solicit reactions to only one part of the proposal at a time.
- Ask for written criticism. It can be less traumatic and can be put aside for a calmer moment.

Source: *Personal Report for the Executive,* Research Institute of America, New York.

Avoiding isolation dangers

Isolation is always a danger for top-level managers. An increasingly volatile business climate makes the calm of isolation more tempting for managers and more of a problem for companies.

Symptoms of isolation:
- Failing to communicate objectives to subordinates, advisers, or the board of directors.
- Bogging down in technical details while ignoring human relations in the company.
- Rewarding only those who go along with management decisions.
- Setting up a management system that filters out what the executive doesn't want to hear.

To avoid isolation at the top:
- Don't pontificate.
- Inform the board as well as the staff of goals and objectives.
- Praise good performance.
- Resist the temptation to make too many changes at one time.
- Guard against complacency.

And an executive who isn't sure whether he's isolated usually is.

Source: Gerald L. McManis, president, McManis Assoc., management consultants, Washington, D.C.

Revitalizing your work day

When work is unrelenting, tension results. A simple change in attitude can revitalize days in the office:

• Think of work as a game. Plan to enjoy it.

• When the day's game is over, put it to bed. In the morning, start fresh for the next inning.

• Maintain psychological distance from the game. You and your work are close, but not identical.

• Cultivate a confidante to discuss your moves, share in your triumphs, and console you during any setbacks.

• If your work (no matter how important) is not fun, take time to figure out how to eliminate the tedious elements. In one case, the owner of a market research firm hated selling but loved unraveling the statistical puzzles of research. He hired a salesperson, although it strained the company's resources at first. As a result, he did better work. The salesperson had more to sell. As a last-ditch move, find a job that will be fun.

Remember, what is the use of being a success if you must suffer to get there? There is very little that is noble about suffering, but many benefits accrue from play and fun.

Source: Arthur Kover, Ph.D., advertising executive.

Recognize your need for stimulation

Individuals' energy levels and their consequent need for stimulation vary greatly. Managers who don't realize this, or who believe their own energy level is the norm, can cause serious problems.

Managers with a high need for stimulation usually perceive conflict as positive. So they regularly seek and provoke confrontations to get the stimulation they want. But what they think is a good discussion is often an exhausting and threatening encounter to their peers or to those under them. Such managers also tend to undervalue lower-keyed, lower-energy staffers.

Managers with low stimulation needs, who are surrounded by highly charged staffers, may mistakenly regard the staff's high energy levels as efforts to compete with the boss.

To avoid problems be aware of your own level of energy. If you have high stimulation capacities, find ways to use up your energy without pouring it out on your colleagues. Physical exercise is excellent. Or look for contact with other high-energy people when you get itchy and feel the need for an exchange of high energy.

Remember that people whose needs for stimulation are modest can still be creative and reflective. And they can effectively complement highly stimulated superiors.

Consider the energy level of each person when assigning jobs that involve a good deal of excitement or tension.

Source: Gisele Richardson, president, Richardson Management Co., management consultants, Montreal.

To avoid worrisome distractions

Consider these tips from Dale Carnegie's book *How to Stop Worrying and Start Living:*

• Keep occupied with productive work. It limits the time and attention avoidable for fretting.

• Save worrying for important matters. Overlook the little things.

• When bothered by the possibility of a disaster, as a source of comfort consider the odds. The worse the disaster, the less likely it is to happen.

• Freely struggle against what can be changed. As serenely as possible, accept the things that can't and make the best of them.

• Once a mishap has occurred, put it in the past and look to the future. Profit from the experience. Resolve not to let it happen again.

Source: Dale Carnegie, *How to Stop Worrying and Start Living*, Simon & Schuster, New York.

How to say no

Say yes quickly. Say no slowly. When a letter or conversation begins with a rejection, the other person usually ignores the rest of the discussion, including the reasons for the negative decision.

The pattern to follow when saying no:

• Review the facts and reasons for the decision without revealing it.

• Build an argument in a step-by-step, fact-by-fact manner.

• Provide information or attachments that support the decision.

• Say no politely.

The goal is to have the other person acknowledge the validity of the rejection.

Always say something good about the rejected idea, organization, or person. Acknowledge the problem and the difficulty of its solution.

Source: William C. Paxson, *The Business Writing Handbook*, Bantam Books, New York.

NEGOTIATING

Picking a negotiator

Chief executive officers should not become directly involved in the early negotiations. Subordinates make fewer concessions and larger demands and have more time available for preparation.

Choose representatives for their negotiating skills, not their availability or seniority.

Traits of a good negotiator:

• Sensitive to the feelings of others.
• Knows how to satisfy the psychological needs of opponents.
• Strongly desires to be liked.
• Listens carefully and looks for the hidden meanings in what is said.
• Will be respected by everyone involved in the negotiations.
• Goal-oriented.
• Displays a logical sense and has shown good business judgment in the past under pressure.

Source: Philip Sperber, *The Science of Business Negotiation*, Pilot Books, New York.

How to negotiate more effectively

• Don't allow the negotiations to be hurried by the other side. Clarify everything that seems fuzzy.

• Have the facts to back up every objective. If no facts are available, use opinions from experts as support.

• Maintain flexibility in every position. It avoids making the other side overly aggressive and always leaves a way out of dead ends.

• Look for the real meaning behind the other person's words. Body language tells a lot. Looking away when discussing a key point can indicate a lack of commitment.

• Don't focus only on money. Loyalty, ego, pride, and independence can be more important than dollars to many people.

• Be alert to the other side's priorities. Don't assume that the two sides are going to have the same priorities. Bending on a point that's important only to an adversary is one of the fastest ways to speed the process.

• Never vent emotions during bargaining. Don't act greedy.

• Get all agreements in writing.

• Don't gloat over concenssions that have been won. Stress that the agreement is a joint accomplishment.

Source: D.D. Seltz and A.J. Modica, *Negotiate Your Way to Success,* Farnsworth Publishing Co., Rockville Centre, N.Y.

A list of negotiating tactics

• Forbearance. Hold back the threat of negative action until the effect will be greatest. Drop the point immediately once the other party has been convinced.

• Surprise. Shift tactics suddenly to throw your opponent off balance.

• Bland withdrawal. Deny everything. Claim a misquote, an out-of-context quote, or say that an employee was unauthorized to act.

• Apparent withdrawal. Deny the legitimacy or authority of the negotiation.

• Fait accompli. Postpone negotiations until the matter has already been completed, at which time it really doesn't matter who wins.

• Reversal. Shift the subject.

• Feinting. Pay lip service, as long as no concrete acts are required.

• Limiting. Put a deadline on the negotiation.

The virtues of nibbling

Nibbling—insisting on a small extra when you negotiate a new deal—often is thought of as cheap, chintzy, or demeaning. Yet nibbling often improves the deal.

The nibbling works because:

• Other party has a strong desire to close.

• Other side's attitude is "most of the deal is done, why waste it now?"

• The bite isn't much compared to the value of the whole deal.

• A long-term relationship may be enhanced by giving just a bit more.

• It isn't bad to let the other fellow feel he's getting a bargain.

On the other hand, nibbles aren't always small potatoes. And they can be stopped. But that can consume too much time, jeopardize the deal, and cause more trouble than it's worth. Each company must know where to draw the line on nibbling, and when.

Using an ultimatum

For it to succeed, especially in the latter stages of a negotiation, the ultimatum must be:

• Presented as softly and palatably as possible.

• Backed by documentation or some form of legitimacy.

• Phrased so it leaves the other side with very few alternatives except to accept or walk away.

Source: Herbert A. Cohen, *Computer Decisions,* Rochelle Park, N.J.

Signs that negotiators are ready to make a deal

It's valuable to know as early as possible that the other side is preparing to settle negotiations. It allows strong points to be pressed home and helps avoid overkill. Clues to look for:

• The discussion shifts focus from the points of contention to the areas of agreement.

• The two sides are significantly closer together.

• The opposition starts to talk about final arrangements.

• A personal social invitation is made. At this point, agremeent is almost always just a formality.

• Other side starts to make notes. Follow through at once, even if nothing but a napkin or envelope is at hand to write on.

But don't handle the signing of the formal agreement through the mail. Both parties should sign it together. This adds importance to the event and helps cement the ties that were formed during the final stage of negotiation.

Source: D.D. Seltz and A.J. Modica, *Negotiate Your Way to Success,* Farnsworth Publishing Co., Rockville Centre, N.Y.

MANAGING THE MANAGERS

Fit the manager to the job

Many companies solve problems short term by opportunistically fitting a manager into an open slot. But the penalties can be long run. Consider a get-things-done executive brought into a troubled department. After setting things right, the executive leaves the company. Meanwhile, the person has alienated so many people that they leave too, and the company is left without an experienced staff. Instead, match the manager to the job.

Lean toward people-oriented managers to keep an already well-run operation in tune. They work very hard and very quickly. And they solve problems pragmatically, though they are not well organized and usually do not like details. Be prepared, though, to work with managers who make decisions at a moderate pace. They need support from superiors. These managers tend to be good at nurturing, but not criticizing, subordinates.

Favor impulsive types for first-line plant managers. They work fast but not hard. They shoot from the hip since they are highly intuitive. Managers above them can expect high performance. But impulsives let everyone know how they feel, whether they want to hear it or not.

Look for sociable and persuasive managers for personnel and public or customer relations. They have a great need to be noticed and stroked by superiors. They also tend to lack clear long-range perspectives and are not especially well organized. But they can advance beyond their abilities due to great social skills or the old boy network.

Source: Dr. Gerald Olivero, vice president, Perception and Preference Inventory Division, PA International Management Consultants, Inc., New York.

Matching managers to products

The manager who boosts a product's market share in a fast-growing market may not be the best person to manage the product once it matures since managers have widely differing strengths, ranging from entrepreneurial talents to expertise in financial and operational controls.

General Electric classifies its products in three phases: grow, defend, and harvest. The managers who are put in charge of each phase are known as growers, caretakers, and, facetiously, undertakers.

Growers are usually entrepreneurial types. They are good at innovation and risk-taking, but weaker on financial controls and organization.

Caretakers tend to be growth-oriented, yet strong on cost-cutting and productivity improvement. They are also good at financial controls and understand the nuances of cash flow.

Undertakers are tough and pragmatic, but not adventurous. They are able to milk every cent of profit from a product after its growth potential has peaked.

But installing a system that matches managers to products has potential hazards. Some of them:

• Bringing in a manager from another division can demoralize subordinates who are expecting promotions.

• Competent managers who are ousted from their positions only because they company's product strategy has changed can become dissatisfied if another challenging position isn't found for them.

• Evaluating a manager's talents can be imprecise and lead to improper assignments. Smaller companies are usually more adept at assessing their managers than bigger ones.

Upgrading production managers

Manufacturing management has long been one of the least popular courses in top business schools. But no longer. Companies will soon be able to draw from a bigger pool of talent as more students sign up for production operations courses. The bottleneck consists of a shortage of qualified teachers. Many schools now borrow engineering professors to teach manufacturing operations courses. Another problem is that some courses lack substance in solving practical problems and dealing with production workers and first-line supervisors.

One barrier to recruitment is that many MBAs do not want to start work on the factory floor. And many of them do not want to live in the smaller towns and cities in which so many plants are located. Students from the Midwest generally take to small-town living better than most.

To upgrade production managers within the company reward top-notch manufacturing managers equally with top people in finance and marketing; make it clear within the company and outside the company that manufacturing management can be a road to the top; and work with older manufacturing executives to overcome their frequent prejudice against hiring MBAs.

Finding good managers

What are the traits to look for in employees who are candidates for promotion? They must:

1. Want to be managers because they're comfortable in the position, not just for money or power.

2. Be able to ease stress for themselves and subordinates.

3. Trust their own judgment enough to work with a minimum of feedback from higher management.

4. Be able to handle difficult situations well most of the time.

5. Channel other people's hostility to solve the problems at hand.

6. Have had successful experience in management positions.

Source: *The Levinson Letter,* The Levinson Institute, Cambridge, Mass.

How to keep executive talent

Important reasons why strong chief executives sometimes fail to hold on to star executive talent:

• They fail to let an aggressive executive know how important he or she is to the organization out of concern that the executive will use that information to bargain. A top-notch executive already knows he is valuable. But he may not know how important he is to that particular company, unless the chief makes that clear.

• They don't always realize the importance of rewarding high performers with both cash and authority.

• They fail to communicate their own awareness of how the organization is changing and what it will mean to aggressive executives' careers.

• They depend too much on feel for talent rather than an executive manpower planning system.

To increase the company's chances of holding on to the best:

• The chief executive must give star performers personal attention and a clearer idea of their potential career within the organization. Speak specifically about potential power, responsibility, rewards, challenges. An exact timetable is not necessary.

• Employ a balanced approach of outside hiring and inside management development.

• Be prepared. A company needs a systematic CEO-directed procedure for pre-screening and advancing talented people on a five-year time frame. Also necessary is a corporate-wide program for assessing overall need for executives. It is particularly important to identify executives most vulnerable to recruitment by other companies by reason of their skills or their inside information on your company.

Source: Kenneth A. Meyers, president, Golightly & Co. International, Inc., New York.

How to cut management fat

Maximize each manager's area of control. A common problem is as companies grow, new layers of management build up over and above what is actually needed. The roots of the personnel glut:

1. Assigning managers to supervise only half as many workers as they normally would when undertaking new tasks. As a result, the change becomes institutionalized and the manager is still supervising only five to eight workers when he could be handling 20.

2. Adding people in an attempt to solve some particular problem.

3. Beefing up staff to help comply with government regulations.

4. Creating jobs for bright new graduates.

Because executives' pay tends to be based in part on the size of their operation, there is little incentive for them to trim excess staff. Also, managers want to assure adequate coverage, so they sometimes build a cushion of extra middle managers to be on the safe side.

Signs of fat management. A large number of assistants (supervisors, managers, vice-presidents, executive assistants) and a staff of specialists. Often they are doing what the managers themselves could be doing (training, problem solving, planning).

What to do:

• Compare the company's unit costs with competitors', as evidenced by price, lost sales, and market intelligence. Comparing the company with a lean competitor may not reveal specific areas where cuts can be made. But it should suggest whether trimming is possible.

• Check each manager's span of control. Some may be supervising 20 people and others only 8.

• The secret. Develop a model plan of how the company organization would look if it were pared down to absolutely essential individuals. (Chart is sensitive information and should be carefully guarded.)

Unless really under the gun to cut costs, reduce the unnecessary middle layers of management gradually (through attrition and reassignment). Avoid sudden amputations that can demoralize the company.

Source: Joseph Eiesenberg, Profit-Improvement, Inc., New York.

How many subordinates can a single boss supervise?

The old formula that says a boss can effectively supervise only six subordinates is silly and erroneous. As a general rule, the more a boss has to intervene with the staff on the job, the fewer subordinates he can supervise. The more job standardization, the more employees he can oversee.

Examples of standardization:

• Employee training sessions, assembly-line and mail-room operations, simple inventory-taking.

• Product managers who report to a single supervisor.

When high boss intervention limits a supervisor's range:

• Frequent exceptions to the norm constantly complicate jobs.

• Many staff groups, in which the manager must work out solutions.

• Top management. The scarcest resource at the top isn't information, but the ability to analyze data.

Signs that a manager is not delegating enough

• Operations slow down considerably when the manager is away.
• Friction, low morale, and lack of initiative characterize the staff.
• Workers defer all decisions on problems to the manager.
• Members of work groups don't come in with new ideas.
• The manager is irritable and complains when a group's work isn't up to expectations.
• The manager sees a worker's status and salary as automatic indicators of how much work to delegate to that person.

Source: Eugene Raudsepp, president, Princeton Creative Research, Princeton, N.J.

Why managers resist new ideas

When people respond negatively to information offered by an outside source, it is usually because they:
• Suspect any ideas that are not their own. The common rationalization is that they are not relevant, not applicable.
• Dislike or don't respect the person that came up with the idea.
• Believe that accepting someone else's idea is an admission of personal inadequacy.
• Fear unknown disruptions may follow, particularly when possibilities exist for job loss, adverse organizational changes, reduced influence.

To overcome resistance, stress the need to compete with outsiders, not co-workers. Build up the credentials of those responsible for new ideas, to create respect and acceptance.

Source: D.E. Zand, *Information, Organization and Power,* McGraw-Hill, New York.

How managers can be more cost-effective

Problem: Two-thirds of today's labor costs are tied up in salaries of executives, technical and professional staffs, and other administrators.

Solution: Ask managers to answer four questions. The responses will improve their cost-effectiveness.

1. What and how well did you do with the manpower, money, machinery and material placed at your disposal last year?
2. What major problems did you solve, and what osbtacles did you overcome?
3. What improvements did you make in the company's products, services, processes, policies, procedures, or practices last year?
4. What can the company now make or do better, faster or cheaper, with less strain on employees, because of your efforts last year?

As a result, managers will reorient their thinking to include explicit cost benefits of the work they do.

Source: Jack Bologna, president, George Odiorne Associates, management consultants, Plymouth, Mich.

When managers' goals are out of line

Unless top management sets the guidelines and the pace, even the best team of managers drifts into contradictory goals, uneven performance, and counterproductive conflicts. Ways to deal with this problem:
• Define clearly the company's direction and emphases.
• Bring incentives into line with the company goals they are meant to promote.
• Lead by example. Policies apply to executives as much as to others.
• Be alert to attitude changes in key employees. Meet with them regularly in an atmosphere

that encourages a review of their assumptions that relate to company policies.

• Explain, in question-answer sessions, the house organ, and memoranda, how the corporate strategy affects employees, and make clear their stake in the strategy's success.

Source: Dr. H.W. Fox, professor, Ball State University, Muncie, Ind.

How to get around circular thinking

Many an executive suite is plagued by circular thinking. George Orwell, the author of *1984,* might have called it *groupthink.* It develops from years of working and associating together. A sure sign is when it's easy to believe that everyone is in agreement all of the time. The trouble is that this becomes a self-fulfilling inhibitor of free thought.

How to identify circular thinking—and avoid it:

• Top-management members pride themselves on their unanimity of opinion. To remedy this, give positive value to constructive disagreement, and enforce consideration of minority views.

• Dissenters are branded obstructionists, or at least negative thinkers. Instead, encourage the airing of disputes and curb any accusations of negativism against dissenting employees.

• Highly regarded executives seek to protect the rest from hearing adverse ideas. See that both the pros and cons of every decision are thoroughly aired. Urge colleagues to play devil's advocate occasionally.

• Managers refuse to rock the boat, and so they fail to point out major problems. The remedy: Separate the discussion of problems from any talk of either blame or solutions. Reward problem recognition even when the person can't offer a solution.

• After reaching a decision, managers rationalize that the negative factors aren't really important. The solution: Look again at how group decisions are made. If rationalization is part of

the process, stamp it out by insisting on a full discussion of all the negatives.

Source: Steven H. Larson, communications analyst, Blue Cross of Northeast Ohio, *Personnel Journal,* Costa Mesa, Calif.

Dealing with political infighting

Don't decide that one of the infighters is "right" and the other is "wrong." That encourages the winner to pick more political fights in the future, while it leaves the loser spoiling for revenge. On the other hand, deciding that neither is right and that they must compromise leaves both parties unhappy and convinced that the boss wasn't fair.

A better solution is to look for a third choice that both parties can live with, without each one feeling that he's lost or that the other one has won. In the ideal "third way," all of the important points of both sides are incorporated. Only the irritants are omitted. The boss, who's led the way in finding the solution, comes out stronger.

Source: *The Effective Manager,* Warren, Gorham & Lamont, Boston.

Crocodiles in business

The company is in trouble. There are too many people on the payroll. The drain on earnings could be fatal. The problem is that many employees are faithful workers who have seen the company through good times and bad. Still, retrenchment is mandatory.

To handle the painful task, hire a specialist, a ruthless manager who allows neither tradition nor sentiment to impede the work at hand.

But this manager could be a Crocodile who

loves the taste of human flesh. That is, the manager enjoys firing people. To satisfy this love, Crocodiles find victims long after all necessary cuts in personnel are made. And crocodiles have been known to devour top managers, and even the boss.

Crocodiles expound the dog-eat-dog philosophy. They also deride weakness or tenderness in others. As managers, Crocodiles are usually productive. But their real pleasure lies in firing fellow employees.

Care and feeding:
• Don't go on vacation and leave a Crocodile in charge.
• Don't give Crocodiles even short-term unsupervised power. They turn any temporary opportunities into a chance to advance themselves.
• Keep Crocodiles in subordinate positions, away from direct personal contact with power sources. Sending this creature to represent management's position to the board of directors gives Crocodiles a chance to be heard. Many end up in the executive suite because their bosses entrusted them on management missions.

Getting rid of a Crocodile isn't always easy, because they are predatory. Sometimes the best weapon is finesse. One boss hired a Crocodile to fire a close employee. The Crocodile and the employee, however, fell in together. They became partners, and the boss then sold them a troublesome branch of the business. The boss rid himself of a losing branch. And he moved two unwanted employees off the payroll. Alternatively, send the Crocodile to industry meetings. He will look good and show off—and may well be hired by another firm.

Never hire Crocodiles unless management is as tough as they are. The best policy is to hire Crocodiles temporarily, during periods of retrenchment.

Source: Martin G. Groder, M.D., *Business Games,* Boardroom Books, Millburn, N.J.

MANAGING YOUR EMPLOYEES

Managing diverse personalities

One of the most precious commodities in business today is the ability to recruit, manage and motivate very different kinds of people. Specifically, creative and analytical types, young, technology-oriented people and older, more seasoned and practical employees.

One reason for the scarcity of managers who can handle diverse groups is that business schools do not teach the subtleties of dealing with highly diverse personality types.

The problem is particularly acute for firms on the cutting edge of technology. The usual problem is that younger personnel understand the latest systems and processes, but the people old enough to understand the economic implications and exercise judgment generally have been overtaken by technological developments. The goal is to achieve a delicate balance between the two groups. Then each group can educate the other and help the company change in desirable ways.

The importance of managers' expectations

A basic concept is that subordinates' performance is strongly affected by what managers expect from them. This theory has been tested and proven among groups ranging from schoolchildren to workers. Act as though there is no doubt that someone will perform well and that person is more likely to do so.

The basic truth is that managers can maximize workers' performance by acting as if they believe the employees can reach the goal, even if they really think the workers will fail.

Other principles, both good and bad, come into play when managers manage by expectancy. *Good:* Employees are less likely to be overwhelmed by the enormity of the goal if intermediate goals based on their present performance are established first. *Not so good:*

• Once managers set expectations, they tend to drive subordinates toward that goal, whether or not it is appropriate to the organization.

• Some managers become dissatisfied if they expect poor performance from a subordinate and the subordinate does better than expected.

• The downside effects of negative expectations are greater than the upside impact of positive ones.

Realities of applying these principles:

• Positive expectations cannot overcome improper training or strong negative conditioning in a poor performer. And high-quality performance is not likely from those who are poorly trained.

• It is more difficult to change people who have learned wrong behavior than to train them from scratch.

Source: Angelo L. Fortuna, vice president, personnel development, ARA Services, Philadelphia.

Hyperfeedback as a management tool

Managers can substantially increase their effectiveness by learning how to recognize and deal with hyperfeedback. Like hyperinflation, it feeds on itself as it gains in intensity.

For example, an employee who detects management dissatisfaction with his work becomes nervous, defensive, and subsequently less effective. This prompts more dissatisfaction on the part of his supervisor, which leads to further deterioration of the employee's effectiveness. Similar destructive examples of hyperfeedback occur between groups within a company and between a manager and division heads who report to him.

Supervisors should learn to recognize hyperfeedback immediately. And get to the source quickly. Then deal with the problem openly in an effort to reverse the direction of the feedback.

To break the hyperfeedback spiral, a manager should single out the best work of an employee and praise him for it consistently. Having won management's confidence, the worker is likely to increase effectiveness in other areas of his work.

By using hyperfeedback positively, a supervisor can upgrade effectiveness to the point where he can delegate authority and not spend time solving morale problems.

Why workers fail

Besides deliberately slacking off, workers often fail to perform properly because:

• Good performance does not really matter. For example, latecomers are not reprimanded. There is no reward for being productive.

• The safest policy is to do nothing. Workers may shirk their tasks because supervisors, out of a desire to retain power and status, may not tell them how to do a job properly.

• Obstacles erected by supervisors make good performance impossible. Example: A secretary who works for more than one boss and must meet their conflicting demands.

• Negative consequences follow the desired performance. Supervisors might urge their assistants to come up with productivity ideas, but the supervisors' common behavior at staff meetings is to dismiss or criticize suggestions.

Source: Bernard L. Rosenbaum, *How to Motivate Today's Worker,* McGraw-Hill, New York.

Recognizing and rewarding employees

There are rewards, other than praise, pay increases, promotions, bonuses, prizes, and trips, that can be used to motivate employees to improve their performance.

Useful alternatives:

• Additional one-on-one (manager-employee) time spent in career-oriented discussion.

• Broadened exposure. Have key employees present proposals to other groups or to executives. Send them to visit other company locations.

• Increased participation in establishing group goals, task assignments, or redesign of work processes.

• Exposure to more company operations. Use task force participation or temporary assignment to another part of the organization or special assignments within the present work group.

• Assignments that more closely fit individual goals and interests and provide a chance to excel.

• Time for special training.

• Time and support for professional activities.

Source: Donald B. Miller, *Working with People,* CBI Publishing, Boston.

Praise and ridicule

Ridicule is a weapon that managers must learn to do without. The certain results of using it against subordinates are loss of enthusiasm for work and lower productivity.

Between management peers, ridicule isn't used often because of the implicit equality of the relationship. Unfortunately, it is used frequently between supervisors and low-level subordinates. That is where it is usually most destructive. The reason: Workers in low-level, dead-end jobs already have a low regard for their own competence. A scathing word such as stupid, lazy, or fat reinforces that feeling. The usual result is even worse performance.

Instead praise workers for routine jobs well done and for routine jobs done over a long period of time.

The conventional attitude is, "Well, that's what they are paid to do." But praise, especially in boring jobs, is one of the proven ways to keep enthusiasm and productivity high.

Source: Dr. Stanley Sherman, head, University Center, Boston.

Managers who undermine morale

Staff morale can make or break a high-pressure effort. But too many managers ruin it by:

• Failing to reward efforts and looking only for results.

• Never giving employees their full attention.

• Confusing workers by frequently changing either instructions or emphasis.

• Insisting that they themselves set the pace for workers.

• Keeping employees in the dark about the goal behind the demand for extra work.

Source: *Reinforcement,* Imperial Management Consultants, Park Ridge, Ill.

Myths about dealing with workers

• Managers think they must be nice to their staff. In reality, their job is to meet corporate goals, sometimes at the expense of personal ones.

• Managers and staff must be part of a team seeking the same goals. Not so. Good management often requires making undemocratic decisions. They are easier to make when managers keep some distance from the staff.

• Staff should understand managers' reasons for their actions. But this is often futile. Attempting to win worker acceptance makes managers seem indecisive or unsure.

• An open-door policy where workers can discuss personal problems is effective. The fact is that knowledge of an employee's personal life will influence manager's feelings about the person's work.

• Managers should be experts on everything in their department or they will lose credibility with the staff. In reality managers who try to keep their hands in every activity are perceived as interfering and robbing subordinates of their initiative.

Source: *Canadian Business,* Toronto, Ont.

Workers' views on what makes a good manager

- Frequently appraises performance.
- Encourages employees to voice concerns.
- Shares information with employees.
- Gives praise as well as criticism.
- Easily accessible to employees. Chats with all employees, not with just a few favorites.
- Doesn't act in an authoritarian manner. Makes orders seem more like discussions.
- Keeps promises.

Source: *Production Magazine*, Bloomfield, Mich.

Planning tips for office routine

Routing lists should be arranged alphabetically. Because this avoids hierarchical irritations that arise because one person's name is placed below someone else's.

If there is a way to avoid written memorandums, use it. Eyeball-to-eyeball response is important in gauging how information is received and how it will be acted upon.

Brevity is the essence of good communications. Boil down ideas and reports to less than one minute, if possible.

Try not to hire assistants, even when the work load gets heavy. Assistants add a layer of bureaucracy, which reduces contact between managers and subordinates. They rarely expedite matters since they cannot make decisions in the boss' absence.

Consider secretarial pools rather than personal secretaries. That way letters can be dictated either to a machine or a person.

Source: Robert Townsend, *Robert Townsend Speaks Out,* Advanced Management Reports, Inc., New York.

Accessibility: how much is too much?

Employees need access: to know the supervisor's values and preferences; to learn what priorities top management has set; and to understand the broader parameters and functions of the tasks they are performing.

Employees often feel they don't know enough about how their boss thinks to make sensible decisions on the work that has been delegated. Only through personal contact can a manager communicate subtle details and fine-tune a subordinate's performance.

And subordinates work most productively when they feel that the boss will be helpful and cares enough about them and their responsibilities to give them some of his valuable time.

There can be too much of a good thing, however. Many subordinates will not learn to make decisions. They will go ahead on a project only when they get the boss's judgment first. Other workers never tire of having the boss's attention. They cling to a higher-status person to solicit favorable comments on how well they are performing.

To ration time with subordinates, keep the door closed at certain hours. Your secretary can intercept calls. Allow interruptions only for true emergencies. Get in the habit of meeting subordinates in their offices for short sessions. It's easier to get up and leave. Keep rough track of how often you see which subordinates. Forcefully wean employees who have been taking more than their share of your time. And make sure to see those who may be too timid to take advantage of access.

Cutting through channels

There are times for managers to break the conventional rules and go directly to subordinates two or three levels below. Direct contact can be useful when:

• Top management needs a clear view of what is going on at lower levels, unfiltered and undistorted by middle manager's perceptions and interests.

• There is reason to doubt that middle managers are portraying top management accurately to those below them.

• Lower-level employees must be assessed for future promotions or demotions. Top management should listen to but not limit itself entirely to a middle-managemer's evaluation.

• Some lower-level employees merit special recognition. Lunch or a private chat with the top manager can be a great motivator of work and loyalty.

But direct contacts like these should be rationed. Unless they are used wisely, their value quickly dissipates.

Consequences of sidestepping the hierarchy too often:

• Middle managers' status and authority can be undermined.

• Top managers are sucked into messy interpersonal and interdepartmental battles that ought to be resolved at lower levels. Getting too involved can damage top executives' reputations and compromise their presumed impartiality.

Top managers should mediate a conflict only after it has smoldered and when high-level intervention seems to assure a quick solution.

Never waste an opportunity to foster commitment

Managers rarely take advantage of opportunities to foster corporate loyalty and commitment and to improve overall productivity. Good opportunities include when a project is finished on schedule, on budget and with good results. Or some difficult task is finally accomplished.

Managers should get all the participants together to bask in the glory. Encourage everyone to express ideas on why and how the work went so well and to compliment one another. It takes only a little time, sometimes as little as 45 minutes. But all the participants will get a large mea-

sure of personal satisfaction and pride. They are bound to feel that they are part of a successful, appreciative organization.

Use each victory for a rite of intensification, an event that reinforces group membership and maintains commitment.

Igniting group creativity

Motivation is generated when employees contribute ideas to improve business and office procedures. Ways to turn employees on:

• Establish a permissive atmosphere at brainstorming meetings.

• Don't reject ideas out of hand. If a suggested approach is unusable, see if it can't be changed so that it can be useful.

• Invite employees to come up with wild ideas. Often this leads to the most original thinking.

New ideas have a way of exciting people, then fading away. Methods of maintaining interest:

• Pump in emotion and excitement by remaining personally involved.

• Organize work schedules so that employees have a sense of directed action.

• Remind everyone of the target. Make it stand out clearly as the common goal among all employees.

• Show respect toward employees by continuing to listen to their comments and ideas to improve ongoing projects.

Source: Craig S. Rice, *Power Secrets of Managing People,* Prentice-Hall, Englewood Cliffs, N.J.

Upgrading staff performance

To get better work, encourage employees in a positive, action-oriented way. Avoid criticism, harangues, and confrontations. They only provoke resentment, resistance, even outright rejection of management aims. The best approach defines acceptable standards.

Upgrade your own expectations. Set clearly defined goals of unquestionable values. (Example: To find the cause of, and to reduce, shipping delays.)

Solicit views from subordinates. Then assemble their relevant information to meet goals.

Plan steps toward achievement so each phase has a definite deadline to be met in weeks, not months.

Communicate your aims clearly. Spell out responsibilities, timetables, satisfactory completion, and accountability.

Monitor progress. Have one individual report in writing about progress, problems, etc.

Repeat and expand the process once the initial goal has been met. Continually upgrade your accepted standards of performance.

Source: Robert H. Schaffer, Robert H. Schaffer & Assoc., Stamford, Conn.

Six ways to reduce turnover

1. Describe the job accurately to the applicants. Disappointment with actual duties is a major cause of turnover.

2. Set realistic minimum requirements. Avoid overqualified applicants who will quickly become restless unless there's a prospect for quick promotion.

3. Keep giving the new employee feedback from the very start on how well he's doing.

4. Check company pay scales regularly to be sure that they're competitive.

5. Watch for sudden rise in absenteeism or lateness, or a drop in productivity. Call the employee in for a conference as soon as any of these signs appear.

6. Cut losses. Let an employee go if the only way to keep him is to distort company policy unrealistically. Otherwise, turnover problems will only crop up elsewhere in a more troublesome form.

Source: *Managing People and Organizations*, New York.

Use transfers to overcome staleness

Employees who stay too long at dead-end, tedious jobs frequently become careless and show other symptoms of poor morale.

Try: Eliminate obstacles to lateral transfers. Some companies unnecessarily restrict transfers that don't qualify as promotions. In their view, too much traffic between jobs lowers productivity.

A short break-in on a new job involving approximately the same level of skill will soon pay for itself in a better feeling about the company and the work. Also, the employee who acquires varied experience may be a candidate for promotion later.

Mediating employee disagreements

Managers should intercede in employee squabbles when the conflicts disrupt day-to-day activities or otherwise impair productivity.

How to intercede effectively:

• See both disputants together. Besides saving time, this forces the squabblers to give a straight version of the dispute.

• Establish ground rules before the explanations begin. Best is to have the individuals tell their sides without interruption directly to the mediator.

• Listen to and accept each party's view. Frequently summarize in simple, unemotional language what each person is saying.

• Encourage the disputants to work out a compromise. Each individual will be much more likely to accept the solution.

• Sum up the agreement before the close of the meeting. Both parties should endorse it. Then set a date for a follow-up meeting. Knowing that they are accountable to management makes the solution binding.

Source: Beverly A. Potter, *Turning Around: The Behavioral Approach to Managing People,* AMACOM, New York.

• Make sure the employee knows his right to appeal a negative judgment.

Source: Louis V. Imundo, *The Effective Supervisor's Handbook,* AMACOM, New York.

Resolving complaints

Efficient complaint-handling improves employees' morale. Resolve as many complaints as possible without outside arbitrators. This builds positive feeling toward management among employees.

Steps in processing complaints:

• Most gripes can be settled simply by discussing them informally with the aggrieved employee.
• If the employee remains unsatisfied, encourage him to write out the specific complaint and what he wants done about it.
• Management should then study the complaint and respond to it within a stated period of time. Management's initial written response must include specific reasons for approving or rejecting the complaint.
• The employee can appeal a denial. Usually, the final arbiter is the director of personnel or the president of the firm. In a unionized company, arbitration is the final step.

The key to the complaint procedure is how the supervisor responds. He should:

• Listen carefully to the complaint and the reason for it.
• Put emotional employees at ease. Give them a chance to unload their grievances, even if it means outbursts of feeling and profanity.
• Assure the employee that he is free from any reprisals.
• Find out the real meaning of the gripe. (An employee complaining about a dirty work area may really be troubled because no one is paying any attention to him.)
• Never get into an emotional argument with a complainer.
• In cases that might set precedents, consult with a higher management before arriving at a settlement.

How to deal with poor work practices

Let employees know that tardiness, a reluctance to work overtime, and other faults are standing in the way of promotional opportunities.

In one case, an employee consistently refused to work overtime. When an opening developed in a higher classification, he applied for it and was turned down. Management's view was that he had the aptitude for the work, but not the right attitude. The job required frequent after-hour machine maintenance to prevent downtime. The ruling was in favor of the company.

In union shops, arbitrators frequently rule that the company cannot deprive employees of contractual benefits (promotion, for instance) as a form of discipline. Make promotion dependent on attitude, work habits, and technical ability.

Source: (73 LA 1215).

Work that encourages drinking

There is a correlation between certain organizational structures and employee alcoholism. Systems that encourage drink:

• Reporting to two or more supervisors.
• Ambiguous performance evaluation standards or goals that are unreachable.
• Joint projects involving another's performance.
• An unhelpful supervisor.

Source: Researchers at the University of Illinois School of Public Health, *S.A.M. Advanced Management Journal,* New York.

Dealing with poor employee performance

The basic reasons for poor employee performance: (1) ineffective guidance from above, (2) inexperience, (3) limited abilities, (4) lack of motivation.

The key to dealing with poor performance is to determine what combination of these four reasons lies at the root of an employee's problems.

Corrective action if the problem is:

• Ineffective guidance. Management needs to better define the employee's job.

• Inexperience. Set incremental goals for the employee. He needs to be coached, then rewarded for effort.

• Limited abilities. Restructure the employee's job.

• Lack of motivation. Determine whether the employee's doldrums are temporary; whether a change or additional challenges will rekindle his interest in his work; or if the best solution is to fire him, or find him a less responsible position.

Source: Robert S. Nadel, partner, Hay Associates, New York.

Warning employees about job performance

A manager calls a subordinate into the office with a warning about job performance and possible dismissal, the atmosphere is charged.

To stay in control:

• Stay in character. If you are normally tough and you soft-pedal your feelings, or vice-versa, you lose credibility.

• Do not sympathize. Sometimes employees are so convincing in their alibis that you get trapped in their problems and end up condoning the misconduct.

• Encourage employees to do most of the talking. Only that way will they reveal the true reasons behind the misconduct.

• Look for compromises when the dispute involves a real difference of opinion.

• Initially, impose a penalty that is less harsh than expected. Employees are more likely to respond to the disciplinary action with improved performance if they feel you tried to correct, not punish.

Source: Edward Roseman, *Managing Employee Turnover: A Positive Approach,* AMACOM, New York.

Developing entrepreneurs within the company

Companies often need managers with entrepreneurial skills, especially ones who work tirelessly for creative innovations in production and marketing. The problem is this executive wants substantial autonomy.

Corporations have consistently lost entrepreneurs who came with acquisitions as well as those developed within the company. Autonomy-minded entrepreneurs find it difficult to live with strict internal controls, staff procedures, and a top management that second-guesses their decisions.

Entrepreneurs usually value the challenge and excitement of making things happen through problem solving and overcoming obstacles; clear credit for achieving results; and the chance to earn large rewards.

Most companies can spawn entrepreneurs by allowing them to control new ventures that are major diversifications. The type of venture best handled by an entrepreneur-manager requires some new technology or product that can be clearly separated from existing operations. To make it work, the corporation bankrolls the new venture when it's still in the idea stage and hands it over to the entrepreneur. About the only constraints the entrepreneur has to deal with are a time schedule and a dollar budget. Support services can be purchased from the parent, but the venture manager is on his own.

If he builds a profitable operation within the specified time, he is promoted to division president and runs the operation. If he fails, he is absorbed back into the main operation.

An alternative is to spin off separate ventures. The parent company keeps some of the stock and either sells the rest publicly or lets it be controlled by the spin-off's top management.

Method. The new company is given a reasonable amount of working capital, and a profit-sharing arrangement is set up with either an existing employee or one hired for his entrepreneurial capacity. Benefits include:

• Top management of the new venture isn't constrained by internal regulations of the parent company.

• If the venture fails, there is little impact on morale in the original company.

• Support services are welcomed rather than resented as an intrusion.

The company that goes this route believes there is great difficulty in having a true entrepreneurial climate inside the corporation. The parent wants to share in the success of the venture. But it also recognizes the value of letting the venture's top management in effect be in business for itself.

Smaller companies use this technique for stretching the managerial capacities of their top executives. Most successful business founders can't resist involving themselves in diversification moves. To force themselves to resist this tendency, they can establish a separate business.

The original company has little to lose. Total compensation isn't much more than it would have been in a closer relationship. Capital infusion can be modest compared with entrepreneurial gain. There is a wide range of compensation schemes, ranging from stock ownership in the new corporation to a straightforward profit-sharing contract.

These organizational devices should be used only where there is a clearly separable product or service that can exist without significant reliance on the parent company. If the new venture can't be run as a separate business, spinning it off by this method can lead only to frustration on both sides.

Source: Dr. Leonard R. Sayles, Columbia University Graduate School of Business, New York.

How to keep star performers happy

• Give them room to operate and live up to their potential.
• Let them take on as much additional responsibility as they can handle effectively.
• Listen carefully when they disagree. (They may have a point.)
• Don't depend on salary and perks alone to keep them happy. Combine financial rewards and recognition with continual challenges to their skills and intellects.

But don't change or alter corporate goals to keep a single superstar happy.

Don't let the perfect employee escape

The better an employee is, the more likely that sooner or later he will have to face problems peculiar to those who excel at anything. Before he is provoked enough to change jobs, his boss should be perceptive enough to see that he doesn't leave the company.

Stay alert for danger signs:
• Jealousy on the part of other employees.
• Deadening containment by immediate supervisors who feel threatened by the achiever.
• Stalled career progress because the good performer is too valuable in the current job.
• A plethora of thankless chores because nobody does them better or as uncomplainingly.
• A negative image, unrelated to his work or attitude because he's not afraid to speak unpleasant truths.
• Pariah status in office politics, because he won't hobnob with the clock-watching, watercooler crowd.

How to deal with these problems:
Management must accept that rules are made to be broken, or at least bent, for the truly exceptional employee. Remember, too, that he's

actually motivated by the need and the desire to excel. Liberal recognition and encouragement from upper management may be all it takes to compensate him for most of the rancor he feels around him. Properly handled, the employee will happily tune out the static.

Source: Jeff Davidson, management consultant, Arlington, VA, *Supervisory Management,* AMACOM, New York.

Encouraging nonconformity

Constructive nonconformists can bring great energy and intellectual drive to a company. And they are efficient problem solvers. But many companies stifle them. To avoid this trap, invite the creative people in the organization to take part in decision-making as well as long-term planning. Don't wait for them to come forward on their own.

Allow those who have shown constructive individualism more freedom in their work. Recognize the achievements that creativity has produced. This may mean modifying the seniority system or the organizational structure.

Encourage departments to exchange ideas without prior censoring of new ideas that seem a little strange at first.

Make groups in the company aware of the ways in which they unintentionally pressure nonconforming individuals to conform.

Brief top management to watch for promising nonconformists. Help insulate them from the conformist pressure that is bound to survive even the most conscientious efforts to eliminate it.

Source: *Chemical Engineering,* New York.

Qualities of a budding boss

Learn to recognize these signs of top-drawer leadership among up-and-coming subordinates:

• Social and emotional poise. Look for self-control, the ability to think on one's feet, self-honesty and the stamina for long hours of brainwork.

• Entrepreneurial talent. Another name for good business judgment and knowing when to take a risk.

• Intelligence. Look especially for the ability to communicate clearly and effectively.

• Effectiveness with others. A broad range of skills, which includes projecting an effective image, being sensitive to other people, and being able to motivate them.

Source: Warren Bennis, University of Southern California, *Technology Review,* Massachusetts Institute of Technology, Cambridge, Mass.

Truly committed employees

Committed employees get a great deal of personal satisfaction from their accomplishments. They totally immerse themselves in a project. And often need a brief break to recover emotionally before a new assignment.

In addition, they:

• Assess the feasibility of a task and speak up when they think the odds are bad. Uncommitted workers take on anything without caring whether it is possible.

• Back up and cover for co-workers and supervisors without concern for who is responsible.

• Understand the underlying plans and objectives of a project. Know how to proceed without checking with supervisors at every point.

• Feel apprehension and anxiety at the possibility of failure. Unhesitatingly ask for help from supervisors when it seems necessary.

Source: W.C. Waddell, *Overcoming Murphy's Law,* AMACOM, New York.

When an employee balks at using the expense account

Newly promoted employees who were brought up to be frugal often are reluctant to make heavy use of their expense allowance. Often they misunderstand the role of business entertaining. Many see it as wasteful, inefficient, and even feel it is dishonest.

Explain to them that their misplaced frugality is keeping them from making contacts and getting to know people who may be important to the company. An expense account is a form of risk capital. It's meant to be invested for the future benefit of the company regardless of any immediate dollar return. It allows an employee to get out to see people, sense trends, exchange thoughts, explore attitudes, and seek out trade information.

Also an employee who scrimps on socializing may give outsiders the impression that the company is cheap or even financially shaky.

Have them pattern expense-account entertaining on what is done by the most successful executives at a comparable level in the company. In many cases, unwillingness to use an expense account properly is read as a serious lack of executive ability.

Source: Betty Lehan Harragan, *Savvy,* New York.

How to manage try-hard employees

Try-hard employees are a special type of complainer. They go to great efforts to make supervisors believe they are trying hard, but actually they avoid rules and subvert the family-company approach. Try-harders make poor managers but can still be useful to a company.

A typical try-harder avoids direct answers; fails to accept criticism, countering it with "Yes, but" excuses; accepts work grudgingly; blames everything and everybody else for his problems; and argues a lot with others.

The best managerial strategy is to joke with the try-harders. Avoid commands: They will tend to rebel. Show them their tactics aren't getting through to you. Don't put them in a key position.

Because they are tenacious and creative, try-harders can be effective in jobs that require persistence but not close human interaction. Divert their energies.

Source: Taibi Kahler, director, Human Development Assn., Little Rock, Ark.

Managing the loner

Employees who don't mingle well at the office need to be handled coolly and firmly. They respond best to definite orders and direction. The worst approach by a supervisor is enthusiastic friendliness, which seems to infringe on the employee's personal space.

Loners need strong direction. It gratifies their unacknowledged need for attention. Following orders makes them become a part of the company family.

Loners are least effective in those jobs that require heavy interaction, such as trouble-shooting, handling complaints or working in the personnel department.

The best jobs for loners are in researching, programming, accounting, or any other job that provides a solitary niche.

Don't be misled by the loner's solitary independence. It merely counters inner feelings of vulnerability and helplessness.

To spot the loner at an employment interview, notice that a loner:

• Has an impassive facial expression.
• Never volunteers information. Waits until spoken to.
• Speaks in an impersonal way that never asserts a sense of self. As an example, instead of saying, I think, they will say, It occurs to me.

Source: Taibi Kahler, director, Human Development Assn., Little Rock, Ark.

Delegate work appropriately to starters and finishers

The starter comes in frequently with ideas and suggestions. He's creative (sometimes a dreamer), sensitive and prone to anxieties. Don't pressure him too much or place too many restrictions on him. The finisher rarely comes up with original suggestions. His personality is more plodding and unenthusiastic. He loves to finish the jobs a starter dropped when he lost interest.

Delegate tasks accordingly. Give the starter the responsibility to come up with solutions to problems. Let the finisher implement the solutions.

Source: *Boss Psychology,* McGraw-Hill, New York.

The insecure employee

Practically every employee passes through an insecure phase when he's new on the job. A great many otherwise competent people never outgrow their insecurity. Turn it to the company's advantage. (The insecure employee typically tries to be precise and orderly and is conscientious in his work.)

To get the most from an insecure staffer:

• Make sure he has complete and unambiguous instructions on what he is expected to do.

• Lavish encouragement and praise on him when he does a task well.

• Be available to give reassurance to the employee when he runs into problems.

• Prepare the groundwork carefully before informing the employee of any changes that will affect his routine. Point out how the new situation will benefit him, if that is indeed the case.

The eager-to-please employee

People chronically disposed to please others can make valuable employees. But they are not good in roles that conflict with their deep need not to offend. Jobs that require them to make quick decisions and to take responsibility for consequences, such as troubleshooting, personnel managing, accounting, or purchasing are usually not suitable for them.

Pleasers' basic problem is their driving need to win acceptance. By refusing to be assertive or competitive, they communicate that they are not adults, but still charming children. Frequently the cause is a pattern fixed early in life of trying to win the parent's attention away from the younger siblings by acting like babies themselves.

Pleasers excel in social jobs without heavy responsibilities and where they can put charm to good use for example, clerical, design, and assembly-line jobs, and especially as receptionists or in public relations.

Pleasers tend to:

• Dress five years behind the times. Appearance is little-girlish for women and flashy for men.

• Smile a great deal, even when angry or unhappy. They have a habit of laughing at themselves at inappropriate times.

• Deprecate their own importance. They are wary of being perceived as taking themselves seriously. They downplay any compliment about their intellectual capacity.

• Be ingratiating and admiring.

Address their feelings instead of their job-related functions in a way that communicates that they are valuable as people. Pleasers have spent their lifetimes looking for approval of themselves as persons. Once they receive the nurturing they want, pleasers are motivated to risk acting like independent adults rather than attention-seeking children.

Source: Taibi Kahler, director, Human Development Assn., Little Rock, Ark.

Employees who steal time

Almost every worker wastes time on the job, if only when taking coffee breaks or chatting with colleagues. But now, personnel experts warn that a growing number of employees are stealing time.

Employees use company time to pursue personal projects, work slowly during the day to get overtime at night, or intentionally arrive late and leave early.

Estimating that 80% of the work force steals an average four hours and five minutes per week, then multiplying the lost time by the average U.S. wage, that time is draining the economy of $98 billion annually.

Come down hard on time stealers to prevent the practice from spreading by stopping senior managers from setting a bad example; singling out time thieves. Tell them to reform or leave; and as a preemptive move against prospective time stealers, launch a companywide campaign to cut down on time wasting.

Source: Robert Half, president, Robert Half, Inc., New York.

Workers who are absent on Mondays

Monday is the day everyone at work has to face. After a weekend of rest and recreation, Monday morning returns the employee to the hard realities of working life. Difficult tasks must be confronted, awkward situations resolved, and reputations once again placed on the line. Most workers accept this challenge by reporting in. Others see Monday not as a challenge, but almost as a prison sentence.

Those among the missing:

• Drunks too hung over to respond to the alarm clock.

• Potheads once again out of touch with reality.

• Hypochondriacs who, after a weekend contemplating all their ills, must rush to the doctor's office first thing Monday morning.

• Depressed people who have collapsed without the work structure.

• Showboaters who have overextended themselves to such a point that they cannot return on time because the yacht is still offshore, the hunting party snowbound, the flight from the tropics delayed by engine failure.

• Aging jocks who have torn themselves up over the weekend trying to prove that their bodies are still in tip-top condition.

• Romantics who have fallen in love again or become so entwined with a mate that they want to continue the ecstasy for one more day.

• Workaholics whose extra job—or the punishing schedule of their work—has taken its toll.

The first step toward a solution is a sensitive interview to discover what is keeping the employee from work. It requires skillful probing. He may not be prey to one of the forms of weakness or bad judgment previously cited. Rather, there could be, for instance, an illness in the family that keeps him traveling long distances over weekends and hampers attendance at work on Monday.

Remember that the employer is the doctor, both literally and figuratively. He is attempting to unearth the disease by discussing the symptoms with the patient, who is the employee who consistently fails to show up for work.

If the worker has a serious, psychologically based reason that leads him to miss Monday, such as alcoholism or drug abuse, enlist the proper help.

If the problem is only that the employee would rather be at play than at work, the time has come for the second step—reprimand or censure. Make it clear to the worker that a high price must be paid for missing Monday repeatedly.

Source: Martin G. Groder, M.D., *Business Games,* Boardroom Books, Millburn, N.J.

Curing the chronically late

Some workers are persistently late arriving at work, getting to meetings, meeting deadlines, and returning telephone calls. Basically, these chronically late employees are rebellious.

They want to determine the routine of their

own lives, and resent the controls placed on them by business regulations and their supervisors.

They show their rebellion by adopting a passive, indirect method. They do what is demanded, but very slowly. These employees spend enormous amounts of time figuring out ways of circumventing systems of control. As a result, the usual correctives such as reprimands and confrontations often fail to work. Instead:

• Make sure the chronically late employee's work can be done within the allotted time and with the available resources.

• If the lateness pattern continues, confront the employee. Convey in no uncertain terms the importance that being on time has to the functioning of the company. Negotiate limits to which he is willing to commit himself. Then hold him to them.

• If the worker continues to rebel by being late, he is not temperamentally suited for work in a supervised situation. Try him on a freelance basis.

• If he can't or won't work independently and continues flouting the timetables, let him go.

Source: Martin G. Groder, M.D., *Business Games,* Boardroom Books, Millburn, N.J.

The chronic complainer

People who are temporarily depressed often feel better after a talk to a friend. The chronic complainer, however, revels in dumping his load of misery on you whenever the opportunity arises. He loves to seek out listeners and leave them feeling worse than he does.

Misery loves company. This insistent unburdening enables the complainer to feel that he is not alone in his plight. By making others worse off then he is, he has proven his power and the fragility of happiness. He proclaims unhappiness is the only reliable element in life. Depression is secure, misery is safe.

To see if the complainer is just a petty griper

or someone with real problems, examine his complaints. Try to help him solve his obvious problems and see how that affects his attitude. If he immediately comes up with fresh complaints, he is a chronic complainer.

Chronic complainers need professional help. Help them obtain it. But if their moaning at work continues, rearrange their schedules to deny them regular access to other employees. Have the complainer tell his problems to a therapist.

Source: Martin G. Groder, M.D., *Business Games,* Boardroom Books, Millburn, N.J.

Workers who never take the rap

Some employees spend much of their working lives making sure they never take the rap. These people constantly cover their tracks. They believe that anything that can go wrong will go wrong. Their goal is to escape blame at all costs.

They write memos by the ton, often opening the memo: "As I have warned in the past..." to establish a blameless position.

Do a file-weight analysis. Employees with the most pounds of paper for their level of responsibility are presumed guilty of playing this game until proven innocent.

In its mild form, this behavior is good for some tolerant chuckles. But, if performed persistently, there are some drains on the company. Specifically:

• The time and effort spent on memos and justification deprives the firm of the employee's productive services.

• If the employees are managers, entire departments can be brought to a halt. When the head people are busy covering their tracks, subordinates soon follow suit. A prime casualty is creativity.

The suspicious demeanor of these employees has a place in the company. But it must be held under control.

Since they are natural advocates of caution and conservatism, the fears they project act as a brake on hasty company decisions. Sometimes they are the only ones to spot trouble. Their role should be advisory. Their fears can immobilize the entire corporation if they hold positions that are too high in the corporate structure.

Also, their pessimistic posture is appropriate for dealing with investigators who are looking for opportunities to cite the business for violations of regulations.

Source: Martin G. Groder, M.D., *Business Games,* Boardroom Books, Millburn, N.J.

How to detect a fibbing subordinate

While otherwise relying heavily on Machiavellian techniques, U.S. business people frequently forget what the Renaissance philosopher cautioned about trusting subordinates. Be on guard.

The rule is a bit harsh for today's management climate, but smart managers should still try to see through employees who tend to stretch the truth to make things seem better than they are. The code words they use to camouflage the bad news:

• "It's nothing serious, but..." Real meaning: A disaster is at hand, but I need more time to cover my tracks before you realize how bad the situation actually is.

• "The customer loved it." Meaning: Problems. If the customer really loved it, there would have been a reorder.

• "All we need are a few adjustments." Meaning: The project has fallen apart.

• "Trust me." Meaning: I'm about to do something that I hope you won't notice.

• "I got it." Caution: Employees who use this phrase in response to instructions probably don't understand them. Advice: Ask them to summarize the instructions.

Don't assume that subordinates are deliberately deceptive. More often, they use the key phrases instinctively to reassure managers, and to keep them from interfering with the work of their subordinates.

Source: Arthur J. Kover, advertising executive, taught Machiavellian philosophy at Cornell University.

Stifling troublemakers

• The tactless one criticizes constantly. Is usually right. Regularly implies that the boss is a fool to let these things happen. Doesn't say so outright. Have heart-to-heart talk about the damage the behavior does. Back up the discussion with the tape recording of a recent staff meeting in which that rudeness was displayed. A course in human relations may be helpful.

• The steamroller never admits to being wrong. Argues endlessly over minor points. Doesn't listen or give up. Cut tirades short by telling him to put ideas into memos. Respond to memos with no more than "thank you" or a past-tense statement of action taken. Avoid an argument or a memo war.

• The sullen one resents job, boss, colleagues ...everything, and performs all tasks grudgingly. Find out what kind of job he or she really wants. Simple praise often helps.

• The lone wolf breaks or ignores all rules. Has no concept of teamwork, hates meetings and other organized events. Go-it-alone determination can make him a top performer. Put him on a long leash. Set clear and demanding goals.

• The old buddy: Started out with the boss but has fallen behind. Uses real or imagined friendship to his own advantage. Tends to embarrass the boss with tales of early years. Create distance from him even if it weakens (or ruins) the friendship.

• The office wit is always poking "fun" at superiors and others. Source of annonymous cartoons, notes, and jokes on the bulletin board. Ignore the antics unless they are upsetting the targets of his jokes. This behavior may be a sign of wasted creativity that can be put to better use.

All subordinates grumble behind the boss's back. Good managers accept this. They ignore the grumbling when they overhear it. It may be time to worry when no one complains.

Source: *International Management,* New York.

Taking the bloom off an office romance

Men and women who work together closely often act as though wed. They play a game of office marriage, which is sexual in fantasy—and sometimes in practice.

The couple are usually devoted, energetic workers. Because they want to be together, they come to work every day. They are rarely absent (even together).

Problems:
- The man and woman are more loyal to each other than to the company.
- The couple can become a closed unit. They exclude influences and information from outside. And they are reluctant to add others to their twosome.

- Their intimacy arouses the jealousy of other managers and employees. A frequent result is efforts to sabotage the relationship with gossip, rumors, and vindictive actions, such as informing spouses. A general loss of morale can ensue.
- The couple resists furiously any attempt by the company to keep them apart.

The best solution is to prevent the relationship from taking hold. But by the time the relationship is apparent to others in the company, it is often too late to nip the relationship in the bud.

Practical guidelines:
- Develop a sensitivity to employees' interests in each other. An early warning system is invaluable.
- Don't think that by ignoring an office romance it will fade away. A delay in action usually makes things worse.
- Limit the frequency and duration of the times that the two same people work together on teams. This lessens the chances of romantic bonds forming.

The best approach is to let it be known informally that employees who are dabbling in office romance will be called in for a serious and frank talk with a supervisor. This serves as a warning that if the liaison continues, termination is a strong possibility. It usually solves the problem.

Source: Martin G. Groder, M.D., *Business Games,* Boardroom Books, Millburn, N.J.

2 MANAGING THE WORK

MANAGEMENT WISDOM

Managing the future

Successful executives traditionally have been expected to know everything that was going on in their business. And it's been even more important for them to exert control over those events. Today, that concept of management is changing quickly. Swift technological changes, consumer reactions, and fast-breaking world events have made it increasingly hard to foresee, let alone control, even the most immediate consequences of corporate decisions.

What companies need is intuitive, people-oriented leaders who can learn about what is going on, sniff out potential problem areas, and sense how best to live with them. Many techniques for this new kind of management already exist: future studies, value-change analysis, strategic management, vulnerability analysis, public-issue scanning. Yet practical use of these tools lags because companies are having trouble incorporating them into the business structure and the traditional patterns of management relations.

The problem is old-style executives. They like to think they know all the answers. Often, they are not very good listeners, which means they no longer even know some of the questions.

The solution is new-style executives. They are geared to learning and listening. They don't ask just to be given the facts. The new breed understands that the situation is much more complicated than generalized, capsulized facts can reveal. Instead, they want all the details, to allow for negative possibilities in their contingency planning.

Nitpickers and idea-killers, long the bane of business activists, may find a new role in corporations. Their function is to build in error-embracing capability, so that as new company policies and products evolve, they are monitored closely and changed if necessary.

New managers should start off expecting uncertainty and change. The idea is to develop contingency plans, and learn from errors. Incentives must be changed to reward people for calling attention to their own errors before they become too damaging, not for hiding them as in the past.

Managers must learn to use a company alert system effectively. When a problem becomes evident, it should be widely discussed and evaluated within the organization. This provides all managers with a valuable lesson that helps them understand uncertainties that are bound to arise in their own areas.

The first applications of error-detection management are:

New-product introduction. Despite the enthusiasm of new-product champions, it is now crucial for companies to face up to and monitor the uncertainties that await a new product or service in the marketplace.

Site selection. Many companies have learned the hard way that it is better to know the worst (as well as the best) about community reaction and involvement before buying land or breaking ground.

Public relations. Some utilities are going well beyond traditional public relations to work with their customers in helping them learn to live with energy costs. Oil and insurance companies are engaging in wide-ranging education programs and addressing more than purely proprietary interests.

Source: Dr. Donald N. Michael, SRI International, Inc., Menlo Park, Calif.

Succeeding when competitors fail

Companies that do well despite overall declines in their industries almost always remain aggressive in hard times. The two best survival strategies are delivering products more cheaply than competitors to gain volume and market share, and producing goods that are markedly different from as well as superior to those of competitors. Remember that winners try to pursue these two strategies simultaneously. Losers switch from one to the other. To keep the company ahead:

• Plow profits back into the basic business. This means ignoring the temptation to milk a mature business in order to enter a newer growth industry. Diversifying out of a mature industry works only when a company recognizes the declines at an early stage and when the company is willing to recommit its resources wholeheartedly.

• Don't integrate vertically as a matter of policy. Instead, invest enough to have the most efficient production at selective stages. The ideal is to find the key areas, upstream and downstream in the operation, where return on investment is highest.

How to plan for uncertainty

Some effort to plan ahead for change and uncertainty is essential. But it demands a different approach from ordinary planning of operations. To plan for change:

• Use generalists rather than specialists. Planning requires thinking big. Most specialists are tactical, not creative, planners.

• Keep the planning unit small and low in profile, to be able to ride out inevitable cost-cutting campaigns when business is off.

• Instruct planners to report directly to top management. That's where any actual decision to make a change must come from.

Source: Milton Leontiades, *Strategies for Diversification and Change,* Little, Brown, Boston.

How valuable is corporate planning?

Planning on a companywide basis pushes managers to improve profitability, a new study of 113 of the country's largest corporations reveals. A plan that simply adds up divisional forecasts, plans, and budgets is not sufficient. Preliminary results of the study suggest that companies that develop long-range corporate plans:

• Emphasize obtaining high market shares.
• Use portfolio analyses to guide resource allocation.
• Report more participative decision making.
• Plan for anticipated product-life cycles.
• Give priority to contingency planning.
• Link planning with managerial performance.
• Structure planning so that board members and chief executive officers are closely involved.

Ironically, the small number of big companies that use no planning of any kind outperform, as a group, those that do. Companies with no planning:

- Are more likely to be in retail and wholesale businesses.
- Have the advantage of being less subject to unpredictable competitive actions.
- Are more often in declining markets and have decided to milk the business for cash.
- Have key decisions made by one or a small group of senior executives.
- Hire more senior executives away from competitors.
- Expect fewer production-process changes.

Source: Noel Capon, John Farley, and James MacHulbert, professors, Columbia University Graduate School of Business.

Making objectives more meaningful

- Focus strictly on results. Don't get into the methods to be used (that's a matter of strategy) or the reasons why.
- Establish a timetable.
- Define objectives in measurable terms whenever possible.
- Confine each objective to a single theme.
- Beware of combining profit and growth objectives. Workers can become confused about which objectives to pursue.
- Set priorities when drawing up the list of objectives. It helps if some have to be sacrificed later.
- Be sure each objective requires a significant effort, to challenge and motivate the employee.

Source: William S. Birnbaum, management consultant, Fullerton, Calif.

Prechecking a system

Use a pilot test before implementing a new system. Reasons:
- The limited cost gives the company a chance to test many forms of the new approach.
- Risk of damage to ongoing operations is minimized.
- Success attracts more attention and enthusiasm elsewhere in the company.
- The pilot may lead to new applications, which may affect the form in which the full project is implemented.
- Success encourages other departments to develop pilot projects of their own. It increases their respect for the benefits of change.

Anticipating changes in technology

Top corporate management that has been misled by unfulfilled promises of breakthroughs in technology sometimes moves too much in the opposite direction and ignores important new opportunities. Make sure a management system is in place to keep top management abreast of new technological advances and gear technology into the corporation's plans.

Areas where major progress now looks certain:
- Robots. Their use is becoming more widespread for repetitive factory operations. Japan is leading. Benefits include upgrading productivity and relieving workers of tedious jobs.
- Computers. Small terminals will proliferate in offices. The terminals will link individuals to inexpensive computer banks and data systems.
- Electronic newspapers. Video units that display news from categories selected by the viewer appear to be only a few years away. But they won't replace conventionally printed newspapers. They will be a complementary medium.

However, widespread computerization of home and business will give additional power to the government, which might not always use it wisely. Keep the company tuned in to diverse and competing information sources. Subsidizing print media or public television may be worth the price.

Source: James Martin, British computer consultant, *Computerworld,* Framingham Mass.

Effectiveness vs efficiency

Effectiveness is getting things done, which is the prime goal of management. Efficiency is using the fewest resources to get a job done. Manager's trap: It's possible to be efficient without being effective. So, first, get things done. Then work on doing them efficiently.

Source: *Sales Manager's Bulletin,* Waterford, Conn.

The benefits of conflicts

Conflicts are inevitable in most jobs, but many managers see only their negative side, and they try to reduce or stamp out conflicts. However, conflicts can help to:
• Build group morale to meet a challenge. Serve as a safety valve within the group for minor disagreements. Drive out disruptive members of the group.
• Spur major changes, innovation and creativity.
• Clarify issues and goals.
• Bring about a faster resolution of a troubled situation. Force managers to face up to a touchy problem that would have been kept under the rug otherwise.
• Speed the breakup of an unproductive working relationship.

Source: Dennis King, organizational consultant, Procter & Gamble, *Personnel,* AMACOM, New York.

Five benefits of failure

At least as much can be learned from a failure as from a success.

Basic questions to ask to benefit most:
1. Can a failed solution be patched up until a new one is ready? Can it be adjusted to increase chances for success?
2. Did the solution fail completely? Are there parts worth saving and reworking?
3. Has it upset anything else—individual growth potential, job structures, work scheduling, interdepartmental interfacing—and can it be corrected?
4. What and where are the solution's strong points—speed, efficiency, interest, enjoyment?
5. What and where are the weak points—wrong direction, cumbersome, disorganized, uninspired, only stopgap?

With answers to these questions, managers learn what to guard against in the future. They also become more flexible in their thinking and planning.

Source: *Successful Problem Management,* John Wiley & Sons, New York.

Don't be shackled by the past

Executives are forced to spend much time, energy, and ingenuity patching up or bailing out the mistakes of past administrations. Solving past problems at best returns you to status quo. Yesterday's successes tend to linger beyond their productive life.

How to find time for the more important responsibilities of positioning the company for the future?

Ask: "If we did not already do this, would we go into it now?" Unless answer is an unconditional yes, drop the activity or curtail it sharply.

Limit servitude to the past by cutting back chores that no longer promise results. And don't commit additional financial or (more precious) human resources to a dying cause.

Source: Peter F. Drucker, *The Effective Executive,* Harper & Row, New York.

Managing walk-throughs

An unscheduled walk through the office or plant to spot-check operations is useful.

For an effective walk-through:

• Evaluate an entire department, not individual employees. The department must continue to function in a normal way while the manager is present. It can't if individuals feel that they are being spied on by a superior.

• Take notes of errors being made. But refer to the errors, not to the people, when reviewing them later.

• Don't hesitate to talk during walk-throughs. But avoid using the personal pronoun *you* when referring to errors or inefficiencies. Instead, refer to this error or this way of doing things.

• Even when criticizing employees anonymously, avoid any references to personal styles. Concentrate on the results that those styles achieve.

• In conducting the review, don't get bogged down in the mistakes observed. Focus on solutions and improvements.

• Use walk-throughs impartially for all departments.

• Don't let the walk-through last more than an hour. Preferably less. After an hour, it's almost impossible to avoid distorting employee performance by the presence of the manager.

Source: *Computerworld,* Framingham, Mass.

Evaluating the need for elaborate management systems

Before implementing management systems that emulate those used by major corporations, entrepreneurial organizations should consider not only what they may be getting, but what is being given up.

There is a trade-off between standardized budget and procedures vs spontaneity and adaptability. Potential problems:

1. Management systems add bureaucratic paperwork which can divert employees' attention from company goals.

2. Because employees know they are being evaluated on the basis of prescribed standards, they tend to burrow into their own niches and not collaborate in those minor ways that often boost profitability.

As a result, management systems may make operations run more predictably, but they also make them less dynamic—the very advantage entrepreneurial companies need to stay ahead in the marketplace.

If the market is a changing one or if the product line is evolving, it's probably better for the entrepreneur to encourage his employees to collaborate in a more informal work environment.

Management systems make the most sense when: (1) work routines are stable and the same thing is done over and over again, or (2) the company is so large that it requires more structure.

Hands-on management

As financial pressures mount, the temptation grows stronger to substitute financial controls for effective management. A symptom of the trend is that nearly three-fourths of the students in major graduate schools of business specialize in finance now. But this development is a gross distortion of the original purposes of such controls. Their prime function is to tell management if the business has adequate cash and to inform shareholders and tax authorities about the company's overall health.

Management by exception, intervening only when a problem shows up in the financial results, has become an excuse for managers who don't want to get their hands dirty finding out what is really going on in the company.

But some things a manager must know can't be learned from financial reports. And errors don't appear in the reports until it is too late to rectify them. Examples:

• Loss of the firm's strongest customers. Sales can be kept high by developing less-valued customers.

• Failure to provide good service. After computerizing its commercial accounts, a large New York City bank tracked the number of errors being made and was satisfied that the incidence of error was normal. What didn't show up until too late was that the mistakes that were occurring were huge ones. The result was the loss of several major accounts.

• Failure to innovate. A good manager spends a great deal of time overcoming obstacles and developing new procedures or organizational approaches. Financial measures do not pick up this capital investment of time, which is costly in the short run but the only way to survive in the end.

• Growing isolation and competition among departments, especially in decentralized companies. Overemphasis on financial results forces each unit to try to maximize its advantages over the rest. The bottom line is departmental efficiency, but at the expense of companywide effectiveness. One symptom is balloon squeezing by managers to make sure costs and/or problems show up in somebody else's department.

A better way is hands-on management. Though a somewhat overworked buzzword, it is a very simple concept. Management must observe directly what is going on, get a sense of the organization and understand the relationships among people and departments. The aim is easy give-and-take among interdependent units rather than defensiveness or an inclination toward one-upmanship.

How to set a hands-on management style for the company:

• On occasion, deal directly with people several levels below.

• To avoid isolation, spend time in the operating units and staff groups. But do not use visits as an opportunity to second-guess managers.

• Give individuals and departments special, tough assignments periodically and watch carefully how they are carried out. Ask managers questions about which parts of the assignment were most difficult, how they went about doing the job, etc. People want cues, and well-framed questions are a way to give direction.

• Ask people questions that can be answered only if they are doing their jobs well. For example, query a purchasing manager on the likelihood of strikes this year and on how many alternative supply sources the manager has lined up.

• Always be curious about how people are handling the discretionary, coordinating, and subjective aspects of their jobs. Problems in these areas are leading indicators that something is wrong. Financial results are a lagging indicator.

By being good hands-on managers, top executives in a company counter the tendency of middle managers to narrow their jobs and do only those things that are measured. By learning how things are done, a good top manager can encourage other managers to facilitate coordination and thereby serve the interests of the company as a whole.

Source: Dr. Leonard R. Sayles, professor of management, Columbia University Graduate School of Business.

Management practices for entrepreneurs

Owner/managers of non-giant companies often succumb to management principles that are inappropriate for their size business and that ignore the critical importance of their special contribution. Major myths and mistakes:

1. Delegate as much as you can. The top manager doesn't do, he plans and evaluates.

Wrong. Usually the man who has started the firm has unique skills and knowledge about the industry, its markets, and certain technical aspects. These strengths ought to be employed at those tasks where he excels. They shouldn't be delegated. The better rule is to delegate the tasks for which the top manager has no flair or special experience.

2. Manage by results. Let people do their work and intervene only after their end results fail to meet preestablished standards.

Wrong. Dynamic newer businesses require a great degree of hands-on management by the owner, who must keep in touch with nearly everything by directly seeing, hearing, and touching. He is the one who must make a constant stream of tradeoff decisions. This pivotal role requires that he know just about everything. The decisions can't wait for the final results of a project to appear at the end of an accounting period.

3. Use written data and reports to evaluate performance.

Wrong. Most written data is distinguished by what it omits and covers up. The way to learn what is going on is to be involved in the day-to-day complexities of the business. The luxury of looking at data can be enjoyed for those operations which have truly become routinized and where there is little chance of surprises. By the time a key objective has been missed by a subordinate, it is often too late for the smaller business to make amends. Thoses losses can be catastrophic.

Source: Dr. Leonard R. Sayles, professor of management, Columbia University Graduate School of Business.

How to succeed as a subcontractor

Working under a prime contractor on a large project requires teamwork, cooperation, and confidence between the subcontractor and the prime contractor. This, however, may be perceived as suppressing aggressiveness or initiative. Therefore, expect regular meetings and plant visits from the contractor. It may even be necessary for the contractor to station someone fulltime at the subcontractor's plant.

Be prepared to temporarily rearrange the management structure to match that of the contractor and other subcontractors.

Resist the normal tendency to point out errors or make suggestions. The contractor is likely to regard this as unwanted interference.

Source: G. Sammet Jr. and C.G. Kelley, *Subcontract Management Handbook,* AMACOM, New York.

Fairness in business relationships pays off

Managers frequently take pride in shrewd deals with suppliers, customers, and employees. That's dangerous. Sharp bargaining can work in a one-time transaction (such as buying real estate from a stranger). The same tactics can be fatal when there is a continuing relationship.

When one partner in a relationship is pushed too hard (he concedes too much or is deceived into thinking he is getting more than he actually is), he looks for an opportunity for revenge. The immediate gain may be dissipated over time in destructive conflict.

Leaders who build successful organizations learn to accept less than they could get in order to build enduring relationships. To earn a reputation for fairness, an effective manager must demonstrate credibility.

It is sometimes important to reveal problems or other weaknesses when negotiating with a valued customer or employee. That creates a basis for trust. The other party is much more willing to take statements at face value. Then, when the manager says positive things (about a product, a new system, company goals, etc.) that have to be taken on faith, the statement is more credible.

The best time to eliminate a job is when it's unfilled

Evaluate the need for job slots in the company organizational chart when they are vacant. It's much easier to eliminate a position, or determine that additional skills are needed, before a job is filled. Checklist of possibilities:

• Eliminate by consolidation. Would it be more efficient to "fill" this position by merging it with other jobs or reallocating it to another department?

• Automate or contract the service. Could it be done better or cheaper by a machine or a system than by a person? Would it be better to purchase this service from an outside agency?

• Overtime for current employees.

• Part-timers.

• Flexible staffing. If this position should be filled by a new staff member, could the job duties be expanded?

• Expansion. Is this job area crucial and demanding enough to justify including more employees?

Source: *Get the Right Person for the Job,* Prentice-Hall, Englewood Cliffs, N.J.

DECISION MAKING AND PROBLEM SOLVING

Rules for better management decisions

One sure way to confront the most important decisions each day is to go contrary to instinct, because the matters that seem most distasteful are probably those that should be the top priorities. Do them.

The second rule of decision-making is to build a 20% pessimism quotient into all expectations. Overestimate by 20% the amount of time it will take to accomplish a plan. Underestimate by 20% the expected results.

Compromise is tempting, whether the decision is between two ideas or two executives. Executives should avoid compromising. Make one manager clearly victorious over the other, no matter how painful it may be. Make sure the loser knows that his case has been fully considered and appreciated.

Implementing company objectives. Before stating the company's objectives, properly define what they should be. Have departmental chiefs write out their two top objectives and what they will mean to the company if accomplished. This way, the chief executive officer gets a good idea of what his managers are up to and can better decide what the overall company objectives should be.

Once the company objectives are determined, the CEO should make sure they are in his mind at all times. Put up a sign in the office that says: "Is what I'm about to do going to get the company any closer to its objectives?" Then repeat the objectives to everyone in the company at every opportunity. This way:

• Employees work much faster and more effectively.

• Diversionary activities, such as going out to lunch with interesting but unimportant (in a business sense) people, are reduced.

• Good ideas that come to the company that are nonetheless outside its main objectives won't divert top management's attention. Before diversifying into new businesses, CEOs should make sure that the existing business has really exhausted all its opportunities because frequently, solutions appear to have run out when the chief executive gets distracted from the company's objectives.

Source: Robert Townsend, *Robert Townsend Speaks Out,* Advanced Management Research, New York.

Decision-making help from the competition

Competitive analysis can be used as an integral part of management decisions and a major factor in all strategic planning.

It's important to keep current on industry statistics. An analysis of the competition usually doesn't require elaborate intelligence-gathering systems. Often more useful is applying common sense to readily available information and asking intelligent questions.

• What do competitors' products show about their understanding of the marketplace?

• Has the competition left a gap between what they are offering and what customers and potential customers really want?

• Are competitors diverting cash or technical resources to new or different product areas?

Approach the marketplace conceptually with

flexible thinking. This tactic might have alerted dairy companies to beware of market losses to soft drinks or warned bread marketers that yogurt was a threat to the traditional lunchtime sandwich. The moral is know where to look for competition.

Source: Connie A. Cox, Cox, Lloyd Associates, Ltd., New York.

Common mistakes in decision making

Flaws in the way managers often make decisions:

• Making unncecssary decisions. All decisions involve risk. It can occasionally be wiser to leave well enough alone.

• Solving recurring problems each time they arise. Resolve them more permanently through new policies, procedures, or standing plans.

• Proposing unrealistic answers. Solutions are not evaluated in terms of cost. Sometimes grandiose schemes are evolved to solve simple problems.

• Delaying the decision. Moving quickly allows more time to correct the decision if it turns out wrong. And it frees the manager to tackle other problems.

Source: Don Caruth and Bill Middlebrook, Caruth Management Consultants, Carrollton, Tex., *Supervisory Management,* Saranac Lake, N.Y.

Problem solving made simple

The first step is to verify that a problem exists. Then, identify it. Many managers waste time setting elaborate problem-solving systems into motion without first verifying that there is a problem or knowing what it is.

For example, if late supplies are slowing production, the temptation is to complain to the supplier. However, before you do, visit the receiving dock to see whether the real problem is supplies arriving on time, but being unloaded late. Also, an inadequate truck entrance or outdated equipment is stalling operations.

The most obvious approach is often the best —when a problem arises, look into it quickly.

Source: Michael Sanderson, *Successful Problem Management,* John Wiley & Sons, New York.

Putting a proposal to the test

It's probably a good business proposal if all the answers to the following questions are yes.

• Do the suggested solutions fit the company's goals and strategies?

• Has the real problem been diagnosed?

• Do these suggestions fit the company's resources?

• Are the alternatives ones that top management is likely to accept?

Traps that inhibit problem solving

Would-be problem solvers often run into trouble because they:

• Cannot tolerate the ambiguity associated with a complex problem and believe all problems must be clear-cut.

• Stick to a preconceived belief and reinterpret inconsistent data to fit it.

• Hesitate to ask questions for fear of appearing ignorant.

• Give in to unrealistic anxiety about failing without systematically doing worst-case scenarios.

• Overemphasize aspects of the problem related to their field.

• Are too logical. Focus on a solution too quickly rather than spending more time analyzing the problem.

• Fail to break the rules. Rely only on tested solutions.

• Rely totally on scientific analysis and ignore common sense. Fail to seek an outside point of view.

Source: H.J. Brightman, *Problem Solving: A Logical and Creative Approach,* Georgia State University Press, Atlanta.

Protect yourself from secondhand information

Managers rarely have the time to validate personally the information they use to make decisions. But if they assume all the information they get from subordinates is sound, they will make critical errors. To validate information quickly and efficiently:

• Determine the original purpose for putting the data together. That purpose may be at odds with the one the information is wanted for now.

• Search for incompatible information within the document. Inconsistencies suggest the material was put together hastily and is unusable.

• Check out one part in detail, looking closely for inaccuracies.

Source: Neil R. Sweeney, *The Art of Managing Managers,* Addison-Wesley, Reading, Mass.

Avoid information overload

Strike a balance between asking for a copy of every report, letter, and memo and receiving only those that would have helped with last week's decisions.

First, identify needs:

• What decisions do I make regularly?

• How timely must the information be to make those decisions?

• What reports would have forewarned me of a recent unpleasant surprise?

Weed out nonessentials with one question: Which reports would I do without if I were charged for them?

Improve the value of the information:

• Specify critical information areas for fully detailed reports.

• For less critical information, improve timeliness and shorten reports by asking for a brief summary.

• When reports from different individuals or departments are inconsistent, the originator must explain the reason for the difference or reconcile it.

Source: Harold W. Fox, professor, Ball State University, Muncie, Ind.

When to make the decision alone

Consensus decision making is often a useful tool. But it can be a mistake when:

• The subordinates are not competent to assist in making the decision.

• The impact of the decision will be great, and the senior manager should have total responsibility for success or failure.

• The options are more or less equal in merit, and the decision can be made on the basis of personal preference.

• Hunches and past experience are the key elements. It is a mistake to water down a strong intuitive sense of what is right or wrong by taking others' opinions.

And individual decision making is faster.

Source: Ray J. Bronikowski, RTE Corporation, *Machine Design,* Cleveland, Ohio.

Group decision making

When a few individuals dominate group decision making, it is important, and often useful, to force participation by the rest. One way is a silent treatment that resembles secret balloting.

To do it, state the problem clearly and have the participants write down their own list of possible solutions, without revealing their identities. No talking is permitted during this exercise. This gives the more reticent group members an equal shot, which the open discussions (perhaps owing to protocol) had denied them.

Then the chairperson selects one idea from each list, records it on a flip-chart sheet, and opens up the meeting to verbal give-and-take on each idea's pros and cons. Finally, every member ranks the solutions, again in a no-talking written exercise, on a one-to-ten scale. After the votes are tallied, the idea with the highest cumulative score wins.

This system is truly participatory decision-making with intensive focus on a single important issue. And it brings about a group result, which is usually greater than the sum of its parts.

Remember, silence is the golden rule at two critical junctures. So the technique hinges on having a strong leader in the chair who can enforce it.

Source: William P. Anthony, Ph.D., *Participative Management*, Addison-Wesley, Reading, Mass.

Basics for a group problem solving session

• Encourage several definitions of the problem before driving toward a solution.

• Do not treat new problems as recurrences of old ones. Direct the group away from comments like "I remember how we handled that before."

• Discourage evaluation of ideas early in the meeting. Criticism inhibits creativity.

• Do not jump at the first good answer. Groups often try to finish their business quickly because unresolved problems create anxiety.

• Seek out dissent and minority opinions to avoid the common group-think trap.

Rules for forming a committee

There's no foolproof prescription for forming a successful committee. Some helpful suggestions which will point a committee in the right direction:

• Three or four members will function effectively. More means members won't feel personally responsible for results. Fewer limits the input.

• Assign definite responsibility to each member.

• Rotate membership on standing committees periodically. That provides a steady flow of ideas and breaks up stagnant thinking patterns.

• Balance membership between experienced employees and relative newcomers.

• Set goals. To solve a problem (rather than merely move it elsewhere), aim for specific results. A committee that isn't expected to produce a substantial result won't.

• Monitor progress. Review level of cooperation. A committee dominated by one member often produces insignificant results and frustrates other members.

• Set a time limit for work to be completed. Get periodic progress reports if the assignment is a multi-stage one.

If committee proposals are rejected, the reasons for that rejection should be explained carefully. If the proposals are accepted, they should be implemented promptly, so committee can see the effects of its efforts.

Making committees more productive

Even the best company committees fall into sloppy habits and become unproductive.

Key questions to ask:

• What is the committee's track record? Are its recommendations implemented?

• If the function of the committee has changed, should its size and composition be overhauled?

• Will a shift to longer, less frequent meetings make the committee more productive and less social?

• Should some newer employees join the committee?

• Do members receive an agenda far enough in advance of meetings to prepare themselves adequately?

• Is the right person establishing the committee's priorities?

Source: U. Merry and M.E. Allerhand, *Developing Teams and Organizations,* Addison-Wesley, Reading, Mass.

Making sure decisions are not made in isolation

Managers who delegate planning to a single, isolated group or task force, and then keep hands off until the final report, guarantee distorted decision making because the project or plan will be out of phase with ongoing functions of the company. It will lack input from managers closest to daily operations.

It is essential to subdivide the problems. Assign segments to different managers or groups to solve. Managers will understand that the effectiveness of their work is dependent on input from others and will read the input critically. This avoids assumptions made early in the process, which are too often accepted as facts.

For example, a budget review group is likely to work with the first sales projections it receives. It soon forgets to ask for alternatives. Or a capital review group will concentrate only on

financial results, out of context with other company needs.

Managers should also keep in touch with a project as it develops, to prevent subordinates from becoming so personally committed that they lose objectivity.

The best ways to keep in touch are to encourage both horizontal and vertical communication about the project. Whenever people need information from another area in the company, they should be able to get it promptly.

Also, integrate planning activities with the work of on-line executives. Encourage interaction. If judgments that define policy are not made by those accountable for results, they lack authority.

Top managers must train themselves to recognize the point at which an irrevocable decision is about to be made. If they think the decision is premature, they must be able to slow down the process.

Source: Pearson Hunt, professor emeritus, Harvard Business School, *Harvard Business Review of Human Relations,* Harper & Row, New York.

A hidden problem with committee decisions

When a committee chooses between two decisions, it generally picks the riskier one. Individuals given the same choice on tests usually choose the safer alternative.

Committees favor more risky actions because:

• No one person is responsible if the decision later turns out to be a poor one.

• Members who advocate risk are usually more influential in groups than conservative people.

• Group discussion tends to make the members more familiar with the pros and cons involved in reaching a decision, therefore the degree of risk seems diminished.

• Group pressure, a force of persuasive power, is often applied to those who oppose chancier moves.

Source: James A. Lee, *The Gold and the Garbage in Management Theories and Prescriptions,* Ohio University Press.

Brainstorming traps

While brainstorming remains a favorite corporate tool for problem-solving, its weaknesses may outweigh its strengths. Remember that brainstorming works best for relatively simple problems; produces a great many superficial ideas; limits quality of output because there is little time to digest and analyze ideas; requires a highly skilled leader to prevent a few individuals from hogging the session; and fails to provide individual priase for ideas generated.

Source: Arthur B. Van Gundy, *Techniques of Structured Problem-Solving,* Van Nostrand Reinhold, New York.

MANAGING A TROUBLED COMPANY

Ten reasons why new businesses go under

The ten most common mistakes made by the managers of new businesses are:

1. Going into a business with little or no experience, and without first learning anything about it.
2. Failing to keep complete and accurate records. Drifting slowly into trouble without being aware of it.
3. Plunging without first testing out ideas on a small scale.
4. Underpricing.
5. Underestimating the time it will take to build a market.
6. Underestimating the competition.
7. Too little capital.
8. Not allowing for inevitable setbacks and unexpected expenses.
9. Extending credit too freely.
10. Expanding too rapidly.

Source: *Sales Manager's Bulletin,* Bureau of Business Practice, Waterford, Conn.

Diversification can be dangerous to company health

Management errors that lead to unsound expansion or diversification are:

• A focus on short-term results at the expense of long-range development of existing operations.
• Discouragement with current performance or problems. Middle-size companies may try to imitate the acquisition strategies of better-financed companies.
• Overconfidence in the executive suite. When the company is doing well, management feels able to make any business succeed. Yet their experience is likely to be inadequate or nontransferable to other fields.
• Pressure of idle capacity in production facilities or underused marketing capabilities.

To keep the company on track, explore opportunities for expanding current activities before looking elsewhere. Determine the most promising sector and focus resources there if the scope of operations is already too broad. Don't let a downturn dictate a sweeping strategy change. The business may need a new marketing approach or increased productivity to remain competitive.

Executives who develop internal resources

creatively should be rewarded. Examples are finding new product depth in an established technical area or gaining market share in a given product or line.

Source: M.C. Lauenstein and W. Skinner, *The Journal of Business Strategy*, Warren, Gorham & Lamont, Boston.

Why reorganization is not the answer

"Professional" general managers tend to propose major reorganization as the solution for all corporate problems, ranging from lagging earnings to nagging operations failures, simply because reorganization is a convenient way to silence critics when management is under fire.

Despite this symbol of decisive action, chances are the organization will later revert to the same old patterns for the same reasons.

A good (as opposed to professional) general manager knows that reorganizations almost never deal with the real problems and that they wreak havoc with employees (as well as lining the pockets of management consultants).

Instead of making any drastic changes, the good general manager concentrates on making the present organization work. That may mean shifts in personnel or procedures, but these changes are almost never as traumatic as a major reorganization.

Source: H. Edward Wrapp, *Good General Managers Are Not Professional*, Graduate School of Business, University of Chicago.

Avoiding the most serious management mistakes

"Happiness is positive cash flow" should be printed in letters a foot high on the wall of every chief executive's office. Cash is the lifeblood of a corporation. Misunderstanding the importance of positive cash flow is by far the most serious management mistake. The most common error is spending earnings to build up more volume and to increase the share of the market. That's not necessarily wise. Ask the right questions first: Is the company increasing its share of the market with a profit? Or is it losing money with each dollar spent?

Another serious mistake is settling for second- or third-rate employees. You need top people and to get them you have to pay a fair price. Entrepreneurs who resist giving away part of their stock end up with stock not worth having. Chances for success of the enterprise increase tremendously when really first-rate talent is in place in each key area. There's a bonus here: top management talent in depth increases the value of the company when it is time to go public or merge.

A third mistake is the tendency of very bright people not to delegate enough. They are so good that they find it easier to do everything themselves. The best way to develop a good manager is to give him responsibility and then act almost as a management consultant for him. A still better approach is to teach him to become his own management consultant. Good managers learn to analyze their own problems as if they were sitting on the opposite side of the table.

Bright managers also spend too little time analyzing markets. Too often they are entrepreneurs in a hurry. They come up with a magnificent new product, but fail to recognize that the market for it is very limited. Failure occurs either because market research is weak, or they spend too much time and money coming up with products that are going to be small rather than taking aim on the major markets. Large markets create large opportunities; small markets create small opportunities. It's that simple.

Evaluating new product ideas is another mistake-prone area. Too often when a manager solicits opinions on a new idea, the inevitable result is a series of objections under the not-invented-here syndrome. A much better approach is to ask subordinates to prepare a one-page analysis of the new product idea, specifying exactly what's bad and what's good about it. Suggest that they start with what's bad, then advance to the good. Avoid presenting a new idea with a strong statement about how good you think it is. The listener's instinctive tendency is to back away. Present the alternatives dispassionately, and encourage the other person to make his own analysis.

Source: Frederick R. Adler, senior partner, Reavis & McGrath, New York.

When operations start to go downhill

Too many managers refuse to face the ugly reality that they are in a dying business. Even when it comes to phasing out a no-longer-profitable product or product line, many otherwise well-managed companies hang on for too long.

The worst offenders are plant or brand managers who recognize the trouble, but can't face giving up their own position or obsoleting loyal workers. Bad news is kept from top management as long as possible.

Even when management knows, however, it may elect to keep a bleeding operation going until the hemorrhage weakens the entire company The usual reasons are heavy previous investment, perhaps not yet fully depreciated; a big difference between book value and liquidation value; fear of image loss in the business community; emotional attachment to the line of business; feelings of responsibility to employees, suppliers, and customers; and fears of customer reprisals against other company products.

One well-managed company handles the problem by asking every manager to make an annual assessment on whether his operation should be continued or phased out. All managers are assured that there will be a place for them somewhere else in the company and that lower-level workers, too, will be retained, if necessary, retrained for other jobs with the company.

The key to intelligent management in a declining industry is to put in enough money so that the company's competitive position won't completely erode. But don't put in so much that the operation gobbles up cash. The best technique is to reward managers of troubled operations on a different basis. Put the incentive on reducing

cash required to run the operation instead of on profit margins or return on investment.

Perils of hanging on too long include: extreme price volatility as companies fight to maintain volume, (overcapacity is a common condition of declining industries); highly uneven financial results; waste of precious management time and talent; sterilization of assets that could be used productively; and a technology lag from which the company may never recover.

Once the decision has been made to abandon the operation, make the transition orderly. One way is to stop making a product, but buy it from a competitor to satisfy the company and customer needs temporarily.

Source: Dr. Kathryn Rudie Harrigan, assistant professor of business and social policy, University of Texas, Dallas.

Turning a company around before it fails

Many companies are prime candidates for turnaround management though they are not even aware of it. The major source of trouble is failure by chief executives or lending institutions to look beyond the bottom line each quarter. Earnings can appear healthy but mask a serious problem. Waiting for problems to surface dramatically is dangerous. The company may register a sales increase while actually losing ground competitively. Use trade-group figures to reckon the competitive position regularly. Be wary of government statistics: they are usually too late, are subject to political influence, and are assembled by inexperienced people.

The company may be using inventory and receivables to finance its operations, or tying up its fixed assets to negotiate a loan. With today's high interest rates, banks are protecting themselves by gathering in more and more of the assets of their customers. This ruins management's flexibility to turn around a company.

The company may be borrowing from the future by failing to replace capital equipment on a scale that relates reasonably to the depreciation being claimed for tax purposes. Make a three- to five-year plan for plant maintenance and reinvestment.

The following are danger signals:

• In-house board of company managers. It won't challenge the CEO. He is cast in the impossible role of omnipotent god.

• No management succession plan. If one person effectively dominates the operation, the company will suffer from lack of leadership at some future date. The older the kingpin, the sooner the day of reckoning.

• No clear idea of the company's basic business. Too often, as growth slows and profits begin to erode, management is tempted into unrelated acquisitions. The choice is not always wise. The new lines divert management from facing the real problems in the core business, and things go from bad to worse.

To stop the slide and restore the company to profitability:

• Stop everything. Make contact with all lenders and litigants. Ask for time to assess a turnaround plan.

• Develop a team that includes everyone with an interest in the situation: directors (in the last analysis, problems are probably their fault), managers, employees, banks, suppliers, technical groups, unions.

• Communicate clearly with everyone, down to the janitor. Tell them exactly where things stand, how the company got there, and what will be done to get the company out of danger. Be confident. Calm any panic that emerges. Employees who are kept in the dark or frightened will usually jump ship. Without them, rescue may be difficult or impossible.

• Review all assets, human and material.

• Get a short-term plan into operation as soon as possible. Day by day, as the company survives, there will be new options and greater maneuverability. Never go in with a preconceived blueprint. Stay flexible.

• Create a war room. Use specific charts to show short-term goals and where the company stands minute by minute. Create a place where turnaround team members can walk in at any time and see just how they are doing (or where they are not performing fast enough). Performance charts should be very specific: Reduce receivables from 72 days to 60 days. Extend payables from 60 to 90 days.

• Be available seven days a week, at all hours,

for 90–100 days. This is the critical life-or-death period.

• Be willing to amputate fast, close the wound, and march on.

There are not many people who can step into a troubled company and guide it toward profitability again. Business schools are not equipping MBAs with turnaround-management skills. Banks are a good place to get help, but company managers frequently hesitate to tell their bankers about their difficulties until things have reached a desperate point. Try asking another bank, perhaps one in another city. Watch the business press for stories of successful turnarounds, and keep names on file. Don't rely on management consultants or executive recruiters to do the job.

Source: John Boudreau, head, Classic Chemicals, Inc., Arlington, Tex.

Where to spend the R&D dollars

Research and development dollars should be spent on (1) improving existing product quality, (2) reducing existing product cost, or (3) bringing out new products. That order of priority generally produces greatest return on investment.

If a company has poor quality in existing lines, that's strong evidence that something is wrong. Getting into a new product line without first getting existing lines in order just spreads the trouble.

Source: Dr. Sidney Schoeffler, director, Strategic Planning Institute, Cambridge, Mass.

Seven questions for managers in turbulent times

1. What kind of planning are they doing? Is it outdated? Does it simply extend present trends into the future? Is it relevant? Can it foresee

coming basic changes that will affect the company? The way to begin relevant planning is to determine what is of value to the company's customers, and to predict what will be of value to them in ten years.

2. What is the company now doing to improve productivity? Companies should be aiming, in general, to double the productivity of capital by 1990, and also to produce 50% more, without increasing their work force.

3. What is the greatest danger to the company? Is it the public's hostility to business? Environmental constraints? Overzealous government regulation? Or is it a deterioration in the company's execution of business fundamentals? Often, it's the business fundamentals.

4. What will it cost the company to stay in business between now and 1990? Only after these costs have been completely calculated, can a company begin to think about profits.

5. What working capital does the company need to withstand a panic or a credit crunch? It should have sufficient liquidity to withstand a crisis lasting 120 days. Even dire crises tend to shake down within this time.

6. What old responsibilities has top management sloughed off or abandoned? It's important to make room for significant new responsibilities. One of the greatest dangers to effective management leadership is a diffusion of energies.

7. Is the marketing strategy of the company directed toward becoming the industry's leader? Or to carve out a noncompetitive niche? If the company's marketing strategy is neither of the above, then management should reexamine its goals.

Source: Peter F. Drucker, *Management in Turbulent Times,* Harper & Row, New York.

Keeping up morale during bad times

Keeping enthusiasm and optimism afloat during recession depends on how the boss reacts to the worsening situation.

• Work hard and insist employees follow suit.

• Keep regular hours. Avoid long lunches and short days.

• Keep up physical appearances. Insist that employees come to work dressed for business.

• Design projects and training programs to prepare for an inevitable pickup in business.

• Praise employees enthusiastically for jobs well done. Delay criticisms until conditions (and morale) get better.

Source: George S. Odiorne, *The 100 Toughest Management Questions,* Westfield, Mass.

Making use of recession opportunities

There's virtually no way management can avoid a revenue slowdown if its markets are hit by recession, but it is possible to plan ahead to minimize the impact. An essential precondition is a detailed understanding of product costs. The better control a company has over its costs, the more it will be able to take advantage of opportunities that accompany economic downturns. Equally essential are an effective cash-management system, and strong inventory controls.

Product lines and services that appear relatively recession-proof should be identified. For example, while consumers aren't buying new cars, automotive dealers build up their business in used cars, spare parts, and service. There are parallel cushioning tactics for virtually every business.

Think of recession as a time to make investments in the company's future. Economic downturns are often the best time to purchase real estate, for example. And many hungry contractors will bid to give the company a good price on needed new facilities. Use the slowdown for preventive maintenance of existing equipment and facilities, too.

Overall strategy consists of reexamining all costs from the ground up, putting a priority rank on every company expenditure, and cutting budgets in areas where the company can't afford to spend or where potential return on investment does not measure up to other opportunities.

Marketing. Trim unnecessary advertising and promotion expenditures, but be prepared now to spend aggressively in areas that will produce future revenues and profits. If competitors are cutting their sales forces, for example, this may be the time to expand the product's share of market so that the company comes out of the recession in a stronger position than it had going in.

Purchasing. Look closely at all long-term commitments with suppliers. Recession offers a golden opportunity to renegotiate and get a better price or more favorable terms on future orders.

Personnel. If the company was not operating lean going into the recession, this is a perfect time to upgrade the work force. More talent is available during a soft economy, and wages are not being bid up by competing companies. Recession provides management with an opportunity to reexamine expensive perks that may have built up in easier times. (If too many people are driving company cars, for example, the list could be cut back without offending. The staff realizes that times are rough.)

Overhead. Wholesale reductions often hurt more than help a company. Be selective. Thoughtful cuts can free up cash to take advantage of the inevitable recession opportunities to buy low and sell at a profit later.

Source: Patterson Krisher, director of management services, Arthur Young & Co., New York.

• Hiring outside contractors to do cleaning, alterations, drafting, landscape maintenance, etc.
• Reviewing decisions to make or buy.
• Leasing rather than buying property or equipment.
• Using public warehouses and common carriers rather than company-owned space and vehicles.
• Changing sales compensation to commission only.

Less integration of the company's operations reduces unit costs during adverse times. The program also allows management to focus its attention and resources on problems critical to profitability.

The company does lose control over the costs it transfers outside. Be wary of transferring to a supplier elements of value added that are critical to long-term competitive advantage. Another possible disadvantage is the replacement cost of fixed assets, should the company decide to reintegrate operations.

Source: Mark Particelli, vice president, Booz, Allen & Hamilton, Inc., Chicago.

Cut fixed costs to increase market share

Most economists predict continued inflation, slow growth, and frequent, though unpredictable downturns for the 1980s. In such a climate, companies that manage costs and margins to anticipate adverse business conditions will be better able to buy market share from struggling competitors.

To keep margins from being squeezed in a weak, highly variable economy, concentrate on reducing the company's fixed costs. Consider:

• Replacing in-house departments with purchased services.
• Selling through commissioned agents.
• Covering the poorest sales territories with manufacturers' reps.

Three ways to cut overhead costs

1. Require overhead departments and divisions (accounting, data processing, engineering, marketing, etc.) to work with the departments they serve to jointly develop cost-reduction ideas. Encourage them to break big, high-risk ideas into smaller, safer ones.

2. Concentrate on reducing workload, even if that means cutting only fractions of jobs. Later, combine the remaining fractions into whole positions.

3. Ask managers of all overhead departments to submit proposals for gradually cutting their budgets by at least 40%. Forcing managers to think radically encourages breakthrough cost reductions.

To really cut unnecessary overhead, don't rely on improving efficiency within overhead departments. Two thirds of overhead waste comes from what the overhead department promises to do for others (and how often), not from how it gets done.

Source: John Neuman, principal, McKinsey & Co., consultants, New York.

A rule of thumb for designing the organization

Strong one-person rule is feasible and most efficient when sales are under $3 million. When the company reaches the $3–$10 million range, delegate real authority to middle-managers. Decentralize the organization at the $10–$30 million level. When the company tops $30 million, an additional shift is indicated. Move toward more formalized departmental planning, the use of cost and profit centers, and increase the quality of objective performance ratings.

Four ways to keep a growth company growing

1. Manage for cash flow, not for paper profits.
2. Look and think beyond the profit-and-loss statement and balance sheet to the way the company's markets are changing. Ask "Where are sales coming from?"
3. Avoid diversification moves that spread the company thinly over unfamiliar ground. They may gratify the owner's ego, but seldom do they satisfy the company's growth needs.
4. Hire senior managers whose strengths are greatest in markets or operational areas where the founding hierarchy is weakest.

Source: M.H. Broudy, management consultant, Baxter, Broudy, Pompan & Storr, Greenwich, Conn.

Warning signs for the growing company

CEOs of small but growing companies tend to spend too much time fighting fires and too little time reflecting and planning. As a result, internal inefficiencies start to sap profits and plunge the company into deep trouble, despite strong sales.

The executive should stay alert for warning signals that indicate problems far more serious than the immediate one, then attack the cause, not the effect.

Signs of growing trouble:

• A bank questioning or delaying an otherwise routine loan.
• Regularly exceeding, ignoring, or never getting around to putting together a corporate budget.
• Accounts payable slipping from 30 days to 90 days.
• Accounts receivable taking a sudden jump upward. (Steadily increasing is dangerous, too.
• Poor or unenforced inventory controls, particularly when coupled with excessive stock on hand.
• Buying on demand, rather than in quantity, or shopping around.
• Excessive scrap, frequent jam-ups, erratic work flow, or idle machinery on production lines.
• Increasing complaints about late shipments, or sudden demands for rush orders.
• Dropping, curtailing, or forgetting production supervisor training.
• Vague answers to simple production questions, such as How long will it take? or How many can be produced in a day?
• Increasing labor costs when calculated as a percentage of sales.
• Sloppy estimating that is revealed by unexplained fluctuations in orders for established products with tight profit margins.
• Discovering that sales reps are being paid excessive commissions by industry norms.
• Insurance brokers who recommend the insurer or program that pays higher commissions over the one that provides more efficient coverage. Counter by using an accounting firm to review the policy. And if the company's accounting

firm is too small to provide expert advice, pay a fee to an expert in a larger firm for an opinion.

• A trusted lawyer because the opportunities for conflict are still great. Lawyers make money in the hours spent on company business. Simple solutions do not pay for them. Or, their advice can be too cautious. It keeps the lawyer from making a mistake, but it may divert the company from a great opportunity. Counter by using one lawyer or law firm for the day-to-day business of the company. But also keep in close touch with another smart lawyer. Pay that lawyer a fee to have lunch with you occasionally. Talk over problems in a relaxed atmosphere. Try out the ideas and advice of others on that lawyer.

The second grim reality about advice is that it is never totally relevant to the company's needs. The only people who can put the pieces of advice together are managers who filter the advice through their understanding of the company's unique position, personality, financial situation, etc.

An essential tactic for dealing with advice givers is to push them to explain the risks and probability of success.

The test of thoughtful advice: Experts volunteer the limits of their knowledge. They say:

• When I say this, I am certain.
• When I say this, I am less certain.
• When I say this, it is pure speculation on my part.
• There are other experts who disagree with me, and they would have this view of the problem.

Understanding these limits is especially important when the advice comes from professionals who stray from their area of authority: The lawyer giving investment advice. The banker rating a market opportunity.

A somewhat sad caution about advice is the closer the business associates, the more cautious a manager should be about accepting their advice. There are great values in long, close business relationships. The level of mutual trust is high. The danger is that manager and adviser adapt so well to each other that the advice-giver accepts as a given what really should be challenged.

Ironically the best outside adviser may resist getting too close to management. Pick up those signals, and don't be insistent.

For example, the chief executive of a fast-growing company has just opened a line of credit with a new bank. Everything is going according to projections. But the chief executive thinks it would be good to know the young banker better. He invites him to lunch. The banker accepts, and then breaks the date. They set another date, fairly far into the future. The chief executive is angry. But there may be a message here: I have to make decisions about you and your company. Don't get too close.

Executives at the top need a relationship with advisers they can trust. But as relationships strengthen, managers may get only reflections of their own ideas or vested interests rather than fresh ones.

One possible solution is to combine closeness with distance by building a network of advisers. Use all the critical intelligence on major problems and opportunities in the business. Put their collective experience to work. Try the ideas and solutions offered by one expert on a specialist from another area of business. By keeping the flow of ideas open, the best top managers make sound decisions. And they avoid most of the major traps of vested interest.

Source: Dr. Leonard R. Sayles, professor of management, Columbia University Graduate School of Business.

GETTING ADVICE

Vested-interest traps

No one gives the top manager of a company advice about the business that isn't somehow affected by a vested interest. That's a grim truth. But understanding it is essential as the manager sorts through reports, ideas, and recommendations from company insiders, outside consultants and lawyers, accountants, bankers, suppliers, and customers.

The specific interest is often hard to detect. Even the person giving the advice doesn't always distinguish between advice that is selfishly motivated and that which is sincerely designed to be helpful.

So put the vested interest on the table. Suggest the conflict if it is apparent. But if it isn't, search it out. Ask what commitments, loyalties, or interests the adviser may have.

Whom to be wary of:

• Professionals with a favorite hobbyhorse. (Academics call it a dominant paradigm.) The greatest dangers are outside consultants, who view virtually all problems from a single vantage point.

• Longtime customers who learn so much about the company's operations that they become competitors by producing the products they once bought.

• Bankers who may push loans when they really aren't essential. And who may set terms that are not as good as are available elsewhere. The company can't change its bank often. But banks too often change the banker who deals with a customer, interrupting normal development of a solid relationship.

• Valued suppliers who try to unload obsolete or less-than-best inventory, and do not explain this maneuver or offer a special rate.

• Major customers and suppliers who detect from the questions asked of them a major shift in the company's strategy before management is ready to tell them.

• Key employees who push for company growth in directions that will enhance their own salaries and personal goals. Check if the growth makes sense at this time and whether the company can profit from a pause.

• Advertising agencies that make more money when the company spends more on ads. But fixed-fee contracts are no easy solution. Then the agency profits from doing as little as possible, and the company may suffer from insufficient advertising.

Selecting the right board of directors

Prestige and financial connections should not be the main criteria in choosing members of a company board of directors. What is essential in selecting a board member:

• Important technical experience. Also, the breadth and wisdom to help make critical decisions, evaluate current performance, and set goals.

• Sufficient commitment to undertake some assignments besides attending scheduled board meetings. Among the most useful are broadening the company's contacts, getting additional experience and knowledge from others, and reviewing managers' reports.

• Enough identification with the organization to care about its future.

• A sensitive relationship with the company's chief executive. The board member must be strong enough to be critical of top management's proposals, and to do so in a way perceived as constructive.

• Personality skills that allow productive interaction with other board members so that meetings are efficient and effective.

A useful board must develop annual self-rating procedures, not unlike those used to measure managers' performance, to assure itself that current board members deserve to be renominated.

An outside director must quiz the experts

A primary responsibility of the outside corporate director is to act as a watchdog over the company's operation. Doing this properly requires close questioning of outside auditors and lawyers about their assessments of the company's weaknesses.

During executive-board sessions (when management is out of the room), ask the accountants about:

• Their biggest area of concern. This provides useful early warning of emerging problems.

• Where they had their biggest disagreement with the company's accounting personnel. This can lead to discussions with a significant impact on reported financial results.

Directors should ask for an assurance from all outside experts that:

• They are being told all they should know.

• The experts have made a reasonable effort to investigate everything they should.

• The directors are acting properly in relation to what they have been told.

The best rule to follow is not to do anything as a director that would be embarrassing to explain on TV. This simple rule is a better test of legality than conforming with current legal requirements, because it anticipates the way the law is moving.

Source: Arjay Miller, dean emeritus, Stanford University Business School, *The Week in Review,* Deloitte Haskins & Sells, New York.

Why it's important to serve on outside boards

Despite the oft-repeated warnings that serving on outside boards of directors is a waste of time and fraught with legal perils, there are real advantages to be gained by sitting on boards. One of the most important is exchanging ideas with top people in the business world. Another consideration is that boards of directors have a real role to play in insuring the health of the business community and the country as a whole by helping management set style, advising them on their responsibilities to shareholders, customers and employees.

What companies get from directors varies with the size of the company. Small companies generally need from directors advice which big companies generally do not need. (Paying a director's fee is a very inexpensive way for a company to obtain skills and expertise of high order.) Other aids are introductions to the right banks, and the best lawyers and accountants. And, advice on how to get the most from each of them. Members of boards have fairly frequent contact with the company's chief executive in addition to the regular directors meetings (which may be four to eight times a year). Company heads always want to know what board members are thinking.

More important than fees to a really good director is the quality of the board. A company which offers a board with a strong leader, whom everyone wants to talk to, is the best compensation. Fees are usually not less than $5,000 a year, though directors will often serve for less. Decent pay is symbolic of the regard for the director's advice. As a rule of thumb, good people (serious, substantial business leaders) seldom stay on boards that don't take their advice.

Another aspect to consider is the problem of picking a board. Picking board members who seem to be "independent" may be a mistake. It's a mistake to think that the "academician" or "admiral" who sits on a board for a fee of $15,000, perhaps a quarter of his annual income, is likely to be a more independent board member than the businessman making $300,000.

Who can profit most by being on a board? People at the top of their organizations. They're seldom well informed by those working for them. Subordinates usually tell the boss what they think he wants to hear. Being on boards provides contact with fresh, independent points of view that shed valuable light on one's own enterprises.

Source: Mark N. Kaplan, partner, Skadden, Arps, Slate, Meagher & Flom, New York.

Advisory board members are customarily paid annual retainers, sometimes with stock options. Occasional meetings at a resort can be another tax-free incentive.

Source: Dr. Leonard R. Sayles, professor of management, Columbia University Graduate School of Business.

The benefits of using advisory boards

When top managers need advice, criticism, or an easy exchange of ideas, they usually turn to their board of directors or outside consultants. An alternative is an advisory board that, though less frequently used, can provide valuable company input.

Advisory boards are often superior to boards of directors for this input, since they do not have the directors' legal responsibilities and their decisions won't affect the tenure of management. Their commitment and continuity make them more effective generally than consultants.

Chief executives need diverse, trusted sources of information who are not dependent on them for salary or promotion. The counsel of insiders is inevitably biased by their economic stake in the president's decisions. Outsiders on contract have a stake, too, but not an overriding one.

Technology-oriented companies regularly use advisory boards composed of top university scientists. Multinationals use such boards to help them deal with distant economic and political climates. Small- and medium-sized companies should consider advisory boards whose members can provide advice for solving their specific problems.

In virtually all communities, there are retired executives, engineers, business-school professors, and self-employed professionals who can be challenged by a commitment to the welfare of a company. After they spend time interacting with each other and senior management, their sense of responsibility usually heightens.

When and how to hire consultants

The biggest mistake clients make is thinking they already know what their problem is. The tip-off is that the client, though he claims to understand his problem, has not been able to solve it.

What the client should do:

• Exchange information with the consultant so he can diagnose the problem for himself. In many cases, the problem turns out to be different than the client thinks it is.

• Recognize that there are no problem-free solutions to anything. A good consultant will try to point out what some of the new problems brought on by the new solution may be.

• Make sure the proposed solution is within the capability of company managers to implement. A weak organization cannot handle a sophisticated solution.

• Have the consultant help implement his solution because the consultant's special skill is the application of the best theoretical solutions to practical situations.

Consultants are of special value because of their industry expertise, independence, objectivity, and ability to transfer workable techniques from one industry to another. But don't use a consultant for industry expertise alone. There's great benefit to a diverse industry background.

Retain a consultant to:

• Gauge the feasibility of a new idea.

• Confront a problem that may require a redirection of corporate strategy. (For example, a significant loss of market share.)

• Solve a specific problem, or fill a special technical need on a limited basis.

Rules for judging good consultants:

1. They should make good business sense.
2. They shouldn't promise anything in the initial meeting.
3. The client should feel comfortable with them.
4. The person who calls on the client ought to be the consultant who will do the work.

Good consultants can be found through referrals from business friends. The Institute of Management Consultants, an accrediting association, can direct companies to reputable consultants.

Consultants ought to be able to give a reasonably accurate projection of the price tag and the time required to diagnose and solve a problem. It's a good idea to have the consultant project the cost in phases. Phase one for diagnosis; phase two for training managers to implement the solution; phase three for execution. After each phase is completed, the consultant should project the cost of the next phase. If the solution is long term, have the consultant give a new estimate every other month. By working in phases, the client is able to keep the cost of the solution in proportion to the magnitude of the problem.

And, a consultant should never be allowed to commit a client's money without approval.

Source: John C. Shaw, head, New York office, Touche Ross & Co.

How to save money on consultants

Some companies gird themselves for recession by cutting off all outside help. A better strategy is to negotiate to cut the consultant's costs. Now is the time the company may need the consultant.

To start, "hire" the company's own employees to work with the consultant.

Before signing a contract, ask the consultant for a detailed proposal of the services to be performed, including a breakdown of how the consultant expects to spend his time. This way you will pay for the consultant's expertise but avoid having an expensive staff collect routine data

and figures that the company's own people could readily provide.

Then, take the consultant's detailed proposal to the company's managers and ask which tasks could be performed by their subordinates. Go back to the consultant and negotiate to remove as much work as possible and reduce the fee accordingly.

For example, many times, consulting firms are engaged to gather data for decision-making. Frequently, much of that data is internal. In fact, employees often complain that consultants are being paid for presenting information that they themselves supplied or could have supplied.

If a consultant is someone the company needs badly for either his independence or his special expertise, leverage will be somewhat weaker.

Next, take a hard look at peripheral areas (copying, typing, telephone charges). See how much of this could be done on company equipment and regular staff time as opposed to having it billed (with a markup) by the consultant. Try to renegotiate the proposed fee without these ancillary costs.

With staff participation, employees develop a stake in the work, veiwing it as a joint effort instead of something imposed from the outside. Assigning the company's own employees to work under a consultant's direction gives valuable training to the company's people (rather than the consultant's), and it provides a constructive way to take up slack time.

Source: Norman Kobert, *Inventory Strategies,* Boardroom Books, Millburn, N.J.

Using a consultant more productively

How to choose a consultant:
• Suggest that the prospective consultant provide a list of his last six clients, then check them out. Some key questions to ask the references: Was the project completed on time? What was the consultant's style? Would you use

the consultant again? What were his strengths and weaknesses? How long has the client-consultant relationship been in existence?

• Talk with the prospective consultant at length. But note that many consultants have an observation fee, which covers the cost of the hours spent with prospective clients.

• When the consultant gives speeches to industry groups, arrange to listen to a couple. Or, if that's not possible, obtain copies of the speech.

Once a consultant is selected:

• Make up an informal contract, defining what is expected of each party. Even penciled memo notes can serve as an informal contract. If the project is an involved one, establish a more formal exchange of letters to define meetings, agendas, content, timetables and fees.

• Make all relevant company information available to the consultant. Where confidentiality is an issue for competitive or other reasons, structure a secrecy agreement that holds the consultant accountable.

• Be careful when introducing the consultant to company managers. Managers may be suspicious of the consultant's function vis-a-vis their roles and missions.

• Evaluate the consultant's effectiveness by questioning managers. Don't worry about some negative responses. Be objective about the vested interests of those making the criticisms.

Source: David Yoho, president, David Yoho Associates/Surfa-Shield Institute, Fairfax, Va.

LEGAL BRIEFS FOR THE MANAGER

Getting the most out of lawyers

You get out of a relationship what you put into it. Some executives view lawyers strictly as technicians, and that's precisely what they get. Lawyers who feel challenged and consider themselves part of the business will be much more productive. Lawyers who know what's going on can keep management abreast of related opportunities and traps in the legal and regulatory worlds. New laws and court decisions present new opportunities for business.

Executives and lawyers should consult one another regularly. The more complicated the business, the more frequent consultations should be. Companies in highly regulated industries need heavy contact with their lawyers. So do firms that are growing fast through acquisitions.

If the company's legal work is being handled by an outside full-service law firm, executives should know both the lawyer and the assistants in different departments who work on the company's account.

A sound rule is to contact the lawyer as soon as there's an inkling of a problem.

If a company has enough specialized legal work to keep someone busy full time, it ought to consider internalizing that function. Legal staffing should be appropriate for the size and type of business.

Some legal services are generally not best covered by the big, full-service firms. Trademarks and patents, admiralty law, labor law, the plaintiff side of negligence, divorce should be handled by a specialty firm.

It's best to let the full-service lawyer recommend and work with the specialist. A good lawyer will be a better judge of the specialist's legal skills. The two lawyers may already have a comfortable relationship.

Source: Mark N. Kaplan, partner, Skadden, Arps, Slate, Meagher & Flom, New York.

More protection for lawyer-company confidences

The realm of confidentiality between a company's employees and the company lawyer has been greatly expanded by a Supreme Court decision. The immediate impact is less opportunity for the Internal Revenue Service to prowl for tax information amid data the company lawyers gather from low-level employees for another purpose. And now company lawyers are freer to make investigations within the company in preparation for private antitrust actions or accident and injury cases.

The Upjohn Co. management initiated an internal investigation, conducted by its general counsel, to uncover evidence of illegal payments to foreign-government officials. The company filed reports on its findings with the Securities and Exchange Commission and the IRS.

The IRS decided it needed more information to determine how the illegal payments affected the company's tax liability. So it issued a summons to the company ordering it to hand over all the questionnaires filled out by employees, plus notes taken by company lawyers during the employee interviews.

The situation was further complicated by the fact that courts in different parts of the country had adopted different rules to govern this type of situation. The two interpretations:

• Control-group rule. The attorney-client privilege exists only between the company lawyer and key executives who are in a position to direct corporate actions.

• Subject-matter rule. The privilege exists between the lawyer and any employee, if certain other conditions are met.

In Upjohn's case, the lower courts applied the control-group rule. Since the interviews and questionnaires were directed at lower-level employees, the company was ordered to produce the papers. It appealed.

The Supreme Court ruled for Upjohn saying the control-group test was too narrow. By making information obtained from lower-level employees disclosable, it could make them unwilling to talk to the company lawyer. That could hinder the lawyer's ability to get information needed to give sound legal advice.

Dealing with the legal department

In-house lawyers are no longer automatic company partisans. Some government agencies are pushing them into becoming enforcers of regulations. So be more guarded in discussing sensitive matters with in-house attorneys. Be ready to turn to outside counsel more frequently.

Source: Detlev F. Vagts, Harvard Law School, *Harvard Business Review,* Boston.

Get a legal audit

Many companies have potential legal liabilities that can be identified through a legal audit and corrected before they become problems. The audit tyically takes two to five days and reviews the company's agreements, procedures, files and published materials. Key managers are interviewed. The cost is $4,000 and up.

Common problems discovered by a legal audit:

• Lack of notations on the front of sales order forms regarding additional information on the back. Customers may claim the material on the back doesn't apply since they weren't informed of it.

• Failure to print warranty disclaimer language in boldfaced type, as required by the Uniform Commercial Code. This negates the disclaimers.

• Prices quoted to customers without an indication that they apply for 30 days only. Customers may claim the quoted rate months later.

Source: Gilbert Kruger, partner, Malcolm & Daly, Newport Beach, Calif.

Identifying legal traps

Make sure the following are reviewed regularly to identify problems or potential problems:

• Company organization. Ownership, trade names, business locations, charter, and bylaws.

• Board of directors. Members, committees, power of board, election and proxy procedures.

• Standard forms. Compliance with government regulations. Are they worded for the company's advantage?

• Financial data. Real property (owned and leased), intangible property (including patents), copyrights, trade secrets, goodwill.

• Financial accounting. Do accounting methods meet standards? What security is held against debts?

• Business operations. Licenses, insurance, product liability.

• Labor. Employee benefit plans, compliance with wage-and-hour laws, affirmative action programs, occupational-safety regulations.

Source: Robert Shafton, Tyre & Kamins, Los Angeles.

Product liability losses

A product made today must be safe for reasonably foreseeable misuse and abuse.

To reduce the risk of being sued, find out who actually uses the product. They may not be the buyers. Parents buy products for children, for example. And try to identify all possible misuses of the product. Courts have been very strict on this. If problems turn up, decide whether to redesign the product, add a warning label or discontinue it.

As an example, ladder manufacturers are frequently sued by peole who stand on the top step and fall off. The manufacturers' choices are to: add a telescoping hand rest for people to hold when on the top step, draw up a warning label not to stand on the top, or stop making ladders.

Warning labels are not required if the danger is inherent in the correct use. No warning is needed on matches saying they can start fires. Essential warning: keep matches out of the reach of children.

If legal action by a product user seems possible:

• Try to obtain an exact sample of the product that was involved in the accident at once. By the time the case gets to court, the product might be unobtainable. Examine it to see how the accident occurred.

• Notify the insurance carrier. It will investigate even when there is only the possibility of a claim.

• Use the information to alter the product or to revise the warning label. The plaintiff's lawyer will try to use the improvement to show that the company was negligent or the product was defective if the lawyer can show the improvement was feasible before the accident. Otherwise, improvements made after an accident may not be used as evidence of the manufacturer's liability.

Where to find experts:

• Human-factors engineers evaluate products in terms of how people are likely to use them. Call the psychology or engineering departments of local universities. Or use the *Human Factors Society Directory and Yearbook,* Human Factors Society, Box 1369, Santa Monica, Calif. 90406.

• Safety engineers apply scientific principles to protect people and property. They can be found through the American Society of Safety Engineers, 850 Busse Highway, Park Ridge, Ill. 60068.

Source: William Kimble, Esq., Lesher, Kimble & Rucker, Tucson, Ariz.

Consumer use of arbitration

Consumer complaints are being settled more often out of court, using the arbitration services of the Council of Better Business Bureaus. Independent panels in local communities resolve disputes that deal mainly with big-ticket items such as cars, major appliances, and building materials.

The drawback from the corporation's point of view is that decisions are binding on companies but not on consumers.

Source: Council of Better Business Bureaus, Arlington, Va.

Keeping company secrets

The Freedom of Information Act (FOIA) has given the public greater access to documents of all government agencies, including the Securities Exchange Commission. Competitive confidential data that the SEC might otherwise keep secret may now become publicly available.

How to minimize SEC leaks:

• When turning information over to the agency, separate the confidential portions and mark each page confidential.

• Include with the material a letter asking that the confidential pages not be turned over in reply to a request under the FOIA.

• Send a copy of the letter to the SEC's FOIA officer.

Companies that follow this procedure will have a chance to object before the SEC decides whether to grant or deny an FOIA request for the material. If the objection is turned down, the company can lodge a formal appeal with the agency. If the appeal fails, the SEC gives companies 10 days to initiate court action before it divulges the material.

Arguments against disclosure should include: evidence that disclosure will seriously harm the business; proof that the company has worked diligently in the past to keep the information secret; and convincing testimony that releasing the data publicly will make it difficult for the company to report similar information in the future.

Showing that the company is serious about guarding its secrets may pave the way for a compromise under which some data is released and the request for more information is withdrawn.

Limiting directors' liabilities

The directors of a corporation are vulnerable to shareholder lawsuits in the event of management wrongdoing. The fact that the directors were unaware of the wrongdoing because they believed what management told them is no defense. Federal securities laws require due diligence in monitoring and supervising company affairs. Directors must be active and independent to ensure that the corporation is run for the benefit of its public shareholders, not for a select group of insiders.

To limit directors' potential liability:

• Hold regular board meetings, at least nine times a year. They should be scheduled a year in advance so that directors can build them into their schedules. All major policy decisions should be discussed openly and candidly at these meetings.

• Establish systematic communications between management and the board. Management should provide the board with regular written reports on its activities. And there should be a way for individual board members to get in touch with key management personnel.

• Form independent committees of outside directors to review hiring policies, compensation practices and auditing procedures.

• Hire outside experts to advise the directors on investment decisions and litigation as well as other complex matters.

• Ensure timely public disclosure of all facts that might have a significant impact on the company's earnings—lawsuits, acquisitions, new-product development.

• Pay directors adequately to compensate them for the greater responsibility they must assume. Otherwise, it may prove impossible to find good people willing to take on the burden.

Source: Mortimer Caplin, former commissioner of the Internal Revenue Service, head, Caplin and Drysdale, Washington, D.C.

Insider sales

An officer-stockholder is usually free to sell his stock without informing the company or giving other stockholders a chance to sell, too. But some courts have held that if the sale delivers a controlling interest in the company, that's more than individual property, it's a corporate asset. Some of the profits may have to be turned over to the company.

Source: 376 NE 2d 1211.

Effects of patent law

For years, more than half the patents challenged in court were declared invalid. The patent reform law that went into effect in December 1980 is expected to change that.

The reform bill allows members of the public to challenge a patent's validity without going to court. An individual can now ask that a patent be returned to the Patent Office for reexamination.

If the Patent Office decides the patent is valid, the administrative decision is final. But the challenger may still go to court if accused of infringing the patent.

If the Patent Office decides that the patent may be invalid, the holder can appeal in court. Then, the challenger is not even a party to the appeal.

A likely result is that courts will be less willing to declare patents invalid after the Patent Office has reexamined and approved them.

While in the past patent challengers have held the upper hand in patent infringement suits, now patent holders may be more favorably positioned.

So patent all technology that might conceivably be proprietary. The law is likely to make challenges to any patents, even patents on weak technology, more difficult. The more patents a firm holds on essential products or processes, the better its strategic position.

Source: Mary Helen Sears, partner, Irons & Sears, Washington, D.C.

Suing the government

A law went into effect in October 1981 making it easier to recover the cost of litigation against the government. The Equal Access to Justice Act (PL 96-481) provides for the award of legal expenses to any party that wins a case against the U.S., as either plaintiff or defendant.

Covered by the act are court cases and adversary administrative proceedings in which the government is represented by counsel. Tax Court cases and the IRS appellate procedures are included.

Recoverable expenses:
• Attorney's fees up to $75 an hour.
• Fees paid to expert witnesses (at a rate not exceeding the highest rate for witnesses paid by the Internal Revenue Service).
• Reasonable costs of any study, analysis or report necessary to prepare the case.

Limitations:
• Expenses won't be awarded when a case brought by the government is substantially justified, even though the government loses. Or when special circumstances would make an award unjust. This means that expenses won't be paid when the government loses its case on a technicality.
• No awards will be made to individuals with a net worth of over $1 million, or to businesses with either 500 employees or a net worth of over $5 million.

Dealing with the unsafe-job protester

The U.S. Supreme Court left some loopholes when it approved the Occupational Safety and Health Administration's regulations forbidding punishment of employees who refuse to perform allegedly unsafe jobs:
• The fear of injury must be bona fide. There must be an objective basis to believe there is a danger beyond the normal job hazards.

• The court's ruling does not sanction wildcat stoppages or the closing of an entire plant because one job may be unsafe.

• Workers who feel they are being unjustly disciplined for refusing a dangerous assignment can seek relief form the National Labor Relations Board or from an arbitrator (as they could before the ruling).

Still unanswered is the question if a worker is permitted to walk away from his job station because he feels it's unsafe, must the person be paid for the time? It's best to transfer the protesting worker to another job while the safety question is being resolved. If a worker must be sent home because other work is unavailable, make it clear that it's not disciplinary.

———

Source: *Whirlpool Corp.* vs *Marshall,* 2/26/80.

3 INCREASING PRODUCTIVITY

PRODUCTIVITY MANAGEMENT

Productivity basics checklist

Before starting a drive to improve productivity, review the company's basic foundation. Any weakness in it could hurt the productivity campaign. Fundamental questions:

• Are there clear, basic company goals? Are they translated into specific long-range objectives?

• Does the chief executive have time for planning and meetings with employees and public contacts? The CEO shouldn't be swamped with details.

• How do rivals compare in technical development? Management strength? Market share? Overall profitability?

• Are there detailed formulas to measure performance? Mere forecasts and budgets aren't enough.

• Do decision-makers have access to full information quickly?

• Is management structured to handle emergencies smoothly? To implement new programs?

• Do customers get quality service on time?

• Are policies for minimum orders and customer credit up to date?

Source: Brooks International Corp., Montvale, N.J.

Worker productivity is only the beginning

Workers alone do not boost productivity. Encouraging increased productivity by labor is still vital, but it should be regarded as routine. The most successful companies: (1) increase the payback from raw materials, equipment, technology, and capital; (2) emphasize effectiveness (meeting market needs) over efficiency; and (3) measure performance against goals, not merely unit output.

How quality and low cost can work together

"Keep the line moving," the primary operating rule for production managers in most American companies, no longer works well enough to keep all those companies competitive. The key problem is the assumption that quality and low cost are mutually exclusive and one must be traded off to get the other. Japanese firms have demonstrated that both are attainable, and they are gaining market shares as a result.

The push for more productivity in a company today must be directly related to a push to upgrade quality. If a company achieves greater output per hour or per dollar of cost, but that production is of poor quality, it gains nothing. If the defect rate is cut by improving quality, however, a company can accept lower productivity and still be ahead of the game. The main reasons for this:

• Reduced rework and repair. Rework can be a huge drain on manufacturing productivity. One manufacturer estimates that 21% of its labor cost goes to correct production mistakes.

• More cooperative workers. They take more pride in their work and feel management is sharing its prerogatives with them.

Behind the new recognition of quality as the key to productivity is W. Edwards Deming, an American statistician whose ideas were adopted in Japan 30 years ago. Deming's work centers on the use of statistical techniques to identify and reduce defects. Much of what he says now has been known for years, but has not generally been applied by U.S. firms the way Deming recommends.

In many American companies, quality control is a separate function from production and is the domain of experts who are usually industrial engineers. When a quality problem arises, the line managers call in the engineers rather than become intimately involved in solving it themselves. Deming's approach is to integrate quality control into the production process itself. Teach workers basic sampling techniques and how to use control charts. Make both workers and managers responsible for quality. If necessary, a worker should be able to stop the line to correct a quality problem. It is essential to get away from the idea that quality is an issue solely for experts.

In the U.S., the tendency among managers is to put the blame for quality problems elsewhere —on suppliers or the workers. Managers often say that if the workers would just work harder or pay more attention to what they are doing, the company would not have this problem. Deming's approach is to assume that the problem is caused by the system, not the suppliers nor the workers. This is true 85% of the time. It may be that workers are not trained properly, or they are poorly supervised, or something else. But usually they have no direct control over the fundamental cause of the quality shortfall.

Some of Deming's other ideas are intriguing, but they are also controversial:

• Eliminating numerical goals. Deming believes these are disincentives if they are not accompanied by detailed plans on how to achieve them. Also counterproductive, in his view are slogans (such as "zero defects") and posters. They are a lazy way out for managers who do not manage.

• Doing away with mass inspections. Many U.S. companies inspect 100% of output, often at several points in the production process. Most have to do this because their defect rate is so high. Deming says that a company using high-quality parts in a high-quality production process with well-trained personnel should not have to inspect everything.

• Eliminating excess suppliers. The conventional widsom is that several sources are necessary to avoid overdependence on any one supplier for critical parts. In Japan suppliers are tied into virtually permanent relationships with their customers. They are secure in knowing they will not be cut off in bad times, unlike even key suppliers to a U.S. company. One U.S. automaker that now has 4,000 suppliers has embarked on a five-year program to cut the number to 800. Toyota has only 380 suppliers, according to Deming.

The new rule for American production managers: quality, productivity, and costs are completely linked.

Source: Dr. David Dannenbring, associate professor, Columbia University Graduate School of Business.

Improving productivity gains

The dismal U.S. record in productivity gains in the last decade is not inevitable for any individual company, however. To counter the trend, top management must identify the company's productivity problems as a priority. If it is relegated to middle management, department by department, support for the improvement effort will lag after an initial flourish. When responsibility is widely scattered throughout the company, the improvement program will be orphaned and eventually abandoned without results.

Give top-management clout to a pilot productivity-improvement program in a single plant or department. Involve that department's workers in finding ways to make operations more efficient, even at the very lowest level.

Set up groups of 10 or 12 (no more) that include first-line supervisors and workers. (They are called quality circles.) Ask each group to tackle a fundamental question: "Why are we producing all these rejects?" Be prepared to deal with hostile replies: "We don't care about the products." But listen for the helpful ones: "You're giving us lousy machines to work with."

This technique can be successful. Sony took over Motorola plants in both San Diego and Chicago, where product quality on the Quasar line of TV electronics had become hopeless. Within a year of using this quality-circle approach with the same American managers and workers who had been in the plants all along, rejects dropped by over 80% and absenteeism almost disappeared. Pay scales went up, and so did job security. These two American plants are now among the most productive in the worldwide Sony manufacturing enterprise.

Adapt all successful ideas (including the one above) to suit the company's special needs. Successful case histories should be used only to suggest ideas that could work. Design a program based on identification of a particular need and analysis of the results of a pilot program.

Guidelines for setting up a company productivity program:

• Integrate the program into company planning and control systems. Don't just tack the effort on to existing procedures.

• Resist the temptation to diffuse the program too fast. Just because a pilot system succeeds in one area, there's no assurance that it can be put into full effect everywhere. Budget snarls could imperil results and discourage management.

• Reexamine the program periodically. It may be that the company has drifted into concentrating on capital improvements when it should be checking materials costs in relation to output.

• Restructure existing manager-performance appraisals in light of the new productivity program. Make salaries and bonuses hinge on pro-

ductivity, not only (or mostly) short-term but over the long haul.

• Set goals realistically. Don't expect overnight success. Develop a system to calculate productivity changes. Use these measures just as the company uses profitability measures. Again, emphasize the long term.

• Consider abandoning piecework incentives, however ingrained that system may be. Under such a system, workers lack motivation to offer ideas that increase output per unit of input, since that merely raises their quota.

• Combine the productivity program with one that pushes the quality of work life. When employees are happy at work, their productivity rises and job satisfaction grows.

• Insist on joint cooperation between labor and management from the program's inception. Union leaders know that everyone suffers when productivity falls off and jobs emigrate to the Far East, Europe, or Central America. Don't push a plan that ignites labor opposition. Usually the price is too high and chances of success too low.

Source: C. Jackson Grayson, Jr., Ph.D., founder-chairman, American Productivity Center, Houston.

Productivity barriers

While government actions greatly affect productivity, U.S. business managers accept most of the blame for poor performance themselves. Chief productivity blocks rated on a one-to-ten scale, with ten the worst:

• Poor management (7.82).
• Government regulations (6.95).
• Training of the work force (6.46).
• Insufficient capital investments (6.36).
• Insufficient R&D (6.06).
• Tax policies (5.77).
• Decline in the work ethic (5.77).
• Quality of the work force (4.84).

Most of the companies surveyed use labor as a measurement of productivity. Some 46% are planning worker-participation programs (one-third already have them).

Source: *Productivity,* Stamford, Conn.

A better way to measure productivity

Measure productivity for each product line separately, even though it entails more detailed record-keeping.

The practice enables managers to focus maximum attention on lines that account for the bulk of sales, and allows them to calculate product strategies more easily because more information is available to them.

Use the specific data to plan the use of company resources more effectively.

Source: David J. Sumanth, University of Miami, *Manufacturing Productivity Frontiers,* Illinois Institute of Technology, Research Institute, Chicago.

Measuring company productivity

• Choose a convenient measure of productivity.

• Tailor the measure to the activity being evaluated. For the production area, consider physical output per worker-year. Alternatively, one large manufacturer tracked real value added per worker-hour and per unit of capital input. For sales consider net sales per payroll dollar.

• If the company is using more than one productivity measure, it should be able to convert units of one measure into other measures. For example, know how many worker-hours are worth one hour of machine time.

• When dollars are used in a productivity measure, keep them constant by making an adjustment for inflation.

Source: Irving H. Siegel, *Company Productivity,* W.E. Upjohn Institute for Employment Research, Kalamazoo, Mich.

How Japanese productivity methods work with U.S. employees

It is often said that the management strategies that have boosted Japan's productivity aren't transferable to the United States because of cultural differences. In reality, Japanese companies with U.S. operations have applied their ideas to the United States extremely successfully. As proof, Sony's best production line for color TV is in San Diego, not in Japan.

Sony's San Diego workers are trained to understand how a TV functions, and to point out production problems. Managers are required to know employees' career backgrounds and goals, meet with them regularly, and listen to their complaints. And workers are guaranteed lifetime employment.

Another Japanese company with operations in California, Fujitsu America, an electronics maker, cites these differences between Japanese management practices and those used by most American companies:

• Job mobility is encouraged in the United States, wasting training efforts.

• Most U.S. workers are unprotected against sudden dismissals.

• Japanese firms have predetermined wage structures with graduated increases. They do not reward on whim, as U.S. firms often do.

• U.S. firms rely on profit-sharing and incentives. Japanese companies disdain these.

• Japanese firms provide greater benefits, including health checkups, company vacation resorts, etc.

Another difference is that Japanese unions organize by company rather than by industry, encouraging identification with corporate goals.

Source: *World Business Weekly,* New York.

The truth about how Japanese factories succeed

The myth about Japanese factories is that all plants are modern. The pace is at a breakneck speed 24 hours a day. Quality circles of workers exert a powerful influence on management. All companies are paternalistic. The reality is somewhat different:

• Factories are usually less sophisticated than in the United States. But in all of them, work and rest areas are meticulously clean and orderly. Workers do regular preventive maintenance and focus on ways to head off disruption. These conditions are fostered by management, not by the workers.

• Inventories are kept very thin, and raw materials are doled out very sparingly. Suppliers often make three and four deliveries a day.

• Most production machines are operated well below maximum levels. The result is fewer breakdowns, and longer life.

• Crisis management is forbidden. Expediting and overloading are not allowed. Production schedules are followed to the letter. To Japanese managers, a crisis is evidence of failure. Many U.S. managers enjoy crises.

• Early-warning and monitoring systems check process flow and signal jams on the line. The gain is that Japanese workers oversee more machines than do U.S. workers.

Source: Robert H. Hayes, professor, Harvard University Business School, *Harvard Business Review.*

Keeping productivity up after a crisis

Most managers have observed the productivity improvement that often accompanies a major crisis. When a new department has to open in three weeks, or when the company is about to lose a major customer to a competitor, there is often an extraordinary spurt of effort and effectiveness.

Studies disclose that crises can produce clear, completely acceptable goals that everyone shares. This result is an unusually high quantity of mutually supportive, reassuring interactions. Departments that may have been feuding ask how they can be helpful to each other. Bosses, instead of barking orders, ask employees for their advice and respond to subordinates' suggestions.

Human beings are highly responsive to an environment in which everyone else is helpful, encouraging and complementary to their own effort. These synchronized interactions release great energy, just as players on an athletic team respond to the sense of what teamwork can accomplish.

To keep the spurt of energy going concentrate on identifying where team play breaks down into bickering and mutual fault-finding; put people into common work groups where they will have to cooperate; and get bosses to be responsive to employee initiatives.

Pitfalls of trial runs

Though it's a tempting strategy, the results are often misleading or inaccurate when a limited number of employees try out a new method for a limited period of time. Because:

• Management's involvement is not typical of the real daily work situation.

• The organizational structure used in the test is often overly simplified.

• Disciplinary problems do not emerge, since people involved in tests are on their best behavior.

• When volunteers are used, the makeup of the test group may not be typical of all employees.

• The informal social relationships that affect regular work situations don't have time to develop.

• Deceptively good results may be obtained because the participants know they can work at a fast pace temporarily, without having that level of production standardized. Once the trial run is completed, they go back to average performance.

Source: James A. Lee, *The Gold and the Garbage in Management Theories and Prescriptions,* Ohio University Press.

Business forms can block productivity

For every dollar a company spends on business forms, an additional $40 goes for expenses such as clerical costs, storage, and disposal. A company can save substantially by reducing the number of forms, designing them more effectively, or retaining a forms management company that will eliminate common mistakes:

• Too many forms. When different departments use several forms that relate to the same subject, consider using a single form, perhaps with separate sections that can be routed to the various departments.

• Using copy machines for reproduction. When business forms are produced on copying machines, the price is 10¢–12¢ each, compared with about two cents for printed forms.

• Too much paper per form. Companies often order 8½- by 11-inch forms when a smaller size would do.

• No inventory control. Business forms are usually ordered in volume to get quantity discounts. There is no analysis to see which ones have become obsolete and no system to warn of impending stock outs.

• Rush printing. It's very expensive. And frequently there are design errors.

Professional forms management companies handle printing, storage, and computerized inventory control. Printing is done at competitive prices, but there is usually a 15% fee for the forms management service. The service includes analysis of company forms to determine their effectiveness and the public image they convey. The process makes executives focus on the problem for the first time. Also, use it to raise morale by including employees in the redesign of the form. For example, secretaries know when forms aren't aligned for typewriter settings and appreciate being consulted.

Conventional forms suppliers traditionally rely on a network of salespeople who are paid straight commissions. They often sell companies more rather than better forms. Business forms management companies are paid to improve and reduce the number of forms that a client uses.

Source: Alfred Jay Moran Jr., president, TJM Corp., New Orleans.

IMPROVING MANAGERS' PRODUCTIVITY

Improving managerial productivity

The nationwide push to boost productivity has led to a rash of new shop floor programs. But in many cases, companies can best improve profits by concentrating on their executives' output.

The most elusive but crucial causes of executive ineffectiveness are failure to set objectives and to establish procedures to make sure those objectives are met.

Management-by-objective is a buzzword. To make the process real, the company chief executive must commit the company to year-to-year objectives; get departmental objectives in numbers; master the debails of senior managers' activities. Then, challenge their plans, steps and timing for meeting the objectives. And be able to measure where the company and each department stand month-to-month in relation to its full range of objectives.

Source: Joseph Eisenberg, president, Profit-Improvement, Inc., New York.

Strengthening middle management

Business managers commonly agree that one of the vital keys to improving productivity is upgrading the performance of middle management. How to do this:

• Develop a new frame of reference for the company's middle managers. Bring in a new middle manager from the outside whose work is clearly superior to the standards presently in force.

• Instruct senior management to stand back as the newcomer learns his way around. Let the new middle manager publicize his superior performance standards himself. Give him an opportunity to describe what he's doing in reports that are generally circulated and in oral briefings at staff meetings.

• Separate the company's veteran middle-management ranks into two groups: Those who have responded by raising their own work standards, and those who haven't.

• Recognize the improved work being done by the first group of veteran managers. Give those in the second group capable of improving their performance, but who have not, an ultimatum—pick up speed, or else. Transfer veteran managers not capable of improving their performance to different functions. Maybe transfer this last group to customer service because veteran managers' familiarity with operations will make them effective in helping customers.

• Once the company's middle management has begun to improve performance on its own, formalize the higher standards with a more demanding budget and sales targets.

This approach should be continual. Top management should periodically inject new blood into the middle-management ranks. Simply transferring old managers to new jobs is not enough.

To make this approach work, top management should not transform each new outsider into a prima donna. To do so will isolate the newcomer from the people whose work he should influence.

Fitting priorities into categories

Even some of the most efficient managers sometimes lose ground because they haven't accurately weighed the relative importance of their activities. To prevent this, categorize activities carefully according to priority, and revise the categories daily.

How to classify work activities:
• Category A. Important and urgent.
• Category B. Important but not urgent.
• Category C. Urgent but not important work. This category is usually the big trap because the crisis nature of the activity makes it seem more important than it is. (Crisis management vs management by objectives.)
• Category D. Neither urgent nor important. For example, cleaning drawers, straightening files.

Since activities will vary in urgency as times passes, it is important to revise the priorities list each day. Most managers don't have enough time to complete all tasks. They should tackle the A and B priorities, and then the C tasks if they have the time. If they never get to the D jobs, what has been lost?

Source: Milton R. Stohl, president, Milton R. Stohl Associates, Farmington Woods, Conn.

Productivity gaps at the top

Computers, word processors, desktop terminals, and other kinds of information-automation have not yet made a big impact on the way managers gather and analyze essential business information. The frustration level is still high, according to a recent survey.

Some 25% of top managers' time is usually spent in nonproductive chores such as traveling, filing papers, or trying to get information by conventional means.

Almost half of their time is spent getting information via the telephone or in face-to-face meetings.

Time wasted on the least efficient ways of gathering information means top managers don't devote enough time to analyzing and planning company operations.

———

Source: Harvey L. Poppel, senior vice president, Booz Allen & Hamilton, Inc.

IMPROVING EMPLOYEE PRODUCTIVITY

Improving productivity from the bottom up

In the current rush to upgrade U.S. productivity, many companies are mistakenly pushing only for harder work from their employees. In the right corporate environment, employees can be sources of creativity and intelligence about organizing production for more efficiency.

Managers, particularly those in production, should ask for and expect more than increased effort. Since most American production workers have at least a high school education, after six months on the job, they understand the details of their work at least as well as their supervisors do, and often better. As a rule, within a 25-foot work space, no one knows how to do the job better than the worker on the spot.

To encourage worker involvement, move away from a top-down, overenergized, aggressive style to a more democratic and bottom-up approach. Some commonsense ways to do this:

• Pay more than lip service to the notion that top management listens to employees. Follow through on good suggestions. Explain why those not used will not work. Take production managers into close confidence. Then let them know they are to do the same with lower-level workers.

• Set practical goals. Make sure production supervisors and workers know what par is for each activity or operation. Then provide some leeway for differing work skills and styles.

• Strip down management layers. The world's oldest and largest organization, the Catholic church, gets along with just four layers. Two are ideal for a company. The goal is to help people do their jobs, not to multiply the number of their bosses, company reports and meetings.

• Communicate directly and clearly. Explain the bad news with, and even ahead of, the good. Communicate face-to-face if possible. Take time to send well-written messages to employees, using nonbureaucratic language.

• Do not let managers throw their weight around. Titles rarely have much to do with getting work done. Managers must lead, not push.

• Resist relying on inspectors to ensure quality. Quality should be the natural aim of every employee. If resentment, misunderstanding, bad judgment, or miscalculation is causing a falloff in quality, quickly open up a new line of communication from bottom to top to remove the block.

• Do not insist on a single way to accomplish something. Many more ways may be acceptable. Let the employee figure out how best to reach a goal.

Training programs can be a powerful incentive. But rely on a manager's instinct that a training program offers a benefit, rather than demand a formal cost justification. When business is slow, retrain in order to ready production for an upturn. Then promote or reward the workers who gain most from the training as an added incentive to increased productivity.

The value of job security is also often underestimated. In fact, workers concentrate best on the task at hand when they are reasonably sure they will have a job tomorrow. Set up a reward pool. Make it uniform for the entire company and distribute the reward as a percentage of income without regard to rank.

Reward employees quickly, preferably monthly, for rising above the average. Let them vote on the payment method. Key to effectiveness—if 70% of the employees do not approve of the incentive plan, change it.

Source: Rene C. McPherson, dean, Stanford University Graduate School of Business, Stanford, Calif.

Motivating employees to better productivity

It's important to get workers involved in any campaign for greater productivity.

The strategy:

• Good planning. Start the productivity campaign with a flair. Finish the effort before employees tire of it. Kick off the campaign with a letter from the boss. Create some excitement, and avoid talking in management terms.

• Settle for immediate gains. Don't press workers for input on a continuing basis. Thirty days is about the limit for a successful campaign.

• Implement good ideas quickly. The same day if possible. Action, not words, convinces employees that management is serious.

• Ask employees for ideas on even the most modest items. Many have ideas from previous employers. One company discovered from an employee that its competitors were recycling corrugated containers. Adopting the idea resulted in an annual savings of $120,000.

• Informality. Complicated employee-suggestion rules should be relaxed for a month. Encourage everyone to take a fresh look at the job. Open direct links to management.

• Recognition. Substitute recognition for money rewards during the campaign. Money prizes can promote jealousy and undercut motivation when they're stopped. Encourage immediate supervisors to recognize contributions. This puts line managers on notice that improvements are expected.

As a result, apart from productivity gains, a successful campaign is likely to renew spirit and improve morale. Most workers want the security that comes from being part of a profitable organization.

Source: George J. Schmidt, president, Industrial Motivation, Inc., New York.

Productivity boosters

Seven insights to help improve an employee's overall productivity:

1. Most employees want to see others succeed —but never at their own expense.

2. Employee change and development are usually slow and subtle. Change is most often visible over a period of months, not days.

3. Each worker has one or two specialties. The manager should learn something about each of those.

4. Some employees will always be jealous of others' success.

5. Every employee, to some degree, resents changes in work patterns or situations.

6. Ease the stress of change by offering the employee more reassurance and encouragement than usual.

7. Most employees have some emotional problems that stymie their progress at different times and in various ways.

Source: Charles C. Vance, *Boss Psychology,* McGraw-Hill, New York.

Mistakes that undermine productivity

• Not giving employees enough to do. Common causes are failing to delegate or to capitalize on an individual's initiative.

• Overworking the best people. Reward employees who carry more than their share of new responsibilities or a bigger staff, not only for a bigger work load. A tip-off that someone's pushed too far is a sudden change in mood or a rash of sick days.

• Failing to live up to promises. A typical case is promising ambitious new workers they will receive training and a promotion for filling a dull or low-level job, but never delivering on the promise.

• Being inflexible. Make exceptions to rules when it's necessary and sensible.

• Moving too quickly with new policies. Changing departmental operations without investigating or explaining them properly can anger and frustrate workers. The biggest problem often lies in calling in outside consultants who promise easy answers to deep-seated problems.

Source: *Supervisory Management,* AMACOM, New York.

Informal ways to measure employee productivity

Alternatives to elaborate, costly time-and-motion studies:

• Short-interval scheduling. Work is assigned and measured for clearly defined intervals throughout the day. It works best in companies with an almost continuous backlog of routine work. Supervisors must ensure a steady flow of work. Both supervisors and workers may object to meeting such rigid schedules.

• Work sampling. Managers make random observations of the work and pay special attention to how long each step takes. It is the most accurate of the informal productivity-measurement techniques. Best used to measure nonrepetitive tasks, determine how much time is unproductive, examine work distribution within a department and find causes of delays. Workers must be told that management is trying to establish standards and that it is not spying. Of course, it's only useful for jobs that are visible.

• Time-ladder studies. Workers keep logs of the time they spend on specific aspects of their jobs. But employees must be persuaded to report their activities honestly and completely. The

logs are easy to conduct and understand. Applicable to many kinds of jobs. But data may be inaccurate. Results can be difficult to analyze.

Source: R.E. Nolan, *Improving Productivity Through Advanced Office Controls,* AMACOM, New York.

Why flextime is paying off

Allowing employees to individually decide when they'll start their work day was first thought of as a morale booster. But flextime is paying another big dividend. Companies using it report sizable productivity increases. Other benefits:

• Lateness and absenteeism (because of personal business chores) are reduced.

• Employees fit their work hours to their own best work times. Output increases because workers are functioning at their peak.

• Employees become more time conscious because deadlines, absences, and meetings have to be individually coordinated.

And flextime forces supervisors to be more careful about work assignments and scheduling.

Source: *Chronolog,* Orinda, Calif.

What's wrong with the four-day week

Four-day work weeks haven't been widely adopted. Only 2.2% of full-time employees work fewer than five days a week. The main problem is that most plants and offices can't close on the fifth day because customers and suppliers would be inconvenienced. And worker productivity was found to drop in many fields because of fatigue from working 10-hour days.

In some companies, employees work nine-hour days every two weeks, taking the tenth day off. A bonus is frequent three-day weekends.

Source: *U.S. News & World Report,* New York.

TRAINING PROGRAMS

Getting the most from employee training

• Be sure training takes place in an environment that is free of distractions. Most common mistakes are bad food, no coffee, incorrect equipment, time limitations, and telephone interruptions.

• Reinforce the initial training. It's estimated that people retain only 10% of what they have learned. Their retention rate can be boosted to 60% with the help of ongoing programs.

• Determine whether it's best to do the training in-house or out-of-house. In-house is good for on-the-job training, one-day job introductions, quick hands-on experience with equipment operation. Out-of-house serves best for intense seminars of more than one day, management training, planning sessions, and for sales, marketing, and product demonstration seminars. Even companies with training centers are going outside the workplace for concentrated sessions with no interruptions.

Training rules

Break down training actions into a number of small steps.

1. Tell what the operation will achieve before showing how to do it.

2. Explain the first step before doing it.

3. Demonstrate slowly.

4. Repeat the demonstration and then have the employee try it.

5. Ask if there are questions before moving on to the next step.

6. After it has all been explained and demonstrated, perform the entire procedure at top production speed to give the worker a goal to shoot for.

7. If the training is interrupted, start over.

8. Follow up by letting trainees know how they are doing. Assist slow learners with the steps that are giving them trouble.

Source: *Executive Action Series,* Bureau of Business Practice, Waterford, Conn.

Problems with management training programs

Managers usually find supervisory training courses stimulating and enjoyable. But there is little evidence that the supervisor's overall effectiveness improves as a result of the training. Usual reasons for failure:

• There is no agreement on what supervisors should be taught. It's not yet clear which supervisory style is best and under what circumstances. Focus on identifying those who seem to know intuitively how to lead.

• Managers find it difficult to transfer training from a classroom to real situations. Usually the expensive course becomes nothing but a fondly remembered experience.

• Supervisors often have little personal control over their management techniques. A dictatorial style is often the solution when the competence of subordinates is low.

The best use of training is to identify those with supervisory skills, teach them the basics, and weed out those who lack leadership potential.

Source: *Work Redesign,* Addison-Wesley, Reading, Mass.

Why most training programs fail

Training that cannot be applied to the job immediately is useless. For employees to use successfully the knowledge acquired in training, they must be able to apply it directly to their jobs and be supported in that use by their immediate supervisors.

The usual reasons training programs fail:
• Real needs are not clearly identified at the outset. A common mistake is focusing the training on overcoming symptoms of problems rather than their causes.
• Too much of the training time deals with theory rather than with practical information and development of skills.
• Follow-up programs are not available.

Source: William H. Franklin Jr., Georgia State University, Atlanta, *Administrative Management,* New York.

QUALITY CIRCLES

What happens when Americans try quality circles

Undoubtedly, the management buzzword of the 1980s is quality circle (QC). This Japanese concept of voluntary worker involvement in management is taking newly productivity-conscious U.S. companies by storm.

QCs' greatest successes so far are with blue-collar workers in plants, warehouses and other facilities. Gaining fast are QCs composed of white-collar employees. Tremendous opportunities exist for improving office efficiency and quality.

Blue- and white-collar QCs operate in essentially the same way;
• A first-line supervisor acts as circle leader, and keeps meetings from becoming complaint sessions by focusing on solvable problems.
• Most companies appoint an overall coordinator (called a "facilitator" in QC jargon). Main functions are to oversee all the circles, monitor progress, serve as a buffer between middle managers and workers, and bring in specialists from other departments.
• In early meetings, the leader asks each member for improvement ideas. All suggestions are taken seriously. A circle is small enough for everyone to participate.
• Once the initial brainstorming is done, the circle votes on ideas to investigate further. The circle must have total freedom to decide which problems to tackle.
• Subsequent meetings focus on possible solutions. Circle members should document the time and/or money required by existing methods and the potential saving.
• Recommendations should be presented to top management by the group as a whole.

Crucial to a QC's success is management's willingness to respond quickly to suggestions—an immediate yes whenever possible; a fully justified no or request for additional information within three weeks. Since many proposals do not fit into existing organizational structures or budgetary procedures, implementation can be slow, even if management approves. QC members may get discouraged, causing the system to founder.

Like any new management technique, QCs have negative aspects as well as positive ones. For example, workers who do not want to join (perhaps 10%–20% of any work group) may feel considerable peer pressure. Most nonjoiners, however, readily accept changes made by QCs. They realize the improvements will help them do their jobs better, too.

QCs can outlive their usefulness. Some experts believe they should be abolished when they have solved most of the problems they identify.

The main difference between QCs in offices and those in plants is that regardless of how educated they are, office workers do not think much about improving operations. They have not been challenged frequently to do things better and faster, as have factory personnel.

And white-collar employees are more vocal, so meetings, can drag on unless the leader maintains control. Participants may feel they have failed if they do not come up with some problems. And efficiencies may be less visible, because they center on speeding paper flows.

A QC program is a time-consuming process. It requires major changes in manager-worker relationships. And QCs can appear to give lower-level employees the right to challenge existing procedures and managerial authority, even though they do not.

Many inexperienced consultants have hopped on the QC bandwagon. Look for consultants who have at least two years experience, a record of success, and workbooks and training aids written on a level appropriate for the workers involved. It will cost $12,000–$15,000, including expenses, for a consultant to get a QC program functioning in one location.

Source: Robert I. Patchin, director of productivity-improvement programs, Northrop Aircraft, Hawthorne, Calif.; Jan Novak, manager, personnel research, Metropolitan Life Insurance Co., New York; and Dr. David Dotlich, manager, employee relations, Honeywell, Inc., Minneapolis.

Helping middle managers deal with QCs

Some companies have found that when workers close themselves off for an hour or more each week to explore ways to boost productivity, managers may get nervous. In fact, regardless of how many briefings are held for middle managers, some react poorly when quality circles are formed in their own departments. They feel they were hired to be problem-solvers, so QCs are unnecessary and even redundant.

Their main fear, that their ability and effectiveness are being challenged because, in the early stages, QCs tend to focus on large issues that managers have already failed to solve, is usually unfounded. But these have no simple answer. For example, tensions between smokers and non-smokers. QCs should concentrate on smaller, work-flow or product-quality issues, rather than those related to work life or the working environment.

A more serious problem is insecurity among managers who feel uninformed and deprived of access to senior management because top managers want to hear the QCs recommendations first-hand, not filtered through middle managers.

The best way to overcome this obstacle is to have the QC coordinator (who should not come from the personnel department if a line employee is available) work directly with managers and reassure them during the critical first few months.

Fear and distrust turn to full support within six months as managers see the QC results support their own goals and enable them to do a better job.

The ideal candidate for QC coordinator is a line person who knows the company well, can communicate with all levels of management and workers, has high energy, and takes minor setbacks in stride.

TIME-SAVING TECHNIQUES

A systematic approach to time management

Effective time management involves an internal and external component. The internal aspect requires heavy doses of self-discipline. The external, a systematic approach to keeping track of how time is spent and how plans to spend it actually work out. A sample system to follow:
- Weed out anything that can be delegated.
- Rank the remaining tasks in order of their importance. Give priority to those items where immediate action will reduce the total amount of work.
- Schedule sequentially enough time for each task.
- Keep a careful log of the actual amount of time spent.
- Once a week, compare the log with the schedule. Evaluate the discrepancies to learn whether enough time was allowed and, if so, what happened to interfere with the schedule.

Hard-nosed approach to managing time

- Concentrate on the best ways to spend time, instead of worrying about saving it.
- Keep an accurate log of activities to identify and define work patterns.
- Have only one chair (besides yours) in your office. Keeping people standing saves time.

- Each meeting should have an announced time limit.
- Have all calls screened. Make a list of who should be put through immediately.
- Arrange office with back to door.
- If someone asks, "Do you have a minute?," say no.
- List tomorrow's priorities before leaving the office today.
- Don't rush needlessly. It takes longer to correct a mistake than to avoid making one.

Source: Merrill E. Douglass, director, Time Management Center, *Marketing Times,* New York.

How to develop good time-use habits

Managers can make more of themselves and their life if they take the trouble to cultivate good time-use habits until they are second nature. Habits automatically steer everyone's lives. When habits become time-thrifty, managers will get better use of their time for the rest of their lives, automatically.

To develop better time-use habits, managers should:
- Pick those habits that are good and drop bad ones. Make a list of times and places to substitute a new habit for an old one. It takes a month or more until a new habit is second nature.
- Concentrate on using the new technique as often as possible. Every time a new habit is used, a mental pat on the back should be given. Otherwise, a mental kick is in order.
- Put weekly reminders of resolves to change

habits on a calendar. When the reminders come up, evaluate the progress. Then list additional times and places to apply the new habit.

• Announce intentions to develop new habits to other people. This strengthens the motivation to finish the job.

Source: Robert Moskowitz, time-management consultant, Canoga Park, Calif.

Personal time-saving tips from top executives

• From a corporate financial planner: I used to spend hours agonizing over tough decisions. Then I realized that hesitation rarely made for a better decision. Now I just gather the facts, then decide quickly. My track record is as good as ever. And I have time for other important matters.

• From a corporate troubleshooter: When I step into an ailing company, I look for ways to put its best resources up against its toughest problems. For example, I put each executive in charge of solving a single critical problem. This combination of concentration and pressure usually leads to top results in record time.

• From a bank executive: I never watched the clock and usually kept staff people waiting 15 minutes or longer to see me. As a result, the staff felt insulted and lost loyalty. Now I keep all staff appointments to the minute. Employees have become more loyal, and they work harder as well.

• From the administrator of a medical center: I feel good relationships with staff are important, but the usual social chatter can take too much time. Instead of trying to socialize with everyone at once, I give a different person each day my full attention for several minutes.

• From the chief executive of a large retailer: I had scheduling problems until I learned the swift task/slow task concept. Now I do swift tasks, like making quick decisions or delegating, during fragmented times of the day. I put slow tasks, like drafting reports or looking at a complex deal, into consecutive-hour time slots, when I can make real progress.

• From the president of a bank: I schedule my work sessions for 90 minutes at a time. That's as long as I can productively concentrate on one project. After each session, I catch up on calls and messages that have piled up. The routine break refreshes me, and soon I'm ready for another working session.

• From an industrial consultant: I can predict efficiency from the look of a person's office. Efficient people show a thin layer of clutter in a neat and orderly office. Cluttered, disorderly offices are strong clues to inefficient occupants. Quite simply, neatness pays dividends in time and effectiveness.

• From an automobile plant manager: With the current push for efficiency, I have adopted a new policy about routine meetings. I never start one unless I know the time it should end. This way, there's pressure every minute to get the business accomplished quickly. And we do.

• From a Midwest attorney: I keep a log of my billable hours. But I no longer do it with paper and pencil. Now I record on a pocket dictation machine the times when I start or stop work on every item. My secretary types up the notes every week and computes the billable time for each client.

• From a theatrical producer: For me, time is money. I have to plan every project and estimate the cost of each phase. At first I lost money on my inaccurate estimates. Now, after practice, I can look at a six-month project and plan it to within a day or two of the actual time required.

• From a top New York advertising executive. It has taken me 15 years to unlearn a bad habit. I always gave my time to anyone who rang the loudest bell. Now I refuse to hear those bells. My time is reserved first for accounts I want most.

• From a vice president of manufacturing: Last year I started eating lunch regularly with my plant managers. After a month, I had heard about three costly situations before they got out of hand. Since then, a dozen more. The meetings save time I used to waste reading reports that ignored the same situations.

Source: Robert Moskowitz, time-management consultant, Canoga Park, Calif.

Setting the right order for tasks

When managers feel overwhelmed they react by leaving many tasks untouched or unfinished. They fail to communicate that the jobs are undone. And then they do low priority items first.

The root of the problem is that they have no master plan for sorting out their tasks. Their work lacks direction.

To regain control:

• Inventory available resources. Include people, equipment, money, or prospects for financing.

• Identify the ways to measure results. Examples: Profit, sales, units produced, letters sent out.

• Be realistic about expected accomplishments. Consider both personal and business goals.

Have a close associate ask the questions. Write down everything important. Be specific. Ambiguities often result from hidden assumptions.

Many offices are snagged by bad communication. Openness is a must in making viable plans, and in changing them if mistakes are made.

Distribute copies of goals to associates to coordinate plans. Ask them to use these as a basis to work out their own objectives in the same way. Many employees do not understand their boss's plans and expectations, so they work at cross-purposes.

Update plans and goals on an ongoing basis. Spend half a day every month with associates, identifying goals and planning how to achieve them.

Once goals have been established, define the specific steps that must be taken to achieve them. Set deadlines for those goals and for intermediate ones, too. Ask:

• How long will it take?
• What will it cost?
• What resources are available?
• From whom can I get the information?

Keep a summary of goals close at hand. Read through it every day and use it. Before scheduling an appointment, be sure its purpose fits in with goals. Focus on productive ideas by noting which techniques and activities were successful during the day.

Source: Howard Schor and Mariana Somer, Creative Communication Corp., New York.

How to find another hour in the day

To add at least 60 minutes to each day:

• Make a list of points to be covered in meetings or telephone calls. Focus on the major concerns of the customer, spouse, boss, or subordinate. The sooner the other is satisfied, the quicker you can move on.

• Set deadlines. Then meet or beat them. Setting specific plans for an evening or a weekend gives incentive to get office tasks finished promptly.

• Identify time buffers, the built-in mechanisms to delay that everyone uses (driving around the block a few times before facing a tough customer, overcommitments, miscommunications, accommodating others unnecessarily). Rather than putting off staff training, for instance, do it. This will free more time later, since you can then delegate more.

• Use your own prime time (most productive period in the day) for your prime projects. Zero in on accomplishing highest-priority goals.

• Be prompt. It minimizes problems with customers, supervisors, peers, and subordinates. And it saves time apologizing and explaining.

• Communicate clearly. It saves time spent in clarifying misunderstandings, correcting errors, rewriting, redoing, explaining delays, and worrying. Use words that are easily understood. Avoid double meanings. Emphasize important points.

Source: David K. Lindo, *Supervision Can Be Easy,* AMACOM, New York.

Dealing with details

When your mind is cluttered with details, use one of these techniques to redirect energy and improve organization:

• Take a mini-break. A short walk, or a minute of relaxation to sip some juice. Or, simply breathe deeply for 30 seconds with your eyes closed (this can help concentration when you shift from one subject to another).

• Keep your schedule on paper. Resist the temptation to keep it in your head.

• Avoid interruptions. Work away from the office and keep your distance from the telephone.

• Delegate details. Rely more heavily on your secretary. Let subordinates handle routine jobs. Let them attend most of the less important meetings.

• Set time limits. If a task isn't completed within an allotted time limit, come back to it later.

Source: *International Management,* New York.

Use commuting time to plan the day

Questions to get started:

• What are the priority items in the current work load?

• What problems can be expected today?

• Which jobs from the previous day need to be cleaned up?

• What special opportunities exist that are particularly challenging or call for special skills?

• What personal contributions to company goals are likely or possible today?

It's best to plan tomorrow the night before.

Open-door problems

How can you be available to subordinates and colleagues, but still avoid constant interruptions. Techniques:

• Set aside special open-door times once or twice a week for anything subordinates want to discuss.

• Encourage (or require) everyone to think through beforehand what they plan to discuss. Ask for a brief outline to help both people prepare for the talk.

• Set a time limit at the beginning of each discussion.

• Occasionally hold talks in other people's

offices, to make breaking off nonproductive conversations easier.

Source: Robert D. Rutherford, *Just in Time: Immediate Help for the Time-Pressured,* John Wiley & Sons, New York.

How not to waste time on committees

• Accept appointments only to committees that are doing work you believe in.

• Restrict your contribution to the area of your professional expertise.

• Whenever possible, delegate time-consuming chores to paid committee assistants.

It is usually flattering to be asked to serve on a committee. What it takes to turn down such invitations is a clear sense of personal direction and a strong sense of security.

Source: Lillian Vernon, president, Lillian Vernon Corp., Mount Vernon, N.Y.

Helping secretaries make better use of their time

If the goal is a team approach that frees managers to accomplish more by having secretaries take over some important tasks:

• Have the secretaries draw up daily plans. Managers should meet with them each day to discuss objectives and priorities. The payoff: Fewer interruptions on both sides.

• Keep secretaries fully informed of daily activities. They should never have to say they don't know where the bosses are or when they will be back.

• Brief them on all upcoming projects. Other managers will be more willing to deal with them on routine matters if they believe the secretaries are well informed.

• Take time to give thorough instructions on new projects.

• Encourage secretaries to organize and schedule their bosses' day. Secretaries frequently see managers' problems more objectively than the managers do.

• Protect the secretaries' time when they are busy. Help them schedule free time for important tasks. Managers should take over routine work, if necessary, such as answering their own phones.

Source: Merrill and Donna Douglas, *Manage Your Time, Manage Your Work, Manage Yourself,* AMACOM, New York.

Start the week right

• Wrap up as many jobs as possible on Friday. It will boost your morale to know these matters have been completed. Before leaving that night, tidy up your office. Encourage subordinates to do the same.

• Reserve the weekend for personal business. Try to get it out of the way. Carrying nonbusiness problems and tasks over to Monday is a double time-waster.

• Set a new goal for Monday. Write it down. Don't make it too difficult. It's fine to devote some of your weekend time to this. Thinking about Monday won't interfere with pruning the roses on Sunday.

• Relax on Sunday night. Schedule your weekend activities for Saturday evening and Sunday afternoon.

• Avoid big jobs on Monday morning. Instead, spread them throughout the week. It makes the thought of going back to work less oppressive.

• Keep troublemakers off the Monday agenda at all costs. Once the week is under way, problems have a way of becoming more manageable, or at least tolerable.

• Plan to break up the week. Schedule something enjoyable on Wednesday. On Monday morning, a midweek reprieve won't seem as far away as Saturday. And it will do wonders to improve your depressed outlook.

• Set an example for your staff. When the boss suffers the Monday-morning blues, the rest of the staff will decide it's okay to do the same, and performance will be off.

Source: *Electrical World,* New York.

How to spot time wasters

To identify nonproductive executive time, do a careful analysis of a typical week's activities.

Make daily time sheets on which each line stands for a 15-minute period. Keep a running record of how each period is spent. It is time-consuming to do, but saves many hours later.

Then, using hindsight at the end of every day, "grade" each activity 1, 2, or 3, according to this guide:

1. The right thing at the right time.

2. The right thing, but at the wrong time. The task might have been more effectively handled later, after something else occurred.

3. The wrong thing, something not worth doing or that could have been done by someone else.

The key to winning the battle against time wasters is to know exactly which high-priority activities to undertake when a time-waster is eliminated. Otherwise, the free time that is created will quickly be dominated by another low-payoff task.

And bad use of time often has an overlooked secondary impact. The negative feelings that result from being forced to carry out a trivial task often create more wasted time (in griping or slacking off) than the original chore.

Source: *Effective Time Management,* Prentice-Hall, Englewood Cliffs, N.J.

How managers waste time

• Doing other people's work. Most managers could improve their efficiency up to 30% if they delegated work more effectively.

• Spending time on phone calls that could be handled by a secretary.

• Working on a favorite chore that might not mesh with the company's priorities.

• Repeating instructions. Give instructions orally to as large a group as feasible, then follow up with a written version of the same instruction. This way, questions can be answered at one time and misunderstandings are less likely to occur.

A simple time-saving axiom: do it now. About 75% of a manager's work can be done right away.

Source: Norman Kobert, Norman Kobert & Associates, Ft. Lauderdale, Fla.

Hiding behind nonproductive activities

The hide-and-seek syndrome grows on you slowly. It makes you hide from responsibility or action and seek shelter behind objections, arguments, or statistics. If you catch yourself early enough, you have a chance to reverse the pattern and become productive again. Warning signs:

• Giving excessive attention to detail. It's not enough to know how many units were sold. You want a breakdown by zip code, even though there's little difference form one area to another.

• Debating without committing. Sometimes this is wise. But in the hide-and-seek syndrome it's the way you maintain an active stance without having to take action.

• Joining committees. You like the way they sponge up responsibility, take a long time to decide, and make easy targets if plans don't work out.

• Making extensive reports. Time-consuming documents can keep whole departments humming without bringing the company closer to action.

The best way to end the syndrome is to look inward to your personal motivations. Find out what you're actually interested in accomplishing. Then take small steps toward your goals until you're more comfortable being active and productive.

Source: Robert Moskowitz, time-management consultant, Canoga Park, Calif.

The lure of low-priority tasks

Although they know better, many managers continue to waste time with trivial chores. This is because they:

• Need to feel busy or wanted, or they need an excuse to justify why they have no time for more risky, difficult activities.

• Are taking the path of least resistance. Low-payoff tasks are usually easy and carry no chance of failure.

• Keep up formerly required chores out of habit although the requirements of the job or personal goals have changed.

• Have relinquished too much control of their time to others who delight in loading them down with low-priority activities.

The only protection against the syndrome is to build in a mechanism that steers them away from low-payoff activities with a limited purpose.

Source: Robert D. Rutherford, *Just in Time: Immediate Help for the Time-Pressured,* John Wiley & Sons, New York.

4 COMMUNICATING YOUR IDEAS

WRITING

Write as clearly as you think

Concentrate on simplifying sentence structure in business writing. It's the easiest way to say what is meant and to make sure the message gets across. Remember three basic rules:
- Keep sentences short. They should be no more than 17–20 words. If an idea has multiple parts, use multiple sentences.
- Vary the length of sentences. The 17–20 word rule is the average. When sentences drone on at unvarying lengths, the reader's attention begins to wander.
- Vary the punctuation. Include plenty of commas, as well as a sprinkling of semicolons, to go with the necessary periods. This improves clarity of communication. Well-placed punctuation is a road map, leading the reader comfortably and accurately through the message.

Source: Paul Richards, "Sentence Control: Solving an Old Problem," *Supervisory Management,* New York.

Communicating basics for a long memo

Before preparing a long memo, ask yourself if this information is:

- Needed at the other end? (If you are not sure, call and ask.)
- Being sent to all the people who can do the most with it?
- Already on hand in another form?
- Generated too frequently?
- Issued not often enough?
- In the simplest and most useful format?

Source: Auren Uris, *Memos for Managers,* Thomas Y. Crowell, New York.

Include traffic signals in your reports

Readers understand a report better when they are carefully led through it. Use the right words or phrases to signal a shift of subject or emphasis:

• Stop and look around. Use: However, but, by contrast, nevertheless, on the other hand, still, despite, notwithstanding.

• Expand the idea. Use: Actually, realistically, at the same time, unexpectedly, perhaps.

• A limitation. Use: Sometimes, to be sure, possibly, to some extent, conceivably.

• An aside. Use: Incidentally, digressing for a moment.

• Move ahead in the same direction. Use: Additionally, also, besides, moreover, furthermore.

• Comparison. Use: Similarly, in the same way.

• Strengthen an assertion. Use: Indeed, in fact, certainly.

• Signal importance. Use: Significantly, notably, remarkably.

Source: A. Weiss, *Write What You Mean,* AMACOM, New York.

Choose your words carefully

Pitfalls you should avoid:

• Using popular but vague modifiers, such as *exceptional* or *efficient,* without defining precisely what is meant. For example, an *exceptional* record can be either *exceptionally* good or bad. Describing something as *efficiently designed* does not say enough. It's better to use facts, numbers, details.

• Exaggerating. Overstating a fact is acceptable (and common) in conversation, but it destroys credibility in writing because readers take it literally. For example, thousands of people at-tended the noon rally in the park. In reality, only a few hundred attended. The others were there eating lunch or passing by.

• Generalizing. Words to avoid: All, right, wrong, true, false, always, never. Instead, say this is true under such-and-such conditions.

• Surface reasoning. For example, "No routine inspection program has been established because of the personnel change every two years." The real reasons for the lack of inspection actually are any number of other factors.

Source: William C. Paxson, *The Business Writing Handbook,* Bantam Books, New York.

How to measure the clarity of your writing

Use the "Fog Index" to measure how clearly letters, memos, and reports are written.

• Count off a 100-word section.

• Count the number of sentences and divide 100 by that number, which gives average words per sentence.

• Count the words with more than two syllables. Add this figure to the average words per sentence.

• Multiply the total by 0.4 to get the Fog Index (indicating minimum school grade level a reader needs to comprehend it).

The lower the index, the better. A score of 11–12 is passable for most business writing. (The Fog Index for this item: 7.6.)

Source: *Time Talk,* Grandville, Mich.

Create your own book of business letters

Business writing can be made easier and faster.

• Save copies of your best letters, memos, report summaries, and proposals.

• Compile them in two identical looseleaf notebooks. They should be organized by topic and numbered by section or paragraph.

• When dictating, give the identifying code for the appropriate recycled words. Add only new material. The typist, by referring to the other copy of the notebook, knows what to pick up.

Source: *ExecuTime,* Newington, Conn.

TALKING AND LISTENING

How to sell ideas

Creative people often find it easier to do original thinking than to sell their ideas to others.

Before presenting an idea to a group:

• Look for reasons why others might oppose the idea.

• Seek out early supporters.

• Decide on goals. Ask yourself if the acceptance of the idea is more important than getting credit for it.

• Downplay originality. Instead, discuss similar concepts that have been successful. Never assume that others want innovation because they say they do. Most people prefer the status quo.

• Play politics. Get an unpopular staffer to oppose the idea. Or point out that competitors might use it first.

• Be detached and appear uninterested. Depriving opponents of a victory reduces their joy in taking the idea apart. Or be the first to point out the idea's flaws, then listen as others solve them.

• Make sure that others' perceptions of the idea are accurate. Otherwise they may reject what they think the innovation is, not what it really is.

• Throw out decoys for opponents to shoot down. Once their negative impulses have been satisfied, bring up the real idea.

Source: Thomas J. Attwood, managing director, Cargill Attwood International, *Management Review,* New York.

Build trust during a discussion

• Begin with a positive statement, for example, "I have been looking forward to talking with you. Joe Smith said if anyone could help us, it is you."

• Avoid pulling rank, making veiled threats, or offering a reward.

• Show yourself to be an expert, and associate yourself with someone the other person respects.

• Restate the other person's opinions or feelings periodically. But do not preface the restatement with "you said" or "you think." The other person may quibble over what is attributed directly.

• Share something personal about yourself if the other person is wary.

• Point out ways the information you need will help you. Indicate ways you can help the other person.

• Make a commitment to action, and then ask for a commitment in return.

Source: Pamela Cumming, *The Power Handbook,* CBI Publishing, Boston.

Using the right words

Simple phrases to help managers detect problems and better motivate subordinates:

• To find out the details of a problem: Then what happened? I see. And then what did you do? Go on. Employees will understand that they are allowed to tell the whole story and that the supervisor does not plan to cut them short.

• To elicit information: Hi, what's new here today? Everything going all right? How's the new clerk in personnel working out? Employees understand that the supervisor is ready to listen to something and is not just saying a polite hello.

• To respond to nonverbal clues: You look concerned about something today. Something tells me you're bothered by the change. I feel you're puzzled by what's happening. Use this technique to draw out the message employees are too timid, too frightened or too angry to volunteer verbally.

Source: Glen M. Morgan, communications consultant, Manitowoc, Wis.

Rules for communicating company policies

Explaining company policies and benefits to employees can be simplified. Keep messages short and lively.

Effective tactics:

• Get out from behind the desk. Becoming more approachable helps to get the message across.

• Call meetings early in the morning. This is the time when workers are most alert and not distracted by other tasks.

• Pass along news of changes as soon as possible, even if all the details aren't known.

• Present the message in terms of what it means to employees or to customers.

• Give both sides of controversial issues. The company's message has to stand up to challenges or it's not worth expressing.

• Avoid overkill. Break complex subjects down. Cover them in several short briefings. Stick to the main points. Fill in details later only for those who are interested.

• Call in an expert when necessary.

• Follow up with additional information. Most effective way: A question-and-answer session.

• If speaking before employees is difficult to do comfortably, enroll in a public speaking course.

• Don't make a presentation until properly prepared. Blundering hurts a reputation and blurs the message.

Source: Norman Berry, Mountain States Telephone & Telegraph Co., *The Effective Executive,* Chicago.

How to give more effective instructions

• Be highly specific, never general.

• Focus on the task at hand, not the circumstances surrounding it.

• Select a time when there are no distractions.

• Don't overload listeners. Present instructions that are complicated or long in a simplified or graphic way.

• Have the employee repeat critical portions of the instructions in his own words.

• Be considerate of the feelings of those receiving the instructions.

Source: Randall S. Schyuler, Ohio State University, *The Personnel Administrator,* Berea, Ohio.

Speaking with authority

When giving orders:

• Avoid weak expletives. Don't use: Darn,

golly, gee whiz, or other trivial expressions. They reduce credibility.

• Don't invite a subordinate to agree with your instructions. The wrong thing to say: This has to be done today, doesn't it? The right way is to confirm authority by saying: You'll get this done today, won't you?

• Don't confuse politeness with authority. Wrong: Will you please do this report? Right: Please do this report. Repeatedly asking employees if they're willing to do their job costs a manager credibility.

• Don't use disqualifying phrases when giving suggestions. Avoid saying: I don't know if this will work, but try it anyway. Instead, simply state the suggestion.

When and how to argue about business decisions

Never start an argument unless the problem is permanent, the situation is serious, and there's a real chance of winning.

Even when these circumstances are in force, don't debate anything that hasn't been clearly and objectively thought out in advance. Arguing and getting angry are totally different things.

The art of arguing:

• Don't get personal. It may win the point but it will create an enemy.

• Avoid overkill. Give the opponent an honorable way to retreat or admit defeat.

• Stick to the issue.

• Argue with the right person.

• Anticipate opponent's position. Plan the counterstrategy.

• State the problem clearly and specify how it should be resolved.

• Listen as well as talk. Rehearse the presentation. Be prepared to answer the other party's responses.

• Concede defeat when there's no chance of winning and forget it. Harping about lost causes

ruins chances for winning a more important matter in the future.

———

Source: W.A. Delancy, president, Analysis & Computer Systems, Burlington, Mass., *Supervisory Management,* New York.

Making the most of office confrontations

One of the most unpleasant parts of being a manager is confronting subordinates who fall short of your expectations. As a result, many executives bottle up their feelings of displeasure until their working relationships with problem employees have deteriorated beyond repair.

Instead, as soon as a subordinate's work falls below standard, have a talk with him about his job performance, with the objective of achieving the necessary improvement in performance from the subordinate and coming out of the talk with both sides feeling better and the relationship intact.

How to do it:

• Prepare for the confrontation. Review beforehand the specific criticism; how it will be presented; what it should accomplish. (It is best to write it out, at least in outline form.)

• Come to the point as quickly as possible.

• Talk about the subordinate's performance in descriptive terms. Don't evaluate. Don't say: You're not trying. Say: You're not producing enough.

• If the employee's behavior provokes anger, tell him or her so.

• Make all statements personal. Don't talk about top management's displeasure. Don't say "we." If the boss personally accepts responsibility for the confrontation, there's a better chance that the subordinate will accept the responsibility for improving his or her performance.

• Take the trouble to undertand the subordinate's point of view. That perspective provides a clearer picture for you of why the subordinate's performance is unsatisfactory.

• Be as specific as possible about the improvement required. Don't say: Change your attitude. Do say: Please stop trying to interpret my instructions. Just follow them.

• Don't conclude the talk until there's agreement on what's been said.

• If something specific should result from the talk, tell the subordinate what it is you're expecting. If this talk is the subordinate's final warning to shape up, let the individual know it.

• Before ending the talk, say something sincere and complimentary about the subordinate.

Learning to express feelings before they become explosive will not end all problems with subordinates, but many executives who learn to speak their minds more freely discover that their fear of confrontation was unfounded and they take more pleasure in their work relationships.

Source: Aubrey Sanford, vice president, The Atlanta Consulting Group, Atlanta.

Becoming a better listener

Becoming a better listener is not easy. Simple techniques that help:

• Relax yourself and the speaker. Give your full attention to what's being said. Stop everything else you're doing. Maintain eye contact.

• Don't let the speaker's tone of voice or manner turn you off. Nervousness or misplaced emotions often cloud the message the speaker is trying to get across.

• Prepare beforehand for the conversation. Take a few minutes to read or consult information pertinent to the discussion. That also helps you to quickly evaluate the speaker and the subject.

• Allow for unusual circumstances (extreme pressure or disturbing interruptions). Judge only what the speaker says given the conditions he's faced with.

• Avoid getting sidetracked. Listen very closely to points you disagree with. (Poor listeners shut out or distort them.)

• Mentally collect the main points of the conversation. Occasionally, ask for clarification of one of the speaker's statements. This shows

your interest and helps the speaker better organize his thoughts.

• Restate what you've heard at the end of the talk to avoid misunderstandings. Emphasize important issues brought up in the discussion.

Source: George de Mare, *Communicating at the Top,* John Wiley & Sons, New York.

Bad listening habits

• Thinking about something else while waiting for the speaker's next word or sentence. The mind races ahead four times faster than does the normal rate of conversation.

• Listening primarily for facts rather than ideas.

• Tuning out when the talk seems to be getting too difficult.

• Prejudging, from a person's appearance and speaking manner, that nothing interesting will be said.

• Paying attention to outside sights and sounds when talking with someone.

• Interrupting with a question whenever a speaker says something puzzling or unclear.

Source: John T. Samaras, University of Oklahoma, *Personnel Journal,* Costa Mesa, Calif.

Less time for listening means more time for work

Listening is usually a very inefficient way to get information. The reason is that most people don't talk efficiently. They don't organize their thoughts. They ramble on, taking about three times as long as necessary, Also, it builds a subordinate's ego when his superior listens to him.

How to save time when listening is unavoidable:

• Insist that appointments and meetings start on time. If people are late, don't wait for them. Do something else.

• For complex problems, insist on written background material beforehand.

• When the speaker rambles, interrupt with questions to bring out the point.

• If a decision can't be made immediately, say, "I'll think about it." Then move on to other matters. Don't waste time rehashing the problem over and over.

PUBLIC SPEAKING

Better speech introductions

Even the best public speakers can be hurt by an overly long or inept introduction. To make sure you are introduced properly:

• Provide the person introducing you with a one-minute written introduction. Do this in advance.

• Bring a second copy in case the first copy is lost.

• Arrive early enough to go over the text with the person making the introduction.

• Be prepared for things to go wrong. Have a few ploys for putting audiences at ease and getting their attention. Good investment: A book on public speaking that gives techniques for handling audiences.

• Keep acknowledgments to a minimum, but say a few kind words about the group. Then move immediately into your prepared text.

Source: William S. Tacey, communications consultant, *The Toastmaster,* Santa Ana, Calif.

Speech preparation

• Find out what common bonds unite the audience so that the speech can be directed to subjects that are meaningful.

• Get a description of the room where the speech will be delivered. It will make it easier to tie in the speech to the specific atmosphere.

• Check on the availability of microphones and audiovisual aids.

• Inquire about travel time and accommodations. Make arrangements for both well in advance.

Source: *The Effective Manager,* Warren, Gorham & Lamont, Boston.

Delivering an important speech

Audience attention drops off sharply after 20–30 minutes, so no presentation should run beyond that. If it's necessary to fill more time:

• Use slides when appropriate.

• Have a question-and answer session after the speech.

Writing the speech:

• Start by tape-recording a spontaneous flow of ideas. Don't attempt to be logical or to follow an outline. This initial tape is the raw material to prepare the final speech.

• Avoid opening with a joke. Most jokes backfire. The best grabbers are a question, personal story, famous quote, vital statistic, comparison, or contrast.

• Use questions throughout.

• Avoid unnecessary phrases such as "Now let me explain...." Or: "The point I want to make is. . . ." Don't ruin the end of the presentation with a turnoff phrase such as: "In conclusion. . . ." Or: My last point is. . . ."

• Be sure the speech is written in oral English. Read it through aloud beforehand. Eliminate words that are difficult to say, lengthy or awkward sentences or phrases that have built-in stumbling blocks. A written presentation that is oral will sound spontaneous.

Source: Roslyn Bremer, president, Communi-Vu, Inc., New York.

Speeches with impact

• Remember that your audience is interested first in people, then in things, finally in ideas.

• Only rarely is it possible to change deep-seated attitudes or beliefs. Aim no higher than getting the listeners to question their attitudes. Avoid alienating an audience by pressing points too hard.

• The most successful speeches state conclusions and call for action.

• When you have to speak extemporaneously, develop a theme early and stick to it.

• Use silence to underline a point.

• End a speech with a short, emotional, conviction-filled summary of the main points.

Source: Michael Klezaras Jr., director of research and planning, Roger Ailes & Associates, Inc., New York.

Effective oral presentations to small groups

at to do:
leet personally as many people as possi-
rehand.
right to the point. The first 15 seconds

is what grabs the listener. Don't start with "thank you" and "I'm very happy to be here."

3. Make eye contact with everyone in the audience at some time very early in the presentation.

4. Support main points with factual information and examples.

5. Repeat the main points to be sure the listeners have gotten them.

6. Look for a creative conclusion—a provocative thought or action-suggesting statement.

Never let a talk end with an answer to a question from the audience. After answering questions, always return to the main point of the presentation. The last word is important. It shouldn't be yielded to a questioner.

Never ask the audience, "Any questions?" If there aren't any, the silence will be embarrassing. Instead, suggest, "There may be some questions." It makes a difference.

Limit use of notes because it inhibits spontaneity. Write out key words or short phrases to jog thoughts. Alternate lines with different color ink to facilitate quick focusing on material.

Rehearsing is usually not recommended. Unrehearsed presentations have the advantage of freshness and spontaneity, which only come from thoughts uttered for the first time.

Source: Dr. Roger Flax, communications training consultant, Motivational Systems, South Orange, N.J.

Using humor successfully

1. Avoid humor when speaking out of doors. The laugh tends to get lost, leaving people with the feeling it wasn't funny at all.

2. Avoid puns, even though they may go over well in a parlor. They almost always cause the audience to groan more than laugh.

3. Leave enough time for the laugh before proceeding. Audiences sometimes react slowly, especially if the humor was unexpected. To a nervous speaker, a second's delay seems like an hour.

4. Be prepared to carry on smoothly and self-confidently if the audience doesn't laugh. The

audience will quickly forget that the speaker laid an egg if he remains calm.

Source: Paul Preston, *Communication for Managers,* Prentice-Hall, Englewood Cliffs, N.J.

Visual aids checklist

Which is best for what:
• Overhead projectors. The best bet generally because they are inexpensive, easy to use, compatible with most materials. Can project to any size. Updated with little trouble.
• Chalkboards. Look amateurish. Hard to read.
• Flip charts. Better than chalkboards. Restricted to handwriting. Like chalkboards, limited in visibility.
• Videotape. Appropriate for meetings in which participants are doing something, for example, role playing.
• Movies and slides. More costly. For presentations that will be repeated many times.

Successful question-and-answer sessions

Every manager must occasionally answer questions from an audience, whether several hundred strangers or a few colleagues at a staff meeting. The key to handling most questions effectively is to paraphrase. Briefly restate the question to the entire audience.

Paraphrase any time a question lasts more than five seconds. After that, at least half the people tune out, and it is difficult to recapture their attention.

Benefits of paraphrasing:
• Gives the speaker a little time to think about the answer. This is the most important benefit.
• Provides the questioner an opportunity to

correct the speaker's misinterpretation of the question.
• Ensures that the whole group hears and understands the question. In a large group, people behind the questioner almost never hear the question unless the speaker restates it.
• Avoids answering the questioner directly. While paraphrasing the question, look at several people individually. When eye contact is established, people listen.
• Allows the speaker to make the questioner feel good and at the same time encourage others to speak. Say: "That's a good question." Then paraphrase it. Encouragement is essential because even top managers often become shy in front of a group.

Source: Dr. Roger Flax, communications training consultant, Motivational Systems, South Orange, N.J.

Facing the fear of public speaking

Eighty percent of the people who give talks are at least a little nervous. It's likely that the other 20% who say they aren't nervous are kidding themselves. Some fear and tension is necessary for a successful performance. Tension gets adrenalin going and helps quick thinking and dynamism.

Virtually all people giving an oral presentation have the same concerns, stony-faced audience members who look hostile, neutral faces that provide no feedback, audience members who shake heads negatively during a talk, and people who whisper to one another and seem to be disagreeing with the speaker.

To cope, bear in mind that most people in the audience want the speaker to succeed. Don't focus on the stony-faced minority, keeping eyes on them, getting defensive, being intimidated by them. Remember, the hostility of a small portion of the audience is mainly in the mind. An audience can seem hostile to a speaker by failing to give supportive, nonverbal feedback.

Warm-up techniques: (1) Meet as many people in the audience as possible before the presentation. (This is particularly useful, and easy to do, in groups of 25 or less.) (2) Get right to the point with a vigorous statement of your purpose. (3) Involve the audience early by asking questions or getting them to speak on the issue.

Treat an oral presentation as nothing more than an enlarged conversation. Dramatic highs and lows of voice, facial expression, emphasis, hand gestures, and body language will then come naturally to enhance the talk.

Source: Dr. Roger Flax, communications training consultant, Motivational Systems, South Orange, N.J.

How to find and use a speech writer

The most important quality in a speech writer is reliability. When an executive has to give a speech on a certain date, it must be delivered, finished and polished, on deadline. So it's important to find the right one.

Get names from executives in other companies, colleagues or public relations firms. Always check a writer's references personally.

Do not rely too much on sample speeches. The speaker may have edited them, or the style may reflect a special relationship between writer and speaker. But samples can reveal how interesting the speech is.

At the first meeting (there should be no charge), see if the writer has done any homework on the company and industry without being asked to. Does the writer have compatible views? How does the writer feel about the industry?

To produce a good speech, the writer needs swers to these questions:

Why did the speaker accept this invitation?
What are the points that must be made to rticular audience?
o is supposed to benefit? The company?
istry? A college? A particular cause or
iew?
ing on the length and the reputation

of the writer, a good speech costs from $700 to $4,000. Expect to pay a premium for rush jobs. Ideal lead time is two to four weeks. If more time is allowed, the material may not be fresh when it is delivered.

Expect up to three drafts. The first is basically for the speaker to react to. Sometimes it is good enough to use as is. The second draft should be close to what the speaker wants. The third should need only slight polishing. The ideas should be well-reasoned, persuasive and forcefully expressed.

Use speech writers on a project basis unless many speeches are anticipated. If a writer is put on retainer, negotiate a volume discount (such as 15 speeches in a year for the price of 12) and an opportunity to get the same speech edited or altered for different occasions.

It's usually wise to accept the writer's judgment when the speaker is not sure what to say. One client required 14 drafts. The final one was almost a duplicate of the first.

And, most speech writers do not write humor. Humor is very personal. If a funny opening line or anecdote seems desirable, try to write it yourself.

Source: Robert Horn Resnick, speech writer, New York.

Once you're on the air

• Set the tone right away. Explain at the outset why subject is important.

• Don't stray from the subject.

• Keep answers tight. Allow time for more questions and answers, and thus more information.

• On television, don't look at the cameras. People are more effective when looking directly at show host.

• On radio, sit close to the microphone. The audience will lose much of what you're saying if you're too far away.

Source: Richard Goldberg, president, *You're On,* Visual Communications Consulting, Brighton, Mass.

RUNNING EFFECTIVE MEETINGS

How not to run a meeting

• Call a nonemergency meeting during non-business hours or on a weekend.

• Have secretary leave surprise short-notice invitations on desks.

• Invite people without regard to their duties or priorities.

• Fail to distribute an agenda in advance.

• Don't announce the subject of the meeting.

• Never reveal who will be there.

• Neglect to bring records along or bring obsolete data. Then it will be impossible to document anything.

• Use technical terms that no one understands.

• Argue and frown a lot to show seriousness. Challenge every statement.

• Always blame someone else for problems (especially in front of customers).

• Run out on the meeting, leaving everyone else wondering what they're supposed to do next.

Source: David K. Lindo, *Supervision Can Be Easy,* AMACOM, New York.

How to chair a committee

• Be aware of every member's interests, hopes, and suggestions for the committee. Meet privately beforehand with invitees to ascertain their points of view. This will insure against unpleasant surprises during the session.

• Handle housekeeping details efficiently. Be sure agendas and supplies are distributed on time. Welcome members at the door to relax them.

• Don't let talkative members dominate and quiet ones fade into the woodwork. Privately urge quiet people to speak up. Or get permission to pass on their views.

• Remain neutral. Avoid granting individual favors or advancing narrow causes. Chairpersons are judged by how their committee performs as a whole, not by personal contributions they might make.

• Stress the blending of divergent opinions into a consensus. Be wary of advancing too many opinions from the chair.

• Check the final report with the full committee before submitting it to make sure it accurately represents the group's findings.

Source: Dr. John E. Tropman, professor of social work, University of Michigan, *Directors and Boards,* McLean, Va.

Rules for more effective committees

• Give the committee the power to act on its decisions.

• Make membership voluntary whenever possible. If it's not possible, encourage members to speak freely.

• Match members' skills to problems. Avoid automatic appointments.

• Choose members of somewhat equal status. Otherwise, the powerful will dominate, the less powerful will agree or don't participate.

Setting a committee agenda

Limit the number of items. Begin and end with the least controversial matters. Schedule seven items per two-hour session. Never have a meeting run more than three hours.

Agenda items one and two should be the minutes of the last meeting and any announcements. This fills time while latecomers arrive.

Items three and four should be fairly simple, with low potential for controversy. At the end of item four, one-third of the meeting time should have been used.

Item five should be the most controversial and the one needing the most time. Allow one-third of the meeting for this matter. Follow it with a break so members can unwind.

Item six should be something that doesn't require immediate action.

Item seven should be a topic on which everyone can agree. That way the members will leave with a feeling of having been part of a consensus.

Source: *Directors and Boards,* McLean, Va.

To keep the meeting lively

• Don't ask questions that can be answered with a simple yes or no, for example, ones that begin with do you, have you, will you.

• Never open a session with "I think." Employees won't offer new ideas when leaders state their positions right away.

• Steer members back to the point whenever they wander. Summarize periodically. A meeting won't go anywhere unless the focus is always on a solution.

• Stress the importance of getting different points of view. This makes it easier for everyone to participate.

• Bring disagreements out into the open so they can be discussed.

Source: Michael Renton, *Getting Better Results from the Meetings You Run,* Research Press, Champaign, Ill.

How breaks improve meetings

Well-planned coffee breaks allow informal one-to-one chats so that meeting participants can work out disagreements and clarify misunderstandings in some privacy. This is especially important when the meeting must result in decisions. To make breaks effective:

• Organize the agenda so that controversial or complex items will be interrupted by a break. It reduces logjams during the discussion.

• Schedule as many breaks as needed (up to one hour). But avoid late afternoon breaks. Some participants may wander off.

• Locate the refreshment table as near to the conference room as possible (outside the door) so that the meeting atmosphere isn't disrupted.

• Duration of the break should be slightly less time than needed for a trip to a coffee shop or back to the desk for a quick task. Remember, breaks are part of the meeting, designed to expedite (not interrupt) the discussion.

• End breaks on time. Get participants back into the formal session by closing conference room doors, ringing a small bell, or both.

Source: William T. Carnes, *Effective Meetings for Busy People,* McGraw-Hill, New York.

Meeting dimensions

• Committee meetings: 30 minutes to 3 hours; 3 to 15 people in attendance.

• Training meetings: 1 to 30 days; 10 to 30 people.

• Planning meetings: 1 to 5 days; 6 to 15 people.

• Information meetings (in which participants are introduced to a new concept or practice and are motivated to use it): 1 to 5 days; attendance can be unlimited.

Too few persons at meetings limit the number of ideas that can be generated. But too many people make agreement and decision-making cumbersome.

Source: Coleman Finkel, president, National Conference Centers, East Windsor, N.J., *Successful Meetings,* Philadelphia.

Ways to save on business meetings

• Deal with hotel sales offices, not reservation centers. Hotel sales reps can be more flexible about group discounts.

• Before setting a date for a meeting, find out when the hotels under consideration have the least business. As a general rule, big-city hotels have the most vacancies (as well as the most negotiable rates) from Wednesday to Friday.

• Pay for open bars at meetings by the bottle rather than by the drink. Request that bartenders pour one-ounce shots rather than free-pour the drinks.

• Ask hotels about their complimentary-room policies. Hotels generally offer one free room for every 50 rooms booked. The policy is negotiable.

• Serve a light buffet lunch rather than a heavy meal. Buffets are cheaper and the lighter fare helps keep employees from falling asleep at afternoon sessions.

• Organize meetings on days of the week that enable the company to take advantage of any available discount air fares.

Source: Stephen Moran, president, Meeting Planners, Inc., Boston.

Meeting site considerations

For the next hotel gathering:

• Examine facilities when they're being used by a group similar to your company's in size and makeup.

• Don't settle for the first price quoted by a hotel salesperson—negotiate. Also shop around.

• Ask about labor relations. Is there a chance of a staff strike during your stay?

• Save on meeting-room rentals and minimize confusion when the general session breaks into small meetings. Have the general session seating on one side of the ballroom; adjourn to setups for small groups on the other side.

• Avoid communication problems with the hotel staff, consider paying for extra help.

• If the company needs special arrangements, ask. Hotels usually can accommodate any request —if the company is willing to pay.

PART II

Financial Management

5 FINANCIAL ANALYSIS AND CONTROL

FINANCIAL ANALYSIS

Pitfalls in the use of ROI

The danger in adopting any new management practice lies in applying it blindly and widely throughout the company, without taking account of the long-range results. A dangerous trend is using current return on investment (ROI) as the chief means of evaluating a manager's performance.

The appeal of ROI:

• It reflects how much investment is required to generate a dollar of profit: *True*. And it's a key way to monitor the company's overall economic performance.

• It's a hard number and it's not subject to subjective manipulation: *False*. Every experienced manager has moved a big spending decision either forward or backward a few weeks to affect a period's return on investment.

A longer-range trap that has now been revealed in a major study of over 200 companies is that overemphasis on ROI discourages investment and new-product development. Plant modernization increases investment and immediately decreases ROI. Research-and-development expenses come right out of profits and push down current ROI.

On average, the research-and-development funds invested in any one year do not turn up as increased profits until four years later.

The simplest alternative is to use ROI, but base incentive compensation more heavily on future performance, for example, stock options (or phantom stock plans for companies that do not have any publicly traded equities). Or executive bonuses to three different profit measures: overall company ROI; ROI for the manager's current unit; and current ROI for the unit the manager last headed.

This way executives have an incentive to make decisions and take sensible risks that might hurt current profits but increase them in the future. And it encourages department heads to pay much more attention to the selection of top-notch successors.

The best technique is to evaluate executives using a combination of measures, with ROI as just one factor. Others are new-product development, sales growth, department productivity and/or major productivity improvements. The usual objection to this approach is that the art of judging managerial performance and persuasively communicating that judgment are among the most important responsibilities of a chief executive. Top managers who shirk the task by relying on mechanical formulas mortgage the company's future to measurable short-term criteria.

———

Source: Dr. Donald Hambrick, assistant professor of business, Columbia University Graduate School of Business.

A financial early warning system

No single financial measure (return on equity, debt-equity ratio, etc.) alerts top management to an emerging financial problem. Closest to such a signal is the Z-Score, developed by Dr. Edward Altman, finance professor at New York University. The Z-Score is useful for manufacturing companies to identify a deteriorating or an improving financial condition when plotted over time. The formula:

$$Z = 1.2x_1 + 1.4x_2 + 3.3x_3 + 0.6x_4 + 1.0x_5$$

$$x_1 = \frac{\text{current assets} - \text{current liabilities}}{\text{total assets}}$$

$$x_2 = \frac{\text{retained earnings (from balance sheet)}}{\text{total assets}}$$

$$x_3 = \frac{\text{earnings before interest and taxes}}{\text{total assets}}$$

$$x_4 = \frac{\text{market value of equity}}{\text{total liabilities}}$$

$$x_5 = \frac{\text{net sales}}{\text{total assets}}$$

To read the results:

• The company is financially healthy when Z is 3.0 or more.

• The company is financially ailing when Z equals 1.8 or less.

• The situation is neutral if Z falls between 1.8 and 3.0.

The Z-Score can be used internally to track the company's financial conditions over time, to compare a company's performance with that of competitors, and to set financial goals.

It can be used externally to perform credit analyses and to help determine an accounts receivable policy.

———

Source: Robert Roussey, partner, Arthur Andersen & Co., Chicago.

BUDGETS

Trimming the fat off budgets

The greater the detail in budget, the greater the waste. The problem is that managers allow a little extra for each item in the budget. As the number of items mounts, the more fat "cushion" accumulates.

This cushion is seldom left in the budget at the fiscal year's end. It gets spent. If it were left over, managers would have to worry about budget cuts the following year.

To trim the fat, require less detail. Allocate expenditures by broad categories. Leave managers some freedom to shift money from one category to another in accordance with need. This cuts the temptation to overbudget. It also reduces the paperwork and administrative efforts associated with budgeting.

Four ways to make a budget more useful

1. Each budget sheet comes with accompany-

ing instructions. Everyone who fills one out follows the same rules.

2. Costs are grouped into categories so that all operating results can be analyzed fairly.

3. There is a clear procedure for midstream revision that includes a definition of what changes justify it.

4. Preparers are accountable for compliance. Their results are periodically examined to judge progress and performance.

Source: *Evaluating Accounting Controls: A Systematic Approach,* Arthur Young & Co., New York.

When formal budgets don't make sense

Many companies operate—or strive for—a system of strict, annual budgets. This is usually counterproductive. The companies that benefit most from rigid budgetary controls are old or well-established firms with a consistent rate of sales growth and a relatively unaltered product line from year to year. Firms that are inhibited rather than helped by strict budgeting:

• Are growing rapidly or erratically—fast one year, slow the next.

• Do not always know which segment of the business will produce the most growth in the coming year.

• Serve widely varying markets, some of which may be very strong one year, while others turn quite weak.

Example: A chemical company supplies products to the automotive and electronics industries. When the auto market is weak, the firm's auto business will be lower than budgeted. Meanwhile, electronics may be doing better than the budget anticipates. To shift more capability into electronics may mean hiring more personnel because electronics is more people-intensive than automotive, which relies more on capital equipment.

Under rigid budgeting, such sudden shifts can be difficult. Managers are normally held accountable for what they had budgeted several months earlier. They would most likely be in trouble if their sales were 5% above or below their projections. They may actually be penalized if they exceed their targets (the electronics manager) as well as if they fall short (the automotive manager). In the final analysis, the budget is keeping the company from taking advantage of changing opportunities.

The chemical company's alternative is ad hoc budgeting. A formal, detailed budget is prepared each year as in other companies, but it is not continually revised with every shift in business conditions. Instead, changes are made in succeeding years' budgets.

One benefit of this approach is that managers know they are not going to be forced to live by the old budget when circumstances change. This permits them to respond to external events and capitalize on opportunities without having to spend time revising budgets.

Another is that the company avoids getting topheavy in its management. The company in question, for example, has a small management group and wants to stay that way. By not repeatedly revising the budget, there is no need for a huge financial department.

And the real world, not the budget, becomes the true control mechanism. Both the board of directors and management use the budget as a guide, not as a bible that tells managers what they can and cannot do.

Ad hoc budgeting lets fast-acting managers change operations without going through numerous formal budget revisions. It gets around the common problem of managers who try to live with out-of-date assumptions rather than go back and change projections.

For example, a company's raw-material costs soar far beyond the budget. Unless the budget is revised (perhaps several times), the purchasing staff goes on buying as scheduled. Meanwhile, the marketing department keeps pricing the product on the basis of the budget because it does not know the actual costs. In extreme cases, marketing may sell more and more and think it is doing a great job, while margins narrow or even disappear entirely.

The company's ad hoc budgeters prevent this by preparing detailed, monthly cost sheets that keep all top managers informed of changes as they occur. Direct manufacturing costs account for 60% of the company's sales dollar. So, the changes reflected in the cost sheets are what the managers use to shift tactics. But this continually updated information is not used to recast the budget, because it would keep managers working on budgets instead of on real tasks.

If a company does not pay attention to the budget, why bother to go through the exercise at all? The answer is it should pay attention to the budget, but as a planning tool rather than an operational control. This company uses its budget to plan in the following way:

• Marketing forecasts where sales will come from in the next year.

• Production determines whether enough capacity is in place to fill those orders.

• Selling prices are determined and costs are estimated to see what is happening to margins.

• Managers project overhead, staffing, and expenses.

• Financial managers project cash flow and figure out whether internally generated funds will be sufficient to finance or whether to borrow.

The key requirement of ad hoc budgeting is an active, attentive management. Managers cannot simply rely on a computer to punch out numbers and put up a red flag if the figures stray a certain percentage from the budget. Managers must look at the monthly cost, production, sales, and other figures intelligently and ask the right questions. The best control is management by people, not by mechanism.

Source: Dr. Herman W. Andre, vice president for finance, and Norman L. Ritter, treasurer, Great Lakes Chemical Corp., West Lafayette, Ind.

PAYING BILLS

Simplifying payables

Check the day's incoming invoices for validity and discounts. Then: Determine the best date to make payment on each and write the check.

Put each check in a separate stamped envelope and code it (rear lower corner) with the required mailing date (allow three days in transit for local, seven days for cross-country).

File envelopes in chronological order and each day, mail those earmarked for that date.

The result: cost-effectiveness equal to any computer-based system.

Source: Ray Martin, president, Microcomputer Applications, Inc., Austin, Tex.

Taking the prompt-payment discount

The 2% discount for prompt payments is usually still worth taking even if it's necessary to borrow to do it. Typical terms are 2–10 net 30. (The amount is due in 30 days, with 2% off if paid within 10 days.) And earning 2% in 20 days is the equivalent of 36% per year.

When the check is for the wrong amount

Deposit a check quickly, even if the amount is wrong, and argue about it later. If the company receives a partial-payment check or a check for an incorrect amount, it's a mistake, at today's high interest rates, to wait until the problem is corrected. Endorse it "Accepted as partial pay-ment." Don't deposit a check for an incorrect amount that the maker has marked "Payment in full."

CREDIT

Smart credit policies

Tightening credit in response to high borrow-ing costs should be done without antagonizing good customers or losing sales. Credit should be more liberal for high-margin products than for low-profit items. If the customer cannot be ap-proved for credit, encourage bank letters of credit, personal guarantees, consignment sales, partial shipments, or liens on assets. Allow volume dis-counts only if payment is prompt. And maintain a bad-debt ratio close to the industry average.

Source: Seidman & Seidman, CPAs, New York.

How to make better use of the credit department

An effective credit department assembles much information that other departments can use—at very low incremental cost. Credit data can help other departments to:
• Forecast liquidation of receivables (finance department).
• Keep top management up to date about bus-iness conditions and trends.
• Profile customers demographically and geo-graphically (marketing department).
• Identify or rate prospects before sales force solicits them.

• Provide specialized data about new markets.
• Evaluate vendors, and find new sources (purchasing department).
• Screen merger candidates.
• Train managers in financial controls.

Source: Dr. Harold W. Fox, professor, Ball State University, Muncie, Ind.

Tightening credit controls in a recession

A recession is no time to continue the stan-dard business practice of making the sales now and worrying about collection later. During a re-cession, stretched-out accounts receivable weaken cash flow, and borrowing to stay liquid cuts into profit margins that are already thinned by weak sales. One result is higher unit costs.

For example, if a company has $5 million in accounts receivable, borrowing $1 million of that at 12% to cover accounts payable costs $120,000 a year. But if the company tightens credit controls at a cost of less than $120,000, and in the process reduces its accounts receiv-able by $1 million, it will come out way ahead.

The key to tightening credit controls is not al-tering credit policy, but improving its execution. This involves accurately analyzing the risk in ex-tending credit to each customer, improving the coordination between the company's credit and sales operations, and clearly establishing the credit manager's authority in regard to how much credit he can extend without top management's approval. Also important is how much bad debt he can pass on to a collection agency or write off on his own authority.

Recommended steps:

• Have the credit manager report to the chief operating officer, not to the controller, in order to draw him into the management process.

• Periodically send credit personnel into the field with salespeople. This gives credit analysts a feel for sales problems, and fosters better working relationships between the two groups.

• Take a critical look at the company's methods for gathering credit information. Review the questions credit analysts ask when calling a customer's bank to see if those questions can be sharpened still further.

Source: Myron J. Biggar, management consultant, Nazareth, Pa.

Shutting off credit

It may be one way to improve the company's cash position in hard times, but regular customers deserve special handling. Besides, their repeat business offers built-in leverage. Save the tough cash-and-carry treatment for infrequent or one-time buyers, at least until a thorough credit check can be made.

How flexible credit terms boost sales

Requiring every customer to make full payment of a bill within 30 days may shut out some otherwise good accounts. Instead; consider offering cash-short customers with good credit ratings a payment plan that lets them pay within an average of 30 days. Flexible formulas include:

• One-third down, one-third in 30 days, one-third in 60 days. The average is 30 days.

• One-half down, one-half in 60 days. This also gives a 30-day collection average.

• One-half down, one-quarter in 30 days, one-quarter in 60 days. The collection average falls to 22.5 days.

Source: Thomas J. Martin and Bruce Trabue, *Sell More and Spend Less,* Holt, Rinehart & Winston, New York.

Using an SBIC to help a customer

If a key customer runs short of capital, reduces buying, and then delays paying for its purchases, the company's sales and profits begin to sag and cash-flow problems result.

To rectify such a situation, use a small business investment company (SBIC) to channel a loan to the customer at favorable rates. The company can use an existing SBIC or set up one itself. The company agrees to step in and make the loan if the customer defaults.

This will build customer loyalty by providing aid in a pinch. The SBIC assumes the responsibility of dunning the customer for overdue payments, freeing the company from this task. The company can usually repossess its goods to cover the balance due if the customer should default. There are also tax advantages.

Details of how to work with SBICs are available from local Small Business Administration offices.

Personal liability for false statement to credit agency

A vendor extended credit to a corporation because a Dun & Bradstreet report showed a six-figure net worth. In fact, the net worth was very small and the corporation went under. In a recent ruling, the owner-officer of the corporation had to make good from personal assets.

Key points were that the creditor showed that it had relied on the false information. And the owner had knowingly given false information to D&B with the intention of deceiving the creditors.

Source: 130 SE 2d 830.

Nine ways to spot credit scams

Scam operators drain $110 million a year from U.S. businesses by buying goods on credit, then declaring bankruptcy or simply vanishing.

Typically, a scam operator will study an industry until he understands its credit policies. He's most likely to look for situations when credit checks are most perfunctory, for example, any seasonal rush period. Also, he will place and pay for small orders. Then, when the time is right, he will place a bunch of big orders, take delivery, and disappear without paying.

Alternatively, a scam artist will buy a small but reputable firm, place large orders, take delivery, and declare bankruptcy.

To avoid getting bilked, check:

1. Unsolicited orders, especially those unrelated to a customer's direct line of business.

2. Trade-show orders, especially the ones taken by suppliers who forgot or couldn't bring their credit files with them.

3. Rush orders from strangers or new customers.

4. Companies that haven't been in business for three years or more.

5. Recent change of ownership.

6. Sudden, large orders.

7. Companies whose names are similar to those of reputable companies in the same area, or use impressive titles such as worldwide or federal.

8. Companies that supply too much unsolicited credit information. Their hope is that this creates instant credibility and won't be checked. Also, check phone numbers of credit references to ascertain their genuineness, as well as letters from CPA firms and other references.

9. Unknown companies that enclose partial payments with first-time orders.

Source: Les Kirschbaum, president, Mid-Continent Adjustment Co., Morton Grove, Ill.

COLLECTIONS

Collection methods that work

Make calls early in the week. Customers who promise on Friday to pay on Monday often "forget" over the weekend.

Be persistent. If customers are out, leave a name and number and request a return call. Ask when they are expected, then call back again, and again. When writing a letter for payment, tell customers these messages have gone unanswered.

Encourage the debtors to commit for a partial payment. Then use that amount to arrange a payment schedule.

When customers agree to pay, immediately send a letter formalizing that agreement.

If a letter threatening use of a collection agency or legal action is sent, don't follow up immediately. Silence makes customers edgy. They will call.

After setting a deadline for payment, stick to it.

Source: Wayne A. Dugger, senior credit representative, Union Carbide Corp., New York.

Bearing down on payment stretch-outs

Businesses share one major problem in today's money environment: not being paid promptly. Accounts that were paid in 30 to 60 days are now being stretched to 90 days and more. To avoid these stretch-outs; establish clear rules concerning payment when the sale is made. Then hold clients to their promised date of payment. If money is pledged for the 15th of the month and nothing is received by the 17th, call. Companies that promise to pay next month could be out of business by then, with bills still unpaid.

It is important to differentiate between old and new clients. On new business, set the terms clearly and firmly. For old clients, use delicate handling, since many are used to being accommodated. Appeal to their sense of fair play: "Let's work together and get through this tough time." Suggest that the customer make a dent in arrearages while continuing to make current purchases.

But avoid a cash-only policy. It can become a mortal blow to your business.

Source: Michael M. Tulman, M. Tulman & Co., Boston.

Four ways to speed collections

To stay liquid in the face of interest rates, many companies are demanding faster payment from customers, while making slower payment to their own suppliers. Smaller companies are often the victims of this strategy. Instead of searching for leverage where there is none, management of smaller companies should streamline accounts-receivable procedures where practical. Specifically, they should:

• Generate invoices faster. Ideally, invoices should be mailed on the same day as the shipment. Try decentralizing the invoicing procedure, or making a capital investment in a computerized accounts-receivable system.

• Study the bill-paying procedures of the company's major customers. Send all necessary information and supporting documentation with the bill the first time. It can be sent in a format that will minimize paying errors by customers.

• Experiment to find the best mailing location for invoices, to cut down on mail time.

• Track accounts receivable day by day (computers make it easy). This puts the company in the best possible position vis-a-vis the customers' other creditors. Few companies can force the giants to speed payments. However, those companies with efficient accounts-receivable procedures will get paid before those with inefficient ones.

Source: W. Barent Wemple, Case & Co., New York.

Dealing with slow payers

Customers squeezed by recession and high-interest rates often stall before paying suppliers. Here are some ways to encourage payments from those who have been good customers but have run into temporary financial difficulties:

• Restrict the customer's credit until all past due bills are paid.

• Use a cash-on-delivery-plus system. Supply goods only on a COD basis. Then add an extra amount from the overdue bill.

• Set up a partial-payment plan.

• Accept a note and personal guarantee of payment from an officer of the debtor company.

• Institute finance charges for overdue accounts. (Consult a lawyer and accountant first. State laws vary on allowable charges.)

• Use these temporary credit arrangements either alone or in combination. Working with a hard-pressed account now may provide a valuable customer later.

Source: Les Kirschbaum, president, Mid-Continent Adjustment Co., Morton Grove, Ill.

The high cost of past-due accounts

Just how much are overdue accounts really worth? Estimates:

Past-due status	Likely recovery (cents on the dollar)
30 days	97
90 days	90
120 days	80
6 months	67
1 year	45
2 years	23
3 years	12

Source: Alexander Grant & Co., New York.

Using a phone call to collect an overdue bill

• Speak to the person who signs the checks. Don't waste time on other employees.

• Make the call as personal as possible. Always address the customer by name.

• Give the customer a chance to explain. There may be a valid excuse for being late.

• Press to learn the real reasons for non-payment. If customer dissatisfaction is the cause, a sympathetic ear or the prompt adjustment of a complaint may be the best way to speed up payment.

• Don't hang up without specifying details of the payment arrangement. Determine what the next step will be—whether it's to pick up the check on a particular day, call back, etc.

Source: *Better Business by Telephone,* Timonium, Md.

Bringing suit for nonpayment

Facing punishing interest rates and dangerous liquidity problems, a number of manufacturers are finally getting tough with slow-paying customers, even if those customers are prized accounts.

Manufacturers are cutting off shipments and threatening lawsuits for non-payment of bills.

Specifically, manufacturers are having attorneys draft letters threatening legal action to customers who lag more than 60 days on 30-day bill payments.

What's precipitating the move to legal action? In addition to a liquidity crunch, many manufacturers foresee further significant price-cutting. With stagflation, slim inventories, and collection policies already steeled with legal threats, price-cutting may be the only survival tactic left.

Source: David Kantes, vice president, Chase Manhattan Bank, New York.

Collecting on default judgments

Employees and consumers have little trouble collecting judgments against employers and sellers. The opposite is not true, though. Businesses find it difficult to collect judgments from customers, individual or corporate, for not paying their bills.

In fact, nine out of ten default judgments never get collected. Half of the remaining 10% get collected only if a business devotes substantial time and money to pursue the defaulter.

Rather than pay a judgment, a defaulter may declare bankruptcy, in which case the business that won the judgment has to stand in line to collect with all other creditors. Or, if the defaulter is a business, its owner may liquidate current operations, then reopen under a new name, making collection difficult.

Debtors may use collection exemptions, which vary by state. In Texas, ranches are exempt from collection. In Florida, boats are.

And the legal proceedings for forcing collection are complicated. They get bogged down in subsidiary issues, and are often presided over by judges sympathetic to debtors. Thus, it rarely makes sense to go to court to win a judgment in the first place. Instead, try to recoup the debt by hiring a collection agent. Collection agents work on a contingency basis. Or threaten a defaulter with a suit, then collect what is offered in settlement. As a general rule, a poor settlement agreed to immediately will usually produce a higher net than a decent judgment collected after a long fight.

If neither of these strategies works and it make sense to proceed in court, the business should familiarize itself with the statutes that aid collection of a judgment. These include:

• Supplementary proceedings to help determine what assets a defaulter has. But even if a defaulter is forced to reveal where the assets are, there is no law requiring that the assets stay there.

• Garnishment statutes allow the business to collect its judgment by going directly to the defaulter's sources of revenue. If the defaulter is an individual, it may not be possible to garnish wages. Only one creditor at a time can do that, and there may be a line of creditors.

• Special receivers in aid of execution statutes permit creditor to try to have the court appoint a temporary receiver for the defaulter's business. The receiver takes over the defaulter's business, temporarily runs it, and turns over all earnings as payment for the judgment.

Taking the first steps in any of the above procedures is often a good way to force a favorable out-of-court settlement.

Source: David Schechner, Esq., Schechner & Targan, West Orange, N.J.

When should overdue bills go to a collection agency?

Focus on collecting past-due accounts within the first 90 days. After that time, in-house collection efforts are almost totally ineffective. It's usually more productive then to turn over unpaid accounts to a collection agency, even though the creditor ends up with an average of only $10 back from each original $100 debt. Pay the agency a fixed fee rather than on a percentage basis to discourage it from pursuing only the largest and easiest accounts.

Source: Richard D. Schultz, president, National Revenue Corp., *Financial Executive,* New York.

Getting more out of collection agents

Some corporate managers instruct their accounts payable departments not to pay bills until they hear from suppliers' collection agents. That buys time because small suppliers can't afford to pay these agents the 28%–50% commission for collecting until it's the last resort. As a result, those suppliers find their cash flow positions seriously undermined. A solution is to find an agent willing to collect accounts on a routine basis for a fixed fee, rather than for a percentage of the bills that they collect. Under this arrangement, the company routinely forwards data on accounts as they become 60 days overdue. The client invests a low fee for a block of the collection agent's services, then keeps 100% of the payments. The company thus pays less for the service, but still impresses its customers with a strict payment policy. And using the service allows the company to use its best inside collectors to concentrate on key accounts.

The collection agent must offer the full range of dunning techniques, give reasonable guarantees, and agree to protect the credit-grantor's goodwill. Without such precautions, some agents might write letters that make the problem worse or alienate future business.

Source: David Allburn, vice-president, National Revenue Corp., Columbus, Ohio.

Delaying-payment ploys that hurt suppliers

Retailers, including some of the most prestigious in the country, are being harsh with suppliers to delay paying them. The most severely affected are vendors so dependent on the retailers that they cannot fight back. A common example is the lost-invoice or lost-proof-of-delivery-document game. One of the biggest and most prestigious retailers kept it up for six months with a particular company.

The cancellation-and-delay ploy is even tougher. The retailer places an order, then asks for partial shipments, delaying the balance, often more than once. At the end, it may cancel the unshipped portion. The supplier has to finance the undelivered part of the order for months, and then perhaps absorb a loss at closeout.

The suppliers' defense is to tighten operations. Be prepared to reduce sales to major retail customers. Or accept the retailers' terms and be squeezed.

Source: Malcolm Moses, financial consultant, Merrick, N.Y.

BANKRUPTCY

Dealing with a company in Chapter 11

With soft spots scattered throughout the economy, many companies are coming up against customers or suppliers in severe enough financial difficulty to file for Chapter 11 rehabilitation, which is far more common than actual bankruptcy that results in liquidation.

Suppliers should use extreme caution in reopening lines of credit with a Chapter 11 company. It is easy to identify such a firm, as it must have DIP (Debtor in Possession) after its name. Although new debts have priority over old debts coming under a Chapter 11 proceeding, there is no guarantee that the company will have enough money even to pay current creditors. Operating problems are not corrected just because the company has filed under Chapter 11.

A good general rule is to extend no credit at all unless there is reason to believe that the company will survive and confirm a plan. Then, whatever credit line the supplier extended before the Chapter 11 filing should be greatly reduced until the company proves that its cash flow is adequate. For example, a pre-Chapter 11 credit line of $100,000 might be reduced to $10,000.

Stay out of the picture during the first 30–60 days after a filing under Chapter 11. It takes that long to learn whether cash flow is sufficient and whether the creditors will stick by the company.

One risk to a supplier is that secured creditors may have a lien on all liquid assets of the company. If this is so, their claims have priority. Such a creditor may choose to cease financing the company, causing liquidation of the company's assets.

Another problem is that payroll, attorneys' and accountants' fees, taxes, and certain claims take priority over repayment of trade debt. Sometimes one current creditor gets a superpriority. For example, a key supplier refuses to grant credit unless it gets special consideration, and without the supplier the company cannot do business. The court and the creditor committee may agree to give that supplier priority over other new creditors.

Even if a company confirms a plan and is discharged from Chapter 11 (at which point it can erase the DIP from its corporate name), the danger period is not over. The credit risk is still high immediately after the company comes out of Chapter 11. In a common situation, a company scrapes together every last penny by refinancing its assets with the creditors' blessing, then it faces going out of business within 90 days after confirmation because of insufficient cash flow. Many of those companies that do survive remain weak for years.

Use the prudent approach. Do not take the company's own cash-flow projections at face value. Instead, assess its debt-payment schedule and its cash requirements, and then determine if cash flow warrants the granting of new credit. In addition to the company itself, sources of financial information about the company are members of the Chapter 11 creditor committee; the creditor committee's accountant (who supplies reports to the committee); and to a lesser extent, the company's bankers. If the bankers will not talk, assume the company's problems are serious.

Customers of a Chapter 11 company face less danger in dealing with it than do suppliers who are waiting to be paid. If the relationship has been a long and fruitful one, stick by the ailing company. But play it smart. Hedge with alternate suppliers in case the company does fold after all.

Source: Malcolm P. Moses, Malcolm P. Moses Assoc., Merrick, N.Y.

How to live through Chapter 11

Most companies underestimate the tremendous opportunities for improvement beyond mere debt restructuring that Chapter 11 offers.

The first step is to find a compatible Chapter 11 attorney, accountant, and perhaps a consultant. Meet all their associates who will be working on the case throughout the proceedings. Then:

• Contact the bank. Inform it of the likelihood of Chapter 11. If it is a secured lender, win its support.

• Manage cash flow so there is enough cash on hand to get through the difficult first weeks after filing.

• Use the opportunity to cut all deadwood operations from the company.

• Terminate all burdensome leases and contracts. (This is legal under the statute). Canceling onerous agreements can be a boon to future operations.

• Liquidate excess or stale inventory. Chapter 11 provides a chance to take the write-offs the company has been avoiding for years because it did not want to hurt its credit standing.

To get new credit, explain the circumstances of the filing to all suppliers and other credit sources. Supply them with current financial information and detailed projections. If the cause of the problem has been alleviated, assure them that they will be paid—but only if that assurance can be met. Many recent Chapter 11 filings have been caused by high interest rates and excessive debt. Once loans are renegotiated, the affected companies often can function normally again.

Finally, keep your customers informed. In most cases, they will try to continue an established relationship.

Alternative to bankruptcy

A small paint manufacturer came close to bankruptcy during the last recession. The owner paid off the small creditors, then calculated that if the business was liquidated the major creditors would get only six cents on the dollar. Instead, he began negotiations with major suppliers for:

• Two years to make good on the debts. During that time, they would be paid in installments.

• Continued flow of supplies, to be paid for COD.

The creditors had nothing to lose. Profit on current COD transactions would be equal to or greater than the interest they would earn on the money they received from a forced bankruptcy. The owner also promised to close shop and liq-uidate immediately if ever behind in these payments on the debt.

The plan succeeded. Using time effectively, the company was in shape to prosper when the economy recovered.

BUSINESS TRAVEL CONTROLS

Controlling travel and entertainment expenses

• Cut back on the number of company-issued credit cards. This will result in some savings on the cards' issue fees, a small decrease in bookkeeping costs and a large saving on T&E costs. Employees without credit cards run up fewer expenses.

• Eliminate or reduce large employee cash advances. Distribute smaller advances weekly rather than large ones monthly. Or use a payable-through-draft reimbursement system.

• Tighten record keeping. Develop a system of controls that tracks an individual's rather than a group's expenditures. This identifies those employees who pad expense accounts.

• Reward the most frugal travelers by giving bonuses to employees in each company category with the best combined record of high productivity and low T&E expenses.

Source: William Shively, vice president, Traveletter Corp., Minneapolis, Minn.

Weighing the costs of business travel procedures

Weigh these alternatives in checking the cost-effectiveness of current travel procedures:

• Per diem vs actual cost reimbursement.
• Charge card vs voucher system.
• Operating a corporate travel department vs dealing with an outside travel agent.
• Negotiating low-rate hotel and car-rental contracts.
• Alternatives to travel, such as electronic mail, computers, closed-circuit TV, private couriers.

Cutting travel costs

A reasonable guideline for business-travel expenses is to keep the last 12-month expenses close to those of the preceding 12 months. Considering the escalation of travel costs, that would be cost-cutting management. A company growing at a rapid clip should not make cuts that could damage sales.

The chief tactic is to reinforce the standard commonsense rules that have started slipping: coach travel, without exceptions; airport limousines to hotels rather than taxis; and good hotels and motels but not the most expensive in town.

Consider negotiating corporate rates, in advance, in cities where many company salespeople or executives go for business. Don't be timid.

Cost-cutting travel management ideas:

• Plan all trips in advance, with a strategy in mind. This can eliminate repeat visits and overlapping trips. And it allows business travelers to use discount fares whenever possible.

• If the company does a lot of business in some areas, consider renting cars at a discount from dealers in those areas. Reserve the cars full time to be used as needed by company business travelers.

• Audit the big spenders on travel. They must prove more business per dollar spent on travel this year than last year.

Preventing expense-account rip-offs

Two new scams that employees are using:

• Car rentals. When returning a car rented on a personal credit card, the employee claims to have lost the contract. The rental agent makes out a new contract, leaving the employee with the original on which inflated time and/or mileage figures can be inserted for reimbursement purposes. To prevent this, have all rental charges billed directly to the company through a company credit card. Forbid employees to use personal credit cards for such business expenses.

• Airline fares. Employee trades in a full-fare ticket for a discounted seat and pockets the difference. Prevent this by tightening up the company's ticket-purchasing procedures to insure that it is getting the lowest fare to begin with. Make sure personnel who handle ticket purchases are familiar with the latest discount and promotional fares—they can save money on lower air fares.

Other rip-offs have been around for years and still work because most companies fail to check expenses under $25.

Old scams that are still widely used:

• Transportation between airport and town. Employee takes a bus and asks to be reimbursed for a taxi. The company should clearly state that the policy is to use the cheapest ride, except under special circumstances, such as rushing to a meeting. Require receipts, but recognize that these may be easily altered. Make it clear that such expenses, even if under $25, will be scrutinized. Then follow through with at least spot-checks.

• Double meal billing. Employee incorporates the cost of a hotel meal into the room charge on the expense account, then puts in for a fictitious restaurant meal. Deal with this by making sure there is a separate line on the expense-account form for room charges and another line for other meal expenses. Carefully double-check the completed form against the hotel bill.

The IRS requires the client to have an itemized bill from the hotel, but many companies never look beyond the employee's expense-account form.

Source: Harold Seligman, president, Management Alternatives, New York.

6 CASH MANAGEMENT

CASH FLOW

How to deal with—and avoid—liquidity crises

The precipitating cause of most company crises is lack of cash, not lack of sales or profitability. Crisis points now arise with astonishing speed as companies do business with 20% or more interest rates and high volatility. The key is faster and more frequent review of basic company controls on credit, purchasing, inventories, taxes, and spending.

• Beef up credit departments. Call the customer at the same time that a 30-day statement is mailed. The traditional practice of three collection letters and a phone call is obsolete for effective cash management under today's conditions.

Reduce the time lag between the day a shipment is made and the day it is invoiced. The current average is seven days; most companies can do better.

Eliminate cash discounts. They are ineffective for stimulating cash flow, when customers are stretching payments because of high interest rates and their own liquidity concerns. Charge interest on the past-due accounts. It's becoming increasingly commonplace.

• Run the company's payables to produce the maximum amount of cash flow, not for the con-

venience of the company's billing department. Relate payments to due dates of the bills.

• Scrap excess inventory. The tax benefits and cash flow may make it worthwhile. The company will also save on rent, utilities, and insurance.

Should the company cut down on its customer-service guarantees? The era of shipping within 24 hours after receipt of an order may be at an end. The cost in inventory is just too much for most firms. And if the company can't afford it any longer, its competitors probably can't either.

• Minimize inventory buildup. Spend the money necessary to install data-processing systems that project the best inventory level. They should be able to update that projection rapidly and often.

• Update production costs. Revise the standard costs that the company uses to measure profitability. The usual practice is to update data once a year. Labor and materials are rising too fast for that now. With computers, it should be possible to revise every three months.

• Going public is an option for many companies right now. Venture-capital groups are eager for sound, growing businesses. And the company does not have to be in high technology. (One nonglamour company found that a stock offering at seven times earnings made more sense than more bank loans.)

Convertible debt has virtues: 15% locked in for 15 years may be a sounder deal for the company than bank loans at three points over the prime interest rate.

• Defer taxes. Use the new installment sales rules as much as possible to defer taxes (and to hold on to current cash). Look for opportunities to use the same technique in overseas subsidiaries, especially in countries where rapid inflation means the taxes will eventually be paid in depreciated currency.

• Get top management involved in monthly and quarterly cash planning. It need not be detailed. But top management should know how much cash is coming in short-term from cash sales, collection of receivables, and other sources, and how much cash is going out short-term to suppliers, for loan repayments, and for other purposes. And it should immediately incorporate potential cash surpluses or deficits into the company's overall strategy.

• Push suppliers to stockpile low-turnover items. Or pool inventory needs with nearby firms.

• Purge customer lists. Eliminate the slowest-payment accounts. Offer to sell them for cash only.

• Stratify suppliers into those that must be paid currently, those that accept late payment occasionally, and those that take late payment as a matter of informal policy.

• Improve cash management by reducing balances in low-interest-bearing savings and checking accounts. Have banks apply funds in company checking accounts against the company's revolving line of credit to reduce interest payments.

• Pay insurance on a monthly basis. The added service charge this incurs is less than the financial advantages of avoiding prepayment of insurance premiums.

Borrow against life insurance policies the company holds on its executives in order to capitalize on low interest rates.

• Toughen tax planning: Accelerate depreciation where possible. Reevaluate the remaining life of company property annually.

• Keep earnings projections current to estimate tax payments more accurately. (Companies in cyclical businesses are thus able to delay tax payments until the high point of their cycles.)

• Buy new equipment late in the year to make maximum use of the 10% investment tax credit.

Source: Nicholas Gallopo, partner, Arthur Andersen & Co., New York City, James Wicker, partner, Peat, Marwick, Mitchell & Co., St. Paul, Minn.

Six ways to improve cash flow

• Prevent bookkeeping from following the comfortable routine of paying all suppliers on one day.

• Negotiate with suppliers for an installment-payment plan.

• Send stamped, self-addressed envelopes with customers' bills.

• Be sure cash is invested quickly in a money-market fund rather than left sitting in a checking account.

• Take precautions against check bouncing. Common ploys are no date, the figure amount varies from the written amount, no signature.

Copier forgeries of checks are a growing problem. They can be recognized by no indentations on the back from writing or typing.

Source: *The Sales Executive,* New York.

How to increase cash availability

For most companies, accelerating receipts to make cash available quickly may be far more important financially than earning the maximum interest on a disbursement float. The challenge is to get all checks and payments processed and consolidated as soon as possible in the company's main bank account.

The first order of business is to sensitize employees to know the difference between big or important checks requiring special treatment and routine receipts. All checks represent cash and should be taken care of promptly.

Rather than holding checks received after 3 P.M. until the next morning, for example, it may be worth keeping employees overtime or hiring extra help to get checks deposited that day. Also, if mail arrives as early as 7 A.M. and the office staff doesn't normally arrive until 9 A.M., it might be smart to add an early shift. Getting checks to the bank by 8:30A.M. instead of in the afternoon may save a day.

Become familiar with the bank's clearing procedures and work around those schedules. (It is valuable information to know that the bank has a 9 P.M. clearing or a late Friday pickup.) Never let receipts lie around when they could be deposited and earning interest or defraying expenses. Most banks will accommodate a company's needs once they have been communicated.

For distant customers, bypass the postal system altogether and ask the customer to deposit funds directly into a local bank, preferably one that has a relationship with the company's main hometown bank. Then the funds can be wired directly bank-to-bank with maximum speed.

Plan ahead for special or very large receipts expected from, say, the sale of a piece of property. Alert mailroom employees and leave instructions that the manager should be notified immediately on receipt of this or any unusually large check.

Even if solid check-handling procedures are supposed to be in effect, make sure they are actually working.

Source: John Carroll, partner, Peat, Marwick, Mitchell & Co., New York.

Check-clearing time is changing

Although the time it takes banks to process checks is generally shrinking, high volume is causing bottlenecks in some areas. For example, Denver banks are processing checks in about two-thirds the time it took them in 1974. But in Milwaukee, checks take an average of nearly a day longer to clear than they did seven years ago.

Cities where out-of-town checks clear in an average of less than 2.5 days: Atlanta, Chicago, Dallas, Denver, Houston, Kansas City, Louisville, Minneapolis, New York, Philadelphia, Pittsburgh, St. Louis.

Cities where checks take longer than three days to clear: El Paso, Helena, Los Angeles, Milwaukee, Nashville, Newark, New Orleans, Omaha, Portland, San Francisco, Seattle.

Source: Phoenix-Hecht, Inc., Chicago.

How to manage the shrinking float

Electronic processing is cutting the time it takes checks to clear. To keep pace with the change, companies must scrap or modify some long-standing cash-management tactics.

New strategies for receivables:

• Use computers to streamline cash management within the company. Many can be linked with the bank's electronic reporting system to give the company an even quicker and firmer grasp of its cash position.

• Offer discounts for payments made by electronic transfer.

• Upgrade lockboxes with a computerized reporting system through which banks notify customers instantly when a check arrives and when it clears. Bank fees for these electronic reporting systems vary widely and depend on what balance the company maintains.

Tactics for payables:

• Begin processing bills no sooner than the afternoon of day received.

• Pay with checks drawn on small banks that do not have electronic data processing or other services that speed check processing.

• Mail checks from clogged postal areas. Checks mailed from midtown Manhattan usually arrive a day later than those mailed from the Wall Street area, for example.

• If the company writes its checks against an out-of-town controlled disbursement point, it should set up at least one other point and monitor the performance of each. Since clearing time is changing in many areas, only trial and error can determine the most efficient disbursement point. And if the company switches disbursement points, it should also monitor the new ones periodically.

Several years ago, the Federal Reserve started clamping down on companies that took flagrant advantage of remote (as opposed to controlled) disbursement points. The Fed's current guidelines discourage companies from using remote disbursement points to make payments to individuals. Companies must also have a reason for banking at the location, such as an office, plant, or branch nearby or a prior relationship with the bank.

Source: George Manning, assistant vice president, Chemical Bank, New York; David Spiselman, consultant, Jamaica Estates, N.Y.

Using barter to strengthen cash flow

About 20% of most company business can be transacted through barter. In fact, more than 60% of the companies on the New York Stock Exchange now use barter for a significant number of transactions. Barter helps companies move inventory, improve cash flow, and open up new markets.

To barter through one of the more than 40 professional barter organizations, a company tells the barter firm what it has to exchange and what it wants in return. For example, a CB radio maker may say that it wants sales meeting facilities in Miami. The barter firm then contacts hotels to see what they want in exchange. It may offer the hotels linen goods that another company wants to barter. Principal barter firms do not normally charge a fee. They make money by selling some of the inventory they collect. A list of professional barter companies can be obtained from the International Assn. of Trade Exchanges in Alexandria, Va.

Smaller barter exchanges, listed in local *Yellow Pages,* also put companies that want to barter in touch with each other. The exchange takes an 8%–10% commission on transactions. It also charges a one-time enrollment fee and annual dues, each of which is usually $300–$500.

Commercial barter is entirely legal and should not be confused with noncash transactions that take place in the underground economy. It is a supplement to cash transactions, not a replacement.

Source: Moreton Binn, chairman, Atwood-Richards, Inc., New York.

Checks and the law

• Stale checks. A bank need not pay a check that is more than six months old. Exceptions are certified checks which must be paid at any time. Note that a bank can pay a check that is more than six months old, but it must exercise due care to be sure that the check is still good.

Source: *Advanced Alloys* vs *Sergeant Steel Corp.,* 12 UCC Rep 1173, 360 NYS2d 142.

• Certified checks normally cannot be the subject of a stop-payment order. However, if the bank is informed by the person who wrote the check that fraud was involved in the transaction, then the bank may stop payment. But it does not have to.

Source: *Lincoln Secs.* vs *Morgan Guaranty Trust Co.,* 8 UCC Rep. 215.

• The statute of limitations on a demand note begins to run on the date the note is due. If the limitation period runs out under local law, the holder of the note cannot collect. For example, a note payable 30 days after demand for payment was made on or after September 20, 1967. The statute of limitations provided for by local law was six years. So the holder of the note could not collect on it in 1974.

Source: *Environics, Inc.,* vs *Pratt,* 18 UCC Rep. 143, 376 NYS 2d 510.

• Letters or telegrams may serve as checks. To serve as a check the letter must be addressed to a bank. And it must state that a specific amount is to be paid on demand either to the bearer of the letter or to the order of a named person. If any one of these requirements is not met, the letter will not be valid as a check. And, of course, the bank will make its usual effort to verify that the "check" is valid.

Source: *United Milk Prods. Co.* vs *Lawndale Nat'l. Bank,* 392 F. 2d 876, 5 UCC Rep. 143.

• Words control figures. When the words and the numbers on a check disagree, the words determine how much the check is worth.

Source: Uniform Commercial Code Sec. 3-118(c).

EXCESS CASH

What to do with excess cash

Enjoying the luxury of a cash-rich company is not a healthy state of mind for any management. Too many managers are simply turning over the cash in short-term money-market funds or CDs, convincing themselves that the money is working hard enough. Yet the after-tax return to the company may be well below the 15% return most successful companies strive to achieve.

In inflationary times, cash is a wasting, depreciating asset, while fixed assets, which accountants are trained to think of as depreciating assets, can really be appreciating assets.

Using seasonal cash:

In investing their excess cash, unsophisticated managers of successful companies make the common mistake of buying CDs from a bank at the standard rate instead of negotiating for a higher rate. Any company that has a history of building up a heavy seasonal flow of cash (say, $500,000 or more) can negotiate a rate 1%–1½% higher than the standard CD rates.

Even higher rates can be obtained from Eurodollars. The rate is about three precentage points higher than standard CD rate. Terms are one, three, or six months. Since many U.S. banks won't handle a Eurodollar transaction of less than $1 million, it's best to go to the U.S. branch of a foreign bank for Eurodollars.

Another possibility is tax anticipation notes issued by localities. They are tax-free and short-term (around three months). At 8%, the after-tax return to a company in the 50% bracket is 16%.

Investing in the company:

This alternative makes most managers comfortable because they believe it is the most conservative thing to do with the cash. But they can be wrong. Make sure the investment in the company produces a satisfactory return. Some of the ways to invest are:

• Buy in company stock. For public and private companies, lowering the equity base by buying in shares gives the company more leverage on its borrowed money. For a privately held company that has gone through two or three generations and now has 15–25 stockholders with very different investment objectives, it can be a way of getting rid of some present and potential problems. (Typically, these minority shareholders can be bought out at net asset value, an attractively low price.)

• Shift the cash into receivables. If done carefully, this can be a very effective way to increase the company's market share. To do it, target important new prospects. Offer them better credit terms than they are now getting from the competition. Don't extend credit terms to weaker prospects who simply can't afford regular terms. The aim is to attract excellent new customers, not marginal ones.

• Build up inventory. This can make sense if the company's recent history and firm forecasts show that the value of its goods and raw materials is going up faster than the rate of inflation.

Acquisitions:

The opportunity to buy a company that is suffering from a cash crunch can be a real bargain. The price will be right, and the acquiring company's cash can be put to good use immediately by the purchased company.

Buying a going concern rather than starting up from scratch can triple the advantages. The buying company should always think in terms of after-tax dollars. Tax dollars and other cash flow can be generated from a smart investment company below book value, at book, or even above book.

Selling out:

Closely held companies with cash in the till make very attractive acquisitions prospects. Either invest the cash before it depreciates, or sell the business. That cash could be extremely valuable to another company.

Source: Robert Levine, Ernst & Whinney; Howard Miller, Peat, Marwick, & Mitchell; Louis C. Moscarello, Coopers & Lybrand.

The importance of money-market funds

It still makes sense to boost company return on investment by putting idle cash into a money-market fund, rather than in a bank deposit. Companies should consider the move if they have heavy seasonal flows of cash into and out of the company, and have no bank loans outstanding and none likely to be needed in the near future.

It also makes sense to keep a compensatory balance in a bank (as a condition for a loan) that is more than 20% of the size of the loan. Take anything over 20% and put it in a money fund. What's left on deposit will adequately compensate the bank for its services.

Money funds have several advantages over other conservative cash investments, such as Treasury bills and CDs. An account can be opened with as little as $1,000, for example, and the money can be withdrawn immediately by check (usual minimum is $500) with no advance notice and no interest penalty.

In addition, company paperwork—and risk—can usually be significantly cut, especially if cash is now managed by an executive on a part-time basis. And there is no commission or fee for putting money into the fund or taking it out. The funds typically take about ¾% out of investment income, however, to pay overhead and expenses.

7 TAXES

CUTTING TAXES

The best way to cut taxes is to plan ahead

Now is the time to review the company's tax strategies for the coming year. Make sure the company is poised to take advantage of every recent change in the tax law.

The greatest change in the new tax law for business is the reform of depreciation rules. Under the new Accelerated Cost Recovery System (ACRS), first-year deductions are larger than ever before. That is significant in the face of high interest rates. For example, a company in the 46% tax bracket acquires equipment in the five-year ACRS category. (Most business equipment is in this category.) The 10% investment credit combined with a 15% first-year ACRS deduction returns 16.7% of the equipment's cost to the company in the first year alone. If financing terms require payment of less than 16.7% of the purchase price in the first year, the result is a net cash inflow to the company.

Timing is the key to best utilizing the ACRS rules. Deductions are worth more when the company is in a high tax bracket. And the first-year deductions must be taken in the year the equipment is placed in service (regardless of when it was acquired). If the company is in:

• Top tax bracket. Be sure the equipment is in service before year-end. That way the company can reduce estimated tax payments now in anticipation of its lower final tax bill. So it gets year-round cash-flow relief.

• Low tax bracket, but expecting to be in a high bracket next year. The company may benefit by not putting new equipment into service until after year-end. The first-year deductions can then be saved to shelter income that would be taxed at a higher rate.

• No tax is owed this year, but heavy taxes were paid in past years. Consider putting the equipment in service just before year-end. Then use the related tax benefits to file for a quick refund of prior years' taxes (file Form 1139). The refund may more than cover the down payment on the equipment.

Commercial real estate is a special case. ACRS rules allow it to be depreciated over 18 years, with larger deductions in the early years. But if commercial real estate is sold before the 18-year period is up, all the previously taken deductions are recaptured and taxed back to the company in one year at top rates. If there is a possibility the building will be sold in less than 18 years, consider electing the alternative straight-line depreciation method authorized under the ACRS. Deductions will be smaller in the early years. But there will be no recapture on the building's resale.

If expansion is on the horizon, be aware of a recent Supreme Court decision that enables growing companies to cut their tax bills. Instead of expanding the business through the formation of a new operating division, form a new corporation. The old owners retain all the stock of the original corporation, but transfer more than 20% of the stock of the new company to a third party (such as a key executive or outside investor). The two companies are taxed as independent enterprises. Each is taxed initially at the lowest (15%) tax bracket. (Under the old law, their incomes were added together. So the totaled amount could reach into higher brackets.)

For example, one corporation with $150,000 in taxable income must pay $48,750 in taxes at current rates. But two companies with $75,000 in income must pay only $15,750 each. The $31,500 total represents a net tax saving of $17,250, or 35% of the original tax bill. If the company operates with a 10% profit on sales, the after-tax gain is equivalent to a sales gain of $330,000.

At the same time, review qualified retirement-plan programs in light of the heavy cash contributions the company might be required to make to the plan. Two possible situations:

If the company is suffering a poor business year, it may be able to obtain a waiver of its retirement-plan contributions. Required: The company must show that it is facing genuine financial hardship and that the waiver saving will help the company through its difficulties, so that the employees will benefit from the waiver over the long run.

If there are excess assets in the plan that are not required to fund plan liabilities, the company may be able to terminate the plan and recover the excess assets. One major corporation is currently recouping $200 million by replacing its defined benefit pension plan with a profit-sharing plan, the contributions to which will depend on company profitability. Caution: Plan termination is a very complicated procedure. Be sure to discuss it thoroughly with the company's advisers before deciding to act.

Also be aware that many companies that now charge off bad debts on a current basis should adopt the reserve method of doing so. Under normal rules, a company can claim a bad-debt deduction only after it has evidence that a specific debt is uncollectible. But under the reserve method, the company can claim a deduction for the percentage of its accounts that it expects will go bad. So it gets the deduction in advance. If company sales consistently grow, it will be able to claim further deductions for additions to its bad-debt reserve each year.

Remember that the company should operate with the tax or fiscal year that yields the most benefits. Typically, the year should end during the middle of the business's slow season. This way executives have more time for end-of-the-year bookkeeping and beginning-of-the-year planning. The company's outside tax advisers may be more readily available as well, since they will not be called on during their busy season.

It is now possible for some companies to change their tax year without IRS permission. The company should consult with its tax advisers about this.

Source: Irving Blackman, partner, Blackman, Kallick & Co., *The Book of Tax Knowledge,* Boardroom Books, Millburn, N.J.

Choosing the best tax year

Every business has the option of reporting its income on the basis of either a fiscal or a calendar year.

A fiscal year, which ends on the last day of any month other than December, is best suited for a seasonal business. Its advantages include the reduced cost of taking inventory because of lowered stocks, and the ease in comparing the operating results of successive seasons. In addition, more time is available to attend to tax and accounting matters because of the low level of business activity, and tax advisers are able to give more attention to quarterly returns.

A calendar year makes sense for a firm with a steady stream of business. It simplifies bookkeeping by corresponding with employment tax periods, which always follow the calendar year. As a result, there are fewer calculations to make at year-end.

A firm cannot change its tax year without permission from the Internal Revenue Service. Permission is normally granted if the firm can demonstrate a valid business reason for the change, and if the change won't distort income to provide a significant tax break.

Tax tactics to increase cash flow

Tough-minded managers who focus on tighter financial controls to loosen up the flow of company cash often overlook one area: tax payments. These, too, can be managed to ease the cash pinch.

It is possible to underpay legally. Make payments that total less than the current year's tax liability. In a good year, base payments on the prior year's earnings. In a bad year, base them on the current year's expected earnings. The company is safe if by the end of the year it has made estimated payments totaling 90% of its actual tax liability.

In a year that starts slowly, base payments on actual quarterly earnings. The result will be small payments at the beginning of the year, and larger payments later in the year when money is coming in.

If the company had taxable income of $1 million in any one of the prior three years, it must make estimated payments totaling at least 90% of the current year's actual tax liability. The exceptions above do not apply to such corporations. They may only use the exception for seasonal earnings.

Request a quick refund of overpaid estimated taxes. File Form 4466 before filing the firm's tax return. The Internal Revenue Service will refund the excess payments within 45 days.

Another opportunity is to pay taxes on the exact due date. Keep the money in an interest-bearing account until then. If the company invests in commercial paper or Treasury bills, time maturity dates to coincide with the dates tax payments come due.

State and local governments are often slow to cash company checks. Delays of three weeks are not uncommon. So pay taxes with checks drawn on a money-market fund. The money in the fund will continue to earn high interest until the check is cashed.

And the company should withhold at the lowest possible rate for executive bonuses. This may be as low as 20%. If near the end of the year it appears that the withholding has been insufficient to avoid a penalty, the executive may have his full salary withheld to make up the shortage. This counts as withholding for the full year. In the meantime, the executive has had use of the money.

Examine the company's accounting methods, and make use of the more beneficial option. Service companies usually have an option to report income on either the cash or accrual basis. The advantage of using the cash basis is that accounts receivable that are outstanding at the end of the year are not included in the company's income.

Manufacturing firms should strongly consider adopting the LIFO (last-in, first-out) accounting method. LIFO will almost certainly cut the taxable income of a firm that holds inventories during an inflationary period.

Also keep tabs on payments to employee benefit plans:

• Medical plans. Form a trust to pay the premiums. Make payments to the trust a year in advance. That way, the company gets a deduction now for premiums that will actually be paid a year from now. And in the meantime, money in the trust earns tax-free interest that can be used to pay part of the premium cost, thus cutting the real cost to the company. The combination may yield more to the company than having the use of the money for that period of time.

• Pension plans. If the company does not have enough cash on hand to make a pension plan contribution, borrow it. Interest paid on the borrowed amount is deductible by the company. And the funds put in the plan earn interest tax-fee until it is distributed. This can be a great advantage to company owners who are major beneficiaries of the plan.

Source: Daniel J. O'Kane, vice president and financial administrator, MMT Sales, Inc., Edward Mendlowitz, Siegel and Mendlowitz, New York.

How to cut payroll taxes

Federal, state, and local payroll taxes, covering the costs of Social Security, unemployment insurance, and disability payments often exceed 20% of the company's total payroll cost before voluntary company benefits are counted in. And these costs are scheduled to rise in future years. There are strategies that can be used to cut this growing tax burden.

Federal payroll taxes are imposed on the wages of employees. So the company may be able to cut its federal tax bill by using workers who qualify as independent contractors instead of employees. This usually cuts the state payroll tax bill as well (though rules vary from state to state). The company does not have to withhold income tax on amounts paid to contractors, so tax and administrative costs are saved.

Candidates for contractor status include salespeople, executives who establish themselves as consultants, car and truck drivers, those with talents qualifying them for special tasks (such as artists and computer programmers). Whether or not a worker qualifies as an independent contractor depends on the facts of each case. That status is supported when workers:

• Are trusted to do the job without close company supervision.

• Provide their own work equipment instead of having the equipment supplied by the company.

• Are paid on a per-job basis instead of a time basis.

• Hire their own assistants.

• Are free to perform similar work for other companies.

• Can perform work off the company's premises.

No single one of these factors determines the worker's status. All the circumstances must be considered. For example, workers who perform on the company premises under close supervision may still be contractors if they perform similar work for other companies.

Drawbacks of using independent contractors:

• These workers usually are not covered by workers compensation insurance. If an accident happens and a contractor is injured on the job, he can sue the company for more than the standard workers compensation award.

• If the IRS determines that workers treated as contractors are really employees, the company may become retroactively liable for employment taxes and penalties.

Be sure to review the company's position with a tax expert before using this tactic.

Another area to examine is whether the business is run through a number of affiliated corporations. When the corporations share employees, they can fall into a tax trap: each pays the employees for services rendered to it, so payroll taxes are duplicated. And while employees can file for a refund of overpaid taxes, the company can never get its excess payroll tax payments returned to it.

Consider having one corporation handle the payroll for all the companies in the group. This will allow for flexibility:

• The paymaster can pay all or some of the group's employees.

• It can pay each employee with one check or issue different checks on behalf of the different companies, whichever method best facilitates the company's bookkeeping.

• A separate company can be set up to serve solely as paymaster, or there can be more than one paymaster.

The only requirement is that each employee paid by the common paymaster must work for more than one corporation.

Also consider paying employees with tax-favored benefits instead of fully taxed salary. Benefits not subject to Social Security taxes:

• Interest-free loans to employees.

• Group term life insurance that is paid for by the company.

• Personal-problem counseling.

• The right to purchase personal items at discount prices.

• Legal-insurance plans.

• Medical-insurance and medical-expense reimbursements.

• Widow's death benefits.

• Reimbursements for moving and relocation expenses.

• Pension and profit-sharing plans.

• Tuition paid for employees under a company plan.

But while all these items are exempt from Social Security taxes, only some are free from income taxation. And some of these items (such as pension plans) are subject to nontax restrictions. Consult the company's professional advisers to make sure that any benefit plan is custom-tailored to meet the circumstances of the company.

———

Source: Edward Mendlowitz, partner, Siegel & Mendlowitz, *Successful Tax Planning,* Boardroom Books, Millburn, N.J.

Minimizing state income taxes

States have been very aggressive in taxing the income of corporations that do business across state lines. To defend themselves, companies must focus on how income is apportioned to particular states and on managing their interstate activities.

Most states measure a company's in-state income on the basis of a three-factor formula keyed to the percentages of the firm's payroll, property, and receipts in the state. In a typical case, ABC Industries has 20% of its property and 40% of its payroll in state Z, and derives 45% of its receipts from the state. The average of 35% is the percentage of ABC's income that state Z taxes.

The formula applies to a corporation's business income. In certain states, investment income—and any other passive income—may be allocated to the state where the investment asset is located or to the company's home state—technically its commercial domicile.

Companies can use various techniques to shift payroll from one place to another. It is worth reviewing the impact on state tax allocations before deciding whether to subcontract work out or hire temporary help.

If the company is planning a major property purchase around the end of the year, time the closing to minimize the tax impact. Generally, consider postponing a year-end purchase in a state with high tax rates and accelerating the purchase in a low-tax or no-tax state.

The destination of goods sold is usually the key factor for states in setting a value on receipts in the formula. Receipts are more heavily weighted in some states than others.

To exclude sales from receipts in a high-tax state, deliver the goods out of the state by mail or by common carrier. If the seller is in a low-tax state, in certain situations it may pay to negotiate the shipping costs and have the buyer accept delivery in the seller's home state.

Generally, goods shipped out of state must be added back into receipts in the origin state if the buyer is either the U.S. government or in a state where the selling company is not subject to income tax.

Sales shipped to a state that has no income tax are usually not recapturable. The destination state must have jurisdiction to tax the corporation's income if it imposed an income tax.

Overseas sales are a gray area. A firm might meet the jurisdiction requirements for taxation in the foreign country but be exempt under a treaty provision. New Hampshire recently took a rigid stand on this issue and is adding back receipts from foreign sales made by companies located in that state. But other states may not.

Companies that overlap in ownership, management, and business operations may be considered a unitary business and be taxed as a single entity under state tax laws. This can help or hurt.

Say a subsidiary has 10% of it assets, payroll, and receipts in state X and has $1 million of taxable income. Its taxable income in the state would be $100,000. The parent has no income, assets, or receipts in state X, but it has $25 million of taxable income. If the parent and the subsidiary are taxed as a unitary business, the apportionment factor might drop to around ½%. But applying this factor to the combined income (½% × $26 million) yields a taxable income of $130,000 (instead of $100,000) in the state.

In a contrary situation, Brother and Sister corporations are both located in state Y, which, like certain states, does not allow loss carryovers. Sister is prospering, but Brother has substantial losses. By qualifying to be taxed as a unitary business, Brother's losses can be offset against Sister's income.

There is no precise standard to define a unitary business. Factors include: overlap in ownership, management, and operation, and how much each business depends on, or contributes to, the other. No consistent formula determines the weight given to each factor. Neither the taxing authority nor the taxpayer may know what the outcome will be without a court decision.

The issue usually comes up when a firm is audited. The auditor's questions generally reveal when unitary taxation is being considered, usually because such treatment will produce more revenue.

If it seems the auditor considered and rejected unitary taxation, the company should review the situation. It is likely that unitary taxation will mean less state taxes. On the other hand, such short-term tax savings should be weighed against long-term consequences.

Most states have a discretionary provision in their rules for apportionment and unitary reporting. Tax officials may disregard or modify an apportionment formula if it does not fairly represent the company's business in the state. It pays to consult a specialist in interstate taxation who is most competent to review the state rules if any planning is to be done in this area or, alternatively, after a state has exercised its discretion.

Source: Richard Krol, director of state and local taxes, and Richard Genetelli, manager of state and local taxes, Coopers & Lybrand, New York.

Year-end tax write-off opportunities

Be careful when taking last-minute tax write-offs. Make sure that the company can justify them to the Internal Revenue Service. There must be proof that the write-off was duly planned, such as prior approval by the board of directors. And the action must be taken before December 31, such as an entry on the company books, or the scrapping of a machine.

Follow through within the organization. For example, if a debt has been written off as bad, salespeople shouldn't continue to solicit the debtor. Fire insurance should be discontinued on property written off as abandoned.

There are specific IRS requirements for different types of write-offs:

• Bad debts. The IRS insists on an identifiable event for deeming the account uncollectible at year-end. Examples are bankruptcy of the debtor, statements by credit agencies, authoritative reports or analyses of other creditors not being paid. Be prepared to demonstrate that the debt wasn't bad at the beginning of the year.

• Casualty loss. Have proof not only of when it occurred, but also how. (Was it really a casualty, or was it the result of nondeductible gross negligence?) Show that there is no possibility at year-end of recovery from insurance, etc. Settle claims with the insurance company or consider dropping them by December 31 to establish the loss.

• Inventory. This is possible only when the inventory is carried on the basis of the lower of cost or market. Have proof of what the year-end market price is for approximately the same number of units. (Examples of proof are quotations, actual sales, offers by other parties.) Also permitted are write-downs of damaged, shopworn, or obsolete goods. The write-down is for the estimated actual realization, less the additional costs of advertising and selling these wares. This does not apply to overstocks of normal inventory.

Remember that any inventory write-down must be brought to the attention of the IRS for verification. The corporate income tax return will ask whether there was any substantial change in determining quantities, cost, or valuations between opening and closing inventory.

• Abandonments. Show the steps that were taken before year-end to dispose of the property or to withdraw it permanently from use. Was it scrapped? Sold for salvage value? Dismantled? Consider deeding abandoned land to the county or city for public use. For patents or other intangibles, surrender the use. Notify the Patent Office that the firm is conveying its rights to public use. Show that costs of investigating and analyzing a business or investment are deductible and not capital expenditures because the attempted acquisition failed or was otherwise abandoned.

• Demolition loss. Have proof that when the company acquired the property, the firm had intended to use it. Show that for reasons then unknown the firm could not do so. (The structure may have turned out to be structurally unsound for the business use the company had in mind.)

• Abnormal obsolescence. Show that business assets have to be replaced before the end of their estimated useful life because of economic, prohibitory law, urban renewal, other causes beyond the company's control, or because another firm has come up with a better, less expensive process for making a product the company sells, and the company can't compete.

How to save money on last year's corporate return

Even when a particular tax year is over, it is not too late to cut the tax liability that will be shown on the corporate tax return that is due March 15. A corporate income tax return is due 2½ months after the close of the company's tax year. That is March 15 for a calendar-year business. If the company uses a different fiscal year, compute the due date and substitute it where March 15 appears in this article. Example: If the company's year ends on March 31, the due date is June 15.

Many deadlines are tied to the date the company's income tax return is filed—the time to make pension plan contributions, the time to make a last-in, first-out (LIFO) election.

When it is useful to stretch out the filing date, the company can get an automatic six-month extension of the time to file its tax return by filing Form 7004.

But a filing extension does not extend the time for paying the company's tax bill. The firm must estimate the tax it will finally owe and pay 100% of that amount 2½ months after its tax year's end. The company may be able to get a payment extension by filing Form 1127. To do that, it must show that payment of the tax on the regular due date will result in undue hardship, for example: The company would be forced to sell assets at a giveaway price to raise funds to pay the tax.

If the company had an unexpectedly poor year, it can obtain a quick refund of estimated taxes that were overpaid by filing Form 4466. The IRS must pay the refund within 45 days. This refund request must be made before the company files its tax return.

When loss carry-backs entitle the company to a refund of taxes paid in prior years, the company can get a quick refund by filing Form 1139. This must be answered by the IRS within 90 days.

It is also possible to extend the deadline for making pension plan contributions for six months by obtaining filing extensions. The company can also amend its pension plan for a particular year (say, to expand coverage or change payment formulas), even though that is over, if it does so before filing the return for that year.

A company that had a poor business year may find that it is difficult to make a big pension plan payment. If so, ask for both a quick refund of estimated taxes and a filing extension. Then use the refund to make the pension payment.

Under the law, the S corporation form of organization is more attractive than ever before. It can be used to eliminate problems resulting from an excess accumulation of corporate earnings; and sidestep the issue of excess salaries paid to corporate officers.

It is also now easier to elect S status because changes in the law eased restrictions applying to the number and kind of permissible shareholders. But an S corporation election must be made within the first 2½ months of the company's tax year. So be sure to discuss the pros and cons of an election with the company's tax advisers before the deadline.

LIFO accounting methods can cut the company's tax bill by reducing its paper tax profits. And new rules have modified the aspects of LIFO that most companies consider to be its major drawbacks (reduced earnings shown on nontax financial statements and inventory valuation adjustments that must be made in the year of a LIFO switch).

The company's LIFO election for a particular year need not be made until the return for the year is filed. So the company can get the extra time it needs to reconsider LIFO by asking for a filing extension.

There is now also a credit for research and experimentation costs. Since many firms now expense research costs under various accounting categories, cull through the company's accounts to be sure that all research and experimental costs are segregated and identified, so that no item qualifying for the credit is overlooked.

The credit is keyed to increases in the company's research expenditures. So now is the time to plan how such expenditures will be handled in future years.

A reduction in a particular year's taxable income (through, say, a LIFO election) may result in cash-flow savings in the next year by cutting estimated taxes. This is because in many cases, estimated tax payments can be based on the taxable income the company reported in the prior year. So a reduction of last year's income will result in smaller estimated payments this year. Also, a company with income of over $1 million during any one of the prior three years may have its estimated payments increased. A company that can reduce its income to less than $1 million may avoid higher payments the following year.

Salaries, bonuses, expenses, and interest payments owed by the company to a shareholder owning 50% of the company's stock, and accrued by the company during a particular year, may not be deducted until they are actually paid.

One problem area is that the company may have declared a large bonus for shareholder executives at the end of a profitable year. The IRS may rule that the bonus was really a disguised dividend payout of corporate profits. So the company will lose its deduction for it.

So set salaries for shareholder executives at a level equaling the total of the previous salaries and bonuses. This will show the IRS that the company genuinely intended to raise executive compensation at the end of the previous year. If, in fact, a particular year proves to be less profitable salaries can be reduced later in the year.

Any loan made between the company and a shareholder should be formalized now with a note, loan agreement, and the terms for repayment, if this has not been done already. Otherwise an undocumented loan's proceeds may be treated as taxable dividend income to a shareholder or as a contribution to the capital of the company.

Keep in mind that adequate records are the key to resolving many tax disputes. So be sure that minutes are complete for board meetings held. Make sure they explain:
• The business reason for accumulating any earnings surplus.
• The reason for a loan arranged between the company and a shareholder.
• The company's salary policy.

Source: Edward Mendlowitz, partner, Siegel & Mendlowitz, New York.

Tax treatment of barters

A television manufacturer wishing to unload inventory may decide to trade TV sets for hotel space for its traveling sales force. A hotel chain seeking to provide services in exchange for inventory may trade hotel accommodations for TV sets, which it plans to install in its rooms.

The television manufacturer must report as income the fair market value of hotel rooms credited to its account, and may deduct the value of the income earned as the rooms are used.

The hotel chain must report as income the value of the TVs as payment for the rooms. And it must begin depreciating the sets immediately.

Source: Charles Bogen, tax principal, Ernst & Whinney, New York.

The power of tax credits

A tax credit is worth more to the company than a tax deduction of equal dollar amount. That is because a credit cuts the company's tax bill on a dollar-for-dollar basis. So if the company is in the top 46% tax bracket, a $1 tax credit is worth $2.17 in deductions.

And the value of the credit goes up, vis-a-vis an equal-sized deduction, as the company's tax bracket goes down. If the company is in only the 15% tax bracket, a $1 credit is worth fully $6.66 in deductions.

FIGHTING THE IRS

How to use private-letter rulings

The problem: The stakes are high and the taxpayer believes the law is favorable but is not sure, before the deal is made, how the Internal Revenue Service will treat a transaction. Ask the IRS for a private-letter ruling, which deals in advance with the tax issues involved. A taxpayer has the right to rely on the rulings contained in a private letter even if the IRS treats other taxpayers differently.

When to ask for a ruling:

• A ruling must be obtained before certain tax-free transactions involving foreign organizations are made.

• One should be obtained when the taxpayer believes the law is favorable and a major transaction hinges on that favorable tax treatment.

• One can be obtained to determine the IRS position when the law is not clear.

When not to ask for a ruling: When it seems likely that the ruling will be unfavorable. That way, the taxpayer can proceed with the transaction without a ruling. If the return isn't audited, the transaction may not be challenged. But a taxpayer who obtains a private ruling must attach it to the tax return. An adverse ruling is sure to catch the examiner's eye and result in disallowance of the questionable item.

How to tell what the IRS position is likely to be: All private rulings requested after October 31, 1976, have been released to the public (with names and identifying details omitted). They are compiled and indexed by the leading tax-reporting services. And while one person cannot rely on a ruling issued to another, or cite it as precedent, these rulings serve as valuable indicators of the way the IRS is likely to approach an issue.

To ask for a ruling, no special form is required. The letter requesting the ruling, which should be drawn up by a tax adviser, must contain all the facts concerning the proposed transaction; explain the transaction's business purpose; and specify what rulings you are asking for.

Send the request to the Commissioner of Internal Revenue, 1111 Constitution Ave. NW, Washington, D.C. 20224. Within 15 work days, an IRS agent will call to discuss the issues involved.

What to expect:

• If the agent says he is inclined to approve the request a favorable letter will follow. It may be in just a few weeks, or it can take months, depending on how busy the IRS office is.

• If the agent says the IRS will rule unfavorably, the taxpayer can withdraw the ruling request and, if he wishes, proceed with the transaction. There is no obligation to inform the IRS about the withdrawn request when the return is filed.

• If the agent is uncertain, a skilled tax practitioner may be able to identify the reservations and amend the ruling request to increase the likelihood of a positive response.

• If matters aren't resolved in this first conversation, the taxpayer can exercise his right to a conference with IRS officials. If the conference results are unsatisfactory, the taxpayer can still withdraw his ruling request.

Source: Edward Mendlowitz, partner, Siegel & Mendlowitz, New York.

The cost of not getting a ruling

The importance of getting a private ruling even when a transaction seems safe is illustrated by this true story:

A lawyer developed great experience in setting up deferred-compensation plans for nonprofit corporations. He used the Internal Revenue Service's own guidelines and also obtained a private ruling for each plan. Except one.

Years later, the IRS changed the rules on how it treated deferred-compensation plans. Those plans protected by private rulings got a chance to adjust to the new rules. But the plan without a ruling had the new rules applied to it retroactively, even though it was identical to many of the others.

It resulted in a whopping tax bill for the employees. And a possible negligence action against the lawyer.

Source: Letter Ruling 8011013.

When the IRS won't comment

The Internal Revenue Service will not issue private rulings concerning these tax matters:

• How estate taxes will apply to the property of a living person.

• Hypothetical transactions.

• Questions of fact, for example, is an executive's compensation reasonable? What is the value of a piece of property?

• Requests from trade associations for rulings on how the law may affect members of the group.

• Issues involving court decisions when the IRS has not yet decided whether to accept or appeal.

• Issues involving code sections for which final regulations have not been put into effect (unless application of the law is obvious or a business emergency makes a private-letter ruling essential).

Recording an IRS conference

Guidelines allow the recording of any conference with IRS collection officers. But three conditions must be met: The recording must be made in an IRS office. The IRS must be able to make its own recording. And the collection officer's supervisor must approve.

IRS browsing rights

Revenue agents often find leads to corporate tax disallowances in the directors' minutes. One corporation said it could not produce the minutes book because the firm's lawyer had it. The lawyer contended the book was protected by the lawyer-client privilege. The court said no. There was no proof that the lawyer had prepared the minutes or kept them in confidence.

Source: *U.S. et al.* vs *Omohundro,* 10 Cir., 3/21/80.

The best way to handle an IRS audit

The chance of an IRS audit of a company return depends on the size of the company. The greater the corporation's assets, the greater the probability of an audit:

Assets	% audited
Under $100,000	4
$100,000–$1 million	12
$1 million–$10 million	40
$10 million–$100 million	50
Over $100 million	75

Audits are more likely still if the company

shows low profits relative to industry averages, or pays salaries or claims deductions that are out of line with its reported income.

There are three kinds of IRS agents involved in audits: Revenue officers usually do nothing more than ask the company to produce income, payroll, and excise tax returns. Revenue officers do not conduct full-fledged audits. Internal Revenue agents (the most common type of IRS representative) may conduct narrow or in-depth audits of corporate and personal returns. Special agents conduct criminal investigations. Consult a tax adviser immediately when a special agent identifies himself.

There are also three types of audits:

• By mail—not true audits. They usually result when the IRS finds minor errors on the return, such as, arithmetic mistakes or improperly claimed deductions. The IRS tries to resolve the problem through an exchange of letters.

• Office audits. The IRS asks the taxpayer to appear at an IRS office to discuss the return. Most audits are of this type, and usually concern only a few items on the return. An IRS letter to the taxpayer will specify which items are at issue. Bring all records relevant to the specified items. Do not bring any other records. If the agent asks about any item not specified in the IRS letter, do not answer. Explain that relevant records must be consulted first.

• Field audits. These are more general examinations of taxpayer records. They usually take place at the taxpayer's place of business and may last for several days.

When faced with an audit, the most important thing to do is prepare. Meet with the tax adviser to evaluate the situation. Ask: What is the IRS interested in? What records do we have to depend on? Then, devise a strategy for handling the IRS's questions. If a large amount of money is at stake, or complicated points of law are involved the tax adviser should meet the agent with the taxpayer. If given a power-of-attorney, the adviser can meet the agent without the taxpayer.

During an audit, act with professionalism. If the records are comprehensive and well organized, the auditor may conclude that it is unprofitable (from the IRS's point of view) to continue. Sloppy records and haphazard documentation encourage the IRS to believe that a fishing trip could turn up something.

It is essential not to display any hostility you might feel toward the tax authorities or the government. If the auditors are personally antagonized, they are in a position to cause the taxpayer a great deal of trouble.

To prevent audit trouble, assume that there will be an audit every year. Consult with a tax adviser at the beginning of the year to devise strategies and keep records as though an audit were sure to follow. The usual result will be less chance of facing a real audit. And should an audit occur, the trouble will be minimized.

Source: Irving Blackman, partner, Blackman, Kallick & Co., Chicago.

Appealing IRS audit conclusions

A company that does not regularly pay tax deficiencies of a reasonable amount is likely to be overpaying its taxes. The company is not taking an aggressive enough position on gray areas of the tax law. To keep its tax bill down, the company must be prepared to fight the IRS on occasion.

The best forum to fight in is the IRS's own appellate division. There, taxpayers who disagree with IRS audit conclusions and who can document their position with sound facts have a good chance of getting at least part of what they're asking for, without going to court.

An appeal to the appellate level of the IRS is handled by highly trained IRS personnel called appellate conferees. It is the conferees' job to settle cases, to see that they don't go to court, while still getting the most they can for the government.

Unlike auditors, who are bound by the regulations and rulings of the IRS, the conferee is entitled to consider the hazards of litigation. That is, the chance that the government might lose in court if it litigates a case. If the conferee feels that the government has a weak position on the facts, or there are cases in the taxpayer's jurisdiction against the government, odds are that the conferee will concede or agree to a settlement.

The conferee has a great deal of leeway. It is

possible for a taxpayer to horse-trade and negotiate on individual items with conferees. Typical is for the conferee to half the tax bill (or insist a third of the bill). The taxpayer will have to concede the other half or two-thirds.

Some issues that are not likely to be settled at the audit level, but which taxpayers have a good chance of resolving at appeal are:

• Cash expenditures that the auditor has disallowed for lack of documentation where those expenditures are common in the taxpayer's business.

• Travel and entertainment deductions that are disallowed because the taxpayer does not have all the support the tax law requires. These disallowances can normally be settled on appeal if the amounts are reasonable.

• Business use of property. A taxpayer uses his car in business 75% of the time, say. But the auditor says he hasn't supported his deduction. If the taxpayer can show that he normally uses his car in business, an appeal should be successful.

• Charitable contributions. Large deductions and those involving hard-to-value gifts, such as stock in a closely held business, become battles of appraisals. These often need to be settled on appeal.

• Inventory issues. Most companies that have converted to the LIFO method of valuing inventory will have disputes of one degree or another with the IRS over their computations. The area is complex, and many questions remain unanswered. Cases not settled at the audit should be appealed. Another candidate for appeal is whether a company's reserves for inventory obsolescence are deductible. The government won a recent U.S. Supreme Court case on the issue. Even though from a financial accounting standpoint companies need to provide these reserves, they often end up being nondeductible.

• Constructive dividends. Are items of expense paid by a closely held company to an officer-shareholder deductible, or are they a nondeductible preferential dividend?

• Depreciation. With the change in the tax law, new company assets must be handled by the Accelerated Cost Recovery System (ACRS) now mandated by the IRS. But for pre-1981 business property, the question of depreciable life may have to be appealed. Repairs are an issue, too. Are they deductible immediately? Or are they capital items that have to be depreciated over time?

But do not go up through the appeal process on a lark, hoping for the best outcome. Prepare a decent case. Get sound professional advice. The conferees are technically competent people. They are not likely to let anything slip by them.

Do not expect to get 100% of what the company asks for. If several issues are taken to appeal, be prepared to concede some as part of the give-and-take negotiations.

Cases that involve questions of fact rather than law have the best chance of being settled because facts lend themselves to compromise. On legal issues, there's less room for negotiation. For every six cases the taxpayer can come up with in support of a legal position, the conferee will have six for the government. There's a standoff, which the conferee will have no choice but to resolve on the principal of hazards of litigation.

The best approach in dealing with an appellate conferee (or an auditor, for that matter) is to give as much factual background as possible. Point out where the auditor was wrong. Support that position with facts. What prevails is a strong factual presentation, forcefully argued.

Source: David E. Lipson, partner in charge of the tax division of the Chicago office of Arthur Andersen & Co.,

After rejecting the auditor's findings

Taxpayers who reject an auditor's findings will be sent a 30-day letter. This is a tentative report that the IRS is disallowing the contested deductions. The taxpayer has 30 days either to sign a form agreeing to the auditor's conclusions (Form 870) or to submit a written protest against them.

Once the IRS receives the protest, the case is referred to a conferee who arranges a meeting with the taxpayer or a representative. This meeting, which is very informal, is called a conference. The taxpayer or the adviser elaborate on the arguments presented in the protest.

If a satisfactory settlement is not reached at the conference, the taxpayer can ask for a statutory notice of deficiency—a 90-day letter. This puts the taxpayer in the legal process of the administration of the tax law. The taxpayer has 90 days either to file a petition in Tax Court or pay the deficiency and sue for a refund in the U.S. District Court or the Claims Court.

After the case if filed with the Tax Court, it goes to the District Counsel of the IRS, where one of the counsel's lawyers reviews it with the conferee. If no settlement can be reached there, then the case will ultimately have to be tried in court.

If the tax is paid and a refund is sought, the case is handled by the Tax Division of the Department of Justice.

The chances of paying less

Taxpayers who fight the Internal Revenue Service have a pretty good chance of obtaining at least a partial victory, according to statistics for the 1981 fiscal year. Of those who appealed an IRS assessment:

• And threatened to go to Tax Court: 83% were able to agree to a settlement with the IRS without actually filing a court petition.

• And actually filed in Tax Court: 57% were able to compromise before going to trial.

Better yet, in those cases that went to Tax Court, the IRS was able to collect only 33.8% of the taxes and penalties it sought.

Source: The IRS Commissioner's Annual Report for 1981.

How to get more time to pay

Corporations can get an automatic six-month extension to file tax returns by filing Form 7004 with the Internal Revenue Service.

Extensions have their uses. One is to delay making payments into a qualified retirement plan. These do not have to be made until the firm's tax return for the year is filed. By delaying the filing date, the firm retains use of the money for a longer period. Another use is time to reexamine the company's inventory accounting methods. Election of the LIFO (last-in, first-out) inventory method must be filed with the tax return. By extending the time to file, the company gets more time to decide if LIFO is the way to go.

The automatic filing extension does not extend the time for paying taxes. The company must estimate the amount of taxes it will owe for the year and pay that amount on the return's normal due date.

If the company underpays, it will ultimately have to make up the difference plus interest. Penalties can also be assessed. If it overpays, it will get a refund. Or the overpayment may be applied against the next year's estimated taxes.

The time for paying a corporation's taxes may be extended by up to six months. But this extension is not granted automatically. The IRS will permit an extension if paying the tax on its normal due date would result in undue hardship to the company.

An example might be that property would have to be sold at a significant loss to raise money to pay the tax. The fact that it is merely inconvenient for the company to pay the tax on the due date is not enough to justify an extension.

When applying for a payment extension, the company must provide the IRS with a written statement of its assets and liabilities, an itemized statement of all its receipts and disbursements for the previous three months, and a full explanation of the hardship that will result from payment of the tax on the normal due date.

Any tax whose payment is delayed will ultimately have to be paid with accrued interest from the original due date for payment.

Note: The time for paying employment taxes and employee's payroll-withholding income taxes cannot be extended.

Source: Irving Blackman, partner, Blackman, Kallick & Co., Chicago.

If there is no money to pay taxes

The Internal Revenue Service is usually lenient to those who are genuinely unable to pay personal or corporate income taxes, provided they cooperate with the IRS in working out a payment schedule.

However, never fail to file an income tax return because the company (or individual) does not have the funds to cover the tax due. That's a crime. Instead, file by the date due, but do not include a check for the amount owed.

The IRS will send a bill. Respond to it immediately. Write to the address indicated on the bill and include a copy of the IRS notice. (The notice is coded to speed the disposition of the case.) In the letter, suggest working out a payment schedule. No detailed explanation is necessary.

Don't delay the response, not even by a few days. The IRS's mailing sequence is computer-controlled. If the system doesn't hear from the taxpayer promptly, it triggers further action.

The IRS will contact the taxpayer to work out a payment schedule that can be comfortably afforded:

• The IRS won't force an individual to refinance a home or sell a car. And it won't force a company to liquidate working assets. But it will force a taxpayer to pay over any assets that are readily convertible into cash, and it will try to get the taxpayer to borrow on other assets (including a second mortgage on a home).

• The entire amount will be paid off in fixed monthly payments.

• Interest is due on the payments (but that's deductible). A nondeductible penalty will also be charged.

• The IRS will reassess the taxpayer's financial position periodically (once or twice year). If it improves, the IRS will ask for a speeded-up payment schedule.

Don't worry if the letter to the IRS doesn't draw a quick response. But if there's no response in three months, give them a call to determine the disposition of the case.

Never ignore a letter from the IRS. Other-wise, they'll assume the worst and could move to seize visible assets.

But a firm that fails to pay the government payroll taxes withheld from employee's wages runs a real risk that the IRS will close down its business.

The best strategy is to resume paying current payroll tax liabilities as soon as possible, before paying any overdue liabilities. The IRS won't close the business if current liabilities are being paid. And they will agree to work out a payment schedule for the old liabilities. Also, a penalty is imposed for every payment missed. The firm will pay more in penalties if it bypasses current payments to pay off old ones.

Source: Edward Mendlowitz, partner, Siegel & Mendlowitz, New York.

S Corporation penalty avoided

A corporation filed an S corporation election, which the Internal Revenue Service accepted. Later, the IRS discovered additional facts indicating that the election had not been filed on time. When the company filed an S corporation return, the IRS rejected it and fined the company for negligence. The finding was that the company did not have to pay the fine. The company owners had relied on the advice of a competent accountant, the accountant had relied on the IRS's initial acceptance of the election. The misfiling was neither willful nor negligent.

Source: *Columbia Steak House II, Inc.,* TC Memo 1981-142.

Low payoff for informers

The Internal Revenue Service promises rewards of up to $50,000 for informants who turn in tax evaders. But few of the informers ever see much reward money. Only one in fifteen received any payoff (during the most recent years analyzed).

IRS figures for a recent fiscal year: $281,367 paid out to 439 of a total of 7,118 informers. The average reward was $641 per informant paid.

Rewards are based on the validity of the information and the amount actually recovered by the IRS. Most informers are motivated by revenge. They include irate employees, feuding neighbors and former spouses. Many are armed with emotion, not facts. Frequently their allegations cannot be proved.

Metered postage is not time proof

Postage meters should not be used when mailing tax documents at the last minute. The date printed by the meter is not proof of when the document is mailed because the meter is under the control of the company. Instead, use stamps, which will be postmarked in the standard way. Even better is certified or registered mail. Get a date-stamped receipt from the post office.

Source: Robert Holzman, *Business Tax Traps,* Boardroom Books, Millburn, N.J.

IRS reaction to the tax revolt

Grass-roots tax revolts have surfaced in virtually every part of the country. In Flint, Mich., in 1981, 3,500 blue- and white-collar auto workers stopped paying income taxes.

The primary tool used by workers: W-4 forms that claim excessive withholding exemptions, so that no income tax is withheld. The Internal Revenue Service's reaction is to prosecute the group's leaders and to instruct rank-and-file workers to correct the W-4 form and claim the proper exemptions.

If a worker refuses, or files a new form that is considered to be another tax-protest W-4, new rules allow the IRS to tell the company how many exemptions the employee is entitled to. The employer must withhold on that basis. The result is the IRS will get its money in advance, and the worker will be forced to file an income tax return asking for a refund of any tax overpayment at the end of the year.

Employers may find themselves caught in the middle of this situation, with their employees telling them one thing and the IRS telling them another. Employers are responsible for withholding income taxes from workers' salary checks according to the information provided to them by the workers on their W-4 forms. If a form is incorrect, an employer must ask the employee to correct it. If a corrected W-4 is not filed, the firm must withhold, according to IRS instructions.

The solution: notify all workers of the firm's policy in handling W-4's that indicate excessive exemptions. Use a pay-envelope stuffer or the employee bulletin boards. Pass no judgment on the pros and cons of the tax movement. But make sure employees understand that the firm will not be put in the middle.

Source: Paul N. Strassels, publisher of *Washington Money Letter,* and coauthor of *All You Need to Know About the IRS,* Random House, New York.

Tougher tax penalties

Recent tax law changes toughened many penalty provisions in the tax code and added some new ones.

The interest rate on tax deficiencies was increased from 90% to 100% of the prime rate. And this interest rate will be adjusted twice every year. Interest is compounded daily.

Excessive withholding claims: The civil penalty for claiming too many withholding allowances on a W-4 form was increased from $50 to $500.

The criminal penalty went from $500 to $1,000.

Negligence penalties were stiffened in general. The old law provided for a negligence penalty equal to 5% of the underpayment. When fraud was involved, the penalty was 50% of the underpayment. In each case, there is a further nondeductible penalty equal to 50% of the interest due on the underpayment.

Tax deposits: A new penalty applies when an employer overstates the amount paid to a government tax depository for Social Security and withholding taxes. The new penalty is 25% of the overstatement.

Penalty for over- or under-valuing property (for instance, the value of a charitable contribution) when it leads to underpayment of taxes. Overvaluation now results in a penalty equal to a percentage of the resulting tax underpayment, as determined by the following schedule:

Size of overvaluation	Amount of penalty
150–200%	10%
200–250%	20%
over 250%	30%

Reasonable cause can excuse this penalty. And no penalty is imposed if the underpayment is less than $1000.

Information returns: The penalty for failure to file most information returns was increased from $1 to $10 per return. The filer of the return is also generally required to furnish a copy to the person to whom it relates. The maximum fine that may be imposed on a taxpayer in one year for failure to file these returns was increased from $1,000 to $25,000.

ORGANIZING THE BUSINESS IN A TAX-WISE WAY

Tax opportunities in buying a business

Record-high interest rates provide an opportunity to buy out the business of a financially shaky supplier, customer, or competitor to broaden the business without the strain of starting a new division or subsidiary from scratch. In some cases, the tax savings can pay the entire cost of the transaction. The tax implications will depend on whether the business has been making money or losing money.

In buying a healthy company, suggest to the present owner that the company redeem some of the shares he holds, paying him cash directly for those shares. Simultaneously, have the owner transfer the rest of the shares to the purchaser. Section 302 of the Tax Code provides the owner with tax-favored long-term capital gains treatment for his profit on the deal, and the seller avoids paying any funds out of pocket.

The purchaser must not commit itself in writing to purchase all the seller's stock, and then use funds taken from the company to make payment. The used funds are a taxable dividend to the purchaser, who winds up paying both the seller and the government.

In buying an unhealthy company, have the old owner put the company into Chapter 11 bankruptcy proceedings before the sale is announced. The liabilities of the company are declared and defined, so the purchaser avoids buying unknown debts. The business's creditors will probably be ready to negotiate a reasonable reduction of their debts, rather than risk losing everything by having the buyer walk away.

It may take some time to turn around a business that has been losing money. But the purchaser gets immediate tax benefits:

• Continuing losses of the company that is bought can be used on a consolidated return to offset the profits of the purchasing company.

• Capital investments made to turn around the acquired business will result in large investment credits and depreciation deductions. These benefits are now larger than ever.

• When the acquired business turns profitable, its post-acquisition losses may be used to offset future gains. The period during which these losses may be carried forward has been increased to 15 years.

When purchasing a company, it may become necessary to give key managers a stake in the business. These employees should not be given more than 20% of the company's stock. Consolidated returns cannot be filed unless the purchasing company owns 80% of the stock of the other. Without consolidated returns, the tax benefits will be lost.

A key consideration in buying a business is assigning a cash value to the purchased company's assets. A high value for the depreciable assets increases the depreciation deductions available in the future, whereas a high value for a noncompete agreement signed by the seller increases the business expense deduction available for its cost. The seller may want little value attached to the noncompete agreement (its price is taxed as ordinary income to him) and as much as possible attached to the goodwill of the business (to qualify for long-term capital gains).

Source: Edward Mendlowitz, partner, Siegel & Mendlowitz, & Rich, CPAs, New York.

Dividing up a company—tax-free

Cutting state and local taxes is often a prod to corporation breakups. A business can profit by incorporating some of its operations in low-tax states. But there are other powerful motivators for dividing up:

• Split liabilities. A retail firm's credit line could be frozen if a large personal-injury lawsuit is filed against one of its several stores. Separate incorporation of each store can help contain the liabilities of each.

• Reduce accumulated earnings. A corporation with $250,000 in retained earnings faces a possible penalty tax. But two corporations with $125,000 each in earnings are both safe, provided there is a business reason (as opposed to a tax reason) for creating them.

• Provide employee incentives. A firm may want to give its branch managers an equity interest in the business, but only in each one's own branch. The solution is to incorporate each branch separately.

• Obtain financing. When a company operates several businesses with different financial needs, the credit rating of one or more might be strengthened by having them separately organized.

• Contain labor disputes. A labor dispute at one plant may result in the entire company being picketed or boycotted. It is easier, legally, to contain a dispute within an operation that is separately incorporated.

• Avoid conflicts of interest. A wholesaler or manufacturer may create a different named subsidiary to begin selling directly to the public without going into direct competition with its retailing customers.

• Settle management disputes. Two groups of shareholders in a mid-size corporation might disagree on management policy and paralyze the company. Dividing the business between two new corporations gives each group control of one.

• Avoid regulation. When one of two businesses is regulated, the entire firm may be subject to restrictions. Similarly, when a firm operates one business in several states, the regulations of one state may affect the entire operation.

The most commonly types of tax-free reorganization is the split-off. The company creates a subsidiary to run part of its business. The parent company's shareholders then exchange some of their stock for that of the subsidiary. The shareholders can vary their interest in the two corporations by varying the amount of stock they exchange. Each can emerge as a shareholder of either company, or of both. Split-offs are often used to settle management disputes and to provide employee incentives.

• In the spin-off, the subsidiary's stock is distributed directly to the parent company's shareholders. No stock is exchanged. The shareholders keep the same proportional ownership of the two businesses that they had when there was one company. Spin-offs are frequently used for financing purposes.

The least common type of division is the split-up. The parent company's entire business is transferred to two or more subsidiaries. Stock in the subsidiaries is distributed directly to the parent company's shareholders. The parent then ceases to exist. Split-ups are used only when there is some reason to terminate the parent corporation.

Certain conditions are essential to qualify the breakup as tax-free. There must be a business purpose to the deal, not just the avoidance of federal taxes. The parent company must own at least 80% of the subsidiary's stock just before the division. A controlling amount of the subsidiary's stock must be transferred to the shareholders of the parent. (There must be a good reason not to distribute all of it.) The subsidiary's business must have been actively conducted by the parent for at least five years—unless the business was acquired in a tax-free reorganization. Finally, if stock is exchanged, the value of the stock surrendered must equal that of the stock received. The transaction's purpose must not be to withdraw earnings from the business.

Source: Dr. Robert Holzman, professor emeritus of taxation, New York University, author of *The Encyclopedia of Estate Planning,* Boardroom Books, Millburn, N.J.

Tax treatment of noncompete agreements

The buyer of a business usually seeks to call part of the purchase price a payment for the seller's promise not to compete for a specified number of years, since he can deduct payments made for that promise. The seller wants as little of the price as possible allocated that way, since money received for such a covenant is taxed as ordinary income. In one case, the seller argued that the amount labeled in a contract as payment for a covenant not to compete should be disregarded as an economic unreality. The seller had a terminal illness and couldn't compete. But the court refused to disregard the terms of the contract. It had not been proven that the seller had been too ill to know what he was signing. Since the contract referred to a big slice of the consideration as payment not to compete, that's the way it had to be taxed.

Source: *Clesceri* vs *United States,* USDC, N. Dist. IL, 11/21/79.

Recapitalizing for personal and tax advantages

If a corporation has only one class of stock, all shares must be treated identically as to dividends, voting rights, etc. But shareholders have different needs. Older ones may require income; younger ones may want growth; not all may be active in the firm's management. The solution is a tax-free recapitalization that allows different shareholders to acquire different types of stock, according to their needs. The standard choices are preferred stock, which usually pays regular dividends, but does not share in the firm's growth, and common stock, which need not pay dividends but increases in value as the company grows. Both common and preferred stock may be classed as either voting or nonvoting.

A typical candidate for recapitalization is a company with only common stock outstanding whose founder is approaching retirement age. The founder owns most of the stock, but all his children own some. Only one child is active in the business.

All the firm's stock is now exchanged. The founder receives voting preferred stock, which becomes nonvoting on his death; the child in the business receives voting common stock; and the other children receive nonvoting common stock. In this way the founder retains control of the business and gets a regular income for life. The children all profit from any future growth in the company's underlying value. And the child active in management gains control of the company when the founder dies.

Here are other reasons for recapitalizing:

• Estate planning. The chief shareholder's estate may be so large that the company may have to redeem much of the shareholder's stock to pay estate taxes when he dies. This cash drain could hurt the business. Strategy: The shareholder exchanges his common stock for preferred. Result: The value of his interest in the business is frozen. Estate taxes are reduced, since future growth goes to other shareholders who won't be taxed on the major shareholder's death.

Income taxes. A firm's sole owner might not want to receive dividends, because they are taxable at rates up to 50%. But the firm may have to pay dividends because of Internal Revenue Service limitations on accumulated earnings. One solution is to create a new class of preferred stock and place it in trust to benefit the owner's children. Since they are in a lower tax bracket, the family as a unit would receive dividends taxed at a lower rate.

• Employee incentives. Key employees may wish to acquire an interest in the business but the value of the firm's stock may be so high they cannot afford it. Solution: The company exchanges each share of old stock for several new ones (common, preferred or both). Result: The value of individual shares is reduced.

• Shareholder harmony. Passive shareholders may want to receive large dividends from the company while those who are actively managing the business may want to reinvest profits. Worse: Active family members may resent working for the benefit of inactive ones. Solution: Inactive shareholders exchange their common stock for nonvoting preferred. Result: Shareholders who actually manage the company get control and the benefits of future growth. They may choose to forgo dividends on the common and invest earnings as they wish. The passive shareholders get the regular dividends they desire.

Before plunging ahead on a recapitalization plan, consider the company's needs carefully with its business and tax advisers. Mistakes can be expensive. A parent might give all the children voting stock in the business, then decide later that only the children active in the business should have voting stock. But the others won't give up their voting interest. A bitter family fight results. Or a shareholder receives preferred stock in exchange for his common stock, then he sells some of the preferred. Under some circumstances, profit from the sale will be considered ordinary income and be taxed at up to the 50% rate. But if the shareholder had received preferred stock to begin with, the profit would have been a capital gain, taxable at a lower rate.

Questions to ask when recapitalizing the company:

• If the business is successful, will it be sold? If so, it may be best to give family members small blocks of stock. Reason: When the business is sold, gain will be spread among family members in lower tax brackets.

• Who will be the company's ultimate shareholders? Possibilities: Near family, distant family, employees, outsiders. What kind of stock should each own?

• Who will ultimately control the company— all the shareholders, or only those who are active in the business? Point: Create voting and nonvoting stock accordingly.

There must be a business purpose for the transaction. Reasons accepted by the Internal Revenue Service are efficient management, shareholder harmony, and estate planning (when the business might be affected by a large redemption). The new stock received by each shareholder must be equal in value to the old stock that was exchanged. And a formal plan of reorganization must be adopted by the company and the shareholders. A copy of it must be filed with the firm's tax return.

The firm's tax adviser might ask the IRS for a private-letter ruling concerning the transaction before it is done. If the ruling is favorable, the company can rely on it should problems later arise. If the IRS raises an objection, the problem area will be known before the deal is completed, and a costly mistake can still be averted.

Source: Joseph Eidelberg, partner, Seidman & Seidman, New York.

When to choose the S corporation

One of the chief attractions of an S corporation is the fact that losses and profits are passed through to the stockholders, reducing the shareholders' taxable income in the case of losses, and avoiding double taxation of dividends in the case of earnings. A recent amendment to the tax law has liberalized the treatment of losses on Section 1244 stock, which is frequently used for corporations starting up. Losses on this stock would be allowed up to $50,000 and, in case of a joint return, up to $100,000.

When starting up a new business, discuss with professional advisers the desirability of qualifying as an S corporation as well as under Section 1244. This can be especially important if initial losses are anticipated. Once the corporation starts making money, it can always terminate the Subchapter S election and become a regular corporation later.

The S election is especially good for companies with high start-up costs for equipment as well as expected losses. A new restaurant venture, for example, might require $50,000 of equipment. If the S is made, shareholders would be eligible for the 10% investment credit. But in an ordinary C corporation with operating losses, there would be no income against which to take the credit immediately. Under the S corporation election, the credit would be passed through to the stockholders of record.

Other times when Sub S makes sense:

• When you anticipate accumulating earnings. In a normal C corporation, the earnings would have to be paid out as dividends from after-tax funds, then taxed again in the recipient's income. For S firms, there's no tax on the distribution at the corporate level.

• For speculative ventures. An S corporation election allows immediate tax write-offs of operating losses up to the amount paid into the company for equity or as loans.

• To simplify some intrafamily transfers. In one case, the owner of an executive recruitment agency wanted to shelter substantial income. He incorporated the business as an S corporation and gave stock to his children. Profits from the business were then taxed in the children's lower tax bracket.

The S corporation election should not be used when the corporation will be using internally generated cash for growth. A C corporation is taxed at a lower rate than high-income individuals.

S corporations can now enjoy the same liberal pension benefits enjoyed by regular C corporations.

Companies that used Sub S to recapture heavy start-up losses and wish to convert to regular corporation status can do so, but once converted, a corporation cannot change back to Sub S for five years unless the termination resulted from circumstances beyond the shareholder's control.

Note: The IRS may grant exceptions to the five-year rule in certain cases.

Source: Sidney Kess, national tax partner, Main Hurdman, New York.

TAX CONSEQUENCES OF BUSINESS DECISIONS

Expensive consequences of everyday decisions

Day-to-day business decisions can have very unexpected tax consequences. The most common mistake is making short-term decisions that clearly cut this year's business or tax liabilities, but which have adverse effects in the long run.

Self-insurance programs, for instance, are sometimes used by companies to cut the cost of insurance premiums. The companies set up a contingency or reserve fund and allocate to it an amount sufficient to cover anticipated liabilities. One drawback is that premium payments for business insurance are deductible as a business expense, but payments into a self-insurance contingency fund are not deductible. And even worse, a cautious company that puts fairly large amounts into a contingency reserve may have part of the reserve attacked by the Internal Revenue Service as excess accumulated earnings subject to a penalty tax.

Insurance claims are sometimes not filed by companies with poor claims records, for fear of having their coverage canceled. The IRS has held that a company that fails to file an insurance claim cannot claim a casualty-loss deduction. So managers have had an unpleasant choice: make the claim and risk losing future coverage, or protect future coverage by forgoing both the claim and the deduction.

Over the past few years, some federal courts have held that a company can claim a casualty-loss deduction when it has a good business reason for not filing an insurance claim. Ask the company's tax adviser whether local courts follow the this rule.

Many types of pension plans require fixed contributions to be made each year on behalf of all employees regardless of the company's profitability. In a poor year, the company may not be able to afford it. And executives may become personally liable if they are deemed to have breached their fiduciary duties as plan administrators.

So make sure that any plan adopted by the company is custom-tailored to meet its circumstances.

Claims against the company should not be conceded without considering the tax consequences. Generally, these liabilities are not deductible while they are being contested. So the company should time the settlement of a suit in order to declare it as a deductible liability for the year in which it will derive the greatest tax benefit.

Casualty losses and bad debts are generally not deductible either, as long as the company has a chance of recovering the loss amount through insurance or other means. So a company that sues to recover a disputed amount delays the time it can claim a deduction for its loss. The IRS rationale is that if the company felt that it had no chance of recovering the loss, it would not sue.

When it becomes apparent that there is little chance of winning a suit, time the settlement to occur in the year when the deduction is most valuable.

Repairing and replacing damaged assets are alternatives with different tax consequences. The cost of restoring an asset to its previous condition is fully deductible. But the purchase price of a new asset is generally recoverable only through depreciation deductions and the investment credit. These tax benefits will rarely add up to the full cost of the new asset in the first year. But businesses can immediately deduct up to $5,000 of equipment purchases each year.

Property exchanges are sometimes arranged by companies to trade assets that are no longer useful for assets that are. Such a trade will qualify as a tax-free exchange.

However, if the property disposed of has a value that is less than its tax cost, the loss incurred on the deal will not be deductible. But the company may trade low-cost property that has appreciated in value in order to avoid realizing a taxable gain on the deal. However, the newly acquired property is depreciable only on the basis of the old property's cost. So future depreciation deductions are forfeited.

Other tactics include abandoning property that is no longer useful to the company. The company is entitled to a deduction for the loss. Establish the date of abandonment in the most tax-beneficial year by ceasing to make payments for property taxes and insurance premiums.

Consolidated returns are often filed by corporations under common control so that one company's losses and tax credits can be utilized to reduce the tax liabilities of the other companies.

But once one company's losses are utilized by the group as a whole, the group may become frozen into filing consolidated returns for all future years. This may result in higher future tax bills, as the group's aggregated income piles up into higher tax brackets. Also, should an accumulated earnings tax be imposed, it could impact on all the corporations, including those that, standing alone, might have been immune.

It is possible to switch back to filing separate returns. But IRS permission is required. And obtaining permission may be difficult if the intended switch back is motivated solely by a desire to save taxes.

Corporate records, such as minutes of directors' meetings, should contain a complete explanation of the business reasons behind any move that will significantly cut the firm's tax bill. But do not let the records emphasize the tax motivation behind the move. The IRS will decide the deal was motivated solely for tax-avoidance purposes and set it aside as a sham.

Tax-refund claims may result in a complete reexamination of the firm's tax return. And the reexamination could result in a higher tax bill. A better way is to review the company's finances at midyear. Make an effort to arrange estimated-tax payments so that the company's year-end tax liability is as close to zero as is possible.

Source: Dr. Robert Holzman, professor emeritus of taxation, New York University, author of *The Encyclopedia of Estate Planning*, Boardroom Books, Millburn, N.J.

The crackdown on inventory write-downs

The inventory adjustment decisions that the company must make at the end of each year became more complex than ever as a result of the Thor Power Tool Co. decision by the Supreme Court and subsequent follow-up guidelines issued by the Internal Revenue Service.

Thor, a manufacturer of hand-held power tools, produced large numbers of replacement parts for each of its tools at the time of original manufacture so as to avoid the high cost of producing parts later on. The result was a large inventory of parts. Using a formula based on the past demand for parts, Thor figured out how many parts would never be sold and wrote them down to scrap value. But Thor kept the excess parts on hand to service customers who still owned the older tools, and made occasional sales of parts at full list price.

Thor's inventory write-down was correct for financial reporting purposes because scrap value was the company's best estimate of the actual worth of the excess parts. But the IRS refused to accept the write-down for tax purposes because Thor was selling the parts at a higher price. The Supreme Court upheld the IRS's position.

Despite the decision, scores of businesses using similar write-downs didn't feel any immediate need to alter their inventory valuation procedures. In order to change an accounting method, even an improper one, a business had to have IRS approval. The IRS acted quickly, however. It granted businesses blanket permission to change from Thor-type write-downs to some other method. And inventory questions designed to force disclosure of Thor-type write-downs were added to corporate and partnership tax returns.

The IRS has also required businesses to adjust their inventory accounts by adding back into income the amount of what it terms improper inventory write-downs taken in prior years. If initiated by the taxpayer, the adjustment can be spread over the number of years the taxpayer used the improper method, up to 10 years. If initiated by the IRS, the total adjustment is taken into account in the year of change. (There are limits, however, on how much a business' tax can be increased.)

The crackdown on inventory write-downs means production and marketing changes for companies as well as accounting and tax problems. In the long run, it will be the consumer who pays. Faced with the choice of carrying unsalable inventory at cost and paying higher taxes, or scrapping inventory prematurely, manufacturers may discontinue the practice of producing large stocks of parts and accessories. Spare parts will become more costly and difficult to procure. Publishers were quick to predict that backlists of quality books would disappear as they were forced to sell off or destroy slow-moving titles to gain needed tax write-downs.

Source: *Thor Power Tool* vs *Comm'r.*, 439 US 522 (1979); Revenue Ruling 80-60; Revenue Procedure 80-5.

The case for LIFO gets stronger

IRS rules have lifted a key restriction that might deter companies from using LIFO (last-in, first-out) for inventories. Formerly a company that used LIFO for tax purposes was required to use it for financial reports to shareholders and creditors, too. And since LIFO reduced a company's apparent profitability, a switch to it made the company look less attractive to investors, banks, and other potential sources of financing. The LIFO statement might also have reduced the compensation paid to top executives who participate in incentive plans that tie bonuses to profits.

Now, however, LIFO firms can include traditional FIFO (first-in, first-out) information in financial reports. The primary financial presentation must still be made on a LIFO basis. But corresponding FIFO information can be presented in footnotes, appendixes, or a supplement. And company incentive plans may continue to use the FIFO basis to establish bonuses even after the company elects LIFO.

LIFO reduces the value of items remaining in inventory by attributing inflationary price rises to the cost of goods sold. An increase in the cost of the goods sold results in lower reported profits and taxes. Each $1 reduction in inventory values (or $1 increase on cost of goods sold) can save a corporation up to 46¢ in taxes.

As a rule of thumb, LIFO will reduce taxable profits by an amount roughly equal to the value of the firm's year-end inventory multiplied by the annual rate of rise in inventory costs. For example, ending inventory is $500,000. Inventory costs are 12% a year. With LIFO, taxable profits are reduced by about $60,000. If the company is in the 46% tax bracket, it saves $27,600 in cash. The saving will be even greater if inventory levels are higher or the rate of inflation in the business is more than 12%. And these savings are cumulative. After a few years, even a small company can save a substantial amount of money.

Many managers believe that LIFO will prove costly if inventory levels are reduced. This is not necessarily so. The dollar-value LIFO method, which most taxpayers use, may provide benefits even if the size of inventory in units is reduced. LIFO benefits are maintained as long as the dollar value of the inventoried items continues to rise.

If a firm shows a loss under FIFO, it will probably show an even greater loss under LIFO. So some companies resist electing LIFO when they anticipate an unprofitable year. But that loss may be carried back to obtain a refund of the previous year's taxes. The refund could help the company through a current cash crunch. The real question is whether the company can use the larger losses that LIFO will generate.

Any company that expects inventory costs to rise should use LIFO. It should not be used by firms that expect inventory costs to decrease. Examples are fast-developing companies or firms in high-technology areas where innovation reduces the cost of production.

Others that should not use the method are firms that cannot use a LIFO-generated loss to offset income in another year, or companies that face the real danger of having the market value of their inventories decrease. Inventories cannot be written down when LIFO procedures are used.

To elect LIFO, send in Form 970 with the company's timely filed tax return. IRS permission is not required to elect LIFO. Still, the technical regulations governing its implementation are very complicated. To gain the full benefit of a LIFO election, seek the advice of a tax specialist who is an expert in the field.

Source: Irving Blackman, Blackman, Kallick & Co., Chicago, author of *LIFO Save,* CCG, Inc., Denver.

Ten-year LIFO savings

The assumptions: A company switches to LIFO this year instead of staying on FIFO and restoring write-downs over 10 years (as allowed by the 1979 Thor Power Tool Co. decision). All write-downs are restored on the first LIFO return. The opening LIFO inventory equals the closing FIFO inventory: $300,000, plus dollar restoration of write-downs as indicated in Column 1. The annual inflation rate: 10%. The annual interest rate: 13%. Savings include interest earned on saved taxes.

Restored write-down (% of inventory)	Annual real inventory increase (%)	50% 10-year after-tax LIFO savings	25% 10-year after-tax LIFO savings
$ 30,000	0%	$353,189	$152,217
(10%)	4	422,194	183,308
	8	506,321	221,394
60,000	0	379,298	164,829
(20%)	4	454,574	198,748
	8	548,350	240,295
105,000	0	418,460	191,806
(35%)	4	503,148	229,967
	8	606,395	276,709
150,000	0	457,623	209,476
(50%)	4	551,715	251,876
	8	666,434	303,809
225,000	0	522,894	238,924
(75%)	4	623,668	288,386
	8	766,512	348,981
300,000	0	588,161	268,374
(100%)	4	713,620	324,905
	8	866,584	394,153

Source: Alan Silver & Associates, Highland Park, N.J.

Tax breaks for equipment purchases

At the heart of the 1981 tax law's business incentives is a revolutionary new method for writing off the cost of business assets, the accelerated cost recovery system (ACRS). It replaces old depreciation rules, including the former asset depreciation range (ADR) system. At the same time, the investment tax credit is boosted, particularly for short-lived equipment.

Under ACRS, most equipment will be eligible to be written off over a three- or five-year period. A few items will have to be written off over a 10-year time period. Three-year property includes cars, light-duty trucks, research and development equipment, and items with a class life of four years or less under the old ADR system, which means special tools, molds, and some material handling devices.

Five-year property takes in most other equipment, except certain long-lived public-utility equipment. Ten-year property is public-utility equipment with a class life of 18–25 years under the old ADR system. Railroad tank cars and theme-park structures are examples.

The percentage of the property's cost that can be deducted each year will depend on the type of property. For three-year property put into service between 1980 and 1984, the yearly write-offs are 25%, 38%, 37%. For five-year property, they are 15%, 22%, 21%, 21%, and 21%. For ten-year property, 8% 14%, 12%, 10% (for 3 years) and 9% (for 4 years).

Catch: When the investment credit is claimed for property, depreciation deductions are reduced by half of the credit. So if a $10,000 machine gives rise to a $1,000 investment credit, the machine must be depreciated as though it cost only $9,500.

Companies with current year losses may prefer to claim lower depreciation initially, in order to preserve deductions for later years when profits and tax liabilities are likely to be higher. This can be done by using the straight-line method. It allows an equal percentage of the property's cost to be written off in each year of its useful life instead of the percentages set out in the tables. Or use longer recovery periods: 5 or 12 years for

3-year property; 12 or 25 years for 5-year property; or 25 or 35 years for 10-year property. For the slowest possible depreciation, use the straight-line method and longer recovery periods.

Previously, companies could depreciate only the portion of an item's cost that could not be recovered if the item were sold at the end of its service life. Now, the entire cost can be depreciated. The prime beneficiaries are car-rental firms, airlines, and other companies that traditionally use equipment for only a fraction of its useful life.

Immediate write-offs. Each year, a company will be allowed to designate a portion of its equipment expenditures to be deducted in full the first year rather than depreciated. The amount eligible for deductions is $5,000 for 1982–87, $7,500 for 1988–89, and $10,000 for 1990 and later years. (This replaces a provision that used to allow an immediate deduction for 20% of the cost of a limited amount of new equipment each year.) There is no investment credit for equipment that is deducted in full the first year.

Investment credit boost. The investment tax credit (ITC) is 6% for 3-year property and 10% credit for 5-year property. (Under the old law, 3⅓% for property with a 3- to 5-year useful life, 6⅔% with a 5- to 7-year life, and 10% with a life of 7 years or longer.) In addition to raising the amount of the credit on some property, items with a useful life below three years become eligible for credit for the first time.

Recapture rules are eased also. Under the old law, if property was disposed of before the end of the useful life used to compute the ITC, part of the credit had to be paid back. The new rules allow a 2% credit for each year the item was in service. Thus if a five-year item is sold after four years, the allowable credit is 8%; only 2% must be repaid.

Excess credits. Some firms generate more investment credits than can be used in a given year because they have little or no tax liability. These credits can now be carried back three years to yield a refund of prior years' taxes. Remaining credits can then be carried forward to offset future taxes. Law: The carry-forward period is extended from 7 to 15 years, beginning as early as 1974. The limit on used property eligible for the credit is raised from $100,000 to $125,000 starting in 1981 and $150,000 starting in 1988.

At-risk rules. The at-risk rules, which used to limit deductible losses on certain investments, will now limit investment credits as well. ITC is available only on the portion of an item's cost that is paid in cash or with borrowed funds for which the buyer is personally liable. Loans from government agencies or from most institutional lenders will be treated as though the borrower were personally liable even if the only penalty for default is loss of the property purchased with borrowed funds. This will reduce the advantage of certain tax shelter deals such as leasing shelters.

Lease or buy: new dimensions

Recent tax law changes have added fresh dimensions to an old question: Is it best for the company to own or to lease its improved real estate (warehouses, plants, garages, etc.)? In different ways, the new law can make either option more attractive than before. More generous depreciation rules allow owners to claim larger depreciation deductions faster than ever before.

When the company wants to acquire a new property, it has the choice of three basic financing methods. Each has advantages and drawbacks. The options:

Cash purchase. This is the cheapest method long term. The company avoids financing charges, has complete control over the property, takes full benefit of the investment credit (where applicable) and gets the fast 18-year write-off allowed under the new tax law. But the heavy cash outlay deprives the company of valuable working capital.

Mortgage financing. It is somewhat more expensive. But the company still gets the depreciation deductions and any investment credit. However, the company's working capital is still reduced by the amount of the down payment (usually about 20% of the total cost). And the mortgage debt will probably reduce the company's credit line.

Leasing arrangement. Here, the company orders construction of the property, assigns its ownership interest to a third party, then leases the property back for a long term (20–30 years). This type of deal usually has the highest total cost. But because the lease payments are spread out and 100% deductible as a business expense, it has the lowest cash-flow cost. But the company gives up its depreciation deductions, any investment credit and the value of the property at the end of the lease term.

There are two critical questions when choosing a financing method. Do the newly increased tax benefits of ownership outweigh the cost in working capital? And is ownership of the property's residual value 30 years from now worth more than the cash-flow savings that can be obtained through a lease deal today?

To save cash, remember that real estate that the company has owned for several years has probably appreciated in value. This may give the company in a profit- and cash-flow squeeze a way out of its troubles: sell the property, and lease it back.

Benefits:

• Cash infusion.

• If the company is incurring operating losses, it shelters the gain on the sale from tax.

• Since the buyer receives valuable tax benefits in the deal, it is usually possible to lease the property back on quite favorable terms.

• Future lease payments will be fully deductible. (If the company is now making mortgage payments on the property, it can deduct only the interest.)

Typically, the property purchaser is a partnership of high-bracket individuals and the current tax benefits through depreciation deductions and any investment credit that may be available, cash flow from the lease payments, and ownership of the property's value at the end of the lease term will be a benefit for them. Pension plans and other institutional investors frequently enter into leasing arrangements as well.

Before making such a deal, company management must make sure it can live comfortably for 20–30 years with the new owners.

Investors are looking for long-term financial strength in the company and the market value of the real estate. Investors do not put too much emphasis on whether the company will be profitable this year. If they are absolutely sure of the company's viability, they will not hesitate to enter a deal involving property that is suitable only for the company's specific purposes. But as they grow less sure of the company's financial status, they want a more versatile property. The terms of the deal depend primarily on these two factors.

Large companies with good credit ratings (typically Bbb or better) can have a deal put together for them by an investment banking firm, brokerage house or insurance company. Smaller companies can get the same services from certain firms that specialize in putting together leasing arrangements. And some companies may be able to use their own contacts, for example, the firm's outside accountant may have some high-bracket individual clients who are looking for a tax shelter.

Leasing arrangements are very complicated, whether approached from the point of view of the company or that of the individual investor. So be sure to obtain expert tax and financial advice when considering such a deal.

Source: Stephen Blank, vice president, Kidder Peabody Realty Corp., New York.

Profiting from R&D tax credits

There is a special break in the tax law for any company developing a new product or improving an old one: a research-and-development tax credit. The company can use it to reduce its tax bill by up to 25% of the increase in its R&D budget. The new credit is available in addition to other, normal R&D deductions. Together, they may cut the cost of the company's research by more than half.

It is important to have the company reexamine its new-product expenditures. Many companies now simply expense these items. But R&D costs should be defined and segregated in the company books, so that creditable items are not overlooked.

Claim the credit for the cost of experimentation and investigation involving the development of a new product or the functional improvement of an old one. It is also available for the cost of applying experimental results to a new plan or design.

The cost of stylistic changes, quality-control testing and inspections that are a normal part of the production process, and consumer surveys are not creditable.

Creditable items. When the company uses its own on the R&D, it can claim the credit for:

• Wages: These include not only salaries paid to researchers but also those paid to their support staffs: a secretary who types R&D reports, an assistant who puts information in a computer, a maintenance worker who cleans R&D equipment. When a regular employee spends only some time on R&D projects, allocate a portion of the employee's wages for the credit.

• Supplies. Claim the credit, of course, for the cost of any supplies used in R&D. But the credit does not apply to the cost of the land or depreciable equipment purchased for the R&D. (Claim the regular 6% investment credit and get a three-year write-off for such equipment.)

• Payments for the use of research equipment. These include lease and rental payments for computers, special laboratory equipment costs and license payments.

When the company contracts out its research, it is not necessary to analyze contract payments to determine what is allocable to wages, supplies and other items. Instead, 65% of the contract payment is considered to be eligible for the credit.

The R&D credit is available in addition to normal R&D deductions. So the company must consider both when computing the real cost of its research work. As an example, if the company spends $1.5 million on research, it will be entitled to a tax credit of $187,500. (Computed: $1.5 million, minus average base-period expenditures of $750,000, times 25%.) But it may also have up to $1.5 million in normal R&D deductions. If the company is in the top 46% tax bracket, these deductions will be worth another $690,000 off of the tax bill. The total tax benefit is $877,500 ($187,500 plus $690,000).

So the research really cost the company only $622,500. And that is just 41.5% of its apparent $1.5 million cost.

The R&D credit is available for any research expenditures incurred after June 30, 1981. The credit can be carried back three years or forward 15 years. Or, of course, a combination of the two. Even if the company ran at a loss last year, the credit can be used to obtain a refund of taxes paid for prior years. Or it can be used to shelter future profits from tax.

Because the credit applies only to increases in the company's R&D expenditures, the timing of a company's research efforts will greatly affect their tax impact. Be sure to consult with the company's tax advisers about this and other technical aspects of the law.

Source: Robert Feinschreiber, partner, Robert Feinschreiber & Associates, New York.

Calculating the credit for R&D

The size of the credit that the company is entitled to is 25% of the increase in its R&D budget for the current year. This increase is measured by comparing the current R&D expenditure to the company's average expenditures made during a base period.

When computing the credit for:

• 1981: The base period is 1980.
• 1982: The base period includes both 1980 and 1981.
• 1983: The base period covers 1980, 1981 and 1982.
• Years after 1983: The base period consists of the three prior years.

Example: Say the company spent $500,000 on research in 1980, $1,000,000 in 1981 and $1,500,000 in 1982. The average base-period expenditures will be:

- 1981: $500,000 (actually spent in 1980).
- 1982: $750,000 ($500,000, plus $1,000,000, divided by 2).
- 1983: $1,000,000 ($500,000, plus $1,000,000, plus $1,500,000, divided by 3).

Limit: Average base-period expenditures will never be considered to be less than half the current year's expenditures. So if the company spent $1 million on R&D in the current year, its average base-period expenditure cannot be less than $500,000 and its credit cannot exceed $125,000.

Make repairs before general renovations

Repairs of business assets are immediately deductible if they merely restore the property to its original operating condition. But if the work materially increases the usefulness or life of a building or equipment, the cost must be capitalized (deducted over the life of the improvement).

If a corporation has a general plan of improvement and restoration of its plant, the entire cost must be capitalized. (This includes replacement of burnt-out light bulbs, refinishing floors, or painting present facilities.) Even if a particular item, considered by itself, would be a deductible repair, it can't be separated from the general rehabilitation plan. The solution is to take care of what are unquestionably deductible repairs before the company puts its renovation plan into operation.

Business real-estate benefits

The tax picture is brighter now for companies that build or acquire new plants or rehabilitate older commercial real estate. Formerly, buildings were typically considered to have a useful life of 40–60 years, and they had to be depreci-

ated over that long period. Now, the law assigns most buildings used in business a uniform depreciable life of 18 years.

The fastest form of depreciation available for business real estate under the old law was the 150% declining-balance method (1½ times the straight line rate). And it was available only for new buildings. Current law allows 175% declining-balance depreciation (75% faster than the straight-line rate). It applies to used buildings as well as new ones.

Combined with the new shorter depreciation period, this yields radically larger depreciation deductions.

The investment credit (10% under the old law) has been made more generous for some rehabilitation projects. The present credit schedule allows a credit of 15% for buildings 30–39 years old, 20% for those 40 years or older, and 25% for certified historic structures (including residential). There is no credit for rehabilitation of a building less than 30 years old.

The investment credit can be taken in addition to depreciation deductions. But when this credit is take, depreciation can be claimed only on a straight-line basis. And the amount of the credit must be subtracted from the building's cost before depreciation deductions are claimed. By claiming both the credit and depreciation, a business may be able to finance the rehabilitation of an attractive older building while putting up little of its own money.

An out-of-state bank account can be costly

If a business fails to report income deposited in a bank, it could be considered careless. That is punishable, at most, by a 5% negligence penalty. But when the omitted income represented deposits made in a bank in a different state, one court regarded the company's omission as a fraudulent, willful attempt to conceal income.

Source: *Candella et al.* vs *United States,* USDC, E. Dist. WI, 12/27/79.

TAX PLANNING FOR A POOR BUSINESS YEAR

Tax-wise ways to prepare for a bad-earnings year

Lagging sales and high costs mean many businesses are bracing for a poor-earnings year.

It is important to devise tax strategies to strengthen the company's cash flow as earnings erode by using the tax code to the company's advantage.

If the company made money in one year but expects to lose money in the next, it can effectively avoid paying any tax that it still owes for earlier, money-making years by filing Form 1138. This extends the time for paying the earlier year's taxes until the date the present return is due. And the loss shown on the return can be carried back to wipe out the earlier year's tax bill.

A company with losses can get a quick refund of prior year's taxes through its loss carry-back by filing Form 1139. The Internal Revenue Service must generally respond to this refund request within about 90 days. It is required that the company must file its regular tax return before the Form 1139 is filed. So file the previous year's tax return as quickly as possible.

Using an S corporation. The S form of corporate organization presents an opportunity for company owners when the company faces a loss. Shareholders of an S corporation can deduct the firm's operating losses on their personal tax returns. So they can use the company's losses to cut taxes on their income from other sources.

A company with 35 or fewer shareholders may consider reorganizing under Subchapter S to take advantage of this break. An S corporation election must be filed in the first 2½ months of the company's tax year. For a calendar-year firm, the deadline is March 15.

But there is a limit to the amount of losses that an S corporation shareholder may deduct. The limit equals the adjusted basis of the shareholder's stock (basically its cost) plus the amount of any debts owed by the company to the shareholder. Owners frequently overlook this limit. Losses that exceed this limit may be carried foward by the shareholder to a year when he has additional basis in the corporation.

When it comes to estimated taxes many firms routinely base one year's payments on the previous year's tax liability. But the resulting tax payments will be too high if this year's income goes down. So be sure the company's accountants base estimated payments on actual earnings as the year progresses. During a stretch when the company is losing money, it need pay no estimated taxes at all.

If business turns good later in the year as the economy picks up, the company may wind up with a large tax liability after all. And the IRS may ask why the company did not make any estimated-tax payments during the course of a profitable year. If this occurs file Form 2220. This shows that the company was actually losing money for most of the year and did not owe the taxes. Make sure the company's bookkeepers examine Form 2220 at the beginning of the year. It will show them what records must be kept to protect the company from tax penalties.

If the company is locked into making large pension-plan contributions this year and is afraid that it may not be able to afford them, plan now to ask the IRS for a waiver of the contribution requirements.

The company must be able to show that it is suffering from genuine economic hardship to qualify for a waiver. And it must show that the waiver is in the best interest of the pension plan's participants. Show that the waiver will help the company regain economic strength and continue in business.

Often businesses are operated through several different corporations. And the swift-changing economic conditions may affect the separate companies differently. Some profit while others lose. Look at the effects of filing a consolidated tax return. The profits of one company may then be offest by the losses of another. And the net tax bill may be reduced. A consolidated return does not have to be decided upon until the normal time for filing the tax return. At that point, with all the good and bad news in, the results of consolidated and separate filings can be compared to see which one produces the best outcome for the company as a whole.

There are two things a company should not do when confronted by financial difficulties. Never ignore an IRS communication about a tax problem. The IRS takes the worst actions when companies are silent. Instead, have the company's tax adviser answer the IRS in a businesslike manner. And never use taxes withheld from employee wages to meet a cash need of the business. That use of withholding is a crime, involving a possible fine and/or jail term.

Source: Henry A. Garris, tax manager, Richard Eisner & Co., New York.

Corporate charity

Even if taxable profits are low because of a slow economy, high depreciation deductions or an investment credit, the company may still want to make a charitable contribution to establish goodwill with influential business and community leaders. But a corporation cannot claim charitable deductions exceeding 10% of its taxable income.

To avoid the 10% limitation, find a business reason for the donation. Business expense deductions have been allowed for donations to:

• Local charities, when lobbying for a favorable community vote on a business license.

• An organization planning a convention that would generate extra business for the company.

• A community group that is engaged in rehabilitating the neighborhood in which the company offices were located.

• A hospital that agreed to provide medical services for the company.

Be sure that corporate records document two things: the business reason for the donation, and the fact that the company expects to receive a return on the expenditure.

Bad-debt write-offs

A debt can be written off for tax purposes as bad only where there is reason to believe that it won't be collected. Slow payments don't in themselves imply uncollectability. Nor does the simple fact that a debt isn't being paid. A tax write-off is limited to accounts that are not paid because the debtor is financially unable to do so. And a loss that results from compromising a debt is not deductible if the debtor is solvent.

The test of reasonable expectation of payment when the obligation was incurred usually rules out deductions on loans to friends or relatives. Money owed by a close relative can be deducted as a bad debt if there was a provable business transaction with reasonable expectation of payment. There must be proof that every effort had been made to enforce the obligation.

If the debt did not arise from a business transaction, it is treated as a short-term capital loss. That's only of limited tax usefulness.

There can be no bad debt if there was no genuine debt in the first place. Examples are gambling debts (in most states) or loans at illegally high interest rates. A cash-basis business cannot deduct a bad debt when its merchandise or services are not paid for, since income had never been reported in the first place.

A bad-debt deduction is allowed only in the taxable year when some identifiable event occurs that indicates the account can't be collected. Such an event might be discharge of the debtor of its obligations by a bankruptcy court. But it needn't go that far. If the debtor's liabilities exceed its assets, there is technical insolvency. If a bank reports that a debtor is defaulting on trade obligations or cancels its own purchase orders, that is an identifiable event.

A bad debt is not deductible at the end of a taxable year unless it can be shown to have been good at the beginning of that year. (The debt actually may have become bad in an earlier year.) Deduct in the year when the debt actually became bad, not in the year when it was discovered to be uncollectable.

If there is real doubt as to whether a debt will be paid, those stuck with it don't have to wait until uncollectability is proven to get a tax deduction. A partial bad-debt deduction can be taken for the portion of the debt that has become uncollectable in that year. If, for example, an experienced attorney advises that there is only a 40% chance of collecting from a certain customer, that justifies a deduction of 60% of the indebtedness as a partial bad debt. (This applies only to business bad debts.)

If a bad debt is written off in one taxable year and subsequently payment is received in whole or in part, the original deduction is not affected. The amount recovered is taxed in the year received, but only if the original deduction created a tax benefit, that is, if the creditor reduced his taxable income by deducting the bad debt. But if the creditor had no income to reduce by the amount of the bad debt, the recovered money isn't taxable.

Recession tax planning

Tax planning can ease the cash-flow problems a firm is likely to experience during any recession. Possible steps to take are:
• Extend the payment time for the previous year's taxes by filing Form 1138, if a loss is expected this year.
• Obtain a quick refund of estimated taxes by filing Form 4466 within two and a half months after the close of the tax year.
• Expedite refunds resulting from net operating losses, capital losses, unused job-credit carry-backs, and investment tax credits: File Form 1139.
• Reduce estimated tax payments by basing them on this year's expected income rather than last year's tax.
• Extend the payment time for this year's taxes to avoid undue hardship to the firm by filing Form 1127.

Source: Deloitte Haskins & Sells, New York.

TAKING MONEY OUT OF THE COMPANY

Making loans to shareholders bona fide

It is very dangerous for the owner of a closely held corporation to borrow funds from the corporation to meet personal cash needs. The Internal Revenue Service may contend that the loan is actually a dividend, and the amount received by the owner will be taxed as investment income at up to the 50% maximum rate.

Furthermore, if a corporation can afford to lend a large amount of cash to an owner for personal use, the IRS may rule that the company had no genuine business reason for accumulating the cash in the first place. The firm might have to pay a penalty tax on its unreasonable accumulation of earnings.

There should be a good reason for the loan, such as an urgent temporary need. (The worst is a loan used to make a long-term investment.) The reason for the loan, and the intent to repay it, should be clearly stated in a separate letter from the owner to the corporation. The board of directors should approve the loan and prepare minutes indicating their approval, before the loan is made.

The borrower should sign a note that is legally binding and provides for a schedule of repayment. The note should require that interest be paid at the applicable federal rate for similar loans. Anything less will make it harder to defend the arrangement as a bona fide loan. Payments of principal and interest should be made on time and by separate check, not by bookkeeping offsets.

Source: Edward Mendlowitz, partner, Siegel & Mendlowitz, & Rich CPAs, New York.

How depreciation rules affect dividends

The 1981 tax law makes it somewhat easier for companies, especially smaller ones, to pay tax-free dividends to shareholders.

A dividend is not taxable if the company that pays it can show that current-year operations have not been profitable, and that total dividend payouts since the company began operations have equaled or exceeded the company's total profits over the years.

If these two conditions are met, the dividend is considered a partial return of the cost of the stock. Thus the dividends are not taxed until the entire cost of the stock has been returned, at which time the dividends are taxed as long-term capital gains.

Depreciation deductions that firms use to compute profits are higher than formerly. Instead of assets being written off over their entire useful lives, the law sets fixed write-off periods. These are keyed to the write-off periods that are provided for computing taxable income:

Write-off period (in years)

For computing taxable income	For determining if dividends are taxable
3	5
5	12
10	25
15	35

When the new write-off periods result in larger deductions to eliminate profits, the company may be able to declare a tax-free dividend.

Justifying a large salary

A large salary can be justified by showing that it includes compensation for work done in past years when an executive received little or no salary. In a recent case, a corporation claimed a $200,000 deduction for salary paid to its president. The Internal Revenue Service said only a $10,000 salary was reasonable. The court agreed with the IRS, but it allowed a deduction of $40,000—$10,000 for the current year plus $10,000 for each of three prior years in which the president received no salary.

Source: *Cropland Chemical Corp., 75 TC 288.*

Traps in intercompany loans

Loans between companies controlled by the same owners may wind up being treated as taxable dividend distributions. In a recent case, two brothers who owned all the stock of two corporations transferred $400,000 from the healthy company to the troubled one. The transfer was ruled a dividend distribution taxable to the brothers because there was no written loan agreement, no provision was made to repay the transferred amount or to pay interest, and the recipient company was apparently incapable of repaying.

Source: *Edward Wilkof vs Comm'r., 636 F.2d 1139, 6th Cir.*

Corporate work on boss' home— taxable dividend

Corporate employees were instructed to do construction and electrical work on the home of the president and chief stockholder. The result: The value of the materials and services was taxed to him as a dividend. The corporation's costs for the work were disallowed. Both the shareholder and corporation were assessed penalties.

Source: *Magnon et al. vs Comm'r., 73 T.C. 980.*

High compensation and the IRS

As an executive gets older and takes more time off, the Internal Revenue Service may claim that he's no longer worth what the corporation has been deducting as reasonable compensation. In a recent case, the full deduction was allowed because it was shown that the corporation's present earnings were in part the result of the work of the executive's earlier service, work that was now paying off handsomely.

Source: *Lundy Packing Company vs Comm'r., T.C. Memo, 1979-472.*

SPECIAL BUSINESS DEDUCTIONS

Tax deduction for employee vacation pay before the company shells it out

Cut vacation-pay costs with a simple technique: Accrued-vacation-pay plans. They are often overlooked as a source of big tax savings.

Most firms deduct vacation pay the year they actually pay it. That means the deduction is claimed on the return filed after the payment is made. But by electing to accrue vacation pay, this deduction can be accelerated by up to 11 months. That's because the pay is them deductible the year the employee earns it, even if it won't actually be paid until the next year.

Example: A company pays its 100 employees $400 each week of their two-week summer vacations. (Total: $800 per employee.) If the following summer's expense is accrued and deducted in December, the company gets an $80,000 deduction for money that won't be paid for another six months.

A company deducting vacation pay on the cash method may be able to increase its deductions for the year simply by switching to the accrual method. In the year of the switch, the company gets one deduction for current cash payments that weren't deducted before and another deduction for vested vacation rights that accrue currently but won't be paid until next year. Catch: IRS permission is needed to make the accounting switch. The IRS may require that the company spread the extra deduction over several years. But even so, the company's deductions are increased while its actual expenses

are not. Caution: Technical rules apply, so discuss this ploy with a tax expert.

Deducting business start-up costs

Start-up cost deductions for a new business are eased by a new U.S. Claims Court decision. But the decision also emphasizes the importance of allocating such costs between operating expenses and capital expenditures.

One partnership constructed an apartment complex and hired a corporation to administer it. The partnership paid the corporation a $35,000 fee and deducted the fee in that year as a business expense. But the Internal Revenue Service disallowed the deduction, since the apartments were not rented until the next year. The partnership was not entitled to a business-expense deduction before it was really in business, the IRS said.

The Claims Court found the IRS reasoning faulty, however. Regular recurring expenses (such as salaries, maintenance fees, and utility charges) can be deducted before a business generates any income. Any part of the fee attributable to such expenses could have been deducted in the first year.

Yet the partnership lost. Part of the fee also covered capital expenditures related to acquiring assets and organizing the business. This part of the fee was not deductible in the start-up year. And since the partnership did not allocate the fee between regular expenses and capital expenditures, no part of the fee was deductible.

Code Section 195 allows businesses to elect to deduct start-up costs of the normal recurring-expense type over a five-year period without fear of an IRS challenge. This U.S. Claims Court decision may make it possible to deduct all such costs in one year. However, a business that tries to deduct all of its expenses in one year and is challenged by the IRS cannot then make the five-year election.

Source: *Blitzer vs U.S.*, Claims Court, No. 426-76, 684 F.2d 874.

Extra deductions from sale and leaseback

In order to deduct the cost of an asset after it has been fully depreciated, sell the asset, then lease it back from the buyer. Deduct the lease payments as a business expense. The time to do it is when an asset's actual useful life is significantly longer than the period over which it is depreciated.

But taxes must be paid on the sale proceeds. A portion of the previously claimed depreciation may be recaptured and included in the seller's ordinary income. Expert advice is required before setting up a sale-and-leaseback deal.

Source: Jack Leonard Green, *Leasing Principles and Methods*, Sound Publishing Co., New York.

Special deduction for product-liability losses

Special tax rules soften the blow to companies forced to pay out large amounts as the result of product-liability lawsuits.

Normally, a company's net operating loss may be carried back three years or forward seven years to reduce its tax liability for those years. But when the loss results from a product-liability claim, special rules allow it to be carried back 10 years. A tax refund paid for those years helps the firm through a financial bind caused by the lawsuit.

For example, a company has a $100,000 loss, of which $85,000 resulted from a product-liability claim, the $85,000 loss may be carried back 10 years, while the $15,000 may carried back only three years.

Product-liability costs include judgments against the company, out-of-court settlements, and expenses incurred while investigating or opposing product-liability claims.

Source: Code Section 172(b)(1)(I).

Benefit-plan deductibles

A firm's contributions to its employee benefit plan aren't deductible until after the plan's provisions are fully communicated to all its participants. The deduction was lost when employees were merely told that a plan's provisions were available for inspection in an executive's office, and that copies of the plan would be distributed at a later date. If a written description of the plan's provisions had been distributed to all employees, then the Internal Revenue Service would have allowed the deduction.

Source: *Engineered Timber Sales, Inc. vs Comm'r.*, 74 T.C. 808.

Deductions can be documented in pictures

Formal documentation of casualty losses, equipment failures, etc., for tax purposes proves the adage that good pictures can often be worth more than a thousand words. And the Internal Revenue Service is encouraging the picture-taking approach. How to do it:

• Justifying accumulated earnings. Show factory aisles clogged with raw materials and spare parts to justify a need for more working space.

• Inventory losses. Show shopworn, smoke-stained, or obsolete items to document write-downs.

• Repairs. Pictures of equipment before and after repairs can prove that the asset merely had been restored to its original condition, meeting the definition of a deductible repair and not a capital improvement.

• Depreciation. If accelerated depreciation is claimed because assets are being subjected to especially harmful use, the camera can support the company's argument. During the reconstruction of a highway leading to a plant, for instance, company trucks had to slog through very rough roads.

• Abnormal obsolescence. Show changes in the character of the neighborhood that have lowered the value of the place of business. Or company equipment can be compared to catalog photos of competitors' equipment.

• Loss on abandonment or demolition. Depict the condition of buildings or equipment that led management to conclude the asset was beyond repair or sale.

• Home-office expense. In cases where a home-office deduction is possible, take photos to show that the claimed office space is just that. (Make sure the photo shows filing cabinets, long-carriage typewriters, duplicating equipment, but no easy chair or TV set).

Incidentally, the cost of photographs used to establish tax liability is deductible for federal income tax purposes.

Entertainment-expense warning

Entertainment expenses are deductible when they are "ordinary and necessary" business costs. But it isn't ordinary and necessary for a business to waste its money. A company's deduction was denied after customers told the IRS that the golfing trips to which they had been invited were not the motivation or even an influencing factor behind their order placement.

Source: *Finney et al.* vs *Comm'r.,* T.C. Memo. 1980-23, January 28, 1980.

Business contributions to political candidates

Direct contributions by business entities to candidates for federal office are not allowed by federal law. Such contributions must be channeled through employee political action committees (PACs).

Some states allow direct contributions for state and local office-seekers, but others bar them even if they are channeled through PACs.

Even when allowed by a state, political contributions are not deductible on federal returns as business expenses, whether for corporations or partnerships.

And when a company does business with the local or state government, a contribution to a local candidate can be considered a conflict of interest, depending on the state and the circumstance. Expensive ads in state political party convention programs are a particular target. Even where ads are legal, no allowable business deduction is permitted for them.

8 HOW TO GET FINANCING

FINANCING STRATEGIES

Strategies for smart borrowing

Basic errors in a company's borrowing strategy often do not become apparent until the company needs money fast. By then, it may be too late. For smart corporate financing:

• Maintain contact with several lenders. If possible, do business with more than one. Relying on one lender is dangerous. A company that has used the same lender for 20 years is extremely vulnerable. If that lender refuses a loan or terminates the relationship entirely, the company will have trouble arranging for alternate financing quickly.

• Anticipate financing needs and make arrangements well in advance. Patchwork financing is an expensive and risky way to operate. Put money on standby whenever possible. A standby fee, if necessary, is cheap insurance against the risk of suddenly running out of money.

• Borrow as much as possible. It is better to have too much than to have too little. Lend out excess funds to reduce net borrowing costs. Large companies view money as a resource to be inventoried, like coal or steel. Smaller firms should too.

• Get all commitments in writing. This includes standby agreements, loans, and increases in credit lines. If there is nothing in writing, the company might not really have what it needs. No professional lender objects to written commitments.

• Never assume that silence is tacit approval of a loan request. Some lenders do not like to say no, so they say nothing. Then when the company inquires about its loan application, usually around the time it needs the money, it suddenly learns that it has been turned down. When applying for a loan, ask when the answer will be ready. Call the lender on that date if there has been no response.

• Do not make the interest rate the major consideration in evaluating a credit. No company wants to pay more interest than necessary. But the most important aspect of a financing is the availability of money—how much and how soon. The second most important is how the deal is structured. Interest rate is third.

• Do not limit sources to banks alone. Too many companies rely on a local bank for all financing needs. This is unfair to the bank, and it restricts the company's growth. Even smaller companies can, and should, borrow from insurance companies, pension funds, venture-capital funds, and other institutions.

Source: Russell Hindin, managing director, Hindin/Owen/Engelke, Los Angeles.

Financing choices

Type of Financing	Typical Use	Typical Sources	Common Structure	Approximate Cost (P = Prime)
Short-term debt	A	Banks	Unsecured notes	P to P + 4
	B	Commercial lenders	Inventory and equipment collateral; sale and leaseback	P + 4 to P + 7
	C	Factors	Receivable and inventory collateral	P + 5 to P + 8
Intermediate-term debt	D	Banks	3- to 7-year self-liquidating secured covenants	P to P + 4
		Commercial lenders	3- to 5-year revolving lines secured (principal paydown not necessary)	P + 2 to P + 6
Long-term debt	E	Insurance companies and pension funds	8- to 15-year principal plus interest, secured or unsecured	Fixed rate (P + 2) plus warrants
		Public offering	10- to 20-year interest only	P + 1 to P + 3
Equity	E	Venture capital	Convertible preferred stock plus common	High
		Public offering	Cash for common	Varies
		Acquisition	Stock swap or cash for stock	Varies
		Joint venture	Cash for common in new venture	Varies
		Private placement	Cash with restrictions for voting common	Varies
Other	F	Various governmental agencies	Long-term. Industrial development at municipal and state levels. Specific applications at federal level. Various special purposes at all levels	Varies

A Ideally used to finance seasonal working capital needs. The borrower should expect the bank to require a compensating balance and annual "clean-up" provisions, when the entire debt must be repaid.
B To finance the acquisition of equipment or inventory. The lender will expect the loan to be repaid from earnings generated by the asset, as opposed to liquidation of the asset, which is the case with seasonal bank borrowing.
C Provide permanent working capital financing for undercapitalized companies or to companies unable to borrow on an unsecured basis. The loan is normally a percentage of the applicable asset (range: 50%–85%).
D Typically a source of semipermanent capital normally expected to be repaid from earnings.
E Source of permanent capital. Additions here support additional borrowing capacity for other types of loans. They are the most difficult forms of financing to arrange as they rest on the ultimate earning power of the issuer.
F Governmental financing (such as a Small Business Administration guaranteed loan) is normally used by a borrower who does not qualify for conventional financing. It can also be used to obtain preferential terms, such as tax abatements.

Source: Jeffrey J. Sands, Peat, Marwick, Mitchell & Co., New York.

How much should a company borrow?

Here's a formula to use to determine how much credit a company can handle. Total borrowings should not exceed the sum of:

10% of net working capital
+ 5% of cash and receivables
+ 10% of one year's net income.

From this total, deduct 3% of the long-term debt. Bankers use this formula to make sure they don't lend too much money.

Source: William G. Torrace, management consultant, Troy, Mich.

What to do when a recession pinches

A downturn in the nation's economy will often be felt by a company as a sudden tightness in cash flow. This problem is followed by other trouble signs: Bills back up. The management spends more time trying to raise funds than it does running the company. The plant is hit by shortages. Fear of talking frankly to banks develops. And concern over meeting payrolls arises.

The usual result is that management becomes paralyzed, and its effectiveness deteriorates. To prevent this, take positive action as soon as the first warning signs appear.

In dealing with banks, don't speculate on the worst possible scenario. (The bank will do that.) Present the data in the best light. If the company has a plant in another city, try a bank there. The bank knows it has a stake in the local payroll.

Use a financial consultant to find nonbank lenders for secured loans. Be prepared for secured lenders to send in their own auditors to make an independent verification of the collateral.

Don't be tempted to borrow short to finance long-term requirements, especially in a recession. And don't pay off a single creditor because he's been yelling the loudest. Chances are he will take the money and cut off credit.

Source: Malcolm P. Moses, financial consultant, Malcolm P. Moses & Associates, Merrick, N.Y.

DEALING WITH BANKS

What kind of bank loan can a company expect?

Bank loans that fluctuate with a highly volatile prime rate can put companies under severe pressure. With the fixed-rate bank loan all but gone, the company may have to settle for a floating interest rate pegged at least 1%–1½% above the prime. Longtime customers of a bank who maintain sizable deposits are the exception; they may be able to get loans several percentage points below the prime.

Also to be expected are payback schedules calculated over 20 years but calling for a complete payoff of the balance (a balloon) after three to five years. As an added requirement, the company may be asked to use other bank services for a fee.

What impresses loan officers

Companies that are successful in obtaining loans are usually those whose management performance is most impressive from the bank's point of view. What loan officers look for:

• A long-term record of solid or expanding market share.

• Concentration in areas of proven expertise.

• Willingness to abandon products as soon as they turn unprofitable, regardless of how long they have been part of the business.

• Company finances that emphasize long-term debt, without undue reliance on short-term financing or collecting accounts receivable.

• Return on capital at 8% or more (allowing for some variation from industry to industry).

• Use of an independent certified public accountant, preferably one of the CPA industry's Big Eight firms.

• A comprehensive company financial plan. Include both short- and long-term projections for cash flow, capital sources, and uses.

• A frank discussion of problems the company faces, and how management hopes to resolve them.

Source: Guy C. Roberts, Massachusetts Life Insurance Company, *Nation's Business,* Washington, D.C.

How to keep your banker happy

In tight money times, don't avoid your banker, call on him. Even better, invite him in to the office for a talk. Present good points, don't hide bad points.

Help him to focus on your company's ability to satisfy pent-up demands when the climate shifts. Prepare samples of the best- and worst-case scenarios and how you'd handle them.

Cash flows and pro forma projections are

closest to his heart. Also give him a projected balance sheet and keep him up-to-date on the back-order situation.

Pump information to him, including your business strategy. Reassure him of top management's character and its ability to weather bad times.

Make sure he is aware of your company in relation to those in the rest of your industry. Put yourself in his shoes by answering questions in a direct and positive tone. Make it easier for him to say yes by supplying the information that's important to him.

Prepare him for bad news. Explain the problem in advance if he is likely to find an overdue notice from his collection department on his desk. If the situation is really bleak, consider suggesting lender's insurance.

Source: T. Patrick Hurley, Jr., Howard & Co., Philadelphia.

The best banking hours

You can get greater attention from bankers by arranging visits to coincide with their least busy period. The best times are between the fourth and the 14th or between the 16th and 29th of the month, and before 11 A.M. or after 1:30 P.M.

Loans that banks don't like to make

Bank boards will rarely approve these types of loans:

• Loans secured by property outside the bank's trade area.

• Construction loans in excess of the bank's limits (usually 60% of the appraised value for business, 80% residential).

• Loans to be repaid by the proceeds of an estate. Exception: if estate and bank attorneys agree on collateral and guarantees.

• New enterprise loans when repayment depends on liquidating assets. Exception: short-term loans secured by equipment with a market value.
• Speculation loans to buy precious metals, foreign currencies, or securities.
• Stock loans secured by shares in a closed corporation with no market value.

Source: Joseph J. Smith, *How to Borrow Money from a Bank,* Global Enterprises, Baxter Springs, Kans.

Lending to S companies

Generally speaking, banks don't care if a company is publicly owned or privately held so long as it is in strong financial condition. An exception to the rule are S corporations (privately held corporations taxed like partnerships) companies. Bankers may insist that such corporations shift to a regular C corporation tax basis to ensure that earnings stay permanently in the company rather than being distributed to the owners individually.

Source: W. Stewart Cahn, vice-president, Chemical Bank.

Recovering from a bank turndown

A common mistake is giving up after the first try. Instead, immediately prepare a new thrust:
Ask for specifics on why the loan was refused. Commonly, the bank is overextended or doesn't know the company's type of business.
Invite the loan officer and one of the officer's supervisors to visit the plant. Build confidence by showing off equipment, facilities, and personnel.
Solicit ideas on how the application can be made more acceptable through financial or accounting changes, tax regulations, government programs, or production changes.
Apply for another type of loan or a different

credit basis. Pledge machinery as collateral, use a third-party guarantee, or borrow against seasonal receivables.
Reapply when the timing is better. Use an upswing in sales or profits to obtain a line of credit, or get close enough to the banker to be informed when the bank has excess funds to loan.
Change banks, particularly to one that is newly chartered and looking for customers. Try splitting a loan between and old and new banks.
Remember that the way the loan proposal is presented can be critical. A friendly banker will advise the company on which documents to present and the best ways to compile financial data.

Source: J.G. Hellmuth, *Finding Money: The Businessman's Guide to Sources of Financing,* Boardroom Books, Millburn, N.J.

Line of credit vs loan commitment

A line of credit with a bank facilitates corporate borrowing but offers less financial security than a loan commitment. The bank can cancel the line of credit at any time. Also, the bank is not required to advance the full amount of the line. A loan commitment, on the other hand, cannot be canceled during its life except under special circumstances spelled out in the loan contract. Note that the company must pay a fee for this assurance of financial availability. There is no fee for the line of credit.

Source: *Midlantic NB* vs *Commonwealth General,* 1980 D.C. App. (4th) 386 So. (2) 31.

Loans from foreign banks

Foreign banks with U.S. offices are aggressively competing for U.S. business, making the same-sized loans as U.S. banks. According to a recent survey, foreign banks now hold more

42% of the commerical and industrial loans booked in the U.S. They are doing business with companies of all sizes.

The most aggressive lenders are French banks. Most of them have fewer capital restrictions than do banks of other countries.

What to seek from a foreign bank: both one-time loans and credit lines. Foreign banks are often willing to:

• Book small loans in hopes that repeat business will follow.

• Offer cut-rate terms, despite a tightening of the U.S. regulations that govern them.

• Make a decision faster than an American bank.

U.S. banks are worried about the hungry foreigners. As a result, if they know a borrower is shopping around at foreign banks, they may make their own offers more attractive.

Source: *American Banker,* New York.

ALTERNATIVE SOURCES OF FINANCING

Alternative lending sources for small companies

In today's world, with the prime rate mainly an indicator of how the price of credit is moving, a favored customer gets the bank's best rate. Although that usually means a giant, well-established company, smaller companies can also get the best rate if they have a solid credit rating and, more important, alternative lending sources. Growing sources of alternative financing are the commercial paper market (generally for sums of $10 million or more) and insurance companies (generally for $1 million or more—a few will lend as little as $250,000).

Another way to strengthen the company's hand in loan negotiations is to talk to foreign banks. They are a new and strong source of competition for U.S banks. Their willingness to shave prices to win customers is helping to erode the prime rate and benefiting corporate borrowers.

In addition, look into the growing commercial paper market. And meet with insurance companies. They are more and more willing to make loans to smaller companies.

Source: Sanford Rose, associate editor, *American Banker,* New York.

Financial futures

As more and more companies with floating-rate loans try to soften the impact of rising interest rates, financial futures are becoming an essential part of financial management. The basic strategy: A company that borrows and wants to protect itself against higher interest rates would sell a futures contract short. If rates go up, the market value of the futures contract will go down. The company will cover the short position and will thereby make money. Those earnings offset the increase in borrowing costs.

The companies that should be protecting themselves with futures are:

• Highly leveraged companies that cannot readily pass on increased interest costs to their customers because of long-term contract commitments.

• Seasonal businesses that borrow short-term for long-term needs.

Futures contracts do not tie up much cash. A futures contract to hedge the interest-rate risk on a $3 million loan requires a cash deposit of about $65,000 for a Treasury bond hedge.

Once top management decides on the use of financial futures, the company accountant or financial manager may initiate and manage all aspects of the transaction except the actual decision of which particular contracts to buy and sell short.

To prepare, define the company's borrowing needs over the next year. Then ask the company's investment banker, its brokerage firm, or its local commercial banker for recommendations on futures contracts.

Source: Harvey D. Moskowitz, director of accounting and auditing, Seidman & Seidman, New York.

Hedging with financial futures

Liquid assets held in the form of government securities decline drastically in value as interest rates rise. It is now considered speculative to buy a long-term bond, no matter how high its stated yield, without hedging against future price fluctuation. This is especially important to a business which might have to sell the securities for cash before the date of maturity.

Margin calls to cover loss on the futures contracts could become a cash drain requiring the company to get short-term financing. Hedging short-term securities with long-term securities may result in a loss when short- and long-term interest rates are out of line or don't follow a normal yield curve. There is no such thing as a perfect hedge, as the cash and futures markets don't always move together.

The completed transactions must take place as close to each other as possible. The more time that elapses between closing out a futures contract and making a cash transaction, the less likelihood that the profit on one will exactly offset the loss on the other. It's best for a company to consult a professional.

Suppose the company expects a heavy cash inflow four months from now and wants to assure getting today's interest rates on that money. The solution is to buy a Treasury bond or bill futures contract. If rates drop in the intervening months, the company will get less of a return on the money it invests then. But it will have made an offsetting profit by selling its futures contract (which will go up in price as interest rates de-

cline). Taken together, the initial yield objective is met.

Or suppose the company is planning for a note or public bond issue. The undewriting process inevitably takes several months, during which interest rates could change. To protect itself against a big increase, the company might sell Treasury bond futures contracts—in effect sell its own bonds short. If interest rates go up by the time the issue goes public, Treasury bonds that the company must buy to deliver on its future contracts will be down in price. And the profit on that transaction will largely counterbalance the increased interest rate the company has to pay.

Management should keep careful track of anyone authorized to trade for the company in the financial futures market, and deal only with substantial brokerage houses and commodity trading firms. Adequate capital is vital, or the company may be at risk.

In addition, make certain that the financial manager monitors activity daily and is flexible in response to market conditions. Finally, be aware that the rules on accounting for financial futures trading are in a state of flux. Consult the company accountant.

While it is prudent to hedge against interest rate increases, it remains to be seen how active the financial futures market will be during a period of falling interest rates.

Source: Stanley Alintoff, partner, Arthur Andersen & Co.

A government loan source

Businesses operating in areas with populations of 50,000 or less can tap the Farmers Home Administration for sizable loan guarantees. Despite its name, the FmHA is not restricted to farmers.

Unlike the Small Business Administration, the FmHA sets no ceiling on loan guarantees. It does not require the applicant to have first sought and been denied credit elsewhere. It will guarantee up to 90% of long-term bank loans. The average amount is $1 million.

Priorities are given to business expansions and to companies in underpopulated areas with no more than 25,000 people.

The agency maintains some 1,750 offices in county seats. Or write to the Farmers Home Administration, U.S. Department of Agriculture, Washington, D.C. 20250.

Cheap loans for firms hurt by imports

Companies injured by imports may be eligible for up to $1 million in loans under the 1974 Trade Adjustment Assistance Act. The law, administered by the Department of Commerce, also provides for loan guarantees of up to $3 million above the initial loan. The interest rate, adjusted quarterly, is designed to be below the prime rate.

To qualify, a domestic manufacturer must show that domestic production has decreased while sales of foreign competitors have increased, and that as a result of the sales drop, the company may be forced to lay off workers.

Note that a healthy financial condition is not the sole criterion for the loan. Some firms in Chapter XI bankruptcy have received loans under the Act.

An applicant company must ask the Department of Commerce whether it is eligible for the program. Expect an answer in 90 days. The company then applies for a direct loan, a loan guarantee, or a combination of both. The decision takes an average of 120 days. The chances of approval are about 50–50. Loans for working capital must be paid back over 5–10 years. Those for fixed assets are paid back over 10–15 years.

Source: Robert A. Ungar, partner, Alton Consultants, Inc., Great Neck, N.Y.

Factoring vs asset financing

Using receivables to replenish working capital is expensive and often the last resort, short of bankruptcy, for ailing businesses.

However, two variations of this type of financing can provide useful options for growth companies lacking access to unsecured funds.

Factoring. An outright sale of accounts receivable. The factor makes cash available as an advance (at 2%–3% above the prime interest rate) against purchase installments collected as accounts mature. A drawback is that customers must be notified of the change and pay the factor directly. To them, it can look like a sign of trouble.

Asset financing (also known as commercial financing). It is secured borrowing, possibly from a bank, but usually from a more specialized high-risk lender, The lender uses accounts receivable or other assets as collateral. Customer notification is not required.

In both cases, sources of receivables financing are not so concerned with an applicant's financial statements. Prime concerns are the quality of accounts and the borrower's previous and projected ability to generate enough cash to pay off the debt.

The advantages of factoring are:

Simplification and safety. The factor assumes responsibility for collection. That, in effect, guarantees customers' credit.

Reduction of overhead. With back-office problems minimized, executives are free to focus their attention on areas for which they are best suited, such as purchasing, production, and sales.

Continuous flow of funds. Once a factoring deal is made, new receivables are batched and sold to the factor periodically.

The benefits of asset financing include:

Nonnotification. Account ownership does not change hands, so the borrower's customers pay their bills directly to the supplier, rather than to a factor.

Cost-effectiveness. The borrower draws funds only as needed. Collections, made by the borrower, are credited daily as they are paid. New accounts qualify immediately as new collateral.

Credit expansion. Besides receivables, the lender may finance inventories, real estate, or any combination of assets. For growth companies, the result is much higher-leveraged operations and greater flexibility.

_____

Source: Robert I. Goldman, president, Congress Financial Corp., Boston.

Accounts-receivable financing

The chief reason to consider raising money against accounts receivable is so the company can borrow only what's needed, day-to-day, instead of meeting the bank's requirements for a larger, fixed amount. This type of financing fine-tunes borrowing to exact time periods, gets the company through seasonal tight spots, and increases working capital turnover. Technical financial assistance from firms that supply accounts-receivable financing can also be useful.

Industrial-revenue financing

A company that needs to borrow money to build a new facility or expand an existing one may be able to reduce the interest cost sharply by using industrial-revenue financing. The company will probably be able to borrow the full amount and will have to put up little or no cash. It works about the same as if the firm got a 15- or 20-year mortgage at 8%–9%, with no down payment. (Interest is tax-free to the lender.) Since red tape and legal fees are considerable, the process is attractive mainly for projects that will cost $500,000 or more. How it's done:

The company finds a community that wants to attract new industry and jobs. It could be a small rural town or a major industrial city, even the city where the company is now located.

The municipality sells tax-exempt bonds or arranges low-interest bank financing to raise the money needed for the facility and lends it to the company. Depending on local law, the deal may cover the building only or the machinery and equipment too. Repayments are set no higher than needed to cover the interest and repayment of the principal. Typically, when the bonds are paid off, the company owns the property free and clear.

Usually, the whole project can't involve more than $10 million. Depending on the complexity of the transaction and the vigor of local legal requirements, it may take five or six months and a lot of management time for meetings and the preparation of many documents.

If the financing goes as high as several million dollars, a public offering of the bonds may be the best financing method. Much of the cost is paid out of the sale of the bonds and is therefore spread out over the life of the issues. The cost of the offering doesn't have to be paid up front.

Some deals, especially those in the $100,000–$1 million range, will probably be negotiated privately with one or two banks or institutional lenders. This way the offering costs less but the terms may be tougher: a faster repayment schedule, or more restrictions on the company's freedom to do other borrowing.

First pick a plant site that is suitable. Then talk to the chamber of commerce or a good lawyer. Local authorities should be eager to help if the facility will create jobs.

_____

Source: Joseph J. Feit, George R. Krouse, and Richard A. Miller, Simpson, Thacher & Bartlett, New York.

Capitalizing on venture capital

Small but growing companies should be looking at venture-capital firms as an alternative source of outside financing. How to proceed:

Draw up a business plan. Venture capitalists are eager to find companies with significant growth potential that are managed by high-caliber executives. They are not interested in inventions or projects. An average venture-capital firm will look at 200 business plans in a year, but pick only a handful.

Sell the plan widely, but don't keep it on the market once a preliminary agreement is reached. A list of the 200 venture-capital firms in the United States and their areas of interest can be found in *Guide to Venture-Capital Sources,* published by Capital Publishing Corp., Wellesley Hills, Mass.

Be prepared to spend time winning the confidence of any venture-capital firm attracted by the plan.

Execute as much of the company's business plan as possible before negotiating a deal. For example, develop a backlog of product orders as quickly as possible. The more a company has to offer a venture-capital firm, the less equity it must surrender to get financing.

Because each venture deal is different, there are no guidelines for what or how much an entrepreneur must give up in return for capital. However, different venture capitalists specialize in various kinds of deals, start-ups, working capital or debt financings, leveraged buy-outs, high-technology or prosaic product lines. Entrepreneurs with attractive business plans should be able to shop within the venture community to determine which group is appropriate for their particular project.

A rule of thumb is that entrepreneurs have to give up considerably more today than ten years or so ago. Venture capitalists can no longer easily turn over their investments by making small growth companies public. They want to be compensated for the longer holding periods.

Source: Alan J. Patricof, Alan Patricof Associates, New York.

Selling bonds

A closely held corporation with pretax earnings of at least $3 million and a minimum net worth of $5 million is big enough to sell bonds. The size of the debt offering should be at least $12 million to attract sufficient market interest and justify the underwriting costs (usually about $200,000).

Three years of audited figures for Securities & Exchange Commission registration, and a specific need for the money, not just a general one must be proven.

An underwriter will closely examine the company's position, history, balance sheet, and management team before agreeing to file the offering. This takes about a month. If snags develop, the company usually is not charged for the evaluation.

But the actual interest rate on the issue isn't set until the day before the offering is made. The underwriter can give a close estimate, but there are no guarantees.

Lowering interest costs with convertibles

An interesting financing vehicle for medium-size companies in a skittish bond market is the high-premium, high-yielding convertible debenture.

A company can save as much as 300–400 basis points (three to four percentage points) on the interest costs of a straight bond issue. And the equity kicker sweetens the deal for investors.

Setting the debenture's conversion rights at a high premium (50% vs the more normal 15%–20%) reduces the potential dilution of company equity. Typically, that dilution is stretched out, since the underlying stock will probably take a while to reach the conversion price.

For example, if a straight bond would have to carry a coupon of 16%, and the company's stock is selling at $20 now, a 50% premium convertible issued ($30 conversion price) could be marketed at 12%. For a $20 million offering, those four percentage points mean an annual cash saving of $800,000.

Source: Leon Black, vice-president, Drexel Burnham Lambert, investment bankers, New York.

Using unregistered securities

One of the quickest and least expensive ways for a private or public company to raise capital is by selling unregistered common stock privately to a limited number of investors. That avoids both registration and underwriting costs.

But selling stock this way, through a so-called investment letter, must be carefully managed. It is easy for a company to unintentionally violate federal securities laws—or state ones, which are sometimes stricter.

The company should try to meet the requirements of SEC Rule 146 on private placements. Lawyers call this the safe harbor rule. A company that can prove that it tried to meet the requirements in issuing the securities can mount a better defense against a complaining investor or regulatory agency.

Unregistered securities should be sold only to sophisticated investors or to those receiving sophisticated advice. Screen potential buyers carefully. Avoid widows, retired individuals (even wealthy ones), and all litigious types. An important limitation is that there may be no more than 35 investors.

The best way for the company to protect against future lawsuits is to require that investors sign a nondistribution letter, such as the following:

> In connection with the purchase of the securities listed herein, purchaser represents that he is making the acquisition without a view to the distribution of such securities.

Other defensive steps include:
• Issuing shares in large denominations, making them hard for the investor to resell. The best practice is one certificate to each investor, whether it is for 100 shares or 10,000 shares.

• Putting a restrictive notice on each security stating that the investor agrees not to transfer it without "approval of counsel for the issuer."

• Obtaining written documentation of each investor's financial status and financial objectives. This "suitability letter" should establish that the investor can afford the risk and is aware of the speculative nature of the investment.

• Listing in detail the information given to the investor to assist in the decision—and getting the investor to sign that he received and read it.

Make sure representatives of the company do not stray from the printed information when they talk to potential investors. The company may lose a court fight if several witnesses testify that they were told the same misleading information.

Source: Dan Brecher, attorney, New York.

Borrowing from within

Borrowing from employees and friends can be an effective way to beat the high cost of getting a corporate loan from a bank.

The chief benefit is that the company pays an interest rate several points below the corporate loan rate. As a bonus, employees become more personally involved wth the company's operations. To sell the idea to employees, it may be necessary to offer a higher yield than the employees could make by investing in the money market.

A food-packaging firm had relied on loans from workers and friends for supplemental funds ever since it was formed in 1948. But the company moved into employee borrowing on a large scale in 1974–75, when it needed cash to research and develop a new food-processing technique. Its bank at the time refused to expand its line of credit. Instead, the company lined up 30 lenders (one-third were employees) and raised $300,000.

Interest rates are adjusted with money-market movements. They also vary according to the size and length of the loan from an employee. The current interest schedule ranges from 12% to 15%. Lenders withdraw their money by giving notice 60 days before the maturity date of their loan. The goal is to replace the company's line of bank credit entirely with loans from employees and friends.

Another company, in the construction equipment business, borrowed from employees in 1979 when it needed $70,000 and its bank said it would charge 33% more in interest than it had previously.

Looking for an alternative, the firm sent letters to all 23 employees asking for loans that would be repaid on three days' notice. It raised $100,000 in a week from 17 employees and their relatives. The company pays a minimum 12% interest on the money. It saves between $15,000 and $20,000 in interest charges compared with what it would have to pay a bank.

Source: Robert E. Laughlin, chief executive, Western Food Equipment Co., Portland; Alfred H. Knief, president, Lincoln Contractors Supply, West Allis, Wis.

R&D partnerships

A growing source of money for companies is the research 'and development partnership. A company joins with a group of outside investors who put up the money to develop a new product. The investors get a tax shelter and share in the profits of a successful product. R&D partnerships can be used by large as well as small companies, and investors are eager to provide cash for a good deal.

Product development in high-technology fields often requires a great amount of costly research over a period of years. If traditional financing methods are used, the company must either pay for the research out of profits, thereby reducing earnings, or borrow the money at high interest rates until the project yields a return. There is a chance that the project will fail and the investment will be lost.

Small companies often can't afford to finance research from earnings, and they may not have the credit standing to borrow. They get their funds from venture capitalists, and the original entrepreneur risks losing control of the company when the backers are paid off.

In an R&D partnership, the company is the general partner and manages the project. The outside investors are limited partners, and if the project is successful, they receive a royalty on sales of the new product.

The risk of loss is placed on the outside investors. And since they are paid off out of product royalties, the owner of the company does not risk losing control of the business.

The attraction to investors is that they invest directly in a potentially profitable product that may prove more lucrative than the stock of a high-technology company. And immediate tax deductions are available to the partners for amounts spent on research.

An R&D partnership is best used when developing a specific product, such as a new sports car or an experimental small plane. It is less well suited for general research. There is no royalty-bearing product to attract investors. And any knowledge that is developed is the property of the partnership and must be purchased by the company, so that it will not fall into the hands of competitors.

Source: Martin Mayer, Peat, Marwick, Mitchell & Co., Minneapolis.

9 MERGERS, ACQUISITIONS, AND DIVESTITURES

ACQUISITIONS AND MERGERS

Guide to a successful acquisition

Before looking for an acquisition, a company should set realistic goals for what it expects from the venture. These goals will vary substantially in each situation. But a buyer should not expect a perfect match between the acquisition's value and present objectives.

The first step is to do careful homework on the acquisition target. Know where it stands in the market and whether it's an innovator. Find out as much as possible about its strengths and weaknesses before negotiations.

Use book value in relation to market purchase prices to determine whether the deal is attractive. A healthy return on equity and a good growth curve will usually insure profits from an acquisition for at least a couple of years.

Keep in mind that acquisitions tend to progress more favorably with the use of a profes-

sional intermediary or investment banker, one with a proven track record and good references. Make sure the actual professional, not just the firm, has the right experience and credentials.

Next, set up an acquisition team to work with the intermediary. The chief executive officer should be part of that team. The final decision should be the CEO's alone.

Don't pursue a company that wouldn't survive a merger. Entrepreneurial companies that rely on a highly personalized management style fall into this category.

Keep negotiations moving at a steady, but not necessarily fast, pace. Lagging negotiations may be taken for lack of interest. Conducting them too quickly, on the other hand, creates an impression of overeagerness and can lead to errors of judgment.

If either side has serious problems, see that they're discussed at the outset. When a company discovers a problem just before the close, it can't help but question the wisdom of the entire deal. Examples are a buyer who doesn't reveal immediately that action can't be taken on the deal for several months, or a seller who delays mentioning that a lease may not be renewed.

Use due diligence in checking on the target company, but don't go to extremes. The term due diligence refers to the acquirer's legal responsibility for performing a full audit, a review of minutes, leases, contracts, etc., and an inspection of plant and inventory. Due diligence can be overdone and mess up the deal. If the target of an acquisition really wants to hide something, it will probably succeed.

Understand the seller's motivation for wanting to be acquired.

Unless the buyer plans sweeping changes in policy and management, it should prepare both teams of executives for the aftershock of acquisition. Except in cases where the company was bought for its plant or inventory, its management should be one of its strongest assets.

Source: Gilbert W. Harrison, chairman, Financo, Philadelphia.

Sizing up a possible acquisition

While a potential buyer should leave full analysis of an acquisition candidate's financial statements to experts, the buyer can sharpen his instincts by looking at those statements for potential danger signals:

• Look at the average age of accounts receivable. If the average is lengthening, find out why. There may be more doubtful accounts than raw figures suggest.

• Check the method by which the company ages its receivables. If that method has changed recently to improve the numbers, beware.

• Are the receivables from related parties significant? Did the deals with related parties take place on terms equal to arm's length?

• Study the company's inventories. If inventories listed as work in process have risen relative to inventories listed as raw materials and finished goods, this suggests a possible slowdown in sales.

• See how labor and overhead have been allocated to inventories. This is one way inventories get padded.

• Closely held companies with unaudited financial statements often reduce their inventory through "reserves." Personally inspect them. Often, they're dumping grounds for unsalable finished goods.

• Scrutinize all contingent liabilities. If the company is a defendant in litigation, or has been threatened with litigation, find out how much an adverse settlement could cost.

• Are the intangible assets overvalued?

• A surplus that the Internal Revenue Service decides is unreasonably retained earnings can sour a bargain acquisition.

If the IRS decides that salaries paid to top management in recent years are disguised dividends, the new owner may face a sizable tax liability.

• Analyze the standard ratios determining the level of the company's profitability. Look for any recent change, then investigate the reasons for them.

• Find out what percentage of sales comes from major customers. Consider including a clause in the acquisition agreement voiding the sale if the sellers don't disclose the number of customers accounting for more than 10% of sales volume.

• Find out what percentage of transactions are with related parties. This includes leases, loans, purchases of property, guarantees of indebtedness, capital transfers, and sales. Beware if the terms of these transactions are hidden or not clear.

• Check maintenance and repair costs to see if they've risen in proportion to sales volume. If they haven't, management may have been running down the capital plant.

Additional points to study:

• Reasons for auditors' qualifications on financial statements

• Reasons for any significant transactions entered into the last year and their impact on earnings.

• Reasons for large legal bills.

• The number of years for which the IRS has yet to close the books on the company's tax returns.

Source: Samuel P. Gunther, partner, Richard A. Eisner & Co., New York.

Eight ways for buyers to evaluate a business

Emotion and other less than pragmatic considerations often play major roles in deciding how much a business is worth. For buyers who want to rely on more logical techniques, there are eight basic methods for evaluating a closely held business with no publicly traded stock and owners who are near retirement:

1. Capitalized earnings. The value is judged according to the previous year's earnings, income over the last few years, or projected earnings.

2. Corporate and shareholder earnings. Both of these are capitalized. This amount is paid out over a period that is usually two to four times the capitalization period. If earnings were capitalized for the previous two years, for example, payment could be over the next four to eight years.

3. Percentage of future profits. The definition of profit can include any items that management determines. Payments can be spread over a number of years and arranged in diminishing stages.

4. Book value. The sum of assets as they appear on the books (excluding goodwill) less liabilities.

5. Adjusted book value. Current values are applied to the balance sheet. For example, fixed assets are valued at either their replacement or their knockdown value rather than as they appear on the books.

6. Book value plus pensions. Consideration is given to retirement plans in effect at similar companies and an equitable compensation program for the retiring sellers.

7. Start-up cost. A buyer who wants to enter an industry will often pay more than a business is actually worth, since the price may still be less than the cost of entering the field from scratch.

8. Industry custom. Some types of businesses are valued on the basis of historic formulas. Dental practices may sell for the previous year's gross income. Insurance brokerages can sell for a price equal to the first year's retained renewals.

Source: Edward Mendlowitz, partner, Siegel & Mendlowitz, New York.

Before buying a small business

Questions to ask in assessing the potential of a business you are thinking about purchasing:

• Was the initial planning effective? To evaluate this, look at lease terms, fixtures and equipment, recordkeeping, advertising, marketing, and site selection.

• What were the start-up costs? Some sellers try to include these in the selling price. A basic rule is that all one-time costs should be absorbed by the owner. Exception: The sale price should reflect the current market value of fixtures and equipment.

• What mistakes did the founder make? Could they eventually kill the business?

• How solid is the current customer base? Avoid any business that depends on strong customer loyalty to the current owner.

• Will the current owner stay on for a few months to ease the transition? This helps transfer supplier and customer trust to the new owner and gives immediate assistance on unforeseen problems.

Source: Kenneth J. Albert, *Straight Talk About Small Business,* McGraw-Hill, New York.

Beware of hidden liabilities

An acquired corporation may have real or potential liabilities it doesn't disclose, even some it doesn't know about, such as product liability suits for products manufactured years before. One solution, but only in certain states, is to buy the assets, not the stock, rather than take over the corporation and its unknown liabilities.

People problems in corporate mergers

Many potentially successful mergers fail because of inadequate assessment by both parties of the human factors.

The most common error made by the buying company is overreliance on gut feelings about the seller's management and organization, and on the seller's past financial performance. People who work effectively in one environment may not do so in another.

High-risk merger candidates are companies in which the entrepreneur/owner is to function as a manager within the merged structure, or companies with a unique image. An example is a small high-technology company, proud of its creativity and independence.

Before making an acquisition, the buyer should know the quality of the seller's management and work force. Look for a diversity of skills and the ability to accept authority.

The seller should ask himself if he will be comfortable operating under the system of the buying company. Before the deal closes, he should clearly determine with the buyer details about reporting and about managerial and financial autonomy.

Sellers who often become unhappy are those in the so-called creative businesses. They frequently get frustrated adjusting to the discipline of the new system. The ideal seller is one who views the sale as an opportunity to turn illiquid wealth into cash, and to grow through the additional resources of the acquiring company.

Source: Arthur A. Rosenbloom, Standard Research Consultants, and Abraham K. Korman, BFS Psychological Associates, New York.

SELLING A BUSINESS

Selling a business aggressively

The most common mistake occurs when a supplier or other industry contact makes an offer for the company. The owners then negotiate with the one buyer to improve the single offer, instead of marketing the company with the same intensity the company markets its products.

The buyer may take a long time to make a decision. Meanwhile, the market changes so that the firm's value is no longer at its peak. The best strategy is to develop the sale of a business by having three or more buyers lined up to assure the highest price and the most expeditious deal.

Bad timing is another mistake that 90% of all selling owners make. They wait until they are getting on in years or the business prospects dim. In almost all cases, the buyer eventually ferrets out the real reason for the sale and succeeds in reducing the price.

The best time to sell a company is when the growth curve is still headed strongly upward. Trying to catch the last bit of fast growth is not really in the owner's best long-term interest.

No business is totally resilient and impregnable to substitutes or competition. Owners must be humble enough to acknowledge bad news on the horizon. It is imprudent to look forward more than 18 months and expect only a rosy future.

Reaching for the last dollar on the negotiating table can ruin a good deal. That's why the most effective strategy to get the best price is to solicit offers from several potential buyers. A realistic benchmark is to compare the expected return to the buyer of the business with what the buyer could get risk-free from Treasury bills.

Sellers should put themselves in the prospective buyers' shoes from time to time during the negotiations. The personal relationship after the merger can be very important. It's best to give buyers the impression that the current owners are amenable to cooperating to solve any problem after the merger is consummated.

Stay flexible on the terms of sale or compensation to the owner. It is unwise to decide firmly before negotiations to take only cash or only stock. So many changes are being made in the tax laws that owners should not refuse to consider an innovative deal that might, in fact, give them a better after-tax gain on the sale of their company.

Don't hold back essential information or try to make the financial statements look better than they really are. There is a big difference between cleaning up the balance sheet in preparation for a sale (for instance, by retiring debt) and understating the real cost of goods. A minor cover-up will break the atmosphere of trust.

Also, owners should not handle negotiations singlehandedly. The selling owner may hope to run the company as a division of a bigger company after a merger. But the negotiations may cause hard feelings at some point. The prospective buyers may then decide they would not feel comfortable having the former owner around. (If the owner has so much time to spend at negotiations, it also raises a suspicion that he is not a key to the company's successful operations.)

Instead, use experienced merger intermediaries. They can use indirection to try to develop a point of benefit to the seller. For example: "There's another company offering much more. If you raise your price just $2 million, I think the owner would go with your company because he prefers associating with your firm's reputation, even at less money."

Playing hard-to-get is dangerous. Many sellers think this puts them in a better light. But when they don't show interest in the buyer, they can't learn much about the buyer's business, policies, or procedures.

Source: Victor Niederhoffer, chairman, and John Hummer, chief executive officer, Niederhoffer, Cross & Zeckhauser, Inc. New York.

Putting the business up for sale

There are four kinds of potential buyers for money-losing businesses:

1. Large public companies with a specific need for products or assets.

2. Risk-playing entrepreneurs with expertise in the industry.

3. Foreign companies looking for a toehold in a particular market in the United States.

4. The business' own management, backed by venture capital.

To find a buyer, figure out which one of these groups will most logically profit from acquiring the business. Then quietly send out feelers to candidates within that group to see if they express interest in acquiring.

If word gets out that the business is for sale, capitalize on the publicity. Use it to flush out as many potential buyers as possible, then pit them against each other.

But publicly putting a business on the block hurts employee morale. If a business is labor intensive, it's generally best not to publicize the intended sale. Labor-intensive companies on the block get raided. The loss of their top talent depresses the business' value.

Make sure you know the strengths and weaknesses of the business. Address both of them openly when negotiating. Don't spread false turnaround tales. When an owner tells a prospective buyer that the business is about to turn around, the buyer will wonder why the owner wants to sell it. This casts doubt on the owner's credibility.

Price the business at least 30% higher than the final acceptable figure. Don't overbluff, however. And keep marginal prospects in the picture to foster competition with the serious potential buyers.

If the sale is not made, liquidate or remove the business from the market for the time it takes to revive it and increase its salability.

Selling the company upon retirement

Despite the temptation to sell out and forget the aggravations of stagflation (especially if a bidder comes along with an attractive offer), many owners of privately held companies will benefit most by staying private and devising a plan that allows them to sell out on good terms when they are actually ready to retire.

Unless an owner wants to make a life or a career change, or believes that the business is going bad, the attractions of selling out are usually less than meet the eye:

• Taxes may take up a large percentage of the profit from selling out.

• Selling out via an exchange of stock with a public corporation is risky in an uncertain market.

• Continued ownership of a privately held company guarantees unique financial flexibility.

An alternative for continuation is to offer selected managers a minority, noncontrolling equity interest in the company. This makes managers into ready buyers whenever the owner wants to sell out, since it gives the managers the borrowing power to come up with the necessary cash for a buyout. As a bonus, equity participation will inevitably improve the manager's performance, which is crucial in the increasingly tough business environment.

If the principal wants to pass on the company to his heirs, the equity participation plan should be structured so that when the time comes to sell out, the owner gets a sizable lump sum with which to retire but keeps enough stock for the family to retain control of the company.

But making managers minority partners changes their relationship with the owners. The change is not necessarily perceived by the principal as for the better. The managers may decide to restrict the owner's perquisites in some unforeseen fashion.

To avoid complications, structure the equity plan so that the owner has the right to buy back the equity of managers at any time. It's important to have a clear and fair formula for determining the price at which the stock will be bought back. This will assure managers they will be compensated for the effort they put into the company, even if they leave. It will also help to avoid bitterness and possible litigation if they go elsewhere.

Finally; structure the plan so that the principal can buy back the stock held by managers if they leave voluntarily, or if they die, to keep the stock from falling into outside hands.

Source: Philip Kimmel, partner, Hertz Herson & Co., New York.

PART III

Marketing and Sales Management

10 MARKETING MANAGEMENT

MARKETING WISDOM

Marketing in inflationary times

Not too long ago, companies that were almost right could usually count on a second chance in the market if they had good trade relationships to carry them through a major mistake. Not so when inflation has raised the stakes. And greater sophistication on the part of both foreign and domestic competitors has reduced the odds for success. To keep up with the shifts, management must avoid inflation pitfalls and make whatever changes are necessary in its comfortable ways of marketing.

Biggest inflationary trap. Looking at the company's sunk cost (the cash already invested) in a product as the controlling factor in marketing it. Beware of the manufacturing mentality in marketing: I sell what I make. We have to find a way to sell more of these widgets. Instead, have the courage to decide that the profitable market for widgets has disappeared. Instead of reflecting on sunk costs, look for ways to use capacity more profitably. Consider getting rid of widget-making machinery in order to: invest in new machinery that will improve productivity for other product lines or switch to products that can be sold at a higher margin because the company has a productivity edge on competitors or the product is more desirable to consumers.

A crucial calculation. Determine costs and profitability on a line-by-line, item-by-item basis. With both inflation and interest rates at near-record levels, it is essential to know which businesses are making money and which are draining resources. Too many companies don't know. Service companies, too, must analyze which clients are profitable.

Get rid of deadwood. That used to mean people. Now it means rooting out anything that is a losing proposition for the company. A major impediment is thinking that what currently is in place is permanent. Almost every company has some product it would be better off walking away from—typically a high executive's pet project that everyone else is wary of touching. Don't worry whether or not some assets can be sold. Simply put a padlock on the door.

Targeting. Marketing research is yielding fewer and fewer distinct answers to marketing questions just when inflation-impacted marketers need specifics most. The old pattern consisted of a single brand-product in the lead, followed by a couple of pretty good brands and a bunch of cats and dogs. Now, the top two or three brands in any category are virtually at parity in quality, image and, often, in marketing approach. Too often, conventional surveys rate one prodduct 4.57 (on a scale of one to ten) and another 4.65. Neither wins. And neither company can make an informed decision.

Find the precise set of characteristics that define a product's bliss point. Then decide how far the company can back down on features and costs before it loses too much consumer appeal. Computer models are being used by national companies to make these analyses. The idea is to search in an open-ended way for the optimum combination of product characteristics. Don't just focus on finding the best of a given bunch of products.

For example, it's wasteful to spend extra money to improve product quality if inflation-impacted consumers of that item are motivated more by nutritional features or price.

Test-market savings and a dramatic reduction in the time required to go from product concept to actual marketing are added benefits. During an inflationary period, this is almost as valuable as more precise positioning.

Source: John H. Lewis, president, Weston Group, Inc., Westport, Conn.

Marketing traps and opportunities in the current climate

As discretionary income is pinched and business levels off and, in many cases, dips, smart marketers are not retreating. Advice:

Don't follow the pack. Expect a falloff in sales, but don't react mechanically with a general cutback in staff, advertising, and promotion. Profits in companies that maintain ad and promotion budgets for strong products during recessions recover faster. Marketing investment in the right product or service reaps the benefit of leverage because weaker (or less smart) competitors cut back spending.

Sharpen marketing focus. Reallocate funds from soft areas to products and services that will produce a better return on investment. Look for products and target customers that are affected least by recession. (Don't make the common mistake of assuming that recession reduces all incomes and all demand.)

Another popular misconception: Price-oriented advertising has the best appeal during hard times. It's more effective to make it easier for potential customers to recognize value. That's what they're really searching for as spending becomes more selective.

Strategy:

• Use price promotions only as a temporary stimulus to sales. Be careful that price moves do not erode a quality image. Customers for a product that has been discounted for too long a time will resist a shift back to the original price. Then, when the recession is over, the company has a lower-profit price brand rather than a value brand.

• Use giveaways, premiums, rebates, and periodic discounts. But do not cut prices to the extent that consumers will believe the cut is permanent. The company will suffer when it then tries to bring prices back to original levels.

• Don't assume that price appeals work for all people or all products. Top-of-the-line brands such as Chivas Regal or Porsche are marketed effectively in both good times and bad as high-priced items.

Recession forces companies to do what they should be doing anyway. Good sales volume conceals many marketing mistakes. When sales are sluggish, ill-conceived moves become more obvious and more costly. "Me-too" products without a clear image or appeal end up losers.

Toughen up. Plan to get more, not less, from advertising dollars during a recession.

• Press the company's agency to monitor continuously the effectiveness of media spending. Jettison any media that don't measure up to the response levels that the agency and the company have set in advance.

• Negotiate for media "extras," such as merchandising help.

• Keep reviewing the ad budget in light of economic and competitive developments. Budgets should not be set and then blindly adhered to. Risks are higher in bad times. Day-to-day and week-to-week decisions can make or break a product. And there may be no second chance.

Source: Arie Kopelman, senior vice president and management supervisor; Paul Paulson, president, New York office; Robert Rees, group senior vice president and management supervisor; Ruth Ziff, senior vice president and director of research and marketing services, Doyle Dane Bernbach, New York.

Recession wisdom for marketers

Management must run an especially tight ship during a recession, but it's a big mistake to inflict false economies on the marketing effort. Instead:

• Hire top sales and merchandising people who may be available from other companies. Fine talent often enters the job market as other companies cut back. Use this opportunity.

• Strengthen sales promotion. Best bets: Price promotions and creative deals. Also look for relatively inexpensive ways to create new excitement (slight changes in product or package design).

• Get more leverage from the advertising budget. Don't drastically reduce it. Companies that keep an advertising presence emerge from recession faster and stronger. Use the fact that the company is maintaining its ad budget to get more and better service and merchandising help from the media.

• Don't be afraid to introduce a promising new product into a soft market. This could help the company establish a solid springboard from which to take off when the market rebounds.

Source: Malcolm Moses, Malcolm Moses & Associates, Merrick, N.Y.

How to win the consumer marketing war

Consumer marketing in the 1980s is more cutthroat than it was in the 1970s because of demographic changes (fewer babies, fewer moves to the suburbs) are flattening out many markets; and because more households are squeezed financially (rising mortgage rates, housing costs, tuitions, etc.).

The losers in the marketing war are middle-of-the-road companies with average quality, service and prices.

To be a marketing success in this environment, companies must pick a strategy to set them apart from the competiton, and pursue it vigorously (from Michael E. Porter, *Competitive Strategies,* The Free Press, New York).

To achieve cost leadership:

• Strive for the dominant market share to boost production and drive down unit costs.

• Budget money to innovate and improve the whole production-management process.

This cost-reduction strategy makes sense for resource-rich firms in price-responsive markets. For example, Texas Instruments in data processing, Goodyear in tires.

To achieve product differentiation:

• Bring to market top-quality products or services that are clearly superior to similar items.

This strategy makes sense for companies with a heavy investment in superior technology and quality control. For example, Sony in consumer electronics, Toyota and Datsun in autos.

To achieve market focus:

• Be quick to identify growing market segments.

• Pinpoint the segments too specialized for the company's competitors, especially the market leaders.

This should be done by smaller and medium-sized companies, for example, suburban newspaper chains that have flourished as city papers died.

When putting this strategy to work, avoid frontal warfare. Exploit a competitor's weak flanks instead. For example, Savin and other

Japanese small-copier manufacturers slipped into the office-products market underneath Xerox. Digital Equipment and Data General used the same strategy against International Business Machines and other mainframe computer makers.

Source: Dr. Philip Kotler, professor of marketing, J.L. Kellogg Graduate School of Management, Northwestern University, Evanston, Ill.

fits, not features. For example, private labels can compete with designer brands only if customers are convinced of the value of the private names.

• Use new marketing tools. Marketing has become more specialized. But so have media and research tools, like data processing, computerized lists, cable television networks as well as test-market innovations.

Source: Robert T. Sakowitz, president and chief executive officer of Sakowitz, Inc., Houston.

Meeting the challenge of consumer marketing

The big difference in big-money customers: In the 1970s, they were young and physical. In the 1980s they are middle-aged and cerebral.

A closer look:

• Demographers predict that in the next ten years there will be a 24% increase in the population of persons 65 years of age or older. The number between ages 45 and 54 will decline slightly at first, then increase 13% in the last half of the decade.

• The Europeanization of Americans is gaining pace in the 1980s. Like Europeans, the U.S. population will come to grips with the limitations on its lifestyle—coping with energy shortages, tight credit, and liquidity problems.

• Customers are becoming harder to reach because they see and hear so many messages that ads tend to blur in the memory. Adding to the problem, some customers don't listen to ads because they know inflation has already undermined their discretionary buying.

For successful marketing response, first, be alert to customer needs. Then specialize more than ever in marketing to customers who have those needs.

Strategies:

• Educate customers. Greater product differentiation makes it essential to show customers the difference between brands in terms of bene-

Price-setting essentials

Companies that can't quickly revise cost estimates and hike selling prices are likely to see their profit margins abruptly erode in today's climate of high interest rates and soaring production costs.

Simplify the price-setting system and review it often. Before setting a price, determine:

• The upper price limit for the product. To calculate the ceiling, use market research to get an accurate reading of what price level is possible. If the research is prohibitively expensive, guessing can be effective. But make estimates on the high side so prices can be lowered later.

• The floor price, which is the minimum that doesn't result in a loss at a specific level of production. Simplify the identification of fixed costs (supervisors' salaries, rent, etc.) that do not vary with production, and variable costs (raw materials, direct labor, etc.) that do. Relate the costs to volume.

• Identify nonprice-related aspects of the product. These help differentiate the product from its competitors so it needn't be sold on price alone. Emphasize other values, such as quality, performance, service, prestige of ownership, warranties, delivery time, and packaging.

Source: Seidman & Seidman, New York.

How to respond to a competitor's price cut

When price competition flares, the worst management move is emotional retaliation. Instead, stay ready for sporadic price cuts by rival companies and exploit the opportunity to strengthen the company's market position.

The first step is to assess the price cutter's position.

• Is the competitor aggressive or desperate? A well-managed rival may be cutting prices to increase market share. That could pose a serious threat and require immediate action. But a drifter in the industry may be liquidating inventory to raise the needed cash. This spoils the market temporarily, which the company may have to live through.

• Does a price-cutting competitor have the capacity and other resources to usurp a significant share of the market? Assess its present facilities and supply sources.

• Does the price-cutter enjoy a cost advantage? Review the degree of integration and comparative costs of labor and transportation. Zero in on a competitor's greatest area of efficiency as a spur to reducing your own company's costs.

Build on knowledge of the market to develop the best counterprice strategy.

• How price-sensitive are your company's customers? Most sellers overestimate the effectiveness of a competitor's price decrease. Astute buyers value long-term relationships above transitory savings. They may even fear that the price-cutter's quality will be poor, the service sloppy or the supply uncertain. Reinforce these apprehensions, if they are warranted. And a temporary deal, cash rebate, or other incentive helps keep customers loyal without remorse.

• Are other competitors starting to discount also? Don't lead the way.

• Can the company's distributors absorb the price differential?

• Does the price cut attract additional buyers or generate additional volume? Be alert to profitable extra business that could be booked at a lower price.

The company's options:

• Do nothing for now. This is probably the best tactic if the price cut is merely a test of the market or a forced liquidation.

• Threats of retaliation or a lawsuit may scare off the aggressor. Avoid letting a competitor maneuver the company into a strategic change solely for defensive purposes.

• Nonprice moves. This could be the most effective strategy if customers prize reliable quality or delivery, extended credit terms or warranties, above all. Most forms of nonprice superiority are more secure from competitive threat than lower prices.

• Put a fighting brand into the lower-priced market to slug it out with the price-cutting aggressor. This keeps intact the company's present price structure and image. (The new entry may even boost the regular brand's volume.)

• Bracket price. Maintain (or even raise) the price of the brand under attack. But offer another brand below the aggressor's price.

It is essential to monitor customers' and competitors' reactions to the company's counterstrategy closely. Have a contingency plan ready.

Source: Dr. Harold W. Fox, professor, Ball State University, Muncie, Ind.

Know yourself— know your markets

Identifying new markets and spotting emerging competitors are often easier if management continually redefines the company's line of business in current terms.

An overly broad definition is useless. Calling a pencil manufacturer a communications company will not help. But defining it as a low-cost writing-instrument maker might be successful.

Test the new definition against this checklist:

• Matches management's values.

• Appropriate for several segments of buyers.

• Distinctive.

- Consistent with the company's experience and image.
  - Fits into other operations.
  - Durable demand under changing conditions.

Source: Dr. Harold W. Fox, professor, Ball State University, Muncie, Ind.

Marketing audits

Marketing strategies in today's fast-changing business climate have a short shelf-life. Just a decade ago, U.S. auto companies were moving ahead with large cars and ever-greater horsepower. The computer industry was geared to producing powerful systems, not the minicomputers prevalent today. What's needed for survival is an early-warning system that alerts the company when its products or marketing approach are heading for trouble. One way is with a marketing audit that:
- Covers the firm's marketing environment, objectives, strategies, organization and systems.
- Is done by someone independent of the marketing operation, either inside or outside the company.
- Uses an orderly investigation sequence rather than random questions that vary from audit to audit.

Before launching the audit, top management should:
- Define the objectives. A primary one is measuring company marketing performance against opportunities, goals, and resources.
- List areas in which recommendations are essential—pricing policy, for example, or how well the sales force executes company marketing strategy.
- Pave the way for auditors to interview customers (most important) and company marketing managers.
- Set a report deadline (six to eight weeks).

Expect the audit to be specific on:
- How well management of the marketing operation is performing. Find out if marketing managers have current information on customer perceptions, preferences and buying habits.
- Best areas for investing future marketing resources.
- Where to cut marketing costs.
- Trouble spots.

Operations that benefit most from marketing audits:
- Production- or technology-oriented companies that grew from a single product or process.
- Troubled divisions that have already been analyzed by general management consultants but have failed to make a turnaround.
- High-performing divisions where growth has outstripped formal management controls.

Source: Dr. Philip Kotler, professor of marketing, J.L. Kellogg Graduate School of Management, Northwestern University, Evanston, Ill.

Getting more out of marketing consultants

Companies should consider retaining marketing consultants to conduct annual audits of overall marketing operations, not just to tackle special problems or projects.

Specifically, hire a consultant for two or three days to (1) review overall marketing operations and (2) write a letter citing the company's marketing strengths and weaknesses.

Ask for an estimate on all the work the consultant believes he could do to improve particular marketing functions.

Alternatively, the next time the company calls in its marketing consultant for a specific purpose, ask him to audit the overall marketing operations as a secondary assignment.

Source: Jack M. Doyle, Jack M. Doyle Advertising, Inc., Louisville, Ky.

Assessing marketing strength

Not-so-obvious questions to ask:

• What percentage of sales volume is represented by products developed in the last five years? If the proportion is high, are the new products sound and prospects for long lives? Or are they faddish? If too few products are new, is the company falling behind the competition?

• What do large customers think of the company and its management? How strong are these large customers? What are their future needs?

• Did the company's growth in recent years come from increased unit sales or from price increase?

• Is capacity available for adding products or services to the line?

for marginal areas. When direct selling is not justifiable, use distributors.

6. Focus more resources on national-account selling.

7. Do not reject out of hand potential selling methods or channels that have not been traditional in your market, such as offering salespeople double or even triple commissions for sales above quotas.

8. Avoid advertising in saturated markets. Concentrate dollars on local media and point-of-sale ads, perhaps shift from 60-second TV spots to 30-second.

9. Tighten control over advertising production costs.

10. Improve product manuals and set up 800 telephone lines so customers can resolve minor service problems themselves or with minimal help.

Source: Earl L. Bailey, director of marketing management research, The Conference Board, New York.

Ten ways to increase marketing productivity

In its focus on production efficiency, top management often overlooks potential improvements in the way the company reaches, penetrates and services its markets.

Aim for a lower cost of marketing as a percentage of revenues and a rate of sales growth that outpaces increases in sales and marketing manpower.

Steps to better marketing:

1. Target market segments and geographical regions more selectively.

2. Increase market leverage and flexibility by strengthening the market information base.

3. Reorganize sales territories to reduce travel time and yet maintain customer contact.

4. Encourage salespeople to specialize so as to serve key market segments or classes of trade better.

5. Minimize sales and promotional support

Four ways to stop a decline in sales

While top management develops an overall strategy for coping with weak markets, middle managers can take these immediate steps:

• Give new twists to old products. Don't wait for R&D to change the company's product line. Find out from field reps what modest product or packaging change would boost usefulness to current customers.

• Recast sales pitches. Have the sales force keep a record of customers' objections to buying. Develop ways to counter the objections that could lead to larger orders. Distribute to sales force.

• Upgrade product knowledge. In good times, products sell themselves. In bad times, salespeople with a grasp on all possible product information and applications do best.

• Explore new markets. Encourage salespeople to do this on their own. Show them what they stand to gain financially from new business —a sales rep who makes ten new calls to land one new customer may spend 30 hours developing that business. Show him what that effort is worth on an earnings per hour basis.

Source: Joseph Eisenberg, president, Profit Improvement, Inc., New York.

Basic marketing errors

• Having undisciplined product policy. To solve the problem, trim away product lines that generate the lowest return on assets.
• Failing to segment markets thoroughly. Instead, position products by geography, product use, and customer purchasing habits.
• Confusing marketing with sales. Do not focus on selling only. This backfires when consumer needs, distribution patterns, or overall economic conditions change.
• Fighting for market share by price-cutting alone. More effective tactics are: improving service, identifying a way to expand the overall market for a product and then capturing that segment.

Aggressive industrial marketing

The persistent threat of recession is locking many manufacturers into defensive postures.
These defensive companies present an opportunity to competitors who remain on the offensive with marketing. Aggressors can win market shares. To follow through, industrial marketers should:
• Resist the temptation to cut promotion budgets. Promotion costs are usually a minimal cost for industrial concerns.

• Establish incentives to encourage the sales force to find new clients.
• Bring marketing executives with consumer products experience into industrial marketing situations. Many consumer-marketing techniques can be adapted to industrial sales.

For example, the Loctite Corp., a chemical manufacturer, went to customers before updating a standard industrial adhesive. Just as a consumer-product company would do, Loctite asked customers how they would like the product improved. Furthermore, they adapted positioning principles from consumer-marketing practices. The result—a new product with a new name, which had sales of $2.2 million in six months. The estimated sales in the same period for the old industrial adhesive would have been $320,000.

Source: John Morris, vice president and director of market planning, Marsteller Research, New York.

Psychological tactics in industrial marketing

Makers of consumer goods have long relied on psychology to boost sales. Manufacturers of industrial products have been slow to learn the game. Recommendations:
• If the seller is small, it can build solid relations with clients by empathizing with the purchasing agent's sense of undeserved low rank.
• Large companies can build similar relations by demonstrating that their vast resources are at the purchasing agent's disposal.
• Dramatize the company's ability to overcome technical problems.
• Show that buyers purchasing the product are really astute.
• Use color and design to enhance the showroom for buyers.
• Even though specifications are in technical terms, present them in human analogies.
• Tailor the sales approach to each buyer.

Source: Dr. Harold W. Fox, Ball State University, Muncie, Ind.

Competing in a soft market

The best approach is to sell the value of a product, not the price. Stress the overall quality of the product being sold; the reliability of the company manufacturing and distributing the product; and the underlying support services.

Case in point: The recession has been weakening the agriculture-implements market. As a result, some suppliers to agricultural-implement manufacturers are beginning to cut prices.

The best strategy in the face of price-cutting competition is to maintain prices and profit margins. Selling points include: (1) the reliability of deliveries, which allows customers to keep inventories low; (2) continuity of service, which means loyalty to the customer; and (3) most important, technical backup services.

Industrial salespeople who keep their customers abreast of technological developments that can cut costs are more highly valued by customers than those who offer discounts in a recession.

Source: Jack Neff, vice president of marketing, Dana Corp.'s Industrial Group, Warren, Mich.

Selling service as you would a product

Over 45% of the typical household budget goes for services (rent, repairs, etc.) rather than goods. Fundamentally, services are a tougher sell than are products, because services are less standardized. They are produced and consumed simultaneously. And services are intangible: they aren't bought as possessions.

One solution is to find a way to market services that lends them a tangible image that buyers can identify and recall.

For instance, credit-card companies direct attention not to the loan they're trying to make but to that tangible piece of plastic. Their marketing focus is on a thing to have and to hold.

Other successful service marketers use a variety of image-provoking techniques:
- Own a piece of the rock...
- Reach out and touch someone...
- You're in good hands...
- The well-scrubbed, fun-filled, colorful ambience of Disneyland and Disney World.

This way, the positive image remains, almost as a tangible possession, reminding the consumer of a service he would buy again.

Source: L. Berry, professor of commerce, University of Virginia; *Business,* College of Business Administration, Georgia State University, Altanta.

The importance of graphic design

Good design work complements marketing by giving a company's products a graphic identity. Design isn't intended to make things prettier. It must solve business problems effectively, contributing to long- and short-range profits. Simply coordinating letterheads, catalogs, and other promotional material can save money through printing economies.

What a client should do:

1. Describe its needs fully to a design firm and ask for a detailed analysis of how the firm defines the problem. When correctly defined, the solution to a design problem usually becomes evident.

2. Ask what services the firm suggests providing within a given time.

3. Negotiate a fee. Most companies want a fixed fee. But even with a set fee it's wise to ask what the hourly rates of different employees of the firm are. Then the company gets an idea what the cost will be for add-ons or negotiated overruns.

Design firms compute fees on a problem-by-problem basis. If the client doesn't like the first solutions, it can pay extra for another. A fixed fee is given for a project, and each possible "extra" is also priced.

To find a design firm, locate the creators of especially good pieces of design work. These pieces may not necessarily be found in your industry. Ask business associates whom they would recommend.

Source: Aubrey Balkind, president, Gips + Balkind Associates, Inc., New York.

Personal taste can be a limiting factor when selecting a new logo. Designs can sometimes be too cute or too complicated. How customers and prospects respond to a new design is the best criterion.

Source: *Private Label,* E.W. Williams Publishing Co., New York.

Importance of the company logo

• Does the logo still look too strong when reduced to the smallest size required for packages and advertising?
• Will it look good big, too?
• How does it look in color? In black and white?
• Will it work in signs?
• Does it stand out from its competitors on packaging?
• Is it easy to read? This is a basic point that's often forgotten.
• Is it visible at long distances?
• Is it promotional?

Picking the right company name

• Keep the name simple and easy to spell and pronounce.
• Try to find a name that evokes an image with market value.
• Make sure the name doesn't violate any existing trade names, trademarks, or copyrights.
• Test the name. A simple and effective way is to make up a sample sign on cardboard and survey customers.
• Make sure a name change is well publicized so that the goodwill associated with the old name isn't lost.

PRODUCT DEVELOPMENT

Finding new technical business ideas

A company's own employees are usually the best source of ideas for new products or processes. But management should also consider other sources. At the very least, outside sources are likely to have fresh points of view.

Long-range ideas that may take 5–10 years to develop can be found by hiring consultants to scout for them and by taping industrial-liason of-fices at major universities. Assign someone to keep in touch with such institutions as the Massachusetts Institute of Technology and the University of California. Alert them to the company's interest in new technology.

Emerging concepts close to commercial development are often licensed by research institutes. For information, consult the Research Centers Directory* which lists all university and nonprofit research centers in the U.S. Venture-capital firms

*Gale Research Co., 700 Book Tower, Detroit, Mich. 48226.

are another good source for companies that want equity positions in new technologies. They are listed in the Guide to Venture Capital Sources.**

Foreign companies are a good source of new ideas ready to go into production. Many are eager to license their ideas under a wide range of financing plans. Visit overseas trade shows or banks and financial institutions to identify the companies with available technology. U.S. embassies abroad and trade associations in high-technology countries can also be excellent contacts.

_____

**Capital Publishing Corp., Box 348 Wellesley Hills, Mass. 02181.

Source: Margaret Pautler, development manager, business research and development, Monsanto Co., St. Louis.

_____

How to evaluate an innovation

Cambridge Research & Development Group, a unique venture-capital operation specializing in the creation of companies to market promising new inventions, has reviewed thousands of new-product ideas, selecting only five in their 15-year history. Their criteria:

1. Does someone really need the product?
Not might like or might buy. Really need.

2. Does a market know that it needs a product?
Even though it may be good for a company, if it has to spend money to convince people they need the product, look for a better idea.

3. Does the market perceive an immediate need for the product?
Not six months or a year from now, but an immediate need.

4. Does the consumer who perceives the need also control the purchase decision? Can he or she come up with the money?
As much as a teacher might perceive the value of your product, for example, the company won't be able to make a sale until the school superintendent or the Board of Education is convinced.

5. Can it be manufactured for 5% or 10% of the selling price?
If a product is really innovative, the company should be able to make a lot of money marketing it. Forget the whole matter if it doesn't promise to earn at least 15¢ after-tax profit on each $1 of sales. Remember, no matter how careful the plan, there will be mistakes made in manufacturing, in hiring, etc. And another 20¢ of every sales dollar will certainly go for general and administrative expenses, which must be spent before the sales dollars actually start to come in. Add another 20¢ (minimum) for sales and marketing expenses. (That's another expense before income starts coming in. The remaining 30¢ or so must cover manufacturing, maintaining the factory, and producing overhead again before any sales are made.

6. Can patents be protected?
Concentrate on a field where patents are respected, such as electronics and chemicals. Avoid the automotive, cosmetic, and textile industries, where patents are either meaningless or nonprotectable.

7. Is there a pool of buyers for the product at the price that produces profit today?
The ability to sell a product eventually for $500 won't help get the company off the ground with a $1,000 product unless there are enough buyers right now at $1,000 to finance future growth.

8. Will product success strain the company's financial, manufacturing, or marketing resources?
Many companies evolve elaborate contingency plans in case of failure but are unprepared for success.

9. Is the environment noncompetitive?
If yes, the product's chances for success are improved, especially if the company gets an edge on the market before similar products arrive.

_____

Source: Lawrence and Kenneth Sherman, Cambridge Research & Development, Westport, Conn.

Assessing new-product risks

Things to make sure about before more money is committed. Will the product:
• Truly fulfill a recognizable need?
• Deliver a demonstrable advantage over competitive products?
• Lend itself to future upgrading and improvement?
• Be cost and value competitive?
Other points:
• Is money available for the product's promotion?
• Is the promotion designed to achieve a valid market trial in the shortest possible time?
• Has research been set up to feed back sales data and compare results with those of the competition?
• Has the company mapped a test-market plan capable of projecting national acceptance?

Source: John S. Bowen, president, Benton & Bowles, New York.

Clues to new-product success or failure

New-product success is likely if:
• The product is unique or superior to what's available now.
• The company knows the market and how to sell to it.
• The marketing and management people understand the product and feel comfortable with it.
• The market is large and growing, and demand is high for the qualities the product offers.
• The product requires substantial investment. That way everyone won't be jumping in to undercut it.
Failure is likely if:
• The price is high, but the product offers no economic advantage.

• The product is new and unfamiliar to the company.
• The market is competitive and customers are satisfied.
• Several similar products are being introduced in the same market.

New-product batting averages

Success rate*	Industrial Products	Consumer Products
	% of companies	
All succeeded	9	18
90–99%	7	4
80–89%	16	9
70–79%	11	11
60–69%	16	12
50–59%	15	15
40–49%	4	2
30–39%	9	9
1–29%	5	4
None succeeded	8	16

Hope springs eternal—nearly two out of three respondents expect a better success ratio over the next five years. Among the reasons claimed: (1) sharper pinpointing of responsibilities, (2) better coordination, and (3) improved sales forecasting.

*The product has met management's original expectations in all important respects.

Source: *New Product Winners and Losers* (a survey of 148 medium- and large-sized firms), The Conference Board, New York.

Choosing product names

The ideal name:
• Communicates the product's main benefit (*Slender* diet drink, *Close-Up* toothpaste).

• Suggests the product's category to help position it in the public mind (*Head & Shoulders* shampoo, *Intensive Care* skin lotion).

• Is almost generic (*People* magazine) but doesn't go over the line and become so general the company loses it to competitors. The classic example of going too far is Lite, which Miller tried and failed to use exclusively as a trademark for its low-calorie beer.

Looking for a common pattern of success in products from the past won't help. Product naming was much more casual then, since there were fewer products on the market and the volume of communication was lower.

Avoid names that are:

• Overly broad. *Time* is a less effective name for a news magazine than *Newsweek*. Similarly, *Fortune* is too general for a business magazine. *Business Week* is better.

• Coupled with a meaningless number (*Breck One* and *Colgate 100*).

• Based on a regional term or a place name.

• Without a specific meaning (General, Standard, Continental). Many such names are widely used, leading to consumer confusion.

Unless the product is the first and only one of its kind on the market, resist the temptation to give it a totally made-up name.

Source: A. Ries and J. Trout, *Positioning: The Battle for Your Mind,* McGraw-Hill, New York.

Assessing new-product consumption rates

Common trap in new-product marketing is letting a good idea slip away because the company mistakenly believes the users will be too slow to consume the product or repurchase it.

One typical failure: An East Coast manufacturer had an idea for a new kind of cleaner. But market researchers dissuaded the company from moving ahead by pointing to the small sales volume and slow use-up of other cleaner products. While the company delayed, a competitor introduced a similar product and created a successful new business.

Success story: Ordinary stuffing is put into a turkey or chicken for special occasions. Marketing managers for Stove Top Stuffing Mix could have been convinced this was a slow use-up product. Instead, they marketed the mix as a potato substitute that can be used once a week or more.

Avoid letting good ideas slip away by separating trial and use tests.

• First determine how many people would try the new product. (The company with the cleaner product should have tested the idea itself first.)

• If the first test proves encouraging, test samples of the new product among people who like the idea.

• Identify the subgroup that would use the product frequently.

Basic rules:

• Don't fall into the trap of evaluating the product on the basis of comments made by people who do not agree with the product idea.

• Don't try to assess how often people are likely to use a new product or repurchase it without letting them try it. (The promotion of the product encourages more frequent use.)

• New products that a good number of consumers show a willingness to try don't come along too often. Don't let a good idea slip away. If response to the idea is good, then figure out how often they will use it. The right kind of research in this area could uncover ways to encourage more frequent use.

Source: Gerald Schoenfeld, Gerald Schoenfeld, Inc., New York.

Revive winning brands before they wear out

Watch out for established, winning products losing their luster in these competitive days. This is happening to even highly successful companies such as Ralston Purina, which recently was forced to reposition its market-leading dog food, Purina Dog Chow.

Some ways to bring back a fading champion:

• Defend continuously against upstart brands. Aim the sales pitch, pricing, and distribution strategy to knock down newcomers before they can get started.

• Don't bring on your own competitive brands too quickly. Let the champion keep its lead. Don't starve its ad budget.

• Don't slice up the top brand's strengths with new products or call attention to an obvious weakness.

• Repackage the old thoroughbred. But do a good marketing survey first. The audience for the product may be different.

• Unroll a new ad campaign with the strength and savvy that befits a champ.

• Don't drop prices too fast on the champ's line.

• Do offer premiums or other promotions. Bargain on prices behind the scene so retailers will push the champion.

• Put the champ on show, in demonstrations, public relations, etc., to demonstrate that new competitors have not taken over.

New life for tired products

Questions to ask management, engineers, production personnel, and customers:

• Can the product be put to other uses? Is there a new way to use it as is? Other uses if modified?

• Can it be adapted? What else is like this? What other ideas does this suggest? What could we copy?

• Can it be modified? Given a new twist? Changed in color, meaning, motion, sound, odor, form, shape? Any other changes possible?

• Can it be magnified? What to add? More time? Greater frequency? Stronger? Higher? Longer? Thicker? Multiply? Exaggerate?

• Can it be "minified"? What to subtract?

Smaller? Condense? Lower? Shorter? Lighter? Omit something? Streamline? Split up?

• What can we substitute? What else instead? Other ingredients? Other process? Other power?

• Rearrange? Interchange components? Other patterns? Othe layout? Transpose cause and effect? Change the pace? Change the schedule?

• Reverse it? Transpose positive and negative? Turn it backward? Upside down? Reverse roles?

• Combine it? How about a blend? An alloy? An assortment? An ensemble? Combine units? Purposes?

Source: Alex Osborn, *Applied Imagination,* Charles Scribner's Sons, New York.

Choosing the right distributor

The length of time a product has been on the market could be a critical factor in choosing the right distributor. For example, middlemen who do the best job during the early market-development stages could be all wrong when it comes to handling more mature product lines, and vice versa. This is particularly important in industrial distribution.

Give top priority to the technical specialist at the beginning stages. That's when the marketplace is adapting the product line to new applications. The technical specialist's emphasis on (a) large end-users, where most new products gain initial acceptance, and (b) engineering levels where the purchase decision is ultimately made.

Consider adding general-line distributors, as market growth flattens out and differences among competing products diminish. If nothing else, by reaching many more small end-users, these all-purpose middlemen help increase market saturation.

Inventory specialists may be best for the company during the later stages of product maturation. These distributors, with their emphasis on large-contract "buys," are most efficient when competitive pressures reach their peak and cost becomes the user's prime buying yardstick.

Source: Frank Lynn, president, Frank Lynn & Associates, Chicago.

Reappraising the package

• What emotional appeal does the package project through color, type, size, shape, and graphics?
• Does it highlight the product's best strengths against competitive products?
• Does it attract attention?
• Is the endorsement linkage between the brand name and corporate name strong enough?
• Are new packaging materials available that may improve appearance, reduce costs, or both?

When to drop a product

Take a critical look at products that produce the smallest sales. Consider whether some of them should be discontinued. Advantages:
• Profits will represent a higher percentage of sales and a higher return on capital.
• There will be lower inventories, thus less cash tied up in inventory and less borrowed.
• Management's time and attention can be focused on more profitable items.
• Management is forced to consider why a product is failing.
• Listen to arguments for giving a slow-moving item one more try, perhaps trying to boost its image by repackaging or reformulating it, or giving the item a new ad campaign. Look for ways to turn losers into winners.

MARKETING RESEARCH

When is research necessary?

A common pitfall is launching a market research project when one isn't necessary.

Stick to the proper use of market research, which is to get information when there isn't enough available.

Situations that justify research:
• To help choose between different strategies.
• To supply more data when management is internally divided on a policy, plan, or goal.
• To find out precisely why the market share is falling or distribution networks are weakening.

• To define the reasons why a particular product or service is doing very well, and to apply the responsible factors to other areas.
• A new product is being considered.
• A new market is being evaluated.

Source: *Sales Manager's Bulletin,* Waterford, Conn.

Market-research strategies

Should mail questionnaires or interviews (individual, group, or telephone) be used?

Use mail when:

• The target group is small, well defined, and has a common identity.

• The research questions can be expressed clearly and simply and are important to everyone in the target group.

• A mailing list is readily available.

Personal interviews are best when:

• The researcher wants detailed, specific information and doesn't know who has it.

• The company isn't sure what it's seeking. A personal interview permits follow-up questions.

Group discussions are best when:

• Vague psychological areas are researched. What's a product's image?

• Fresh ideas are being sought. In a group, people encourage, react to, and build on each other's ideas.

• The focus is on exploring complex or hidden motivations.

Telephoning is best for:

• Measuring of ad impact.

• Quick, informal studies of short, specific answers.

• One-shot checks of product recognition and brand preference.

• Specialized studies involving a small number of trustworthy respondents.

Source: G.E. Breen, *Do-It-Yourself Marketing Research,* McGraw-Hill, New York.

What research costs

Research services can tap outside computerized data banks, their own libraries and computer files, and government sources, and they can conduct individualized marketing studies. The big question is how much to pay. Follow these guidelines:

• A rock-bottom package for $50–$100 will buy broad statistics on the market size and the names of the leading companies. It's best used for quick, general information about a specific topic.

• For $500–$1,000 you will get more specific statistics, a general listing of published articles, studies, and copies of the most important documents. Best used for background information, speech writing, reports, early stages of planning.

• A $5,000–$10,000 package will provide limited telephone contact with trade sources, a 20–100 page profile of the subject, complete search for all published material. Size of market, companies, distribution, pertinent regulations and other significant factors. Best used for initial stages of a new-product study, new venture or projected acquisition.

• For $15,000 and up you will get full-scale market and industry studies, including projections on potential and limitations. It's best used for advanced stages of product-introduction planning and acquisition exploration.

Information searches are based on time. Be specific, in order to avoid charges for needless material.

Source: Andrew P. Garvin, *How to Win With Information or Lose Without It,* Bermont Books, Washington, D.C.

Questioning the questionnaire

The average market-research questionnaire is never justified beyond the usual explanation: "It's always been done this way."

Watch out for the almost universal temptation among researchers to add extraneous questions. These merely complicate tabulation and delay giving managers the few basic answers they need before going into test markets.

A typical example: A new product description, followed by a choice of five boxes:

☐ Definitely would buy.
☐ Probably would buy.
☐ Might or might not buy.
☐ Probably would not buy.
☐ Definitely would not buy.

But with this approach, the results are too vague. One division or company (not noted for new-product development) might be discouraged by only 24% "definitely would buy" responses and might drop its plans. Another more aggressive company might add together the 24% "definites" and the 31% "probables" and forge ahead, overconfidently thinking it had a 55% mandate from consumers. Still another manager might conclude that the 24% "definites" were solid, but that perhaps only half of the "probables" should be counted.

What the manager really needs to know is whether consumers would *definitely* (not probably) buy or try the product (not repurchase or switch brands). Or would they not? Other categories just confuse the respondent and becloud the results.

Other common mistakes are questions that lead consumers to assume they are being asked to switch brands. The actual purpose of the questions is to find out whether or not they would *try* the new product. Avoid questions such as: How would you rate this product for economy? How do you think this product would compare with your present brand? They are patently absurd, since the true answer is: "I don't know. I haven't tried it yet." If the respondent guesses, how valid is that judgment?

The worst abuse is questionnaires burdened with downright mischievous open-end comments, which must be transcribed verbatim and so take months to collate and analyze. By that time, no one cares to read the results.

The ideal new-product questionnaire is no more than one page long; exposes respondents to the product concept quickly, before they become bored answering questions; and then it asks in simple terms: "Would you buy this product or not?"

Beyond the answer to that question, the only other helpful information is the factors that were important to the consumer in making the decision.

Source: Gerald Schoenfeld, Gerald Schoenfeld, Inc., New York.

Don't ask salespeople to do market research

Salespeople often have personality traits that can subvert a good research interview. Specifically, they are outgoing, tend to dominate the conversation, and often aren't as analytical as is necessary.

Salespeople are trained to concentrate on what is right about a product, not to uncover what might be wrong.

Excellent salespeople always put selling duties first. Research chores may be performed haphazardly or grudgingly, if at all. Such an approach can bias results.

Source: G.E. Breen, *Do-It-Yourself Marketing,* McGraw-Hill Book Co., New York.

Business data from states

Free information on business conditions in 20 states is available through toll-free telephone services. The services, designed primarily to give information to tourists, also provide material on taxes, licensing laws, plant sites, etc. Most also suggest state agencies and bureaus to contact for more details.

The telephone services:

State	Number	State	Number
Alabama	(800) 633-5761	Montana	(800) 548-3390
Arkansas	(800) 643-8383	Nebraska	(800) 228-4307
Connecticut	(800) 243-1685	New Mexico	(800) 545-2040
Delaware	(800) 441-8846	North Dakota	(800) 437-2077
Georgia	(800) 241-8444	Oregon	(800) 547-4901
Idaho	(800) 635-7820	Pennsylvania	(800) 323-1717
Kentucky	(800) 626-8000	South Dakota	(800) 843-1930
Maryland	(800) 638-5252	Utah	(800) 453-5794
Minnesota	(800) 328-1461	West Virginia	(800) 624-9110
Mississippi	(800) 647-2290	Wyoming	(800) 443-2784

Source: *The Information Report,* bimonthly, Washington, D.C.

MARKET SEGMENTS

Targeting tomorrow's consumers

Changes to tune in to:
• Consumers are getting older. Less than 40% of the population will be under 25 by 1985.
• Only about 20% of the country's households now have annual incomes over $25,000. By the mid-1980s, the proportion is expected to be 27% (not allowing for inflation).
• Americans will have more leisure time than ever before as the average workweek slips to 35 hours or less.
• The population itself will grow by about 20 million.

Source: Arthur W. Schultz, chairman, Foote, Cone & Belding; *Marketing Times,* New York.

• Construction of multiunit rental housing will decline sharply. Demand for single-family houses will remain strong, although construction of these, too, will slack off.
• Purchases of household goods will begin to fall in the late 1980s, following the housing trend.
• Rising prices of cars and fuel, if coupled with possible improvements in public transportation, could put the U.S. auto industry in a permanent decline.
• Service industries will continue growing.
• The new generation is increasingly likely to rebel against mass-produced products, leading to a resurgence of small, specialized businesses.

Source: William A. Cox, deputy chief economist, U.S. Department of Commerce, *American Demographics,* Ithaca, N.Y.

Preparing for the baby-bust markets of the 1990s

Business executives must prepare now for major demographic changes that will reshape the markets of the 1990s. There will be significantly fewer adults than there are now, and their buying habits will differ from those of their parents.

In the new market:

Family changes mean marketing changes

The average U.S. household now numbers just 2.7 persons, down from 3.1 ten years ago. Over half consist of only one or two individuals. They account for 25% of total consumer expenditures today.

Each newly separated couple splits one household in two, in effect doubling the market for a wide range of low- to medium-priced consumer products and services.

Family units headed by single men have incomes almost double the average. There are about 1.6 million of them and 40% have one or more children.

The over-65 market: myths and realities

Myths: Older people have limited needs, little money and little inclination to spend it. Many are institutionalized or confined to home by ill health. Most are victims of severe inflationary pressures.

Realities:

• Per capita spending by those over 65 exceeds the national average in many categories. Prime examples are vacation travel, women's hair care, gifts. Spending for food is higher than in any other group.

• Per capita income for households headed by someone over 65 is only slightly below the national average.

• In the over-65 group, fewer than one out of twenty are institutionalized. Only 5% are confined at home. About 70% of families in this group own their own homes, and 80% are fully paid for.

• Incomes are keeping closer pace with inflation than in most other groups. One reason is that Social Security payments, a prime source of income, are indexed to inflation and are not taxed. The percentage of those over 65 who are poor is smaller than for most other age segments.

For almost 70% of senior citizens, the quality of life is as good as when they were working.

Source: *American Demographics,* Ithaca, N.Y.

The importance of older consumers

After an era of concentrating on the 18-to-34-year-old age group, business has discovered the 45-to-64-year-olds.

Reasons for their importance: People today live longer than their predecessors. They are healthier. They don't feel obligated to leave their sizable estates to others. A number of older women are getting jobs after their children leave home. And people who are 45 to 64 years old have substantial spending appetites, and the disposable income to satisfy them. This group makes up one-third of all the household heads in the U.S.

Use 45-to-64-year-olds in planning the company's marketing, sales, and advertising. Identifying the product with an older celebrity is a helpful tactic.

Leisure marketing in the future

What to expect:

• Expanding markets for athletic products as sports activity by both sexes continues to increase. Another hot spot is sports-related personal care markets—foot care for joggers; skincare preparations for skiers; hair products for swimmers. Athletic fashions will become even more popular.

• Growing opportunities for products and services that make home living more enjoyable. As the baby boom generation matures, it will spend more leisure time at home. The increase in working women means that convenience products will do well and more people will be eating out.

• Do-it-yourself products will proliferate as consumers try to combat inflation and participate in the trends towards conservation and spending more leisure hours at home.

• More interest in the arts, education, hobbies, entertainment, travel, gourmet foods, and fine wines, resulting from attitudes that emphasize enjoyment and self-improvement.

• More products and services designed to tap growing markets for developing new minority segments, for example, Hispanics, handicapped, overweight people.

What to be wary of:
- Consumerism will grow stronger—and with it litigation will soar.
- A backlash against the blurring of sex roles. Macho and traditional feminine images will be more effective in advertisements.

There will be changes in marketing techniques: traditional methods of marketing—telephone solicitations, door-to-door sales, and direct mail—will be less effective because the new adult generation has strong feelings about privacy. More marketers will utilize cable TV, electronic catalogs, and at-home-shopping systems.

Source: *The Coming New Environment for Marketing Leisure Goods and Services in the U.S.,* Weiner, Edrich, Brown, Inc., New York.

- Sell components and parts to the do-it-yourself market.
- Extend credit terms to help stimulate sales of high-priced items.
- Add factory-outlet distribution.
- Develop no-frills or generic product lines.
- Discount prices to liven up sales.

Remember that price-cutting strategies must be accompanied by realistic resetting of profit goals.

Source: Avraham Shama, marketing consultant, *Marketing News,* Chicago.

Selling to the inflation poor

A greater proportion of middle-class income now goes for basic food and shelter items, especially those perceived as durable, functional, or economical. What to do to sell other products:
- Modify existing products so they sell for lower prices. One way is to eliminate manufacturing steps, such as assembly or finishing.

Do-it-yourselfers

Do-it-yourselfers are a fast-growing market. About 85% of single-family households have at least one do-it-yourselfer. These tend to be white-collar workers earning an average of $25,000 annually. They are spending an increasing amount of disposable income on home repairs. Almost half the homes in the survey reported that the woman of the house helped make do-it-yourself buying plans.

Source: Survey by Market Facts, Inc., Chicago.

MARKETING TO THE GOVERNMENT

Breaking into the federal market

First steps a seller should take:
- Purchase a copy of the *U.S. Government*

and Sales Directory, which lists federal purchasing agencies and the products and services they buy. It's available from all regional government bookstores and the Government Printing Office, N. Capitol and H Sts. NW, Washington, DC 20401.
- Register with the free federal Procurement Automated Source System (PASS), which in-

stantaneously transmits information on products and services available from businesses for government purchase. Any regional office of the Small Business Administration will be able to help.

• Make direct contact with the procurement officers or prime contractors that use the products or services in the company's area.

A key source of information can be the business advisory programs that are now mandated for all federal procurement departments. Check which areas the Department of Labor has designated for preferential treatment because of high unemployment.

Other helpful publications:

• *Commerce Business Daily.* Lists items for which government agencies are seeking bids. Available from Superintendent of Documents, Government Printing Office, Washington, DC 20402.

• *Selling to the Military.* A good source book. Available from regional government bookstores.

• *U.S. Government Manual.* Provides code names and item classification numbers used by the government. Available from regional government bookstores.

What to do before seeking a federal contract

• Read the printed Request for Proposal (RFP) carefully. Note all timing, sequence, and factual support requirements. Note the evaluation criteria that will be used.

• Contact the agency to resolve any inconsistencies or ambiguities.

• Even if there are no problems, get in touch with the agency, talk to key people about the RFP. Find out what kind of firm they're looking for and how they want the work to be done. Try to establish an identity so the proposal will be recognized when it comes in.

• Study the agency itself. Be aware of its

problems and other outstanding contracts. One source of information: *Catalog of Federal Domestic Assistance,* Office of Management and Budget, Room 6001, New Executive Office Bldg., 726 Jackson Pl., Washington, DC 20503 (annual plus updates).

Get on and stay on government bidders' lists

Every government procurement office maintains a list of bidders it will notify when an appropriate contract comes up. But government personnel may not recognize that the firm can handle a particular contract. And they may not send out the notice even if they do recognize suitability, if 50 or more prospective bidders are already on the list.

Solution: (1) Request specific "bid set" (listed in the *Commerce Business Daily* or discovered through any other source), and file form (Standard Form 129) with the procurement office. (2) Once the bid set arrives, respond to it, and to all subsequent bid sets that the office sends. (3) If not interested in making a specific bid, send in a "no-bid" message. It's important to state a desire to continue to receive future bid sets. The procurement office will usually continue to send bid sets automatically as long as it keeps receiving responses from the bidder.

Source: Herman Holtz, *Government Contracts,* Plenum Publishing, New York.

Metrics make selling easier

Selling to the government will be easier for companies producing goods to metric measurements.

Instructions to all federal agencies from the Interagency Committee on Metric Policy tell buyers to pick metric over nonmetric products as long as the choice does not mean an unreasonably high cost.

Changes in government R&D rights

Research and development projects for the federal government have become much more attractive.

Companies now get the exclusive right to market commercially any discovery or invention they come up with during the project. Previously, Washington retained all rights and would not issue exclusive licenses. Few companies were willing to work or spend money on research and development projects that they were then prevented from exploiting commercially.

Small companies can sue

Small companies that lose out on a government contract intended for a small business may be able to sue under state law if the job actually ends up in the hands of a big firm.

A large company that has misrepresented its size in order to win government business earmarked for small companies has actually defrauded the smaller concern that would have gotten the job. The loser can call the profits unjust enrichment and use state tort law to get relief. If the plaintiff and defendant companies are in different states, the suit can be filed in federal court, but state law will still apply. And the original contractor still has the obligation to complete the government job, without a profit.

Iconco vs *Jensen Construction*, CA Eighth, 6/12/80.

EXPORT MARKETING

How to find export markets

Unlike large corporations, many small companies don't have the resources to pursue overseas sales. There are several low-cost steps that companies that are not exporting can take on their own or with the help of export-assistance organizations to explore international possibilities.

How to tell if a product can attract a foreign market:

• Find out whether competitors are exporting. If they are, chances are good that there's more room in the overseas market.

• Consult the company's trade association. Most have economists who are familiar with foreign markets. A few have export specialists.

• Tap the Commerce Department's information system. It lists products being exported and countries that are buying them.

When a company believes it has a potential export market:

• Determine the price range of the product overseas.

• At several possible price levels, get estimates of production, marketing, and shipping costs. Remember that higher export overhead often makes the initial return on investment lower for a company's overseas sales.

• Begin making contacts with prospective buyers in target countries.

Professional assistance is available from:
• State and local government agencies. Many have offices that help companies develop export operations. The Regional Export Assistance Program, a division of the World Trade Center, offers low-cost assistance to companies in New York and New Jersey.
• Marketing consultants. Most large U.S. firms also work in the international field. Many of their knowledgeable staff members are available after hours. Retired export managers in the U.S. and overseas make good consultants.
• The U.S. Department of Commerce's Worldwide Information and Trade System. It can put U.S. companies in touch with specific foreign companies that are likely prospects.

When a company isn't big enough for its own export division, consider hiring an outside export manager who knows the major foreign markets and relevant shipping and tariff regulations. The National Association of Export Management Companies, 99 Church St., New York, NY 10007, puts American manufacturers in touch with export management companies. There is no charge.

Source: Gregory Landenburg, international marketing consultant, New York.

Before you venture into a foreign country

The proper way to handle business dealings abroad differs, often sharply, from country to country. But there are basic steps every company must take well before it actually ventures into any foreign market:
• Study the country and its business customs.
• Know the market potential. (One U.S. company actually started a frozen food venture in a major country in the Far East before it realized that most homes in the market area did not have freezers.)
• Accurately assess the competition. Newcomers from the United States often don't realize the strength of rivals already on the scene.
• Most companies don't establish an interna-

tional business until their sales reach the $30–$50 million level. Exceptions are that some high-technology businesses may have a strong international market from the outset. And some service businesses never go international.

The best source of information is the Commerce Department. Also helpful are the Export-Import Bank, Small Business Administration, and the Overseas Private Investment Corporation.

Get to know the export market

Before wasting time and money trying to crack international trade markets, there are simple questions to ask. Specifically:
• Which countries restrict your company's products because they are produced locally?
• Could customs duties price goods out of the market?
• Is franchising or licensing an effective alternative?
• What U.S. financing is available to potential foreign customers?
• What is the likely profit margin and profit potential?

Several government and trade organizations will assist anyone trying to export products. For those addresses and further details, send for the free publication *How to Export—A Step-by-Step Guide,* Washington Researchers, 918 16th St., NW, Washington, DC 20006.

How to get organized for selling abroad

Essentials if the company is preparing to take its first plunge into international waters:

• Foreign-language ability. Set up an international section in the customer-service department. At least one staff member must have a full (reading, writing, and speaking) capability in each new market's native tongue.

• Foreign-currency savvy. Prepare to accept foreign currency in payment of invoices. If marketing plans include East European countries, where all local currencies are nonconvertible, develop a rapport with a key currency broker in Vienna.

• Foreign-sales personnel. Post native company-trained employees in each territory. Top managers must be at home there. Other staffers should at least be ex-residents. Knowing nuances of local culture, idiom, and politics can be as vital as language expertise. Count on the competition (foreign and domestic) to know this. Foreign nationals hired after the sales program is underway (without company training) could be worse than none.

• Metric systemization. Whether or not the company has converted to metrics for U.S. marketing, it's a must in markets that use nothing else. Metrication of product specifications, invoice data, transshipment distances, and all forms of communication involving numbers is required.

Source: Textile World, New York.

How the Japanese view U.S. firms as world competitors

An internal report prepared by the Japanese Foreign Ministry identifies these soft spots:

• Prices. American companies believe that the changing value of the dollar will greatly affect their market share overseas. What they fail to recognize is that non-price factors are more and more important. U.S. firms are losing ground to foreign competition in market familiarity, salesmanship, product quality, after-sales service, and credit terms.

• Ineffective management. U.S. management attributes the Japanese leap ahead in productivity and quality during the 1960s and 1970s to the difference between Japanese and American workers. But Japanese managers who have spent time in the U.S. debunk that explanation, blaming U.S. industry's problem on the quality of management.

• Technology. High-technology products bolster U.S. exports, but most of this technology was developed with government research funds. The plateauing of government funding for research has not been matched by an upsurge in spending by companies. The consequent drop-off in American technological superiority has been made worse by stiffer regulatory pressures on new-product introduction.

• Earnings pressures. Management's accountability to the stockholders of the giant multinational corporation (which account for 85% of all U.S. exports) leads to ultra-conservative investment decisions. Quarter-to-quarter earnings gains are put ahead of investment in new equipment, technology, and overseas marketing efforts.

• Weak sales effort. American impatience in business is a big handicap in developing new customers overseas, especially in Asian markets. The American approach is just the opposite of the painstaking perseverance required to penetrate difficult but profitable markets with complex distribution systems.

• Ignorance of overseas markets. The United States is the biggest and most indifferent exporter. Only 25,000 to 30,000 American firms export at all. And 95% of these firms are small and medium-size, exporting only 15% of the total.

An additional 30,000 small companies, say the Japanese experts, could export successfully but do not do so because of management's inexperience or ignorance of world market opportunities. The domination of American exports by giant companies holds down successful expansion of the export trade by a wider variety of firms.

Doing business in Canada

Though still potentially profitable, it is getting tougher because of the Canadian government's attitude of discouraging U.S. ownership of Canadian businesses. Canadian-owned companies are being favored for government contracts for example, and the government is selling oil to Canadian-owned companies at about half the worldwide price. Companies in U.S. government-related or energy-intensive industries may have difficulty competing with native Canadian outfits. Other areas of the economy are relatively open.

Help for the business traveler abroad

Officials at the U.S. Embassy in a foreign country can help collect bills, provide briefings on local business, supply names of local busi-ness agents, receive mail, and point to the right bureaucrats in the host government or even personally intercede. It may take some prodding, but it can be worth it. Have your congressman write the Embassy to give them time to prepare for your arrival. A list of key officers of Foreign Service posts is available from the Superintendent of Documents in Washington, D.C.

Business travelers should check foreign countries' holidays before scheduling a trip. Many countries have public and bank holidays unknown to Americans, or they celebrate common holidays on uncommon days. Travelers may find business closed on a day planned for heavy activity.

And when using an interpreter:

• Don't look at (or address) the interpreter. Instead, establish eye contact with the person you are talking to.

• Express only one thought at a time. Pause while the interpreter makes the point, and then proceed when the audience shows that it is ready for the next point.

• Meet with the translator beforehand to brief him on the content of the presentation. Give him copies of all charts, tables, and other visuals.

A point to consider is that using an interpreter roughly doubles the length of any speech or negotiations.

Source: *Industrial Marketing,* New York.

MARKETING AND THE LAW

Six ways to minimize product liability risks

• Strongly warn users against any possible product abuses that could result in injury.

• Periodically review all product claims for misleading statements.

• Establish a consumer complaint procedure and explain it carefully to all employees who handle customer telephone queries and letters.

• Handle all complaints systematically. Errors made by switchboard operators and other clerical staff in handling complaints can increase a company's vulnerability in a product liability suit.

• Set up worst-case contingency plans for receiving product liability complaints.

• Distributors should negotiate hold-harmless agreements to put liability for distributed products on the manufacturer.

Source: Richard S. Betterley, D.A. Betterley Risk Consultants, Inc., Worcester, Mass.

New direction in antitrust

The economic line in Washington always has an impact on antitrust activity. The guideline for government antitrust action is: Does a company's trade practice promote economic efficiency and production? If it does, it may not be restrained by the antitrusters even though the practice has some anticompetitive aspects.

But do not take the line coming from the Department of Justice and the Federal Trade Commission as a green light to pursue risky trade practices.

In 1977, the Supreme Court ruled that it was not automatically illegal for a manufacturer to prohibit a dealer from reselling products outside the dealer's specific territory. But many companies incorrectly read that decision as complete freedom to add prohibitions to all their dealership agreements. Some of those companies have since faced serious consequences because the agreements were held to be illegal even under the new, easier rule of reason set by the Supreme Court decision.

A new danger is more private antitrust suits. An expanding business may act overaggressively if it calculates that the government is less active in policing the law. A threatened company may sue to defend itself. Private antitrust suits can be harmful to the company that sues because the disclosure procedure forces it to reveal confidential company information.

Source: Richard Givens, partner, Botein Hays Sklar and Herzberg, New York.

Criminal antitrust violations

Corporate antitrust violations are criminal offenses. The executives can be sent to jail. Criminal antitrust actions brought against individuals have increased 300% since 1977. The average fine in 1980 was $27,000. The average jail term was three months.

Offenses most likely to result in criminal action are price-fixing, allocation of territories or customers, boycotts, tying agreements, and willful violations of the law.

The best legal strategy for a defendant is to quickly convince the prosecutor and court that the offense is regretted and will not be repeated. Then try to plea bargain. The prosecuting attorneys will not initiate discussions about plea-bargaining. They are more likely to accept a deal offered by the defendant before they have spent a great deal of time developing the case.

Source: Robert P. Beshar, Esq., attorney, New York.

Preventing illegal pricing practices

Courts now punish top corporate officers for negligence when subordinates collude with competitors on prices. An established preventive system may impress a judge with top management's effort to abide by the law:

• Have lawyers tell salespeople what the laws allow and prohibit. Make the sessions constructive and realistic. Stress what can be done under actual field conditions.

• Help price-setters observe the law. Explain and enforce specific codes of conduct. Reduce pressures to maintain a particular price.

• Avoid opportunities for collusion. Centralize pricing. Control contacts with competitors.

Source: Harold W. Fox, professor, Ball State University, Muncie, Ind.

Proving intent in price-fixing cases

Court rulings and judicial rebuffs make it tougher to harass and convict business executives. The government now has to prove not only that criminal activities did take place, but that defendants also intended to curb competition.

Exchange of information is not proof of price fixing and can even serve legitimate busines purposes, at least as far as federal antitrust law is concerned. But be aware that some states have tougher laws.

Pitfalls in fighting foreign competition

The government has streamlined the procedure for fighting foreign companies that dump goods on the American market. But U.S. companies should be careful in using it. If a trade association gets into the act, a complaint against dumping can look like an effort to curb foreign competition, and that is illegal. The Justice Department may become suspicious if:

• The trade association denies membership to the subsidiaries of foreign producers.

• Dumping charges are brought merely to harass the foreign companies.

• Signals go out to overseas producers that U.S. companies will not complain as long as foreign prices remain above a specified level.

• Illegally restraining competition can result in making the company vulnerable to a treble damage penalty. Convicted companies are also exposed to liabilities for loss of sales to U.S. distributors and from customers who paid higher prices.

Source: Carl A. Cira, Jr., U.S. Justice Department, the World Trade Institute.

11 DIRECT MARKETING

DIRECT MAIL MARKETING

The public's reaction to direct mail

How the public really feels about direct mail:
- Most people enjoy receiving a variety of mail.
- They separate their mail into six categories: personal, incoming money, bills, magazines, catalogs, direct-mail advertisements.
- Many people enjoy getting "junk" mail and use the term generically.
- Consumers don't mind being on mailing lists. They're quite willing to throw away mailings they don't want.
- The most popular kinds of direct mail: catalogs, free samples, coupons. Least popular: requests for donations, duplicate mailings, advertisements that have nothing to do with the recipient's interests.
- Catalogs are seldom thrown out without being looked at.
- Bill inserts are read with interest.
- Contests, while popular, arouse hostility in some consumers, particularly men.

- The person handling the mail in the home usually also pays the bills. In most American homes, this is a woman.

Source: Goldring & Co., Chicago.

Sales-letter basics

- Begin with the strongest point or the best promise. Fire the "big gun" first.
- No paragraph should be longer than seven lines.
- Fill the letter with "you" references.
- Use an occasional handwritten note in the margin (or underline).
- Be personal and informal. Write the way people talk.
- Single-space the copy. Skip an extra space between paragraphs.
- Use a P.S.—everybody reads a P.S.

Source: *How to Make Your Advertising Twice as Effective at Half the Cost,* Nelson-Hall, Chicago.

More effective selling letters

Use direct-mail experience to improve business letters. Specific suggestions:

• Use an opening that promises the reader a benefit (a free booklet, time or money saving, etc.).

• Ask a question that gets the reader to agree with the points in your letter.

• Get news into the message.

• Keep the opening paragraph short. Alternate long and short paragraphs.

• Address the reader as an individual.

• Get to the point quickly.

• Don't annoy the reader—and lose him—by telling him obvious things about his own business.

• To carry a reader through the entire letter, use conjunctions liberally. They work particularly well at the opening of sentences and paragraphs.

• Keep the tone personal, low-pressured, friendly, sincere, informal.

• After writing the first paragraph, ask yourself: Is that what I'd say after the handshake if I were calling in person?

Source: John D. Yeck and John T. Maguire, *Planning and Creating Better Direct Mail,* McGraw-Hill Book Co., New York.

What makes a mail-order catalog successful?

• Merchandise that's useful, interesting, attractive, and with easily perceived value.

• Prices that are as low as possible. But higher prices can be charged when the merchandise can't be found elsewhere or convenience outweighs the cost.

• Products with a common theme. Merchandisers should appeal to a particular interest group or a specific life-style. L.L. Bean's outstanding catalog of out-door-oriented goods is a perfect example.

• Merchandise that's artfully displayed. Color isn't necessary. Factual descriptions are.

• Money-back guarantees.

• Testimonials from satisfied customers.

• An order blank that's easy to fill out according to simple instructions in easy-to-read type.

• A free service for phone orders. As a plus, the order-taker can suggest other items while the customer is on the line.

Source: Julian Simon, author, *Direct Marketing,* Garden City, N.Y.

Don't use directories for direct-mail lists

Don't copy names from a trade or professional association directory for business and professional mail promotion, because every directory is substantially out-of-date as soon as it is published. (Rates of address change in some directories vary from a few percent to over 50% in a single year.)

Best strategy is to rent the list directly from the trade association or professional society. The rental cost is usually about $40 per thousand.

Source: *Book Marketing Handbook,* R.R. Bowker Co., New York.

How to get mailing lists from government offices

Thousands of lists of potential customers are tucked away in government offices. But government officials do not think of them as mailing lists and do not market them. The way to get the lists is through the Freedom of Information Act.

After identifying the market to be reached, determine which government forms are regularly filed by people or companies comprising the market. Trace these forms to the office or agency that receives the filings.

Contact the managing official in charge of the project directly. Public relations departments and Freedom of Information Act officers take more time or give less than optimal results.

For best results, use bureaucratic jargon. In particular, mailing lists are referred to as data bases or information bases. The purpose of the request is market research.

To order a list, submit a formal Freedom of Information Act request. The request will be confirmed in two to three weeks, and a magnetic tape will be delivered in several months.

Lists protected by federal law (IRS, Social Security, National Security Agency), names listed at home addresses and lists used by the Government Printing Office for its own mailings are not available.

Examples of lists that are available:

• 18,000 paid subscribers to *Energy Update,* from the Department of Energy.

• 150,000 foreign business firms that have expressed an interest in doing business with U.S. corporations.

• 80,000 education, health, and welfare organizations that have received grants from the Department of Health and Human Services or the Department of Education.

• 17,000 federally chartered savings and loan associations with 15,000 banks with current data for assets.

Source: Philip Dismukes, head, Marketing Services for Information Products, Arlington, Va., quoted in *DM News,* New York.

The direct-mail elite

Highest rentals are for lists with the names of customers who have bought collectibles by mail at an average price of $50–$60 per 1,000 names. The cream of this crop goes for as high as $100.

Names of those who have responded to TV offers, by contrast, rent for only an average of $30.

Source: Jack Oldstein, president, Dependable Lists, New York.

Direct-mail briefs

Timing a mailing. Mail delivered on Mondays, Fridays, and Saturdays is at an obvious disadvantage. Also badly timed are the letters that arrive around any holiday or vacation period. Avoid the first and fifteenth of the month, because of the distractions of bill paying.

Signing direct mail. Direct-mail promotional letters signed by the company president sometimes don't draw as much attention as expected. Most recipients tend to disbelieve the signature —and the content. Also, the title sales director is often a turnoff. One solution is to have letters come from the vice-president.

Business reply envelopes usually add significantly to direct-mail responses. For consumer mail BRE's improve returns 99% of the time. Two exceptions are (1) high-priced items, where need for postage contributes to snob appeal and (2) charitable solicitations, to give the impression that all of the contribution goes to the cause.

Direct-mail response rules of thumb. Half of the total response to first-class national mailings comes in five days once it starts. With third-class mailings, half comes within the first 13 days of return. Slower returns can be expected in the summer and at Christmastime. Faster returns come with regular-size envelopes (No. 10), rather than the larger ones.

Postal-meter ads

For about $25, companies can imprint an advertising message and an illustration on metered mail. The ad appears next to the postage-meter imprint. For example, an insurance company ad asks, ''Are you fully covered?'' And it shows a person in bed with his feet sticking out from under a short blanket. For details, contact a local post office.

Source: Pitney-Bowes, Inc., Stamford, Conn.

More effective direct mail

• Hand-stamped mail impresses the general consumer. But metered mail is fine when directed to corporate managers.
• Type recipient's name on reply card to increase response rate.
• Processed letters are often as effective as individually typed ones except for charity appeals or very select mailings.

Source: *Planning and Creating Better Direct Mail,* McGraw-Hill, New York.

A pair of aces—direct mail and phone

Direct mail and phone can be a powerful combination. One-quarter to half the customers use a toll-free 800 number (now a vital part of most direct-mail campaigns) to order or to get more information about the product before ordering. Be sure the phones are staffed with people trained to deal with consumers, solve problems, provide necessary information, and close a sale. Don't neglect your customer-service operation. A customer's question and/or complaint can be turned into a sales opportunity by skilled telephone representatives. Telephone work is difficult and turnover is high. Be prepared to absorb training costs.

Tandem mail and phone technique works well

when the aim is to get an apopintment with the prospects and one or more of these conditions exist:
• The product or service being sold requires a large investment and/or a demonstration.
• The offer is complicated. Buyers will respond better if they've seen written materials.
• The list of prospects is very good, or small, or being used by competitors.
• Buyers are hard to call because the market is saturated with unwanted phone solicitations.

Source: *Better Business by Telephone,* Kirkley Press, Timonium, Md.

Third-class mail problem

The post office often returns as undeliverable bulk mail that is marked ''return postage guaranteed.'' But much of it could have been delivered. As a result advertisers do not contact all their customers and they pay return-postage costs unnecessarily.

Doubleday & Co. discovered that 82% of a recent third-class mailing returned as undeliverable was really mishandled by the post office. The company found this out be sending first-class letters to the addresses the post office had just reported as no good. Only 18% of the first-class mail sent out in the follow-up test came back as undeliverable.

Source: *DM News,* New York.

Playing ''bingo'' cards . . . to lose

Those stiff, small pages in trade magazines, which readers checkmark to request further information and then mail in to the magazine for forwarding to the advertisers, are not called bingo cards for nothing. The reason is that shrewd sellers of goods and services play them to win new customers and business.

But the game works for the advertiser only when cards received are acted on promptly. Failure to respond in good time actually is counterproductive.

Unfortunately, the laggards are the rule, not the exception. Bingo-card senders usually wait about seven weeks to get supposedly preset answers on the ads in question. Barely a quarter of all card-mailers receive any follow-up calls, even though two-thirds of these potential buyers state that they are requesting data for current needs.

As a result for 43% of all respondents, the information eventually arrives, but it's too late to be effective. Another 18% claim it never arrives at all.

Six of every ten sales leads originally turned on by advertising are turned away by the marketer's inexplicable neglect. Most turn up somewhere else, as good customers bringing new business to a competitor.

Source: *CMC Study of Advertising Inquiries,* Advertising Research Foundation, New York.

The profit potential in company mailing lists

Any company that generates a mailing list of customers is generating a potential profit center, too. About 10,000 companies rent their mailing lists to direct-mail marketing companies. And a growing number of these lists are being generated by companies, both large and small, that are not engaged in the direct-mail business themselves.

A typical list prospect is a company that gives warranties for the video equipment it sells, so it has a list of customers who have video record-ers, cameras, etc. Prospective customers for the list would include companies that want to sell video cassettes, peripheral equipment, magazines and other products to customers whose lifestyle includes owning video equipment.

Profit potential:

• Lists rent for $30–$80 for each 1,000 names.

• Costs are low. A list broker assumes the promotion costs and gets a 20% commission. The company must pay only to computerize its list so it can be handled easily. (Cost per 1,000 names about $40–$50.) Sometimes the broker will advance that money and deduct it from the rental income.

• A small list (25,000–50,000 names) might generate an additional $100,000 in yearly earnings. A good large list (50,000 or more names) might earn as much as $1 million.

What makes a marketable list:

• Clear definition of the prospects in terms of their interests as indicated by products and services they have already purchased.

• Freshness guideline. Customer lists should not be more than two years old. Names of warranty holders or buyers who responded to sales promotions should not be more than six months old.

To determine whether the company's mailing lists are worth renting, prepare a sample of the list on a computer. Give the information to list brokers. If the sample generates enough income prepare the entire list for rental. For names of brokers:

• Contact the Direct Mail Marketing Association, 6 E. 43 St., New York, 10017.

• Read the trade publications such as *Direct Marketing* and *DM News.*

Note that companies maintain control of how their lists are used. They see in advance all pieces of mail going to the people on their lists. And they should exercise the right to withdraw their lists if they disapprove of the material. Also they "seed" the list with names of company managers so that any fraudulent use of the list will be detected.

Source: Rose Harper, president, The Kleid Co., Inc., New York.

TELEPHONE SALES

Using the telephone to save $

With the cost of making personal sales visits on the increase, timely telephone calls to good customers about small problems can pay off. Some examples:

• Price increases. Call with an explanation as far in advance as possible. Offer the customer a chance to stock up at the old price.

• Minor complaints. Phone the customer the day the letter of complaint arrives. Such contact is more effective, faster, and cheaper than a letter of explanation.

• Delayed shipments. An immediate call gives the customer time to adjust to the delay—and vent his frustrations. But it's a mistake to make false or optimistic promises on the new delivery date. Be honest and call with progress reports.

• Countering competition. Reacting to new products or pricing changes from competitors by phone brings the counterproposal to the customer's attention quickly and cheaply.

Source: *Better Business by Telephone,* Kirkley Press, Timonium, Md.

The basics of telephone sales

Selling by telephone, as old as the technique is, is still in its infancy. But a pattern of success has already emerged. The elements:

• Calls should be made only to prospects on carefully compiled lists. These should include only prospects with a high probability of making a purchase, given the relatively high cost of phone selling. Use clerical employees to get the phone numbers of the prospects from operator information. Making random calls seldom pays off.

• The product should ideally be reasonably priced and familiar. New products do not sell well by phone.

• Success of the phone campaign is often determined by how well the product is matched to the age and sex of the person called.

• Callers should use short scripts.

• The pitch should be made to the person on the list, not to anyone who answers.

• Some days and times are better than others. Friday night and Sunday morning are generally poor.

• Add-on items lend themselves to phone sales.

• Offers should have a money-back guarantee.

• Orders should usually be verified by a second call. That cuts merchandise returns.

There is generally no way to know in advance whether a phone sales program will be successful. The best method is to work up a sample script and test it for 30–40 hours of calling. Or hire a professional phone marketing firm at a cost of $1,500–$3,500 to write and test a script, about $25 an hour per operator to make calls after the test. A professional caller with a good list can reach eight or nine prospects per hour.

Source: Joseph J. Libman, president, Ring America, Chicago.

Planning your message

Plan and tightly organize the sales message. The working and progression of the message are even more important in telephone marketing than in print, radio, or television selling. When a canned phone pitch is boring and insincere, the problem is that it has been poorly planned and delivered, not that it follows a set format.

• Begin by grabbing the listener's attention and getting past the natural tendency to say *no* right away. Use the listener's name several times within the first few seconds. Ask an easy question, to which the listener must answer *yes*. Example: Can you hear me okay?

• State the reason for the call within 15 seconds, the time when the prospect's attention begins to wander and the person wants to hang up. Be brief and phrase the reason so it offers a benefit to the listener.

• Ease into the fact-finding phase, the heart of the call, with closed-ended, easy-to-answer questions that help the salesperson control the conversation. Then, shift to open-ended questions to find out the prospect's attitudes.

• Recommend and explain whatever course of action seems best to follow up the call. Example: Let me suggest that I call you monthly to keep you up to date on what's coming on the market.

• Close with a firm question designed to win the prospect's agreement to the recommendation.

Source: Bill Good, president, Telephone Marketing Associates, Salt Lake City, *Real Estate Today.*

The supervisor's role in telephone sales

Good supervisors can make or break a telephone selling program. One major supervisory function is to control the salespeople so that they don't promise too much and don't deviate from the prepared sales pitch.

The best telephone sales supervisors are experienced sales representatives, are naturally steady, and understand management's reasons for doing things. To keep supervisors effective, give them hiring power. Screen job applicants on the phone.

Source: Tom Moore, circulation director, *Army Times,* Washington, D.C.

Handling marginal accounts by telephone

When credit is tight, it makes less sense to pursue marginal accounts. But marginal accounts are important for their growth potential, so handle them by phone. The average cost is only $10 per sales call. Select telephone salespeople who can:

• Speak in a logical, straightforward manner.
• Establish their credibility quickly.
• Identify with customers without being disloyal to the company.
• Gain adequate product knowledge.

When selecting salespeople, interview applicants, at least in part, over the phone. A good source of telephone salespeople is the company's customer-service staff. They know the company's products, are experienced in dealing with customers over the phone, and may be motivated by the chance to take on a more financially rewarding job.

Since a person's telephone personality reflects his working conditions:

• Put a working supervisor in charge, someone who does more than simply watch others.
• Provide adequate backup material (catalogs, price sheets).
• Don't make telephone selling a dead-end job. Give the most successful telephone salespeople a chance to move out into the field.

Measure the results by recording:

• New accounts added by telephone sales.
• Before-and-after sales volume in marginal accounts serviced by phone.
• Before-and-after profitability in marginal accounts.

Source: Robert B. Friedman, manager of customer service, Thompson Medical Company, Inc., New York.

Promote shopping by phone

The high price of gasoline and the increase in the number of women who work are encouraging telephone shopping. Promotional aids:

• Make up ad copy and illustrations so that they give a complete picture of the products. (Photos are better than drawings.)

• Give telephone salespeople complete details of advertised items. And they should be trained to upgrade orders by suggesting other purchases.

• Get the customer's account number (or credit-card number) at the outset to enable a quick check on credit rating.

• Part-time employees, such as students, working mothers and retired people, often make good sales personnel. Their flexible schedules can fit peak call-in hours.

• A no-questions-asked refund policy builds confidence in shopping by phone.

Source: James Atkins, publisher, *Telephone Marketing Report,* in *Zip,* New York.

Keeping phone order levels up

Customers frequently order products by telephone, but salespeople are not always available to take the calls to upgrade the order. Ways to keep up the sales effort automatically:

• Quote a minimum phone order size, providing a saving for customers but requiring buying in large quantities to reduce the frequency and cost of delivery.

• Train phone order clerks to suggest a replacement for items that are out of stock. And they should also recommend a move to the next higher price or weight level and push related products.

12 ADVERTISING AND SALES PROMOTION

ADVERTISING STRATEGIES

Market-testing a new ad campaign

Market-testing is the only sensible way to determine whether additional advertising, a switch in media, or new copy will boost company sales. What to do:

• Develop a new theoretical advertising plan. Company managers decide how much they are willing to risk on growth. For example, a company with $20 million in sales and a $4-million gross profit may be willing to spend $2 million on advertising. Industry average advertising-to-sales (A/S) ratios are usually dependable standards to make sure the budget is in line. To introduce a new product, increase market share, or combat competition, the firm may consider exceeding the industry A/S ratio.

• Work out a test-market translation plan. Normally, this is a 10% microcosm of the national plan. Budget $200,000 (instead of $2 million). Target six cities that cumulatively represent 10% of the country, as a whole, and offer fairly typical demographic characteristics. Age, income, geographic location and city size should be well mixed. (Cities widely used for

such tests are Syracuse, Denver, Phoenix, and Madison, Wis.)

• Test and monitor results. Measure product sales six months before and six months after the test is run (impossible for new products) in order to provide a more accurate projection of results if the national plan is put into effect.

Results may seem less promising than they really are if the company does not have many distribution outlets in the test city. To strengthen distribution use the TV ad schedule for the upcoming test to convince store buyers to stock up for the campaign.

Source: Jim La Marca, president, La Marca Group, New York.

Executive involvement in advertising decisions

Few bosses spend time on advertising in proportion to the size of the advertising budget. Yet the best way to ensure that the company is getting the best advertising for its dollars is to get involved. This can be accomplished by personal contact with the creative people at the ad agency doing the work. They need the benefit of the chief's familiarity and experience with the products. But remember, there can also be too much participation in advertising by the chief executive officer.

Remedying ad failures

Just because the pre-market tests document high memorability of ads and the company uses media that reach the largest target audiences doesn't mean ads are producing maximum sales, because frequency and exposure intervals of ads may affect consumer response more than creative impact or media selection.

Careful tracking of response to various frequency and exposure patterns are needed for cost-effective advertising: On a market-by-market basis, use different approaches with the same media budget and audience rating level. Extend or shorten periods in which the ads run. Intensify or dilute concentration of ads during specific periods. Compare sales patterns in each market. Keep on fine-tuning to maximize results.

Source: Gene Dewitt, media services director, McCann-Erickson, New York, *Advertising Age,* Chicago.

• Have the company's advertising agency cost-justify its strategy. Question everything. (One question: Why isn't the company using more radio and less TV? Many media experts believe radio is the biggest media bargain around.)

• Narrow the demographic focus of the company's target audience.

• Tighten the focus of the advertising copy's appeal, too.

• Reduce industrial advertising. It's possible to reach key industrial buyers by cheaper means —personal letters, for example.

Be wary of emphasizing value in advertisements:

An overemphasis on value often leads to an unintentional focus on price. The reverse is also true, by overemphasizing promotional offers, a company runs the risk of undercutting its product's reputation. Instead, stress the product's benefits.

At the retail level, offer limited-time discounts. This will bring about a better long-range result. Instead of feeling that they are economizing when they use the product (which lessens the product's value), customers will believe they're getting a bargain.

Consider increasing ad budgets once the company's advertising presence has been carefully reevaluated. (The companies that maintained or raised ad expenditures in the last recession generally increased their market share.)

Source: Jim Durfee and Martin Solow, partners, Creative Services, Inc., New York.

Increasing ad effectiveness during a recession

Assume that a recession is more than a normal cyclical downturn and that it marks the beginning of an era of tougher choices and narrower limits.

Go for increased effectiveness.

How to evaluate a co-op ad program

Key questions:
• How much of the co-op budget is actually spent?

• Are the people staffing the co-op department as talented and as well paid as those running the national campaign?

• What proportion of retailers participate?

Which ones are using the co-op ad with the most effectiveness?

• Is there a difference in purchasing volume between those who spend the co-op funds and those who don't?

• Should all retailers have equal access to the co-op budget? Or would it be better if only certain stores used it? Be careful, this strategy can violate antitrust laws.

• Should co-op ads be limited to certain markets?

• Are retailers using the most effective media for the product?

• Are the co-op dollars allocated to the proper product lines?

• Is it preferable to have retailers create their own ads? Or is it better to do the job for them?

Source: Ed Crimmins, co-op advertising consultant, New York.

Setting an ad budget: how much is enough?

Although there are definitive rules, there are useful criteria that can help financial and marketing executives determine how much to spend on advertising. It's important to listen to an ad agency's advice, but formulate overall strategy at the company.

The basic problem: In general, the more money spent on effective promotion, the greater the sales. But there is a point of diminishing returns, at which extra ad dollars will not produce additional profitable sales. And there is no way to measure the precise effects of advertising spending.

The size of the ad budget is affected by a variety of factors: the size of the geographic market, distribution of buyers, type of product advertised, and competitive spending.

Most companies use one of the following approaches:

• Percentage of sales. The budget is based on last year's sales or anticipated sales for the coming year. It is a popular and easy method but not always the best. Trap: It lacks the flexibility needed to take advantage of unusual marketing opportunities that may arise.

• Fixed amount for each unit produced. It has the same defects as percentage of sales, except more money becomes available as more units are produced.

• Competitive spending. A useful guide when the average is based on a number of competitors, but competition may be wasting money. A copycat company may commit the same mistake.

The best method is based on identifying both advertising objectives and tasks.

First determine the communications objectives an advertising campaign is to achieve.

They should:

• Be specific and quantitative. For example, an 8% increase in sales, 12% increase in market share, 40% brand awareness.

• Include a position in the advertising media best suited to convey the brand message.

Once management agrees on the goals, estimate the cost of these tasks. The total appropriation can be adjusted to fit into the company's financial resources by modifying objectives.

The objective and task approach is the most logical method to determine an ad budget. The difficulty lies in estimating the level of effort needed to achieve objectives. This can be overcome by experience and by measuring productivity. Systematic testing of results at varying budget levels would be helpful.

Percentage-of-sales is still the simplest and most widespread method used by companies to arrive at an ad budget. (Often, it is expressed as advertising-to-sales ratio—A/S.) Advertising as a percentage of sales varies greatly by industry and product:

• Industrial products, airlines, autos, oil, utilities and retail chains have low ad budgets relative to sales (usually under 2% of sales).

• Convenience and package goods: Soft drinks, tobacco, soaps, drugs, cosmetics and toiletries generally have high ad budgets as a percentage of sales (can go as high as 25%).

Source: James La Marca, president, La Marca Group, media consultants, New York.

Budgeting for ads as sales slow

A recent study shows many companies that maintained ad budgets during the last recession escaped sales slowdowns. But this analysis was made by the American Business Press, a trade association with a vested interest in advertising.

One major advertising agency points out that while the study is undoubtedly accurate for some companies, it is not thorough enough to establish a general pattern. Few advertisers responded, and the results were not broken down by the type and size of business. That makes it impossible to determine whether sales were retained at the expense of a decline among nonadvertising competition. Instead, stick to the tested approach of not cutting back on ads as long as expenditures bring profits, except for ads for products known not to sell in a recession.

Common mistakes that waste advertising dollars

• The ad budget is allocated to national media when the company's sales are geographically more limited.

• One broad marketing plan is used for all markets when individual ones should be developed based on brand-development potential on a market-by-market basis.

• Seasonal purchase patterns are ignored.

• It's not known which media best influence target customers. Rectify this by including media usage questions in all consumer research.

• The company's media buyer overpays for broadcast time when it is highly negotiable.

Source: James La Marca, president, La Marca Group, media consultants, New York.

When to use comparative ads

Stacking a product directly against the competition's brand in a comparative ad can confuse and mislead consumers. Still, such ads can be effective if used carefully.

As a rule, products with practical rather than psychological benefits are most suited for comparative ads. The ad should depict the benefits in normal daily use.

Use comparative ads when:

• A new or unknown product needs public awareness. Demonstrate advantages over the market leader; psychologists have found that a low-status object gains in importance when compared to a high-status one.

• The goal is to plant doubts about a rival product. If the ad is convincing, loyal users of the competing product are likely to try the challenger at least once.

• A product has good distribution but low market share. Strong comparative ads can make the item better known but usually at the expense of other brands, not the market leader.

Avoid comparative ads when:

• The product is vulnerable to counterattack by the market leader.

• Its only advantage is price. Rivals can neutralize the entire ad campaign simply by lowering their prices.

• The product's benefit is one of marginal consumer interest.

Don't plan a comparative campaign on the assumption that it will attract attention merely by tackling the leader. The novelty of comparative ads has worn off. What they say is the key.

Source: *Advertising Age,* Chicago.

Nothing but the truth in endorsement ads

The Federal Trade Commission is continuing to set stricter standards for ads built around celebrity endorsements. The basic rules are:

• All product claims must be able to be substantiated.

• The copy must represent the celebrity's honest view of the product.

• If the celebrity says that he uses the product regularly, that statement must be able to be substantiated.

• Consumers must be advised if they cannot reasonably expect the same results as the celebrity.

Using stars in ads

Here's what their agents advise:

• Match the product's image with the star's. Joe Namath in panty hose attracted a lot of attention, but who remembers the brand name?

• Be prepared to share the celebrity. Exclusive contracts are very expensive. Avoid stars who oversell their time and names.

• Don't take advantage of the star. Most are willing to sign autographs and pose for pictures. Ask, don't demand.

• If the celebrity is to meet with customers or salespeople, do it in an office. Avoid restaurants and nightclubs, where autograph seekers and public gawkers constantly interrupt.

• Have an ad agency or market-research firm determine how the public views the star. Hiring the boss's ideal can backfire.

• Black and Puerto Rican celebrities who are very popular with the public as a whole have extra appeal to minorities.

• Use famous people on tape. For much smaller fees, they will record a sales pitch.

• Imitation celebrities are effective, too, par-

ticularly at sales meetings. The top impersonators also work well in ads.

• If using the star on a sales call, make the star of that sales call the salesperson, not the celebrity.

The major reason for using a star is to boost sales-force morale. Focus on the celebrity's involvement as often as possible in sales bulletins.

Source: *Sales & Marketing Management,* New York.

Making a splash with celebrity look-alikes

Models impersonating famous people are being used increasingly in ads and promotions for a wide range of products and services.

Advantages. The cost is only 2%–3% of what the celebrity would charge, if that person were available. Look-alikes are attention grabbers and rarely project a negative image.

Typical costs. $1,000–$1,500 for an eight-hour day at a sales convention for a Reagan look-alike. Other political impersonators run slightly less. Nonpolitical stand-ins charge about $750–$1,000. Expect to pay extra for speeches, gags, special assignments.

Costs also vary according to the amount of time involved, location, type of ad or promotion and the professional status of the look-alike. For example, a doctor who portrays Henry Kissinger charges more for his time than does an unemployed actor.

A wide range of political, historical, and entertainment figures is available. Current favorites include: Prince Charles and Princess Diana, Burt Reynolds, Robert Redford. Perennial favorites: Almost any president, Elvis Presley, Farrah Fawcett, Muhammad Ali.

Be cautious. Celebrity images are highly volatile. If a celebrity is suffering image problems, be wary of using a look-alike in a promotion.

Reputable look-alike companies insist on printing a disclaimer or making a public announcement such as "Celebrity look-alike provided by Company X." They also will not allow their models to be used in a way that would disparage or ridicule the celebrity.

Source: Jaeson Cayne, executive vice president, Ron Smith's Celebrity Look-Alikes, Los Angeles.

Should the boss be in the ad?

Frank Borman. Cal Worthington, the California car dealer. And Frank Perdue, the chicken salesman. There have been enough successful TV advertisements featuring company presidents that other firms ought to consider the technique.

It can create an atmosphere of sincerity and trust. Perdue's dinstinctive looks and the unpolished delivery of most of these company chiefs help their ads stand out.

The best situations in which to feature the owner are in service industries and where quality and reliability are key sellings points. The chief executive is willing to face customers and to personally guarantee the product's quality. And it can cost as little as $5,000 for a locally produced 30-second TV ad spot.

But vanity can be a dangerous motivation. If the owner doesn't project well, find another technique. Commercials can be copy-tested before a full commitment.

Source: Jim La Marca, president, La Marca Group, media consultants, New York.

WORKING WITH AD AGENCIES

Rating ad agencies

Key factors:
- Past record.
- Related experience.
- Ability of personnel on the account.
- Agency fee.
- Time needed to launch campaign.
- References from other clients.
- Importance agency attaches to satisfying clients.
- Awards and other professional recognition won by agency.

Assign points to each criterion on the basis of how important the company believes it is for a project. A company may feel that a good track record is worth 10 points and creative ability is worth 15.

Source: Bob Chang, Harshe-Rotman & Druck, *Sales & Marketing Management,* New York.

Choosing a new ad agency

- Ask the agency what it feels makes great advertising. It should be similar to the customer's view.
- Review projects done specifically by members of the team who will handle the new account.
- Determine how past creative work met a customer's objectives. Did it stand out from the clutter?
- Weigh the advantages of an out-of-town agency with a strong creative service against the negatives of working only via telephone, plane, and mail.
- Evaluate the charges beyond the 15% agency commission on ad space or the 17.65% fee on services.
- Run a background check to be sure the

agency pays suppliers promptly, since top talent may be unwilling to work for a slow-paying outfit.

• Identify the long-term clients and review for steady growth. A heavy client turnover could be a sign of agency problems.

Source: Rich Flaskegaard, Minnesota advertising executive, *Advertising Age,* New York.

Why clients switch ad agencies

Major contributing factors:

• Dissatisfaction with billing procedures. A major complaint is inaccuracy. Financial misunderstandings usually occur when the agency operates on the fee system. When a client starts to complain about billings, it is a signal of unhappiness with the agency's overall performance.

• Frequent turnover of agency personnel leading to continual changes of key employees.

• Lack of creativity. Another major complaint is lack of innovation by the agency.

• Poor agency management. The advertising agency is perceived by its clients as lacking in depth and in the managerial resources it needs for growth.

Source: Robert Boyd, Northern Arizona University. Flagstaff, Ariz., *Ad Week,* New York.

What ad agencies need from clients

• Early consultation, before plans and ad budgets have been firmed.

• Prompt, accurate responses to the agency's questions.

• Treatment with respect, even when differences occur.

• Reasonable deadlines and the willingness of clients to meet their own deadlines.

Source: Don Hauptman, creative consultant, *Direct Marketing,* Garden City, N.Y.

Getting more out of agencies

Companies can use their advertising agencies as marketing consultants to conduct annual audits of overall marketing operations, not just to handle advertising production and placement.

Specifically, have the advertising agency, working as marketing consultant, spend two or three days to: (1) Review overall marketing operations. (2) Write a letter citing the company's marketing strengths and weaknesses.

Ask for an estimate on all the work the agency believes they could do to improve particular marketing functions.

If the company's advertising agency doesn't offer this service, the next time the company calls in a marketing consultant for a specific purpose, ask him to audit the overall marketing operations as a secondary assignment.

Source: Jack M. Doyle, Jack M. Doyle Advertising, Inc., Louisville, Ky.

ADVERTISING COPY

Principles of effective copy

• Get attention by stating a believable promise in a few words. Or illustrate the product and its advantages in a photograph.
• Hold the reader's attention with subheads, illustrations and a good first paragraph.
• Create desire by piling up product benefits.
• Make copy believable. Include specific figures, testimonials and guarantees.
• Prove it's a bargain by giving specifics on price reductions and building up the value of the product.
• Create a reason to buy now. Use a special offer for promptness.
• Close ads with a paragraph that makes it easy for customers to act. But shopworn phrases like ''Write today'' or ''Order now'' are too weak. What stirs prospects to action? Coupons (especially those offering a premium); 800 numbers; explicit buying instructions, including the actual words to use in the response; details about an easy-payment plan.
Not every ad can contain all elements, but aiming for them is the first step toward copy that works.

Source: John Caples, vice president, BBD&O, New York.

Basic advertising appeals

Universal human desires motivate people to read, to believe, and to buy. Build advertising appeals on these basic wants: to gain, to save, to do, and to be.

People want to gain health, popularity, praise from others, pride of accomplishment, self-confidence, time, improved appearance, comfort, social and business advancement, security in old age, leisure, increased enjoyment, and personal prestige.

People want to save discomfort, risk, money, worry, embarrassment, work, and doubt.

People want to do things that express their personalities, satisfy their curiosity, and attrack others' affections. They want to be able to resist domination by others, emulate the admirable, acquire or collect things, and to improve themselves in a general way.

People want to be creative, efficient, recognized authorities, good parents, up to date, first in things, gregarious, sociable, hospitable, proud of their possessions, and influential over others.

Holding a prospective buyer's attention

Good advertising headlines may grab the reader's attention, but only momentarily. To hold the prospect so he'll read the main copy:
• Quote a celebrity, even if the quote isn't a direct endorsement of the product. One ad that sold millions of copies of Dale Carnegie's best-selling book bridged the title, *How to Win Friends and Influence People,* to the text with John D. Rockefeller's advice on the value of ''the ability to deal with people...''
• Point out the disadvantages of competitive methods. A direct-mail piece for a weight-reduction belt (which ran for 10 years) made the transition from a straightforward headline into copy with these words: Diet is weakening—Drugs

are dangerous—Strenuous exercises strain your heart. The advertised weight-reduction belt (made of "reducing rubber") promised safe results equivalent to those of sessions with a skilled masseur.

• Repeat the idea stated in the headline. Head: "Who wants a whiter wash—with no hard work?" The bridge: How would you like to see your wash come out whiter than hours of hard scrubbing could make it?

• Spin an incredible story, but tell it believably. Example: "They laughed when I sat down at the piano." The bridge: Can he really play? He never played a note in his life. This is going to be good. This ad led to the sale of thousands of correspondence-school courses, and it started a new school of ad writing.

• Come right to the point, which is the product information that is of direct value to the buyer. An ad ran for 40 years under the headline: "Do you make these mistakes in English?" It held reader attention by answering that query with a free (one-paragraph) lesson in basic English, followed by 1,100 words of highly successful hard sell.

Dated examples? No question of that. But they certainly are techniques that continue to prove their selling effectiveness.

Source: John Caples, *Direct Marketing,* Garden City, N.Y.

ally associated with Pepsi-Cola ads, are now imitated by many other companies with the result that consumers don't distinguish between products being advertised. Some advertisers end up supporting the opposition.

Why the USP is important today. As the economy gets tougher, advertisers will have to focus increasingly on the consumer's need for the product.

Main focus of the USP. It demonstrates what the product can deliver that no other product can. A common mistake that companies make is to limit the emphasis of their advertisements to the product, without a broader regard for larger consumer interests.

Strategy. Say the company makes furniture. Instead of representing itself as being in the furniture business, it should project the image of being in the home-environment business.

The difference. In the new definition (along with an offer to give customers decorating advice), the company is selling a reassurance that the consumer's choice of purchases will be expertly guided. In addition, the manufacturer is promoting the belief that its customers' homes will be more beautiful and fashionable as a result of buying the company's furniture.

Source: Jan Hedquist, president, Rosser Reeyes, Inc., New York.

Making advertising more meaningful

Successful advertising should hinge on the unique selling proposition (USP), i.e., the particular merit that distinguishes a product and makes it meaningful to consumers, for example, the "Think Small" theme of Volkswagen, one of the most successful unique selling proposition campaigns in advertising history.

Current advertising tends to focus on mood and feeling, rather than on the quality of a product. Also, the emotions that are projected tend to be similar. For example, the scenes of happy old people, teenagers, babies, and dogs, gener-

Using negatives positively

There have been many admonitions about the use of negative copy. Conventional wisdom says it does not sell products. Truth: Think again.

The halitosis ads were one of the best advertising campaigns. The ads didn't say: "Listerine makes your breath sweet." They said: "If you have halitosis, even your best friend won't tell you...or your boyfriend won't love you...or your children won't kiss you. So use Listerine." The ads attacked rather than stroked.

Being self-conscious, and not being able to detect halitosis, the consumer used Listerine, and kept on using it, despite its taste. That's a negative working in a positive fashion.

There's another good word, one that every person in advertising would like to cry out to every reader or viewer: STOP! That's a negative if ever there was one. A copywriter would be hard-pressed to think of an affirmative word that has the impact of STOP!

Source: Milton H. Biow, *Butting In,* Doubleday, Garden City, N.Y.

Humor in advertising—advice from a master

Humor in advertising is what David Ogilvy of Ogilvy & Mather is now advocating. That's a complete turnaround for him. But research now shows that it works when it is concentrated on the product.

More Ogilvyisms:
• Don't be cute in headlines. Instead, put in the product name and a promise.
• Give the brand name in the first ten seconds of a TV or radio commercial and repeat it over and over. Even play funny games with it.
• Avoid showing couples walking through the woods, happy families at dinner, sunrises and sunsets.
• Quit worrying about not hatching the really big idea. (Ogilvy says he has had only nine in 30 years, and that, he finds, is more than most people.)

Source: *Advertising Age,* Chicago.

Outstanding headlines

The ones below were selected by John Caples, BBDO Advertising:
• Great new discovery kills kitchen odors quick—makes indoor air "country fresh."
• Have you these symptoms of nerve exhaustion?

• Five familiar skin troubles—which do you want to overcome?
• "Here's an extra $50, Grace—I'm making real money now!"
• Here's a quick way to break up a cold.
• How I became popular overnight.
• How I improved my memory in one evening.
• How I made a fortune with a "fool" idea.
• How I raised myself from failure to success in selling.
• How to do your Christmas shopping in five minutes.
How do your company's headlines compare?

Source: John Caples, *Direct Marketing,* Garden City, N.Y.

Unforgettable tag lines

Advertising tag lines, those repeated slogans used to identify a product or a company, work wonders only when their catchy recall establishes the product and leads prospects to it repeatedly.

Three forgettable flops:
• Ford wants to be your car company.
• NBC: Proud as a peacock.
• Because the wine remembers. (Can you remember which wine?)
Ones that work:
• Don't squeeze the Charmin. (There are more consumers who perceive Charmin to be softest than there are those who don't.)
• Merrill Lynch is bullish on America. (The biggest bull market in U.S. history brought Merrill Lynch Pierce Fenner & Smith the sharpest growth any stockbroker ever experienced.)
• Have a Coke and a smile. (Inviting and memorable.)
How to create a winning tag line of your own? Don't force it. And do not dream it up first, then build a campaign to fit it. A good tag line is likelier to turn up by chance in a campaign that is already under way. It's often hidden somewhere in good copy or in a headline and needs only to be recycled.
But face the prospect that a really good tag

line may not be forthcoming. A tag line is good only if: (1) it can significantly strengthen the marketing strategy and (2) it can stand alone to suggest the campaign to your market in a kind of shorthand message.

Timing is essential. Unforgettable tag lines, good or bad, don't achieve that status overnight. And never without careful multimedia planning plus hefty spending. The keys are repetition, longevity, and wide exposure. It's a tough task without big spending, but not impossible. Low-budget campaigns that are stretched out can bring it off. A combination of packaging and point of sale (where appropriate) is helpful.

Source: James I. Greene, president, Creative Associates, Inc., Dallas, *Adweek,* New York.

Traps in using pictures in ads

Misleading consumers through the use of photographs can get an advertiser in trouble just as readily as making deceptive claims in copy.

Generally prohibited:
• Illustrations implying a product has parts or characteristics it doesn't have.
• Pictures of higher-priced models in conjunction with prices of lower-cost models.
• Illustrations of products not readily available for sale.
• Enlargements used to create false impressions.

Effective trade advertising

• Get the real prospects to indicate their interest in your company's product or service far in advance. The best way to do this is to offer free literature. It takes very little ad space to make the offer. And every company has something already written to offer in the ad.

• Make it easy to respond. Offer a toll-free or collect telephone number. It makes the prospect feel that the advertiser wants to do business.
• Show names of salespeople. Customers prefer calling a person. And salespeople appreciate the ego massage.
• List the company's telephone number and address. No matter how big or well known the advertiser is, chances are the customer does not know the company's phone number and address. Make it easy for the real prospect to make contact.
• Know the ad's target. It costs the same to reach both the big and little firms. Ads that work pick up where the sales force can't go, because of some geographical, financial, or another reason.
• Use the word "free." It is magical. Don't take it for granted that everyone knows ad literature is free—say so.
• Don't bury the company and the offer. Make sure the offer, address and phone number are in large enough type to be read easily.

Source: Freeman R. Godsen, Jr., president, Smith & Hemmings, Los Angeles, *Adweek,* New York.

Advertising established products

When advertising to purchasing managers, stress company performance, not the product, because the purchaser already knows the product line. He needs to know about the company's capacity to follow through on delivery, quality control, availability of supplies and spare parts, and the like.

How to test advertising effectiveness

• Does the ad get through the "clutter" of

other ads? Does it rivet the viewer's (or reader's) attention within the all-important first three seconds? A common error is the failure to recognize that the ad's true competition is other ads, not other products.

• Does it zero in on just one or two ideas to leave with the viewer? Frequently, the ad lists so many reasons for buying the product that the viewer becomes confused and doesn't remember any of them.

• Is it relevant to the way the viewer sees himself and his own needs and desires? Be careful though, running an ad written for one need where customers have entirely different needs.

• Does it leave the product's name clearly in the viewer's memory? Or is the ad so "cute" that people remember the cuteness but forget the name of the advertiser?

Source: Nicholas VanSant, VanSant Dugsdale Advertising, Baltimore, *Marketing News.*

Print advertising checklist

• Most important point—does the headline clearly promise a well-defined benefit? Readers respond to simple, direct information. They tune out headlines that are cute, boastful, or exaggerated. *Good headline:* Eight attractive ways to solve your storage problems. *Bad headline:* It has everything.

• Is the ad cluttered or hard to read? Don't use light type on a dark background and don't superimpose words on pictures. Lines of type should be short enough to read easily. Avoid fancy type, copy or art that's tipped at an angle, color for color's sake.

• Without being clever or mysterious, does the body of the ad tell the reader how, what, where, when, and why?

• Do the illustrations back up the sales point? Many ad professionals strive for creativity above all else. But flashy ads usually don't work.

Source: Robert B. Parker, *Mature Advertising,* Addison-Wesley Publishing Co., Reading, Mass.

What copy-testing can't measure

Copy-testing a proposed ad can indicate its ability to convey concrete benefits and information. But it is an ineffective way to measure these key intangible elements of an ad:

• Emotional or psychological benefits that affect irrational or impulsive responses to buy.

• Visual distinctiveness.

• Competitive uniqueness. Ads that imitate a successful competitor score high on copy tests, but not in the marketplace.

Source: Shirley Young, executive vice president, Grey Advertising, *Marketing Communications,* New York.

CHOOSING AND BUYING ADVERTISING MEDIA

Guide to advertising media

	Benefits	Audience	Advertisers	Usefulness	Limitations
Metropolitan Newspapers	Sense of immediacy. Credibility and authority of message. Space for extensive copy. Mass medium reaching all ethnic groups.	Highest concentration among upscale, higher-income, better-educated adults. *Education a definite factor:* 81.8% of college graduates "read a paper yesterday."	Major ones are food, tobacco, appliances and travel companies. Most papers have special sections (Travel, Home) which are good for coupon and sale items.	Specific advertising in special sections is far more appropriate in terms of both audience demographics and editorial content. Space flexibility heightens ad's impact.	Color advertising varies from newspaper to newspaper. The cost of national coverage is high. Low pass-along readership.
Local Television	Sight and sound mean dynamic and personalized selling. Both mass-market and select-market appeal. Cost-efficiency. Programming directly tied to audience demographics.	*Daytime programming:* Female audiences, low income, low eduction. *Prime time:* Upscale in income, not education. *Weeknight viewers:* All family members. *Weekends:* Mostly men.	Essentially all product categories, including automotive, food and beverages, pharmaceutical and household products.	Specified program format and dayparts (programming times) provide key environment for maximum reach of well-defined audience.	High out-of-pocket cost. Short life of commercial message. Limited availability of *right* time and program. Advertising clutter. Loss of audience attention.
Local Radio	High demographic selectivity. Low out-of-pocket cost for time and production. Personality identification. Exceptional reach during times people are driving.	Audiences highly fragmented. Highest reach among young (teen) audiences. Important to pick the station with the right demographics.	All product categories. Mostly used by local advertisers.	Relative flexibility of program format lends itself to creative media planning. Careful selection of format will ensure reaching desired audience.	Clutter of competing advertisers. Fragmented audiences. Fleeting messages.
Cable Television	Varied programming and reach. Growing rapidly. High level of community interaction. Regional and local capabilities. Flexible commercial lengths.	*Estimated penetration:* 22%–28% of all U.S. television households. Concentrated in metropolitan counties with 150,000 or fewer people. Households upscale, younger, with children.	No longer solely regional, but include national hotel chains and car, beer and oil companies.	High coverage of select audiences and specific geographic areas at a low out-of-pocket cost. Attention must be given to the right program environment.	Research is unrefined. Uneven national penetration. Short life of commercial message as in all broadcast media. Appeal is still to a narrowly defined audience.
Surburban Newspapers	Local emphasis and impact. Geographic flexibility. Production and copy flexibility. Short closing times.	Readership is uneven. Suburban papers tend to be upscale and concentrated in more affluent communities. Reliable demographic data unavailable, but audience is mainly female and older.	Most newspaper advertisers, but much less national advertising. Banks, car dealers, restaurants, local theaters are heaviest users.	Best way to reach local communities. Heightens neighborhood identity. Local advertisers include supermarkets, banks, dealers, stores.	Market-by-market review is necessary. Editorial content can be unsophisticated and lack prestige.

	Benefits	Audience	Advertisers	Usefulness	Limitations
City/Regional Magazines	Local editorial content and increased involvement of readers. Publications are geared to specific reader interests. Upscale demographics. Long life.	Upscale, trend-setters, involved in community life. Audience research still unrefined but improving as magazines gain in importance.	Mostly local advertisers showing high-priced luxury items (cars, clothing, liquor and jewelry) as well as travel destinations and entertainment establishments.	Good editorial and physical environment for luxury goods and services. Stock of paper often lends itself to outstanding color reproduction.	Long closing dates. Lack of immediacy. Advertising clutter because of small-space ads. Uneven and unaudited circulation.
Outdoor (Billboards)	Strong brand identification. Sustained presence. High visibility, high coverage, high frequency. Geographic flexibility. Cost-efficient. Strong support medium.	Mass medium for broadest exposure. Reaches over 80% of demographic groups.	Mass-market products, including cars and tobacco, liquor and restaurants. Some public-service advertising.	Broad audience reach. Strength lies in delivering straight, clear, graphic messages. Location of boards is significant.	Length of copy limited. Unreliable research as to audience delivery. Relatively high out-of-pocket cost. Limited recall.
Yellow Pages	Local coverage, reaching the neighborhood buyer. Provides same-product proximity. Long life of message.	Local households with telephones.	Virtually all retail and wholesale advertisers use the *Yellow Pages*.	Provides clear, direct information on locally available goods and services.	Too localized. If broadly used, checking procedures to determine success of campaign are laborious.
Trade Publications	Editorial environment targeted to a specific market. High coverage of well-defined audience.	Highly selective as well as highly defined. Total audiences are generally small, but the percentage of desired types of readers is high. Demographics linked to editorial content.	Highly specialized and narrowly focused.	Provides the latest in industry information. The marketplace and showcase for company news and developments. Proximity of same-product categories.	Unreliable research on effectiveness of advertising. In smaller books, low editorial quality.

Why local media are a good buy

Advice for advertisers whose budgets are keeping pace with the inflation in media costs or whose product sales are falling short of targets: Fall back from national or regional advertising support to a local-marketing approach.

Concentrate advertising dollars in areas where business is strongest and where the company will get the best payoff on its investment.

Spot TV is relatively soft right now. The biggest bargain is the late fringe viewers, between 11:30 p.m. and 2:00 a.m.

Radio is also hot. Strengths:

• Power to deliver good levels of a target audience.

• Reach and frequency are excellent for a reasonable out-of-pocket cost.

• It sells.

However, the radio audience is so segmented that no one station delivers a meaningful number of potential customers. Therefore, the advertiser must buy at least four stations in major markets to get meaningful impact. In certain markets, 10 or 11 stations are sometimes needed to do the job.

As an example, to reach 60% of the women between 25 and 54 years of age in the New York metropolitan market five times within a four-week period, time must be bought on five to seven stations.

The cheapest way to buy TV and radio times is to use buying services that own banks of time on desired stations, which they can sell at attractive rates.

But this trade time can usually be preempted if the station finds a cash buyer for the same time.

Solutions:

• Write tight specifications, with penalty clauses, into the company's deal with the buying service.

• Monitor the service closely to assure that the purchased ad time is being delivered.

• Tie a trade deal with a cash purchase to give the company some insurance against being pre-empted. The station will generally treat an advertiser who pays some cash better.

An economical way to buy print is through 3M's Magazine Network, Inc. (MNI). It has been around for a decade, but is now catching fire. MNI offers advertisers selected editions of many magazines (including *Time, Newsweek* and *U.S. News & World Report)* on a market-by-market basis. The cost is a fraction of what it costs to buy the entire circulation.

MNI delivers a wide range of special-target audiences such as high-income individuals, working women, urbanites, executives. The company also provides similar TV services.

___

Source: Bruce Hoenig, senior vice president and director of media, Avrett, Free & Fisher Inc., New York.

Shrewder newspaper advertising

• Ask for a discount if the ad will run more than once. Papers usually give a reduction of 5%–15%, depending on how often the ad appears.
• Don't automatically buy a full-page ad when seeking maximum impact. If well designed, even a quarter-page ad can dominate a page.
• Always include the company logo. Leaving it out squanders much of the benefit that comes from advertising frequently.
• Think position. For an extra fee, many papers guarantee space on a page with proven high readership. Or negotiate the premium position without a premium charge.
• Ask the newspaper sales representative for readership survey information to help decide which section of the paper is best for the ad.

___

Source: S.L. Dean, *How to Advertise: A Handbook for Small Business,* Enterprise Publishing Inc., Wilmington, Del.

Matching the ad to the reader

Personalized magazines could soon be a reality, using a computerized collating system that assembles each copy according to the subscriber's profile. Example: Cigarette ads would be automatically withheld from copies going to nonsmoking readers. Computer time-sharing could reduce per-copy cost to 15¢ to 80¢ range. Advantages: Sharper segmentation for advertisers. Lower paper and postage costs for publishers. For further information contact: U/Stat Inc., 730 17 St., Denver, CO 80202.

Remnant space—an ad rate bargain

Advertisers can save up to 75% on remnant space. That's unsold space the magazine must fill as an issue's deadline approaches. To reserve the best tell the space sales rep to put the company account on the remnant buyer list. The usual saving is 40% of rate card. Be prepared though. Remnant space must be filled quickly. Have ads ready for the moment when space is available. There are even some brokers in remnant space. Remember though, that remnant space is not available to current advertisers and there's no ad-agency commission.

How to save TV dollars

Advertising dollars can be stretched by as much as 30% if advertising agencies can be induced to negotiate on TV spots. But few companies are aware that the TV market is highly negotiable. They accept whatever quotes their agencies give them. But agencies earn a straight commission on whatever they spend, so they lack incentive to negotiate for better prices.

Ask the ad agency to buy spots through an outside media buying service. (Most small agencies do this anyway.) The media service assesses the prospective ad budget and makes a bid to cut it by, say, 25%. The advertising agency gets the first 10% as its fee and shares any additional saving evenly. The saving is then reinvested in more advertising. But ad agencies are often resistant to incentive buying because it cuts their profit.

Effective animation use

Animation in TV ads can be more effective than photography, but only when used correctly. Consider animation when exaggeration helps make a sales point, when it is useful to explain visually how a product works, or when humor can strengthen the sales ptich.

Source: Hooper White, president, Hooper White Co., *Advertising Age,* Chicago

Local advertisers taking to grade-B productions

Tacky, low-budget, do-it-yourself TV commercials are becoming standard viewing fare. The pitches, for anything from used cars to discounted home appliances, make Madison Avenue purists scoff. But in terms of doing what a good ad should (boost sales, increase product recognition at lowest cost), many are exceptionally effective.

Several advertisers pitch their own merchandise rather than buy professional talent. A number also write their own copy. They've learned the ins and outs of media buying (i.e., how to buy time at 60% off or more). And they use inexpensive, small TV production studios. The typical budget is less than $1,000 to produce two or three ads. Another $10,000 for station time.

Start slowly. Test some spots and measure the results before plunging into a major schedule.

Don't expect immediate miracles. It takes time to create the commercial that clicks.

SALES PROMOTION

Promotion pays off

Cents-off coupons, cash refunds, sweepstakes, and other promotions have been growing almost twice as fast as national advertising during inflationary times.

The reason is that promotion is very price-oriented. And inflation drives consumers toward every possible way to save money at the supermarket. Some 70% of households send in for cash refunds, as compared with 40% a few years ago. Fully 80% regularly redeem coupons. And this is not a low-income phenomenon. Families with over $25,000 in income and relatively high education levels are the smartest shoppers. They also are more apt to see the newspapers and magazines in which coupons appear.

To promote effectively:

• Recognize that consumers are eager to try brands that offer coupons, but they are simultaneously moving to nonbrand generic products (now 14% of supermarket sales) if the product is used in quantity and if there is little real difference among products.

• Use cash refunds to load up customers with several packages of a product instead of the single package they usually buy.

Source: Louis Haugh, managing partner, Westport Marketing Group, Inc., Westport, Conn.

Sales promotion ideas

• Sampling. Free samples distributed by mail or door-to-door.
• Coupons. In the product package, by mail, or in newspapers and magazines.
• Trade coupons. Offered by retailers rather than the manufacturer.
• Trade allowances. Special payments to retailers for advertising and displaying the product.
• Bonus packs. Such as buy two, get another free.
• Price-offs or cents-offs. Should allow at least 15% off the regular price to be effective, more for weaker brands.
• In-, on-, and near-packs. Such as packaging the product in a reusable drinking glass, or several brands of cereal packaged together.
• In-the-mail premiums when one or two labels are sent in. Can be free or with an additional charge, usually less than $5.
• Contests (including sweepstakes).
• Mail-in refunds. A customer who sends in a label gets either a cash refund or a coupon for another purchase.

Source: William A. Robinson, William A. Robinson, Inc., Northbrook, Ill.

Sales promotion tactics for hard times

Basic promotion techniques that are right for uncertain times:

• Premium offers. Stick with brand names. Use premiums that build from ongoing advertising program. Offer realistic values.
• Sweepstakes. Stick with cash prizes. In times of inflation/recession, cash does best. Desirable alternatives are prizes that look like money but really aren't, like a shopping spree at a famous store.
• Point of purchase. Stick with displays that are best for your company's best customers. Use display contests to encourage retail support. Don't be afraid to provide the retailer with a display that can be used later for his brands. Retailers remember.
• Price-offs/bonus packs. Offer loyal customers a combination cash refund and money-saving coupon for multiple purchases.
• Trade promotion. Use value-added promotions in lieu of cash discounts. Although retailers always welcome allowances, they like promotions that increase store traffic even better.
• Trade shows and exhibits. Probably the best promotion bargain around if properly used. Trade show costs have not gone up as much as other advertising and promotion costs. But make sure those who run the booth have special training. Follow up those leads.
• Sales meetings. Now is the time for close-to-home, shirtsleeve, working meetings. Cut the number of days by a third, drop nonproductive recreation sessions. This will enforce the message that these are serious times.

Low-cost promotions

Few companies have promotion budgets as large as those of Procter & Gamble, General

Foods, or Philip Morris. Those others, though, can develop productive promotions by imaginatively downscaling some big-spender techniques. It is essential to adopt a positive attitude, confidence that the promotion budget can be effective. Suggestions:

• Be shrewd. Develop a willingness to bargain over every aspect of the promotion. If a promotion gimmick is available at $10 per unit, find out whether it can be bought directly from the manufacturer for $9 or from a discount vendor for even less.

• Pay attention. Become closely involved in each aspect of the promotion. Chances of saving money increase when managers keep tabs on printing, artwork, copy, display, premiums, specialties, etc. Former Chicago White Sox owner Bill Veeck was a whiz at shoestring promotions, largely because he handled the events himself.

• Challenge. Think in terms of adapting, eliminating, combining and modifying. P&G might use a full-page ad in 1,200 newspapers. But another company can deliver a sweepstakes with a small space ad combined with in-store displays. P&G might offer a $100,000 grand prize. But a smaller company can effectively offer a prize worth $10,000 and get it as a trade-out with the manufacturer.

• Stand firm. Stress good relations with vendors, but do not let them railroad the company into buying more than it needs. Let them know that if the promotion is a success, they are likely to get future business.

• Think ahead. Plan the promotion with the longest possible lead time. Short leads invariably result in higher costs because mistakes have to be corrected with rush orders and because vendors cannot always fit the job into their best time slots.

• Accommodate. Aim for a team spirit between company and vendor staffs. Put things in writing as the project develops in order to avoid confusion. After the promotion is over, ask for suggestions on how to save money the next time around.

Source: Louis J. Haugh, managing partner, Westport Marketing Group, Inc., Westport, Conn.

When it's okay to break the rules

Sales promotion rules aren't engraved in stone. Here are six that can be broken on occasion, when the product, and the reason, are right.

1. Promotions are always short-term. Maybe, but long-term promotion can build a franchise, too. What is Cracker Jack without the prize?

2. Samples should include a cents-off coupon. Cents-off may actually hurt the brand's price position. A better method is to introduce the product with advertisements and sample sizes. Offer the discount coupon later.

3. Always test a promotion first. Trusting your instinct is better. If the promotional tactic is familiar and only the creative element is different, or, if promotion is tied to a one-shot event (the World Series, for example), go ahead.

4. Sweepstakes don't always build sales. Alternate means of entry do make sweepstakes problematical. But with the proper theme and a good involvement device, they can lead the consumer, especially the new one, to a brand. The trick is to make sweepstakes simple, yet involving. Offer great top prizes, skip the boxcar runner-up awards. They don't motivate entries and are a nuisance to send out.

5. Use a name brand as an incentive or premium. Use the brand name when there's a choice. But, if possible, try to create a product with a higher perceived value to the consumer. Some brand names are sold at discount, thus a premium offer may not be very attractive. But a created premium using your company's brand name reinforces consumers' identity with your product.

6. It's important to sell the product, not the premium. True, but make the premium so much a part of the brand that it encourages the use of the product (a coffee offering coffee cups, for example). Remember, the closer the relation-

ship between brand and premium, the better the promotion.

Source: Louis Haugh, managing partner, Westport Marketing Group, Inc., Westport, Conn.

Premium considerations

• The most effective promotions are those that tie the premium to the sponsoring product. For example, tea bag manufacturer using an automatic-dispenser vacuum bottle; breakfast food and a digital alarm clock.

• Customizing (the consumer's name on a shirt; favorite football team on an athletic jersey) increases the premium's appeal. But that's only if it doesn't stretch delivery time out too far.

• Price—for self-liquidators, do not charge more than 50% of retail value.

• Offering a number of premiums in the same ad can backfire. Ad ends up looking like a mail order catalog. The better way is to focus on the most appealing one.

• Consider shipping costs. Consumers don't like paying postage and handling charges in addition to the basic price. Low-value items that are heavy or fragile to ship are a bad idea.

• Trends: (1) Higher prices. (Recent analysis: Price to customer was over $5 in 37% of the cases.) (2) Longer delivery times. (Average now is 39 days.)

Source: *Incentive Marketing,* New York.

Saving on premiums

Low-priced premiums that are cleverly presented can be as hard-hitting as costly, high-quality premiums. For example, a fast-food chain used a giant treasure-chest display to dispense penny charms to children.

What conquers the consumer is the vehicle through which the premium is presented—the packaging, print work, store display, tear-off coupon, etc.

Source: Jeffrey K. McElnea, president, Einson Freeman, Paramus, N.J.

Basics of promotion advertising

Promotion advertising differs significantly from consumer franchise-building advertising. The latter is long-term in nature and aimed at giving customers reasons to buy. Promotion advertising is short term. It pushes for the order by providing incentives (coupons, rebates, premiums and contests).

Print is the usual medium for promotion advertising. Some big-budget companies use broadcast advertising to get consumers to look for the promotion at stores or in newspapers.

As a general rule, resist the inclination to include extraneous points in the promotion ad. Focus on a simple call to action. Including other ad copy is dangerous.

Typical calls to action:

• Redeem this coupon and save money.
• Buy this product and get a $2 refund.
• Win $100,000 in the product sweepstakes.
• Buy this product and get this other item for only $4.95.

Remember that a sweepstakes cannot legally require a purchase. It is generally used to focus attention on the brand and reinforce key copy points. A sweepstake's ability to move products at retail is limited, but it can lead customers to make a purchase.

Most promotion events are price- or value-added-oriented. As such, promotion copy must appeal to the wallet rather than emotions. But this doesn't mean the ad can't look like the franchise-building ad. Graphics should retain the brand's inherent appeal to its target group. Most promotion ads have higher readership scores than straight brand-sell ads. A promotion ad generally attracts a wider audience to the product.

It's essential to keep the offer simple. Example: Save 25¢ now with this coupon. To be avoided: Save $1.50 when you purchase six of the products/sizes listed and send in proofs of purchase with two cash-register tapes from a supermarket. (To say the least, consumers would be confused.)

The art, copy, and terms in promotion ads should get the same clarity and attention to detail that other advertising does.

Source: Louis J. Haugh, managing partner, Westport Marketing Group, Inc., Westport, Conn.

Fighting a sales slump with cash refunds

Cash refunds can be useful tools for fighting a sales slump. Some pointers:
• U.S. households exploiting rebate offers tend to be higher-income, larger-family bigger spenders than the national average.
• Effectiveness in promoting supermarket trial purchases ranges from 51% for soap to 83% for cigarettes.
• Refunds spur buying even by consumers who don't request money back.

Check successful refund campaigns in similar product categories before making advertising-media decisions.

Sweepstakes planning

Sweepstakes can range from a simple shoe-box promotion in which customers fill out entry blanks to win some small item to a $500,000-or-more campaign heralding fabulous prizes.

The difference between a contest and a sweepstakes is that a contest requires some level of skill

or involvement, such as completing a sentence or answering a question. It draws fewer entries. The sponsor can require the consumer to purchase something actually or submit a proof of purchase. Sweepstakes cannot require proof of purchase.

Advantages of a sweepstakes or a contest. It generally adds interest or excitement to a promotion event. Most sweepstakes ads are more widely read than straight brand-sell ads. They provide an extra selling message to revitalize a brand or company's image, or to tie in with a highly recognized event, such as the World Series. The promotion can be linked to a product or service. It can be aimed at a specific consumer group through selection of prizes, or can build in-store traffic or tie in with displays.

Some of the drawbacks. Because no proof or purchase can be required for a sweepstakes, additional sales as a result of the promotion are hard to prove. there are professional sweepstakes "contestants" who may not be prime customers. Sponsors must comply with a variety of federal, state, and local regulations.

If the company decides to launch a sweepstakes or a contest:
• Determine objectives: Sweepstakes or contest?
• Plan advertising support.
• Estimate the cost of the prize structure, judging, media support, complying with legal requirements.
• Clear ad layouts, entry blanks with postal authorities.
• Decide if outside professional, legal, judging assistance is needed.
• Make sure the sales force and trade understand the promotion. Should a companion promotion be aimed at them?
• Write the "official rules." Make sure they are understandable. Publish the list of winners.
• Get wide distribution of in-store materials because most entries will come from point of purchase rather than ads. And in-store promotion is more likely to generate sales.
• Limit the length of the sweepstakes to two months at most.
• Provide enough room on the entry blank. Spell out an alternate means of entry. For example, a 3-by-5 card instead of a coupon.
• Make sure the handling of all entries is safe

and secure and in compliance with regulations. Set up a method of handling consumer inquiries.
• Deliver prizes promptly.

Source: Louis J. Haugh, managing partner, Westport Marketing Group, Inc., Westport, Conn.

Coupon fraud

Grocery store coupons that appear in newspapers are widely counterfeited and turned in for redemption. The estimated cost to manufacturers to redeem counterfeit coupons is $250 million annually. In a rather startling case, 25¢ coupons for a fictitious detergent were once run in three newspapers. More than 2,000 grocery stores in 40 states tried to redeem the coupons.

Having a
profitable party

Parties are a big part of promotion programs in some companies. Use them to introduce new products and line extensions, to explain a new marketing thrust for an existing product, or to tout mergers, acquisitions, promotions, and anniversaries.

Keys to successful business entertaining:
• Planning. Allow at least six weeks.
• Liaison. Only one person should have the authority to coordinate all services needed for the event.
• Objectives. Spell out the intent of the party.
• Communication of message. Exploit all opportunities. Indicate in the invitations what guests can expect. Display company products. Offer giveaways bearing the company logo.
• Control costs. Hold the event in the company's headquarters or showroom. Use in-house graphics, public relations, and printing

services. Company personnel can be hosts and hostesses.

Source: *Marketing Communications,* New York.

The status party

The right party will upgrade the status of the company as well as launch the new product or the new model year by mixing uniqueness with taste.

A common mistake is having huge, crowded parties full of gate crashers and friends of friends. Keep guest lists small. Limit attendance only to those invited by name.

Get away from the traditional showroom cocktail party, with the usual complement of girls in short skirts. Instead, hold the party at a good club with handsome facilities, one to which you are connected. Ideal locations are the Arts Club in Chicago, the River Club in New York.

Clubs provide quietly elegant tone, which companies would want identified with themselves and their product. The paintings and other art works on view there can be impressive and serve as an added attraction for guests. Disadvantages include cost and club restrictions on press attendance.

The evening should include the unusual and exotic. Make sure people remember the evening and the company responsible for it. Perhaps have an Oriental theme for the evening, or jazz harpists, barbershop quartet, etc.

Invite company's top customers. All company salespeople can be invited to a pre-dinnner cocktail party, but not necessarily to the dinner.

All customers as well as press people invited should receive press kit (with photos) telling the story. Buyers should see the material to understand the mood that the company is trying to create. The presentation can take place during dinner. Keep it dignified and keep it short.

Costs vary from city to city. Here are rough averages for a first-class show for 100 people. The public relations firm gets (and pays for) the entertainment, makes arrangements with caterer, arranges press coverage and publicity, $15,000. Food and drinks for 100 people will cost roughly $7,500 at a posh place in New York. Press kit costs are about $4,000. Invitations (engraved) will cost about $1,250. A party designer (includes purchase of centerpieces, decorations, favors, linens made to order, and fee for putting it all together) will charge $5,000. The total cost will be $30,000–$35,000.

Source: Letitia Baldridge, Letitia Baldridge Enterprises, New York.

Getting the most out of big-draw trade fairs

• Reserve hotel rooms at least six months in advance.
• Select accommodations within walking distance of the exhibition halls. Valuable time will be wasted in traffic snarls if you must take a bus or taxi. Or take hotel space outside town but near rapid transit.
• In cities reputed to have fine food, book reservations at renowned restaurants at least three months in advance.

• Arrive a day or two early. Overcome jet lag and get settled in before the hectic days of the trade fair itself begin.

Avoiding trade-show rip-offs

Defensive strategies: (1) Arrange for unloading and assembling of equipment beforehand. Schedule work precisely, hour by hour. (Enables those in charge to detect goldbricking, etc., and possibly head off extra charges.) (2) Make early contact with the show manager and local service unions. They have the power, not the exhibit hall staff. (3) Attend exhibitor meetings and discuss mutual problems. Solidarity gets better results than individual complaints. (4) Construct displays with safety devices such as unbreakable plastic cases for valuable items. Weld working parts of vital equipment. (5) Sell marketable items at the end of the show to reduce thefts.

Source: Ron Hardaway, AT&T, New York, and director of the National Trade Show Exhibitors Assoc., Rolling Meadows, Ill.

13 MANAGING THE SALES FORCE

HIRING

Ads that bring in the right salespeople

Before writing the ad, develop a simple job description of the activities that the salesperson should be willing and able to perform.

Next, try different classified newspaper ad approaches. Vary the day of the week occasionally (Sunday is almost always best). For future planning, keep copies of each ad with dates, number of inquiries it drew, number of applicants interviewed, and how many were actually hired.

Effectiveness of different types of ads. (1) Direct-answer ads get the fastest responses. (2) Blind ads entice, but give little direct information beyond a number to call. (3) Least effective and most time-consuming is the write-in ad, which tends to attract lots of compulsive resume mailers.

Tips on ad composition:

• Use a brief headline surrounded by white space.

• Words like "Attention" or "Advancement" catch the reader's eye and sometimes assure good position in papers that arrange ads alphabetically. Other unusual headlines: Stop-Look-Listen; Now; TNT—Today Not Tomorrow.

• State only absolute requirements like "car essential." Leave factors like experience as flexible as possible.

• Mention benefits, compensation (salary plus commission), and training where these are attractive.

• Strengthen company image by tying it to a specific industry via comments such as, "We are part of the rapidly growing telecommunications business."

Sample direct-answer ad for inexperienced sales personnel:

IT'S A FACT
The biggest money and the fastest promotion are found in well-organized sales work. We are tops in our field and are equipped to train from the ground up. Our very successful salespeople include former farmers, retail sales clerks, cab drivers, engineers, secretaries, as well as salesmen. Experience is not necessary. Prefer married person with a car who is interested in an absorbing and permanent position. Salary and bonus basis for those selected. Apply...

Sample blind ad:

ATTENTION
Trainee to work with manager for four weeks' training to prepare for position with large local

concern. Salary, pension plan, group insurance. Sales background not considered necessary if personable and neat. Age no barrier. Complete details will be given during interview. Car necessary. Phone for appointment 10 a.m.–1 p.m. Tuesday or Wednesday.

Sample write-in ad:

SALES EXPANSION

Large local company with full-scale expansion program needs two persons. Those selected will be given thorough office and field training. Promotions available as soon as qualified. All large-company benefits, salary, and incentives. *Qualifications:* Car necessary, aggressiveness, record of stability, desire to be in outside sales and assume responsibility. Address Box...

Train operators in precise procedures for taking telephone responses from the ad. They should get information on respondent's name, marital status, brief work history, availability, etc.; then set up an interview date and time.

Most respondents will try to elicit information from operators about the company and the job. Operators should be courteous but firm in saying that further information will be forthcoming only at the interview.

Source: David Yoho, David Yoho Associates, Fairfax, Va.

Sales-force hiring standards

Never hire anyone there's the slightest doubt about. Candidates who raise questions in the interviewer's mind will do the same with customers.

Immediate turn-offs are poor appearance or a manner of dress that clashes with norms of the employer or customers; shifty looks or poor eye contact; sloppy language; job hopping.

Standards a prospect salesperson must meet (failure in just one category is a sufficient reason for rejection):

- Enough maturity to be fully responsible and accountable.
- Bachelor's degree or equivalent successful business experience.
- Dependable, ethical member of the sales community.
- No excessive debt, or convictions for misdemeanors or felonies (except for traffic violations).
- No serious or continuing domestic problems.
- Sound physical and emotional health.
- Intellectual capacity equal to the demands of the position.
- Enthusiasm about the job and its responsibilities.
- Willingness and ability to devote all the time, effort, and energy necessary to fulfill the job's requirements.
- Pleasing but strong personality. Projects an air of confidence and respect without humbleness. Able to get along with all kinds of people on all levels.
- Understands importance of conforming to company policies and procedures, yet is flexible enough to accept changes.
- Firm belief in private enterprise and high profits.
- Interested in making long-term commitment to company.
- Sufficient general business experience as well as knowledge of the employer's specific industry.
- Able to handle rebuffs properly. Accepts criticism and uses it for self-improvement. Full awareness of the importance of accountability to superiors.

Candidates who meet these criteria must also successfully complete several more steps in the hiring process:

- Reference check. Phone former employers to verify that candidate's reasons for leaving agree with ex-employer's answers. The most important question: "Would the company hire him back?"
- Physical exam. Pay for a physical to learn if the applicant has sufficient stamina and emotional stability to fulfill job and is free of undesirable personal habits, such as drinking to excess or drug use.
- Size up the spouse. Must be willing to accept frequent and long absences, if that's part of

the job, help out with phone messages and paperwork when the salesperson works out of the home. Spouse must indicate that all other demands of the job and their impact on home life are acceptable.

• Approval by immediate supervisor. Omitting this step or overruling negative recommendation immediately sets up new salesperson for possibly serious problems in the future.

Initial screening time-savers. Don't bother to see people with poor or incomplete resumes. Conduct initial interviews by phone. Recruit from within, particularly from customer services and telephone-order departments.

Source: William Wachs, Sales and Marketing Executives Workshop, New York.

Was the application form, for example, filled out completely and per instructions? Was the candidate on time?

• What motivates the applicant? Keep probing with open-ended questions. Be understanding. Never indicate disapproval.

• Can you (and your customers) cope with the candidate's personal habits? Best to face it up front.

• Does the candidate have the stability to hold a job? Watch out, not only for unexplained gaps in employment record, but also numerous jobs or residences.

Source: Davod Yoho, David Yoho Associates, Fairfax, Va.

Qualities to look for in sales personnel

• Initiative and perseverance.
• Reliability, including honesty with management and the capacity to win the confidence of customers.
• Ability to deal with unexpected obstacles and to recognize shifting customer and market conditions.
• A willingness to travel.
• Skin thick enough to repel rejection.
• Good emotional balance, which allows a salesperson to handle, without getting personally involved and defensive, the type of treatment he or she is likely to experience.

Good reasons to hire saleswomen

• Women are good listeners with stronger verbal skills than the average male. They often can give compliments more easily than men.
• Curiosity works in their favor, at least right now. Most male prospects wonder how a saleswoman operates. Also, women have an easier time getting by secretaries.
• There are many highly qualified candidates at salary ranges in which there are relatively few males.

Source: David King, president, Careers for Women, New York, *Sales Manager's Bulletin,* Waterford, Conn.

Some questions that need answering

Get answers to the not-so-obvious questions:
• How organized is the candidate?

Hiring mistakes

Considering only persons with at least three to five years' experience in the industry is self-protection for the personnel manager, but it is not the best way to find top salespeople. They must be personable, persistent, and able to work on their own, which are traits that can be found outside the industry as well as inside it. For example, a teacher whose job requires working through problems and persuading might make an excellent salesperson despite a lack of experience. Often unrecognized is the fact that many prospective salespeople have the wrong kind of experience within the industry.

Other hiring mistakes:

• Ignoring employment patterns. Few companies actually check references anymore. If they did, they might see a pattern in the reasons a prospect left recent jobs.

• Overemphasizing physical appearance. Salespeople should be neat, but they need not all look alike.

• Overselling the job to the candidate. Giving unrealistic expectations is a sure way to breed dissatisfaction.

Questions to ask prospective salespeople:

• Why do you want this job at this company? First-rate applicants, even if they were attracted by an ad, should have done a small amount of research on the company. They should be able to give a reason for wanting the particular job available.

• Do you have any questions about the job or the company?

• What makes you think you will succeed in this job? A good prospect ought to be able to cite past experiences and qualities (such as tenacity and independence) that make a good salesperson.

• In what areas will you need initial assistance to help you succeed? A good answer matches the company's ability to provide that support.

Satisfactory responses often help identify likely prospects, even those without prior selling experience. But hiring should not be based exclusively on a candidate's answers. Some potentially superior salespeople may not yet have developed the skills needed to do well in an interview.

Source: Dr. Barbara Pletcher, president, National Association for Professional Saleswomen.

New-hires survey results

About three-quarters of the firms in a recent survey said more than half their new hires for sales openings are college graduates. Other findings:

• The national sales manager is responsible for recruiting and hiring in about 50% of the companies. Regional and local sales managers draw that task in about 30% of the companies. In another 8%, it's a function of the company's personnel department.

• Turnover of salespeople is high. Nearly 40% of the companies report a turnover rate of 11%–20%. Another 28% of the firms said turnover is even higher than 20%.

Source: Sales and Marketing Management, New York.

Cutting turnover of sales recruits

Sales recruits are most likely to stay with employers and be productive when they are put into a sales-training program within weeks of joining the company.

In addition, it is important for them to develop good working relationships with their supervisors. Finally, sales recruits will thrive when the company places a strong value on the contributions of all members of its sales department.

Source: Edward Flanagan, executive director, Sales Executives Club of New York.

Independent sales reps vs staff salespeople

Consider contracting with an independent

sales agent, rather than hiring new staff sales-people, if:

• A new product is aimed at markets outside the company's established channels of distribution. Sales reps with solid contacts in the field can put it across quickly.

• A territory's potential volume is too small to support a full-time company salesperson. The agent, representing several suppliers, will be making regular calls anyway.

• Customers order infrequently, but they must be called on often by the sales rep.

• Sales are volatile. An agent is paid only for sales made, so when volume slackens, costs will too.

• A product line requires specialized or technical knowledge. Sophisticated reps come cheaper than hiring technically savvy salespeople full-time or training staff.

• It's a new business, and management needs to devote all its time and effort to matters more

crucial than supervision of a start-up sales force.

• The product, after succeeding in the home territory, is being readied for expansion to new regions. Experienced agents will know the territories beforehand, and they can move faster.

Staff salespeople are apt to prove more cost-effective when:

• Volume per customer runs high. A sales rep's commission is unvarying, while those of an in-house sales force are adjustable.

• Service is a key element of sales. Agents, paid only for orders, have no incentive to spend time on servicing nor on selling a product that requires it.

• Projecting a corporate image is important to a company's marketing strategy.

• Sales campaign timing is crucial. Reps can't be time-controlled the way staff can.

———

Source: *The Professional Report,* Scarsdale, N.Y.

TRAINING

Breaking in a sales apprentice

Let the apprentice learn by doing. A survey by the Small Business Administration shows that trainees remember 50% or less of what they learn from lectures. But in real-life cases, they remember 70%–90% of the lessons picked up through experience.

The best approach is to assign an apprentice to a top pro. They should make sales calls together. The experienced rep should let the apprentice make the pitch, and critique immediately afterward.

Caution: (1) Don't force the trainee into a predetermined mold. (2) Don't look for high sales volume in the learning period. (3) Stress the

importance of organization for selling early and often.

———

Source: *Industrial Distribution,* New York.

How to make training sessions popular

Turn groans and frowns into more welcome expressions by offering real benefits during training. Techniques:

• Stress usefulness. Don't use the cure-all approach or present a management-knows-best attitude. Instead, present training as something the staff might be able to use.

• Concentrate on specific problems. Instead of a general session on how to handle objections, offer help on specific problems that are giving top performers trouble, for example, price resistance.

• Never tell the sales force it needs training or is mishandling situations. Everyone will deny he's at fault. Sell training as providing new, better, or easier techniques.

• Keep it pleasant. Don't overstate problems or use long, dull lectures. Instead, use experienced professionals as instructors or panel members. They know what the problems are and can identify solutions.

• Talk up training in the field. When a complex problem comes up, tell the salesperson that it will be handled at the next training session.

• Offer something new every time. Use surveys and suggestions from the field to keep training relevant.

Evaluate the results. Distribute a questionnaire after each training session. But be prepared, answers aren't always what you might expect.

Source: *Marketing for Sales Executives,* New York.

How to boost sales in a sluggish economy: sales retraining programs

Sales at Pitney-Bowes, Inc., the office-products manufacturer in Stamford, Conn., dropped 25% in the second quarter of 1980 from the first-quarter results. As a result of a sales retraining program, Pitney-Bowes' sales climbed 15% in the second half of 1980 over the first half, erasing the weak second-quarter performance. How the sales retraining program worked.

The purpose of the program was to increase the rate of new contacts (new accounts, or new business from old accounts) made by local sales representatives.

Sales managers paired off with sales representatives one-on-one. They set a target for the day: X number of new contacts to result in Y dollars of new business.

Then, sales managers and sales representatives went into the field together. The sales manager took charge of the first call to demonstrate the sales technique. Then he observed while the sales representative practiced the technique. And the manager made suggestions right on the spot to improve it. The day the program ran in Philadelphia, Pitney-Bowes salespeople initiated contacts that resulted in $80,000 worth of new business!

Why the program worked:

• It demonstrated management's commitment to support the local sales representatives.

• Sales managers showed, rather than told, sales representatives how to improve their techniques.

• The program nudged sales representatives into setting higher goals for themselves, which subsequently raised overall productivity.

Recommended:

• After a sales manager has gone into the field for a day with a local sales representative, maintain contact with that salesperson. A mentoring relationship develops, which supports increased effort and better performance.

• Repeat the program once a year to rekindle enthusiasm.

Source: Michael J. O'Connell, vice president, Pitney-Bowes, Stamford, Conn.

MANAGING YOUR SALESPEOPLE

Setting sales budgets

The basic method is for top management and operating sales managers to submit their own proposed budgets. Where there are great variances, differences are analyzed and a compromise is worked out. Areas of common agreement are automatically accepted.

But using the costs of the existing sales force as a starting point in budgeting doesn't take into account changing company objectives or marketing considerations.

Not allowing for enough time lag between sales efforts and the initial order is a common error. Expenditures of time and money don't always show up in actual orders within the same budget year.

An "investment" approach to sales budgeting rather than an "expenditure" approach is a good solution. This way management can use return-on-investment in appraising sales efforts. The cost of training and the nonproductive period of new salespeople can be more accurately measured over the longer term. The cost of selling new products and entering new markets is extended over a longer payback period.

Source: *Checking Up on Your Sales Force,* The Sales Executives Club of New York.

Cutting the fat from sales budgets

Don't assume that belt tightening will hurt morale. Sales personnel are aware of economic conditions. Cutting costs to strengthen profits is reassuring if it's presented positively.

How to do it:

• Boost the productivity of, or fire, marginal or unprofitable salespeople.

• Give bonuses to salespeople who improve their expense/sales ratios.

• Reduce travel and entertainment costs by making fewer supervisory trips, cutting down on evening and spouse entertainment. Use cheaper hotel rooms, buses instead of taxis or limos to and from airports.

• Have the odometers on all cars that earn mileage allowances checked by the service station. Most are 10% off in the wrong direction.

• Use a scale for mileage allowances rather than flat amounts, allowing smaller payments for heavy car use.

• Tighten up on reporting and reimbursement for private use of company cars.

• Pare down the number of home-office staffers who serve as liaison between sales and internal departments. Instead, have field force make direct contact with payroll, shipping, credit, etc.

• Purge mailing lists of deadwood.

• Use manufacturers' representatives to cover thin territories.

• Review the need for national sales meetings. Look at alternatives such as regional meetings, more central locations, and less entertainment.

• Cut back on sales contests and merchandise incentive awards. Replace them with cash, a greater motivator in inflationary times.

• Get tough about long-distance phone calls. Substantial telephone savings can be realized if all correspondence is answered in writing.

Source: *Marketing for Sales Executives,* Research Institute of America, New York.

A better approach. Since most such analyses are prepared by computerized equipment, program the computer to focus on those items which deviate significantly from previously established norms.

Source: *Total Participation for Productivity,* AMACOM, New York.

Sales quotas that work

Past sales figures continue to be the best guide to quotas. Six factors that are also important:

1. Economic trends (national and regional).
2. Number of competitors selling in each territory and their performance.
3. Size of the actual and potential market. Whether or not the count is increasing or decreasing.
4. Anticipated levels of sales promotion and advertising.
5. Plant capacity and probability of production slowdowns.
6. Amount of time it takes to reach customers, close the sale, make the delivery, and collect.

Source: *The Effective Manager,* Boston.

Sales analyses—control by exception

How it works: Most monthly sales analyses contain reports on many hundreds of items. Management needs this analysis to counteract problems or take corrective actions in areas that deviate substantially from previously established quotas.

The problem. To find the trouble spots among all those items reported, the manager has to spend too much time digging.

Beefing up the inside sales force

Problem: Rising cost of field sales calls.

Standard solution: (1) Encourage outside salespeople to use the phone more, (2) plan daily routes better, (3) make better use of time in general.

Innovative solution: Encourage increased performance from the inside sales force, who in the past have served as simple order takers. Put them on a bonus system.

The economical way to cope with rising costs of sales calls is to sell more to existing accounts. This can be done by pairing inside and outside sales forces.

The outside salesperson continues to cover the territory, and to provide each account with a personal contact. Meanwhile the inside salesperson handles specific account assignments and assumes more responsibility for (1) providing immediate service to accounts and (2) researching.

The company thus effectively double-teams each account, and increases its chances of penetrating existing accounts more deeply.

Recommended:

• Develop guidelines for measuring the performance of the inside sales force.

• Set up a bonus system for inside salespeople that doesn't discourage the outside ones. Begin modestly (90% base salary, 10% commission on increases in business).

• Set a higher bonus for new business brought in by outside people, to offset grumbling that bonuses now earned by inside people should have gone to them.

Source: Jerome A. Colletti, Sibson & So., Inc., Princeton, N.J.

Improving sales performance

Salespeople can often turn in a good performance simply by focusing on their strengths or coasting on the regular orders of a limited number of good customers.

The problem is that management is satisfied and neglects to search for areas of potential improvement.

Even top performers may be ignoring potential customers in their territories. Or they may be downplaying less popular items in the company's product line. Suggestions:

• Consider assigning additional salespeople to search for new customers, even in a star performer's territory. They may be able to develop new accounts without taking a penny from the regular salesperson's commission.

• Make joint sales calls routinely with the salespeople to be sure they aren't ignoring products or sales techniques. Be wary about barging in on customer negotiations. It could undercut the salesperson's authority.

Source: William Exton Jr., William Exton Jr. & Associates, New York.

How to get more from salespeople

Selling is not all the fun it's cracked up to be. The salesman's lot includes three of most people's greatest aversions: being alone; being thrown into new situations; and facing the possibility of rejection.

Managers must realize the tremendous stresses on their sales force from constant travel, production and delivery problems, and hostile receptions on cold calls.

There's no single solution to these problems. But managers can improve conditions by being totally honest about the difficulties and the po-

tential for failure. They should give salespeople frequent opportunities to ventilate their frustrations.

• Listen sympathetically. Focus on the very real rewards of getting the order. Don't gloss over the difficulties of the sales effort.

• Arm salespeople with everything possible in the way of product information. Train them to present it effectively. Equally important is to rehearse their answers to all the possible reasons not to buy. Salespeople should be prepared for the negative reactions they will inevitably get. It's vital to teach them how to close the sale.

A key motivational technique is to have salespeople grade each prospect or current account on the basis of potential dollar volume. Example: A $100,000 account might be an "A"; $75,000 a "B"; $50,000 a "C"; and $35,000 or less a "D." Then, within the "A" category, create subclassifications: "A-1" now buys $100,000 from the company; "A-2" is worth $100,000 but currently buys only $60,000 from the company; "A-3" may buy only $40,000 from the company; and "A-4" perhaps $25,000 or less. Once each customer is graded for potential, salespeople can recognize the challenge in trying to build up that account.

For the best result, give salespeople a frank analysis of the profitability of each of their accounts. Structure compensation plans to favor profitable business rather than sheer volume.

Smart salespeople will want frequent reviews by their managers to be sure they're on the right track. For managers, of course, this is time-consuming. If bimonthly reviews are not possible, quarterly is a good compromise. At the very least, salespeople need an annual performance and compensation review.

Source: Dave Yoho, Dave Yoho Associates, Fairfax, Va.

Spurring input from the sales force

A useful check on top management's marketing priorities is to query the sales force regularly for ideas from the field on obstacles salespeople face in the marketplace, company procedures that hinder sales, company promotions and advertising that are useful, and so on.

Consider having an outside consultant prepare the questionnaire and tabulate the results. The likely cost is $8,500–$20,000. And employees will be more candid and helpful to management if they are assured of absolute anonymity.

The basic questions are: How do customers respond to the company's new products? What are the chief obstacles to completing sales? What are their opinions about sales support and training, sales leadership, etc.? Open-ended questions on how business looks in their territory over the next six- to twelve-month period. Ask what major changes they would make in sales strategy and management.

Source: Donald B. Waite, Jr., Sales Staff Surveys, Inc., West Redding, Conn.

Basic sales leadership styles

Three styles that work:
• Take charge. Makes and implements all plans, solves problems, tells salespeople what to do, how to do it, how quickly to get it done. Demands obedience. This has special value with insecure salespeople and beginners.
• Let's work together. Acts as captain of the team, suggests goals, involves sales staff in decision making, periodically checks up on performance and builds interdependence and cooperation among salespeople. This motivates hard workers who try to cooperate to display more aggressiveness. Gives satisfaction to those who want to work with a friendly, closely knit group, particularly ex-athletes.
• Self-starter. Gives salespeople free rein to plan and carry out sales and merchandising programs. Encourages initiative. Assists in problem solving only when asked. Gets best results from the show-off or highly individualistic

salesperson. Only choice with loners who can deal with no more than one person at a time. Modify this approach when the hands-off style creates resentment within the sales force. Try to involve the loner in some group activities.

Source: *Managing a Sales Team,* Lebhar-Friedman Books, New York.

How to increase sales-force morale

Salespeople at some of the country's largest companies were asked what they would do if put in charge of sales management. Their response: Remove the layers between top management and the people in the field. Reason: To help higher-ups recognize real needs of the sales force. According to field representatives, too often no one seems interested in listening to them. And, say the field representatives, their opinions are not even taken seriously.

Source: Don Waite, president, Sales Staff Surveys, W. Redding, Conn., *Sales & Marketing Management,* New York.

Don't undercut salespeople's confidence

Managers who accompany salespeople on customer visits risk undermining employee efforts.
Keep in mind:
• Your purpose on the visit is to help improve the company's image, not to measure the performance of your personnel. You can do that by looking at the numbers. Be sure the salesperson knows your reasons for tagging along.
• You're probably not the world's only sales executive with all the answers. Be open to learning from your sales force.

• Let the salesperson think you're accompanying him on a routine basis, not because he's in trouble. Don't let him believe his future depends on the success of the calls he makes while you are with him. You'll only throw him off stride and damage company relations with customers on his rounds.

Much good can come from your showing of personal interest—in customers, in your own people, in the way things are done by the company. Just remember not to let your presence interfere.

Overcoming the summer sales doldrums

The apparent problem is that customers are away on vacation. In reality, a recent survey of business executives, it was reported that 94% were available in June; 89.6% could be seen in July; and 88.1% in August. The real problem is that salespeople slough off in the summer, too.
Solutions:
• Reschedule the salespeople's calling time so that more calls are made during midweek. This will help them to avoid missing customers who are away on long weekends.
• Compile a list of vacation periods of key customers and alert salespeople about their customers' vacations ahead of time. This will enable salespeople to call on customers just before they leave and immediately after they return.
• Ask the company's top executives to help team-sell. Executives can see customers who might otherwise sidestep routine calls.
• Offer an extra incentive to top performers. Extra vacation time, for example (but not during the summer).
• Produce leads for salespeople that will keep them busy selling all summer.
Also, dealers and distributors complain that the summertime presents special selling problems.

Solutions:
• Answer these complaints by compiling information on summertime buying preferences.
• Adjust the use of the media and merchandising aids to meet summer demands of dealers and distributors, as well as customers.

———
Source: William J. Tobin, president, Salesmakers' Syndicate Services, Wilton, Conn.

Sales managers' biggest mistakes

Because most sales managers were once salespeople, many of them believe their job is to manage sales instead of the staff. Their real job is to manage the selling skills of others through motivation, training and supervision. Most common mistakes:
• Using the sales force to collect data from the field. In fact, letting a salesperson, who is one of the most expensive employees in the company, do anything but sell is foolhardy.
• Using call reports as a form of control rather than a communications tool. Example: insisting that salespeople make out a report for each call. Instead, reports should be made out only when a salesperson needs to give the manager data about the call.
• Imposing too many standards. Instead of standardizing sales efforts, managers should train salespeople to expect specific efforts to yield specific results.
• Mismanaging territories by using geography rather than sales potential. To do the job of dividing up territories right, managers must be involved in market research and maintain a broad overview of sales operations.
• Failing to manage their time effectively. Too many managers get bogged down in administration. They ignore supervising the development of the sales staff.

———
Source: Dr. Robert F. Vizza, dean of the School of Business, Manhattan College, Riverdale, N.Y.

Why well-paid salespeople quit

Turnover continues among salespeople even after the compensation program is made highly competitive. Where the real problem may be:

• Salespeople perceive there is nowhere to advance in the company because: (1) all sales territories are considered equal; (2) the path to management appears to have far more candidates than openings; (3) higher positions seem to offer only more work and, often, insufficient income. Solve the problem by creating clear career paths. When salespeople are focused on their next promotion, their earnings in a particular year are less important.

• Management sends the message that it considers manufacturing priorities ahead of marketing needs. Typical signs may be sales quotas are set to reflect production capacities rather than the demands of the marketplace in each territory; the sales force is viewed as a cost center, with an emphasis on minimizing selling costs. Instead, view sales as an investment and reinforce its importance.

Source: John K. Moynihan, Towers, Perrin, Forster & Crosby, New York, *Sales & Marketing Management,* New York.

How to handle freewheeling salespeople

Some of the best salespeople operate in a freewheeling fashion that totally ignores standard office practices and plays havoc with company routine. What to do?

The best approach is to praise their results and resourcefulness in thinking up new uses for the product, etc., and thereby increasing sales.

After praise has been digested, mention matter of factly some of the problems their freewheeling behavior has created for others. Cite specific examples. Ask for their suggestions or solutions.

Because productive freewheelers know they can easily find jobs elsewhere, it's more important to appeal to their respect for the company, its products, and product support than to come down hard on them for not following regulations precisely.

Source: *Sales Motivation,* National Sales Development Institute, Waterford, Conn.

What to expect from top industrial salespeople

• A consistent flow of new ideas, especially for cutting costs.
• Enough technical expertise to help customers' engineers with design problems.
• Involvement in quality control.
• Commercial as well as technical know-how.
• Makes the case for any necessary change in materials or methods by taking it to top management.
• Willing to get hands dirty on projects. (The salesperson may organize seminars for customers, make plant tours, etc.)
• Has a record of 100% on-time delivery.
• Immediately jumps to the rescue if there's a problem.

Source: *Purchasing,* Boston.

INCENTIVE PLANS

Incentives vs salary

Put more weight on incentives for sales personnel when:
- The job requires a high level of skill.
- The company is not well known.
- The product price is high.
- Competition is keen.
- Advancement possibilities with the company are low.

Put less weight on incentives and more on salary when:
- Sellng is more a team effort.
- Advertising and promotion are used extensively.
- The product or service requires little sales effort.

Keys to successful sales incentive programs

- Specific, realistic goals.
- Sales quotas that give all the salespeople an equal opportunity to win.
- Time limits that are adequate for salespeople to cover territories and get maximum sell-through.
- Simple and comprehensible rules.
- A theme that reflects how the program works, for example, a sports theme for a plan that groups salespeople into competing teams.
- Enthusiasm-building (use meetings, mailings, phone calls, ads, and items in the company newsletter).

- Frequent progress reports.
- Meaningful awards when participants qualify.
- Publicity for results. Note that recognition may be more important than actual awards.

Source: *Sales & Marketing Management,* New York.

When to introduce new sales incentive plans

It's best to introduce new incentive plans during good times. The sales force will be quickly convinced of its value when they reap immediate benefits. Incentive plans introduced during recessions usually turn out to be too generous to the salespeople when good times return.

Source: Richard C. Smyth and Matthew J. Murphey, *Compensating and Motivating Salesmen,* University Microfilms, Ann Arbor.

Improving sales incentive plans

- Determine the company's sales and marketing objectives. Examples: Increase dollar volume, multiply sales of the most profitable products, push new products, secure larger average orders, acquire new customers, reduce customer turnover, make more calls per week, improve follow-up service to existing customers.

• Choose only two or three primary selling objectives. Then build financial incentives into the salespeople's compensation plan to encourage them to spend more time on those objectives. Example: If the goal is acquiring new customers, the salesperson is rewarded for all new accounts, regardless of size, on the theory that small accounts can eventually be upgraded to large accounts.

• Determine how much time the salespeople now actually spend on each sales function.

Source: Richard C. Smyth and Matthew J. Murphy, *Compensating and Motivating Salesmen,* University Microfilms, Ann Arbor.

When to review the sales compensation plan

A review is apt to be both costly and time-consuming and to cause counterproductive anxieties among salespeople. Nevertheless, it should be considered when:

• Good salespeople are leaving for competitors—even when the new jobs are not promotions.

• Most of the sales effort is concentrated on a few products.

• Some territories have become much more productive than others.

• A number of salespeople aren't making a decent income even though they are meeting quotas.

• One person is increasing earnings much faster than the average or than others of comparable ability.

Source: John K. Moynihan, *Designing an Effective Sales Compensation Program,* AMACOM, New York.

Setting a commission plan for salespeople

In many situations, a commission plan based on a sliding or variable rate is preferable to one that rises evenly with volume.

A variable plan can provide a fairer reward for the salesperson's true efforts. And it gives the company greater flexibility to control the selling flow, including power to speed up, slow down, or shift emphasis of the flow.

Three common variable plans:

• Accelerating commissions. Provides higher compensation for sales above a given quota. Best to use them when fixed costs are high compared to selling costs, and selling costs are variable because the last dollar of volume is hardest to sell, but it's the most profitable to the company, so the sale should be rewarded at the higher rate.

• Decelerating commissions. The rates drop after the quota is passed. Useful when a company wants to limit volume during a period of short supply or start-up, or when one product threatens to become overly dominant in the sales mix. Also when repeat business or larger order sizes are easier to achieve than new business.

• Varying rates by product. Three advantages: (1) It provides a higher commission and a greater incentive to emphasize products that are hardest to move; (2) it can focus on products that have the highest profit margins; (3) it boosts volume for products important in the company's long-range marketing strategy.

Source: John K. Moynihan, *Designing an Effective Sales Compensation Program,* AMACOM, New York.

Controlling incentive commissions

Commissions based on volume and used as part of a salary-plus-incentive plan risk becoming excessive, particularly where sales are volatile. There are worse problems for management than runaway success. But it should not be sought at any cost.

Devices used by companies to avoid runaway commissions:

• Set a cap on the amount that will be paid above salary.

• Limit the volume on which commissions can be earned.

• Put a ceiling on windfalls from any one order or customer.

• Reduce territorial size.

• Scale down commission rates beyond a specified volume level.

These devices are motivation dampers, so set limits that everyone regards as liberal. One company still finds it cost-effective to cap commissions at 100% of salary.

———
Source: *Effective Sales Incentive Compensation,* McGraw-Hill Inc., New York.

Advances on commissions when the salesperson quits

What happens to commission advances when a salesperson leaves the company? Unless salespeople sign a prior agreement, they are under no obligation to refund advances when they terminate.

Traps to avoid in setting a sales-quota system

• Paying incentives for simple quarter-to-quarter sales improvements. Problem. Salespeople may slack off in one quarter, concentrate on setting up sales, then close them in the next period.

• Rating individual salespeople on total sales from their territory. Problem: One exceptional account may be providing the bulk of sales while the salesperson neglects other accounts. Solution: Assess potential of each territory to measure sales performance accurately.

———
Source: *Sales and Marketing Analysis,* New York.

Striking a balance in sales compensation

Overcompensation of salespeople usually results in morale problems and high turnover among the company's managers (who see themselves earning proportionately less than the salespeople). And it's hard to recruit experienced salespeople for other tasks within the company (marketing, management, etc.), which may pay less.

Undercompensating salespeople, even when a company's products are easy to sell and other salespeople are available, is also a bad idea because: (1) the best salespeople will probably leave the company and the poor ones will stay on; (2) the company's customers often want continuity of contact once they have accepted a salesperson they feel understands their problems. (They may even follow the salesperson to a new employer.)

Recession and inflation— impact on salespeople

The combination of inflation and recession makes compensation decisions especially difficult when they involve salespeople.

Key questions:

• Should commissions and quotas be adjusted because of rising prices? Or because of falling demand?

• Has the recession made real earnings insufficient to keep the top salespeople?

• Are there now more managers partly due to inflation, than are needed in a recession?

Running a sales contest

Basic rule: The success of a sales contest is usually in direct proportion to the number of awards and the amount of promotion to the staff.

Recommendations:

• Give each contest a specific theme that the staff can relate to. Dramatize the theme with strong promotion.

• Broadcast the leaders.

• Use categories of awards (such as the most improved salesperson).

• Give interim prizes.

• Award prizes that an entire family can enjoy. Keep the range of prizes broad so that every contestant sees that there is a real chance of winning.

Source: David D. Seltz, *How to Conduct Successful Sales Contests and Incentive Programs,* The Dartnell Corporation, Chicago.

14 SALESMANSHIP

SALES METHODS

The intelligent way to prospect for clients

Too many salespeople approach a territory with the notion of selling to every possible account. But the servicing of smaller accounts and all-inclusive prospecting is too expensive today. Instead, identify and go after a segment of the market. That's more productive than all the various individual accounts that might buy a product.

A segment is a group of users and prospective users that differ in size but are in the same general business. It's better to concentrate on selling to the segment that offers the highest sales potential than to try selling to all businesses in a territory that might buy.

Identifying the best segment to prospect, and getting to know its particular needs and product uses, sharpens the sales effort significantly.

Questions to ask when prospecting segments:
• What new segments or categories of business can use the product?
• What is the company's present share of the market in each segment?
• Which segments represent the greatest potential?
• What businesses within the segment haven't been sold yet?

Always do as much research beforehand as possible to avoid the soaring costs of making personal calls to find prospects. It's often possible to identify the accounts and determine their needs and ability to pay before contacting them.

Get supportive market data. The kind depends on what sort of product is being sold. For consumer goods, get population and income data. For industrial goods, sales and employment data. Best data sources are the U.S. Department of Labor, Bureau of Economic Analysis Data (available from the U.S. Department of Commerce).

Once customer contact is made, be sure to determine who has the authority to buy. In today's complex organizations, more people are getting involved in buying decisions.

Source: Dr. Robert Vizza, dean, Manhattan College's School of Business, Riverdale, N.Y.

Using the mail to generate sales leads

More and more, industrial and consumer products companies are using the mail to qualify prospects for their salespeople.

Mailings can be designed to elicit responses in which sales prospects ask for more information, agree to see a salesperson, or accept a trial offer of a company's product or service. If a prospect checks a box that suggests serious interest in the proposition, a top-notch salesperson is assigned to follow up. If a prospect checks a box suggesting he's only vaguely interested, a second-rank salesperson is assigned.

The key to an effective mailing package is the right combination of features to maximize both the responses and the conversion rate of responses into sales.

To increase the responses:
• Offer something free or at a substantial discount.
• Promise that no salesperson will call. If sales calls are not part of the company's selling strategy, be sure to say so.
• Include an easy response device, like a prepaid reply card.
• Make the mailing package short. Pique the prospect's curiosity to prompt him to send for more information.

To increase the conversion rate of responses into sales:
• Ask for a telephone number. (This information can also be used as a credit qualifier.)
• Ask for other qualifying data, such as financial information.
• Show the product's price.

Following up on mail-generated leads:
• Distribute leads to the sales force by phone or wire, rather than mail.
• Get weekly rather than monthly call reports from salesmen.
• Reward salesmen who convert leads into sales.

Recommended: Limit the time a salesman has to convert a lead into a sale. Send a second, direct-mail selling package to his leads if he hasn't converted them into buyers within 60 days.

Source: Edward L. Nash, executive vice-president, Rapp & Collins, New York.

How to evaluate leads that come in the mail

The best buying prospect who responds to a print campaign is the person who calls on the phone. That person is almost always eager to buy. Follow up fast. But responses that arrive in the mail differ in interest. These questions will help focus on the better prospects, people who may be worth calling before sending sales material:
• Are phone numbers included? Then people responding expect a call.
• Are job titles given? If so, the people are probably more interested. They are asserting their importance.
• How big is the company? Responses from smaller companies often lead to quicker sales because the inquiry is usually from top management.
• Where is the inquiry from? Those from branch offices may not be as solid as those from headquarters.
• Is the inquiry form complete? If not, the interest level is lower.

Source: Rene Gnam, marketing consultant, *Zip,* New York.

How to sell more to current accounts

Broaden contacts with customer personnel. People at different levels in a company see its needs differently. Once uncovered, the various viewpoints can be used by the salesperson to develop more persuasive selling strategy.

Make sure to identify everyone affected by the purchase of specific products (or services). This means, for example, identifying the financial manager responsible for the budget line out of which payment for the product is made, as well as the proper purchasing department liaison and product users.

Meet with each person in the customer company with a stake in the buying decision. If turned down, try for a group demonstration. If rebuffed again, shape sales proposals to the people with a stake in the buying decision. A salesperson will eventually get access to everyone in a customer company whose needs he satisfies.

Help customers visualize additional product applications. Salespeople are usually quick to recognize new uses for their products. But often they mistakenly blurt out their theories too quickly. They try to close a sale before the customer understands what it is that's being sold or how it can help.

A better approach is to help the customer help himself. Ask questions: What would happen if you started doing this? What would happen if you stopped doing that? The adroit questioner can close an additional order without having seemed to settle it.

Use inside allies to overcome obstacles to bigger orders. Once a salesperson develops an ally in a customer company, he needs to understand that ally's motivation. Example: The ally hesitates to press his point of view with his superiors. The salesperson's response should be to show the ally why there is no risk involved in pushing it further and/or that there is a risk involved in not doing so.

The basic approach of a salesperson in working with an ally inside a customer company is to give him all the information that may be useful.

Source: Don Hammalian, senior product manager, Xerox Learning Systems, Greenwich, Conn.

Strategy for selling through large retailers

Close coordination between salespeople (in the field) and the sales brass (calling at the executive-suite level) is important.

Selling takes place at all levels. An effective sales effort requires a relationship between the selling company and the customer starting at corporate level and covering all points down to the contact between route salespeople and retail-store managers.

Participatory management. With selling going on at all levels, the seller's executives need input from the field level to be effective in their own presentations. They need feedback to adjust future presentations. More important, they need to know what goals are achievable. Goal-setting begins in the field where the real problems and the real answers are. Executives find out, for starters, the amounts of their products that could be sold under ideal conditions, and what those conditions would be.

To handle this, salespeople are motivated to do well individually, and motivated to be part of a team. The key is to balance individual and team bonuses.

Study the customer's style and blend into it. Learn how each customer approaches its market. Does it sell by price cutting? Quality merchandising? Who are the customer's competitors?

With this knowledge, you can put forward a unique sales proposition. Example: The seller has a new promotion idea, but the customer is short on warehouse space. If the customer trusts the seller, during the promotion it will allow shipments direct to the retail outlets (circumventing the warehouse). The key is trust.

Earn partnership status with the customer. Then sales calls are transformed into business review meetings. Instead of trying to sell the customer, opportunities are explored for both parties to grow.

But too often, the price and terms become the entire basis of a company's relationship with its customers. A successful consumer sales operation will try to provide each customer with ideas, benefits, and maximum profitability. A company must keep its sales promotion fresh. This means staying current with more than price and terms.

Develop a working relationship. If a company is selling at all levels, involving all the decision makers, and has won the confidence of its customer, it can develop a plan detailing how the company will be serving the customer for a year ahead. The plan will get revised, of course. But once the company and the customer both agree to it, they will use it as the basis for their working relationship.

Source: Robert E. Randolph, vice president, western region, Del Monte Sales Co., San Francisco.

Cutting low-profit sales

When a large percentage of the company's customers are providing only a small percentage of its profits, the company is wasting time and effort that could be better spent.

Steps to consider:
• Stop calling on occasional buyers, and reduce the number of products in the product line. Concentrate on selling the most profitable items to the biggest buyers. Then deliveries and inventories can be simplified and service to the most important customers improved. Also, hike minimum-order sizes. Some small customers may agree to up their orders.
• Stay away from poor payers. High-risk customers are those who are 30 days behind in payments, or owe the company 20% or more of net worth. Collect from them before supplying more goods.
• Piggyback orders on short-run sales. When one order does not justify a profitable production run, contact other customers using the same product to see if they will also order. It may be necessary to offer speedier delivery or lower prices.
• Identify the break-even point for all accounts. Determine whether each account is profitable, not how much volume it represents.

Source: Thomas J. Martin and Bruce Trabue, *Sell More and Spend Less*, Holt, Rinehart & Winston, New York.

What to know about your accounts

What to know about an account before the next call on it:
• Its business, products, market, and primary customers.
• How big it is. Its ranking within the industry.
• Who does the actual buying? Who makes the decisions to buy? Who influences these decisions?
• How often the company buys. Quantities ordered.
• Total sales for last year.
• Its primary competition. Approximately how much business your company is doing with them.
• The financial standing of the account.
• What plans it has that could affect the use of the products being sold.
• What problems immediately concern it.
• What value customer places on the products now being bought.

What to know about the person being called on:
• Job responsibilities and purchasing authority.
• The business problems the buyer needs solutions for.
• Where the buyer fits in the organizational structure.
• Some of the buyer's personal interests and his business background.

Source: Robert F. Vizza and Thomas E. Chambers, *Time and Territorial Management for the Salesman*, Sales Executives Club of New York.

Industrial sales

The rules for industrial selling are simple: (1) Know the product, (2) know the customer, (3) know the competition, and (4) master the basic sales techniques.

Knowing the product means knowing more than the product's features. It means knowing how the product is used by customers, as well as the benefits it brings when integrated into the customer's operations. Salespeople should spend time in a customer's facility to see how the product is integrated into operations. Then they will be able to dream up ways for greater and more effective use.

Knowing the customer involves reading the trade magazines the customer reads, paying attention to the customer's corporate public relations and product literature. It also involves noticing their key people, the buzz words they use, their business philosophy. Faced with stiffening competition, is their instinct to cut costs or stress quality? Knowing this is crucial in tailoring a sales pitch. Also, it helps to be on a friendly basis with the decision-makers two and three organizational levels above the person with whom the salesperson regularly deals.

Know the competition. The first rule is to assume that the competition is intelligent. Then see how the competition's products are integrated into the customer's operations. Try to learn from customers what the competition is planning to do. Then a salesperson can hit the competition where it's most vulnerable.

Master sales techniques. All too often, despite what he's been taught, a salesperson will walk in and flat out blast a customer with how great his product is. That's not what a customer wants to hear. The customer wants to know how his company's problems can be solved. Use whatever selling techniques are appropriate. Offer solutions and options to the solutions. Don't make commitments beyond what's possible. If an answer will be delayed beyond the period promised, advise the customer immediately.

Stay fresh. This is a big problem. A good sales manager will promote or reassign a salesperson every three to five years, if not to a new territory, at least to a new function in that territory (switching the salesperson to bigger accounts or asking him or her to train younger people, too). The best way a salesperson can keep fresh is by growing through his or her customers. Ask them periodically what more the company can be doing. Understand their markets and market strategies. Know how their business is evolving over the years.

Source: R.J. Steele, general manager, Telecom Division of AMP, Inc., Harrisburg, Penna.

Landing subcontracts

Companies looking for subcontracts from a major corporation can make an approach cold by identifying the small business liaison in the corporation's purchasing department. The liaison will explain:

• The corporation's philosophy in dealing with subcontractors.

• Which divisions are potential customers.

• The projects within those divisions that have reached the procurement phase.

• How much assistance he can offer in shepherding the small-business representative around.

But pushing too hard at this point is a mistake. Liaison people are go-betweens, not buyers. Information to spell out: (1) characteristics of any proprietary products, (2) capabilities of the company, (3) other company customers.

Next, ask the small-business liaison to set up meetings with actual buyers. Promote the company's full line of products or services, and the company's management in general, since major corporations are constantly looking for new subcontractors.

Once a corporate purchasing agent gains confidence in a subcontractor, he will introduce him to other buyers within the corporation. A valued subcontractor can even get technical and management assistance. The giant will work to make sure a valued subcontractor survives.

Source: Bryce Smith, manager, Small Business and Economic Utilization, Rockwell International, Inc., North American Aircraft Division, El Segundo, Calif.

Selling by seminar

During conventional sales calls, prospects block out much of what they hear. At seminars, however, they remain open in anticipation of learning. Thus, seminars can be a cost-effective way to close sales.

Selling via seminars is especially useful when:

• There is a perceived complexity to the goods

or services being offered: computers, financial services, new industrial technologies.

• Buyers are young, business-school educated and trained to act on information rather than personal contacts. Therefore, a seminar must inform rather than pitch or it loses its credibility.

When planning a seminar:

• Use a hotel meeting room instead of a company hall.

• Arrange for outside experts to appear as part of the program.

• Invite salespeople to attend only the closing cocktail party. Insist that they pitch to no one.

• Follow up by sending transcripts to all who attended and all those invited who did not come. Mail responses to all unanswered questions from the seminar.

• Use seminar experience to evaluate the needs and level of interest of potential customers.

Source: Michael J. Enzer, president, Saxton Communications Group, Ltd., New York.

Using sales literature more effectively

Mail reprints of ads to customers before sales calls. Make notes in the margin (use a colorful felt-tipped pen) to point out important product features.

Turn ads into visual aids during sales presentations. Open the magazine to the ad rather than using a reprint. This increases impact.

Point out product claims and guarantees in advertising copy to substantiate selling points. Ad copywriters are expert at translating product features into simple and compelling language.

Follow up sales calls with reprints marked to highlight points made during the visit.

Mark catalogs according to individual customer's interests. And attach a business card to a catalog left behind or mailed to a customer.

Search house organs and other company information for news that can be passed on to customers.

On price tags, list the product's advantages, instructions, sales tie-ins and other reasons to buy it. This will increase customer understanding of the product.

Source: *American Salesman,* Burlington, Ind.

Avoid being priced out of a sale

When a longtime customer announces that its next order will go to a competitor that has offered a better price, don't fall into the trap of immediately rushing to meet or beat the other firm's offer.

Instead, recognize that the customer is under heavy pressure to cut costs right now. Raise the question of false economy, reasoning that if the other firm's product is cheaper, there's a good chance that it's of lower quality, too. Can it really do the job? If it fails, what would be the consequences and the costs? How do potential damages compare with the "savings" offered by the untried supplier?

Another consideration—will the competitor provide any special services?

If the product has been specially formulated to meet the customer's requirements, bring up the times your company's technical people helped solve its problems.

Explain precisely why your company's product was made to a specific quality level. Ask whether the customer's product has changed in some way so that the same quality level is no longer necessary.

Then, if all has failed, and only then, offer to see what your people can come up with in the way of a lower-priced product.

Source: *Sales Motivation,* Sales Development Institute, Waterford, Conn.

Reasons for lost sales

To turn a weakening sales situation around, know what's causing the trouble. The first step is to isolate the problem. Key questions:

1. Are sales of all products down? Just a few?

2. In which areas are sales down? Use specific breakdowns such as urban, suburban, rural, residential, college, inner city, recreational.

3. Are sales down for all types of accounts? Is the decline limited to chains? Independents? Some other classification?

4. Where did the business go? Was it lost to a competitive product? Another size of the same product? One of the company's own products? A cheaper product?

5. When did the decline start?

6. How serious is the drop? Is the change due to seasonal factors? Did a similar decrease occur at the same time last year?

Source: *Managing a Sales Team,* Lebhar-Friedman Books, New York.

THE SALES CALL AND FOLLOW-UP

Planning more effective sales calls

• Decide on the objective of the call. ("Make a sale" is not good enough unless all the preliminary groundwork has been done. Asking for the order at the wrong time is as bad as not asking at all.)

• Review everything known about the customer (purchases from competitors, results of previous calls).

• Identify the product benefits that are not available in competitors' products and are special to the prospect.

• Focus on the selling points that will best illustrate product benefits. Write them, in advance, in a logical order.

• Prepare a file of spec sheets, photos, testimonials, test data, etc., that fully supports the sales story.

• Anticipate general areas of resistance. Plan how to counter each one.

• List all the specific sales objections the customer could raise. Arrange them in order of importance.

• Prepare at least two answers for each anticipated objection.

• Write out the pre-closing summary. Decide on the closing strategy to use.

Source: *Sales Manager's Bulletin,* Waterford, Conn.

How to work with a prospect

Selling means one thing: getting out and talking to prospects. This entails a constant push. To spur yourself, keep records of the number of sales calls made daily. There should be at least four. These records track your activities.

Example: 70% of sales are made on the first call, 23% on the second and only 7% on the third. But most salespeople spend half their time chasing that 7%. Forget those timid repeat calls and concentrate on the first and second.

Other steps:

• Make appointments. This shows that you value the prospect's time.

• Be prepared. Make notes to help keep the focus on key issues. Memorize as many of the supporting facts as possible. But don't be ashamed of referring to the notes to keep the interview from straying.

• Ask questions. This starts the prospect talking. It helps bring his ideas into focus. He then can make clear what really interests him.

• Arouse fear. Two emotions motivate people: Desire for gain and fear of loss. A sense of fear never fails to make clients ponder their company's needs and deficiencies.

• Make your points boldly. Be demonstrative: beat your fist in your palm, jump up to make a point, use a prop to grab attention. Show your enthusiasm and interest.

• Create confidence. Imagine the prospect is your boss. Muster all the excitement you can to please him. (People don't like to be sold to; they like to buy.)

• Make your prospect feel important. But be sparing. Too much praise is worse than none.

• See things from your prospect's point of view. This helps you appreciate what is best for him.

Source: Frank Bettger, *How I Raised Myself from Failure to Success in Selling*, Cornerstone Library, New York.

Sales-call strategies

Successful salespeople in the 1980s will recognize that they must become sustaining resources for the customer. Techniques:

• Request only 15 minutes of the prospective customer's time on the first appointment. Be prepared to leave when the 15 minutes are up.

• Ask the prospect short questions, and listen to the responses. People love to talk about themselves and their activities.

• Rely on aggressive listening, not fast talking.

• Don't present the service or product until the prospective customer's objectives are completely understood.

• Never begin a sales call with a presentation.

It establishes only one-way communication, rather than dialogue.

• Point out only those features and benefits of the product to which the prospect can relate. Focus on the specific value the product will have for this prospect.

• Encourage resistance, and deal with it openly and honestly.

• Make sure the initial sales call includes at least one request by either the salesperson or the customer for a small favor. This builds an ongoing relationship.

• Maintain a continuing dialogue with the prospect. A call every other month is generally not sufficient.

• Present new and useful information to the prospect each time you make a call.

• Make it clear that any information that's not readily available at the meeting will be quickly forwarded.

• Start to make the sale when the prospect's head starts moving up and down in agreement.

• Close the sale with an offer to begin service or shipment, not by offering to send the customer a proposal.

• Don't try to close the sale at every opportunity. Wait until it is determined that the product or the service meets the objectives of the prospective customer.

Source: Kenneth A. Meyers, president, Golightly & Co. International, Inc., New York.

Making a major presentation

The basic rules:

• Don't get up unless you really have something to say that is not generally known.

• Talk about something the listeners need to learn about and are interested in knowing.

• Understand the presentation's purpose. It is not to get agreement or write an order, as in selling. It must give the listeners basic information they need to know.

The most effective start is to tell the audience

some interesting or surprising new fact rather than recite a tired joke. Jokes have a place, especially in after-dinner speeches. But too much humor in a serious presentation indicates that you don't put a very high value on the listeners' time.

Think of the presentation as a coat rack. Hang all the important ideas on it. Relate everything to the single most important message you want to get across.

Invite questions. They indicate that the audience is involved. But try to relate all answers to the central point you want listeners to remember two or three days later. Everything you say should serve that purpose.

Be crisp. It's important to let the listeners know that you value their time and don't intend to waste it. Bring your wristwatch out at the beginning and get agreement from the audience as to how much time you will take. Starting off with an arresting new fact reinforces the point that you are not intending to waste anyone's time.

Maintain eye contact at all times. Don't use props that draw attention away from you. Personal contact is much more effective in holding an audience than slides or charts.

A common mistake is to begin at too high a pitch. This leaves nothing to which you can build up. It's better to start on a low key, even make the audience strain to hear you. The most effective way to quiet a noisy crowd is to speak softly. Persevere until the audience gradually becomes more attentive.

The best way to end is to reinforce or repeat something important that was said in the beginning. Tie together various aspects of your main point. (The Russian playwright Anton Chekhov made the same point nearly a century ago: if you show a revolver in Act I, it must go off in Act III.)

Source: Gerald Schoenfeld, Gerald Schoenfeld, Inc., New York.

The customer never forgets. Follow through on all commitments.

2. Don't knock competitors. It's counterproductive. Most buyers become intrigued with a product under assault.

3. Don't question a customer's final decision to buy competitive merchandise. Instead, increase your own selling efforts.

4. Don't get too close to buyers. Habitual socializing can be risky. When a buyer begins to expect such treatment, withdrawing it becomes painful.

5. Don't complain to buyers about job or domestic problems. Complainers quickly change from friends to nuisances.

6. Don't overwhelm buyers with technical information. They are more interested in what a product or service can do for them, not so much how.

7. Don't try to impress customers with professional qualifications, education, social status. Some buyers resent those who appear to be snobs. Learn about each buyer's personal history and adapt the conversation accordingly.

8. Don't ignore personal sensibilities. Never smoke unless a buyer lights a cigarette first. Do the same with drinks at lunch. If a noontime nip with a key customer is necessary, be careful about seeing other key customers after that.

9. Don't overdress. Extreme fashions call attention to the wearer. Conservative clothes are always safe.

10. Don't be a gossip. They are universally distrusted.

11. Don't use canned presentations. A prepared pitch is best, but try to preserve spontaneity.

12. Don't misrepresent the product. Know the warranty terms and how much backup to expect from the supplier.

Source: P.J. Koerper, *How to Talk Your Way to Success in Selling,* Prentice-Hall, Englewood Cliffs, N.J.

Twelve keys to positive selling

1. Don't make promises that can't be kept.

Understanding buyers

The common personality types among buyers

and purchasing agents, and how to deal with them:

• No-decision buyer. He never says yes or no. An inexperienced salesperson may waste time on repeated calls, without any chance of getting an order.

• Reputation buyer. He's more impressed by others who have bought the product than by the product itself. You should come to him armed with testimonials from satisfied users, preferably big names in the buyer's field.

• Aggressive buyer. He won't sign a contract until he has driven the hardest possible bargain on price and other terms. This type is the most discouraging for new salespeople and leads newcomers to give up selling.

Identifying buyer attitudes

It helps to match the sales pitch to the customer's attitude and personality. Basic customer attitudes to identify:

• Mainly concerned with the product itself. Usually wants substantial proof of its usefulness, quality and value. Bone up to provide all this information.

• Prefers buying from a salesperson he likes. Win his confidence.

• Indifferent to both product and salesperson. Earning his trust might result in a sale.

• Tentative. Buys only generally accepted or status items. Focus on the product's reputation.

• Concerned with making a sound purchase from a trusted salesperson. Logical presentation. Answer questions with facts.

Source: *The Grid for Sales Excellence,* McGraw-Hill, New York.

Purchasing executives rank bad traits of a salesperson

1. Overly aggressive.
2. Lacks problem-solving skills.
3. Talks too much.
4. Poorly attired.
5. Inadequate knowledge of seller's business.
6. Calls at inopportune time.
7. Substitutes sympathy appeal for straight talk.
8. Lacks knowledge of competitive products.
9. Inadequate knowledge of customer's business.
10. Uses entertainment as a crutch.
11. Fails to keep commitments.
12. No interest in helping customer.
13. Fails to listen.
14. Lacks planning ability.
15. Not punctual.
16. Lacks persuasive abilities.
17. Lacks understanding.

Supersalesmen use the soft sell

Contrary to most popular conceptions, the supersalesman is a softseller, not a hardseller. He says and does the unexpected and, as a result, gets the customer to reveal what he really wants. Then he tailors his pitch to meet those wants and makes the sale.

Marks of the supersalesman:

• Brings up objections before the customer thinks of them.

• Doesn't try to impress the customer about how much he knows about his product. Concentrates completely on what will make the sale.

• Spends the first part of the sales meeting

asking questions about the customer's problems.

• Spends most of the rest of the time getting the customer to suggest how the problems might be lessened.

Then he makes the sales presentation, tailored to customer's needs.

• If the customer is hostile, he gently tries to neutralize him. If that doesn't work, doesn't try to sell, but lays the foundation for a callback.

Source: David H. Sandler, sales seminar trainer from Stevenson, Md., *Baltimore,* Baltimore.

• Anticipate objections. Prove that the product can solve them before the customer brings them up. At the least, the purchaser is impressed by the salesperson's understanding of the situation.

• After the sale. Show a continuing interest in the customer.

• Attack headon any post-sale problems. If the boss complains that the salesperson worries more about the customer than the company, show how it works both ways. Confidence earned helps the salesperson in the future, and thus enriches the company.

Negotiating with buyers

A negotiating session is an exercise in persuasion. Sellers who do their homework enhance chances of success. Before making proposals to potential customers, consider:

• Personality. Introverts generally require details. Extroverts may be bored with them.

• Behavior. The buyer's actions in previous negotiations.

• Age. If the buyer's is very different from the seller's, some values are also likely to differ. For example, people who experienced the depression of the 1930s tend to drive for security all their lives.

• Need. The extent to which the buyer needs the item being sold.

Source: John J. McCarthy, *Electrical Wholesaling,* New York.

Fielding questions from customers

Salespeople who really know their product well should resist the temptation to dismiss a customer's question out of hand. Rules of the game:

• After listening carefully to the customer, pause to give him the impression that you're thinking about his query. Paraphrase his objections.

• Avoid showing resistance or disdain. These may offend the prospect while a mild show of surprise followed by a confident answer can suggest that his doubts are groundless.

• Question him tactfully on those parts of his argument that seem weak. Doing so may lead him to take back all objections.

Source: *The Skills of Selling,* AMACOM, New York.

Winning over a customer

How to win the customer's faith, and how not to lose it:

• Avoid exaggerated claims for the product or unrealistic promises.

Responses to four common sales stalls

• I haven't had time to think about it. Response: I know how busy you are, but just a few minutes can clear the whole thing up. For example...

• I've got to talk it over with my partner. Response: Fine, a wise decision. Now let's get the whole thing boiled down so your partner can clearly understand it.

• The price is too high. Response: I know some companies that sell for less, and I'll explain why they do.

• Business is bad right now; I'll have to wait. Response: I'm sorry to hear that, but we certainly can work out satisfactory terms. Tell them how to make business better.

Source: *How to Sell in the 1980s,* Prentice-Hall, Englewood Cliffs, N.J.

Ways to combat the silent treatment

Customers often remain silent when salespeople finish presentations. Sometimes it's a negotiating tactic to throw salespeople off the track, but there are other reasons, too.

Buyers clam up because they:

• Do not want to reveal their ignorance. If you push to close the deal, it forces them to ask for more information.

• See no need for what is being sold. Use direct questions to smoke out the reasons. Sample: What do you need to know that I omitted?

• Can't afford the product. So scale down the size of the order, or offer them a trial period. Make absolutely sure that money is the issue before offering to cut back.

• Don't have the authority to buy. Present all the facts, and suggest another date to discuss the purchase. This provides them time to talk with their boss.

• Are taking time to think the deal through. Keep quiet. Let them think.

• May be annoyed by salespeople's presentations or simply dislike particular personalities. If necessary, eat humble pie and ask politely for their objections. The best tactic is to leave the offer with the customer. Then tell the sales manager of the personality conflict.

Source: John J. McCarthy, *Electrical Wholesaling,* New York.

How to deal with an angry customer

• Stay calm. It's tempting to fight back, but that only worsens the situation. Instead, empathize with the customer's viewpoint.

• Isolate the real reason for the complaint. Often, it's a misunderstanding that can be settled by facts and logic.

• Don't assume the customer is being intentionally nasty. The actual attitude may not be the one that's being projected.

• Conciliatory comments help defuse the tension. For instance, you and your company have always been very fair. But you may be a little unjust right now without realizing it.

Don't use an angry customer as an excuse for not pursuing a sale or holding onto an account. That's avoiding the situation, not coping with it.

Source: John J. McCarthy, *Electrical Wholesaling,* New York.

Common objections to price hikes and how to counter them

• *I don't believe costs have gone up that much.* Defense: On the first visit, show solid data demonstrating the product's cost structure.

• *I don't have the profit margin to meet an increase.* Defense: Don't be swayed by emotional appeals or unsubstantiated facts. Show that the company has not increased its own profit margin on the product.

• *We will accept the price increase, but we also want new nonprice benefits.* Reaction: Be prepared to offer cheaper alternative products or suggestions on more efficient ways to use the current one.

• *I don't have the authority to accept the increase.* Reality: The buyer is stalling and has no better defense. The hike will go through eventually.

• *We'll switch vendors because of the price hike.* Reality: This is a desperate move by the buyer, which probably cannot be carried out precipitously. Reason: Research and development approvals and production trials cost money and take time.

Source: Roger Clark, industrial products division of Johns-Manville Sales Corp., *Industrial Marketing,* Chicago.

Using warranties as a sales tool

Aggressively publicize the company's warranty program. Show how it will cut customers' purchase costs. Demonstrate its superiority to competitors' warranties.

Avoid extending warranties—either in time or breadth of coverage—without accurate projections of added costs. Warranty programs should be projected as a percentage of sales.

Companies that extend warranty programs to boost flagging sales in a recession often end up with smaller profit margins, which defeats the purpose of boosting sales.

The company's warranty program will be most cost-efficient if it's a logical extension of a quality-control program. Companies turning out high-quality products can offer the best warranties at the least cost. Traditionally, strong warranties are used to offset premium prices that are charged for products that are top of the line.

Keeping warranty costs down. Identify high-warranty areas and take corrective action to redesign the product accordingly.

Recommended: Companies committed to using warranties as a sales tool should offer to cover the labor costs as well as the parts cost. Then they have something to promote.

Source: Fred Bartholomew, marketing-administration manager of the special-products division of Raymond Corp., Greene, N.Y.

Questions to ask about the competition

• Who got the customer's last order? Why?

• What are the weaknesses and strengths of the salesperson who represents the competition?

• Does the customer sell to the competitive firm (reciprocal buying)? Does the customer feel obligated to continue to buy for that reason?

• How badly does the competition want the sale? Is it a pilot purchase by the customer that could lead to much more future business?

• Can the salesperson match whatever additional services the competition can supply the customer?

Source: John J. McCarthy, *Professional Sales Situation Management,* McGraw-Hill, Inc., New York.

Putting down the competition—a bad policy

Attack a competitor's products indirectly, if at all.

Your best bet is to concentrate on the superiority of the company's product in comparison to the competition's.

Why put-downs are risky:

• Disparaging comments are likely to be discounted as biased even when they are valid.

• The prospect might be friendly with the competitor and be personally offended by any direct attacks.

• If the prospect is using the competitive

product, critical comments may impugn his own judgment.
• If a prospect chooses to focus on the competitive product, agree with its merits, then switch to the virtues of your own product.

Source: Roger W. Seng, *The Skills of Selling,* AMACOM, New York.

What closing a sales call really means

A common misconception is that closing a sales call means simply getting the order. In reality, closing is accomplishing the objective of the sales call. That may or may not be to get the order on that call. Other closing objectives include:
• Getting approval to survey the company's needs.
• Presenting a written proposal.
• Demonstrating the product.
• Answering objections.
• Finding out the firm's buying and decision-making structure.
To be sure all the objectives of the call are met:
• At the end of the call, agree on the aims of the next one with the buyer. Some salespeople rely on their flexibility and experience instead of planning the next call.
• At the beginning of the next call, restate the agreed-upon objective. This tactic heads off any problem if either the buyer or the salesperson is unable to deal with the matter that day.
Before setting the objectives, analyze the decision process the buyer has to go through. What does the buyer need to know and do? Who else has to agree to the purchase? This will establish call objectives most likely to advance the buyer's decision-making process.
When it comes to time spent on calls, more is not better, particularly on a call where a decision to buy has been made. This often produces conflict and anxiety. The longer the salespeople stay, the more likely buyers will change their minds. Anything the salespeople say may provide an excuse to back out.

When the moment for the sales close comes, maintain silence. It makes buyers focus on the fact that it is their move now and time for a decision.

Source: Dr. Robert F. Vizza, dean, School of Business, Manhattan College, Riverdale, N.Y.

When the prospect is ready to close a sale

Salespeople must be able to recognize when a prospect is leaning toward a purchase so they can put the most effective closing strategy into play. Buyers are probably about to say yes when they:
• Reexamine the product or return to a point in the contract with evident interest.
• Say they want to buy but follow with an emotional reason why they can't. Example: It's a good product, but too expensive.
• Begin to agree with minor sales points.
• Ask about details of service, such as shipping or delivery times.
• Spar for a concession or start to ask hypothetical questions.
If prospects begin to hesitate, seem to stall, or say they need to consult a third party, they can often be won over by a repetition of the product's strong points and the key reasons to buy.

Source: William J. Tobin, *Salesmakers Syndicate Services,* Wilton, Conn.

Faster sales follow-up

A centralized dictation system can speed follow-up correspondence while saving field sales representatives' time.
Following the sales calls, the rep phones a transcribing and word-processing center and dictates letters and instructions for materials to be mailed to the prospective buyer. The message is recorded

on tape. Telephone lines are open after-hours and on weekends. The use of standardized letters, where appropriate, can cut dictating time to as little as a few seconds.

A practical alternative is to use a mini-cassette pocket dictating machine. Mail in the tapes at least once a day.

Quick response to customer requests

Prompt response is a winning sales tactic too often neglected by U.S. businesspeople. A successful executive who recently returned from five years in Europe has been struck by the low level of responsiveness here. One of his most productive selling tools is making sure promised information is delivered to a prospect exactly when due.

Subtle ways to lose a sale

Personal mannerisms can create problems. Specifically:
• Handshake. Is it dead? Is it too lively?
• Speech. Too fast to be understood? Does it falter? To test, tape-record one salesperson selling another in practice sessions.
• Talking too much. It never pays to win the argument and lose the sale.
• Superiority. Implying that the customer is stupid.

• Inattention. Not concentrating on the prospect. Letting eyes wander around the office—or the workers.
• Irritating gestures. Shoe tapping, playing with pencils, poking the customer with an index finger to drive home a point.

Source: *The American Salesman,* Burlington, Ind.

What to do when the customer says no

Basic rule: Go back to a prospect as many times as it may be worthwhile. Use potential dollar volume from the account as a guide.

Find out why the customer is resistant. Often the problem is timing. A product that is being rejected now could be well received a few months from now.

What has to be overcome in subsequent calls:
• The customer has a previous supplier and is reluctant to shift sources without a significant gain in price or quality.
• The potential buyer has enough stock but indicates that the price is good. (Return later for the order.)
• The customer doesn't have inventory dollars to spend right now.
• The dollar volume of a potential order is large, so other company managers have to be consulted.

To avoid wasting time, make the first visit short and make it constructive. Treat the person you are dealing with diplomatically.

Find out who makes final buying decisions. Direct future efforts to that person.

Source: Harry Bell, Harry Bell Sales Co., Wyckoff, N.J.

15 PUBLIC RELATIONS

DEALING WITH THE MEDIA

Getting local publicity

Getting an article in the local newspaper (particularly in smaller towns and the suburbs) is easier than most people realize.

A phone call to the city desk or business editor about a special promotion, new product line, store expansion, or other event may well generate a useful item.

Writing news releases

Don't be clever or cute. Get all the basic information (what, where, when, why, who, and how) in the first paragraph. The news editor going through the stack of releases often reads only the first paragraph.

When using photographs, vertical shots are best. They fit in better with newspaper and magazine layouts. Contrasts should be very sharp (some detail is always lost in newspaper reproduction). The 5″×7″ photo is big enough. A

larger size costs more to print, mail, and is easily damaged.

Timing of releases

Chances are better of getting a release printed in the newspaper during slow news days. Best are Saturday, before noon, if there's a big Sunday paper (especially if there are photo possibilities); February (traditionally a slow month); August (as staffs are reduced because of vacations); holiday issues (Thanksgiving, Christmas) for feature pieces.

But don't send releases the month before contested local political elections or near local government budget- and tax-setting deadlines.

Sharing news releases with employees

Company news releases should be distributed

to employees the day they are sent to the media. Workers will be better informed and their morale will be boosted because of being included in the information network.

When the news release is about a special achievement, attach a congratulatory message thanking the work force for a job well done.

Source: George F. Trueli, *Building and Maintaining Your Non-Union Organization,* Drake Beam Morin, Inc., New York.

What to do about media mistakes

If the error is relatively insignificant, ignore it. If the general tone of the story is unfavorable, a retraction brings up the whole issue once again, increasing visibility.

If the story was favorable, write a memo correcting the error, and post it on company bulletin boards. Don't send it to the media.

In case of a serious error, request a correction. The media will probably print the company's side in the letters-to-the editor column.

Source: *The Corporate Communications Report,* New York.

How to get along better with the media

• Don't stonewall. If an answer can't be given, explain why.
• Never lie. Reporters are likely to discover the truth.
• Respond quickly. Journalists almost always are on a deadline.
• Assure accessibility by distributing other office or home phone numbers where the press can make after-hours contact.
• Maintain contacts with reporters even when

they're not working on a story about the company.
• Assign appropriate executives to be available for answering questions after a press release is issued. Be prepared with background information or leads for reporters who ask for them.
• Be aware of the biases of the different media.
• Don't play favorites among reporters. Also don't hold grudges.
• Work to educate the press. One company hosted seminars on computers.

Source: *The Corporate Communications Report,* New York.

How to say "no" to the media

In general, avoid saying no comment. It sounds defensive. A straightforward no is preferable. A better tack is to say that a comment at this time would be inappropriate. It's helpful but not essential to give the reason.

If the company chooses not to respond to the media, consider passing on the names of spokespeople from other companies who might be more willing to speak up.

Never say the company can't comment because the corporate spokesperson isn't available at the moment, unless that's truly the case and not just an excuse. The reporter may simply offer to postpone the story.

Source: *The Corporate Communications Report,* New York.

Dealing with the media in a crisis

Many executives regard reporters as busybodies with a personal bias against business. They don't like to answer questions from the media.

But this is unavoidable in a crisis. Suggestions:

• Give all the details of what happened. Stick to the facts. Avoid half-truths. Don't try to cover up.

• Designate a group of high-level executives as spokespeople. Give their names and business numbers to the media. Also, get reporters' names and numbers. Monitor coverage and speak up if there's a mistake.

• Anticipate questions reporters might ask. Draft statements beforehand.

How a company reacts can determine how the public will.

Source: *National Thrift News,* New York.

The need for a company spokesman

Pick a crisis spokesman now, before something goes wrong. If the company has no public relations department, select someone from upper management. This person should know the line managers and understand the production processes. He should be someone who is usually at the office.

As groundwork, prepare a set of written plans for handling accidents, strikes, recalls, layoffs, suits, and other negative events. Plans must cover internal communications, police, fire and medical officials, community leaders, and the press.

COMMUNITY RELATIONS

Improving the company image

Dollars aren't the only way to build community support for a company. Alternatives (in order of their popularity):

• Donate materials and services.

• Lend personnel to act as staff for short-term fund-raising and other projects.

• Allow employees days off with pay to work as volunteers.

• Give company recognition to those who volunteer for community work.

• Encourage company executives to serve on boards of volunteer organizations.

• Sponsor community events on the company grounds.

• Organize companywide fund-raising drives.

• Allow organizations to recruit volunteers in areas such as the cafeteria.

• Give social-service leaves, with full pay and benefits.

• Match donations by employees to community groups.

Source: K.K. Allen, *Worker Volunteerism: A New Human Resource for the 1980s,* AMACOM, New York.

Helping consumers means better business

There are many reasons for a company to take positive steps to help consumers. Two of the best:

1. In addition to good public relations, a strong consumer policy builds morale. Employees take pride in working for a company that

shows a high degree of responsibility and public-spiritedness.

2. Companies that are responsive to consumers don't have to invest heavily in complaint mechanisms.

Simplification of bank-loan forms and using larger type on such records were important gestures from business. By offering loan forms that make very clear to customers what their responsibilities are, banks weed out people who should not be borrowing in the first place. To take people to court for defaulting on a $500 loan is expensive.

Another example: Bristol-Myers showed concern by publishing a booklet on drug products. It informed consumers what they could and could not realistically expect from each drug. Bristol-Myers also bought useful poison-control ads, warning consumers of the dangers of substances in everyday use.

The business community is not indifferent to consumers' rights. On the contrary, the business community has shown itself to be remarkably positive, even eager, to take steps beneficiary to consumers. What it needs most is guidance.

It is essential for a business to have a complaint mechanism that works well, and is run by people who are patient and polite.

———

Source: Bess Meyerson, former New York City commissioner of consumer affairs.

LOBBYING CONGRESS

How to lobby in Congress

By phone, find out which aide in the senator's or representative's office is handling the issue the company is concerned about. By letter, outline the company's position to the aide. Tell the aide that the company president or other officer will phone later to set up an appointment with the legislator during a specified week. The date should be a month or so away. That makes it difficult for the lawmaker to refuse.

Follow up with the call to make the meeting appointment. In that conversation, repeat the point of view that the company wants to get across.

Go to the meeting with:

• A list of the legislator's key constituents who share the company's position, or with signed petitions. Show how jobs will be lost in the state or in the representative's district unless the desired action is taken.

• A short document that gives a tight argument for the company's position.

• A file of material to show the representative constituent support for the company's point of view, for example, letters to the editor clipped from the major newspapers in the lawmaker's district.

———

Source: *Legal Times of Washington,* Washington, D.C.

Getting action from Congressional staffers

Staffs of senators and representatives (as well as Congressional committees) are an overlooked source of information and influence for business executives.

How to find them. A phone call to the committee or legislator's office is the easiest method. Members of small staffs follow many areas of interest and Congressional bills. Those on larger staffs specialize. The *Congressional Staff Directory,* is useful, but many staff assignments change soon after new editions are in print.

Ground rules for dealing with staffs:

• Meet with them before asking for a favor, if

possible. Then maintain contact on a regular basis.

• Flatter staffers by asking them for advice.

• Keep track of conversations with staffers by writing short summaries that include an address and phone number.

• Be frank, especially about the opposing viewpoint. Business executives who intentionally mislead a staff member usually have a hard time gaining access again.

Lobbying by mail

A personal letter from a top company executive to an elected official can be a persuasive lobbying tool. To make the letter effective:

• Show thorough knowledge of the subject and the current status of the legislation. Refer to the bill by its number.

• Mention the official's vote on a recent issue to demonstrate awareness of the record.

• Be specific about what you want the official to do. Give reasons why, citing personal experiences or observations if possible.

• Ask a direct question about the official's position on the matter. This forces the legislator to answer clearly, not send back a form letter.

• As a general rule, keep the letter brief and cover one issue only. Be helpful rather than threatening. Offer to provide further information.

Source: *Grass Roots Lobbying,* AFL-CIO, Building and Construction Trades Dept., Washington, D.C.

Congressional pressure on business

Senators and representatives often pressure business groups without passing legislation. Bills may be introduced that have no chance of passing, but the hearings generate negative publicity for an industry. As a result, the industry makes changes to placate Congress, which then drops the probe or legislation.

Don't overreact when self-interest is threatened. Instead, call or visit congressional members. Ask them to place the situation in perspective and assess the chances for passage.

Business interests now have high credibility in Congress. When serious threats are made, banding together can be very effective. Seek out senators and representatives who oppose the changes. Work with them to use nonlegislative devices such as press releases, alliances and hearings to overcome the smoke screen.

Source: Richard L. Ratliff and Bob Benedict, University of Utah, *Sloan Management Review,* Cambridge, Mass.

How to testify before Congress

Congress holds thousands of hearings a year on subjects vital to business. Can a company hope to influence legislation by testifying? Chances are against it. But testimony can sometimes make a difference, particularly on a subject with which legislators are unfamiliar. And a company can raise its profile if an appearance before a Congressional committee is covered by the news media.

The first step is to write a letter asking to appear to the committee chairman, whose name appears in the *Congressional Directory.* Focus on the company's expertise. Point out that the company's views differ from those already presented. To cover themselves, committees look for a cross-section of views.

Next, submit a detailed summary of testimony for committee members to review before the hearing. (Some committees require it 24 hours in advance.) At the hearing, limit testimony to two or three major points, then open it up to questions. The impact of testifying lies in the face-to-face exchange with committee members. Brief testimony is more likely to be covered by the press.

To improve chances of being asked to testify, keep in touch with committee staff members, listed in the *Congressional Directory,* and the representatives from states where the company does business. Also useful is the *Congressional Record,* which gives advance notice of hearings.

Source: *The Directory* and the daily *Record* are available from the Superintendent of Documents, U.S. Government Printing Office, Washington, DC 20402.

WORKING WITH PR AGENCIES

Choosing a public relations agency

Public relations is changing its image and expanding its realm. Considerations in picking an agency:

• Look for an agency that has a background in dealing with your company's type of business.

• Set desired PR goals.

• Keep an open mind when listening to proposals. Don't miss out on a fresh idea from a good agency.

• Select a product (or service) area to concentrate on.

• A year of PR work can cost as little as the price of a full-page ad in a national magazine or a 30-second prime-time network TV spot.

What to look for in an agency

• Talk to three firms of different sizes.

• Be very specific in identifying the company's needs.

• Don't volunteer all information about the company. What an agency asks for shows how much initiative it has.

• Set a reasonable deadline for the agencies' proposals.

• Have the person who will serve as the account executive attend the proposal presentation. Evaluate one of the programs he did for another company.

• Don't choose a firm simply because of its experience in a certain industry. PR firms generalize; one major strength is applying what they know about one industry to another.

• If the agency doesn't learn quickly about the company, don't expect it to do so later on.

Source: *The Corporate Communications Report,* Corpcom Services, New York.

PART IV

Administration and Office Management

16 THE EFFICIENT OFFICE

OFFICE SPACE— PLANNING AND DESIGN

Designing the office

With office rents skyrocketing, many companies are asking designers for ways to put more employees comfortably into less space.

Good design reduces employee turnover and boosts productivity. For example, studies show that carpets, in preference to vinyl tile, reduce absenteeism and the correct light level makes the employee work more efficiently.

Another advantage of a good design is that office ambience enhances the company's image among employees and customers. A futuristic design may stimulate a creative mood among employees of a high-technology firm. Elegant offices enhance the image of a cosmetics company.

Office warmth can be created by color, texture, and enough furnishings to make the office space look like it's being fully utilized. Sometimes a large picture or bookcase can substitute for some furnishings.

Use a sensible approach. Many companies try to standardize offices and furnishings according to rank. Instead, tailor the design to the individual executive's tastes, but standardize elements such as desks and carpeting. Give the executive some choice in upholstery, wall color, artwork, and accessories.

Money-saving luxuries:

• Reduce overhead lighting. For a 40,000 square-foot space, a company might spend $12,000 or more a year on electricity. But thousands of dollars could be saved by switching to low-bright ceiling lighting, and most offices are overlighted anyhow.

• In open-space designs (i.e., areas of large, unobstructed spaces, with no built-in offices), let some of the window light filter into the inner areas. Daylight is humanizing. It makes employees feel like performing better.

Open-space design:

• Pro: Allows for greater density.

• Con: Makes privacy more difficult.

Originally, the open-space concept used plants to separate work areas. But sound carried too far and offices looked like tangled jungles. Thus, movable partitions were installed to break up open spaces. One aid: Build rooms where sensitive meetings can be held in privacy.

Source: Jack Lowery, Jack Lowery Associates, New York.

Fitting more workers in the same space

Most workers realize that a tight realty market and difficult business conditions make office squeezes inevitable. Few of them will gripe as long as space is reduced intelligently.

The best approach is to start with communal spaces around copiers and other office equipment. Next, computerize records to minimize storage area. Down-size mail rooms. Consolidate typing pools. Study office traffic flow to reduce corridor space to a minimum.

Reduce private offices by redefining their function. Replace individual conference areas with a single, common one.

Compensate for lost space by adding well-considered amenities—a larger desk, always welcome, can accommodate chairs for small meetings.

While compressing space, use the opportunity to work toward greater flexibility. Consider task lighting and modular partitions and furnishings. And reduce office costs in other ways. Avoid unneeded pieces of furniture and showy frills.

Source: Barry Wilke and Julian Davis, principals, Wilke Davis Associates, New York.

Minimum office space size requirements

Guide to space requirements:
- Top-executive offices—270 sq. ft. (15′ by 18′).
- Middle-executive offices—196 sq. ft. (14′ by 14′).
- Supervisors' offices—120 sq. ft. (10′ by 12′).
- Specialists' offices—72 sq. ft. (8′ by 9′).
- Work stations with 30″ by 60″ desk and chair—25 sq. ft.
- Drawer-type file cabinet—10 sq. ft. (additional).

- Main aisle widths—5 ft.
- Intermediate aisle widths—4 ft.

Designing an office to increase productivity

The easy steps:
- Put the right co-workers next to each other.
- Place the appropriate support staff with the right executives so that communication is easy.

The hard choice: Whether to have a traditional closed office or an open-plan office. Aside from the basic benefit of an open plan (it does accommodate more workers in less space), designers disagree over whether it increases or decreases productivity. In general, this depends on whether:

- The workers need to interact or need to maintain privacy to do their jobs most efficiently.
- The increased motivation that the democratic atmosphere of an open plan generates outweighs the inconvenience of interruptions and loss of confidentiality that result from open offices.

To maximize productivity in open offices, make sure to set aside some private conference rooms for meetings that require confidential discussions.

Source: Susan Orsini, partner, Feinberg Orsini Associates, New York.

The office chair

Three out of four people work seated. The chair's fit affects health hence productivity.

Checkpoints: (1) Backrest should be open at the bottom, with a slight inward protrusion just above, for best posture and least back strain. (2) Seat should be front-rounded (to prevent thigh numbness), not too softly cushioned (to permit normal squirming that prevents muscle spasms), and height-adjustable, so feet rest firmly on the floor (rather than dangling or forcing knees to jackknife). Experts say proper design can add 40 productive minutes to sedentary jobs.

Source: *Progressive Architecture,* Stamford, Conn.

When to build and when to renovate

Before a company decides to refurbish its existing quarters or build new ones, consider:
• Comparable costs. It's a common misconception that rehabilitation always costs less than new construction. In practice, it often costs more. Underpinning, reroofing, repointing, and the hidden expenses of working with outdated parts and outmoded designs all add to the cost of renovation.
• Time. There is no point opting for new construction if plans do not call for longtime residency.
• Work schedules. Rehabilitating disrupts routine work. New construction rarely does.
Renovation generally saves only 10%–15% of the cost of new construction. The margin is often not wide enough to be the sole determinant for the decision.

Source: Michael Federman, vice president, Federman Construction Consultants, New York, *Civil Engineering,* New York.

Avoiding cost overruns when remodeling

For remodeling jobs of under $1 million, there is no valid reason for the contractor to exceed the budget. Of course you must allow an extra 10% for contingencies that cannot reason-

ably be foreseen. There may be rotted inner walls hidden by outer ones. Or sudden delays in deliveries of essential materials.
Ways to keep the contractor in line:
• Use an architect, especially if this is a first experience with contractors. The architect provides a cost estimate and mediates disputes with the contractor.
• Get bids from five or six contractors. These provide an average cost for the job, and they are free.
• Do not jump at the lowest bid. Beware of one more than 10% lower than the average of the others. It is likely to be swelled by overruns.
• Specify a job completion date in the contract. Contracts that carry penalty clauses for projects not completed on time also usually require bonuses if the contractor meets the deadline.
• Stipulate that disputes will go to arbitration. It is cheaper and resolves disputes more quickly than going to court.

Renting office space at a business center

The cost of opening and operating an office can be cut by two-thirds if a company sublets furnished space and uses office personnel provided by a business center. (Look under "Office and desk space rental services" in the *Yellow Pages.*)
The company rents space from a business center and shares reception area, conference rooms, switchboard, telex operators, and clerical help with others.
Points to check when negotiating with a business center:
• Exactly which facilities and services are included in the rent. Is furniture included?
• Additional rent for secretarial space, if the company plans to employ its own clerical staff.
• How the company is identified in the lobby directory and on the door to reception area.
• How (and by whom) the company's telephone is answered.

- Hours of access to the office.
- Sublet rights.
- What happens to company's mail if it moves. The business center should forward mail weekly for a month at no charge; forward it more frequently and for longer period for a small fee.

Source: Alan L. Bain, president, World-Wide Business Centers, Inc., New York.

Taking the pain out of an office move

There are four steps involved in an office move:

1. Site selection. Use as many sources as possible to see what is available. Aside from brokers and published information, tune in to upcoming moves of other companies through the corporate grapevine. Ask all your contacts for suggestions.

Don't judge new premises on raw space alone. Have a preliminary sketch showing how the company can adapt that space.

2. Lease negotiations. Since office space is generally scarce, companies have little leverage in negotiating basic terms. But there is room for negotiating what alterations a landlord will make at its own expense. Many landlords will invest in construction to please a new long-term tenant. (How much? Depends on the expertise of the company's negotiator.) Improvements and quality tenants increase the worth of a building.

Detail the alterations to be made by the landlord (for example, auxiliary air conditioning) in a work letter. (If the previous tenant left something useful behind—a paneled conference, room, full-height doors, etc.—stipulate in the work letter that these features should not be altered.)

3. The alterations. Unsupervised contractors and improper scheduling are major causes of cost overruns in a move. Minimize them by working very closely, every day, with the architects and contractors involved. Plan so that no time is wasted and nothing has to be done twice or on overtime.

4. Physical move. Plan well in advance. Those who don't plan wind up taking everything with them. The result can be unnecessarily high moving expenses.

Source: Walter King, president, Corporate Controlled Moves, Inc., New York.

OFFICE EQUIPMENT

Using electronic equipment effectively

Many companies that invest in electronic equipment (computers, word processors, etc.) don't get the improved productivity they expect because the type of equipment purchased often doesn't fit the company's needs or is not being used properly.

First, look for ways to raise productivity by improving the company's existing operations.

Develop specific applications for hardware. Experiment before a purchase is made. Too many companies get educated at the wrong time, when the equipment is already in place.

Look for ways to share equipment among departments.

Train operators and support personnel in how the equipment works so they can fix it if anything goes wrong. Vendors no longer provide the kind of service they once did. In addition, train some people well enough so they can adapt the equipment for other company needs.

And, of course, make sure managers really need the new equipment they request. To many managers, new equipment is a corporate status symbol, not a vehicle for solving problems.

Unlike capital spending in plant, investments in electronic equipment do not guarantee increased production. Simply raising a secretary's output of lines may not make her more productive. That depends on what she does and how she uses her time, too.

Source: Robert A. Shiff, president, Naremco Services, Inc., New York.

Make sure you really need that new equipment

There is a continuing problem in allocating glamorous new equipment. For both status and job satisfaction reasons, there will always be pressure on management to purchase more units of whatever is the newest, most glamorous type of office equipment. In the past, this meant copiers and push-button telephones. Now the status symbols are word processors, desk-top terminal, CRTs (cathode ray tubes), and minicomputers. These are all important, productive pieces of equipment.

Review requisitions to separate real need from desire. Get to know the data used to justify a purchase.

The electronic office— not here yet

The electronic office (also known as the office of the future) cannot be expected for several more years. Individual functions exist separately (word processing, electronic mail, electronic filing, teleconferencing, etc.). But no one vendor is expected to produce an effective, integrated system, in the near future.

Reasons for the impeded development of the office of the future include human limitations, mismatching of work performed, lack of communication standards, and incompatibility of products. The current focus is on improving typing and editing productivity of office-support workers. Next to be concentrated on will be clerical tasks. Each of these improvements helps in containing costs. The big payoff will be in increased productivity of management (and professionals) whose salary and related expenses are the greatest office cost.

Source: Hambrecht & Quist, Institutional Research Department, San Francisco.

Reducing copier costs

A common mistake is trying to lower copying costs by reducing the volume of copies. But it often takes a massive drop in the number of copies to achieve significant savings, since copier vendors usually charge on a sliding-fee basis. As the volume of copies increases, the cost per copy drops to as little as ½-cent. On a high-volume copier, a 20% cut in copy volume may mean only a 5% drop in costs.

A better approach is to control the cost per copy. Limit the number of copiers in use. The same copy may cost eight times more to make on a low-volume machine than on a high-volume one.

Reassess the need for special copier features such as collating, reducing, or printing on both sides. On a low-volume machine, each can add 50%–100% to average copy cost. If special features are necessary, limit them to the high-volume machines.

Buy some copiers and lease others on a long-term basis, rather than rent all short-term. A good mix is 50% owned or on long-term lease, 25% on two- to three-year rental, 25% on one-year rental. The savings will be 15%–25% over the cost of renting all for one year.

Source: Jerrold J. Eisen, president, Office Sciences International, N.J.

Office copier: rent or buy?

Low-volume copiers. Generally, these should be purchased. Make sure the dealer has an established reputation for properly servicing the machines.

Medium-volume copiers. If purchased, amortization should be no longer than four years, and preferably only three years. Constant usage wears out even the most durable copiers during that period of time.

High-volume copiers. If they cost more than $10,000, buy them outright only when usage exceeds 30,000–40,000 copies per month. With lower use, outright ownership of an expensive copier isn't justified, especially in view of the industry's track record of constantly coming out with improved, more efficient machines.

Source: Datapro Research Corp., Delran, N.J.

Judging word-processing operations

Productivity standards for word-processing operations can be hard to establish by conventional time and motion techniques. The equipment is so much more expensive than standard typewriters that quantitative evaluation is more desirable.

Useful rules of thumb:

1. Set a standard unit of productivity for an average mix of original, revisions and repetitive materials. In ordinary commercial business use: 125 six-inch lines, with 12 characters to the inch (12-pitch printer element).

2. Pick a standard time-frame: Four hours to turn around 50% of the work, eight hours to turn around 95%.

3. Quality standard: Two format errors per draft page, but none in grammar or spelling. (Permissible errors: names, technical jargon.) Final copy should contain no errors of any kind, including formatting.

4. Using these standard units, a satisfactory one-day performance (six working hours) would be:

original copy	100 lines per hour	600 lines per day
revisions	150 lines per hour	900 lines per day
repetitive copy	200 lines per hour	1,200 lines per day
repetitive copy with automated paper feed	300 lines per hour	1,800 lines per day

Source: J.R. Little, Reg Little & Associates, Fairfax Station. Va.

Choosing the right word-processor supplies

Paper. Many offices use a higher quality than necessary for the job at hand. Always buy in quantity.

Printing wheels (used to print out texts onto paper). Plastic wheels are faster, quieter and less expensive (about $3 each when bought in volume) than metal. Metal printing wheels, which cost up to $30 each, last only four to five times as long. Golf-ball printers, used on IBM and some other typewriters, are extremely long lasting and can be repaired and reused.

Ribbons. Fabric ribbons can be reused. They provide up to 800,000 character impressions. The ribbons are suitable for some correspondence. Multi-strike ribbons provide a high-quality impression, are more expensive, and provide up to 300,000 impressions. Single-strike ribbons, which provide about 80,000 impressions per cartridge are the top of the line. And most nylon ribbon cartridges can be reloaded for a significant saving.

Floppy disks and tape cartridges. Unless special features are desired, ignore brand names and buy on the basis of price because most so-called magnetic media on the market are made by a few reputable manufacturers and sold under a variety of brand names. Tapes and disks should come packaged in a plastic box rather than the traditional paper box. More damage is done by poor handling than by actual wear.

Source: *Word Processing Systems,* New York.

Dictating machines vs secretaries

It makes more sense than ever to prepare business letters automatically. The cost of letters is escalating more rapidly now. And the spread is widening between the cost of dictating to a secretary versus dictating to a machine.

Including such factors as the cost of executive time and fixed office charge, the price of a face-to-face dictation now averages $6.07, compared with $4.18 for a machine-prepared letter.

Tracing the cost of a letter prepared by a secretary:

1930	$ .30
1935	.52
1940	.72
1953	1.17
1960	1.83
1964	2.32
1973	3.31
1977	4.47
1980	6.07

When being a dictator pays

Executives can dictate up to six times faster than they can write, and up to three times faster than they can dictate to a secretary. Secretaries can transcribe machine dictation twice as fast as shorthand notes, and with fewer errors.

Source: Dartnell Institute of Business Research, Chicago.

SECRETARIAL SERVICES AND PAPERWORK

Avoiding boss–secretary misunderstandings

When hiring, don't overemphasize office skills. Instead, look for tact, dependability, loyalty, discretion, initiative, stamina, and friendliness.

Common causes of secretary flare-ups:

1. Inadequate direction. Make sure to meet with the secretary for 15 minutes at the beginning and end of each day to go over routine chores. Use the time on Friday to plan the next week. Hold monthly sessions to evaluate any procedures that need to be changed. Also, be sure to let the secretary know where the boss, his superiors, and his staff fit into the company structure.

2. Brooding resentments. Show concern at signs of anxiety or listlessness. Both the secretary and the boss need to forgive and forget frequently.

3. Improper criticism. Balance criticism with praise when it's justified. Don't criticize the secretary in public.

Source: E. Manns, a secretary, *Toastmaster,* Santa Ana, Calif.

What secretaries dislike the most

• A disorganized boss. Or, even worse—a boss who throws projects on their desks toward the end of the day.

• Several supervisors who all want their work done first.

- Insufficient or hurried instructions.
- Faulty copy machines.
- Nit-picking tasks that delay important assignments.
- Work that must be done for the family of the boss.
- The role of personal servant.
- No opportunity to take on more responsibilities.
- Extra work that is given because their regular work is finished so quickly.

Source: Dr. Roger E. Flax, Ph.D., executive director, Motivational Systems, South Orange, N.J.

Coping with secretarial shortages

Many firms experience shortages of secretaries even when there is high unemployment. Personnel experts think the situation will get worse. The number of job openings, even with improved technology, keeps rising relative to other kinds of work.

Secretarial jobs repel many bright people because they are often dead-end positions. Yet executive secretaries require a wide variety of administrative and interpersonal skills. They also get to know the nuances of organizational life. One way to avoid the secretarial shortage is to use the job as a selection mechanism for a range of administrative posts. Management would have to assure new hires that they weren't being treated as permanently low-paid job holders.

Another part of the solution is to make these jobs attractive to men and to think of men as part of the labor pool for secretarial jobs. Traditionally classified as low-paying, no-promotion female jobs, these jobs were shunned by men. Changes to make the job into a rung on a promotion ladder would change its image. Further, the increasing technology associated with secre-

tarial work (word processors, CRT displays, computers) makes the job more attractive.

As equal opportunity catches hold, this is a good time to make secretarial work available to both sexes. Possibly, the job title itself will have to be changed. Titles such as administrative assistant can communicate a new business position.

Running an office without secretaries

Most managers depend so heavily on secretaries that it seems impossible to run an office without them. In fact, many types of businesses actually operate more efficiently when the straight secretarial function is eliminated or reduced.

They include advertising agencies, technical- and management-consulting firms, other types of service companies. In some situations, secretaries can hinder a smooth relationship between managers and the inside operations staff.

Case history. Juhl Advertising Agency, a Midwestern advertising firm, had six secretaries in 1970. Now it has none. In the meantime, it tripled its size (to 56 employees) and boosted annual billings similarly. Though managers now make their own phone calls, none find the chore burdensome. With the money the firm saved by not paying for high-priced, hard-to-find secretaries, it has been able to hire college graduates (manager trainees) who are eager to enter the business and are not bothered by handling their own letters and phone calls.

Consider reducing the number of secretaries when overall communications require sophisticated language ability or other expertise or executives need to stay in frequent, personal contact with clients.

Alternatives to secretaries are typists who use high-speed word-processing equipment combined with junior employees who keep projects moving in the right direction. In this system, more details are delegated to trained specialists. Managers write rough drafts and give them directly to professional typing centers.

Source: James J. Dominello, senior vice president, Juhl Advertising Agency, Inc., Elkhart, Ind.

Simplified filing systems

Organize files around the function they serve. Keep in mind that too few classifications results in systems that are overloaded, but too many categories confuses users. Ask the people who do the filing for ideas on how the system can be made more workable.

Most frequently needed categories:
• Activities supervised.
• Reports received.
• Reports generated.
• Correspondence (filed either by name of correspondent or of company, whichever is most efficient).
• Support and background material.
• Interdepartmental activities.

Keep files uncluttered by following a master calendar of dates to cycle documents into inactive storage or destroy them.

Source: Louis B. Lundborg, *Execu-Time,* Lake Forest, Ill.

Mechanics of filing made easier

Staple all letters, replies, and related papers together. Remove paper clips. They add bulk to the file, slip off, and catch on other papers.

Write (or type) the folder's heading prominently in the upper corner of the top sheet to insure its return to the same spot.

File the most recent papers in the front of the folder. Most requests are for the latest material.

In removing papers from a file, pull the folder up. Do not remove it—folders are easily misfiled when returned to cabinet.

Keep a record of material removed from the file. Don't try to remember such details.

Allow three to four inches of work space in the drawer to avoid tugging at and damaging the folders.

Source: *Office Administration Handbook,* The Dartnell Corp., Chicago.

How to reduce clerical errors

Few managers know what it really costs to correct a mistake in keypunching, order processing, billing, or other clerical operations.

In insurance companies, the average cost of correcting a routine processing error is $56 by one estimate. Another estimate is between 5% and 15% (and sometimes more) of total payroll and related overhead expenses is spent on rectifying clerical errors. And it takes at least five times as long to correct an error as to do the work right the first time.

To reduce errors:
• Identify contributing factors such as boredom, poor lighting or ventilation, noise, rumors, gossip, unpopular supervisors, etc. Then, correct any obvious deficiencies in working conditions, supervision, and training. Incompetence is rarely a primary cause of errors.
• Inform clerks of the cost of errors and the individual error rates.
• Make them responsible for correcting their own mistakes.
• Vary tasks to reduce boredom, and consolidate clerical functions to minimize fragmentation of work and buck-passing.
• Move supervisors out of their office and into the clerical area. Have them function as on-the-spot trouble-shooters who can prevent mistakes or correct them as soon as they happen.

Source: William E. Exton, Jr., management consultant, New York.

TELEPHONE SYSTEMS

Cutting telephone costs

The first step is to analyze whether it's more economical to rent or buy telephone equipment. Check the company's equipment rental charge (first line of the bill). It may be as much as 60% of the phone tab. (1) All the equipment may not be needed. (2) There may be charges for equipment that was removed months (or years) ago. That adds up to a huge credit. (3) Similar, or better, equipment may be purchased at less cost from a non-AT&T supplier.

Buying suggestions:

• Deal only with a consultant willing to sign a noncollusion contract. (Consultant should be paid by client or vendor, but not both.)

• Buy directly from vendors to avoid the chance of purchasing stolen equipment. To check a vendor's reliability, ask to see the firm's financial statement and also those of the equipment manufacturer it represents.

• Avoid buying equipment that's designed to work only within one proprietary system. If the business outgrows the system, the only thing salvageable is the cable.

• The most important factors in determining which telephone equipment to buy: (1) Incoming volume of calls. (2) Outgoing calls: Where are they going and with what frequency? (3) The internal communications needs of the organization.

How to save on nearby calls:

• Install a system that confines calling to a certain radius which results in employees making fewer personal calls. Calls for the weather, time, Dial-A-Joke, etc., can be blocked.

• Use a "lud" list which shows where every local call is made. The phone company provides this list for a small fee.

How to save on long distance:

• Make department heads or specific employees accountable for their long-distance phone use by having the phone company bill their extensions or departments separately.

• Have long-distance needs of the company analyzed by a consultant to see if a WATS line or other "bulk" long-distance service is appropriate.

Source: Robert De Rosa, Bridging the Gap Through Communications, Blauvelt, N.Y.

Use the PBX to cut phone costs

Consider PBX (private branch exchange) switchboard add-ons to give the company more control over phone costs.

Station Message Detail Recording (SMDR). For good-size businesses (at least 200 extensions on the PBX), where productivity of calls carries high priority. The system collects taped data that identifies the originating extension of each call and shows utilization of WATS or tie lines. It gives management the ability to review call data, sort and prepare reports, to improve telephone usage. Management can compare order-takers' average phone times against order volume to determine who is most efficient, then trains others to use that person's techniques. Optional equipment connected to PBX is available for around $12,000.

Automatic Number Identification. For large organizations (hospitals, universities, etc.) with more than 300 telephone units. It provides a separate phone bill for each extension, making it possible for management to identify heavy telephone users (and abusers), and assign the costs accordingly. There is a moderate charge, depending on how much work the telephone company must do to set it up on their central office switch.

Automatic Route Selection. For firms equipped with distributed locations and at least three alternate routes (for example, WATS, tie lines, network trunks) to remote company locations. The system automatically selects the most economical way available to reach any phone number a user dials. If that route is busy, it computes the next best. Then it computes whether the advantage lies in switching over or holding and waiting for the cheapest route. The cost will be $25,000–$30,000 for computer hardware and software.

Source: Richard Carr, marketing vice president, Harris Corp., digital telephone systems division, Novato, Calif.

Two ways to eliminate telephone cheating

1. Most credit card bills show the time of day, length, and cost of each call charged. Audit the company bill each month for lengthy evening calls (especially if residence-originated) that may be disguised personal employee calls.

2. Check the credit card bill for "third party" calls. Ask the phone company's business office to provide the name of the people or organizations making, and receiving, the calls. If they're unfamiliar, don't pay them. It's up to the telephone company to prove that the calls were properly charged.

Source: Frank K. Griesinger, president, Frank Griesinger & Associates, Cleveland.

Choosing an 800-code service company

Advertisers who use the 800-code numbers for responses should pick an answering service to respond to the calls on the basis of these key questions:
• Are there enough supervisors, and do they work well with the operators?

• Are the operators able to handle a variety of order situations? Check their training and reference manuals.
• Can supervisors and clients randomly listen as operators handle orders? If so, check for politeness and efficiency.
• Does the company specialize in the selling medium to be used?
• Is it staffed to meet peak demands? Services that handle both print and TV should be able to segregate the two types of incoming calls to minimize busy signals during peak TV hours. And beware of services that claim their operators can handle up to 50 calls each per hour.

Both computer and manual operators have their own advantages. Don't buy on the basis of gadgetry.

Source: George Smith, Avis Rent-A-Car, *ZIP,* New York.

Holding down phone bills while traveling

Resist the temptation to use credit cards to charge telephone calls. They can increase the price of a call by as much as 500% over the direct-dial method. One reason is that the initial charge on a credit card is three minutes, not one minute.

Develop the habit of calling WATS information at (800) 555-1212 before phoning a hotel, airline, or other large service company. Information knows if a company has a free 800 number.

Take advantage of free local calls that can be made from many VIP lounges at major airports.

Look into Bell System competitors, whose cheaper service extends to out-of-office calls, for example MCI Telecommunications (Execunet), ITT-U.S. Transmissions (City-Call), and SP Communications (Sprint V).

Don't charge in-state calls to a hotel room. A hotel usually adds a service charge to them, which it cannot legally add to interstate calls.

Source: Frank K. Griesinger, Frank K. Griesinger and Associates, Inc., Cleveland.

MAIL SYSTEMS

Effective mailing techniques

• Close the daily mail cycle at 2 p.m. rather than 5 p.m. The mid-afternoon deadline encourages employees to handle correspondence early. Mail put into a mail box after 2 p.m. often is delivered no earlier than if mailed the next morning.

• Insist that all business reply mail be delivered by the Post Office daily.

• Send pre-addressed envelopes with all bills. This prevents delays due to misaddressed payments or payments sent with the wrong ZIP Code.

• When sending packages, check rates of United Parcel Service and other major private parcel carriers before using parcel post.

• Where possible, drop bulk mail away from major metropolitan postal centers, especially New York City-area post offices. They handle more mail daily than all of Britain. Avoid them if you can.

Source: John Jay Daly, Daly Associates, Inc., Washington, D.C.

Interoffice mail

For mail to branch offices or subsidiaries of the company:

• Use zippered bulk pouches made of nylon. They are reusable, stronger, safer, and lighter than standard manila envelopes.

• Monitor arrival times. Packets sent after Tuesday or Wednesday may not arrive until Monday, along with the Friday packet. Consolidate them into one mailing at the end of the week.

• Mail sensitive material directly to individuals' homes. That increases privacy and reduces need for handling at the receiving end.

• Send only the contents of reports and printouts, not the binders to avoid extra postage.

Source: *ZIP*, New York.

Effective use of electronic mail systems

Mail can be transmitted electronically the following ways:

• Telexes have been around for years, but are often overlooked. They are an effective, economical means of transmitting pricing information, policy changes, and personnel announcements. Rental and use of a telex from Western Union costs about the same as rental and use of phone equipment.

• Slow facsimile machines are an efficient way to transmit key documents occasionally. These machines average one page of text every six minutes. They cost about $5,000 to buy and $100 a month to rent. Manufacturers include Xerox, 3M, Qwip, Graphic Services.

• Fast facsimile machines are well suited for the frequent transmission of documents. These machines average one page of text per minute at a cost of $10,000 to buy and $300–$400 a month to rent. Top manufacturers are Rapicom, Panafax, 3M, Graphic Services.

• Computer-based message switching centers are used primarily by multinational companies with global office networks. Base price for installing a system with ten terminals and a central-computer bank is $100,000. A practical first step is to rent time on other companies' systems to try out this form of electronic mail without making a capital investment,

• Communicating word processors can be used productively by any company requiring quick turnaround and wide distribution of documents, and increased productivity by typists. A typical grouping of five word processors, two printers and a memory bank costs $65,000. There are about 25 companies offering word processors, all with good reputations.

Source: Victor Krasan, Peat, Marwick, Mitchell & Co., New York.

Assuring facsimile compatibility

At least 16 different manufacturers have machines in wide use. Unfortunately, many transmitting and receiving facsimile units operate at different speeds. To avoid problems, transmit facsimile copies to a service (listed under Facsimile Transmission Services in the *Yellow Pages*) that retransmits on compatible equipment. Use of such a service also means that companies with high-speed machines can batch transmissions and always use the fastest mode, cutting toll charges.

The new convenience of electronic messaging

An important communication innovation is electronic messaging for executives on the road. An important advantage is that users receive a printed copy of the communication.

Electronic messaging devices weigh one to fourteen pounds. Depending on the model, they have a keyboard, liquid-crystal displays and a printer that delivers messages.

To use the portable units, the message sender goes to a telephone and places the handset into a device on the messaging unit. (Any phone with a standard handset can be used.) The sender keyboards the code of the person who is being called and then types the message. The message goes to a storage computer.

To receive the message, traveling executives put a phoneset into their unit. The machine displays the message on the liquid-crystal screen (cheaper units) or prints it out on hard copy (more expensive).

It will cost $450–$1,000 to buy a portable unit, plus about $160 a month to rent computer time. Texas Instruments, Data General, Digilot and Nixdorf make and sell protable messaging devices. GTE, Computer Corp. of America and Tymshare rent computer time.

But messages can only go and come from companies or individuals who subscribe to the system, and some users find the larger messaging devices to be cumbersome.

Source: Dr. Howard Morgan, professor of decision sciences at the University of Pennsylvania's Wharton School and chairman of Advanced Office Concepts, Bala Cynwyd, Pa.

17 COMPUTERS

BUYING A COMPUTER—HARDWARE AND SOFTWARE

Too many computers?

Nearly half of the computers operated by U.S. businesses are not paying their way. They are just not economically viable. Computer installations either don't do their proper jobs—or there are other ways to do the same job better, faster, or cheaper.

How did this state of affairs come about? Much of it is the result of management ego: "If my competitor has a computer, why shouldn't I? After all, we're smarter, more progressive etc." No matter what the facts are, once the top man decides he needs a computer, cost estimates, investment priorities, application plans —all are subtly adjusted to support the president's decision. They are fed some fast figures and blue-sky stories by computer salesmen—and by their own people who are either trying to make the boss happy or saving face for themselves and him. Computer expenses can be hidden in any number of accounting nooks—written off in any number of ways.

The critical time comes about six years after the computer has been purring along. Clearly, it's not doing what it's supposed to do. Now management must decide: Should it dump the thing or get a newer, bigger, more sophisticated machine to do the job? Pressure to get that big computer is enormous. Reports of other businesses with great computer successes mount. Meanwhile, the company's computer staff is pushing for the new hardware. They have to save their jobs and, if they intend to move on to better ones, they'd like their resumes to show they operated the biggest, latest, most sophisticated computer. If the whole computer idea is scrapped after costs are calculated, enormous expense is involved in revamping the entire operation. And the original mistake must be admitted. The decision is clear: Get the bigger system. And the business finds itself in a deeper hole than before.

Most of the bad decisions about computers are neatly hidden. Only the multimillion-dollar mistakes are too big to hide.

Of the three levels of business computer applications, only one—the largest—is anywhere near approaching its potential. That is on the operational level (payrolls, billing, etc.), where the computers are operating at 40%–50% of expectations. In the area of providing information to middle management (sales quotas, inventories, etc.), operations are 10%–20% of potential. Top management gets only 1%–5% of expectations.

Management information system (MIS) is the buzzword of management. That's the carrot that salesmen use to lure management into a big computer purchase: MIS will not only give management the tools for making decisions—it can be a decision-maker, too. But the truth is, it'll never work that way. Eighty percent of an executive's decisions are based on information he must get from outside his company: politics, government actions, competitors' actions, etc. That leaves 20% for the computer. But, again, expecting to exploit a computer's full potential is unrealistic, because systems are designed from the bottom of the management pyramid. First, the bookkeeping department gets its hands on it. It devises programs to do its job. Then, step by step, the applications move up the line. By the time it reaches top management, the system is too complex and too basic to the needs of the operating level to be really of help.

A critical problem is that every time a middle manager changes jobs, the computer operation is changed to provide him with what he thinks he needs from the machine. The higher he is in the organization, the more changes will be made—involving more money, time, and effort—but rarely more useful information.

Many firms turn to a computer consultant, thinking that will solve their problems. It's a dream. These computer experts know how to make a computer do things, but they don't know anything about business, which is an inherently unstructured affair. They create problems by trying to impose a structure on an unstructured situation. Fifty percent of the work in solving a major computer problem (including the question of whether the firm needs one in the first place) requires total management involvement.

And don't let equipment salesmen arrange a computer feasibility study. They naturally have a built-in bias. So do many consultants and management service divisions of accounting firms. If you buy the machine they recommend, they'll have their hooks into you for some time.

Source: Dick H. Brandon, Brandon Consulting Group, Inc., New York.

Do you need a minicomputer?

A minicomputer becomes practical for most small companies when sales exceed $200,000 a year. Companies that maintain heavy inventories or do extensive mailings could use one even sooner.

But home computer systems in the $3,000-and-under range won't stand up to business use. Software for them is limited. Instead, a company should buy a $6,000–$12,000 system that can be expanded, and that comes equipped with sophisticated software.

Source: *The Insider's Guide to Small Business Computers,* Data General Corp., Westboro, Mass.

Buying a minicomputer

• Hire a consultant with small-business experience to protect against overbuying and to assist in selecting five or six systems for serious consideration.
• Look at the systems in operation in actual installations.
• Expect computer salespeople to explain their systems in plain English. Don't deal with those who can't.
• Base 50% of the buying decision on the knowledge and willingness to help of the sales and technical people. (There are few differences among most hardware and software.)
• Retain the old system or service bureau for at least six months to allow ample time for installing and debugging.
• Free up one person from top management for two weeks to attend vendor-run seminars that teach how to install and run software packages.

Source: *Computerworld,* Newton, Mass.

How good are handheld computers?

Handheld computers (HHCs), which are slightly longer than a paperback book and weigh about a pound, are amazingly versatile. When extended with portable (optional) peripherals, such as a printer, HHCs can run a wide variety of programs. They can communicate with large mainframe computers, too. They can do whatever much larger, stationary personal computers can do. HHCs can be hitched to a color television set for visual display or to a telephone for transmission.

The leaders in the field are: Hewlett-Packard HP-41C, Sinclair ZX80, Radio Shack/Sharp, Panasonic/Quasar.

Source: *Byte,* Peterborough, N.H.

Buying a used computer: pros and cons

The computer that one company trades in when it upgrades its computer capacity (over 40 new computer models are now introduced each year) may be just the right unit for another company to buy used. Consider the option of a used unit when adding to the company's computer capacity (or when buying a computer for the first time). But recognize the risks, too.

Advantages of a used computer:

• Software. Any widely popular model, after years in the field, has a vast array of proven, working programs that are time-tested. They cover a wide array of applications. Against newly developed software for newer equipment, this is a big plus—the most significant.

• Backup. Experienced workers are available who know the older models inside and out, allowing reduced training and recruitment costs. Fewer learning-curve problems.

• Price. Expect to pay 20%–45% of the original list for a four- to six-year-old computer. To make a fast price check, use *The Computer Blue Book,* published by Computer Merchants, Inc., Chappaqua, N.Y.

Most users consider price the main advantage. That may be illusory. As in most competitive markets, list prices are meaningless. New computers sold to volume distributors are discounted 10%–40%, and some of that discount is often passed along to the end user.

Disadvantages of a used computer:

• Leasing. The long-term deals at favorable rates that lenders often make on a new computer cannot usually be negotiated for secondhand models.

• Vendor support. Original-equipment manufacturers don't generally sell used computers, so there's no manufacturer's warranty. Equally troublesome is the fact that there is no easy access to the manufacturer for documentation on technology, bugs, improvements, etc.

• Maintenance. Some manufacturers hike charges for servicing older machines. Or they require an upfront, costly reconditioning program before agreeing to a maintenance contract. You might try a good independent servicing organization.

• People. The biggest problem. Most technicians prefer jobs involving the newest technology. While there is that large pool of experienced talent, it may not be available for work on older models, except at premium wages.

If the pluses still add up to more than the minuses, the company buying a used computer should:

• Obtain all needed software and vendor support beforehand to make sure it's available.

• Line up the poeple who will program and run it beforehand. And keep them fully informed. Consider ordering a new computer, too, for indefinite future delivery. Let the computer staff take training courses for it as a morale-booster and to prevent staff attrition.

• Insist on a warranty or maintenance contract in writing, without penalizing preconditions, cancellable only by the buyer.

• Buy a popular-model computer, so that the advantages of buying a used one don't suddenly disappear, along with spare parts, backup equipment and peace of mind.

Source: Dick H. Brandon and Sidney Segelstein, *Boardroom's Complete Guide to Minicomputers,* Boardroom Books, New York, N.Y.

Buying or leasing: tax considerations

Acquiring a computer generates many of the same tax questions as acquiring any major asset. But software adds to the complications. Important tax savings are possible because software can often be treated differently (and more favorably) than hardware. It is therefore wise to consult qualified tax counsel before the contract is signed. Considerations:

Federal income tax:

• The purchase price of the computer and any simultaneously purchased software can be depreciated in five years, without residual value. All acceleration methods are usable.

• The software can be expensed. But the price must be separately stated (or otherwise provable for tax purposes). Most software "purchases" are single-payment, perpetual license fees, which can be treated either way.

Purchased software must be treated for tax purposes identically to software developed in-house: either deduct entirely in one year as a current expense, or depreciate as a capital investment. If there is no in-house software development to serve as a precedent, the tax treatment of the initial purchase will generally govern.

• The 10% federal investment tax credit is applicable to purchases of software if the software is purchased as a package with the hardware. The credit (a dollar-for-dollar reduction in taxes owed) is allowed no matter what the company's previous treatment of software for tax purposes. The credit is also applicable to any sales taxes paid if you elect to capitalize sales tax. If the credit is taken, software must be depreciated along with the hardware and 50% of the credit must be subtracted from the cost basis for depreciation. Alternative: Reduce the investment credit to 8% and use full cost basis for depreciation. Software cannot be deducted in one year as a current expense.

• Used computers. An investment credit is allowed on used-equipment purchases. All types of equipment, not only computers, are applied to an overall limit of the first $125,000 ($150,000 after 1987). But a knowledgeable computer expert can sometimes make it possible to treat software as new, even if it is obtained with a used computer.

Local taxes:

• In some states sales taxes are applicable only to the hardware. If software is included in the package price for investment tax credit purposes, have the vendor provide a separate statement of the hardware and software price.

• Property taxes are only applicable to that portion of the hardware price which relates to the actual components. If the "hardware" price includes any software (such as operating system) or vendor service and advice, installation, education, documentation, etc., that portion of the hardware price is not subject to property tax.

Check rulings in the local tax jurisdiction and others to determine what percentage of the hardware list price should be subject to property tax. Tax counsel can obtain this information.

Leasing or renting a computer has similar tax consequences:

• A company that rents its equipment to another firm pays property tax only on its manufacturing cost (typically 18%–25% of the purchase price).

• Most vendors will pass through the investment tax credit, or reduce lease payments accordingly. This is negotiable.

• Lease payments are generally deductible as a current expense, unless the lease is structured as an installment purchase. Many complex deals can be made with a computer purchase, such as through a leveraged lease. In any of these, it requires a qualified professional to optimize the benefits.

Recommended: Include a provision in the lease

giving the firm the right to dispute legitimately any property or sales tax that might be levied.

Source: Dick H. Brandon, Brandon Consulting Group, Inc., New York.

The basic computer languages

FORTRAN. A scientific language. Avoid business programs that are written in it.

BASIC (Beginners' All-purpose Symbolic Instruction Code). Easiest to understand, learn, and use. The accepted language for small computers, it dominates the field. But there are many versions of BASIC and not all programs are interchangeable. So ask which computers will accept the BASIC that this program uses.

COBOL (Common Business-Oriented Language). Best use is for programs handling large amounts of information because it's faster than BASIC. Its use in business is increasing. Some computers run on programs written in COBOL as well as in BASIC.

PASCAL (named for the French philosopher). Expected to become the business language of the future because programmers must work in a logical manner, which reduces errors. But make sure any program written in PASCAL has been debugged in actual use.

Source: Brian R. Smith, *The Computer in Small Business,* Stephen Greene Press, Brattleboro, Vt.

How to talk to computer salespeople

Effective managers often feel very ineffective and overwhelmed by technical details when they start shopping for a small computer. All it takes to ask the right questions are a few basic terms:

• Expansion. The cost and modifications necessary to add terminals, storage capacity, or a different printer.

• Upgrading. Once expansion limits are reached, are the terminals, software, and peripheral equipment compatible with more powerful models?

• Word length and bits. The bit is the smallest unit of information a computer can recognize. Word length refers to how many bits of information it can handle in a single operation. The longer the word length, the faster and more expensive the equipment must be. A 16-bit word length is the minimum for most business uses. (Most home computers have 8 bits.)

• Memory size. The main random-access memory (RAM) stores software and programs. A business-system memory needs 64,000 bytes. (eight bits equal a byte.) This can be augmented by disks (auxiliary memory-storage devices). The number, size, and type of disk storage is dictated by needs, for example, one 4½-inch floppy disk holds 250 customer billing files.

• Ruggedness. The computer runs most of the business day and will be jostled on occasion. Is the chassis sturdy? Are the circuit boards easy to remove for servicing? Do the exterior panels protect against spills and dust?

• Terminals. These are the television-like devices on which information is displayed. Cathode-ray-tube models are the best. The display panel should be large enough to show 24 lines of 80 characters each. (Five-inch models are impractical for anything but hobby use.) The keyboard through which the user can change the copy should be set up the same as a regular typewriter. A separate calculator-style keyboard speeds numerical entries.

• Printers. These type out information on paper. Letter-quality models give a typewriter-like appearance but are more expensive. Less-expensive matrix printers form letters out of dots and sometimes require special paper. A letter-quality printer is better in business. The results look better, and it's cheaper in the long run to buy one outright than to upgrade later from a matrix type.

And small computers don't need to be specially located. They will function anywhere an electronic calculator will.

Source: *The Insider's Guide to Small Business Computers,* Data General Corp., Westboro, Mass.

How to find the bugs before signing the contract

A standard computer-equipment sales contract provides that the equipment will be deemed accepted by the buyer when it has been installed and minimally tested. The average buyer tries to anticipate potential bugs by negotiating rougher tests before acceptance.

He usually falls into a trap—negotiating by going down the seller's contract line by line. Remember that the seller put a lot of work into formulating that contract and knows it intimately.

A better way is for the buyer to consider carefully what the equipment will be used for and how it should perform. He should then formulate his own tests of acceptance. Offer these to the seller as the basis for negotiations.

Source: *Computer Negotiations Reports,* Winter Park, Fla.

Computer sales scams

Small business computers are highly price-competitive. Shopping around pays. But how can you tell an honest bargain from a bad deal? Be on the lookout for these scams:

• The super-saver. An exceptionally low-price should be an automatic danger signal that the computer is being misrepresented.

• Bait and switch. In this scam, the salesperson sells the company a small system that cannot do the job, then cashes in when the company is forced to upgrade.

• Flagship account. The vendor offers to custom-design a system that it says it can use as a model for other users. The outcome is seldom satisfactory. The vendor rarely puts enough time and money into the effort. Moreover, new software packages require a long shakedown.

• The promise of full testing. If a computer system has not been fully tested for the company's application, the shakedown period can be costly. Do not rely on the vendor's word that the computer has been tested. See actual results.

• Easy conversion. Here, the salesperson assures the company that a software package can be easily converted to a different type of hardware. In reality, conversion is difficult and time-consuming. Get written assurance that the vendor will stick with the job until the system works to the company's satisfaction.

Source: Thomas K. Christo, *Medical Economics,* Oradell, N.J.

Why buyer and seller relationships break down

It's almost impossible to buy a computer and simply plug it into an organization. Therefore, the working relationship between the vendor's trained specialist and the new buyer is a critical one.

Problems that can interfere with the relationship:

• Failure to define responsibilities. At the outset, it should be clear who will do what. The contract (or proposal) should specify exactly what the tasks are, who will do them and what schedule has been established.

• Emergence of hidden costs. The user typically budgets the amounts proposed by the vendor. But when other costs show up (for transportation, power, supplies, cabling, insurance, sales taxes, travel expenses, installation, rigging, communications, air conditioning, etc.), the user is upset and the relationship suffers. Spell out these costs in advance.

• Perception differences. The user regards its needs and its computer applications as unique. The vendor wants to supply a standard package, to minimize customization efforts. The user assumes it will get everything it needs. The vendor can only afford to supply the basic package.

• Inadequate personnel. The more successful the vendor, often the less trained its personnel will be, especially if the vendor has grown rapidly. And computer vendors too often use their best people in selling, rather than in fulfilling agreements.

• Performance. Computer-system performance, such as terminal reponse time, deteriorates as volume builds, since vendors will low-bid the system's configuration, hoping to add more equipment before or immediately after delivery. The computer's performance will often be disappointing unless the user spends more money for hardware.

• Reliability. Computer systems are very reliable, and monthly maintenance costs typically run about 1% of the purchase price. But when the computer does fail, vendors often cannot repair it quickly. The user's system must therefore provide backup. This is often not included in the system's design or in the up-front cost quoted originally.

• Ethics. Many computer-system suppliers, especially software sellers, turnkey-systems houses, and service bureaus, are undercapitalized and struggling to survive. They will compromise their ethics to keep going. The frequent result is customer mistreatment.

Three solutions:

1. Deal with reliable, reputable vendors. Check their references with other customers.

2. Screen offers carefully. Eliminate bids that are so low that the vendor's margins have to be impaired. Lowballing will result in poor performance, poor reliability, low quality, or a sizable increase in operating costs.

3. Spell out everything in detail, either in a contract or another document. Define the system's responsibilities, scope, performance standards, reliability standards, maintenance service, hidden costs—everything about the relationship.

Source: Dick H. Brandon, Brandon Consulting Group, Inc., New York.

Shopping for computer software

The number of companies that produce programming is increasing rapidly. Computer owners who want to expand applications should comparison-shop rather than simply rely on the manufacturer or on a single software source. A good program must be:
• Advanced technologically.
• Easy to use.
• Continually updated by the supplier.
• Capable of modification and up-grading to keep up with state-of-the-art developments.
• Created by a team of programmers rather than assorted individuals or outside experts.

Source: *Computerworld,* Framingham, Mass.

Software choices

Making the right computer decision means matching the right combination of hardware and software. Amid the confusing array of software options, the basic choices:
• Packaged computer programs. They perform standard business functions (payroll, inventory control, billing) and are available for all the better-known computer systems at a cost of $500–$1,500 per package. All but the newest have been debugged and proven through extensive use. They are designed for operators with little or no training. They use questions and instructions that appear on the terminal screen to guide users.
• Modified packages. Designed to accommodate special needs through relatively minor changes made in standard packages at a cost of $1,500–$7,000, based on the time involved. The best approach is to modify an off-the-shelf-program after testing it extensively so all changes can be made at once.

• Custom software. The only answer for businesses with unique requirements. It will cost $10,000–$20,000 if done in two weeks by a single programmer. A detailed study of the business is necessary before designing a specialized program. Only go the customized route as a last resort. Use a software house recommended by others, a dealer, or the manufacturer.

Source: *The Insider's Guide to Small Business Computers,* Data General Corp., Westboro, Mass.

What to look for in desk-top software

When considering buying a small business computer, look at software before choosing any system because most programs are designed to run on only one type of system. A good program has:

• Written directions that appear on the terminal screen and can be followed without referring to the instruction book. It's best if the computer explains mistakes with on-screen messages.

• An instruction book written on the seventh-to eighth-grade level and clearly illustrated.

• A minimum of disk switching and flopping when the system is in use.

• Protection against losing information (or the entire program), known as error tracking, when a wrong key is struck.

• A brief code to stop work. Some programs require long sequences to be run after even a simple entry is made.

• Use of a single one- or two-letter code to initiate routines.

Source: Robert L. Perry, Rochelle Park, N.J.

Guarding against software traps

Ways to check on your company's expert and protect your company from the vendor:

1. Describe personnel support the vendor will be required to supply, including both the number of people and minimum qualifications.

2. Tie any progress payments to clearly defined milestones in the contract.

3. Have the vendor warrant title to the software and agree to indemnify the user against any loss sustained in an infringement claim.

4. State delivery deadlines.

5. Include detailed specifications for program acceptance.

6. Include "license to user" that spells out the right to duplicate tapes and documentation, multiple-site usage, rights of assignment and sub-license.

7. Clarify the vendors continuing maintenance and repair obligation including response time.

Try to avoid agreements that refer to specifications "to be mutually agreed upon" at a later date, unless the contract allows the user to cancel at no obligation if specs can't be agreed upon.

Source: *Computer Negotiations Report,* Winter Park, Fla.

Drawing property lines on software

The proliferating market for computer software packages is producing some potentially dangerous areas for the unwary purchaser. Since the typical software package is copied and sold to many people, title to the software is not transferred with the sale. Normally, the user obtains only a license to use the package. To avoid problems with this legal relationship:

• Be sure that the vendor owns the program or is authorized to grant licenses for it. A warranty to this effect must be written into the contract. It should also have a hold-harmless clause running from the seller to the buyer, because if part of the package was developed for another user, that user may be the rightful owner. Legal danger for the new user—a charge of receiving stolen goods.

• Retain all rights to your own company's modifications of the program. Agree to strip them out upon termination of the license and before returning the package to the owner.

Avoid giving the seller rights to any modifications in advance. (Most standard contracts give the seller rights to any modifications.) In one case, a licensee made changes in a program, gave them freely to the seller and was sued by another user when the modifications did not work.

When a program is custom-tailored:

• Obtain a warranty from the designer that the package does not infringe on any previous ownership rights. Include a hold-harmless clause.

• Have the vendor mark that it is the purchasing company's property on all work papers, on the source code (human-readable version of the program), and on the object code (machine-readable version). Have these handed over as part of the contract.

• Restrain the vendor's future use of the program. One way to do this is to negotiate a noncompete agreement into the contract to stop the vendor from reselling parts of the program. For less sensitive programs authorize the vendor to license or reuse parts of the package, but arrange to receive royalty payments for this. Allowing others to use, rather than develop, the material can give them an unwarranted competitive edge, especially in complex management and marketing areas.

Basically, deal with a reputable vendor. Have a knowledgeable attorney or contract specialist examine any agreement in this tricky area before signing.

Source: Dick H. Brandon, Brandon Consulting Group, Inc., New York.

Time-sharing and service company hazards

Computer time-sharing (direct access through an on-premises terminal) and service companies (batch processing on a daily basis) have grown into a multibillion-dollar industry.

But many companies offering these services are undercapitalized and make lowball bids to beat out the competition and stay afloat. This can mean that all of your company's financial records may be entrusted to a firm that could go bankrupt without warning.

Worse, even many financially stable operations deliver bad service. Before signing an agreement, talk with current and former users. Look for these common traps:

• Loss of information through inadequate backup systems and sloppy handling.

• Poor or nonexistent security procedures limiting access to client files and records.

• Delays in processing information and delivering regular reports.

• Too many errors, due to poorly trained and underpaid operators.

• Unwillingness to cooperate after the agreement is terminated. Talk with former customers about delays and hidden charges.

Source: Dick Brandon and Sidney Segelstein, *Business Computers,* Boardroom Books, Millburn, N.J.

COMPUTER OPERATIONS

Starting up a computerized operation

Computer cost overruns, delayed start-ups and line management's lack of commitment to results, have soured many executives on the potential of computer processing. Recommendations on how top management can ensure that computers will contribute to profits:

• Critically evaluate each proposal and its alternatives before putting part of the company's operations on computer. Determine return on investment by comparing projected savings (or benefits) with the total cost of the change (or its alternatives) and of the additional costs of running and maintaining the proposed system.

• Hold line management responsible for the projected savings.

• Control costs by defining objectives clearly up and down the line and fine-tuning schedules.

(If line management is likely to change features of the system during development, add an appropriate factor to the cost estimate.)

• Make sure the final decision to computerize a part of the business is not made by a computer specialist (whether an insider or an outsider).

• Let computer programmers and analysts know that there will be a post-switchover audit of all projections of costs and benefits. Job performance will be measured by the accuracy of their projections and results.

• Avoid dotted-line and dual-line relationships between computer and line management.

• In the computer department, eliminate any one-on-one reporting. An ideal span of control is six to eight subordinates for each supervisor.

• Structure computer department jobs so that a career path is clearly defined. Different computer specialties tend to obscure the hierarchy in computer departments. As a result, computer workers have little incentive to work hard to advance themselves. Instead, they advance their salaries by going to work for another company.

Source: Joseph Eisenberg, Profit Improvement, Inc., New York.

Before computerizing a function

Before a particular function or operation in the business is computerized, answer the following questions:

• How often will the program be run? It takes four to six times as long to create a program as it takes to do the job once, without a computer. If the job isn't done fairly often, it may not pay to computerize it.

• Can data be entered into the computer easily? The more work that's involved in collecting, keying, and proofreading the data, the fewer the advantages of computerization.

• How complicated is the job? The more complex the work, the greater the potential savings from automating.

• How many different ways will the information be used? The more outputs required, the greater the advantages of using a computer.

Source: Computer Programming for the Complete Idiot, Design Enterprises, San Francisco.

Integrating computers into a company's operations

The objective is integrating a computer into the company's overall business systems to get largest payback possible.

The company will realize the biggest single payback by computerizing its entire sales order processing.

A company should not computerize order entry, fulfillment, billing, accounts receivable, credit, commission accounting, or sales analysis in a piecemeal fashion. The piecemeal approach can be more costly in the long run. Computer vendors will undersell companies adopting piecemeal approach, just to get their foot in the door. Then, as the company expands its computer operations, it will have to buy expensive add-on equipment or a totally new system.

Smaller companies may also get a good payback by computerizing manufacturing operations. Here, the piecemeal approach makes sense.

Computerizing the company's general accounting system generally offers little payback. However, if the company has other operations on computers, it may make sense to put this on line too in order to improve overall financial controls.

Source: J. Richard Fleming, System Planning Associates, Westfield, N.J.

Getting more from the company's computers

It's critical to get the manager of the computers to think like a top manager. Scrap the idea that the company's computer division only responds to management requests. The company's top computer manager should be offering solutions for the company's most pressing problems.

Improved use of computers is the key to better information management, which is the best way to improve white collar productivity.

Source: James J. Crenner, chairman, Dun & Bradstreet, New York.

Preparing the staff for the computers

Establish good relations between computer technicians and line management. Jointly enroll computer technicians and key line personnel in a seminar on business applications for computers. Have computer technicians work for a week in the departments whose functions they will be putting on line.

Prepare company personnel well in advance for the changes that the computer will bring. The computer will affect the nature and content of work for everyone in a small company.

In testing the software for the company's newly computerized operations, don't use computer technicians. Use the managers and clerical staff who will actually be working with the software. As these people see how the computer changes their jobs, get them involved in redefining their work assignments.

Go on line only when everyone is satisfied with the new system. Allow at least three months more for employees to adjust to working with the computer. Shift personnel only after this phase-in period is completely over.

Systematize the company's paperwork flow around the capabilities of the computer. Most companies concentrate on getting the computer working first, then tackle the problem of rerouting paperwork. This is a mistake. Once the company makes the decision to computerize a function, management should immediately rethink department paper flow. Design improvements into the system and inefficiencies out of the system.

Don't underestimate the cost and complexity of computerizing a company operation. Putting the company on the line takes six to nine months of preparation, conversion, and integration. Then it takes another three to six months to absorb changes fully and to reap the revised system's benefits.

Source: J. Richard Fleming, principal, System Planning Associates, Westfield, N.J.

When to decentralize computer operations

As minicomputer prices fall and sophistication grows, it becomes advantageous for some companies to switch from using one central computer. Benefits of using a number of small systems:

• Different departments can get programming and services tailored to their specific needs. And they will make more use of the system.

• Backup systems are cheaper and easier to provide.

• Conflicts over sharing are reduced, and low-priority jobs no longer get put aside.

• Reliability increases. Unscheduled interruptions occur more often in shared systems.

• Simpler system designs become possible.

• Overhead costs are assigned to departments on a fairer basis.

• Transmission and storage of unnecessary data, which occurs with a centralized system, are eliminated.

Computer professionals use the term *distributed data processing* for a decentralized system.

Source: *Computerworld,* Framingham, Mass.

OPERATING COSTS

How to trim data-processing costs

Troubled times make it easier to reduce the data processing costs that seem to rise routinely. Overall strategy: Trim judiciously. Minimize impact on morale.

Areas where cost reduction is usually possible:

• Number of terminals. Reduce them by strategically locating shared or pooled terminals. If you have ten or more terminals, look for at least a 15% reduction. But be aware that some employees consider terminals status symbols.

• Review of total equipment. Buy, or third-party lease, hardware rather than rent it. (A leveraged lease provides low money cost.) Consider peripheral equipment from off-brand suppliers as well as used equipment (which typically sells for less than half its original list, even if it is only three or four years old).

• Paper. Print eight lines to the inch instead of six. Saving amounts to over 20%. Limit printing of test results. Use both sides of stock paper for tests. Sell used cards and paper to a waste dealer.

• Program packages. Buy off the shelf where possible, even if it means compromising some requirements. When packages are bought together with hardware, both may be eligible for the investment tax credit under current law.

• Computer facilities. The company may be able to use outside air for cooling in winter and also benefit by ducting computer-generated heat through the building. Further saving may be possible by increasing temperature in the computer room by 5°, cleaning it less often, and enforcing the ban on smoking and eating there.

• Training. Eliminate conference attendance and temporarily reduce training programs. This technique reduces costs and eliminates opportu-

nities for job shopping. But entry-level personnel and terminal operators must be trained. A 10%–15% productivity improvement is generally possible.

• Development projects. Review each one on a return-on-investment basis. Eliminate any that don't provide at least a consistent 30% return.

• Research activity. New equipment can wait. High-paid personnel who perform this type of evaluation can be more productively used in development work.

• Staff reduction. Aim for 10% or better. The least productive employees are usually known to fellow workers. Their termination often boosts morale.

• Salaries. Continue giving raises to deserving performers. Keep in mind that legitimate cost reduction eliminates deadwood, luxuries, perquisites, and ineffectiveness. It does not mean steps that reduce productivity or lessen gains.

To help morale, ask for suggestions from the staff. Make them participants in the process of restructuring a leaner, more effective organization.

Source: Dick H. Brandon, Brandon Consulting Group, Inc., New York.

Costs of operating small computers

Hardware and programs are not the only expenses a company must consider before buying a small computer. Other costs:

• Site preparation. Computers need to be protected from changes in temperature and humidity. Electrical circuits should not be shared with other equipment. Computers must be protected against electrical surges and brownouts.

• Space preparation for storing tapes, disks, and supplies.

• Supplies. Initial costs for tapes and disks add to start-up costs.

• Special equipment. In addition to desks designed to hold terminals and racks and cabinets to store tapes, the company must pay for disks, printouts, and a fireproof storage facility for duplicate copies of all records.

• Manuals and instructions. Most users eventually prepare their own simplified instructions. Emergency procedures must be developed in case of fire or other disasters.

• Service and maintenance. Contracts or per-call agreements are essential. Employees in charge of the data-processing operation should belong to appropriate professional organizations, attend seminars, and subscribe to trade publications.

• Hidden costs. These include sales and property taxes, freight charges, staff travel, and legal and consulting fees.

Source: Dick H. Brandon and Sidney Segelstein, *Business Computers,* Boardroom Books, Millburn, N.J.

• Determining which company records are important enough to be fed into the computer's memory banks. Because 30%–70% of most paper documents are inactive, this often takes longer than managers expect.

• Translating paper documents into computer language creates a danger of loss or mistranslation of important records.

• Indexing the stored data. If users don't have easy access to records, all the speed of the computer system will be wasted.

Overlooked utility costs

Computer vendors often understate the significance of energy costs to run data communications equipment. Power costs to operate some devices over their life cycle equal or exceed the equipment's initial costs. Proposed utility rate increases for some cities could add significantly to annual operating costs for larger data communications networks.

Hidden costs of installing a computer filing system

To hear a sales representative tell it, installing a minicomputer is the solution to any company's record-storage and retrieval problems. But before a data system can work efficiently, some very expensive tasks are necessary. Records must be reviewed, information fed into the computer, and a filing system developed.

What's involved:

The cost of human errors

Human errors in programming, keypunching, or other computer operations cost business far more each year than do computer crimes. Use security software so that the computer ignores commands from anyone who isn't certified as competent on a preprogrammed list.

Source: *Security World,* Culver City, Calif.

COMPUTER BACKUP AND MAINTENANCE

Cautions on computer maintenance

Maintenance charges by vendors are getting lower as computer systems get cheaper and more reliable. But with low maintenance charges, the quality of repair suffers, resulting in lengthier and more frustrating computer downtime.

Types of maintenance:

• Routine operator maintenance. It's best performed by the company's own staff, using instructions (and possibly materials) supplied by the manufacturer.

• Preventive maintenance by the vendor. Becoming increasingly rare, it usually is performed only four to six times per year.

• Remedial (and emergency) maintenance for malfunctions.

• Engineering changes or field upgrades. They're necessary when the original manufacturer changes the design.

A principal barrier to swift repairs is that almost all computer systems have separate components supplied by different manufacturers. This can result in "finger-pointing" and delays if the error diagnosis is not exact when the system initially breaks down.

Essentials of a good maintenance agreement for computer systems:

• A single vendor to accept responsibility for a system. No matter what caused the failure, the initial call is made to one vendor, who in turn may call others.

• Fixed-cost maintenance is generally far cheaper and less risky than service on a time-and-materials basis. Or a fixed-fee maintenance coverage for one shift only. Use "on-call" maintenance for odd hours or less critical shifts.

• Start the maintenance contract at the end of the warranty period. For certain types of components, such as terminals, where spares may be available, the company may be able to do without maintenance coverage in the first year or so.

• Response-time guarantee. Most vendors will agree, depending on location, weather, traffic, to an average response of two hours with a maximum of four hours.

• Special problems. If a particular maintenance engineer is unable to fix a problem in three or four hours, he will call someone on the next higher level for assistance.

• "Lemon" clause. Something that fails consistently, or has downtime in excess of $x\%$, is replaced by the vendor.

• Computer's environment requirements. Spell them out ahead of time. Then the vendor can't blame that for frequent failures. Insist on specifications for temperature ranges and changes, humidity, dust level, maximum power fluctuation, and equipment access.

• The original manufacturer should agree to provide all engineering changes as soon as they are issued to the field, regardless of who maintains the company's computer.

• Check the vendor's facilities near the computer site. Where is the staff? The nearest spare-parts depot? Does it contain all parts needed for the system? If not, where are they? How long will it take to get them?

• What parts will the vendor store on the company's computer site? What tools will it keep on company premises? Will it keep blueprints or wiring diagrams with the computer or at the vendor's office?

• Is a backup system available in the event a failure lasts for more than some defined critical period?

• Continuity guarantee. The vendor agrees to make available maintenance for a number of years. This could be coupled to maintenance price protection (increases are limited to a known percentage, or to changes in the cost-of-living index).

• In the event that your company expects to sell the system as a used machine in the future, get a vendor guarantee that reconditioning or resale will not be a requirement for maintenance continuity, so long as the system has been continuously maintained. (This eliminates a poor practice, in which some vendors attempt to control the used-equipment market in their products.)

• Negotiate for credits for system malfunctions in excess of a defined percentage.

Plan ahead. Obtain some rights to blueprints and/or training in maintenance techniques, if the company is large enough or skilled enough to consider doing some of its own maintenance in the future.

Source: Dick H. Brandon, president, Brandon Consulting Group, Inc., New York.

Selecting a data-processing backup

Although there is no alternative to safe, off-site storage of programs, tapes, and documentation, a company has several options for a backup facility. The choices:

• Empty shell. Prepare for setting up a duplicate facility from scratch, including floor plan, utilities, security, and equipment. Negotiate short lead-time contracts for replacement equipment from suppliers. The cheapest approach is often best, but it's not recommended for companies heavily dependent on data processing in their daily operations.

• Fully equipped backup. This is the most expensive and best insurance for firms that will go under if data-processing capability is destroyed.

• Cooperative plan with one or more other companies. Draw up firm agreements on configurations and space and time availabilities, which will allow all companies to operate in case of an emergency.

• Commercial backup facility. It's an alterna-

tive for most businesses. Before signing a contract, investigate: How soon can the backup be available? During what hours can it be used? Does the service supply operators, a 24-hour hot-line, and free-of-charge test time to determine systems compatability?

Source: *Computer Decisions,* Rochelle Park, N.J.

Disaster plans

Adequate preparation is the only defense against a fire, flood, and other emergencies that put the company's data-processing system out of operation. A data-processing manager should ask:

• Who heads the recovery team? And who are the members?

• Where will the emergency control and planning center be located?

• What notification procedures are to be used to call the team together? One mistake is keeping the list in the computer facility.

• Has emergency transportation been arranged?

• Are the equipment inventory and documentation complete and safely stored?

• Have arrangements been made for security, communications, backup facility staffing, and utilities?

• Are all changes in programs and equipment routinely duplicated by the backup facility?

Source: *Computer Decisions,* Rochelle Park, N.J.

Protecting computers from electrical damage

Computers are increasingly vulnerable to damage from static electricity generated by items made of synthetic materials. An employee wearing crepe-soled shoes and a synthetic-fiber sweater can generate enough of a charge in a dry room to destroy a computer's printed circuit boards or its memory devices. Other static-makers are carpets, and plastic envelopes and bags.

Preventive steps:

• Maintain computer rooms at the recommended humidity level. (Electricity builds up in a dry atmosphere.)

• Keep all unnecessary plastic items out of the room.

• Equip all carts, dollies, and other pieces of movable equipment with conductive wheels. Never drag these pieces of equipment.

• Prohibit the use of waxes or aerosol sprays. Both help conduct electrical charges.

• Consider installing an air-ionizer to stabilize the balance of charges in the room's atmosphere.

Source: *Computerworld,* Newton, Mass.

PROGRAMMERS AND OTHER PERSONNEL

Selecting the right data-processing manager

When hiring a data-processing manager, narrow the field down to those who (1) demonstrate ability as project managers and (2) are technically highly qualified. Then hire from among the finalists the one with the most political savvy.

We've moved beyond the super-technician-as-manager stage. Candidates should have records of success in:

• Translating a business's data processing needs into understandable language and plans.

• Resolving user complaints and conflicts.

• Justifying budgets and cost overruns.

• Convincing management to change or expand data processing systems—with profitable results.

When checking references, go beyond immediate superiors at past jobs. Find out what top executives thought of the data processing operation as well as the applicant.

Source: *Computerworld,* Newton, Mass.

Hiring computer personnel

Companies recruiting new graduates with credentials in data processing should prove what they actually learned in school. Commercial schools offering data-processing degrees often teach antiquated computer languages on antiquated computers. Universities too often concentrate on theoretical computer science, not very applicable to business world.

Recommended: Hire away data-processing personnel already trained by other employers. Then offer prime compensation to keep that talent on staff.

Source: John Kirkley, *Datamation,* Barrington, Ill.

Recruiting in-house

Recruit in-house from among clerical workers who display such aptitudes as attention to detail, math skills, and ability to work alone. Training builds loyalty and is often cheaper than frequently replacing job-hoppers in the current marketplace.

Simplify lower-level computer training

Often novices can't begin to learn from complicated manufacturers' manuals.

Instead, set up a barebones training program, using simple instruction sheets prepared from the manuals by experienced operators.

• Teach one operation at a time. For example, how to do a mailing list.

• Give instructions on how to do that job and nothing else. Too much information given too fast confuses any student.

• Teach successive steps in the same way, introducing new terms and techniques only when necessary to complete the step being learned.

Source: *APC Tablet,* Alltech Publishing Co., Pennsauken, N.J.

Avoiding built-in problems with programmers

Computer programmers are often inherently inefficient. To maintain an appearance of use-fulness, they tend to design programs that require their surveillance rather than programs the user can handle independently. And many programmers don't keep abreast of developments in their fields.

To avoid such problems, make program simplicity one of the main goals of the programming staff. Insist that programmers keep up with the times by reading the latest literature and attending important technical seminars.

Source: Richard Hamming, adjunct professor, U.S. Naval Post-Graduate School, quoted in *Computerworld,* Newton, Mass.

Aiding computer-terminal workers

Work at the video terminals of computers entails long periods of concentration. Ways of easing the burden:

• Solicit suggestions from employees about improving work conditions.

• Have mandatory break times.

• Avoid bright lighting. The glare makes the video screen hard to read.

• Lessen screen glare through special coatings and hoods.

• Buy adjustable chairs and a movable keyboard to enable the operator to find the most comfortable positions for work.

• Institute training programs so workers learn to handle equipment efficiently.

• Don't place terminals too close to one another. It will distract the operators.

COMPUTER SECURITY

What management must know about computer security

The biggest security problem today is management's failure to recognize that computer operators are actually handling money. If those people were physically shuffling cash, companies would be much more careful about screening them.

The best protection is to build appropriate safeguards into original computer programming. The cost ranges widely, of course, depending on size and complexity. But it is worth the expense to avoid the huge cost of a rip-off and the inconvenience of reconstructing computer records.

The best time to start a security program is when the company relocates to new quarters. Security hardware must be laid out with the electrical system. Wiring is difficult later.

The most common computer crimes:

• Creation of fraudulent payroll checks, usually done by adding non-existent names to the payroll. An old crime, but one made easier by computers.

• Preparation of fraudulent checks to phony vendors. Another old scam, but harder to detect in the computer age.

• Electronic transfer of assets. A new game, potentially devastating, as many companies are finding out to their horror. The only defense is more sophisticated auditing.

The best way to improve auditing procedures is to establish norms for key business ratios , for examples, labor to sales, inventories to sales, etc. Those are programmed into the computer in such a way that abnormalities, such as a too-high monthly payroll, show up immediately. But since computer printouts appear authoritative, figures that might be questioned if typed or written seem inviolate on a printout. They are not.

To promote computer security:

• Limit access to the computer. Program it to keep track of who keys in what instructions and when they are entered. This provides a trail.

• Also limit the ability of any one computer operator to do tasks such as initiate checks or cash transfers.

• Follow up internal audits with an objective outside review. Personal relationships within a company often make it difficult to blow the whistle. And if culprits are only warned, they will probably just cover their tracks more carefully.

• Check out computer operators as carefully as bank tellers. In states where it is legal, give a lie-detector test before hiring and periodically thereafter.

• Watch for emotionally unstable people as well as dishonest ones. Vindictive employees may deliberately sabotage the company's operations.

• Remember that the higher people are in the firm, the more they are able to embezzle or divert.

In one case, a vice president of an apparel company set up his own manufacturing operation (which his wife ran) three blocks away from his employer's plant. Not only did he divert materials, but also several employees (after punching in at the legitimate plant) were instructed to spend the rest of their day at the "satellite" operation. It cost the employer over $1 million in two years.

Source: Saul D. Astor, president, Management Safeguards, Inc., New York.

Safeguarding computerized accounting systems

Rules that help cut opportunities for fraud:

• All transactions must be recorded. No exceptions.

• All data recorded must be examined before key entry to make sure there's been a real transaction, not a fictitious one.

• Every time a transaction is entered, simultaneously enter the dollar amount assigned to it.

• Transactions should be entered within a specified time after they've occurred. Require an explanation whenever this time limit has been exceeded.

• Provide controls to ensure that every transaction is entered in its proper account classification.

• The summaries of transactions used to figure all calculations should be automatically checked for accuracy before the calculations are undertaken.

• The system provides checks to ensure that transactions are posted correctly, so when data are transcribed from one record to another, the transfer is accurate.

Source: *Evaluation Accounting Controls: A Systematic Approach,* Arthur Young & Co., New York.

Preventing the crime

Over 50% of major U.S. corporate assets are controlled by computer. This is breeding a new kind of criminal who out-thinks the system and gets away with an average of $500,000 per incident (compared with $10,000 for the average armed robbery). What to do:

Retain an EDP consultant to assess the company's vulnerability to computer crime and to determine the security needed. Install an appropriate security system and have the consultant follow up regularly to see that it's working.

Keeping an eye on departing programmers

When it's necessary to fire a computer programmer or engineer, don't let him near the computer room again. If he holds a grudge, he can do enormous damage in a minute or two. The same thing applies if he resigns with ill-feeling. Make sure he is closely watched as he gathers personal belongings.

18 PROTECTING YOUR COMPANY

PLANT AND OFFICE SAFETY

Fire-detection devices

Key point in choosing fire detectors: A fire should be detected as early as possible, before heat builds up or flames break out. A developing fire produces invisible gases and smoke first. The detector should spot these.

A heat detector or flame detector may be worse than none since it provides a false sense of security. It allows the initial signs of a fire (invisible gas and smoke) to go undetected.

Invisible gas detectors:
• The high-voltage detector uses radioactive material to ionize the air.
• The low-voltage detector ionizes without radioactive materials, using a solid-state amplifier instead.
• The photoelectric cell units measure the level of light given off by a built-in source. If smoke blocks lessen the intensity, the alarm is triggered.

Remember though that all types of detectors have false-alarm problems, especially during a crowded meeting or cocktail party when many smokers are present.

Chemical fire protection

Besides sprinklers, these chemical systems are effective fire fighters:

• Halon 1301. A colorless, ordorless gas that is safe to breathe during evacuation. Best for delicate machinery, computers, other electrical equipment. Leaves no residue.

• Carbon dioxide. Useful for stopping localized blazes in large areas subject to flash fires. Relatively inexpensive. But people must be evacuated from the area first.

• Expandable foam. Its best use is to stop fires from spreading in large warehouses, machine rooms, etc. Can fill a 1.5 million cubic foot warehouse in seven minutes. Will not damage paper. Inexpensive.

• Dry chemical. Used primarily in fire extinguishers or in large systems mounted on trucks. They are available in two types, for electrical fires and non-electrical ones.

Get expert advice on installing devices that use these powerful chemicals.

In-house fire brigades

Few industrial manufacturers can afford to rely solely on local fire departments. The first five minutes of a fire are crucial because control can best be exercised at that time. But few fire departments respond that quickly. The answer is to organize an in-house fire brigade.

Appoint a safety director with full responsibility for fire prevention. Local fire departments and fire-insurance representatives will give helpful advice. Schools offer fire-fighting courses for a fee.

Essential equipment. In addition to the necessary sprinklers, hoses and extinguishers, protective clothing stored in strategic locations throughout the plant.

Personnel. Maintenance, construction, security, and supervisory workers. They are likely to be in good physical condition, and training them usually does not disrupt production. Typical brigade size should be 10–12 people per shift. Include an electrician, a pipe fitter, and someone who knows how the sprinkler system works.

Source: *Professional Safety,* Park Ridge, Ill.

Policing the plant for safety

Prime causes of industrial accidents and injuries:

• Unauthorized use of tools, machinery, or vehicles.
• Not giving warning signals when starting up equipment.
• Unusual work (or line) speeds. Tools should be passed, not tossed.
• Inoperative, or ignored, safety devices in hazardous areas.
• Unsafe loads—overloading tractors, feeding parts into machinery too fast.
• Working in unsafe positions.
• Failure to secure valves, tools, switches, and

other equipment against unexpected movement.
• Working on dangerous or moving equipment. Includes jumping on or off moving vehicles. Performing maintenance on still-running equipment.
• Horseplay.
• Failure to wear standard protective devices (masks, aprons, shoes, goggles, and gloves).

Source: *Plant Engineering,* Barrington, Ill.

Common causes of plant accidents

• Improper guards. Are machinery guards inoperative? Do they interfere with work?
• Defective tools, machines, materials, etc.
• Inadequate warning systems.
• Hazardous storage of goods, materials.
• Hazardous procedures. Do the standard operating procedures expose workers to accidents?
• Improper illumination or ventilation.

Source: *Plant Engineering,* Barrington, Ill.

Eye injuries

Objects smaller than a pinhead cause the greatest number of on-the-job eye injuries. Two out of three injuries are due to flying or falling objects. And most of those objects are less than one-half millimeter in diameter. Over half the injuries are minor scratches to the eye. Contact with chemicals or liquids accounts for a quarter. Others are caused by objects swinging from fixed positions (tree limbs, ropes, chains) or objects, such as tools, during use. Sixty percent of those injured are not wearing eye protection at the time of the accident. Most employers provide such eye protection at no cost.

Source: U.S. Department of Labor survey.

Safeguarding workers' lungs

Of all occupational illnesses, lung diseases account for half the deaths. Some safeguards:
• Maintain a good ventilation system. Be sure grilles are not clogged, ducts are sound, and fans are operational.
• Provide protective equipment, such as mouth-nose masks, for workers in dangerous areas.
• Solicit ideas from employees on safety. The better ideas for precautionary measures come from workers exposed all day, every day, to the risky conditions.

Smoking bans at work

Smoking bans have to be worded carefully. In one case a total no-smoking rule throughout a plant that did not manufacture flammable products was ruled unfair by an arbitrator. What to do:
• Designate certain times and/or places where smoking is permitted.
• Be prepared with evidence that cigarette smoke is harmful to the health of nonsmokers. This line of reasoning is winning increasing acceptance by courts called on to review arbitration decisions.

Source: 79-2 ARB Par. 8398; 368 A2d 408.

Preventing office injuries

Statistically, one of every 27 office workers is injured on the job every year. And one of every 22 workers' compensation claims is for an office injury. Offices are booby-trapped with safety hazards, which many companies don't correct.
To make offices safer:

• Appoint a safety director to work with the insurance carrier to reduce hazards.
• Carry out regular safety inspections throughout the premises.
• Remove any penalties or stigmas associated with reporting hazards.
Common office hazards:

• Coffee spills and other items dropped on slippery, uncarpeted floors that might cause falls.
• Wastebaskets, desk or filing drawers, and other objects left protruding into aisles.
• Doors without glass panels to show what's on the other side (for example, a person standing there unseen, risking collision).
• Steel files that can fall forward because they are not bolted to the floor.
• Damaged or weakened file ladders and stools.
• Electrical extension cords stretched across aisles or between desks, frayed extensions, and broken plugs.
• Fans, coffeepots, and other appliances used by workers.

Source: *Modern Office Procedures,* Cleveland.

SECURITY MEASURES AGAINST THEFT

How employees steal

How thievish employees get loot off the company premises:

• Products are turned into "scrap" and then easily repaired after a worker is permitted to take the "spoiled" merchandise home with them.

• Company property is concealed in scrap barrels.

• Gas is siphoned from company trucks into private cars.

• Oversized lunch boxes hide company goods.

• Small items are concealed under clothing. In one case an arbitrator upheld a rule requiring men to tuck shirts inside their trousers before exiting via a guarded company gate.

• Valuable material, copper wire, for instance, is taken through the plant's gates on delivery trucks. The driver then hides the loot for a later pickup. Even dumpsters carried away by contracted sanitation companies have been used this way. Such scams always involve collusion.

• Merchandise is taken from a customer's order, so they don't get all the goods for which they paid. The belief is that the customers won't check their shipment. In the aggregate, the small amounts stolen from a customer develop into large ones for the thief.

• Drivers leave products at a customer's house "by mistake" and retrieve them later. This involves telephoning the receiver immediately from a pay telephone before he has a chance to check the delivery and call the company about the mistake.

• A hole is dug under a fence. Merchandise is then pushed outside and picked up after dark. But no theft has occurred until someone takes possession of the material outside the premises.

Successful prosecution may require surveillance until the offender picks up the merchandise.

• Shipping clerks send packages to confederates.

Source: Discharge arbitration hearings.

Employee theft patterns

Worker immaturity plays a surprisingly large role in employee thefts as well as sabotage.

Key findings from a recent study:

• Young, unmarried workers are responsible for more thefts than any other group.

• Potential thieves are often workers who believe that management is unethical.

• A high percentage of company thefts are committed by employees who believe they've gotten a raw deal from a supervisor or lower management.

When a good man steals

What should a company do when good managers engage in casual theft of company property?

In a recent case, a foreman at a tableware factory shipped some boxes of silver-plated utensils to a customer. He then billed the customer for less-expensive stainless-steel items. When confronted, the foreman admitted the scam. His motive was to give a break to the customer, who was a friend. The foreman begged for leniency, citing 23 years of loyal service.

The boss' decision was to fire the foreman without references. The company's logic was that failure to take disciplinary action against a known in-house thief, even one with long years of service, leads to an erosion of morale among honest workers. And allowing theft would set a bad example for those easily influenced.

Source: *International Management,* New York.

How to use undercover agents to detect internal theft

To pinpoint the cause of unexplained inventory losses, consider placing an undercover agent in the company plant or warehouse to watch for internal theft.

• Get recommendations from other businesses.

• In a small- or medium-size city, ask the local police department which are the reputable firms. The owner of the agency will probably supervise the job personally.

• If neither business nor police advice is helpful, use a big national agency such as Pinkerton's or Wackenhut.

To measure the cost/benefit:

Project current losses out a few years to see if an investigation will pay. The fee is usually $1,000 per month over the agent's salary as an employee, plus expenses for gambling, drinking, union dues, and buying drugs.

When interviewing agencies, make sure to specify that the company is interested in undercover work. Don't accept agency recommendations for surveillance. The only way to watch someone closely on the job is through undercover. And surveillance costs as much as $50 per hour plus car-rental fees and other expenses. Surveillance can work when management suspects who is stealing, but doesn't know how they are getting rid of the goods or where they

are being fenced. It also works when the thefts are occurring off-premises. For example, a truckdriver has aroused suspicions by making unusual stops.

The agency should be able to provide an undercover agent from the community, but engineers or computer programmers may be difficult to find locally.

How long it takes to get results:

Three to six months. What prolongs the investigation:

• Unions.

• Wary employees (because the company has used undercover agents in the past).

• Management has alerted employees that it suspects theft and has already applied pressure to stop it.

Never hire an agency that:

• Guarantees results.

• Bases charges on a percentage of recovery (an incentive to inflate losses).

Precautions in using an agent:

• Ask to have the prospective agent take a polygraph (lie-detector) test from a polygraph expert who is not affiliated with the security agency. It will cost $30–$50. If an agency balks at this, find a different agency.

• Get a signed agreement of indemnification from the agency to cover both workers compensation and any legal claims that the undercover agent might make against the company.

• Inform associates of the investigation on a need-to-know basis only. Have the agent come into the company through normal hiring channels. And don't try to find out who the agent is.

• The agents may induce disciplinary action by the company to enhance their status with suspects. Don't hesitate to enforce the company rules.

What to expect:

Daily and weekly reports sent to the responsible manager at home, detailing on-the-job stealing, gambling, drinking, drug use, violation of safety or work rules or poor supervision. Read the reports and forget them. They are simply proof that the agent is on the job.

Expect nothing to happen until the investigation is completed. At that time, the agency will give management a complete report, revealing who the offenders are and what they are doing. At a minimum, expect to be able to fire the offenders. Recovery of losses through prosection may be possible. A court may order restitution as a condition of probation. Or the company may hire a collection attorney. Some states provide for double damages.

Never tell the judge that the company is prosecuting to get the money back, because the court will not act as a collection agency. If the company prosecutes simply because someone committed a crime, the court often demands restitution.

Source: J. Kirk Barefoot, *Employee Theft Investigation,* Butterworth Publishers, Woburn, Mass.

Tracking the real inventory thief

Manufacturers may think that theft is responsible for their inventory shortages. Most likely, it's not. Principal causes of shrinkage are undetected bugs in the accounting system, such as inaccuracies in bills and imprecise reporting, and may account for 80% of most inventory shrinkage.

Effects of inventory shrinkage:
• Loss of profit.
• Distortion of true material costs. One product may be the source of the problems, but the loss is spread across the board. Management is handicapped when it comes to making intelligent cost-control decisions. Selling prices are raised to offset the inventory loss. In turn, the company's market position can be undermined.
• Shaking of management's faith in its control system.

What to do first: Take proper security precautions.

If shrinkage is a new problem, start by making sure the last physical inventory was properly costed. And re-examine the accounting system.

What to look for:
• Inventories transferred to a new branch, but which are still on the books of the main office as well.
• Changes in cost accounting.

If shrinkage is a persistent problem, in-depth analysis is necessary:

• Determine the total shrinkage dollar value.
• Brainstorm the possible causes (engineering, manufacturing, accounting, sales, etc.) to determine where the most serious problem exists. (The average manufacturer has about 50 possibilities.)
• Prune the list to the 10 most likely possibilities.
• Investigate each problem area to determine the cost and time needed to correct it.
• Decide whether corrections make cost-benefit sense.

Problems with in-depth analysis. It occupies a great deal of executive time. Objectivity is difficult to obtain. For example, computer programmers may not want to admit the fault lies in their area. In such cases, outside specialists may have to be brought in.

The special problem of unreported scrap. Because there is nothing to look at in investigating unreported scrap, it is hard to get a handle on the problem. Try to make comparative tests with competitors. Ex-employees, company controllers, and trade-association people often can supply rough scrap figures.

Organized theft. If the company is a target of organized crime, inventory analysis probably won't pick it up. Professional thieves are sophisticated enough to reprogram computers, too. Special expertise in crime detection is necessary to pinpoint the problem.

Source: Robert J. Shaw, Peat, Marwick, Mitchell & Co., New York.

Some counterattacks against employee theft

The favorite tactics of employee pilferers, and effective countertactics:
• Heavy on-the-job breakage claims. Workers must show a supervisor the broken item when the claim is made. Otherwise the employee might take home or sell items reported as broken.
• Delivery shortages to customer. Require

written customer verification of quantities. Investigate any shortages.

• Shipments to nonexistent customers. Use consecutively numbered shipping records. Spot-check inventories, especially at the unloading docks.

• Unrecorded sales from delivery docks. Reconcile stock withdrawals against sales records. Identify locations plagued by shortages. Sell only from register-equipped sites.

Source: Harold Davidson, *Beverage World,* Great Neck, N.Y.

Stop rip-offs in the shipping department

Problem: Shipments of goods to phantom customers, with the connivance of accounting, shipping and delivery personnel. A six-step program to cut this risk:

1. The billing department prepares sales invoices after the shipping department (or an independent shipper) returns the complete shipping documents.

2. Customers must sign shipping documents (showing acceptance).

3. Prenumber and independently match sales invoices against shipping documents. The object is to identify customers, quantity, nature of goods, and time of shipment.

4. Have all records checked at least once a month by someone who is outside both the billing and the shipping departments. Object: To guard against duplicate invoice numbers.

5. At least once a month, reconcile the quantities shown on the invoices against the quantities sent out by the shipping department. This helps spot uninvoiced shipments or inflated quantities.

6. Send customers monthly statements for balances due. Investigate customer complaints for nonreceipt of goods promptly and thoroughly.

Source: *Evaluating Accounting Controls: A Systematic Approach,* Arthur Young & Co., New York.

Thwarting cargo thieves

The first step is obvious but not always done. Report a suspected theft at once (even if there's a chance that the material is only lost.) The information may give the police an opportunity to spot the stolen goods if they are still in the terminal area.

Additional security aids:

• Plain brown wrappers. An unmarked carton deters impulse thefts, by not calling attention to what's in the box.

• Keep manifests out of sight. If cargo-identifying documents are not plainly visible to every passerby, the number of people who do know the contents of a container is reduced. So are the risks of a large-scale loss.

• Secure cargo cribs. Even when locked up tight, storage bins inside consolidation sheds must be kept in mint condition. Solidly built, top-quality cribs are worth the investment.

• Use seals. Inadequate seals, even no seals at all, are a commonplace in every port. Use seals on each container. Even though determined thieves can get around them, seals are effective.

Security-guard checklist

What a contract with an agency providing security guards should include:

• List of duties to be performed in detail.

• Minimum training for guards and their supervisors.

• The right to remove individual guards for poor performance.

• Thirty-day, or less, option to cancel contract.

• Liability insurance that protects in case of false arrest. Also, require 30 days' notice if insurance is to be canceled.

• Fidelity bond greater than maximum possible losses.

• Spell out when overtime goes into effect.

Source: Warren, McVeigh & Griffin, San Francisco.

A simple system for restricting keys

Divide all areas into four security groups, with the following key restrictions:

• Group 1: The lowest-level security areas. Keys to these areas can be duplicated commercially by any competent locksmith.

• Group 2: More sensitive areas. Keys can be duplicated only by a locksmith who participates in the security program with the company.

• Group 3. High-security areas. Key duplication is possible by the lock manufacturer only.

• Group 4. The highest security classification. No duplication of any keys to Group 4 facilities is possible. If an original key is lost, replace the whole locking system.

Source: *Security Management,* Washington, D.C.

Burglary-prevention checklist

• Fences. Erect sturdy fences along the perimeter of the grounds. Keep surrounding area free of debris, other hiding places.

• Alarms. Rig alarms to all openings in buildings. Periodically test them and their power sources.

• Lighting. Install lights at fence gates, entry points to buildings, in alleys, and at rear of buildings. Wire alarm to go off if any light goes out.

• Doors. Install pry-proof door frames. Use cylinder locks and pry-resistant hasps. Recess cylinder ring of locks. Use wire mesh to prevent glass panels from being pushed in. Use sheet metal on basement doors. Control access to keys.

• Windows. Grate most vulnerable windows and all skylights, ventilators, fire exits. Where possible, use glass bricks for windows.

• Safes. Bolt lightweight safes to floor. Change

combinations regularly. Illuminate them so activity in their vicinity is visible from outside.

Source: *How to Develop an Effective Security Program,* Dartnell Corp., Chicago.

Mark company property against theft

Engraving Social Security numbers on personal property is the best way to make it difficult for thieves to get rid of their loot. Businesses can do the same thing, using the Federal Employer Tax Number. Remember to add zeros to the front of the number to total nine digits. That makes it compatible with police-computerized lost-property systems.

Indoor security systems

Indoor devices should be placed wherever high-value material or proprietary processes are located. Most widely used systems:

• Ultrasonic motion detectors. Protect areas up to 25 feet by 35 feet by producing ultrasonic patterns that react to motion or noise. Although drafts, hissing radiators and moving machinery can cause false alarms, it is the least expensive device for small areas.

• Microwave sensors. Cover areas up to 70 feet by 100 feet. But the beams can pass through glass, thin wood and plasterboard walls. So it's not useful where passersby or movements of machinery are not adequately screened by thick walls. Does provide low-cost coverage of large, open areas.

• Passive infrared sensors. Cover large areas by picking up the infrared energy radiated by an intruder, but cannot be used where levels of sunlight change. Most expensive.

Other options:

• Audio sensors that are set off by strange sounds in unoccupied areas.

• Listening systems that permit guards to hear intruders.

• Sensors that detect vibrations or human proximity to metal objects.

———

Source: *Plant Engineering,* Barrington, Ill.

How to spot a fake ID

The best identification is a photograph, physical description, and signature. Employees who inspect identification cards should also use these safeguards:

• Repeat some information from the ID card back to the holder, but make a small mistake in repetition. Example: Is your address 733 Lake Drive? (743 is the real number). Imposters are often unfamiliar with details.

• Don't accept IDs that have the name of the state or issuing agency typed instead of printed. A typographical error is almost always a sign of a fake.

• Check wear patterns on old cards. A genuine card will be worn mostly around the edges from handling. Some forgers artificially age cards, which gives a uniform look of wear all over the card.

• Look for raised edges around photographs, which is a sign that a substitution has been made.

• Feel for flaws in laminated cards, another sign of tampering.

• Compare the typewriter face on various parts of the card. Reject it if there is a mismatch.

• Check the holder's signature against the one on the ID.

Birth certificates are poor IDs because they fail to describe the adult using them. A driver's license, passport, or credit card (that can be checked to see if stolen) are better forms of identification.

———

Source: *The National Notary Magazine,* Woodland Hills, Calif.

Vandalproof fencing

Fences made from expanded metal provide excellent security. Intruders have great difficulty getting a handhold or toehold because of the fencing's close, sharp-edged mesh construction. It is also very difficult to cut through, wears well and looks attractive.

Expanded metal is a solid sheet of galvanized or stainless steel that is die cut and stretched, producing sharp diamond-shaped openings.

Expanded metal can also be used for antiscaling barriers, storefront gates, screening for secure areas inside factories, grates for drainpipe openings.

The cost is slightly more than traditional fencing. But they have a longer life, require less maintenance, and have a better appearance.

———

Source: Expanded Metal Manufacturers Assn., 221 N. LaSalle St., Chicago 60601.

WHITE-COLLAR CRIME

Countering white-collar crime

The first line of defense against white-collar crime is never to trust any employee, especially not long-term workers who handle money or finances. If the company is up front about this, the boss and employee will work together better.

Basics of an antitheft system:

• Make sure receipts are quickly posted against specific invoices at all cash-collection points.

• Have two people deposit money in the bank at least twice a day.

• Cross-check deposit balances, slips, and receipts.

• Review the books on a regular basis, and make surprise checks.

• Require everyone to take vacations. For those in critical money spots, consider ordering surprise time off so procedures can be checked.

• Set up a paper trail whenever possible, with easily checkable invoices, check numbers, dates, etc., so that embezzlement charges can be made effectively.

Computer crime is on the rise. Prosecutors still do not have a handle on all the techniques. One common crime is clerks at computerized point-of-scale cash registers erasing cash receipts from the computer tape.

Computer safeguard efforts should start with programmers. If there is only one, hire an outside consultant to check that employee's work. Have printouts run with computer balances so a paper record is available. Reconcile balances often. Have supervisors check on computer operators. Check the supervisors, too.

Surprise audits by the firm's auditors are a good idea. It may also be smart to cross-check the auditors if they have been working on the books for a long time.

But if managers make charges they can't back up, they lay themselves open to a lawsuit. Therefore, call in police at the least suspicion, and let them quietly make a case. Then, don't be afraid to file criminal charges against the thief. Examples work wonders, especially in larger workplaces where everyone seems to want to get into the siphoning-off act.

Embezzlement sometimes starts with padded expense accounts. It is a good idea to be clear and tough about accounts. Require weekly reconciliation against advances, even if the employee is out of town.

Source: Lawrence V. Christ, assistant district attorney for consumer fraud, Johnson County Court House, Olathe, Kans.

How to guard against embezzlement

Be suspicious of embezzlement when bookkeeping employees:

• Are excessively sensitive to routine questions or protective of records.

• Continually work overtime.

• Refuse to take vacations or reject promotions.

• Allow ledgers to fall behind.

Suspicious cash-flow and production patterns:

• Collection of receivables declines without apparent reason.

• Debts are written off without good explanation.

• Raw-materials use increases but production does not.

Suspicious outside relations:

• Creditors ask to deal with a specific person.

• When absent, the employee receives many

odd calls or visits from people who are reluctant to explain their business.

Source: *Alert,* New York.

White-collar crime tip-offs

U.S. companies are losing over $40 billion a year through kickbacks, embezzlement, and other so-called white-collar crimes. A substantial percentage of them can be traced to purchasing departments and could have been prevented if management had been more alert. Early-warning signals:

• A buyer dealing only with a few suppliers. Big orders go to only one or two of them while other potential suppliers complain.

• Refusal of a buyer to delegate his duties when he's absent.

• Sole evaluation of suppliers left up to a single buyer.

• Supply costs that have risen faster than the inflation rate for the industry.

• Purchasing records that are difficult to locate.

• Loading-dock scales that often malfunction.

• A purchasing officer's life-style that is conspicuously above that of similarly paid employees.

Source: Jules B. Kroll, president, Kroll Associates, Inc., New York, *International Management,* New York.

Management styles that encourage crime

Top management can create an environment that discourages or encourages white-collar crime. When the management style is bad for security, even the best internal controls fail. Avoid:

• Obfuscation, the deliberate attempt to con-fuse tax and insurance audits. This is commonly done by keeping poor records or secret books, making phony transfers or setting up dummy corporations. If middle-level managers see that top management winks at the law, they may spot and take advantage of embezzlement opportunities. Efforts to prosecute the embezzlers can be blocked by blackmail threats. And the firm's poor record-keeping hinders prosecution.

• Favoritism to relatives or particular employees. The worst situation is letting such people help themselves to company products, services, supplies or petty cash. This creates a psychological climate in which all workers feel entitled to help themselves.

• Crisis management. If a company regularly operates in a frantic manner, good management practices fall by the wayside. A typical bad directive: Forget the paperwork. Just get the goods out now! When managers encourage workers to disregard control procedures, security slips. A frequent result is routine loading of extra merchandise, that is, theft.

• Self-delusion. Managers refuse to acknowledge loss figures that signal employee misbehavior because of what these numbers say about their competence.

Source: Saul D. Astor, president, Management Safeguards, New York.

When managers handle money

Pay special attention to financial control systems during periods of rapid growth. They are often stretched thin at this time.

Require that all outside business dealings with customers of the company be disclosed.

Prohibit financial managers from visiting the office during vacations. A few minutes may be all they need to keep a computer swindle going while they're away.

Once an employee has been told he is under suspicion, don't let him leave the office until he is fully questioned. He may disappear. The faster the investigation proceeds, the more money is likely to be recovered.

Source: *Security Letter,* New York.

How to cut cash pilferage

Splitting cash functions among two or more employees is the best way to deter thefts of cash. Collusion is still a problem, but it cuts the risk significantly. Eight points at which functions can be split:

1. *A:* Handle cash. *B:* Annotate cash ledger.
2. *A:* Collect from delinquent accounts. *B:* Credit the account.
3. *A:* Authorize petty cash payments. *B:* Disburse the money. *C:* Record the disbursement.
4. *A:* Accept an order. *B:* Send the goods.
5. *A:* Work the cash register. *B:* Audit the register tapes.
6. *A:* Make bank deposits. *B:* Review the slips.
7. *A:* Approve payments by check. *B:* Review the checks.
8. Have someone from outside the department (or even the organization) take all physical inventories.

Source: *Security Management,* Washington, D.C.

PROTECTING COMPANY SECRETS

How to protect company secrets

A common problem is that many employees aren't sure what's confidential and what isn't. Have someone in the know classify documents and stamp the degree of confidentiality on them. Other ways to tighten procedures:

• Beware of those employees most likely to let secrets slip. Best candidates are those who socialize with competitors, compulsive talkers, and people who boast when drinking. Keep them off the list for classified documents.

• Don't discuss plans or developments with colleagues in nonsecure places. There's no way of knowing who's listening.

• Require that all desks be cleared of confidential information at the end of each day.

• Account for every key to the office. Change locks when an employee who has had access to a key leaves the company.

• Don't throw sensitive material into office wastebaskets. Take it home and throw it out

there. It's cheaper than buying a paper shredder.

Source: *The Effective Manager,* Boston.

Routine safeguards

• Shred all rough drafts of important documents. If they're only torn up manually, they can easily be retrieved from wastebaskets and pieced together.

• Destroy old typewriter ribbons. Cassette-type ribbons can be read as easily as a finished document.

• Create special in and out boxes for confidential memos. Handling such material the same way as routine paper flow leaves it vulnerable.

• Clearly mark all confidential data, for legal purposes.

• Don't leave keys to important drawers and files in an unlocked top drawer.

• Periodically check phones and data-transmitting and dictating equipment for bugs.
• Screen custodial and maintenance crews carefully.

Source: Ira A. Lipman, president, Guardsmark, Inc., New York.

rial. For total security, use a disintegrator or a pulper. Material destroyed in these cannot possibly be reconstructed.

Source: *The Office,* Stamford, Conn.

Is the office bugged?

Someone impersonating a telephone-repair worker can install an eavesdropping device in minutes. The devices can also be easily hidden in offices, elevators or rest rooms. And spike microphones can be driven into the walls of neighboring offices to pick up conversations.

If bugging is suspected, a full electronic sweep may be necessary. This involves hiring outside experts to look for microphones, wiring or transmitting bugs with a variety of detecting devices. Searchers trace all electrical and communications wiring. They pry apart molding and paneling, take up rugs, unscrew fixtures and thoroughly examine office furniture.

But bugs that are extremely small, operate on low power, or are not in use at the time can escape even the best sweep.

Other defenses:
• Do not discuss confidential information on the phone. If it is unavoidable, play a radio loudly in the background.
• Vary the location and setting of important meetings so there is no pattern for a potential eavesdropper to pick up.

Source: *Occupational Hazards,* Cleveland.

Shredding confidential documents

Shredders that slice paper, microfilm documents and computer printouts into ¼-inch strips are adequate for most confidential office mate-

Bonding employees

Bonding is an agreement by an insurance company to reimburse a firm if an employee steals money or other property. But there is no way to designate classes of people who may steal or embezzle from the company, so the best policy is to bond all employees. The smaller the company, the greater the need for bonding. Since small firms usually cannot withstand significant losses.

The rate is determined by:
• Type of business.
• Annual sales.
• Marketability of product. The more marketable, the greater the possibility of loss. Television sets are easier to turn into cash than are carburetor parts.
• Loss history. Retailing, warehousing, and trucking have higher-than-average losses.

There are three Ds in bonding. They stand for dishonesty, disappearance, and destruction.

This policy covers any of five kinds of loss:
• Employee dishonesty. Loss of money, securities, or other property, which is caused by dishonesty or fraud involving any employee or officer acting alone or in collusion with others.
• On-premises losses. Loss of money or securities from the company's premises or bank safe-deposit boxes.
• Off-premises losses. Loss of money or securities while being transported by a messenger or armored-car company.
• Counterfeit currency. Loss due to accepting counterfeit U.S. or Canadian currency in exchange for merchandise.
• Forgery. Loss through forgery or alteration of checks, drafts and other specified instruments issued by, drawn upon or purporting to have been issued by the company.

A blanket-crime policy covers the same five

areas as 3Ds but requires the insured to take all five and accept the same limit or liability for each.

Kinds of bonding coverage not as widely used are single-fidelity and single-forgery policies. They have been replaced by the broader types of coverage.

Deductibles. These should be set by the insured firm, based on the losses it can afford. In a company with up to 300 employees, the deductible might range up to several thousand dollars.

Comparison shopping. Contracts are almost all the same. Differences among insurance carriers are in the way they interpret the factors that go into the rate structure. Prices vary at most by 15%.

Filing claims. Report losses as soon as possible, and file an affidavit within four months. If the insurance company disallows the claim, file suit against it within two years. The vast majority of cases are settled without suits.

———

Source: Vincent J. Borelli, vice president, Marsh & McLennan, Inc., New York.

Reporting bonded losses

Suspicions about a dishonest employee should be reported to the bonding company immediately. Fidelity bonds normally cover only losses discovered while the policy is in force. The company could lose out even if the loss occurs during the policy period, if the insurance is cancelled or switched to another company before the incident is discovered.

Also, some policies have a time limit for notifying the insurance carrier after the discovery of the theft. If it's only a suspicion, the information must be handled very discreetly to avoid a libel suit.

———

Source: 581 P 2d 744.

How, when, and where to use lie detectors

Lie detectors come in a variety of forms. The standard polygraph measures breathing patterns, blood pressure, and skin resistance to electrical current. Newer polygraphs concentrate on only one of these physiological changes. The focus now is on those detectors that measure changes in voice vibrations.

Claims of accuracy vary for each type. But the consensus is that standard polygraphs, which proponents say are right 90% of the time (and critics say are right 50%-75% of the time), are the most reliable.

The key to accuracy of standard polygraphs is an experienced operator. Since a polygraph measures bodily changes, the operator must ask right questions, and interpret the machine's record of physiological changes in reaction to questions.

Some subjects "beat" polygraphs by staying up all night before a test, drinking coffee before hand, or tensing muscles during a test.

Legal status of lie detectors: Few courts will admit polygraph tests as evidence. Seventeen states ban use of lie detector tests as a condition of employment.

And some union contracts rule out any employer use of lie detector testing.

———

Source: Robert Ellis Smith, *Privacy,* Anchor Press, Garden City, N.Y.

Using exit interviews to cut worker theft

Exit interviews can give employers a new perspective on their security programs. Ask departing employees:

• Are there any problems of which security managers should be aware?

• Do you have any comments about our security program, or the ways it could be improved?

• Have you ever observed anyone taking merchandise?

• Do you have any information concerning thefts, theft rings, or dishonest employees?

• What is your opinion of the security program here?

• Do employees respect the security program?

• If you had to find a way to steal anything, how do you think it could be done?

Source: G.A. Lapides, western regional security manager, McKesson & Robbins, *Security Management*, Washington, D.C.

THREATS TO PERSONS

Telephoned bomb threats

Whether to evacuate an office after a telephoned bomb threat is a decision for top management. Training switchboard personnel in these procedures will help:

1. Identify background noises (traffic, machinery, other unusual sounds).

2. Try to determine the caller's sex, approximate age, race, and any accent or unusual speech pattern.

3. Ask what time the bomb is set to go off.

4. Ask for the bomb's location.

5. Notify management and *then* call the police.

Heeding your instincts

Thefts and physical attacks can be headed off if managers and employees learn to trust their suspicions. Hesitancy to run or call for help is an intruder's best friend.

Robberies and assaults are often committed by people who know their victims. A person you have seen before is not necessarily above suspicion.

Don't assume that a stranger in the office is there on business.

Don't be influenced by stereotypes of attackers. They come from all ages, races and classes.

Be alert to suspicions of others. Take employ-

ees' feelings for trouble seriously. Encourage them not to shrug off suspicious incidents.

When in doubt about someone, run away at once. Don't be afraid to seem rude or paranoid.

Source: Tamar Hosansky, partner, Safety & Fitness Exchange, New York.

Practical personal defense

Unless a company is a target for terrorists or fanatical special-interest groups (still not a common problem in the U.S.) it is probably unnecessary for top executives or owners to take extreme precautions.

Simple, commonsense measure are always advisable:

• Maintain a relatively low profile in the community.

• Don't follow exactly the same route or routine each day.

If a company believes its top executives are vulnerable to attack, the best form of personal protection is the individual bodyguard/driver. Select someone trained by the armed forces, the Federal Bureau of Investigation, Secret Service or state or local police. Check references carefully. Insist on a lie-detector test.

Highly qualified, personable driver/guards are hard to find, because they must be ready to lay their lives on the line, but it is essentially a boring job. Expect to pay $30,000–$40,000 a year plus benefits. Contract a personal-guard service to do the paperwork, screen and bond the people, and take responsibility for always having someone available. But it will not usually be the same person.

Source: Saul Astor, president, Management Safeguards, Inc., New York.

Security precautions for working late

Follow these safety measures when working overtime:

• Work after hours only when there are others in the office or in nearby areas.

• Stay near a telephone. Keep phone numbers of security guards and police close at hand.

• Distribute whistles to employees who work late. Call the police as soon as anyone hears a whistle.

• Stand close to an elevator's button panel. In the event of an attack or threat, press the alarm button and as many other floor buttons as possible to make the elevator stop at the next floor. But don't press the stop button, which will trap you between floors with the attacker.

• Familiarize yourself with emergency exits and fire stairs. Don't run into an elevator or locked stairwell if someone is chasing you. It might provide the kind of privacy the attacker wants.

Source: Tamar Hosansky, partner, Safety & Fitness Exchange, New York.

How to behave if taken hostage

While the idea of being taken hostage may seem farfetched, it's happening with disconcerting frequency in many big cities, especially in banks, liquor stores, and airplanes. To get through it safely:

• Concentrate on following instructions exactly during the first 15-45 minutes. This is the critical period, when the terrorist is emotional and trigger-happy.

• Keep quiet, and speak only when spoken to. Don't try to be friendly, phony, argumentative, or hostile.

• Don't make suggestions. Captors will suspect a trick.

• Be wary of attempting escape. If it fails, it's likely to bring violence.

• If you are released ahead of others, closely observe everything that goes on in order to help police.

• Treat the hostage-takers like royalty, but try not to be overly condescending.

• Expect to be frisked or even treated roughly by police when released. Cooperate fully—police aren't sure who is who and don't take chances.

Source: Frank Bolz, captain, New York City Police Hostage Negotiating Team.

19 INSURING YOUR BUSINESS AND EMPLOYEES

INSURANCE— WHAT YOU SHOULD KNOW

What to expect from a broker

• Renewal proposals made well before the original policy expires. The company should have at least 30 days to review a proposal. If necessary, an extension (binder) should continue coverage during the review.

• Renewal policies received within 30 days after approval and signing.

• Workers' compensation claims. Approved within 24 hours for serious injuries.

• Medical claims paid within four working days.

• On property claims, major damage inspected by broker and adjuster the same day. Reimbursement within 10 days after approval of claim.

The broker should also prepare a market comparison to help the company take advantage of those insurance prices that have declined.

Securing coverage after the loss

When the MGM Grand Hotel in Las Vegas burned disastrously in November 1981, its owners did not have enough liability insurance to cover the claims filed against them. One month later, however, they were fully insured. Twenty underwriters joined to sell MGM retroactive insurance.

Any company that is underinsured and faces substantial losses can buy retroactive insurance. Underwriters assess the probable loss and the probable time it will take to settle. They then calculate the premium they need to pay all claims and make an investment profit.

The cost of the coverage depends on how long the underwriters think it will take to settle the case. (Litigated cases can run seven to eight years.) Coverage for long-running cases may cost only 30% of the probable loss—say, $300,000 on a $1 million claim. In cases that will be dispatched quickly, the premium may be 100% of the loss. The advantage to the company is that the insurers handle all the claims.

Retroactive insurance makes the most sense when the company itself cannot determine the size of the probable loss. If the company is fairly confident of what its losses will be and the length of settlement time, there is no benefit in buying more insurance. It is advisable to consult a claims expert before approaching a broker.

Source: Michael Cox, partner, Touche, Ross & Co., Stamford, Conn.

Keep policies on hand

Fire and casualty policies should be in hand (on file) before the full premium is paid. One firm, after finding its plant burned to the ground, didn't have the policy it had paid for. Though it produced the canceled check to the broker, its claim was disallowed. The wise course is to buy insurance as you would an automobile: Give the broker a small deposit, but don't pay up until the policy is delivered.

Opportunities in deductibles

By taking higher deductibles on selected insurance policies, even small companies can derive many of the financial benefits of self-insuring. Premiums are reduced because a business loss is tax deductible, the government shares some of the risk the company assumes in the higher deductible. And making fewer claims often leads to lower premiums or broader coverage.

Taking higher deductibles makes sense in all types of property insurance. The deductible range should be $1,000–$10,000; the precise figure depends upon the type of protection and the company's situation.

Higher deductibles also make sense in bonding groups of employees (a deductible may make the insurer more willing to underwrite this type of insurance) and in automobile insurance (by raising the deductible from $200 to $500, fleets may realize substantial savings on collision premiums).

The higher deductibles should not be used in liability insurance. Premium credits for liability deductibles are usually quite low. And it must be determined who handles claims—the company, the insurer, or an agreed-upon third party.

If the company has a great deal of risk in one geographic area, higher deductibles again are not desirable. If ten company stores in an area get flooded, for example, and the property insurance is written so that each store has a $10,000 deductible the company stands to lose $100,000. A better approach is to get an aggregate overall deductible written into the policy. That way, the maximum sustainable loss to the company is known and manageable.

In choosing the deductible, average the company's insured and uninsured losses over the last five years to get an idea of the historical risk to the company. Then check the effect of the deductible on cash flow and earnings. Finally, compare the potential premium savings to the likely deductible expense.

After a certain point, going for a higher deductible stops making sense. There's little difference in savings to the company between a $5,000, $50,000, or $100,000 deductible if the underwriters have an irreducible premium minimum regardless of the deductible's size.

Source: Marvin Sameth, president, Kurtis, Sameth, Hill, Inc., New York.

INSURANCE COVERAGE FOR THE BUSINESS

What risks should the company insure against?

Musts: fire, business, liability, auto liability, workers' compensation.

Valuable but not vital: theft, vandalism, business interruption, glass, rent, key-executive life insurance.

Competitive employee benefits: group life, group health, disability, retirement-income insurance.

Bad-debt coverage

The slow economic recovery and high interest rates have spurred more companies to buy bad-debt insurance. The biggest buyers are companies with less than $50 million in annual sales, which are least able to risk defaults. The cost is an average 0.2%–.033% of annual sales. Companies usually absorb normal bad debts but need insurance to protect against catastrophic defaults. Policies typically cover only a company's most important accounts. Some creditors are covered automatically, others only if named, and then only to certain limits.

Advantages of having bad-debt coverage include:

• These insurance policies help keep lines of credit open at the bank.

• The underwriter's periodic investigation of insured accounts gives the company what essentially amounts to credit checks on its customers.

• The fee charged by the insurer for acting as a collection agent is less than the average fee charged by commercial collection agents.

Source: Robert E. Parmelee, senior vice president, American Credit Indemnity Co., Baltimore.

Property insurance traps

Company property insurance policies should contain endorsements protecting against:

Early lease terminations. Many leases stipulate that landlords have the right to cancel obligations in the event of fires or other mishaps.

Added reconstruction costs. Forced to replace damaged property, many companies face stricter building codes. Property insurance rarely covers the added costs of meeting the new building codes within a specific endorsement to that effect.

Source: Richard Hess, executive vice president, Schiff Terhune of California, Inc., Beverly Hills.

Cutting fire insurance costs

Installing fire extinguishers cuts insurance premiums. A 2½-gallon extinguisher for each 3,000 square feet of plant area can mean a 5% premium saving on a building and its contents. For a bigger savings, install approved, self-closing fire doors in fire walls. Use of this compartmentalization can prevent a total loss.

Source: *Business Insurance,* Chicago.

What business interruption insurance covers

The kind of business interruption insurance a company needs depends on the type of business, its location, and its ownership structure. Five types of coverage are available:

• Gross earnings protection. Pays the equivalent of earnings plus payroll during shutdowns. It can be modified for the length of the company's shutdown, exclusion of payroll, and other deductibles.

• Business earnings insurance. Pays owners the monthly net profit during a shutdown.

• Valued business interruption. This is on a per diem basis. Payments are negotiated in advance, based on the business' projected financial statements.

• Additional expense coverage. Covers the cost of housing workers after a fire, leasing delivery vehicles to replace those destroyed, or the extra costs of subcontracting normal manufacturing operations.

• Rent insurance. Needed when the lease keeps running uninterruptedly despite a work-stopping fire. It also can cover the excess cost of renting alernative space during rebuilding.

_____

Source: Bruce M. Bradway, *Protecting Profits During Inflation and Recession,* Addison-Wesley Publishing Co., Reading, Mass.

INSURANCE COVERAGE FOR EMPLOYEES

Dangers in health-care rebate plans

The increasingly popular attempt by companies to cut health-care costs by paying employees not to file claims can easily backfire.

The basic concept is that the company fixes an annual health-care claims budget. If claims for the year do not exceed it, the balance is rebated to the employees.

Two techniques that have serious flaws:

• Individual employees receive the unused portion of their claims account at year-end. But high claims by some employees plus rebates to others can cost more than no plan at all.

• Employees are all in group accounts and benefit only if the group as a whole makes fewer claims. There is thus little incentive for individuals to reduce their claims, since co-workers may eat up the rebate fund. A variation that can benefit the company: if the account is overdrawn, employee contributions are raised for the following year.

Programs most likely to succeed:

• The budget is split into individual accounts for each employee and one overall group account.

• If an individual's account is overdrawn, additional claims come out of the group account.

• If the group account is overdrawn, additional claims are deducted proportionately from the remaining individual accounts.

Individual incentives to cut claims are therefore high. At the same time, the goal of reducing group overutilization is kept clear to the employees.

_____

Source: Philip Alden, vice president, Towers, Perrin, Forster & Crosby, management consultants, New York.

Minimizing health insurance outlays

As health-care costs rise and employees visit doctors more frequently, premiums for employee medical coverage can become a significant drain on earnings. Medical insurers estimate that 50%–70% of doctor/patient contacts are unnecessary.

One recommendation is to motivate employees to use the doctor only when necessary by rewarding those who file no medical claims in a year.

For example, one national bank recently started a program to test the concept. Bank employees who file no medical claims in a year will receive free medical coverage the following year. Note: The bank's employees now contribute $120–$300 toward their medical insurance, depending on the number of dependents they have.

Companies considering a pilot program should consult the insurers underwriting their medical policies. Insurers support the stay-well concept and may have applicable experience.

Health maintenance organizations get good marks

People who have switched to a health maintenance organization (HMO) for company-paid medical care are generally happy with the decision, according to a nationwide survey. In an HMO, the subscriber is entitled to unlimited medical care from a group of doctors for a flat fee.

Key findings:

• Of those surveyed, 86% said they are satisfied with the quality of the doctors, even though under the HMO concept they don't get to pick their physician.

• Complaints about long waiting times and impersonal service were not any higher than those voiced by a similar group of workers not in an HMO program. Of those responding, 13% complained about waiting time and 12% about impersonal care.

Companies are increasingly pushing HMOs because they have found they often cut reimbursed hospital costs.

Companies should actively promote the HMO alternative to their employees. The survey found that only 7% of HMO subscribers signed up without prodding from their company or their spouse's company.

Source: Survey by Louis Harris & Assoc., *Business Insurance,* Chicago.

Rejected medical insurance claims

If a medical insurance carrier refuses to pay all or part of a claim, it is often helpful to file an appeal. The problem may be only in processing of the claim or failure of the doctor to supply enough information on the form. (All medical insurers have a procedure for appeal (ERISA) requires it.) There is a good chance that an appeal will succeed.

Better deals on dental plans

Many companies shy away from employee dental insurance because the plans are relatively more expensive than other medical insurance. This is because insurance carriers know that employees will use them heavily initially for overdue dental work.

Within two years, most employees will be caught up on dental repairs. At this point, the company should renegotiate the cost of the plan downward. Steps to take:

- Compile the records that show dental costs have peaked.
- Set up a companywide preventative tooth-care program to minimize future dental bills.

Source: Donald A. DiGiulian, DDS, publisher, *Dentographics,* Branford, Conn.

Pregnancy coverage

Companies that provide medical insurance for wives of employees do not have to pay for their pregnancy-related disabilities. A federal district court said only female employees are legally entitled to this coverage. The court ordered the EEOC to stop implying that companies are legally required to cover wives of employees.

Newport News Shipbuilding Co. vs *EEOC* U.S. Dist. Ct., Eastern District of Va., 25 FEF 5.

Look to other insurers to reduce cost of disability pay

Accident and sickness disability pay should be reduced by amounts employees are eligible to receive from other insurance. For example, many states now provide "no-fault" auto-accident insurance which pays hospital expenses of persons (pedestrians or motorists) injured by motor vehicles. The company's obligations should (where allowed) be reduced by what is paid by no-fault.

But workers sometimes neglect to apply for no-fault auto-insurance benefits because their employers have generous disability policies. Disability plans should be designed to offset insurance benefits receivable, whether actually received or not.

No-fault laws can reimburse employees for 80% of wage loss while disabled. Administrators of wage maintenance plans should take that into account.

Are your premiums for workers' compensation insurance too high?

Some companies pay only half as much for workers' compensation insurance as others of the same size in the same industry. The difference is that they monitor claims carefully and challenge those that are exaggerated or phony.

You should be suspicious if a worker claims injury happened at work but doesn't report it until the next day.

The most important value of monitoring is the deterrent effect. If all injured workers are questioned closely about details, word gets around. As a result, fake claims drop sharply.

Self-insuring to reduce workers' compensation costs

Relatively large companies have long been able to cut costs on workers' compensation by self-insuring. Now, about a dozen states allow smaller companies to form self-insurance pools that give them many of the same advantages big companies enjoy. Other states are likely to move in this direction before long.

How the pools work. A nonprofit organization is set up to accept businesses as insureds and employ specialists to adminster the fund. Compensation claims are paid from members' premiums. The fund also buys supplemental insurance to cover catastrophic claims.

Advantages:

• Lower rates. Premiums after advanced discounts are typically 5%–10% below the state-approved rates (the basis for the premiums charged by private insurers that offer compensation coverage).

• Rebates. Some pools return a percentage of the premiums to companies with low losses. A company with a high premium and very low compensation claims might get back 50% of its premium at the end of the year, after all claims have been filed and covered.

• Emphasis on prevention. Some funds employ loss-control specialists to work with members to develop prevention programs. Some also employ rehabilitation nurses to work with the worst compensation cases to get them back to work faster.

A major disadvantage is that members are responsible for remaining debts if premiums, reinsurance, surpluses and reserves run dry. Be sure the pool screens applicants carefully to eliminate high-risk companies with bad claims records.

One caution though, the pool must carry adequate catastrophe stop-loss insurance and maintain reserves.

Source: Gilbert Waters, administrator, Florida Construction, Commerce and Industry Self-Insurers Fund, Sarasota, Fla.

Who's covered by group life

Does the company's group life insurance policy cover part-timers, consultants, or those who have independent-contractor status? What about an employee who retires from full-time work but continues to serve the company as a consultant? For answers, check the language of the policy. The typical policy covers everybody who works at least 30 hours a week. But changes that occur during employment can cause problems. For example, a retiree-turned-consultant thinks he's still covered but isn't. He dies, and the insurance company refuses to pay. In that case, the estate might sue the employer for failing to let him know in time to convert to an individual policy.

Source: 570 SW 2d 213.

How to avoid group insurance overcharges

Some insurance companies may be overcharging their group insurance customers—slightly. Because buying group insurance is so automatic, and complicated, the insurers usually can get away with it. But by knowing what the group contract really is and how to negotiate with their carrier, most customers can cut costs by as much as 10% or more. Remember, the rate is not the annual cost of the insurance, it is only the advance premium, as a breakdown of the premium charges will show. One area where overcharge could occur is carrier retention. Only one out of a hundred insurance brokers really understands what goes into these surcharges, which are intended to cover a broad range of miscellaneous carrier costs. Insurers aren't eager to teach brokers either.

Some of the costs included in retentions are carrier processing, the insurance company's profit, contract and booklet printing, carrier administrative service, late payment, pooling and conversion, state premium taxes, commissions, and claim determination and processing. Many of these items should rightfully be picked up by the insurer.

Another common overcharge area is reserves. Often as much as one third of a year's premiums are held in reserve by the carrier to protect itself against the time when the customer terminates the policy.

Very often, the carrier pays little interest on this money. Two ways to earn higher interest, or get the entire reserve refunded, are to negotiate a lag time for premium payments equal to the amount held in reserve, or to offer the carrier a letter of credit that guarantees payment for claims filed after the company switched insurers.

The following are signs that your company may be overcharged:

• A retention percentage above 10% of annual premiums. Retention rates commonly vary between 8% and 12% of the annual premiums. In some cases, the higher retention is offset by a lower premium rate. Frequently, however, it is a gross overcharge.

• A reserve that exceeds 30% of annual premiums, or one on which little or no interest is being paid.

• A large number of small claims. It may indicate that a plan is misdesigned.

• A consistent retrospective charge, levied by the carrier to compensate for an excess amount of claims. Negotiating the retrospective trigger level from 75% of premiums to 80% can save $5,000 on a $100,000 annual premium bill.

• A customer is dealing with a captive insurance agent of a specific company. No matter how smart the agent may be, the likelihood is that the agent is partial to his own carrier. Have an independent broker examine the policy to see if there's a better deal elsewhere. The typical fee is $80 per hour. Depending on the size of the account, the total fee cost may be $1,500–$3,000.

<hr>

Source: Arthur Schechner, president, Schechner Corp., insurance consultants, Millburn N.J.

<hr>

Permanent (not term) insurance for key executives

When buying permanent insurance for key executives, do not debate the merits of term and whole life insurance. In the long run, term simply does not do the job.

While term insurance is cheaper to buy, it best serves short-term needs, such as insuring that a debt is repaid. It is also appropriate for providing employee groups with protection, because the group insurance protects employees only during their working years.

But these advantages disappear when the object is to provide permanent insurance on the life of key employees. A corporation's life is perpetual—it presumably outlives its employees—so it must inevitably gain on its investment in a whole life policy that is kept in force until the insured's death.

For example, a company buys a $300,000 policy on the life of a 45-year-old executive. The policy is paid up when the executive is 65. The company pays a $10,000 premium out of capital each year for a total cost of $200,000. Having been issued by a mutual life insurance company, the policy pays nontaxable dividends (partial refunds of premiums), which are used to buy additional, paid-up life insurance.

When the executive is 65, the policy's cash value (which is counted as part of the corporation's capital) is $250,000. The insurance protection, including the additions bought with dividends, is $433,000. The corporation would receive that sum tax-free if the executive dies at this point.

Annual postretirement dividends of $8,000–$10,000 after age 65 continue to buy paid-up additions. The insurance amount grows to $525,000 by age 75, and $600,000 by age 80.

This return on the corporation's $200,000 investment cannot usually be topped by any buy-term-and-invest-the-difference argument.

The company can use the policy to entice the executive to remain with the company until retirement. Offer the executive the chance to name a beneficiary for part of the policy's proceeds. Or offer supplemental income at retirement, perhaps a corporate tax-deductible consultant contract. The net cost of the income supplement is offset by the insurance proceeds received at the executive's death.

<hr>

Source: Arthur Schechner, president, Schechner Corp., insurance consultants, Millburn, N.J.

When a key executive is disabled

A type of coverage, called key-man disability insurance protects the company's bottom line until the executive is replaced. The policy pays benefits to the firm to replace the profits the executive formerly contributed. The cost is 1%–3% of the amount of protection purchased. For example, if the executive is responsible for $500,000 per year of after-tax profits, a policy for that amount costs $5,000–$15,000 annually. It varies with the person's age. After a six-month waiting period, the policy pays monthly benefits for two years. It is expected that by then a successor will be in place.

Key-man disability insurance is available from several large U.S. mutual life insurance companies and Lloyd's of London. Contractual provisions can significantly differ with each carrier. The company should be careful to get the best contractual provisions possible, to avoid problems later.

Source: Paul Fierstein, Paul E. Fierstein & Co., New York.

20 MANAGING REAL ESTATE

REAL ESTATE BASICS

Real estate: an overlooked company asset

On the average, 10%–30% of a corporation's assets based on book value is tied up in real estate. At the market value, these holdings can easily rise to 50% of assets. The problem is that most managers, including entrepreneurial ones, have neither the experience nor inclination to be in the real estate business. But they are in it, like it or not.

Real estate can help the company generate cash without incurring new debt. Especially with land, where the book value is typically small, returns from a development deal can be great. Also often overlooked are underutilized plants, undeveloped factory sites, and warehouses. Most can be recycled into more profitable use, with a minimum downside risk.

Financial restructuring offers other opportunities. For example, privately held companies can usually profit when the owner assumes the real estate assets and leases them back to the company. Lease payments are, for tax purposes, a cost of doing business. With the real estate assets removed from the balance sheet, the company's return on invested capital looks much better. Meanwhile, the owner, because of tax benefits derived from the real estate, needs to take less out of the company in the form of salary and perks.

In publicly held companies, managers have a duty to shareholders to make maximum use of corporate assets. When a company has surplus property, managers can breach their fiduciary responsibility if they sell it without first studying the alternatives. There are typically three or four types of buyers for real estate, of whom each will pay different prices for different reasons:

- Speculators pay the least. They assume the risk of being able to put together a salable package.
- Land developers pay more.
- Builders are still better payers. They tack higher land costs onto the end-product price.
- Users pay the most. They have a definite and immediate need for the property.

Almost any acreage size can be developed into an attractive package. It is usually easier to find several small users to lease building space than one big user to buy it. At first, it is better to lease real estate. It's the best way to establish the true worth of property. (Appraisals can vastly underestimate true market value.) Less marketing effort is needed for parcels of 50,000–100,000 square feet, since in almost all parts of the country there is demand for property this size.

It is best to work with a professional real estate specialist on a fixed-price basis or a monthly retainer instead of commissions of contingency fees. The professional starts with an objective study and analysis of the property. The market is researched to see how external factors (building ordinances, demographic trends, economic conditions) affect potential new uses.

The next step is packaging for market appeal, including discussion with potential tenants to suggest appropriate layouts. To help prospects visualize the end product, prototype drawings are used as marketing tools. Target prices are based on projected new uses and the costs of implementing the development plan.

Approval of necessary variances in zoning or building ordinances is essential, as is preparing answers to possible community objections. When the company leases its property and then mortgages it, the owner has tax-free use of the borrowed funds and still retains title. As the property is depreciated for tax purposes, it generally appreciates in the marketplace. If necessary, the property can be sold later, after its value is proved.

Recognize that real estate activity is dynamic. To profit, companies must be flexible enough to seize opportunities on short notice or to pull back when conditions change. Unanticipated competition, development costs, or changes in highway construction plans can change the picture suddenly. The best approach is to plan big, but start small in terms of cash outlays.

Source: Howard P. Hoffman, president, Howard P. Hoffman Associates, Inc., New York.

Defining market value

Market value should be fully defined when it is used in determining rental values in long-term leases.

One automobile dealer signed a 40-year lease in which rent increases were determined by appraisers' judgments of the market value of the property. However, the judgments of the appraiser were based on the highest and best use of the property. The rent jumped, and the tenant challenged it in court and lost.

If market value is a factor, it should be based on the company's use of the land, not the highest possible use.

Source: *Real Estate Law Report,* Boston.

Renting office space: lessons learned in New York

Tenants with leases expiring in two to three years should be negotiating new leases now. Despite the recession and slow-growth forecasts long-term, rental costs will rise with the economy's underlying inflation rate.

Small-business tenants should avoid subletting from major ones. In tight realty markets, sublets go for premiums, and often tenants must move when sublets expire. It's better to have a longer-term direct lease.

Don't rent extra office space that is apart from the central office area, even when it's cheaper. Employee proximity is usually worth the extra rent. The cheapest perk for employees is a good working environment.

Hire a real estate consultant and a space designer before looking for new premises. No matter what real estate brokers say, they work for landlords. A consultant works for the tenant and will survey current market conditions. He will then negotiate the best rent, escalation clause, and remodeling and maintenance arrangements.

Don't hire real estate lawyers because they are with large, prestigious firms. The real estate departments of these law firms usually work for mortgage lenders, not for tenants. A better bet is to hire smaller firms specializing in the tenant side of real estate law.

When possible, avoid moving. On the average, direct and indirect moving costs add up to a year's rent.

In the office rental market now, tenants have leverage only when they are occupying at least 30,000 square feet of space and their credit-worthiness affects the landlord's ability to refinance his property.

Source: Frederick P. Rose, president, Rose Associates, Inc., New York.

Taking advantage of an older lease

With downtown office rents soaring, an older lease with rents below current market rates and more than five years to run is a significant company asset. It has an easily definable value that can be converted into cash immediately or used as a powerful negotiating tool.

If the lease permits subletting, move and sublet the space to someone else at current rents. A growing company can often acquire more space in another building at no extra cost by applying the profits it makes from the sublease.

An alternative for a company that needs cash now is to move, sublet, and sell the rights to the cash flow from the sublease to a third party. A lease with 10 years to go that has an aggregate rental value of $10 million might be sold now at a 60% discount. The company selling the rights to the lease receives $4 million now. The customers for such rights when the potential profit is $1 million or more include tax-exempt institutions, buyers with excess depreciation, or any company with a tax loss carryforward.

To calculate the current value of a long-term lease, multiply the market rent per square foot by the size of the space by the years on the lease.

If the lease forbids subletting, bargain with the landlord. Offer to move and sell the lease back for cash.

To benefit from an older lease while remaining in the same space, instead of waiting for the lease to expire and then negotiating a new one, renegotiate now. The aim should be a 15-year extension on terms more closely resembling cur-

rent market conditions. Landlords often agree because they get an immediate boost in their cash flow from the building.

If the company needs more space in the current location, bargain for that with the lease. Offer to pay more for the existing space in return for a break on the desired new space.

Principals of the company are not the best ones to handle negotiations over an older lease. Landlords and tenants have opposing interests. Consult a real estate expert who knows if the current market really allows the landlord to command the rent he is asking for the space.

Source: S. Donald Friedman, executive vice president, Huberth & Huberth Inc., New York.

Coping with lease escalation clauses

Escalation clauses for long-term leases are the rule. There are no exceptions. The only defense for companies in the market for rental space is to negotiate hard for as limited an escalation clause as possible.

For example, the landlord may demand rental increases pegged to the Consumer Price Index. The tenant should agree, on the condition that if the CPI goes up 10% a year, the rent will go up only a quarter of that, or 2.5%. (Only a portion of the landlord's costs go up. The financing, for instance, is long-term, and doesn't vary).

Tenants should also resist escalation clauses that allow for both pegged rental increases and a straight passthrough to the tenant of tax, energy, and wage increases, or other expense variables.

If a company is being hurt by rental costs generally, it may make sense to buy space rather than rent it. Companies with sufficient liquidity to buy space can make inflation work for them as the value of their real estate appreciates.

Source: Donald Schnabel, Julien J. Studley, Inc., New York.

If disaster strikes a commercial site

Commercial property leases should define what the landlord is required to do after a fire or other disaster. It should stipulate:

• Whether the landlord is obliged to rebuild.
• How soon.
• Whether the lease will be automatically extended, and for how long.
• If rental payments continue during reconstruction.

Alternatives to renting

Companies attracted to the idea of office condominiums as a way to control escalating commercial rents, but uninterested in using working capital to purchase real estate, have an option: looking for a limited partnership that wants the real estate as a tax-sheltered investment.

How the deal works: The partnership buys the office condo, then leases it to the business. The partnership gets the tax benefits of ownership, plus the advantages of a stable, long-term tenant. The business gets a fixed, long-term lease on favorable terms.

Source: Edwin J. Glickman, senior vice president, Sybedon Corp., New York.

SITE SELECTION

Choosing a plant site

The land bought as the site of a new plant should be, as a rule, at least five times the area the actual plant will cover, to meet needs of future expansion, parking spaces, storage, and other related purposes.

A new-plant-site checklist

• How close is it to major suppliers? Proximity assures an uninterrupted flow of goods, plus savings in shipping costs.
• Is it near other firms in the same general business? Already established supply lines would be an advantage.
• Will trucking companies serve the prospective site? Will the service be limited by restrictions on road weight? Will delivery costs go up because of small-load or less-than-load surcharges?
• If a rail spur is needed, will railroad and local governmental regulations allow it?
• What's the existing mail and telephone service like?
• What sort of police and fire protection is available?
• Are there hotels near the site? What's public transportation like? What about banks, shops, restaurants, hospitals?
• What do firms already in the area say about the site? Are there any hidden handicaps that would hinder the company more than its neighboring businesses?

Source: *49 Things to Check Before You Locate and Build Your Plant,* Continental Illinois National Bank and Trust Co. of Chicago.

The best states for tax and energy costs

Wide differences in state taxes and energy costs make a decision to locate a plant on one side or the other of a state border worth checking into.

The best choices on the tax front, according to a recent survey, were Alaska, California, Colorado, Hawaii, Idaho, Maine, Michigan, Minnesota, Oregon, and Wisconsin. This listing is based on a ranking of state tax policies by the Coalition of American Public Employees (CAPE). States listed were found by CAPE to be the most "unfair," meaning that they were most favorably disposed to business at the expense of other groups.

The best choices on the energy front were Arkansas, Colorado, Idaho, Kentucky, Louisiana, Maine, Montana, Nebraska, Nevada, Ohio, Oklahoma, Oregon, South Carolina, Tennessee, Texas, Utah, West Virginia, and Wyoming. These states were found to have relatively low average industrial power costs.

Changes can be expected ahead. The advantages of the Gulf Coast and Southwest may be coming to an end as current low-cost gas contracts expire and as stack gas scrubbing is increasingly required on electrical or heating plants using low-sulfur Western coal.

Source: *Chemical Week,* New York.

Before moving office premises

Many companies, squeezed by soaring midtown rentals and pushed by short-term leases and costly escalator clauses, are moving to neighborhoods that used to be considered marginal. The average saving is 25% over the life of the lease. Before moving, determine the suitability of local transportation facilities, local support services, and the interest of local property owners in upgrading the neighborhood.

Source: Michael Safko, J.G. Haft & Co., New York.

PART V

Operations Management

21 PURCHASING

PURCHASING WISDOM

Getting the most out of purchasing

Without regular attention from top management, a company's purchasing department is apt to fall into a rut. The buyers place their orders routinely. They call for upper-echelon help only when problems develop. To minimize that, check the operations' efficiency level by asking these basic questions:

• How often is a real effort made to find new vendors and fight price increases? Simply ordering from established suppliers is lazy, and often not cost-effective.

• Is management delivering the message that purchasing is an important corporate function? Is it provided with high-level guidance before problems crop up?

• Is there an amply budgeted training program? Buyers need to stay abreast of new developments to be effective. Seminars, conferences and special classes pay off.

• Is value analysis being put to use? This involves nothing more than determining which goods are needed and which materials or processes are best. And it will result in low-cost substitutions, more realistic specifications, avoidance of duplication.

• Does purchasing have easy access to engineering and other technical personnel? Without such in-house assistance, buyers can overwrite specifications or misjudge quality standards.

Source: Lawrence D. Miles, *Purchasing World,* Barrington, Ill.

Factors to weigh in a make-or-buy decision

Reasons for retaining tasks in-house:

• Proprietary design ideas or manufacturing techniques are confidential.

• Special-purpose equipment is available in-house.

• Production requires close personal control.

• No other acceptable source or product part is available.

• Keep expensive machinery operating or keep employees busy.

• Lower cost.

• Product development is continuing concurrently with the production run, with the design not yet completely firmed up.

Reasons for placing work outside:

• 343 •

• In-house shop has neither the facilities nor skills to do the job.

• Outside facilities are available that can do the work with little or no tooling.

• To satisfy legal or contractual requirements (e.g., buying from small business, minority, or foreign sources).

• Too many unknowns in projecting cost of doing work in-house.

• Overall labor costs are lower because fringe benefits are fewer.

• Efficiency is higher because the owner of the outside firm is on-site.

Source: Robert N. Huntoon, *The Challenge of Profitable Procurement,* Robert N. Huntoon Reports, Redding, Cal.

What to bargain for on a big-ticket buy

When purchasing major capital equipment—a sizable computer system, for example—check all matters requiring manufacturer support before finalizing the purchase contract or making any payment.

What to bargain for:

• Reasonable delivery time, to avoid costly renting, borrowing, or making do without equipment while awaiting delivery. But delivery schedules vary by industry. Computer manufacturers consider nine months to be reasonable. If urged, some Original Equipment Manufacturers (OEMs) will arrange with a competitor to fill the lead-time gap, even absorbing the expense.

• Rapid installation, to avoid disrupting other operations. Speed up the time it will take for the new asset to go on-line full-time. Check the labor-contract status of the supplier. In the unlikely event of an ill-timed strike, who is liable?

• Conversion of related equipment, to accelerate integration of in-house systems (if they are not being scrapped) toward a total cost-effective operation. New vendors may be hard bargainers. They want to replace old equipment.

• Adequate operator training, to ensure that current employees master the equipment quickly, while avoiding problems that could cause breakdowns later. The OEM may offer resistance by pointing out coverage in the maintenance contract (see next point), but the company's concern is to minimize downtime.

• No-loophole maintenance contract, to fix future maintenance costs and service-check routines and to ensure immediate attention in case of a breakdown. This must be in writing and signed prior to the closing of the sale. It's the only pledge that will remain in force after installation of equipment is accepted.

Purchasing used equipment

Some of the big pluses of buying used equipment:

• Prospective buyers can usually inspect the equipment while it is installed and in operation.

• Purchasers are able to discuss actual performance and maintenance needs with the current owner.

• Helpful items such as foundation drawings and spare parts are usually available.

• The price of the used equipment is probably lower, because the owner does not incur major selling costs.

The drawbacks of purchasing used equipment:

• Units sell on an as is basis. The hardware is not reconditioned or otherwise improved.

• Sellers don't offer engineering assistance to potential buyers.

• Dismantling and transportation are the purchaser's responsibilities.

• If the equipment doesn't exactly match a buyer's needs, the buyer must determine whether necessary modifications are possible or worthwhile to the company.

Source: *Chemical Engineering,* McGraw-Hill, New York.

Lease instead of purchase?

The basic advantage of a lease is that it requires a smaller immediate cash outlay than with a purchase. The company then can use the extra cash in ways that add more to revenues and profit than the purchase of equipment. The lease arrangement does not add to the company's debt burden, either. That means credit lines can be used to buy capital equipment not available for leasing (or more profitable to buy).

Cash-flow bonuses include the fact that the investment tax credit is available to lessees, and the cost of the lease can be deducted from ordinary income.

And leasing for a fixed monthly or annual cost gives the company a chance to pay for future use of the equipment with cheaper dollars.

Source: Jack Leonard Green, *Leasing Principles and Methods,* Sound Publishing Co., New York.

Adjusting product specifications

As a rule of thumb, the looser the product specifications, the lower the costs, usually. So make sure tight specifications are necessary and not just an engineer's whim. What to do:

• Avoid nonstandard items. Use readily available components.

• Control only the critical factors (mounting dimensions, envelope size, weight, electrical values, etc.). Leave maximum latitude in unimportant areas.

• Make specifications simple.

• Where possible, specify quality control methods that don't require use of special or expensive tools, equipment, or procedures.

Encourage buyers to solicit supplier recommendations on changes or modifications that would reduce costs. Do that before the specifications are final. (And, of course, check out those recommendations with designers.)

Foreign producers can provide bargains

U.S. companies that need quick delivery of machine tools are turning from domestic manufacturers to overseas competitors. Even U.S. auto companies are buying the imports, particularly from Japan. Problems for the domestic machine-tool manufacturers go beyond delivery times. Foreign makers have also upgraded quality and increased their service capability.

Chinese products are improving in quality and becoming extremely cost-competitive. Examples are textiles, chemicals, pharmaceuticals, metallurgical supplies, and light industrial products.

COST-CUTTING METHODS

How much bidding is enough?

Is your company getting competitive bids regularly? Even for basic products from well-established vendors? Standard reasons for not getting bids:

• Earlier bids are already on file. However, those bids may be too old. Or the order quantity may be different and now qualify for a lower price.

• Quality and delivery are more important than competitive pricing. But the statement that the chosen vendor gives better service must be substantiated with specific benefits.

• All standard items are priced alike. However, there is price competition on most standard items. Also consider service, terms, size of orders.

• The product is patented. But engineers may not have been queried or presented with alternatives in some time. It's also likely that engineers have not kept abreast of alternatives.

• Customer specifications. But the customer may no longer care for the detail.

Source: *Purchasing,* Boston.

Cheaper ways to buy capital equipment

Most equipment manufacturers publish price lists from which they don't normally deviate. Some ways to get special prices:

• A minor alteration can be construed as making the equipment a "special" machine.

Thus the manufacturer can negotiate without violating its price schedule.

• Offer a trade-in for a substantial allowance.

• Costs of transportation, installation, and training can add substantially to total cost. They may be negotiable.

• Push for delayed or extended payments or a low-interest, time-payment contract.

• Warranty, service, and spare parts inventories are generally open to discussion.

Cost-reduction reminders

• Materials. Look for materials that are cheaper to buy, easier to fabricate, offer a product improvement.

• Specifications. Consider eliminating manufacturing operations, cutting scrap, reducing rework, widening tolerances.

• Purchasing. Investigate quantity buys, market fluctuations, open contracts, any financing concessions from suppliers.

• Packaging. Costs may be reduced through redesign, new materials, different sizes, different quantities.

Source: *Purchasing Factomatic,* Prentice-Hall, Englewood Cliffs, N.J.

Coping with price increases

• Complain immediately. Call, and complain in writing, too.

• Give suppliers an opportunity to break the

new price by providing technical assistance or other in-house help.

• Retaliate. Switch vendors as long as the alternate source isn't more costly.

• Switch to f.o.b. price quotes. Arrange your own shipping when more economical.

• Expand supplier list and let existing vendors know about it.

• Search specs for ways to substitute materials or use alternative processes. Relax tolerances.

• Make spot buys to keep pressure on contract sources.

• Increase order size. Renegotiate quantity discounts and shipping costs.

• Demand the cost/price breakdowns. Pay particular attention to the popular excuses for price increases—the vendor's rising energy and labor costs.

• Promote your firm as a good one to do business with. Stress growth plans and future opportunities for suppliers that control costs.

Source: Dr. Chester L. Karrass, *Purchasing,* Boston.

Four ways to fight a price hike

• Send the supplier a substantial purchase order, but specify the old price, as if the announced hike had been overlooked. The implied threat—accept these terms or risk losing the whole order, perhaps even the whole account.

• Ask for a reduction in price, without any reference to the proposed increase. This may lead to an eventual compromise at or near the old level.

• Acknowledge the hike, but claim an inability to pay more than the former price for this current order. The vendor probably will agree to continue with the old price, at least for a time.

• Turn the raise down, out-of-hand. Say that the company will go elsewhere unless the increase is rescinded. This is risky, even if the vendor feels forced to go along, because of the resentment stirred by the take-it-or-leave-it ultimatum. Then what? Someday, when the vendor

holds the bargaining leverage, expect a move to get even.

Source: Dr. Chester L. Karrass, *Purchasing,* Boston.

Ways to water down escalation clauses

When sellers insist on a clause permitting them to raise prices during the life of a contract, buyers should push for these contract provisions if prices are raised.

• Seller's costs must be increasing by more than a specified minimum.

• Goods already in the seller's inventory pipeline are not included in the increase.

• Does not apply to late deliveries, back orders, certain goods, commodities, or services, etc.

• An increase will not be allowed during the final six months or so of the contract.

• Increases will not be allowed for the first so-many months of the contract (or within so many months after the last increase).

• They must be cost pass-throughs on a dollar-for-dollar basis only; nothing may be added to the seller's profit.

Source: Dr. Chester L. Karrass, *How to Fight a Price Increase,* Karrass International, Inc., Los Angeles.

Price-protection clauses

Three possibilities:

• Peg future increase to the seller's costs, seller to pass through higher costs on a dollar-for-dollar basis without tacking on a profit margin.

• Use a most-favored-customer clause. Specify that the seller can't charge any more than the most favored customer. Even if there's no easy way of actually checking, the seller can't be sure that the buyer won't accidentally find out. This possibility helps.

• Insert a downward-adjustment clause that allows the price to go down as the market does. This gives the buyer a chance to get something back if prices seesaw during the life of the contract.

• The seller locks up the business. Competitors can't get any of it for a year.

• Profit on the sale does not have to be taken into income and declared for taxes until the goods are actually accepted by the buying company.

Consignment buying: how it cuts costs

A company that has some clout with its suppliers should consider buying on consignment. Basic tradeoff: The buyer agrees to purchase a certain volume of goods over a specified time. In return, the vendor stocks the order, at its expense, on the buyer's property.

This way the price is locked in, typically for one year. Inventory and carrying costs (including insurance) are paid by the seller. The buyer has immediate access to the goods.

When consignment works best:

• The buyer is able to estimate closely the amount needed over the period covered.

• The product has a long shelf life and will not become obsolete or need redesign.

• The order is large enough to be worthwhile to the seller.

Suppliers often don't understand the consignment method and rarely suggest it. But buyers should point out that consignment is a trade-off.

Advantages for the seller:

• Because there's an assured sale of a sizable order, the supplier may seek quantity discounts from its suppliers and may save by having one long production run.

Ways to cut carrying costs

Top industrial purchasing managers estimate it now costs at least 24% a year to carry inventory. That's up 6–9 percentage points from several years ago. Strategies for coping:

• Cut down price hedging. Some 80% of the buyers in a recent survey reduced purchases aimed at beating announced price hikes. In many cases, savings are offset by sky-high carrying costs.

• Purchase more from distributors. This shifts some of the inventory back onto suppliers.

• Look more closely at leasing alternatives. These are often the only way to avoid locking the firm into high long-term charges in order to finance investment of essential machinery and equipment purchases.

• Reappraise payment options. More and more purchasing managers say they think twice before taking a small discount for prompt payment. Each 30-day delay in paying the bill knocks 1%–2% off overall procurement costs.

Source: *Purchasing World,* Barrington, Ill.

WORKING WITH SUPPLIERS

Using suppliers' knowledge

One advantage to a business slowdown: Faced with declining sales, suppliers will be more eager than ever to provide ideas and expertise. Be sure to encourage this knowledge sharing. One way is to post a sign prominently in the reception area soliciting their ideas. Be specific. Tell vendors to:

- Ask the company's buyers about the why and how of specifications. As specialists in their fields, suppliers know the factors governing quality and price.
- Tell the buyers if they should be ordering different quantities or whether a standard part can substitute for a special part.
- Show advantages of their suggestions in terms of lower prices, longer life, use of readily available materials, etc.

Be sure suppliers who make solid suggestions reap some benefit.

Source: Somerby R. Dowst, *More Basics for Buyers,* CBI Publishing Co., Boston.

Secrets key suppliers should be told

Letting select suppliers in on closely guarded company data can pay off. Suppliers do a better job when they understand the company's short- and long-term needs. Tell them about:

- Long-term materials needs. Suppliers can then make necessary investments to meet projected buyer needs for five years or longer. In return, the buyer should get an early warning of any supply problems.
- Historical data on stocking levels. This will help shift inventory responsibility to suppliers.
- Product planning. This can help you to tap design ideas and other suggestions that help create the best possible product. If a product will be dropped, suppliers can make adjustments in their own planning.
- Production requirements. Suppliers who stock or handle critical parts know by parts number what must be supplied for the next six months.

Source: Dr. Chester L. Karrass, *Purchasing,* Boston.

Open house for vendors

Invite existing and potential suppliers to an open house to discover new sources and cost-cutting ideas and to improve communications.

Give participants a packet at the door that details purchasing procedures, quality standards, and special situations or problems that the buyer faces. Set up displays that give annual needs and parts numbers so vendors can request specs. Include plant tours and corporate information seminars as part of the open house.

One company estimates that its open house generated almost 150 cost-cutting ideas. And many current vendor may discover other goods that they could be supplying. Also, minor problems between buyer and supplier can be informally ironed out.

Source: *Purchasing World,* Barrington, Ill.

Profiling suppliers

Prepare a profile of each supplier to the company. Include list of items, prices, quantities, delivery dates. Note all shortfalls, delays, defects, and other problems. List potential alternate suppliers (after checking on their financial stability). Try out the most promising from time to time. Let current suppliers know about the profile, even if no switch is planned.

Setting up systems contracts with suppliers

Systems contracts* can cut inventories, paperwork, and other related costs. But they often misfire.

When setting up workable systems contracts with the company's vendors, start with clear, quantifiable objectives. Decide how much inventory the company's going to cut. Set a dollar and a unit goal. Also set a dollar goal for savings in expediting and order processing. Measure performance.

Don't bastardize the concept. The aim is to negotiate lower costs (not prices) by getting the vendor to do some of your work. The company isn't trying to get him to give it a volume discount on a bunch of items. Stress to suppliers that reliability and speed will be the criteria for selection.

Propose systems arrangements only to vendors with known track records for performance. Stress that competitive—not necessarily the lowest—prices are required.

Systems contracts mean that the company will be dealing with fewer vendors. If this is unacceptable, then forget the systems idea.

*Vendor agrees, for guaranteed annual volume, to stock supplies until the customer needs them, and delivers quickly upon request.

Make sure adequate volume exists. Unless the company can deliver good volume for the vendor, there's no way he can cover his costs and deliver the kind of service the company is seeking.

Don't spread a contract over too many items. A large number of small orders can't be handled efficiently by anyone.

Get a commitment from top management. Systems contracts wipe out vast amounts of paperwork that often is near and dear to accounting, stores, production, and finance. Unless the top boss understands that old procedures will have to be modified and is willing to accept these changes, the idea won't work.

Make sure the company's buyers know and understand systems contracts. Their aim is to cut inventory, paperwork, and expediting. Simple release systems have to be set up, and order matching eliminated.

Audit the purchasing department periodically. Look for: (1) instances of continued expediting, and (2) continuation of old work procedures. Unless there is a marked reduction in both, something is wrong.

Watch out for squirrels. Normal tendency for production people is to set up sub-inventories. This undermines the systems approach completely. Find out from production what items they are worried about. Make sure vendors know about these worries. Then check regularly to make sure vendors are performing as promised. It's essential that vendors know from the start that you are going to level with them on needs.

Drafting the contract after negotiations

A big edge goes to the party who actually writes it up after negotiations.

Reasons: (1) greater familiarity with every element in the agreement, having done the detailed review that was necessary to prepare it, and (2) the basic approaches, the fine print, even the language itself favor the person doing the drafting.

The other party must ask that something be inserted after the fact, or object to something else already written in. That gives the nondrafts- man the psychological burden of having to undo a fait accompli.

Source: Philip Sperber, *The Science of Business Negotiation,* Pilot Books, New York.

PURCHASING AND THE LAW

Arbitration—alternative to a lawsuit

When a business deal turns sour, a lawsuit is not the only answer. If both sides are willing, an impartial arbitrator that they choose can decide who's right. The award will be legally enforceable in most states.

Advantages of arbitration:

1. It's not necessary to retain a lawyer. However, attorneys' costs for an arbitration hearing are much lower than they would be for a court proceeding.

2. The arbitrator can be a person particularly familiar with the industry. This can be important if the issue is the quality of merchandise.

3. An arbitration hearing can usually be arranged within weeks.

4. Because arbitration is private, neither the public nor government regulatory bodies are alerted to facts about trade practices or credit standing.

There are disadvantages as well. Arbitration may not be the answer where a very large sum of money is involved. The finality of arbitration is great for the winner, but bad for the loser if an appeal is blocked.

Also, if important legal issues are involved, court proceedings may be better in the long run. In a patent infringement issue, for example, the patent owner may want a court decision to stand as a warning against other potential violators.

The fact that commercial arbitration awards are not routinely published thus becomes a disadvantage to the patent holder.

The first step toward arbitration is to contact the local bar association or the American Arbitration Assn., 140 W. 51 St., New York 10020.

Arbitration over defective goods

An arbitrator's award in a dispute over defective goods may not be as final as it seems.

In a recent case, Firedoor sold door frames to MacFarland Builders for $7,600. MacFarland refused to pay, claiming the frames were defective. In arbitration, the price was cut by more than half. The basic problem was that the paint had peeled, and all the doors had to be refinished. More than a year later, MacFarland initiated another arbitration proceeding, alleging new defects. Firedoor sued to block further arbitration.

The court ordered more evidence taken to determine when MacFarland found out about the additional defects. If it did not know about them at the time of the first arbitration, a second arbitration would be justified.

Source: *Firedoor Corp. of America* vs *MacFarland Builders, Inc.,* 185 NYLJ No. 65, p.1.

When a contract isn't binding

Oral contracts involving more than $500 are generally unenforceable. However, even a simple confirming memo that identifies the parties, the item, the quantity, and the price may be enough to establish a written contract.

A recent Iowa Supreme Court case upheld an oral contract, for much more than $500, between two parties who had done business that way for many years, on the ground that the buyer relied on it. But that was unusual and most courts would not allow it.

Service contract protection

Contracts for services are not covered by the Uniform Commercial Code unless the contract says so. To bring a service contract under the code, add language such as:

"The parties to this contract recognize that the Uniform Commercial Code does not normally apply to the performance of services as distinguished from transactions in goods. However, the parties agree that the Uniform Commercial Code shall apply to this contract, and any dispute arising under this contract shall be resolved under the provisions of the code."

Construction contract traps

Construction contracts generally provide for a performance bond or other financial guarantee by the contractor that the construction will be done as specified and on time. But clients can unwittingly invalidate this guarantee by materially changing the contract. Contracts frequently contain a clause which stipulates: *All changes must be approved beforehand by the surety* (the bonding company or other third party making the guarantee).

Even without the clause, if the contractor's performance bond does not specifically include the terms and conditions of the contract, the surety may only cover costs for work left undone, and not for the bills unpaid by the contractor for completed work.

Source: Marc J. Lane, attorney, Chicago.

Signature substitutes on contracts

Substitutes for signatures are now accepted on legally binding contracts. Acceptable and binding:

• Facsimiles produced on copiers or over phone lines.

• Imprints on large-volume forms.

• Codes or symbols agreed upon by buyer and seller that computers can read.

• Initials.

• Trade names if used instead of a written signature.

The Uniform Commercial Code, Section 1-201 states that any symbol used by someone with the intent to make a writing authentic qualifies as a signature.

The UCC makes it clear that the key to the validity of a signed contract is that the signatory be positively identified by oral evidence. Section 1-205, dealing with trade usages, requires that the signature be consistent with accepted practice in the field.

Source: Dr. Russell Decker, professor emeritus of legal studies, Bowling Green State University, Bowling Green, Ohio, *Purchasing*, Boston.

Consequential damages: the costly truth

When a new piece of machinery breaks down, all sorts of trouble can break loose. Other equipment is damaged, orders are lost, downtime spreads like shock waves. Eventually, somebody must pay for the loss.

Such havoc is called *consequential damage.* The party liable for this chain reaction, which may cost more to correct than the initial defective equipment, is rarely the equipment supplier.

While courts often stretch a point for unsophisticated consumers in comparable circumstances, commercial buyers aren't well protected. The reason is that sellers restrict their obligation to repair or replace defective parts, excluding consequential damages. And contracts between business firms are, of course, binding.

To avoid problems, require a nonexclusionary warranty on new purchases. In a soft capital-goods market, suppliers should be willing to assume some consequential damages.

Source: 587 F 2d 1363.

Altered provisions on purchase order

The buyer sends a printed purchase order. The seller sends back a printed acknowledgment form with different provisions. The goods are shipped, accepted, and paid for.

Later a dispute arises over the transaction, but the two forms differ as to warranty terms, arbitration criteria, or other provisions.

The usual rule is that buyer is stuck with seller's terms unless it had given notice of its objections, or unless the seller's terms materially change the contract.

Source: 380 NE 2d 239.

Relying on a seller's advice

Buyers have special rights if they rely on a salesperson's recommendations in selecting goods, and the seller knows how the goods will be used. Even though there's no written warranty, a buyer may collect damages under an implied warranty that the goods were fit for a particular use.

Keep correspondence and notes based on conversations with the seller to show that the seller knew how the item would be used and recommended it for that purpose. But your case may not stand up if the purchasing documents contain no-warranty disclaimers.

Source: *Purchasing,* Boston.

Legal problems with bulk sales

When buying all the inventory of a business that is closing, the buyer could be liable if the seller hasn't paid his bills.

Buyers usually aren't responsible for what the seller does with the money. But the law recognizes that it's common for a business to close its doors, sell its assets, and leave creditors hanging. So in a bulk sale the buyer must be sure that the seller has paid. It isn't enough to have the seller promise in the contract to pay all debts.

Before paying, the buyer should make sure the seller's creditors have been paid. Or put purchase payment in escrow rather than pay seller directly.

Source: UCC Article 6; 25 UCC Reptr. 1424; 25 UCC Reptr. 1427.

Protecting inspection rights

A buyer can take a reasonable time to examine a shipment and still reject it if the merchandise is unsatisfactory. What's a reasonable time? As little as a few hours or as much as several months for complex equipment that takes repeated adjustment to get it working.

Signing the trucker's receipt does not constitute acceptance of the goods as satisfactory. It merely acknowledges that something was received. The buyer can decide after inspection whether to accept or reject the shipment.

What buyers should do to protect their rights:

• Be sure not to use the item if it doesn't meet the specs. Using it can constitute acceptance and the buyer would then have to pay for it. If part of the shipment is acceptable, notify the seller before use that part of the shipment is acceptable but part is being rejected.

• Don't delay informing the seller of rejection. A buyer who fails to give notice of rejection, within a reasonable time, is deemed to have accepted the shipment and will have to pay the seller for it.

• Don't pay if the goods are unsatisfactory. It's still possible to reject after payment in some cases. (For example, C.O.D., where the buyer is required to pay before inspecting.) But many buyers who paid before learning of the defect have lost when they sued to get money back.

The buyer also must act in good faith. If the goods are perishable, the buyer must take steps to avoid spoilage. But, if time is crucial, he may cover his needs by buying replacement goods elsewhere. The buyer can then sue for the extra costs.

Source: Dr. Russell Decker, *Purchasing,* Boston.

When delivery is in installments

If the seller under an installment contract makes one shipment that is late or defective, the buyer can reject that shipment even while accepting others.

What if the buyer wants out of the contract, and uses the bad shipment to claim breach of contract. It depends on how serious the defect is and how the buyer handles it.

In one case, one seller contracted to deliver concrete ready for pouring every morning. Repeated late deliveries forced the buyer to work into the evening and pay overtime to its employees.

The court ruled that the repeated lateness impaired the value of the contract to the buyer. It could legally refuse further deliveries and turn to another supplier for its needs.

In a second case, several deliveries were late. The buyer never complained about the lateness but found a more reliable vendor.

The court ruled that there were no grounds for the buyer to break the contract.

Handling a single defective shipment

Occasionally, the company is unhappy with one shipment from a regular supplier. It doesn't want to pay for the goods. But it does want to continue buying from the vendor.

So send earmarked checks until the dispute is settled. Specify on the back of the check that it is in payment of a particular invoice (an undisputed one). Include the number and the date of the invoice. Otherwise, the supplier may credit the payment against the bill that is in dispute.

But don't rely on verbal instructions to the seller's bookkeeper. Make a written notation on each each check that is sent.

Source: 462 S.W. 2d 321.

KEEPING BUYERS HONEST

Warning signs of purchasing fraud

Be suspicious of collusion between company supplier and purchasing representative when:
- Buyer's working files are not readily accessible or so disorganized that a given transaction can't be tracked.
- Buyer consistently uses verbal bids instead of formal, signed bids, always pleading lack of time.
- Orders are smaller than they should be for no logical reasons. (The buyer's logic is that small orders command less attention.)
- Purchase-order amendments authorizing changes in price do not have supporting explanations or approval signature higher than the buyer's. (Price renegotiation is one of the most fertile areas of fraud.)

Source: Robert N. Huntoon, *The Challenge of Profitable Procurement,* Redding, Calif.

"Yes men" buyers can be dangerous

Beware of buyers who turn into yes men (giving in too readily to demands from in-house or outside).

Signs that buyers are bowing to inside pressures:
- Weak reasons for source selection on contract-approval forms being sent to top management for final okay. (Example: They've always had this business from us.)
- An excessive number of rush orders.
- Too many small orders.

- Supplier complaints about unfair test methods on new products.

Signs of saying yes to outside pressures:
- Too many price increases.
- Excessive reject rate.
- Sudden increase in late deliveries.
- User complaints about the suppliers' lack of follow-through.

Source: Somerby R. Dowst, *More Basics for Buyers,* CBI Publishing Co., Boston.

Issuing a company code of ethics

Keep them honest.

Put the company ethics code in writing. Studies show a positive correlation between the ethical performance of buyers and the written ethics policies of their firms. A written code lets employees know what's expected of them. And it sets the same standards for suppliers' salespeople who will then offer fewer gifts to purchasing agents.

The ethics policy must apply to all employees to be effective. A double standard with exceptions for the top rank builds resentment and leads to trouble.

Source: National Association of Purchasing Management, New York.

Buyers' ethics

Seventy percent of the purchasing agents surveyed said they would accept meals from vendors. Only 60% felt that accepting theater or sporting-event tickets is ethical. Barely 50% felt accepting modest Christmas presents is okay. A vendor-financed golf outing is acceptable to 47%.

Overwhelmingly disapproved are gifts of appliances, cars, loans, or vacations.

Source: Survey by the Center for the Study of Ethics in the Professions.

22 FACILITIES AND EQUIPMENT MANAGEMENT

EQUIPMENT

Keep new equipment running smoothly

To minimize service problems with new high-technology equipment, make full use of the pre-installation training which almost all manufacturers offer. Stock the full range of spare parts likely to be needed for the most common repairs and provide the constant preventive maintenance that complex systems need. Assign operating employees to the equipment early. And make sure that senior management is aware of the importance of a vigorous maintenance program.

Source: *Production Engineering,* New York.

Using capital equipment more efficiently

Effective planning for machinery replacement requires that these records be kept for each piece of machinery: (1) complete identification (serial numbers, size, etc.); (2) date of manufacture; (3) date bought; (4) price paid, including any extras; (5) installation cost; (6) location in plant; (7) record of use (number of shifts, etc.); (8) annual maintenance expense; (9) rebuilding record (what was done, when, cost). In addition, make an annual physical inventory of all machinery (some will have been moved, some idled, etc.). Alert foremen and workers to watch for signs of deterioration, obsolescence, etc.

Source: Dr. Lawrence Hackamack, management professor and consultant, Northern Illinois University, De Kalb, Ill.

Saving with older machinery

Old machinery can often be rebuilt to perform better than it did when first purchased, at costs well below the price of replacing it. Retain valuable portions (bases, frames, drive shaft, consoles). Replace old motors, bearings and controls with modern components that perform far better than the originals.

A typical saving is to rebuild an obsolete wire-drawing machine for $157,000 (the cost of a new model: $245,000).

Source: *Production Engineering,* New York.

Buying spare parts

• Eliminate items used less than once a year.
• Keep inventories lowest on parts that can be bought locally on comparatively little lead time.
• Where possible, stock entire assemblies rather than individual components, especially if the assembly tends to break down as a unit.
• Each part should be easily identifiable.
• Use the same spare-part code in maintenance, production, and the stockroom.

Source: Kenneth J. Vargas, Eldorado Nuclear, Ltd., *Chemical Engineering,* New York.

Costly mistakes with new technology

When companies shift over to a technological innovation, they quite often:
• Underestimate the time for getting the new equipment installed and functioning efficiently.
• Overestimate use rates, productivity increases or savings.
• Misjudge the degree and extent of adjustments necessary to existing equipment and procedures, and fail to realize the number of older facilities and machines suddenly made obsolete.
• Fail to anticipate problems with worker acceptance and use.
• Improperly project increases in costs, prices and productivity.

• Assume that cost reduction will translate directly into profits.

Source: *Evaluating Technological Innovations,* Lexington Books, Lexington, Mass.

Before replacing people with machines

A great variety of advanced automated equipment is coming onto the market. But many companies are poor candidates for large-scale automation and are likely to suffer a decline in profits if they rush in.

Key criteria for success:
• High relative share of market. Companies with more than a 60% share (relative to competitors) are strong candidates. Those with less than 25% are weak ones. Market leaders are usually economical producers, have flexibility in pricing and can withstand surges by competitors. These strengths are necessary to best absorb the cost of automating and to weather temporary setbacks resulting from it. Firms with small shares don't have enough value-added per employee. They can go into a tailspin from the huge expenditures required for effective automation.
• Low reliance on new products. The best candidates derive less than 1% of sales from new products. Those with more than 10% should be wary. Start-ups add costs on top of the original capital outlays for automation hardware.
• Little unionization. Companies less than 20% unionized are more likely to do well than those with over 65% union employees. Union work rules slow new production methods. Union members tend to resist automation in the belief that it always leads to job loss.
• High plant utilization. Good candidates use more than 85% of plant capacity. Those with under 70% utilization are bad candidates. At high operating levels, fixed costs are spread over a large volume of output, usually reducing unit costs. Profit margins and return on investment tend to increase swiftly at full capacity.

• Good market growth. Real sales industry-wise are expanding by more than 6% a year.

• Highly standardized products. Companies that produce to order are least likely to benefit from mechanization.

How to automate:

• First, design a strategic plan that relates the area to be automated to the total business. Involve operating managers, too. Top management must participate in the follow-through.

• Have productivity benchmarks in place such as value-added per employee. The goal should be to guard against excessive investment for automation. Set output-per-worker benchmarks for each business unit for which automation is planned.

• Don't automate until the profit picture is clear early in the process. Provide a reserve to insure staying power once automation begins.

• Work intensively with employees. Work rules may have to be changed ahead of time.

If productivity and profits begin to fall, be willing to try shop-level tactics, especially worker motivation. It is probably the strategic plan that needs drastic revision.

Source: Bradley T. Gale, director of research, Strategic Planning Institute, Cambridge, Mass.

The economics of buying a robot

A general-purpose assembly-line robot that replaces one worker can pay back its costs in one-and-one-half years if used for three shifts. Payback for one-shift operations occurs within five years. The robots cost $20,000–$60,000 each and have an anticipated life of seven to eight years.

Other costs of using a robot:

• Installation, tooling, and start-up equal one-half the purchase price.

• Programming and routine engineering services are an additional 5%–10%.

• Annual maintenance runs 5% for one-shift use, 7½% for two shifts.

Total first-year costs are an additional 60%–75% of purchase price.

Intangible benefits are real gains from lower waste rates, improved quality and fewer injuries. But these are difficult to measure, and they vary among plants.

Source: Thomas E. Lipinski and Charles S. Skinner, manufacturing technology specialists, Booz Allen & Hamilton, New York.

Robot pros and cons

Every manufacturer is going its own way on design. As a result, there is almost no robot standardization in equipment or computer language. A problem for users is trying to base long-range planning on robot usage.

Robots are not economical for one-shift operations, but they can often be cost-justified for two shifts. Basic advantages over humans are: while people can produce a superior product for a period of time, robots can produce high quality throughout the work period, and they can be used in work environments dangerous to people and for jobs people find distasteful.

Source: *Machine Design*, Cleveland, and *Modern Materials Handling*, Boston.

PLANT ENERGY COSTS

Comparing energy costs

Use the table below to compare your company's energy costs to the industry's average and to assess energy inflation impact on items that the company buys.

Industry	Energy cost as a % of shipment value
Blast furnaces and steel mills	8.5
Petroleum refining	2.4
Industrial organic chemicals	7.5
Paper mills, except building paper	10.3
Paperboard mills	4.5
Cement, hydraulic	6.0
Industrial inorganic chemicals	5.7
Primary aluminum	10.0
Nitrogenous fertilizer	1.4
Plastics materials and resins	20.8
Cyclic crudes and intermediates	13.7
Glass containers	13.2
Motor vehicle parts & accessories	15.4

Source: Census Bureau.

Plan ahead for energy needs

Do not wait for utility bills to determine how much energy is being used at a plant. Instead, have the plant energy manager take weekly utility-meter readings and calculate fuel inventory.

This way the manager can pinpoint areas needing improvement and keep on top of the conservation program.

Source: Robert R. Cooke, energy manager, Coca-Cola Co., quoted in *Facilities Management,* Washington, D.C.

Pros and cons of independent power

Faced with rising electricity bills, a growing number of companies are cutting loose from the big utilities and generating power independently. On-site diesel generators produce usable waste heat as well as electricity. Electricity is produced for about seven cents per kilowatt-hour, including the initial investment, operating costs, and diesel fuel bills. The waste heat can be used to make steam for manufacturing processes as well as for heating and air-conditioning.

Saving: Utilities charge as much as 5 cents per kilowatt-hour more than it costs to generate electricity independently. But the initial investment is sizeable, an average $200,000 per diesel generator.

If a local utility opposes independent power generation, there may be other pitfalls. The utility may charge high rates for standby electricity, which a company might need if its generators break down or if it must meet peak demand; pressure local government to tax private power plants as real property instead of depreciable capital; or raise environmental objections to private power plants.

Source: Herbert Wishengrad, president, Seal-Kap Packaging, Inc., Long Island City, N.Y.

In-plant energy conservation

To reduce the impact of rising energy costs and fuel shortages:

- Develop multifuel capacity.
- Burn waste oil.
- Use computers to monitor and regulate power consumption in heating, air conditioning, lighting, and machine operation.
- Meter each department's consumption of electricity, natural gas, compressed air, and hot water to implement an energy-cost-accounting program and to provide conservation incentives.
- Tailor lighting to specific functions. Cut back where appropriate.
- Appoint an energy manager to be responsible for monitoring fuel consumption and implementing alternative energy technologies.
- Anticipate equipment maintenance. Replace parts before deteriorating machine efficiency wastes fuel.

Source: *Industrial World,* New York.

Keeping out the cold

Covered windows are one of the easiest and cheapest factory energy savers. Where neither light nor visibility is needed, cover the windows with 3-inch panels of compressed fiberboard and polystyrene insulation. Users report saving up to 35% on fuel bills, more than enough to offset the cost of installation. A further advantage —fewer windows to clean.

Warehouse heating

How to reduce costs.
- Interconnect heating unit with shipping and garage doors so heat shuts off automatically when they are open. As a result, employees will keep them shut when not in use.
- Adjust garage door height to eight feet by hanging a vinyl curtain from the ceiling.

- Install full-height transparent strip-curtains in shipping entrances.
- Use time-delay buzzers that are activated when doors are not closed after a predetermined time.

The most light for the least cost

Recommendations for saving energy (and money) in lighting, while still providing enough light for worker comfort and job needs:
- Aim the light on the work—a desk lamp instead of overhead fixtures; strong lighting on a machine tool rather than illumination from the ceiling, high above the equipment.
- Don't go overboard on savings. The most efficient light sources (in terms of the amount of light for a given energy-consumption level) are blue and yellow. But they could annoy and disorient workers. Some efficient lights must be replaced often, adding to maintenance costs.
- Light sources should be easy to clean (factory dust cuts light output).
- Fixtures should allow easy changing of bulbs or fluorescent tubes.
- Use the heat produced by lighting equipment. Direct it into heating ducts or radiator vents, if at all possible.
- Maximize reflection of light in the fixtures.
- Incandescent lamps are slightly more efficient in the higher-wattage ratings. Use larger lamps and fewer of them.
- Provide light switches. Turn off lamps when the space is not in use.
- Control window brightness to enhance heat savings, comfort, and visibility.
- Balance daylight with artificial lighting for versatility and lower overall cost. The more daylight, the fewer lamps needed, and those lamps can often be high-efficiency types producing harsher colors (the daylight makes them less annoying).
- Set maintenance schedules for lighting fixtures.
- Provide operating and maintenance instruc-

tions for lighting fixtures. (Get them from the fixture manufacturer; installers often throw them away.)

Source: *Electrical Construction and Maintenance,* New York.

be stored? Local regulations on fuel storage can be strict. Diesel may not require underground storage, however.

Source: *Energy Management Report,* Old Saybrook, Conn.

Improving boiler efficiency

Install a second, smaller boiler for off-peak periods, when energy needs are below the main unit's low-fire range. The large unit is no longer repeatedly cycled on and off, while the unit is allowed to run for long stretches at top efficiency.

The initial investment is usually returned within two years.

Source: *Plant Engineering,* Barrington, Ill.

Consider buying a standby generator

Fuel can be the most important consideration when selecting a small emergency generator to protect a limited installation in a plant or office against a power failure. The pros and cons of generator types:

• Gas. Engine life is long because the units are generally easy to maintain and to run efficiently. But gas fuels vary considerably in the heat they deliver, so the generator's output might sporadically drop below minimum needs.

• Gasoline. The least expensive units, and easy to start at low temperatures, but they are less efficient than either gas or diesels.

• Diesel. About 40% more efficient than gasoline and low on maintenance (can be half that of a gasoline unit). However, small diesel units are more expensive to install than gasoline.

Where will fuels for the emergency generators

Avoiding coal freeze-ups

Help is available for companies that have recently switched back to coal. To keep the coal piles from freezing into a solid mass:

• New chemicals such as Dow Dowell Division's Agent M185 are added to coal as the shipper loads it into hopper cars.

• Chemicals to seal coal piles against outside moisture can be added at the plant site. Alternative: Careful compacting of piles to keep water from penetrating, then freezing solid.

Also useful are runoff ditches around stockpile to divert rainwater and melting snow. Avoid sites near rivers, especially those where flooding has been a recurrent problem.

Problems with solar-energy systems

Though solar heating and cooling systems offer the possibility of significant savings for industry, the current generation of equipment is full of problems because performance data from earlier solar experiments were improperly disseminated. Communication has been inadequate among researchers and developers, as well as the solar technology's end-users.

Typical problems:

• Basic plumbing and engineering requirements are ignored by designers who overemphasize the experimental nature of the field.

• Systems are overly complex. Those with

both heating and cooling capability are especially troublesome.

• Collectors and storage tanks are the wrong size.

• Inefficient or overly expensive back-up systems are installed, which negate the cost-effectiveness of the overall solar energy system. For example, boilers to supply extra power for a solar absorption chiller use more power than a conventional chiller to meet the cooling load.

• Installers are inexperienced, because of scarcity of solar installations. Base your selection on expertise, not price.

• Many systems are still prone to leaking, freezing or corroding.

Source: *Energy User News,* New York.

Time to think about windmills

Wind-power systems are shaping up as a realistic and economical source of electricity for heavy power users located in windswept areas. Major manufacturers such as General Electric, Hamilton Standard, Westinghouse, and Boeing are working on prototype systems for general pro-

duction. And once a windmill is installed, it generates electricity with almost no operating expenses.

It costs $1.5 million to $2 million to install a typical one-megawatt system. This produces roughly 2 million to 3 million kilowatt-hours of electricity a year. Wind-system costs decrease as development continues. Businesses with electricity costs of $20,000 a month or more that are located in a favorable area should consider a windmill. The best sites are on both the East and West coasts and in the Midwest. Hawaii is best of all. But even New York City is windy enough.

The site must be chosen precisely. Wind speed varies greatly within small areas, and a one-MPH average difference can boost a system's annual output 30%. A typical one-megawatt system involves a 150-foot tower and two propellerlike blades each 100 inches long. Problems to watch for:

• Wind conditions that don't match power needs, for example, for a plant on a daytime schedule in an area with good evening winds.

• TV reception interference. Some wind machines can disrupt TV signals for over a half-mile.

• Low-level noise. Wind systems sometimes produce a low-pitched rumble, which can annoy neighbors.

For more details, contact the American Wind Energy Assn., 1609 Connecticut Ave., NW, Washington, DC 20009.

Source: Roy Stoecker, vice president, Energy and Environmental Analysts, Inc., Garden City, N.Y.

OFFICE ENERGY COSTS

A four-stage approach to conservation

First stage: Increase awareness of the need to save energy by appointing an employee conservation committee. This will get employees to take individual responsibility for saving energy.

Second stage: Cut the company's electric bill. In an average office building, lighting accounts for 40% of a company's electric bill. One-third of that can be cut easily. Switch from blanket overhead lighting to task lighting. Illuminate brightly only those areas where employees are actually working. Use timers to control office air conditioners automatically. Install reflective blinds on windows. Check existing equipment for efficiency. Check heating and cooling controls to see that they are properly calibrated.

Third stage: Analyze overall energy use. The Department of Commerce's analysis of the average energy requirements for various manufacturing processes can be a helpful resource.

Study utility rate structures. Reschedule work loads to take advantage of off-peak rates. Before adding capacity, look closely at what this will do to the company's utility bill. If you are billed on a survey basis, request a new survey after making changes.

For example, a candy manufacturer bought a $2-million electrically powered manufacturing line for added seasonal capacity. The added electrical load, however, pushed the company's peak demand into a penalty range. As a result, the profits from the sales resulting from the added capacity were offset by the penalty charges.

Fourth stage: Look into generating energy on-site (co-generation). For co-generation to be practical, a company must be able to use the heat thrown off in generating electricity either to warm a space, create steam for manufacturing, or both. In the summer, rejected heat must be used for cooling purposes, utilizing appropriate steam- or hot-water-driven refrigeration equipment.

Rule of thumb: Any existing building with more than $250,000 in annual energy costs is a prime candidate for on-site generation.

Source: Peter Flack, managing partner, Flack and Kurtz, New York.

Where to look for big energy cuts

It's relatively easy to reduce energy use by at least 25% in almost every building constructed before the late 1970s. It's done through simple engineering changes that usually pay off in three years or less. These big improvements are possible after the company has already made such basic energy-conservation moves as removing unneeded lamps and limiting hours they're used in the office.

The effective steps are usually expensive though.

It is often difficult to get top management to realize that the initial investment will quickly benefit the bottom line. Controllers are not receptive to plant engineers who want $1 million for a lighting program.

In reality, investment tax credits and depreciation sharply reduce the purchase cost of conservation equipment. And the changes usually result in an identifiable contribution to cash flow.

An added incentive can be for the engineering consultant that plans the program to guarantee energy savings on a money-back basis. Typically the consultant guarantees 20% annual return on each dollar spent for the program over five years, resulting in a guaranteed simple 100% payback in five years of total program costs.

An alternative would be for the consultant to find investors who will pay for the new equipment. They lease it to the company under an attractive fixed-cost lease because of the guarantee.

Conservation essentials:
• Lighting. Accounts for 40% of total energy costs in most offices, 26% in plants. Lighting waste can be avoided by modifying existing fixtures. Reduce light bulb wattage or find lighting fixtures requiring fewer bulbs. Replace frosted diffusers with polarized ones that do not disperse the light. Be sure that separate rooms have separate light switches. Average annual saving on electricity: 35¢–40¢ per square foot.
• Fans. Run them year-round at one fixed speed in most buildings to move heated or cooled air and increase ventilation. These can be converted to run at two speeds, the lower one providing 70% of the air flow at one-third of the cost.
• Absorption chillers. Widely sold to cool air at a time when natural gas was priced very low to boost summer usage. Today, they are regarded as totally inefficient and should be replaced.
• Pressurized steam systems. Often operated at unnecessarily high pressure. They can be easily equipped to operate at lower pressure for part of the day or during nonwork cycles. And leakage drops sharply at lower pressures.

When choosing a consultant be aware that some energy consulting companies in the field make promises they don't keep. Check their credit ratings.

Expect the consultant to specify equipment that is compatible with the level of skill of the workers who will operate and maintain it. The consultant shouldn't give untrained workers a computer to operate, but should recommend improvements that can work with the mid-range abilities of the operating group.

Source: Michael Munk, manager of energy conservation engineering, Ebasco Services, Inc., New York.

Low-cost energy savers

Many areas are overlooked in cutting back on energy use. Where to find them:
- Outdoor air dampers that aren't airtight.
- Dirty air filters.
- Thermostats that aren't adjusted for cloudy days, evenings, weekends, or little-used areas.
- Signs that are too bright or lit at unnecessary times.
- Oversized or improperly maintained electrical motors.
- Equipment that runs when not in use.
- Off-peak electrical rates that are not fully taken advantage of because of improper scheduling.
- Steam or hot-water boiler leaks.
- Gas pilot lights that stay on in warm weather.
- Steam-pressure or water-flow rates that are too high.
- Efficiency analyses that aren't run daily.
- Hot water that's used unnecessarily.

Source: Wayne C. Turner and Carl B. Estes, Oklahoma State University, *Modern Materials Handling,* Boston.

Psychological climate control

Heeding the psychological aspects of climate control can increase productivity and reduce complaints:

Color helps. Switch to cooler blues in spring. Deep, rich browns, and other earth tones create a mental image of warmth. In winter, create psychological hot spots by hanging paintings or posters of vivid reds in open areas.

Insulate outer walls with draperies. Use a lighter-colored set for spring and a dark-colored set for the fall. And noise levels will be reduced.

Ask staff members their personal temperature preferences. Shift desks so that the polar bears sit in the coolest areas and the shiverers get the warmth they need.

Relax the dress code to allow lightweight garments in summer and boots, pants, and heavy sweaters in winter. Encourage management to dress down occasionally to show that the new policy is real.

New thermostats save fuel

Thermostats in most buildings are designed to hold the temperature within a three-degree range. The problem is that huge amounts of fuel are wasted when the furnace is triggered to raise the temperature during cool periods in normally warm months, and when the air conditioner comes on during warm days in cold months.

A new breed of thermostats is helping to solve the problem. A floating-space temperature control thermostat triggers the furnace or air conditioner only when the temperature is outside a specific acceptability band.

The idea is to keep the temperature within the 65°–78°F range mandated for federal buildings.

In one test, the University of California spent $640,000 to fit 12 older buildings with the new system. Fuel consumption dropped to 65% of what is was in 1972–1973. Cost will be recouped in less than three years.

And it's better to work in environments where temperature variation is greater than three degrees, say the health experts.

Source: *Heating/Piping/Air Conditioning,* Chicago.

Saving by controlling ventilation

The amount of air brought into a building through the ventilation system drastically affects the heating and cooling load. Controlling ventilation can translate into a large saving.

Keep outdoor dampers airtight when closed. Verify that indicators accurately show closed and open positions.

Install remotely adjustable outside dampers in areas where the number of occupants is large or fluctuates greatly.

Use baffles to keep wind from blowing directly into the air intake.

Cut off the direct indoor air supply to rest rooms. Instead, ventilate with air from other areas, allowing it to come in through the door grill and go out through the exhaust system.

Source: *Facilities Management,* Washington, D.C.

How to reduce lighting costs

• Turn off the lights whenever an office is vacant. As short a time as 15 minutes with fluorescent bulbs, or three minutes with incandescent, is worth the effort.

• Reduce after-hours and outdoor lighting. Customers and the public are highly conscious of waste and an overlighted building.

• Remove bulbs in fixtures and reduce wattage wherever possible.

• Use photoelectric switches to regulate the hours of security lighting and parking-lot lighting according to the seasons.

• Replace standard fluorescent and incandescent bulbs with high-efficiency fluorescents. New bulbs give the same light output for $\frac{1}{3}$ to $\frac{1}{2}$ of the electricity.

• Switch from overhead lighting in large areas to lights over individual work areas.

Myths about artificial lighting

• Electricity bills can be cut by taking some bulbs out of fluorescent fixtures. Reality: This only works if the ballasts are also disconnected.

• Turning off the lights when leaving the room saves money. Reality: This is true for incandescent lights but not necessarily for fluorescent lights. Turning a fluorescent lamp on and off shortens its life. Unless the intervals are more than five to fifteen minutes (depending on the cost of electricity), the cost of the more frequent replacements will outweigh the electricity savings.

• Fluorescent bulbs with partly clear glass give more light per energy dollar than fully frosted bulbs. Reality: This just isn't so. Fluorescent lamps emit a lot of energy in the invisible ultraviolet range. This is converted into visible light by the lamp phosphor (frosting). A lamp that is clear of phosphor at certain points on the glass actually gives out less visible light.

Source: *Plant Engineering,* New York.

New lighting controls

The first lighting control systems shut off all lights at once and did not permit lighting levels to be varied. Now more flexible systems are available.

Personnel sensors. They detect when people enter and leave a room by using heat or sound waves, and they turn lights on and off. Cost: $150 per control.

Photoelectric dimmers. A light-sensitive cell detects available natural light, and the dimmer system adjusts lighting output to maintain a uniform level of light. Cost: $100 each.

Voltage reducers. Manually adjusted from a control panel as daylight changes, they maintain light levels and reduce power demand. Cost: $1,000 for 90 40-watt bulbs.

Programmable lighting controls. These allow the user to create a time-of-day program that automatically switches off and on different groups of fixtures or lamps within fixtures at different times of day. Cost: $20,000 and up for 200 fixtures.

———

Source: *Energy User News,* New York.

ENVIRONMENTAL ISSUES

Steering a course to meet environmental regulations

Companies should not take an administration's pledge to deregulate as an automatic signal to relax environmental programs. Deregulation is unlikely to affect the bulk of pollution-control, hazardous-waste-management, solid-waste-management, product-safety, and occupational-health statutes.

A prudent approach is to set up an environmental auditing program. It should aim to:

• Help a company's efforts to stay abreast of changes in regulations as they occur.

• Keep the company in full compliance with environmental regulations. But a company can be fined for not obtaining permits from the Environmental Protection Agency that they did not even know were necessary. And failure to comply with certain regulations leaves company officers open to personal liability lawsuits.

When reviewing the company's environmental records and procedures, find out whether directives from headquarters are reaching the plant floor. (They often don't.) Also find out if record-keeping is complete.

Periodic environmental audits of this type provide the company with data that can be vital if it has to defend itself in court or at an enforcement proceeding.

———

Source: J. Ladd Greeno, Arthur D. Little, Inc., Cambridge, Mass.

23 INVENTORY AND MATERIALS HANDLING

INVENTORY MANAGEMENT

Inventory strategies for troubled times

Every business manager must reduce the amount of time it takes to turn over inventory assets in a dangerous economic climate.

The biggest inventory mistakes are first made in company sales forecasts. These forecasts are anything but an exact science. Be conservative. Recheck all assumptions. Try to get verification from industry experts. Poll a portion of the company's customers to determine their buying intentions. But stay aware that they can't guarantee anything either.

Strategy goals:
• Get the best possible sales information you can.
• Update it frequently.
• Think of the sales forecast as being dynamic, not static. Keep checking actual sales against projections.

Key management strategies to keep inventories in line:
• Try to get day-to-day information on sales without overburdening salespeople with reporting requirements that keep them from selling. One way is to develop an internal reporting system that is generated automatically by sales invoices.

• Reevaluate all lead times, both within the company and from suppliers. Remember that orders are delivered faster in tough times. As lead times shorten, it becomes necessary to review inventory more frequently (weekly instead of monthly). Pay special attention to expensive materials and those used in great quantities. And don't overlook outstanding purchase orders. Stretch out some or cancel them.

• A common mistake is ordering a stop to all purchases or sharply cutting back on the purchases. It is much better to scale down purchasing on a planned basis to bring it in line with changing sales forecasts and manufacturing needs.

• Build in signals to alert management whenever day-to-day figures vary from the planned levels. A sudden falloff in orders should trigger an immediate management review so that production schedules and purchasing plans can be cut back.

Financing strategy:
Take a close look at the trade-offs involved with reduced purchases. Quantity discounts may be forfeited, bringing unit costs up to a level that no longer covers the cost of borrowing money. If that danger point is reached:

• Reconsider offering that item.
• Raise the price, if possible.
• Use the first available cash to resume quantity purchases.

To move inventory out as fast as possible:
• Communicate with the sales force more frequently and more honestly than ever. Each salesperson must understand clearly what items need to be pushed off the shelf.
• Consider shifting to different sales motivation techniques. These can range all the way from extra compensation for meeting new goals to increased competition between salespeople. (Too few companies do this effectively.) Now is the time to adopt some of the newer sales motivation programs being offered, which give the company the benefit of outside thinking and approaches.

When banks are financing the company's inventories:
• Expect them to be looking over the shoulder of top management. Keep cool and try not to panic or overreact. Listen and take bankers' comments under advisement, but also rely on the company's own experience and the business judgment of its management team. Bankers are undoubtedly comparing the company with other clients in the same business or industry norms. Only the company's management knows what is best for its actual circumstances.
• Don't be stampeded into paying off loans prematurely (the company will need all the cash it can generate) or into dumping salable inventory. Move cautiously. Even if the inventory is moving slowly, it still represents cash.

Liquidating inventories:
• Keep it orderly. And keep the bank informed of the company's plans. Don't give the bankers any surprises!
• First balance out the inventory. Try to avoid carrying ten of one component and seven of another when you will only be able to sell five finished items.
• Investigate the possibility of returning goods to some suppliers in lieu of payment. Many manufacturers would rather take goods back, even after a year, than get into a wrangle about collecting. They may well have another customer waiting. Or, inflation may have increased the value of the goods.
• Make deals with competitors by selling off excess inventory to balance each other's stock.

For example, one distributor has 5,000 type A gaskets and distributor Y has roughly the same amount of type B. By swapping half of their inventory, each is in a better balanced position, without cash outlay.

Don't be tempted to lower credit standards in order to move goods. The company may wind up swapping goods for bad debts.

Source: Stephen B. Zimmerman, CPA, partner, Arthur Andersen, New York, and Malcolm Moses, head, Malcolm P. Moses & Assoc., Merrick, N.Y.

Useful inventory ratios

Inventory represents 40%-50% of the current assets of the typical manufacturing company (followed by receivables and cash). The key management tool is the inventory ratio. A common mistake is misunderstanding the components of the ratio and then making decisions based on the wrong assumptions.

The basic ratio is inventory turnover. It is best computed by dividing the annual sales at standard cost by the average inventory cost. Define sales carefully. Be consistent about using gross sales or net sales, sales at actual cost or sales at standard unit cost. (Dun & Bradstreet's yardstick, which many companies use for comparisons, is net sales. That figure is readily available on published financial statements. The standard unit cost or the actual cost of sales is not.)

Be consistent about the inventory measure also. Is it the beginning-of-the-year inventory, average annual inventory or average monthly inventory? One company had either a 5.3 or 3.6 turnover ratio, depending on which method it chose.

For effective financial control, be sure the components of the inventory ratio, and what they imply, are clearly understood by all managers. Above all, be uniform in reports.

Other useful inventory ratios:
• Inventory to current assets. Take into account seasonal and economic aberrations when applying this ratio.
• Inventory to total assets. Total assets are the sum of current assets plus fixed assets. Compa-

nies often compare this ratio to the overall company return on assets.

• Number of months' supplies. Operating personnel often relate better to inventory measures if they are expressed in terms of months of raw materials on hand.

• Number of days' sales. Sales and marketing people get a better handle on inventory when it is expressed in terms of number of days' worth of finished goods on hand.

• Inventory to net working capital. Net working capital (current assets minus current liabilities) is a key measure of a company's basic health The inventory to net working capital ratio adds a good reading of liquidity. If net working capital is less than inventories, inventories are probably too high.

Source: Robert A. Bonsack, principal, Peat, Marwick, Mitchell & Co., Newport Beach, Calif.

Carrying-cost formulas

There are costly traps in "quickie" formulas for calculating the right amount of goods to order. The Economic Order Quantity formulas can lead to overbuying because many managers are plugging outdated numbers into them.

Inventory holding costs (carrying charges, warehouse labor, pilferage, etc.) have been rising fast. For example:

$$EOQ = \frac{2 \times \text{annual usage} \times \text{ordering cost}}{\text{holding-cost rate}}$$

There's a tendency to assume that holding costs are keeping to the 15% to 24% that was typical a few years ago. In reality, in many industries they've zoomed up into the 30%–36% range. Using a 15% holding-cost rate when the real rate is 30% will lead to an order size more than 40% too large. Inventory turnover will be slowed by a third.

So recalculate holding costs, taking into account the indirects such as labor, as well as the more obvious interest charges.

Source: Lele & Co., Evanston, Ill.

Signs of inventory problems

• Competitors' prices are lower.
• Slow-moving items are reducing cash available for new inventory.
• Odd and nonstandard sizes are overstocked.
• Too many seasonal items are carried over.

Inventory aids:

• Arrange for quick delivery from suppliers for seldom ordered goods. (This can mean an extra charge.) An alternative is an informal borrowing system with friendly competitors.
• Grade inventory according to profitability. Ensure 100% availability of biggest profit-earners. Stock down or out on all slow-selling items.
• Color-code bin or package labels to indicate month of receipt. This provides visual identification of slow-moving merchandise.
• Establish a monthly schedule of returns of excess inventory. Hit minor suppliers once or twice a year, major ones on a more frequent schedule.

Source: Bruce M. Bradway and Robert E. Pritchard, *Protecting Profits During Inflation and Recession,* Addison-Wesley Publishing Co., Reading, Mass.

The high cost of inventory

It costs at least 25¢ to carry one dollar's worth of unsold inventory for a year (15¢ or more for interest, 10¢ or so for space, handling, utilities and insurance). And if the item becomes obsolete or goes out of style, the obsolescence loss increases the cost even further.

How to keep inventories down:

• If customers stretch out delivery dates, move fast to cut production and delay orders of raw materials.
• Check customers often to find out how fast they are selling the product.
• Sell obsolete goods fast and at distress prices to cut inventory holding costs. Losses will

be partly absorbed by income tax saving and write-offs.

Source: Selwin E. Price, Partner, Alexander Grant & Co., Chicago.

How to achieve lower inventories safely

The most common barrier to trimming inventories is the fear that customer service will be sabotaged. Not necessarily, if there is closer coordination between marketing, manufacturing, and inventory-control managers.

The first step is a regular review of inventory base levels to update the most cost-efficient combination of manufacturing lead times, inventory control, and customer-service standards.

In a typical situation, the company has goods on hand to fill orders promptly 95% of the time but sees a great saving if it can reduce the figure to 90%. Solution:

• The manufacturing manager decides whether lead times can be accelerated enough to help compensate for lower inventory levels.

• The marketing manager asks customers to increase safety margins when ordering.

The second step is for the three managers to coordinate plans for occasions when base inventory levels must be temporarily changed, in preparation for a sales promotion, for example.

Marketing must let the manufacturing and inventory departments know far in advance what increase in orders it expects during the promotion. With help from the finance department, the three managers plan the most efficient way to meet the surge without disrupting computerized inventory-control systems that have been set to maintain the base level.

Inventory requirements are also a function of the company's distribution system. The cure is to analyze the distribution system regularly for inefficiencies.

It is typical for distributors to cut orders across the board to trim costs, resulting in spot shortages. Rather than change inventory levels to meet these shortages, the company should use its expertise to help distributors with their own inventory problems.

When distributors manage their inventories better, they may reduce orders slightly. But product-cost reductions in manufacturing will be far greater than the cost of reduced orders.

Source: Robert Burrows, Booz Allen & Hamilton, Cleveland.

Reducing excess stocks

First identify specific excessive stocks. Next, determine the cause of overstocking. Excessive inventories are imbalances between what is purchased and what is used, what is manufactured and what is shipped, what is put on distributors' shelves and what they are actually able to sell to retailers or end-users. Imbalances can also arise where, say, three components go into a product. If supply runs short on one component, supplies of the other two are useless at that time.

Common causes of imbalance:

• Engineers and design people insist on having immediate access to many components they use or might use. If the company has a large engineering and design department, or is technologically oriented, look here first.

• Irregular demand. Assumed inability to forecast precise demand encourages larger-than-necessary initial orders.

• Lead time is out of whack. Because delivery times in recession tend to grow shorter, chances are the company is purchasing and receiving in advance of actual need. Revise purchase orders on basis of current lead-time experience.

• Usable supplies may be low, relative to the total amount stocked. This often happens with a new product when tolerances have not been fully worked out.

• Supplies in the pipeline are not being taken into consideration before reordering. As a result, reorders are placed too soon.

• Excess sitting time. If the components for 1,000 products come in each week and 1,000 finished products are shipped out, it is not necessary to maintain inventory levels of 5,000. Cutting to 4,000 would leave an adequate cushion.

• Decisions made in affluent times may not be appropriate in recession. For example, "We will never again run out of this item." "Let's keep several suppliers on this component." "We'll sell more typewriters if we also offer a full line of cases and supplies."

Reexamine these premises. Now is the time to reconsider the benefits of working very closely with a single source. Have the sales department reevaluate how important a full line is.

• Too-specialized components. If standardization of parts has never been tried, consider the idea. Do a commonality analysis to identify product applications where various functions could be performed by the same component. Also, discourage all special-order items.

It's a good idea to make materials lists available to engineers and designers before they write up specifications. Get purchasing people and engineering department to cooperate in cutting manufacturing costs without hurting product quality.

Source: Norman Kobert, Kobert & Associates, Fort Lauderdale, Fla.

Protecting inventories

• Store materials out of reach of damage from traveling fork trucks, oil and water leaks, and other common hazards.

• Prevent doctoring of records in advance of normal checks. Also, count materials on hand irregularly, when time permits.

• Date all labels to assure first-in, first-out usage of age-sensitive items.

• Use protective security to limit losses from pilferage.

• Clearly label all items to avoid accidental openings, misuses, and spoilage.

• Install temperature and humidity controls.

Source: Edward J. McNesby, *Systematic Control of Factory and Manufacturing Costs,* Prentice-Hall, Inc., Englewood Cliffs, N.J.

Coping with shortages of critical raw materials

Uncertain supplies of critical raw materials have joined high interest rates, inflation, and declining productivity as facts of life for business in the United States.

In the long term, we can expect continuing volatility in supplies of critical raw materials because many of the critical materials are found in countries with unstable political regimes and the U.S. government is not able to foot the bill for emergency stockpiles of all materials.

The company should be no more dependent on critical materials than competitors are. If some companies put themselves in a much better position than competitors, Washington may be tempted to step in during an emergency and equalize the situation.

Positive steps to take:

• Stockpile enough critical raw materials for an unexpected short-term shortage but not a protracted crisis.

• Step up research for substitutes for critical raw materials.

• Redesign products now to reduce the need for raw materials in tougher times.

• When developing new products, minimize their dependence on critical raw materials.

• Improve inventory management of tools and equipment containing materials that could be recycled.

Common mistakes in resources management:

• Panic buying at the first hint of shortages.

• Excessive capital commitments in resources from countries that are unstable.

Source: Bruce Lane, senior staff member, Resource Consulting Group, Arthur D. Little, Inc., Cambridge, Mass.

How to cut down on spot shortages

When caught flat-footed or forced to buy quickly, investigate to find out the cause in each case. Determine how shortages can be avoided in the future.

The outlook is for more spot shortages, particularly in petroleum-related products, as vendors cut back on unprofitable lines. Ways to insure supplies:

• Horse-trade. Level with suppliers on current needs for commodities in tight supply. Release unneeded materials in exchange for priority goods.

• Be a visiting fireman. Meet with the top brass of critical vendors and subcontractors in their offices. Set up the visits in advance. Be prepared to discuss long-range needs and how projected conflicts can be resolved.

• Help with cash flow. Nowadays, simply paying bills on time earns hero status. Offering to help with cash flow problems, particularly with distributors, is powerful protection against shortages and long lead times.

• Give long-term orders. And get firm commitments.

• Standardize. It really does help.

• Reassign buying responsibilities. Have headquarters handle purchasing of goods with national sourcing. Have the buying staff concentrate on specific types of vendors, not commodities. For example, one group buys from manufacturers, another groups buys from distributors, and a third handles subcontractors.

• Use Murphy's Law. Test possible substitute materials before what can go wrong does go wrong, particularly with long-lead-time items.

Source: *Purchasing*, Boston.

How to count your stock accurately

• Use two squads that alternate between taking the initial count and making the recount.

• Minimize opportunities for the two teams to communicate.

• Appoint an inventory auditor to collect the tally sheets and make surprise visits.

WAREHOUSING

How to make warehouse sites efficient

A good site layout reduces truck turnaround time, yard congestion, security problems, product damage, and accidents.

Desirable features:

• Provide for future increases in truck sizes. Make berths five feet longer and six inches wider than current equipment requires. Allow one foot extra in service-road widths.

• Make one-way service roads at least 12 feet wide. Widen them on approaches to intersections or turns.

• Locate sidewalks at least six feet from roads. Install curbs or barriers.

• Have road structures and materials strong enough to carry expected loads and designed for adequate water drainage.

• Separate truck and pedestrian gateways.

• Make truck berth doors wide enough to allow trucks to get in and out easily.

• Provide adequate visitor parking to discourage parking in receiving and shipping areas.

Locate this space near office to minimize walking time and turn space over faster.

• Design berths so trailers can back in from a counterclockwise position. Lay out roads with only left turns.

Here are some design guidelines for the structure itself:

• A square is the best shape. It minimizes exterior wall space, is energy efficient, and increases supervisors' efficiency by keeping interior distances and walking time down.
• Design the structure around pallet dimensions and their stacking limitations.
• Plan column spacing for pallet size, storage, proper aisle width, and location of conveyors.
• Locate ducts, pipes, and electrical conduits to permit optimum vertical clearance near handling and loading activities.
• Align doors with aisles whenever possible. (Turns cause accidents, product damage, and increased handling time.)
• Locate permanently installed equipment, utilities, cooler space, etc., with expansion in mind. It is costly to move them when extensions are added.
• Make aisles as wide as possible. Narrow aisles reduce handling efficiency and increase accidents.
• Improve security by fencing the visitor parking area or locating it at a distance from loading docks. Design and locate shipping/receiving offices so no outsiders have direct access to the warehouse.
• Provide enough illumination. A loaded warehouse requires more lighting than an empty one.

Source: *The ABC's of Warehousing,* Marketing Publications Inc., Washington, D.C.

Alternative to the wooden pallet

An alternative to hardwood pallets is the slipsheet, made up of rigid fiberboard sheets sandwiched between layers of kraft paper and waterproof plastic film. The package rests on top surface of slip-

sheet in fashion similar to palletized freight.

It is low in unit cost, lightweight, and takes up little space.

The disadvantages include: cost of slipsheet packaging equipment—all stations in the company's physical distribution system must be converted. It may cost $8,000 or more to convert a forklift run so that forks can be slipped beneath sheets. And it's not appropriate for certain uses—for example, heavy loads.

Faster unloading

Use a time clock to stamp on the paperwork accompanying each load the arrival and departure times of drivers delivering shipments. It will encourage time-wasters to tie up another company's loading dock. Inform dispatchers of key carriers about the time stamping so that they can police their own drivers.

Source: *Electrical Wholesaling,* New York.

Stretch-wrap vs shrink-wrap

Plastic stretch film, which is applied under pressure and then secured around a load of goods (stretch-wrap), is generally better than shrink-wrap, a different type of film that's tightened around a load through the application of heat. Stretch-wrap costs less, requires less energy, and is easier to apply.

Shrink-wrap is best for irregularly shaped loads or material that must be protected from the weather, provided it's not affected by the heat used to make the wrap tight.

Source: *Modern Plastics,* New York.

SHIPPING

Freight savings with computer models

Deregulation is making shipping rate structures even more complex. But computer-based models are now available to provide cost estimates based on the type of freight, carrier, and proposed route. Estimates can often be used by the shipper as leverage to negotiate better rates and services with competing carriers.

Shipping-cost models can also:

• Forecast future transportation bills (estimates from 5–10 years out are available).

• Evaluate the costs of carrier service levels, providing information on service-vs-cost trade-offs.

• Identify locales better for establishing new facilities because of low transportation costs.

• Provide data for negotiating favorable rate escalation agreements.

• Evaluate private-fleet vs regulated-carrier operations.

• Conduct competitive mode and routing analyses.

Typical cost might be $15,000 per year plus $45–$65 for each estimate. Discounts may be available for more than 350 estimates per year.

Source: *Purchasing World,* Barrington, Ill.

Holding down freight costs

Ideas to put a lid on industrial freight costs, which are rising a lot faster than the general price level:

• Standardize shipping instructions based on urgency. When the lack of an item threatens a production shutdown, specify small-package or priority airfreight. When the lack could cause a stock outage, specify nonpriority (two to three days) airfreight or LTL (less-than-full-truckload). Specify a truckload or rail shipment for items for regular stock resupply or normal reorder.

• Consolidate inbound freight. Have the carrier consolidate two or more shipments from a single vendor (or even from several vendors) into one. Advantages are weight breaks and minimal delivery charges.

• Think total cost. Direct shipping charges (rates, packing, crating, insurance) aren't all. The final cost decision on mode must include indirect shipping costs such as capital that is invested in inventories, carrying charges, warehousing, cost of damage, theft, pilferage, etc. In addition, intangible considerations, such as system flexibility, competitive advantage, and customer goodwill.

Source: *Purchasing World,* Barrington, Ill.

Avoiding unnecessary charges

When the company uses regulated common carriers, watch for extra charges that are legal but avoidable:

• Single-shipment charges. Assessed when only one shipment is picked up. Therefore always contract for more than one load, or use carriers that do not charge for this service.

• Pickup and delivery charges. Assessed to cover unusual or difficult situations, usually in big cities (particularly New York). Instead use companies that specialize in serving congested areas at regular rates.

• Arbitrary charges for freight tonnage imbalances when a truck returns empty from a trip. Use carriers that regularly service the delivery area and do not make an arbitrary charge.

Handle as many shipping chores as possible in-house. For example, provide return bills of lading, use proper labels, and do necessary repackaging. The freight firm will charge extra for these services.

Source: Donna Behme, Behme Assoc., *Sounding Board,* Cherry Hill, N.J.

Deregulation causes pitfalls for shippers

Motor-carrier deregulation has imposed major new responsibilities and costs on shippers.

Traps to watch for:

• Insurance against cargo loss and damage. Previously this was the responsibility of the carrier. It is now negotiable.

• A carrier may now refuse cargo specially liable to damage. The alternatives are higher rates or limits to carrier liability.

• The shift of responsibilities to shippers may lower trucking companies' incentives to keep up their loss-control programs.

Remember, easier entry into interstate shipping opens the way for organized crime. Deal only with well-known firms, even if their prices are somewhat higher.

Source: *Business Insurance,* Chicago.

Avoiding billing losses on rush shipments

A big danger on rush shipments is that the company's controls frequently slip and it fails to bill for a shipped order. What is needed is a final check at the loading dock to make sure that the bill of lading matches precisely the sales invoice that is used to bill the customer.

When a sales invoice is missing, for whatever reason, the loading dock should make up an exception report. This triggers a search for the missing invoice. Meanwhile, another sales invoice is generated, and made it out to correspond to the bill of lading.

Matching the bill of lading to the invoice provides a second check on the spelling of the customer's name, the accuracy of the address and account number, and whether the right merchandise is being shipped. It's better to remedy a mistake like this before the goods leave the premises.

Another technique to consider is to use prenumbered customer order forms that record orders in sequence as they are received. Follow up any open order numbers to detect unbilled shipments.

Source: John Mullarkey, director of auditing standards, Touche Ross & Co.

Collecting freight claims

Immediate inspection and specific reports of damages improve chances of collecting on a claim. One common, and costly, error is inspection is not made at time of delivery and the receipt is signed, "subject to further inspection." Such notations carry no legal weight in claims against the carrier if damages are later discovered. So note condition of shipment in detail.

Proper documentation is essential. Include: (1) original bill of lading or certified copy; (2) original paid freight bill or certified copy; (3) invoice; (4) carrier inspection report; (5) documents substantiating repair costs, extra freight charges, etc.; (6) delivery receipt showing exceptions noted at time of truck delivery or inspection document for open-top railcar shipment; and (7) pictures of damaged goods and packaging.

Railroad freight safety record

Railroads' safety record for hauling freight is improving steadily. The number of claims by shippers for losses and damages hit a 47-year low. The ratio of payments to revenues (1.08%) was the lowest in 30 years. The record has grown progessively better over the last decade, the result of railroad revitalization and a special campaign.

Source: Association of American Railroads, Washington, D.C.

Shipping by rail—economically

With diesel-fuel prices destined to keep rising, over-the-road haulers' prices will keep increasing, too. The likely result is a resurgence in railroad shipping. To get the best rates:

• Ask about piggybacking (loading goods into truck trailers, then loading the trailers on railroad flatbeds). Piggybacking is the chief way that many railroads take market shares away from over-the-road haulers. Bargains are available. For volume traffic, it offers lower-than-truck rates and the convenience of truck pickup and delivery.

• Buy in railroad carload quantities when possible. Take delivery of a shipment at the railroad terminal over several days. Buying in carload quantities means volume transportation discounts. The railroad will usually arrange for a truck delivery from the terminal and provide free storage until delivery.

• Agree to unload the railcars carrying your company's shipments in a shorter time than normal on the condition that the railroad splits the savings it realizes with your company.

Source: *Purchasing,* Boston.

When air freight is essential

• Shipment time eats up selling days (seasonal merchandise) and cuts turnover of expensive merchandise.

• Transportation delays discourage orders and reorders.

• Speed is required to beat or meet competition.

• Important markets are long distances from vendors.

• Inventories must be lean because of cash or space limitations.

"Priority" air freight— a rip-off

Many carriers are billing their new guaranteed "Priority Air Freight Service" as the long-awaited answer to the shipper's dream. This service carries a 30% surcharge. Customers are encouraged to believe that they get speedy delivery.

What's really guaranteed is only shipment on the flight specified on the air bill, with no responsibility for safe arrival at any particular time. The carrier's liability for failure to "prioritize" the shipment is limited to refunding the surcharge only, not the full payment. Even this liability is excused if the delay arose from a list of common causes, including bad weather and mechanical troubles of the aircraft.

Source: *Freight Claims in Plain English,* Shippers National Freight Claim Council, Huntington, N.Y.

$\mathbf{24}$ FLEET MANAGEMENT

TRUCKS

Owning your own fleet

Deregulation of the industry could significantly disrupt the operations of common carriers. Volatile rate changes are possible. Bankruptcy for some carriers can't be ruled out. For companies that do substantial shipping, it may be opportune to consider a company-owned truck fleet.

A private trucking fleet provides quicker service, more flexibility and security, less damage to goods, and better control over costs and cost increases.

However, any company that creates a trucking operation is apt to find itself the target of a union-organizing drive by the Teamsters.

Questions to weigh in considering a private fleet:

• How much of the time would company trucks be running empty? If it's more than 20% of their mileage, they would not be cost-effective.

• Are company products distributed in bulk, which would favor private shipping? If they are distributed in small loads, using a variety of common carriers is probably still the best bet.

• Are there overlooked opportunities to make additional use of a private trucking fleet for transporting material among the company's own facilities?

• Do the products require specialized han-

dling or equipment during shipping that a common carrier could better provide?

Truck leases: which to use and when

• The capital lease. It's generally long-term. The accumulated payments nearly equal the truck's purchase price. Companies can use the capital lease as a substitute for a loan to purchase. If a fleet is being leased, the interest charges may be well below the prime rate. But the lessee must be willing to maintain, operate, and dispose of the trucks involved.

• The operating lease. The lessee pays only for the use of the truck when he needs it. The lessor provides the maintenance and insurance and disposes of the truck when the lease expires. However, the truck is not counted on the lessee's books as an asset, although this may be negotiable. Operating leases are generally more expensive than capital leases because of the services provided.

A lessee should always shop around and bargain for the best price. Successful leasing is based on negotiation.

save 240 running hours and up to $4,800 in truckers' salaries and make customers happier.

For better tractor-trailer mileage

• Air deflectors. They cost $350–$600 and provide a fuel saving of 4%–8%. Payback is usually under one year.

• Radial tires cost 20% above bias plies for purchase, but 3% per mile less after one recap when used on drive wheels. Fuel saving is 3%–10%.

• More efficient axle ratios, temperature-controlled fan clutches, and speed-control devices that lower horsepower demands. Fuel saving is 6%–30%. Also available are programmable tachographs that automatically print out incidents of excessive speeding, engine revolutions per minute (RPMs) and idling time.

Also helpful:

• Retrain drivers to avoid unnecessary speed changes and shifting.

• Tighten up air-cleaner maintenance and tire-pressure checking. Tires inflated to 100 pounds per square inch save 5% in fuel costs versus those inflated to 55–65 pounds per square inch.

Source: Study by the Voluntary Truck and Bus Fuel Improvement Program, *Oil & Gas Journal,* Tulsa, Okla.

Ease up on the pedal...maybe

Researchers simulated a 450-mile truck trip at the legal 55 mph and at the illegal 65 mph. Because of traffic, road, and weather conditions, the 65-mph highballer averaged only 58.6 mph (vs 51.3 of the 55-mph truck).

The slower truck used 15% less fuel. Over 100,000 miles, driving slower would save 2,500 gallons or about $2,500. But going faster would

Lower-quality diesel fuel

Major problems and how to cope:

• Higher sulfur levels. Can form sulfuric acid, especially in engines that run cooler than normal. So drain engine oil more frequently. Control engine termperatures by shutting down during pickups, deliveries, lunch, etc., rather than idling.

• Wax formation in colder weather. Clogs the fuel filter, stopping fuel flow. Install a fuel warmer to combat the problem.

• Water contamination. Clogs fuel lines, can damage injection nozzles in cold weather. Install a fuel-water separator.

• Elimination of winterizing additives formerly put in by refiners in all seasons. As a result, fuel bought earlier in the year and stockpiled for use in winter must have additives put in by the user.

Source: *Automobile International,* New York.

Using synthetic oil

The higher price of synthetic oil is justified only for vehicles used for long-distance highway driving, towing heavy loads, or operating in temperature extremes. Less-expensive conventional oil is preferable for vehicles used in stop-and-go driving or through hilly or dusty areas.

Under less-than-ideal driving conditions, the improved mileage and longer oil-change intervals possible with synthetic oil are canceled out.

A recent finding indicates that only 16% of all drivers operate their vehicles under ideal conditions.

Source: Dave Bowman, Fram/Autolite technical service manager, quoted in *Automotive News,* Detroit.

Keeping drivers cool

Truck air conditioning makes drivers more alert, less accident prone. In addition, closed cab windows keep out distracting road dust and traffic noise.

Roof-top models are the easiest to maintain, don't add a complex heating function, and provide larger but less concentrated air volume. Their major drawback is that they are more easily damaged than under-the-hood types.

Source: *Fleet Owner,* New York.

Safety and maintenance tips

Simply applying reflector strips, at a cost of about $100, along the bottom and sides of trucks and trailers cuts nighttime accidents sharply.

The safest color for trucks and cars is yellow. It is most visible under almost all traffic conditions, particularly in fog or hard rain and at twilight. Second best is light green. Both yellow and light-green vehicles are two to four times more visible than dark-colored trucks and cars during poor driving conditions.

Truck maintenance costs for small, company-owned fleets are usually lower if the company buys a guaranteed maintenance plan from the truck maker instead of hiring a mechanic, buying tools, etc. As a rule of thumb, one mechanic can handle ten to 15 trucks. If the fleet is smaller, do a cost comparison. The cost of a maintenance plan varies with truck size, annual mileage, driving conditions, and so on.

Install fuel heaters in diesel trucks. Cold-weather starting problems are increasing because changes in the refining process are adding to the fuel's wax content. (Using kerosene as a wintertime fuel thinner is too expensive.) Heaters mean cheaper and more plentiful number-two diesel can be used all winter.

One overlooked problem with truck batteries is maintenance costs (mainly for adding water once a week) amount to about twice the purchase price of a truck battery over its life. Try one of the two improved batteries on the market, which have sharply reduced watering requirements. One uses an alloy to reduce water loss, cutting required watering to two or three times a year. The other incorporates a system that adds water to each battery cell through a single opening. This will save up to 35%. The purchase price is $350 extra, but watering costs drop from $1,800 (over five years for a comparable conventional battery) to $108.

Recapping tires is almost always cost-effective since the casing accounts for 75% of the total cost of a new tire, it pays to use it more than once. But always insist on a warranty against separation.

Antifreeze used the year round prolongs the life of water pumps in trucks. Replace the pump only when it shows signs of wear, not at predetermined mileage.

Trailer specs to consider: (1) maintenance problems minimized if there are a sufficient number of hinges on the rear doors: (2) protective coating for outside wiring reduces damage caused by tree limbs; (3) extra-strength flooring. Also parts that require frequent checkups should be easily accessible. Get input from drivers on special loading and unloading requirements.

Sources: *Commercial Car Journal,* Chilton Co., Radnor, Pa., Minnesota Department of Safety; Ed Boone, Sun Oil, *Fleet Owner,* New York; Edward Larkins, Plainfield Super Valu, Plainfield, Ill., *Fleet Owner,* New York; *Traffic Management,* Boston.

What's down the road in truck design

• More diesel engines. Half of all medium-duty trucks are likely to be powered by diesels by 1985.

• Smaller engines. Only 15% of light trucks are expected to use V-8 engines by 1990.

• Turbocharging, which uses exhaust gas to

increase engine combustion. It will be used more often to offset engine-size reductions.

• Front-wheel drive. Increasingly popular on automobiles, it will appear in light trucks and vans as well.

• Improved cab designs and trailer aerodynamics. Estimated MPG increase by 1990 due to better wind resistance: 10%–15%.

• Computerized controls and diagnostic systems. Now used on a growing number of autos, they will be widely adopted for trucks.

Source: *Truck and Equipment News,* Peterson, Howell & Heather, Inc., Baltimore.

CARS

Cars: buy or lease

Leasing rather than buying automobiles almost always costs more (about 40%) than buying a car for cash. Leasing costs 10%–15% more than buying a car on a 35-month installment plan. But as interest rates remain high, the difference between leasing and installment buying diminishes. And leasing can be attractive, anyway, for three basic reasons.

• It ties up less capital than buying. Thus, it makes sense for individuals and companies that have other things to do with cash.

• Leasing agencies are expert at maintaining and reselling cars. So a lease with a maintenance clause can reduce, for a price, the headaches that go with maintaining and reselling on your own.

• Cars obtained through operating leases rather than capital leases can be treated advantageously for business-accounting purposes. Under the provisions of an operating lease, the leasing agency, not the company, assumes the risk involved in owning and operating cars. So companies obtaining cars through operating leases need not enter them as liabilities on their balance sheets (except in memorandum form). Thus, a company can acquire a fleet of cars without adversely affecting its debt-to-equity ratio.

Leasing fundamentals:

• There are two types of long-term auto leases: (1) open-end, in which the lessor and the lessee agree beforehand on the resale value of the car at the expiration of the lease; and (2) closed-end,

in which the lessor agrees to take back the car and sell it for whatever he can get at the expiration of the lease.

Monthly payments for open-end leases are lower than for closed-end leases. However, those opting for open-end leases must make sure that the agreed-upon resale price is not unrealistically high. If the car sells for less than the agreed-upon price, the lessee has to make up the difference.

• Leases vary in length from one to five years. Average length is two years.

• The maintenance clauses in leases come in a variety of forms, and should be negotiated vigorously.

• Categories of leasing agents include: nationwide car-rental companies (Hertz, Avis, and National); independent leasing companies (Enterprise; Peterson, Howell & Heather; and Gelco); and local auto dealers and banks.

Experts recommend for leased cars traveling between 10,000 and 20,000 miles a year, closed-end non-maintenance lease. For leased cars traveling more than 25,000 miles a year, a closed-end full-maintenance lease.

Restocking the company auto fleet

Instead of standardizing on a single new model, consider a fleet of various sizes of models, in different fuel-economy categories.

With demand rising for smaller cars, delivery time for them is running longer. Adding some larger vehicles to the mix will assure a steadier flow of replacement cars through the year.

If the smaller-car trend reverses, a mix of models will provide a hedge against any steep decline in fleet value on the resale market.

Gradually stepping back down to smaller cars each time the fleet turns over will ensure continued annual improvement in overall fuel economy well into the future.

Source: Peterson, Howell & Heather, Baltimore.

Savings for fleet buyers

Fleet car buyers hard-pressed by the profit squeeze should take a look at used cars. Savings in ownership and operating costs:

Age when purchased	Cost (cents per mile)*
new	38.0
one year old	34.7
two years old	27.0

Put another way, a one-year-old model saves about 9%. The saving is closer to 30% with a two-year-old model.

*Based on a used intermediate-sized car driven 10,000 miles per year for three years.

Basics in fleet cost cutting

• Reward employees who achieve the largest cuts in gasoline usage.
• Switch to smaller cars. They are cheaper to buy and operate.
• Consolidate sales territories.
• Encourage telephone sales for customers whose business doesn't justify face-to-face visits.

Source: Robert H. Kastengren, Runzheimer & Co., *Sales & Marketing Management,* New York.

Liquid-petroleum gas for fleets

Converting gasoline-powered auto or light-truck fleets to run on liquid-petoleum gas (LPG) is starting to make sense. Propane, the most common LP fuel, costs 40¢ a gallon less than gasoline and delivers almost the same mileage. Fuel and other savings can easily pay back the cost of conversion ($900–$1,500 for an average delivery van). Note that diesel engines cannot be converted.

Other advantages of LPG:
• Smoother, more powerful engine performance from the fuel's higher octane rating.
• Lower maintenance costs. LPG burns cleaner and more completely than gasoline, so spark plugs last five times longer. Smoother combustion puts less strain on engine parts, and produces little carbon buildup.

Drawbacks:
• Fuel outlets can be hard to find (10,000 LPG stations vs 160,000 gas).
• LPG-powered vehicles can't be operated in tunnels because of possible leaks. Mileage with LPG is about 5% lower than with gasoline.

Conversion includes installation of the carburetor, vaporizer-regulator, filter-fuel lock, fuel lines, and tanks set up for gas use. Most customers install one central tank at headquarters.

Business chauffeurs

If a company has an executive car pool, it's likely that the pool will also supply chauffeurs.

These drivers ferry senior managers to and from business meetings and, if corporate policy permits, on some personal trips.

Top managers in companies that don't have car fleets, but who need chauffeurs, often make the mistake of hiring a single driver full time. This will cost a minimum of $200 a week plus overtime. And the company will be paying someone who will be idle for long stretches. And there will be rapid turnover.

Better bets:

• For executives who need a chauffeur for a limited period, use limousine-rental services at a cost of about $10 per hour plus tip, two-to-three hour minimum.

• For executives who need a chauffeur permanently but only occasionally, tag someone in the company's mail room to be avilable when needed and to keep the car maintained and gassed up.

2. Reimburse on a formula based on fixed costs for the vehicle, as well as the per-mile cost of driving.

3. Weigh the formula to recognize important cost differences in different drivers' territories (weather conditions, for example).

4. The cost formula should assume that everyone is driving the same car, however, regardless of which cars the drivers may actually choose to drive. This allows employees to choose their own (more expensive) cars if they choose to while the company's low-cost fleet operation is preserved.

5. Update the allowances and reexamine the formula regularly.

———

Source: *Survey and Analysis of Business Car Policies and Costs,* Runzheimer and Co., Inc., Rochester, Wis.

How to design a car reimbursement plan

Reimbursing employees who regularly use their own cars for business travel requires a system that's fair and efficient. Build it around these five elements:

1. Keep the plan simple. Once the plan is set, the only thing the employee must report is actual mileage driven.

Are employees' cars covered?

Check company insurance to see if only company vehicles are covered for liability. Employees often use personal cars on business. But some policies don't cover against comprehensive liability unless the vehicle is company-owned. Excess liability coverage also won't apply. Add non-owned vehicle coverage. Premiums are quite low.

PART VI

Personnel Administration
and Labor Relations

25 HIRING AND FIRING

HIRING WISDOM

How to avoid errors in hiring

Many mistakes in hiring employees are obvious and can be avoided easily, specifically: failing to describe jobs adequately to prospective candidates, hiring overly qualified people. Other mistakes, however, are often difficult to avoid.

• Too little information in help wanted ads. Include required skills, duties, type of business and location, benefits, advancement opportunities and name of specific person to contact.

• Failure to prescreen applicants before scheduling interviews can result in time wasted interviewing unsuitable candidates, while good prospects are overlooked.

• Inadequate interviewing. This is a task for someone with plenty of skill and time. Interviewers should explain the interview purpose and company policies and encourage applicants to ask questions. They should not ask for information which may be negative without first allowing the applicants to establish their strengths.

• Unchecked references. This applies especially to those who claim success in previous jobs.

• Rejection because the applicant might not stay a long time. Good employees benefit the company even in short stays.

• Delays in making the hiring decision. If an applicant is going to be rejected anyway, the company should use its time to find other prospects. If the applicant is going to be hired, delay cuts productivity.

• Hiring friends or relatives who are not qualified. A uniform hiring policy boosts morale among those employed.

Source: Alan Leighton, vice president, Cole Associates, management consultants, Short Hills, N.J.

Hiring dangers

• Favoring a candidate who *looks like* the kind of person who belongs in the organization.

• Lowering standards after talking to a series of mediocre candidates, then picking the best of a bad lot.

• Finding a candidate with strengths in one area, and projecting those qualifications into all areas.

• Overselling the job to a strongly qualified candidate who is not really interested.

Source: Darlene Orlov, personnel consultant and president of Orlov Resources for Business, *Business 1981,* Chicago.

Don't take "no" for an answer

Employers turned down after making an offer to a particularly attractive job candidate should not give up easily. If the person was worth offering the job to in the first place, he should be worth pursuing. Wait a month, then call to chat. Don't immediately sweeten the company's offer. Simply listen to see if the executive has had any second thoughts. If so, reopen negotiations by asking why he or she turned down the original offer.

Avoid mismatches

Don't assume that applicants who were fired from their last job are unqualified. As few as 10% of all firings, according to some estimates, occur because of inadequacy on the job. The real reason for most separations is poor selection procedure, leading to a mismatch between the hiree and the job or the company. Missing from the usual hiring decision is a clear idea that the candidate, even if perfectly qualified, will remain motivated to do the job within the company's particular environment.

Source: Donald H. Sweet, director of employment, Celanese Corp., *Personnel Journal,* Costa Mesa, Calif.

Creating useful job descriptions

To profile the ideal candidate, answer these questions about every new job:

• What specific skills and talents are required?
• Which of these skills and talents are most critical to job performance?
• Which portions of the job will require personal supervision and which can be delegated?
• How much training and experience are necessary?
• Is familiarity with the company's organizational structure and management system important?
• Does the job primarily involve developing new plans, or following through on established plans?
• How many people will be supervised? What degree of supervisory skill and experience is required?
• How knowledgeable does the person have to be about the industry? Is specialized experience essential or preferred?
• Where does this job fit into the personnel and management structure?

Source: Toby Clark, Toby Clark Professional Recruitment, *Advertising Age,* Chicago.

How to spot idea people

Hiring employees who are original thinkers is important for all companies, but it's absolutely crucial for growing firms in highly competitive industries.

But screening people for creative potential is much more difficult than testing for more measurable skills. Look for the following traits:

• Observant, highly alert.
• Ability to concentrate fully despite distractions.
• Excellent reasoning power. Well organized in seeking solutions to problems, even though other work habits may not be methodical.
• Always ready with numerous suggestions.
• Resistant to narrow job specifications.

The most creative employees are often *not* the most manageable. They're frequently uncooperative in following company procedures.

Source: J.G. Mason, *How to Be a More Creative Executive,* McGraw-Hill, New York.

When to broadcast help wanted ads

Since radio and TV reach virtually every household, they are very effective at reaching job prospects who aren't actively looking for work.

Broadcast help wanted ads when:
• There are multiple job openings, or the can-didates must be screened and a large response is needed.
• A major impact is needed quickly in order to get to top candidates before they learn about other openings.
• The company wants to build image and awareness. As a side benefit, current employees and customers get a reinforced positive message.

Source: *Personnel Administrator,* Berea, Ohio.

FINDING PEOPLE

Consider retirees and housewives

Because of a drop in the U.S. birthrate in the 1960s, fewer young people will enter the labor force in the 1980s, therefore employers will need to hire more retirees and housewives reentering the labor force. Start hiring from these groups on a small scale now. Anticipate a significant number of new hires coming from these groups by the mid-1980s.

Beef up community contacts with social or-ganizations catering to retirees and housewives, to identify the best candidates in these labor pools.

Consider adjusting work schedules to accom-modate the needs of these labor pools. For exam-ple, an early morning shift of retirees. A midday shift of housewives who work while their children are in school. An evening shift of more retirees.

The convenience of this schedule to retirees and housewives will attract the best workers from both labor pools. Part-time employment will allow employers to keep the costs of fringe benefits low.

Source: George Brown, secretary, Conference Board, New York.

Employee referrals

Use incentives to get the company's work force to become a good source of new person-nel. Give a referring employee a bonus of 5% of what the newly hired employee earns during the first 13 weeks on the job.

Some guidelines may be necessary to make the program feasible. Job applicants must show up for the first interview with a note of introduc-tion from the employee (the personnel department can prepare cards for the purpose). No bonus is paid unless the new worker proves satisfactory and stays on the job at least 13 weeks. Consider restricting the plan to a limited number of hard-to-fill jobs, for maximum cost-effectiveness, with minimum fuss.

Take note that the Equal Employment Oppor-tunity Commission has said that filling jobs by employee referrals tends to perpetuate the existing racial balance of the work force. But there should be no problem where minorities and women are already employed and where employee referrals are the exclusive way to recruit.

Rehiring ex-employees

As turnover rates have jumped, attitudes about rehiring ex-employees have changed. Now, there's a good reason to hire back familiar faces. But before doing so, ask these questions.

• If he goes back to his old job, will there be room for advancement?

• What new skills does he have now? How can the company best use them?

• Why did he leave his job here before? Why is he leaving where he is now? Earlier jobs? (Similar reasons are a tip-off to chronic malcontents.)

• Will the rehire stay long enough to make a contribution? Is he only looking for a familiar spot that will tide him over?

And check references to find out if major changes have taken place in behavior or work habits.

Source: *Electrical World,* New York.

Investigate drop-outs

Many highly qualified professionals have dropped out of corporate life, but want to come back to work occasionally. These *drop-ins* offer creativity and productivity far superior to the average daily full-time employee. They may have a wide range of experiences and may bring new approaches to old problems.

To pick a winner:

• Openly discuss the project, anticipated problems, and how long it will take. Also discuss whether or not the drop-in's knowledge and style mesh with the company's needs.

• Check references carefully to determine if the applicant made a real contribution to previous companies during past short-term jobs. Focus on results rather than likability or other personal traits sought in full-time personnel.

• Accept some negative comments from references, particularly those who are the drop-in's peers. They may take exception to his favored status, aggressiveness, etc.

• Draw up an agreement specifying exactly what the job entails and how long it will take.

Source: Charles J. Sterin, Community Mental Health Center, Palm Beach, Florida, *Canadian Business,* Toronto, Ontario.

College recruiting

College recruiting is expected to become even more fiercely competitive. Start laying the groundwork now for a successful recruiting program. Some suggestions are:

• Company executives should make themselves available as guest speakers to student and college alumni organizations.

• Give employees time off to help the school's fund-raising activities.

• Reserve some summer jobs for promising undergraduates.

• Contribute full or partial scholarships, even as little as $50.

Source: Dr. Warren D. Ross, University of Texas, Arlington, Texas, *Personnel Administrator,* Berea, Ohio.

Choosing your campus recruiters

• Personnel specialists are often the best informed about the company as a whole and may be the best experienced in evaluating potential executive material.

• Technically trained staff (ideally from the discipline that interests each prospect) can best gauge a student's special skills.

• Combine strengths—send a technical person with a personnel expert. A recently hired college graduate who can relate to the student can also be useful as a recruiter.

MBA schools as talent sources

Chief executive officers of the country's largest companies ranked business schools as sources of talent for their own companies in the following order (the percentage indicates how many chose that school as number one):

1. Harvard (33%)
2. Stanford (18%)
3. Pennsylvania/ Wharton (7%)
4. Michigan (5%)
5. Dartmouth/ Tuck (5%)
6. Chicago (4%)
7. Texas (4%)
8. Northwestern (3%)
9. MIT/Sloan (3%)
10. Purdue (2%)
11. Columbia (1%)

A Master of Business Administration from Harvard is the most widely held degree among the participating CEOs themselves.

Nearly 60% of those surveyed think MBAs contribute more to management than non-MBAs, but 40% rank MBAs and non-MBAs as making equal contributions. In industrial companies, the split is almost 50-50.

Source: Arthur Young Executive Resource Consultants, *The Chief Executive, Background and Attitude Profiles,* New York.

MBA disillusionment

More companies are finding the degree-holders *not* worth their cost. Often they have general training but still need to learn the way businesses really work, and many of them expect too much power too soon. Eager liberal arts or engineering graduates who train on the job are cheaper and work out at least as well.

The best justification for an MBA-hire plan is finding those few special gems that a company needs for future growth. The problem is that the company must hire and fire many before finding those few who really fit.

SUCCESSFUL INTERVIEWING AND FOLLOW-UP

Better interviewing— better hiring

Two out of three employees are either underqualified or overqualified for their jobs. The situation not only leads to rapid employee turnover but is costly in terms of an interviewer's time, agency fees, preemployment physicals, possible relocation costs as well as training time.

To address this problem, interviews should:

Clarify any confusion in the application, for instance, years not accounted for.

• Test the truthfulness of the applicant to the extent possible. (Do oral responses coincide with the information that is written on the job application or resume?)

• Evaluate the personality of the candidate in terms of the job to be filled.

• Explain the job's requirements. Include any conditions of employment.

• Make the applicant eager to work for the company.

Some interviews fail because the person conducting them does not:

• Establish rapport with the applicant.

• Question the responsibilities of the applicant's past and present jobs enough.

• Adequately explain the prospective job to the applicant, including skills, work environment, and responsibilities.

• Determine what the applicant has been paid to do and is capable of doing.

• Maintain objectivity whether or not the candidate is likable.

A realistic assessment distinguishes what is ideally desired from what is in fact required. For example, does the candidate really need a college degree in order to do the job?

Interviewing basics:

• Make the applicant feel comfortable. Establish trust. Interview in an informal atmosphere where the interviewer devotes full attention to the applicant and is not distracted by phone calls or other interruptions.

• Use nondirective questioning. After an applicant has answered a question, the interviewer should pause to give the applicant time to fill the silence vacuum. The interviewer can then observe when the candidate is not giving a pat answer to an expected question.

• Ask why the candidate is seeking the job. Encourage the applicant to ask questions about the company, future advancement, colleagues, etc.

• Tell the applicant to expect feedback within a given time, whether hired or not.

References:

A previous employer is required only to answer questions about an applicant's work record. A company that catches an employee stealing cannot legally divulge that information if it does not prosecute the worker. Since the company will often give the employee the choice of being prosecuted or resigning, the application may show the person left a previous job voluntarily. And a reference check will only confirm it. The interviewer must then follow up by asking if the company would rehire the former employee.

To get qualitative information from a previous employer, interviewers must establish a friendly, nonthreatening conversational tone. Next, seek confirmation of observations rather than answers to specific questions.

How to conduct a revealing interview

• Do all necessary research before a job applicant's interview. Study the applicant's re-sumé. Match it against the job description. Is it a good fit? Do any special questions arise from the resumé that you want answered during the interview?

• Do basic reference checking in advance. At a formal interview, having specific information on a candidate's possible weaknesses allows for sharper questions.

• Set the stage. Put the candidate totally at ease by having absolute privacy and not receiving telephone calls.

• Avoid interviewing tricks. No high chair for interviewer and stool for interviewee.

• Be punctual and pleasant. Establish immediate rapport. Talk about the weather, commuting, etc.

• Get the applicant to commit himself. Seek his point of view on such issues as welfare, the family, the impact of the women's movement.

• Let the candidate talk. You will learn more from listening than from talking.

• Ask open-ended questions that require ongoing discussion. What has he been doing with his life? Who has had the greatest influence on him? What are his goals? In what does he think he succeeded? Failed?

• Don't give any more time to an unsuitable candidate than is necessary. Just say you will need to study the resume along with the others being considered. Whichever way it goes, let him know where he stands and what and when the next communication will be.

Source: John Wareham, *Secrets of a Corporate Headhunter,* Atheneum Publishers, New York.

Traps when several people meet an applicant

When a string of managers meet with a job candidate, their impressions often differ because they lack experience in interviewing and use different, often inappropriate, techniques. Untrained interviewers commonly:

• Make a decision in the first few minutes of the interview, long before sufficient information is developed.

• Talk for most of the interview.
• Ask irrelevant questions, allowing each interviewer to end up with different information about the applicant.
• Tend to see an applicant as all good or all bad, or give one characteristic undue weight.

Source: Terry W. Mullins, University of North Carolina, and Ronald H. Davis, Carolina Steel Corp., *Personnel Administrator,* Berea, Ohio.

Using tests in applicant evaluations

Good tests are time-consuming and expensive to develop, validate, and learn to use, but they can result in more objective prediction of job success (especially for applicants who are not sufficiently skilled verbally to "sell" themselves well in personal interviews). Better-qualified candidates can be pinpointed. There is less turnover of newly hired employees. Initial output and quality of work by the newly hired are higher. Training costs are lower. Employees are placed in positions better suited to their skills.

Further, testing contributions to initial employee motivation and confidence, since each employee knows that he was carefully selected for the position because of his skills and abilities.

Source: *Get the Right Person for the Right Job,* Prentice-Hall, Englewood Cliffs, N.J.

Showing the applicant around

Working conditions are often better demonstrated by a tour through the office or plant than by an oral briefing.
Specific advantages:
• Candidates may discover they can't work in the company environment. (It may be too hot,

too isolated, too noisy, too crowded, etc.) Better to find out before.
• Nagging but unspoken questions can be answered for the applicant. Will I be the only female in a work force? Will I be isolated in one of those cubicles where I'll die of boredom?
• Rumors or vague fears regarding cleanliness, safety, work pace, apparent morale, type of supervision can be personally checked out.
Also, a tour gives an opportunity to gather additional information about the applicant.

Source: *Get the Right Person for the Right Job,* Prentice-Hall, Englewood Cliffs, N.J.

Questions to ask a job candidate—legally

Five questions to avoid: (1) What is your religion? (2) Do you have school-age children? (3) How long have you been living at your current address? (4) Are you married? (5) Were you ever arrested?
What to ask instead: (1) Will there be any problems, if you have work on a weekend? (2) Are there any reasons why you might not be able to make an overnight business trip? (3) What is your address? (4) Defer questions on marital status until after the employee has been hired. Then they are completely proper if asked in connection with such purposes as insurance, etc. (5) Were you ever convicted of a felony? (Ask only if the question is job-related.)

Source: Hunt Personnel, Ltd., New York.

Avoid sexist language in employment records

Employment interviewers often score applicants on a numerical scale for factors such as appearance, manner and bearing, height, comprehension and presentation of ideas, attitude and overall capability.

A woman turned down for a city job in Oregon filed a sex-discrimination suit and subpoenaed the forms filled out by three examiners. On the forms she found the following words, which she thought showed a sexist attitude: *medium-sized; attractive; college gal; cute; easy on the eyes.*

Outcome: A federal judge ruled against the woman because there were nondiscriminatory reasons for not hiring her. But, he said, some of the comments she objected to might well have indicated a demeaning attitude toward women.

The art of checking references

Most managers are unwilling to make even slightly negative comments about former employees. To combat this tendency:

• Avoid vague questions that can be met with equally vague answers. Instead of asking, "What kind of guy is Ed?," ask for concrete instances of what Ed did. For a marketing director applicant, ask "What was Ed's contribution to any new products put out during his tenure?"

• Listen carefully to the former supervisor's tone of voice over the phone. Hesitations or false heartiness may be warning signs. But do not jump to this conclusion. Many managers are unused to giving recommendations and they respond awkwardly.

• Do not settle for a reference from the personnel department. It knows almost nothing about the applicant's day-to-day performance.

• For key positions, take the reference source to lunch, if possible. Frankness is likelier in a face-to-face situation. Do not solicit references by letter or request written responses.

• Double-check an overly negative response to a reference call, since the supervisor may personally dislike the applicant.

Source: Harry David, principal, H.D. Associates, recruiters, Washington, D.C. *Nation's Business,* Washington, D.C.

Background checks

Some companies are going beyond traditional reference checks and having full-fledged background investigations run on applicants.

In addition to information on the job candidate's character, habits, health, and finances, employers get knowledgeable assessments of the candidate's job performance, planning skills, and business experience from a wide range of previous employers and clients.

Reports are typically three to four pages long. They include the job applicant's personal background, education, work history, financial situation, and (in the parts of the country where it's still possible) a police check.

Private investigators cost $20 to $30 an hour, or they charge a flat rate of $50 to $75 per person checked if working on an annual contract.

Source: James H. King, Jr., vice-president, Hooper Holmes, Inc., Basking Ridge, N.J.

Preemployment physicals

A limited medical exam is definitely worthwhile for the final candidates for a job. It may cost as little as $20 for companies that send many people to a doctor on contract.

Physicals can screen out:

• Job misassignments. Supply the doctor with a job description for each applicant to prevent such mismatches as hiring a color-blind person to assemble electronics devices with color-coded wiring.

• Legal liabilities for the company. An applicant who could infect others and open the company to a lawsuit may be detected.

• Chronic medical problems at an early stage. Recommending treatment now will head off later medical insurance claims and cut absenteeism.

• Serious, undetected current medical problems. If such a problem is discovered, the physician should break the news to the applicant rather than pass the details on for personnel to disclose.

The physical should be relatively thorough but not time-consuming. To speed the process, instruct applicants to fill out in advance a medical history checklist composed by the doctor. Key question: How much time were you out of work because of illness or injury in the last two years? Include authorization for the doctor to ob-

tain any of the applicant's past medical records the doctor may need. Serious job applicants don't hesitate to sign whatever waivers are necessary.

To protect against applicants who conceal previous problems, warn in the job application that serious misrepresentations will result in dismissal no matter when the facts come to light.

A few states give applicants or employees the right to be examined by a doctor of the same sex.

DISCRIMINATION TRAPS

How to minimize discrimination charges from walk-ins

First, recognize that this is a growing problem, especially for companies with the most enlightened hiring policies and the best working conditions.

A typical case: Although no job vacancy was announced, a woman or a member of a minority group walked in looking for work. The individual was permitted to complete an application but was told that no jobs were available. Weeks later, the company hired a white male, and the walk-in applicant charged discrimination, despite the time that had elapsed.

A court's decision: A vacancy need not have existed on the precise day the application was filed to establish a *prima facie* case of discrimination. If a person fills out an application, it must be considered within a reasonable time.

To avoid problems:

• Explain that the application will be held for consideration for a limited time (say, two months) and that it is the applicant's responsibility to renew it. Include on the application a printed statement that fully explains the policy.

• Inform the applicant that jobs are filled on the basis of ability and that any opening that oc-

curs may be advertised or announced to current employees.

• Consult the personnel office's active files before hiring anyone, and interview any applicant who seems reasonably qualified.

Phillips vs *Joint Legislative Committee et al.,* 5th Circuit Court of Appeals, 25FEP 120.

Legal traps in saying "no"

• Don't confuse job experience with personal qualifications. For example, the requisites for a receptionist don't have to be previous work experience, or any work at all. But the person should have the right personality traits, such as neatness, a friendly manner, clear speech, and so on, to deal with the public.

Don't tell a rejected applicant for an unskilled job that you need someone with more job experience. A woman rejected by a department store because of "lack of experience" as a clerk sued the store after they hired a woman who had no more job experience. Court testimony revealed that the claimant was turned down because she seemed immature and made a poor impression during the interview. The judge awarded damages. A better course would be to tell the applicant that another candidate has personal qualifications more suited to the job.

If the circumstances are not favorable for a pleasant interview, ask the applicant to come back another time. One Hispanic applicant, who showed up late in the day, tired from job-hunting, was interviewed by a person who was distracted with other business. A court held that, in this unfavorable atmosphere, race may have been a contributing factor in the decision not to hire her.

Persons applying for entrance-level jobs usually have little experience in being interviewed. Make allowances for this.

———
21 FEP Cases 1664.

Affirmative-action dangers

Reverse discrimination (and the lawsuits it can bring) are becoming an increasing threat to companies. According to a study by the American Psychological Association, many personnel managers are too eager to comply with affirmative-action programs. As a result, the personnel managers unintentionally discriminate against nonminority job applicants.

When discrimination against women isn't illegal

A company that refused to consider a woman for an international marketing position didn't violate the law, a federal court ruled. The job in-

volved dealing with business executives in South America and Southeast Asia, who would have been offended by the idea of a woman in a high executive position doing business out of a hotel. *(Fernandez* versus *Wynn Oil Co.,* Federal District Court, Central Calif., 20 FEP Cases 1162.)

Said the Court: "Quaint as the notion appears to the American mind, it is a very real and formidable obstacle to the success of any business enterprise in South America."

Courts have previously held that, except where personal privacy is involved, the preference of domestic customers for dealing with persons of a particular race or sex is a mere "business inconvenience," not a business "necessity." Typical exceptions: retail clerks selling lingerie may be women; salespersons of men's suits may be men.

Discriminating in favor of age

It's a common misconception that federal law protects employees of any age from discrimination. In reality, the Age Discrimination in Employment Act protects only those between 40 and 70. Bias favors the elderly.

For example, it's legal to advertise for employees *over* 40 but not *under* 40. Exception: When youth is necessary to the job itself, such as teenage modeling.

Statutes apply to discrimination on the job as well as help wanted ads.

Case in point: a utility company excused workers over 55 from shifts that ended at midnight. Younger employees took legal action on the basis of the company's discrimination against them. The wage-hour division of the Labor Department upheld the company policy on the grounds that federal law doesn't protect employees under 40.

———
Peoples Gas/Light & Coke, 256 AAA 12.

Discriminating against age

A company that unlawfully fires an older worker may not necessarily be ordered to hire the person back. Although courts may award monetary damages, they won't always order reinstatement if the elderly employee is also incompetent.

Ginsberg vs *Burlington Industries,* USCA So. NY, 10/27/80.

On the subject of firing

Never tell job applicants the company fires workers only for good cause. Saying this can create a contract promising job security.

Be sure the company's policy booklets and employee manuals don't suggest in print that firings are only for good cause.

Toussaint vs *Blue Cross,* 48 U.S.L.W. 2826.

TAPPING TOP-LEVEL TALENT

Mistakes to avoid in hiring key executives

Most companies spend too little time defining what they want in a new key executive and preparing the way for the recruited executive's entry and smooth integration into the firm.

The first essential step is to assess the existing management's strengths and weaknesses honestly. Define what aspects of top management the newcomer should either complement or counterpoint.

Common mistakes to avoid:

• Failing to inform employees that a search is going on to fill a top slot. Instead, prepare people on the inside when someone new is coming. That defuses jealousies and the sense of being passed over. The danger of secrecy is that some good key employees may become apprehensive or discontented enough to leave. Before beginning a search, tell inside executives that they are not quite ready for the higher position, but top management is keeping an open mind and, quite possibly, after looking at outside candidates the company may conclude that the choice *should* be made from within.

• Failing to spend enough social time with the outside prospect before hiring. Top managers must get beyond superficial good chemistry with a candidate. That can only be done over time. Arrange a weekend breakfast with a prospect, play tennis, go sailing, have dinner a number of times. Meet the prospect's spouse over dinner and determine how he or she feels about the move to another company, or a relocation.

• Propelling a new executive straight into a division or even corporate presidency without a period of testing and adjustment. The ideal situation would be to bring a new key executive aboard for six months in a visible but understudy position. Natural leaders and high-caliber managers will be recognized as such and their skills will be sought out by others in the company. It's not easy to get a top-notch executive to leave a company for a situation where he will be offered a top job only after he proves out. One way to do it is to make the contract terms especially attractive.

• Failing to check references carefully. Most people at the top tend to give positive references. It's important to be alert to anything less. Watch for neutral remarks, they are an important warning signal. Probe further.

• Promoting a new executive into a higher-level position than he had at the former company. The new executive must learn a great deal, besides having to adjust to the new company.

This makes the risk of failure higher. Incoming key executives should have more experience than is actually required for the immediate job.

• Not being willing to pay the market price for the best person. Excellent executives are never available at bargain prices. As in everything else, you get what you pay for.

Source: Millington McCoy, Gould & McCoy, executive search consultants, New York.

Wooing top talent from giant companies

A recent news item reported that several senior Superior Oil executives (earning over $300,000 plus stock options and other benefits) left their jobs to join various smaller companies. Why? To be on top—to be truly in control of a company.

Smaller companies can offer an enormous, often irresistible, lure to super-executives—the chance to run their own show. A useful sweetener is equity in the company. It can help make up for a lower salary and provide a powerful incentive to make the company grow and prosper.

Most likely to take the bait are entrepreneurial executives in large companies who feel stifled by bureaucracy.

The truth about hiring managers from the outside

Myth I: The best executives hop from job to job frequently, as they move upward.

Reality:

• A systematic review of studies of effective managers by a business research group, the Conference Board; executive recruiters Korn-Ferry; accountants Arthur Young; and *Fortune*

magazine revealed that 70% of managers identified as effective had spent their entire careers with one employer.

• A recent two-year, in-depth study of 15 well-regarded managers in nine U.S. companies, ranging in annual sales from $10 million to over $1 billion, showed that 12 were still with their original employers.

Myth II: Good executives are adept at managing any number of situations because of basic professional skills.

Reality: The very best executives rely on detailed knowledge of their businesses and cooperative relationships with many colleagues, inside and outside their organizations.

The best executives share specific skills and character traits:
• The will to achieve.
• Analytical ability.
• Interpersonal ability.
• Optimism.

The study of 15 effective managers revealed that most of them made important decisions in uncertain, unstable organizational environments. And they had to implement decisions despite limited authority.

To operate effectively, given these conditions, the managers counted on:

• Intimate familiarity with products, technology, markets and the history of their businesses to make the right decisions.

• Their friendships, credibility, and track records to influence others to line up behind their decisions.

Recommended for management development:

• Discount the premium placed now on hiring financially oriented managers who focus on short-term results and those who favor aggressive acquisition programs.

• Concentrate outside hiring on situations where skills and relationships can be mastered quickly. Or where work experience is transferable and key contacts are external. Or where the need for added managerial talent is immediate.

• Pay less attention to college degrees and prior jobs. Focus on developing specifically relevant knowledge and a network of good relationships.

Source: John B. Kotter, associate professor of organizational behavior, Harvard Business School.

Objectively evaluating top-management candidates

Bringing in an outsider to fill a top-management position in the company is always a delicate task. The most common mistake companies make in such recruiting is to select the manager too hurriedly from three or four candidates introduced by a recruiter or identified as prospects by company managers.

Consider using a professional consultant or other person familiar with the company and its top managers to help match the job with a prospect.

The most important task for the consultant is to assess the duties of the job and the important relationships in the company with which the newcomer will have to deal. Against that assessment, evaluate each candidate in terms of those requirements developed by the job analysis.

Let the consultant know why the position is available, and also tell the consultant what happened to the last person who held the position.

Source: David Goodrich, Ph.D., senior consultant, Rohrer Hibler & Replogle, Inc., Stamford, Conn.

When and how to hire an office manager

Some operations need an office manager when they have only 10 employees. Others with 30 workers can get by without one. When too much time is being diverted from productive work to nonproductive official administration it is a sign that an office manager is needed.

The best candidate is a person with accounting experience and the ability to get along with people, because once the office is running smoothly, a manager mostly faces people problems, and accounting skills are helpful so the operations manager can supervise bookkeeping.

There are two major pitfalls of which you should be aware. One is assuming that former military personnel and professional accountants make the best office managers. In fact, the failure rate is highest among those with a background in rigidly structured jobs. Also automatically promoting from within may cause problems. Even though a secretary or administrative assistant might have the right skills, it may be difficult for either to command respect from associates who remember them when they were humble beginners.

One caution though, there is a danger of boredom among office managers. One way of alleviating this is to let the office managers decide on their work methods as frequently as possible.

Source: Bradford W. Hildebrandt, chairman, Bradford W. Hildebrandt, Inc., Union, N.J.

How to avoid hiring high-level incompetents

Incompetents operating at high levels of authority are much harder to recognize than those at lower levels. Everyone assumes they are competent because it is more difficult to accept that a person with status and power is at heart a loser. And the consequences of high-level mistakes may take years to reveal themselves. As a result, incompetents usually succeed in holding on to high-level jobs after they show unmistakable signs of who they really are.

High-level losers give themselves away by:

• Misdirected energy. They share the energy of winners, but they use it to avoid catastrophes coming their way, not to win.

• Gallows humor. Tell incompetents that they are doing well and they are likely to respond: "Ha, ha—hope it lasts." Incompetents almost invariably feel at some level that they are headed for disaster (the reason that their energies go to warding off or concealing trouble). Listen carefully to what makes them laugh. Gallows humor often points to insecurity, guilt or a sense of impending tragedy. Jokers fear the area they joke about.

• A history of many small incompetent acts. None individually may amount to much, but if examined together, they create a pattern that should make a prospective employer or partner uncomfortable. That intuitive discomfort should not be ignored.

• Subtle criticism of other people. Their description of events implies that they are more intelligent and farsighted and that they would have avoided errors in judgment that others made. This temporarily provides the reassurance incompetents badly need.

• Long series of previous jobs and business involvements. When these involve a failure, incompetents invariably explain how it was the fault of others, or the situation. Before hiring someone who talks this way, check out the person's history with someone who was there and find out what really happened in each case. Also check out what the person was planning and predicting five years ago. Then see how accurate the judgment was.

Source: Gisele Richardson, president, Richardson Management Associates, Montreal, Quebec.

HANDLING LAYOFFS

Reducing the work force in hard times

Periods of economic downturn provide a good opportunity to eliminate overstaffing that has crept into company operations during good times. In many cases, companies find they can cut staffing by 20% more than required by scaling back of operations and still maintain the same production level.

To do it, don't make seniority the exclusive determinant of who is kept on and who is laid off or fired. Instead, use rules violation records and poor-performance evaluations to weed out ineffective workers. Make exceptions for very talented younger employees who are likely to become major assets to the company in the future. (Many union contracts allow management to exempt about 10% of the work force from seniority-based protocol for layoffs.)

Don't scrap seniority considerations completely, even where possible. Such a policy will weaken morale. Employees expect the company to show loyalty to veteran workers. Any indication that their future may be in jeopardy will cause some good employees to desert the company at the first opportunity.

Other considerations in implementing a cutback include moving swiftly and making the cutback criteria clear. Uncertainty breeds rumors that the worst is yet to come, and erodes productivity as employees spend time worrying —or looking for other jobs. Tell laid-off workers approximately when and in what order they'll be rehired.

Handling recession layoffs humanely

While more and more large companies are using outplacement services for top executives, most middle managers, support personnel, and production workers get little besides a pink slip.

Outplacement is expensive (about 15% of each departing executive's annual salary). But for much less it's possible to provide basic support services for all lower-level "terminated" employees. Such assistance can make a world of difference in how employees feel about themselves and the company. It also has a positive impact on the morale of those who are still employed but fear they may be the next to go.

An orderly procedure, with clear-cut reasoning, helps everyone concerned. And avoids lawsuits from those who feel they were unjustly singled out for dismissal.

Lay out parameters (minimum profit dollars that must be "turned up," maximum number of employees that can be laid off and still keep company's vital operations functioning). Develop basic criteria (seniority, etc.) to be used in decision making. Whatever the criteria, make no exceptions, unless they are essential to operations and can be documented as such, for example, a recently hired specialist. Spell out such exceptions and the reasons for them. Keep written back-up material on file in case of future challenges.

Remember that without advance preparation, sheer paperwork alone could swamp the personnel department. For example, elimination of a shift will mean changes and transfers in all of the remaining shifts.

Be sure to make a big enough cut the first time around. Unpleasant as a big reduction is, it's preferable to a constant chipping away.

• Do it quickly and decisively. Post notices stating the size of the force reduction, the economic reasons for the cuts, the date they will become effective, and the criteria used.

• Coach supervisors on termination interview techniques. It is essential that: (1) news should be delivered in private and (2) stated factually and forcefully before employee has a chance to argue or to leave the room; (3) it is not a negotiation; it is a *fait accompli.* (4) The supervisor should conclude by giving clear instructions about what comes next ("See the personnel people about your benefits," etc.).

• Follow up with a letter to terminated employees thanking them for service to the company, reiterating economic reasons for the layoff, and offering supportive references. This costs little and gives the departing employee something positive to show to future employers, family, and personal contacts.

Source: Daniel N. Adams, Jr., president, The Learning Pyramid, Inc., Westport, Conn.

How to lay off workers at minimum cost

Government red tape and by-the-book union contracts often make necessary layoffs complicated and expensive.

Get workers involved in planning the company's layoffs. This will minimize worker animosity and allow the company to hire back laid-off workers when the economy recovers.

What to do:

• Determine what percent of the company's work force must be trimmed for what minimum period. Spread the word through department heads. Invite layoff volunteers.

Often, those workers willing to stop work for three to four months will be those closest to retirement, with the most seniority. They must know that when the period is over, they can get their jobs back.

• If the company needs to lay off more workers than there are volunteers, let each department arrange its own layoff policy. Some will opt for job sharing. Others will choose to take every fifth week off. They'll also create their own system. To the extent workers decide for themselves, the layoffs will go more smoothly.

By spreading the financial consequences of layoffs among the maximum number of workers, the company will force fewer workers to quit. The financial impact on both employees and the company will be minimized. (The company can save on severance pay, accrued vacation time, pension vesting and future recruiting and training costs.) If laid-off workers go on unemployment, the company's obligation for future unemployment insurance will increase.

This strategy will not work for companies that plan to use recession layoffs to weed out unproductive labor. The strategy assumes that management has been weeding out unproductive labor, all along.

Source: George Raymond, president, The Raymond Corp., Greene, N.Y.

The importance of minimizing layoffs

Management has traditionally seen layoffs as the quickest way to cut costs in a recession. That can now be considered a partially counterproductive strategy, especially in view of antidiscrimination laws and the existence of the Equal Employment Opportunity Commission.

Firings should actually be viewed as a last resort. In fact, laying off large numbers of employees is often more expensive than carrying them along for a few months.

Real layoff costs:

• Severance pay, typically a week's wages for each year of service.

• Accrued vacation time.

• Pension vesting.

• Higher unemployment insurance in the future.

• Programs to help fired employees to relocate or adjust.

• Antidiscrimination-suit liability.

• Future recruiting and training.

• Delays in gearing up for the upcoming cycle.

After adding up these costs, companies will realize that there are many options:

• Cut staff by attrition.

• Extend plant shutdowns.

• Reschedule vacations to coincide with the slowdown.

• Postpone pay increases and reduce fringe benefits.

• Cut salaries.

• Share the work load.

• Retire employees early.

A company that's willing to invest time in analyzing its financial position may hit on a cost-cutting system that leaves personnel virtually unscathed.

Best strategies to improve the company's financial position:

• Improve the cash flow by establishing tighter controls, collecting receivables faster, and slowing down payables.

• Improve inventory levels. Stall on purchases and speed up deliveries.

• Consolidate activities by selling off some facilities and reducing fixed charges.

• Revise marketing strategies, perhaps by making short-term cuts in advertising budgets or adopting a new pricing policy.

• Cut overhead items such as training and management programs.

• Monitor expense accounts more closely. Reduce allowances, too.

The potential for a company's success at cost reduction, using these tactics, will depend largely on how well managed it was before. But for nearly all companies, tighter controls and cash management will forestall layoffs for some months.

Capital-intensive companies are, of course, better positioned to trim costs because they can cancel or defer major projects. For labor-intensive companies, the day of reckoning may come much sooner.

After deciding what volume of expenses should be cut, determine how much of it can be accomplished through attrition and encouraging early retirement.

Nonunion companies should zero in on the least-productive and highest-paid employees. Unionized companies should be communicating the problems to union leaders now. This may pave the way for options such as work-sharing. Some states offer partial unemployment benefits to workers on reduced schedules.

Consult lawyers on ways to avoid violating the Equal Employment Opportunity Commission's regulations. Seniority considerations, for instance, may be mandated in union contracts, but using them for layoffs may violate government regulations if women and minorities have been the last hired. Courts now tend to consider the result of layoffs, not the method used to implement them. Regardless of how fair a company's layoff policy might seem, it may be in violation of EEOC regulations if women or minorities are hurt more than others.

Public-relations problems. A company almost always loses some prestige in the community after mass layoffs. The loss may even make it hard to hire workers when times improve.

Make a clear explanation that the survival of the majority of jobs is at stake. On the other hand, a company can chalk up a public-relations victory by keeping people on and using them for slack-time projects. Jobs such as reorganizing a warehouse and overhauling files rarely get done when business is booming. Also, use downtime to explore new markets and to develop mid- and long-range plans.

Source: Donald Law, partner, Arthur Young & Co.; James A. Giardina, principal in Arthur Young & Co.

Taking steps to retain skilled workers

Hiring back skilled workers after a recession layoff is difficult and expensive. The right strategy is to take steps now to keep them on the payroll through the next downturn.

• Promote highly trained employees into the more senior job categories that aren't immediately affected by economic downturns.

• Make plans to move skilled workers into standby jobs or even jobs that aren't essential. Rather than lay off highly skilled employees in

its plastics machine-tool division, Cincinnati Milacron recently moved them to its regular machine-tool operation. As a result, it incurred the slight expense of overstaffing, but key workers were still on the payroll when orders revived for the plastics tool division.

• Temporarily transfer some key workers to company branches in areas less affected by recessions. Most workers prefer temporary relocation to being laid off.

• Seek union cooperation to avoid having to lay off apprentices in skilled categories.

• Plan a public relations program to cushion the impact of layoffs when they must be made. Bendix Corp. paid for newspaper ads to publicize its efforts to find other jobs for laid-off workers at its Kansas City plant. Workers remained in the area, and when the recession was over, many were eager to go back to work for Bendix.

By keeping skilled workers on the payroll during a downturn, companies help them to maintain seniority. The effort goes a long way toward solving the problem of having to lay off skilled employees with little seniority. In general, companies should work with unions toward a personnel structure where skill and seniority are both important.

GUIDELINES FOR FIRING EMPLOYEES

Firing policies

It is important that a company make a clear distinction between layoffs and firings for cause. Firing workers who do not measure up is a continuing management function, in good times as well as bad. The main problem is that managers shy away from giving errant workers clear warnings on job performance. As a result, company record of trying to assist workers is poor, creating union grievances or general morale problems.

There are four progressive steps to a sound and effective discipline policy:

1. First, an oral warning by the supervisor, citing the work rule or job-performance standard that is being ignored.

2. Next, a written warning that becomes part of the employee's permanent record.

3. If no improvement, a penalty (such as a temporary suspension).

4. Final action: dismissal.

But serious offenses may warrant an immediate discharge. Theft, drug use, falsifying records, destroying property are examples. Other serious first offenses may deserve a penalty short of discharge.

It's management's responsibility to make sure employees know the rules. Ideally, posted rules should be supplemented by oral explanations reminding the violator of the probable penalty (so long as they don't sound like threats). When rules exist, but their enforcement has been slipshod or nonexistent, they lose the force of a warning. An arbitrator could rule that most disciplinary action under such unenforced rules is discriminatory.

To get maximum effect, problem-prone employees must associate a penalty with wayward behavior. Supervisor must not put off the penalty until it is convenient for operations. Use suspensions when the facts are not clear but the infraction is serious enough to warrant discharge. Tell the employee that the penalty will be determined after investigation.

It is important for the employee to realize that it is unsatisfactory behavior or performance that is being punished. The supervisor must make sure that disciplinary action (including an interview to explore the employee's side of the case) is not tinged with subjective emotions. Temper, shouting, and bawling out, or quiet apologies and timidity, will all be interpreted as the boss's problem, not the subordinate's. It is important not to condemn an employee personally. After the penalty has been imposed, the supervisor should treat the person fairly.

Establish clear, predictable limits. Employees who know what is expected are more likely to respect the rules. A likable employee should receive the same treatment as others. An offense during a critical period when the employee is needed merits the same penalty as an offense committed during a slack period.

Has management tried hard enough to help the worker overcome problems?
- Has the company given enough credit to the employee when tasks were well done?
- Is a replacement likely to do much better?
- What will be the reaction of employees who have been associated with the worker? How will that reaction affect the company?
- Has the worker shown interest in another area?
- Could the investment in the employee be salvaged by transfer to other work?
- Will it be troublesome if a talented and trained person winds up working for a competitor?

Newly promoted? Don't start firing . . . yet

An executive promoted from within is likely to have negative opinions about at least one former colleague's performance, capacities, or work habits. Before taking tough measures, such as firing:
- Reexamine the colleague from your new perspective. He might have been producing better results than you suspected.
- Determine priorities for change.
- His views about the company's needs and priorities might be similar to your own. It's possible that the old regime frustrated him.
- Work out a plan of action that is mutually agreed upon. Put it in writing. Keep a record of his progress. Success warrants a reappraisal of your earlier attitude. If he fails, your efforts and records support a decision for firing, probation, or transfer.

What to ask yourself before firing anyone

- In what ways has the employee failed?
- Is part of the failure the company's fault?

Can you get rid of a constant complainer?

Yes, under certain conditions. A nonunion employer can fire a malcontent whose complaints involve personal grievances in which the other employees have no interest.

In a recent Court of Appeals case, a secretary who did not get an expected promotion began to complain that too much vacation was given to a newly hired worker. The National Labor Relations Board ruled she could not be fired because that action was protected by the labor laws.

But the Court reversed the decision, because the evidence showed her purpose was to advance her own interests and did not concern other workers.

Koch Supplies, Inc. vs *NLRB*, 8CA, 4/17/81, 107 LRRM 2108.

What employees owe the company

Courts have repeatedly held that employees owe loyalty to the company. If they badmouth the company or its products, or act against its interests, that is grounds for discharge, possible withholding of monies due, and perhaps damages, too.

It's not uncommon for a salesperson to tell customers of plans to leave the company and ask if they will go with him to a competitor. That's permissible after he leaves (unless he's signed a non-compete agreement).

In one case, a departing salesman tried to get fellow workers to defect, too. It was ruled that the company was justified in refusing to pay commissions he had accrued because of his disloyalty to the company.

306 NY 172; 211 F. Supp. 835.

When a resignation is not a resignation

It is not an uncommon scenario: The company wants to fire an employee for cause, but it

hesitates because of possible litigation. Instead, the worker is pushed to quit by such techniques as demeaning criticism or transfer to unpleasant surroundings.

Courts, arbitrators and the National Labor Relations Board regard resignations encouraged in this way as constructive discharges. Then the employer has to prove just cause after all.

As a general rule, if the company deliberately makes an employee's working conditions so intolerable that the employee is forced to quit, the company has made a constructive discharge. It is liable for any illegal conduct in the same way it would be if the employee had been formally discharged.

Related case. Does a worker who walks off the job in a fit of anger actually intend to resign? The question is important, because hasty acceptance of resignation where none was intended may also be considered a constructive discharge.

But an employer can demand the immediate discharge of an employee who has given two weeks' notice. Here, courts say, there is no question of constructive discharge, since the employee clearly announced his intentions by giving notice. There is no obligation to keep malcontents on the job.

Young vs *Southwestern Savings and Loan Association*, 509 F. 2d and *Bourque* vs *Powell Electrical Mfg. Co.*, 5 CA 22 FEP 1193.

Fired for refusing to take psychiatric exam

An employee whose behavior was erratic and disruptive but who refused to be examined by a psychiatrist was fired. The court upheld the firing. The judges' view: employers can require psychiatric as well as medical exams to determine an employee's fitness to perform the job.

It's important to note that this employee's behavior was bizarre. It is not clear that courts would approve a demand for mental testing of workers whose behavior was closer to normal.

466 F. 2d 1366.

Supervisor's misconduct affects decision on assault case

The arbitrator revised the discharge of a worker who ignored three direct orders to perform a certain task and then physically assaulted the foreman who issued the order.

A supervisor of Mexican-American laborers was in the habit of uttering racial slurs. After several specific complaints from workers, the employer transferred the supervisor to a different shift. Although he issued proper orders to a worker at the new post, he punctuated them with an insulting remark about the man's race. The worker responded with his fist and was fired.

The arbitrator's opinion: "Employment contracts contain an implied promise that employees shall be respected as persons by the management. And management has a responsibility to take all steps necessary in its own ranks to guarantee integrity of such covenant." The arbitrator said the grievant deserved only partial back pay, however, because the man should have obeyed the order before the insulting remarks were made.

Looking for new job may be considered a resignation

Turned down for a raise, the employee made it plain that she would start looking for another job. As a result, she was terminated immediately. The court held that making such an announcement was the equivalent of resigning and that the company had no obligation to keep her after that.

Since she was terminated for good cause, she was not eligible for unemployment-compensation benefits.

576 SW 2d 218.

Don't fire without looking

A worker showed up drunk and collapsed immediately after clocking in. The company dismissed him for violation of work rules. But the arbitrator ordered reinstatement.

Background. It was the worker's normal day off. A foreman had called him at home and offered a full day's overtime. He had two hours to report, but was too drunk to decline prudently. Discharge under the circumstances, said the arbitrator, amounted to discipline for an activity engaged in on the worker's own time.

Recommended course. Follow a "rule of reason." Suspend the employee, pending investigation and final decision.

249 AAA 3.

Discharging a slob

Arbitrators and courts will usually allow the firing of workers whose personal habits are offensive to everybody around them. The key is that co-workers must unanimously agree the person's habits are disgusting. If some testify that "he's not all that bad," there could be a problem.

402 A 2d 308; 60 LA 366.

Avoiding abusive-discharge suits

Nonunion companies, which employ 80% of all U.S. workers, are facing a new threat to their traditional right to fire workers at will. Courts in several states have already heard cases where non-union employees, working in no-contract companies, charged abusive or malicious discharge.

Some of the reasons nonunion employees brought suit:

• The firing was prompted by a desire to save a bonus payment. (The employee won.)

• The employee was fired because he served on a jury. (The employee won.)

• An employee asked permission to go to law school at night and was dismissed. (The company won.)

Potential costs to the company:

• Reinstatement of the employee with back pay.

• Punitive damages if the claim charges that the company maliciously fired the worker.

Lawyers anticipate that employees will begin to sue nonunion companies for other slights, such as being passed over for promotion or a bonus, or when job duties are shifted.

To avoid abusive-discharge suits:

• Check with a lawyer about the possibility of a complaint of abusive discharge before firing. Consult a labor lawyer familiar with the legal precedents and the direction the law is going in that state.

• Make sure the reason for firing is carefully thought out and defensible. Be rational, fair and nonretaliatory.

Good reasons for firing are as important as not having a really bad reason to fire a worker.

Remember, though, that even if the company wins the suit, it wastes time and incurs the expense of a trial. Canny lawyers for workers have begun to use abusive-discharge suits to stretch out litigation when the statute of limitations runs out on discrimination suits (charging that the firing was for age, race, sex, etc.).

Source: Alfred T. DeMaria, partner, Clifton, Budd, Burke and DeMaria, New York.

Are there ways to fire tactfully?

• Keep the firing brief, 10 minutes at most. State the reasons for dismissal clearly and simply.

• Choose a neutral site such as a conference room or an empty office away from the employee's staff and co-workers. Leave the worker time afterwards to compose thoughts and emotions.

• Don't wait until Friday, which gives the employee all weekend to agonize about the dismissal. Monday and Tuesday are the best days.

• Don't procrastinate once the decision is made, because the news may leak out and the about-to-be fired worker could do damage to the company.

• Offer suggestions and leads on where new employment can be found. Pass along the names of executive recruiters, or use an outplacement service.

Dos and don'ts of firing

• Don't blame the dismissal on a reorganization if inadequate performance is the real reason. The employee might demand, and sometimes get, extra severance pay and other benefits. Give the real reason and also tell what kind of recommendation the company will give.

• Don't duck the firing responsibility. Handle it yourself or delegate it to the employee's immediate boss.

• Don't talk openly about a firing beforehand. Tell the employee as soon as the decision is made, and discuss how the news is to be broken to co-workers.

• Don't fire someone without first giving a warning. Make the warning specific in terms of what needs to be improved. Set a deadline.

Source: Ruth Macklin and Tabitha M. Powledge, Institute of Society, Ethics and Life Sciences, *Savvy,* New York.

GETTING RID OF EXECUTIVES

Why executives get fired

Executives are fired in the vast majority of cases because they have personality problems with their superiors, not because their performance is inadequate. One major problem is that many executives expect their worth to be recognized automatically. They don't promote their own successes to their higher-ups.

carry him as long as it can. In some cases, the company can promote the discharged executive to help facilitate his job search. (But make sure he understands why he is being promoted.)

What to do about reference calls: Always answer questions about the discharged executive as positively as possible without being dishonest. Don't volunteer information. Remember that no chief executive officer knows how effective a discharged executive will be in another context. It's always possible one of the reasons things didn't work out is the CEO himself.

Source: Robert Townsend, *Robert Townsend Speaks Out,* Advanced Management Research, New York.

Firing a top man

Frequently there's a person in the top ranks of a company whom almost everyone hates to work with—and with justification. Firing such a person can be better for organizational morale than giving everyone a raise.

What to do:

• Tell him that operations are being restructured and that despite his intelligence and skills, he doesn't fit in.

• If he's old enough, give him early retirement. In some cases, it's better to pay him his full salary just to have him stay home so that his office and his job can be filled by a better executive.

Tell him to leave the company that same day. Otherwise, he may become a morale problem.

Fair severance terms:

• Have the company's operator take messages for the fired individual, telling callers that the person is out of the office.

• Don't give him a set deadline to find another job. Instead, tell him the company will

When contract employees don't measure up

Can he be fired before his contract expires? It depends on how the contract is written. If it merely requires full-time services or best efforts, he could collect damages.

As an employer, specify contractually just what is expected (a sales increase of X%, for example), and stipulate that duties must be performed to the company's reasonable satisfaction.

Inadequate-performance cases remain tenuous. But worst cases don't. Where negligence, disloyalty, or criminal actions are involved, firing is almost invariably justified no matter what the contract says.

193 F. Supp. 163; 397 A. 2d 1323; 486 F. 2d 39, cert. den. 415 U.S. 919; 314 N.E. 219.

One way to replace veteran managers

Problem: A company has a long-time employee whose work is as good as it ever was, but now falls below standard because the rest of the company has moved ahead. The company wants to replace the manager in his job. But there's no obvious place to transfer him. And there are no clear grounds to fire him.

Solution: Offer the manager a consulting job for three or four years at half his previous pay. The company thereby lives up to its obligations to the veteran, while replacing him, and still gets the benefits of his long experience with the company. The veteran gets some work and a base from which he can pick up other consulting clients.

Source: Sherman Lurie, corporate director of marketing, Cadence Industries, West Caldwell, N.J.

Compulsory retirement at 65 is possible

Executives and high policy-making employees with retirement plan benefits of $27,000 a year or more can be forced to retire at age 65 (instead of 70) under federal law.

New EEOC regulations, under Sections 12(c) and 12(d) of the Age Discrimination in Employment Act, limit the exemption to top-level executives and to high-policy-making employees who play a significant role in the development and implementation of corporate policy. They must be in such a position at least two years immediately before retirement.

The $27,000-or-more pension has to be made available within 60 days of retirement and be unconditional during retirement. Retirement income from Social Security, employee contributions, and prior employers cannot be included in the $27,000. But plan payments in lump sum or in some other form, whose value equals the cost of a single life annuity yielding at least $27,000, qualify.

A legal alternative to forced retirement may be a lesser, or part-time, position, if accepted by the employee.

Source: David L. Hewitt, vice-president, Hay Huggins, Philadelphia.

Cushioning the shock of dismissal

Advantages of outplacement to the company:

• It helps counteract the bitterness of the fired employee. That's an important consideration, since the fired executive often seeks a position in the same industry and could surface as a commercial enemy.

• It eases conflicts for the top manager who does the firing.

• It counteracts the loss of morale among fired employee's colleagues.

Mistakes companies make in terminating executives:

• Vague, euphemistically phrased dismissals that don't actually communicate the hard fact that the employee is fired. The phrase "start looking around" can result in an executive simply wandering around the executive corridors for months postponing the inevitable. What compounds the communications failure: Fired employees are too upset to retain most of what is said to them at the time. (Research indicates they retain less than 40%.) An added problem may be that the person doing the firing is often tense and communicates poorly.

• Postponing the dismissal. Keeping an executive on when dismissal is inevitable saps his morale and damages his chances of finding another position. This is particularly true of the 50-and-over executive, for whom every year's delay is costly in terms of his market value.

• Overgenerous severance allows the fired executive to postpone the painful process of going out to look for a new job. It undercuts motivation and may even encourage the executive to sink into apathy, sickness, and depression—at the company's expense.

How outplacement works:

• Companies usually use outplacement services for individual dismissals at the $30,000 + salary range. Different outplacement programs can be used right down the line when an operation is closed down.

• The consultant helps the client firm structure a brief, direct (about six-minute) termination interview in which the employee is told that he is "redundant" and that a consulting firm has been hired to help him look for another job outside the company. Words must be thought out and tactful without being evasive. Only the executive and the person being fired are present at this talk.

• The dismissed employee is introduced to the outplacement consultant. The consultant encourages a "ventilation period" to vent the employee's emotions of resentment, bitterness, and confusion. The first two days or so after termination is the peak danger time for fired employees. Precipitous acts and outbursts can permanently damage their reputations and endanger their chances for new employment. Another danger is that they may try to set up job interviews before they are prepared to present themselves properly.

• Counseling helps with personal problems, such as how to handle family and neighbors.

• The employee's skills and achievements are assessed in discussion with the consultant. Keep the fired employee focused on the future. Teach him how to reenter the job market. Advise him on how to handle job interviews, negotiate salary, write an effective letter, respond to the question "Why were you fired?" Most important: An outsider with contacts in many companies can help a fired executive recognize opportunities elsewhere.

Fee for outplacement services: Cost to the company is approximately 15% of the employee's annual salary. (It's tax deductible.) Some consultants also charge an additional flat fee for office expenses, secretarial services, etc.

Source: T.B. Hubbard, chairman, and E. Donald Davis, president, THinc Consulting Group International, Inc., New York.

26 PERSONNEL POLICIES

SETTING COMPANY RULES

Foul-weather policy

When snow starts falling early in a shift, some employees will want to leave early. Obviously, closing down too soon disrupts operations, but delaying too long may endanger some employees.

Establish procedures for monitoring the weather every hour or half hour with local weather bureaus. Perhaps keep a radio tuned to a station that issues bulletins.

Watch school closings. Some employees customarily pick up their children after work and drive them home from school. Let them leave early when schools close, even when others are kept at work. It may be useful to ask employees who may be affected by school closings to register with the personnel office. Inform all employees of procedures for resolving the work-or-close question. Be prepared to make exceptions in individual hardship cases.

Note that to the extent that employees resort to car-pooling, as they are encouraged to do, the company may expect a "domino effect" when one or two employees leave work early.

Winter-weather closings

When storms force closings, management may want to make up for lost time by having employees work late on other days or by scheduling weekend work. That raises problems.

• Nonunion shops. The law does not require premium pay after eight hours per day or on Saturdays and Sundays, as such. Time-and-a-half is required only after the 40th hour of work in a week. Catch: Employers of nonunion shops who have customarily paid the premium on a daily basis or for weekend work may have to do so, not for the sake of compliance with law, but for the sake of good personnel relations.

• Union shops. Nine out of ten union contracts provide for premium pay for work outside of normally scheduled daily hours, or for the sixth and seventh day of the work week, regardless of the number of hours previously worked. This means, in most instances, that labor costs will be higher for working unconventional hours. (Exception: If the union can be persuaded to waive contractual requirements.)

Jury duty pay policies

Deduct jury fees if workers are paid for jury duty. Require workers to report for work when excused from court duty early in the day.

Special problems may occur on grand juries: In some states these juries use volunteers, or jurors are nominated by organizations. Pay arrangements must be different. These jurors were not summoned and not required to serve; service may be much longer than on trial juries.

One company's solution to grand-jury problems:

1. Hourly workers who are called are paid regular wages.

2. Those who volunteer to serve must ask for unpaid leaves of absence. Leaves may be denied if their absence would require the hiring of temporary replacements, or the scheduling of excessive overtime.

3. Managerial employees who volunteer for grand juries are paid regular wages. They are expected to perform as much work as they can. As grand juries often function in afternoon or evening hours, managers are usually able to keep an eye on things at work.

Doctors' notes: reading between the lines

Family physicians sometimes tell less than the whole truth when a patient suspects that too-frequent absence is putting his job on the line.

For example, a worker called in sick on a day he knⁿ w he was scheduled for some unpleasant chore. Company rules required a letter from a doctor in his case because his absentee record was poor. His note read: "Patient has been under my care for a sinus condition." Further inquiry revealed that, although the employee did see his family doctor from time to time, he hadn't seen the doctor on the day in question and there was no proof he had been ill.

Medical examinations

Personnel policies usually require employees returning from extended leaves for health reasons to undergo physical examinations before restarting work. Employees should be told of the rule when they apply for leave.

Case. An employee was discharged after a seven-week medical leave because it appeared that she refused to complete the blood chemistry part of the physical examination. In the course of litigation, it was discovered that she was not concealing drug abuse (which had been suspected). She was simply terrified of the blood test. Twice in her life she had given blood samples, and on each occasion she fainted.

The cost and the trouble could have been avoided by a candid talk with the employee when the leave was requested.

79-2 CCH Par. 8453.

Demanding early notice of pregnancy— legally

It's legal to require female employees to inform management as soon as they know they are pregnant only if there is a business reason for such a rule.

Good business reasons: (1) protecting pregnant woman from exposure to radiation or toxic substances; (2) special lead-time problems in finding a suitable temporary replacement.

Recommended: Require all employees to report medical circumstances that may require them to take leaves of absence in the "near future."

4th Circuit Court of Appeals, 19 EPD 9257.

Traps to avoid in maternity leaves

Recent legislation requires employers to regard maternity as a form of temporary disability. This means disability of the mother, not the child. Congressional sponsors of the legislation specifically stated that a leave for nurturing the child was not required by the law.

Problems arise because some women who request three-month leaves from the eighth month of pregnancy through the second month after delivery find that they would like to stay home longer with the infant and still have the guarantee of the same job when they reutrn. Companies that didn't hire temporary replacement then are handicapped for a longer period than expected.

Whether an extension must be granted depends on the physical condition of the mother, just as it would depend on the physical condition of any other employee, male or female, who wants sick leave. A note from a family doctor should be read critically. They are notoriously obliging to new mothers. If in doubt, insist upon an examination by a company physician or neutral doctor.

A compromise may be to allow the mother who wants to extend her maternity leave to do so with the understanding that she would not necessarily return to her regular, or even to a comparable, job.

Testimony before Congress showed that 95% of women are able to work until the eighth month and return six weeks after delivery. Therefore, a three-month leave for maternity can be presumed to be for disability. Longer maternity leaves should be documented by medical advice.

If you hire a woman who is already pregnant, it's illegal to ask about pregnancy on preemployment applications or on personal interviews. But it's within the law to limit the benefits of disability leaves (and the guarantee of return to the same job) to men and women who have worked for the company less than a full year, except for any workers who are disabled due to on-the-job accidents.

Source: Morris Stone, retired vice president, American Arbitration Association, New York.

Company day-care centers

Advantages:
• Increase the size of the labor pool from which employees can be drawn.
• Make working for the company more attractive (even if pay is less).
• Lower rates of absenteeism, lateness, and turnover.
• Improve employee morale.
• Keep workers on the job through a full shift.
• Generate favorable publicity for the company in the community.

Before setting up a center, determine the number of children whose parents might want to use it. Also calculate the number of nonemployee parents who would pay to use the center.

Then set up a budget. Most company-run centers charge for the service but also subsidize part of the cost. In addition, government money is usually available. Remember that one of the chief reasons company day-care centers fail is because of unpredicted increases in costs.

Source: *Personnel,* New York.

Better company sports programs

• Separate serious team players from employees interested in general recreational activities. Many employees who only want to maintain their physical fitness wouldn't go into a company sports program if it meant having to become part of a competitive-team activity.

• Encourage all recreational activities, not just the popular sports. This way more employees participate. Workers discover new skills.

• Involve employees' families and the community in the program. Wide participation enchances good will and yields inexpensive promotion for the company.

• Recognize participation with trophies and awards banquets. Doing so boosts morale by giving recognition to ordinary employees who might otherwise go unheralded.

Pay for changing clothes

Question. A job requires special clothing. Must the employer pay for the time it takes to change from street clothes in the morning and back again later?

Answer. Yes, if clothes-changing must be done on the premises. No, if the worker engages in this activity in the plant for his own convenience, or if changing time is minimal.

Example. Workers exposed to lead and acids wear coveralls furnished by the company. The clothes must be decontaminated in the plant every few days. It would be potentially harmful to workers and their families if they wore the coveralls home. Showering and changing clothes thereby becomes compensable time, unless the time involved is minimal.

But if workers customarily shower and change into street clothes before going home, and management does not require them to, they need not be paid for this time, even if it exceeds the minimal level.

Appearson vs *Exxon Corp.,* U.S. Dist. Ct., Eastern District of California, 24 WH Cases 372.

Employee education

Companies used to be concerned with improving work-related skills. The trend now is toward encouraging employees to take courses in general communication and social skills, such as English, reading, and math.

The lures: 75% of companies surveyed by the Conference Board (all had 500 or more employees) offer in-house courses, mostly during working hours. Three-quarters of the corporations authorize higher-level employees to take outside courses during working hours at company expense. Tuition-aid or tuition-refund programs exist in 89% of the companies. Benefits include higher-skilled, more productive employees, better morale, and lower recruitment costs (employees qualify to be promoted from within the company).

Company parties

Some companies still give wild bashes during the holiday season. Employees drink too much and for the only time in the year get on a first-name basis with their bosses. Much better ways to use holiday office parties include developing company friendships across the department and authority lines that reinforce good employee relations and building goodwill with important resources outside the company.

Companies that recognize the opportunities have radically changed the style of the holiday office party.

The trends are now:

• Less alcohol. More important is that management mingle with employees and show that it cares about their well-being. It doesn't matter whether champagne is served or coffee. What counts is an attitude that shows positive feelings toward employees. Heavy drinking on company premises gives tacit approval to an essentially negative practice.

• Outings and breakfast parties. Outings bring employees' families together in a holiday spirit. Breakfasts can be a memorable diversion from the routine party, especially when something more imaginative than bacon and eggs is served. (Try a hearty English breakfast with kippers, etc.) Use the occasion as a morale-booster by starting the workday an hour or so later than usual.

• Employee-organized parties outside the office are good because employees take a vested interest in making the affair a success. Management doesn't feel obliged to stay to the end. Specifically, the entire staff may feel more relaxed and uninhibited at a hotel or country club.

If the company's party is a large gathering with outside guests, organization can be the key to success.

Recommended procedures:

• A receiving line near the door. Include the top executives (without their spouses). Guests feel more important when they're immediately greeted by the top brass.

• A staff member at the entrance to identify guests for top company executives.

• Name tags that aren't gimmicky. Use first and last names and the company name in easy-to-read type. Avoid name tags with smiling faces that say "Hello."

• Dinner and luncheon parties given with a flair. Too many companies have the chief executive's secretary telephone a hotel banquet manager for dinner for 50. Instead, challenge the kitchen to come up with something special. Use an outstanding florist to create impressive table settings.

At informal office luncheons or dinners, consider drawing lots for seats. Morale usually gets a big lift when a messenger sits by the CEO. On formal occasions, consult an etiquette guide for proper seating.

Source: Letitia Baldrige, head, Letitia Baldrige Enterprises, Inc., N.Y.

Harsh penalties can backfire

When an employee commits an offense punishable under two different rules, don't always apply the harsher penalty.

For example, according to a company's rule book, the first instance of unjustifiable absence called for a warning. But insubordination was punishable by a one-day suspension.

An employee was denied permission to take an unpaid day off but took the day anyway. For this, the employee got a one-day layoff under the "insubordination" rule.

After this incident, employees called in sick or stayed out with no excuse and only got the warning letter.

Avoid actions that discourage responsibility. The suspended employee did, after all, show concern for the company initially.

Solving the profanity dilemma

The general loosening of standards and liberalizing of life-styles in recent years has led to a significant increase in the use of foul language in offices and plants.

Swearing can serve a useful function, as a safety valve for anger and frustration. In general, it is more acceptable than other forms of release such as crying, screaming, laughing hysterically or becoming physically aggressive.

When dealing with equals or supervisors, mild obscenities need not be forbidden or discouraged. Reserve them for strong provocations, or they lose their power. And the strongest words do not have to be used to defuse anger.

When dealing with workers, do not curse. Studies show that people react negatively when those in authority use profanity. Foul-mouthed managers generally do not rise far. Do not go too far in the opposite direction and demand that workers never swear. Workers are not justified in cursing when they drop a pencil. But allowing them to release their anger when they drop, say, an expensive piece of equipment, is humane.

Source: Dr. Reinhold Aman, editor and publisher of *Maledicta, The International Journal of Verbal Aggression,* Waukesha, Wis.

Easing impact of relocation on employees

When transfers create the most serious problems:

• Midlife crisis. A relocation that coincides with a period of personal transition adds to the emotional confusion of an employee who is already trying to cope with changes in life goals and lifestyle.

• Career-oriented spouse. There is a good chance the working spouse will greatly resent the career interruption and show it. One solution is to help the spouse find rewarding work at the new location, or help pay for more education.

• Adolescent offspring. Children of other ages cope better with a move than do teenagers.

• Repeated relocations. Even an adaptable family resents the moves when they occur every few years.

The company can alleviate the problems by encouraging families to discuss their reactions to the transfer openly; helping them make a clean break; bidding fond farewells and having informal send-off parties; providing extensive information to the family on their new area; checking in with the family after the move for a progress report.

Source: *The Effective Manager,* Warren, Gorham & Lamont, Boston.

Helping executives move

Companies increasingly must underwrite housing costs to encourage their executives to relocate when it means giving up a low-interest fixed-rate mortgage.

Three ways to help:

1. Cover the loss the executive suffers from trading the old mortgage for a new one.

For example, an executive sells a house with a $50,000 balance on a 7% mortgage. The executive then buys a new house with a 15% mortgage. The company reimburses the executive for the extra interest, usually for the next three years. Calculation: $50,000 (old mortgage balance) times 8% (difference in interest rates) equals $4,000 a year. Total payout: $12,000.

2. Finance the home purchase of the relocating executive through the company. It can offer interest rates below market levels but high enough to minimize losses.

3. Purchase the home jointly with the executive and share the profits from its future appreciation. This is similar to a bank's share appreciation mortgage.

Making up the difference in interest is less costly in the short run than the alternatives, but more expensive over the long run. This approach is best if high rates for home mortgages are temporary, but most expensive if high rates are here to stay.

Source: Patricia E. Matteson, marketing director, Merrill Lynch Relocation Management, Inc., White Plains, N.Y.

Relocation costs

Relocating an executive making $60,000 a year now costs an average of $26,700. This includes moving costs, upfront bonuses, differential payments if mortgage rates are higher and miscellaneous house-hunting expenses.

Not included in that figure are special allowances for moving to areas where living costs are high and payments to handle the sale of the executive's house.

Source: Survey of 200 companies by Eastman & Beaudine, Inc., executive recruiters, Chicago.

Keeping a tight rein on unemployment claims

Many companies pay more than they should in unemployment insurance premiums. Major savings can be achieved by monitoring applications for unemployment compensation, and challenging unjustified ones.

The rule is that a worker is eligible for compensation only if the company lays him off despite a good record. The problem is that borderline cases outnumber instances of clear-cut eligibility.

Recent cases point to how officials are ruling in these gray areas. Benefits were denied to a worker who quit because his car broke down, an employee who knew when he started that he would leave to return to school, and another who left because sitting at a desk made her legs swell.

On the other hand, even though one claimant was guilty of excessive absences, benefits were granted because permission for the time off had been given. Another claimant, whose car had broken down, waited four hours for a tow truck without notifying the employer. That was ruled not disqualifying conduct.

Source: Philip Kaplan, Reed Roberts Associates, Inc., Garden City, N.Y.

Dealing with unemployment cheats

Companies can be unfairly charged with "credit weeks" by state unemployment-compensation agencies when a laid-off worker earns wages elsewhere. To prevent this:
• Make sure all laid-off employees know they are eligible for unemployment only while they are out of work.
• Explain how cheating affects the company. This blocks the worker's defense that he cheated only the state, not the company.
• In taking any disciplinary action, charge the worker with violating a widely publicized rule, not with a theft. (An arbitrator will want a much higher standard of proof if theft is alleged.)
• Be prepared to show that a formal prohibition was required because so many employees accepted benefits wrongfully.
• Report improperly granted benefits immediately to the unemployment agency and ask that the company be credited with a lower claim incidence.

COMMUNICATING POLICIES TO EMPLOYEES

Effective personnel manuals

When putting together a manual of company rules and policies for employees, start by:
• Looking at manuals published by other companies, especially those in the same industry.
• Surveying current employees as to what they want and need to know.
• Getting the opinion of an outside personnel consultant.

• Seeking the views of new employees. They are the ones who will have the freshest ideas on the orientation and training program.

What management gains from policy handbooks

• Employees' sense of security is increased by the existence of a published policy. (It can be as modest as several sheets stapled together.) This is good for morale and productivity.

• Unions are less likely to try to organize workers who enjoy fair and equitable benefits that are clearly spelled out.

• A published policy saves the CEO time and worry.

• It protects against claims of discrimination and EEOC violations.

Myths and realities about communicating with employees

Pragmatic research shows that many commonly held ideas about communicating with workers are untrue. Sorting out the facts:

• Myth: Employees are not concerned about their company, except for shoptalk, trivia, or social news. Reality: Employees do have a vital interest in company policies and developments, even when these don't directly affect them.

• Myth: Unions have the inside track to reach workers. Reality: Many employees give equal weight to company-originated news.

• Myth: Messages must be short if they are going to be read. Reality: Workers have a huge appetite for detailed information about areas such as pay scales and benefits.

• Myth: Management should avoid controversial issues. Reality: That can't be done and isn't expected.

• Myth: A good company publication requires plenty of money for staff and flashy production. Reality: What's most important is a straightforward presentation of information, which requires creative skills plus careful supervision.

• Myth: The effectiveness of reading matter can be judged by the number of people who pick it up and carry it away. Reality: Effectiveness depends on how well the material is written and presented, and communicated.

• Myth: Trick headlines or fanciful introductions are needed to make workers read about serious subjects. Reality: Sugar coating serious subjects often turns off readers.

Source: Survey by Opinion Research Corporation, Princeton, N.J., quoted in *The Gold and the Garbage in Management Theories and Prescriptions,* by James A. Lee, Ohio University Press, Athens, Ohio.

Using a personnel manager

A company with fewer than 100 employees may have trouble keeping a personnel manager busy. If so, assign additional work to the underemployed personnel manager, which other employees may not have the time or skills to perform. Examples:

• Most supervisors do a poor job of orienting new employees and of explaining company policies, benefits, and payroll systems.

• After about three months, all new workers should be interviewed to determine how they are adjusting.

Source: Frank L. Nemeyer, North American Publishing Co., *Folio,* New Canaan, Conn.

Improving orientation

Even some of the best orientation programs fall short because they don't take into consideration a new employee's limitations in absorbing information. To avoid the pitfall:

• Keep orientation and training sessions short, not more than two hours at a time, especially for lower-level employees.

• Hold at least one follow-up meeting not more than two months after the worker has assumed his duties. Use it to refresh his memory and to answer questions that have come up since his prejob briefing.

Intracorporate communication

Employees need information from two sources: (1) job-related information from immediate supervisors, (2) organizational information from top management.

If the grapevine is the sole source of organizational information, there is too much distance from the top ranks—and considerable distortion. As a result, employees feel the company discourages openness, lacks incentives and advancement opportunities.

Source: Study by State University of New York at Buffalo professors Gerald Goldhaber and Richard Lesniak.

Reports for employees

Annual reports for employees are worthwhile. The report should spell out details of the company's pension (or profit-sharing) plan, as required by the Employee Retirement Income Security Act (ERISA), and explain other benefits as well.

Without such reminders, employees tend to forget the value of fringes. That leaves the benefits short of the value to employers (better work attitudes, etc.) that they are designed in part to foster.

What to report:

• Company and employee contributions, and the number of participants, in each program.

• Amounts paid out.

• A financial statement and a list of the assets in which the pension funds are invested.

• A summary of fund performance compared with the stock market or other economic indicators.

Source: *Pensions & Investments,* Chicago.

Fringe-benefit trap

Companies that itemize all benefits in a special annual publication to dramatize their total value must be careful in handling discretionary ones. In a recent case a company was ordered to give its workers a picnic every year because it listed a previous picnic as a benefit in a letter sent to each worker's home. An arbitrator ruled that the letter transformed the picnic into a contractual obligation.

If such gifts are included in a benefit roundup, add a sentence or two in the printed matter saying that there is no promise that the gift or benefit will be offered in the future.

Glen-Gery Corp., 260 AAA 13.

Making fringe benefits cost efficient

No matter how much a company spends on health and life insurance and other nonwage benefits, these perks won't motivate employees unless employees believe they're getting a good deal.

Properly handled, nonwage benefits can increase employee motivation without costing more money.

The key is to sell employees on the company's nonwage benefits plan, by distributing a full information kit on the benefits package. First lay out everything each employee is getting, and then provide details on eligibility and filing procedures. Tabulate each employee's nonwage benefits as a percent of salary, and tell him how much extra he is being paid.

If the company's benefits program is superior to the industry average, let employees know. Then prove it.

Source: Carson E. Beadle, director, William M. Mercer, New York.

EVALUATING EMPLOYEES

Performance appraisals that work

Informal appraisals of employees go on all the time, but they often seem unfair to many workers. Reason: There is usually no balance between criticism, praise and inquiry into the employee's ideas of how to do the job better.

The advantage of formal appraisals: Employees recognize that their work is being evaluated by standards that they themselves can understand. Formal appraisal systems, however, don't always succeed because management sees them as a one-time effort instead of an ongoing process.

To use the appraisal system as a way to achieve greater productivity, link appraisals to compensation in a way that is clear and fair to employees. How to do it:

• Clear up the basis for salary ranges (skills, experience, responsibility, marketplace for the worker's skills, etc.).

• Set specific criteria for promotions, demotions, terminations.

• Make clear how often performance appraisals will be done and salaries reviewed. (Semiannually or annually is best.)

Useful guidelines for raises:

• When appraisal is commendable, raise salaries up to 20% more than average.

• When appraisal is adequate, make the raise average.

• When appraisal is unsatisfactory, give no raise. Instead, issue a warning that a second unsatisfactory review will result in dismissal or demotion.

Top management must take the performance-appraisal system seriously for it to have any impact on worker performance. Instruct managers to:

• Keep the appraisal sessions free of interruptions.

• Listen to employees. Allow them to give a self-appraisal first.

• Tell employees what they are doing well and ways they can improve.

• Assume employees are creative and want to contribute. Ask them for suggestions.

There should be no surprises for an employee during an appraisal session. Don't appraise too much. Set two or three primary objectives at most. Once primary objects are consistently met, add new objectives—but only one at a time.

Source: Norman Auslander, group vice president and general manager, Miracle Food Mart, a division of Steinberg, Inc., Rexdale, Ontario.

Use a variety of performance-rating systems

Companies should have a variety of performance-rating systems in use, since no single one is effective for all occasions.

Four widely used approaches:

1. Rating personality traits. This could include effort, initiative, job knowledge, etc., rated on a range from outstanding to unsatisfactory. Although easy to administer and everyone is rated on the same scale, the traits are general

and don't relate to specific job-performance results. They also don't reflect the greater knowledge and performance expected of a higher-level manager. They're useful for raises that depend on personal effort rather than proficiency. Reviews of low-level workers for whom it's impractical to set targets.

2. Rating by responsibilities. Measures how well employees carry out all the responsibilities identified for their jobs on an outstanding/superior/average scale. The ratings are tailored to each job, but the scales are the same for each employee. Where performance standards are included, workers can see a direct tie between their efforts and their ratings. Defining all jobs in such detail can be a burden. The best application is for positions where many people are doing largely repetitive jobs. Useful for salary review, but not for assessing whether someone is promotable, because the ratings apply only to the present job.

3. Management by objectives (MBO). Rates employees on how well they have achieved business goals agreed on at the start of the year. MBO focuses directly on results, not personal characteristics. By setting new goals every year, the system has the flexibility to take account of both fluctuating business conditions and the employee's personal development. But every employee is rated on different criteria, which raises the possibility of inequities. The system is also difficult to install, time-consuming to administer, and demands extensive training in goal-setting. Use for senior-level positions and deciding incentive awards.

4. Free-form evaluations. Supervisors rate employees using little or no prescribed format. Usually a narrative describing overall performance, strengths and weaknesses, and perhaps behavior in critical instances. This way supervisors aren't tied down to standards they may find inadequate. They can focus on a worker's special efforts or note when the employee failed on a crucial occasion. But evaluations are totally susceptible to differing standards. Such a system is best used for assessing candidates for promotion or for working on employee development. They are not good for salary reviews.

Source: John D. McMillan and Hoyt W. Doyel, A.S. Hansen, Inc., compensation consultants, *Personnel,* New York.

Mistakes to avoid

How to make fewer errors in evaluating employees:

• Avoid judging an employee without knowing the details of the job. Your concept of the job may differ from the employee's.

• Measure performance against what was done by others in the position rather than against a mythical perfect standard.

• Recognize that an employee's performance reflects his reaction to many situations. Some of these are beyond his control.

• Don't let personal feelings color your judgment.

Source: *Office Administration Handbook,* Dartnell Corp., Chicago.

For valid appraisals

• Evaluate employees in terms of job-related factors only. For example, do not rate a worker on initiative if the job does not call for that.

• Do not let personal feelings influence judgments, even though there is a natural tendency to favor those who are well liked.

• Judge for the entire period. Do not give undue weight to one incident that may be inconsistent with the employee's total record.

• Base appraisals on objective data (production figures, sales records, chargeable accidents, etc.).

• Do not assume that an appraisal is inaccurate merely because it differs from someone else's previous judgment. The employee's work attitude may have changed.

• Avoid attaching undue importance to any single factor. A worker who is superior in willingness to accept responsibility may be deficient in judgment.

• Disregard length of service. A worker who has been satisfactory for many years may now have slipped below average.

• Be suspicious of any appraisal system that gives similar or identical ratings to all. If there is no opportunity to observe an employee's performance, it is better to skip that appraisal altogether than to give a meaningles routine passing grade.

Surveys that evaluate executives

Don't put an executive on the spot simply because his subordinates rate him harshly on a survey. He may be the victim of politically motivated underlings. To check the accuracy of a negative response:

• Go over survey answers with the manager's subordinates. Can they support their contentions with specifics?

• Focus on questions that reveal whether some people are stirring up resentment against the boss to strengthen their own power base.

• Ask the executive who he feels are potential rivals or manipulators. Whom does he distrust? Why?

Think of survey results as a first step, not as the last word.

Source: *The Levinson Letter,* Cambridge, Mass.

Five ways to improve performance-rating systems

All employee performance evaluation systems suffer "score inflation" sooner or later. Often it's because raters believe that high scores make subordinates and departments look good.

It's time for a change when average performance scores move near the top range.

To make ratings realistic again:

1. Change rating scales, categories, and names of categories. Usually only a temporary solution.

2. Set quotas for the highest rankings. Limit the top 5% rating to no more than 5% of employees, for instance.

3. Use behavioral scales. These award points for traits desirable for each type of job rather than for general performance.

4. Bring in outside raters, but remember that although it increases objectivity, it removes managers from evaluation process.

5. Measure performance strictly by success in meeting management-by-objectives goals. However, this system makes no judgment on the value of the goals to the employer.

Source: *The Personnel Administrator,* Berea, Ohio.

Personalize the appraisal interview

Questions to ask before an appraisal interview with an employee:

• What sort of person is the employee? How will he react to criticism? How should I respond to his reponse?

• What detailed instances can I cite to back up my criticisms? How did these specific instances affect the employee's overall job performance?

• What training is available to help the employee develop needed skills?

• What can I praise about the employee's performance?

• What follow-up should there be on the appraisal interview?

Acknowledging the evaluation

Both the supervisor and the employee should initial the final evaluation report. Reasons:

• It certifies that the report was, indeed, discussed by both parties (and not merely inserted into the record).

• Indicates the employee was given an opportunity to challenge the report's conclusions. Space for the employee's comments above the signature on the report further ensures that objections are noted.

• Commits employee to the goals set up in the interview. It also subjects him to appropriate penalties for failure to meet them.

• Lessens the possibility of future disagreement over what was said at the evaluation.

Source: *Working With People,* CBI Publishing Co., Boston.

PROMOTION POLICIES

Moving from supervisor to middle manager

Many companies take pride in the policy of promoting from within rather than hiring outsiders for management jobs. But they often find to their disappointment that capable, ambitious first-line supervisors fail when promoted to middle-management jobs. They don't recognize that middle managers need other skills to face problems significantly different from those of lower-level managers. Most management-selection processes and training programs do not take the differences into account.

The most obvious contrast is that first-line managers lead followers. Middle managers lead other leaders. This requires very different management styles. Lower-level workers generally respond to a leadership-dominant style (known as pressure-compliance). But the more assertive, independent types the middle manager works with require a much more interactive (or persuasive-collaborative) approach.

Other key differences between first-line and middle management:

• Planning. First-line supervisors typically implement plans made by others. They direct the efforts of one small work group. Middle managers, on the other hand, formulate plans and often coordinate the work of several groups.

• Problem-solving. Most first-line problems are repetitive. Problems are solved by either applying set guidelines or tried-and-true solutions geared to the particular situation. In contrast, middle-management challenges are often new, more complex and risky because they can require untested solutions. The pressure on middle managers is also more intense, because top management expects them to make these novel solutions work.

• Information-gathering. First-line managers can find out most of what they need to know by personal observation and direct questioning. Middle managers, on the other hand, must rely on secondhand sources (reports, computer printouts, standard forms, and conversations with lower-level personnel). Middle managers must learn how to validate such information. They must ask the right questions in the right ways, because first-line supervisors are wary of giving information they think can work against them. New middle managers must develop the skills that are necessary to detect suspicious facts or figures.

Middle managers often find themselves caught literally in the middle. They face scrutiny and criticism from both below and above. First-line supervisors complain about bosses who are not flexible enough or who cannot sell ideas to top management. Senior executives criticize middle managers for making demands they deem unrealistic or for interfering with high-level decisions. Finally, the middle manager must contend with constant and often cutthroat competition from peers.

To improve the situation:

• Start with the job description. Make it as

complete and accurate as possible. Recognize, however, that only experience on the job will reveal whether top management really wants aggressive managers. Does it encourage these people to look for trouble spots and propose correctives?

• Make training programs more responsive to the requirements of the job. For example, a key middle-management challenge is to motivate first-line supervisors to work as hard toward company goals as they do toward their own career and personal goals. But many managers complain that training programs simply rehash material they learned when being trained as first-line managers. Areas in which they want better training include motivating and decision-making.

• Do not expect quick changes. Traditional patterns are sometimes hard to break. If the previous holder of a middle-management position was required to have all decisions reviewed, it will take time to foster more autonomous decision-making.

In the final analysis, there is no clearly defined role for middle managers at many companies. Each individual must work out a personal style for the job and then sell it to others in the organization.

Source: Neil R. Sweeney, management psychologist and national training director, Seagram's Paul Masson Vineyards, Saratoga, Calif.

Advantages of promoting from within

Promotion from within has even more pluses than most managers realize. Obvious advantages include big saving in personnel costs (advertising, interviewing, etc.), and less break-in and orientation time.

Less obvious advantages:

• As a safety valve. A good worker may be in the wrong spot or be having a personality conflict with a supervisor. If not transferred, the worker may leave.

• Discovering underutilized talent. Every company has employees with untapped potential.

It's a good idea to let everybody know when a vacancy opens up anywhere in the organization. Carefully consider all applications, even those from left field. (Let the plant foreman who wants to join the sales force explain why he thinks he can do the job.)

Temporary tryouts for supervisory positions

Vacations and other temporary absences of supervisors and leadmen provide opportunities to give rank-and-filers some on-the-job training or unofficial tryouts for managerial jobs.

The tryout lets the worker know that management regards him highly. It gives management an opportunity to judge potential. Also, since, the upgrading is known to be temporary, no ill feeling results when the worker, who may turn out not to be a good leader, returns to the ranks.

In some instances, unions will forbid workers from accepting out-of-unit assignments on the ground that this creates "divided loyalty." But the First Circuit Court of Appeals declared that a union's rule against accepting temporary supervisory positions is an unfair labor practice.

Problems when line managers are promoted

Many promoted line managers miss the hands-on involvement of their former jobs. They are uneasy because they:

• No longer get direct feedback on performance.

• Must face a new ambiguity in dealing with higher-level abstractions.

• Are increasingly dependent on how well others perform.

• Find it more difficult to confirm their success or capability in direct ways.

To aid in their adjustment, help them establish new benchmarks for performance. Give them the chance to talk over the loss of their former image.

Source: Harry Levinson, *Executive,* Harvard University Press, Cambridge, Mass.

When employees are passed over

• Tell them the news personally, right after informing the winner. This lessens their disappointment. Don't let them learn through the grapevine or through a general announcement.

• Don't overapologize for passing them over. They will see it as hypocrisy.

• Let them talk, even if they are angry. Don't interrupt or try to change their feelings.

• Answer only questions asked. If the employee asks why he was passed over, give him a straightforward recital of the reasons. Examples: The promoted individual had more experience, training, etc. Tell the runner-up what steps he should take to get the promotion the next time around.

• Pay extra attention to the runners-up for at least a month. Encourage them to keep up their efforts. Follow up later on promises made for opportunities to develop skills and talents.

Source: *International Management,* New York.

PERSONNEL POLICIES AND THE LAW

Who owns employee inventions?

Usually, invention ownership is determined by the employment agreement.

The employee owns it if the invention is made on his own time, using his own facilities and equipment.

Most employment agreements provide that the employee owns the invention if he uses the company's facilities or time but the invention process is outside the scope of his job. In this case, however, the company has shop rights to the invention. That is, the company can use the invention free of charge regardless of whatever the employee decides to do with his patent.

The company owns the invention if the employee's invention falls within the scope of his job. Therefore insist that employees sign an agreement which says that part of their job is to make inventions. Avoid overly broad language in the agreement, which could be interpreted as preventing the employee from ever competing with the employer. If there's a legal dispute between employer and employee, the court would invalidate any covenant that thus overreached the company's lawful claim on employees.

A special problem is patent ownership in a new high-technology company. For example, an engineer, a venture capitalist, and an MBA combine to start a company based on new technology. The company fails, and the principals split up. The engineer, working on his own, refines the technology, then finds new partners to launch a second company, which succeeds.

How, if at all, do the original venture capitalist and MBA profit from their ex-partner's success? The answer depends on the original assignment of patents covering the new technology.

Executives and engineers involved in a new high-tech company should insist on a written agreement to specify assignment of patents.

In the absence of such an agreement, keep a diary recording any oral agreements that have been made, the development of the new technology, and the contribution to the fledgling business based on that technology.

Source: Mary Helen Sears, partner, Irons & Sears, Washington, D.C.

What departing employees must leave behind

A recent court ruling gives a company the right to keep anything containing confidential information when an employee leaves to go to work for a competitor. The court held that the employee's desk calendar, with customers' and prospective customers' names written in, would have to be returned to the company. To take it would represent a breach of trust on the employee's part.

To avoid problems, when hiring employees, have them sign an agreement that they will return all confidential data when they leave.

Source: 182 NYLJ 66.

Garnishees vs assignees

An employee voluntarily assigned a portion of his wages to a bank to pay a loan. Later, a finance company got a court order garnishing his wages. The problem: Who gets paid? The ruling was a creditor with a garnishment order takes precedence over an ordinary creditor. But a party with a wage assignment isn't an ordinary creditor, so the finance company had to wait until

the bank was paid. The bank got there first.

Source: *Associate Financial Services* vs *McClendon,* 376 So. 2d91.

Incompetence protection

It may be possible to collect on a fidelity bond when an employee covers up mismanagement by filing false reports. Usually an employee bond only covers stealing or fraud, not incompetence. But courts have held that concealment of mistakes can be a kind of dishonesty that requires the bonding company to pay.

Case I. A manager concealed weekly cash shortages with false reports. The shortages were apparently caused by mismanagement rather than stealing. But the false reports prevented the company from discovering and stopping the losses.

Case II. The claim was justified when a manager lied about the high death rate of livestock, thus preventing the owners from learning about the losses and stopping them.

Source: 266 N.E. 2d 365; 569 P 2d 857.

Workers' compensation rules

A worker cannot sue the employer on any other grounds when an accident or injury is covered by workers' compensation. In a recent case, a woman worker on the night shift was raped by another employee in the company parking lot. She sued the company for damages, claiming that it was negligent in not keeping the lot secure. The danger for the company is that a jury's award for damages could be far larger than any payment under workers' compensation. The court's decision was that the incident took place during the worker's course of employment and was covered by workers' compensation. So she could not sue the company on other grounds.

Source: *Helton* vs *Interstate Brands Corp.,* 271 SE 2d 739.

27 COMPENSATION

WAGE POLICIES

Setting a wage policy

The advantages of operating without a formal policy on salaries:

- Individuals can be rewarded with merit increases without setting precedents.
- The annual raise does not become automatic. Instead, employees know they must demonstrate that they deserve more.
- There are no rules to break.

Advantages of a written policy:

- Salary costs are protected from overinflation. Easier budgeting.
- Employee turnover is lessened because compensation levels stay competitive and rewards for advancement are known.
- Legal problems over discrimination are less likely.

Source: Stanley B. Henrici, *Salary Management for the Nonspecialist*, AMACOM, New York.

Pros and cons of salary grades

Advantages:
- Performance evaluations are simplified.
- Job status is easily identifiable. For example, when employees applying for transfers are told that the new position is Grade 6, they immediately know whether the job is an advancement.
- Promotions are easily noticeable when workers advance to the next grade.

Disadvantages:
- Managers lobby to upgrade jobs, particularly those close to qualifying for the next level.
- The grade structure quickly becomes public knowledge, which leads to overly simplified job comparisons between and among employees.
- Grades complicate the creation of new jobs because the level becomes more important than the responsibilities. Example: The job has to be a Grade 9 to attract the right person.

Too many grades are better than too few. A multigrade system appears to offer more opportunities and create fewer complaints about inequities. Common practice is to establish between 10 and 30 grades, depending on company size.

Source: Stanley B. Henrici, *Salary Management for the Nonspecialist*, AMACOM, New York.

When inflation hurts motivation

One of the most serious effects of continued inflation is the undermining of carefully constructed compensation policies.

Incentive programs can rarely be changed fast enough to keep pace with the inflationary spiral. Many companies find it hard to finance merit increases for good performers because a disproportionate share of revenues goes for cost-of-living raises and employee-related costs (benefits, travel, relocation allowances, etc.).

Inflation has also raised the ante for new hires, creating strains within the existing pay structure, resulting in lower morale and the danger of performance falloff.

What to do:

• Initiate new challenges. When opportunities for salary advancement lag, find new challenges for restless achievers. Enlarge their areas of responsibility or increase their independence, or try quasi-promotions.

• Publicize performance. Company and trade publications are good spots to applaud superior work. Outstanding achievers can also be assigned to key roles in meetings or to prestigious projects.

• Establish better training programs. They will enable employees to become more professional.

• Consider increasing the ratio of managers to staff personnel. Managers can develop more leads on prospective sales and hold more frequent meetings to encourage feedback from the field.

• Offer career-path counseling so stalled personnel can see where they're heading.

Source: Mary Lynn Miller, "Motivating the Sales Force," *The Conference Board Information Bulletin No. 64*, New York.

Simplifying compensation complications

Employees are often more concerned with their pay in relation to others' than with dollar amounts.

Considerations that can help company establish fair salary schedules and policies:

• The size of a pay increase for a promotion should always be larger than a normal salary increase given to someone who remains in the same position.

• The size of the raise relative to what someone else got. Employees do share salary information no matter how much management would like it kept secret. If an employee believes his performance is better than another's, he won't like getting a smaller pay increase, even if his overall pay is higher.

• If an employee's performance has been rated higher this year than last, he expects his raise to be greater.

• Pay should be directly related to responsibilities. Sometimes problems that arise can be solved by explaining to the employee why another job (which he sees as lower than his) actually has greater responsibilities or training requirements.

It is the manager's responsibility to explain the company's pay policies to subordinates who feel they are being paid unfairly (if the manager feels the present pay is just), or to fight for an adjustment in the employee's pay level (if the manager believes the subordinate's complaint is justified).

Paying for productivity

Don't let cost-of-living increases blunt an effective incentive-pay program. Instead, calculate total funds available for salary increases. Allocate no more than half of the funds to cost-of-living raises.

Apportion 70% of the remainder to the 20% of employees who are most productive and 30%

to the next-most-productive 30% of employees.

Every incentive-pay program makes some workers unhappy, but who better to be discontented than the lower 50% of the company's performers?

Source: Theodore Cohn, management consultant, West Orange, N.J.

Cost-of-living adjustments

Give employees transferred to a high-cost area a lump-sum pay adjustment. Then, when the person is transferred again, to a lower-cost location, no adjustment need be made in regular compensation. Reductions, even if understood by employees as cost-of-living adjustments, are frequently felt to be pay cuts and can be demoralizing.

Source: *Executive Compensation Letter,* Arthur Young & Co., New York.

How compensation can boost productivity

Inflation-inspired pressures for sizable pay hikes, even in the face of declining (or flat) productivity, is a continuing problem. To break out of this cycle, managers must alter their approach to compensation strategies. Specific suggestions:

• Put teeth into merit programs by giving merit raises and bonuses only to the best performers. By giving fewer but bigger bonuses, management encourages continued high performance of recipients, and makes clear to other workers what their stake is in increasing output. This step requires tight control over the company's definitions of performance. It demands that managers rate their subordinates' performance accurately.

• Change the pattern of raises by granting fewer routine increases. Instead, keep workers on the same base salaries longer, and reward outstanding performance via bonuses.

• Emphasize current rather than deferred dollars. Pay workers higher salaries but offer them fewer deferred benefits. This takes some of the sting out of inflation, and makes sense given the fact that inflation will erode the value of deferred benefits anyway.

• Be flexible in offering non-cash benefits. Without increasing the cost to the company of worker fringe benefits, management can increase the value of those benefits by letting workers choose their own fringes.

For example, a worker with young children wants maximum medical coverage, while another with college-age children prefers a maximum tuition-support program. Workers allowed to choose these benefits cafeteria-style will feel better compensated. But cafeteria-style benefits increase administration costs and, in some cases, insurance premiums.

• Reward workers most who use costly fringe benefits the least. Example: A company covers all its workers with the same medical insurance. One worker costs the company $1,000 in medical expenses over a year. Another worker costs the company nothing in medical expenses. If the company rewards the worker with no medical bill by giving him a small cash bonus, this will encourage other workers to use the company's medical plan more sparingly.

Source: Robert S. Nadel, partner, Hay Associates, New York.

MERIT PROGRAMS

Merit raises

There is no need to give raises year after year until salaries are far above the going rates. There is a correct salary for every person. To calculate it, look at salaries at other companies and the internal wage balance within the company.

Although experience counts, it's not overriding. More important is how much the employee has done beyond the call of duty to help the firm.

Getting the most out of merit raises

Granting merit raises once a year to all qualifying employees destroys the raises' motivating power because workers come to expect them.

Better alternatives:

• Tie the pay increases to each worker's regular performance appraisal to reinforce the improvement and achievement.

• Vary the periods between merit raises. This way, star performers can be given increases fairly often.

• Link merit raises to corporate earnings, rather than to some arbitrary annual schedule.

• Grant a partial merit increase to a worker who is being promoted for good performance before the base salary is upgraded.

Source: Stanley B. Henrici, AMACOM, Saranac Lake, N.Y.

When not to give a raise

One key to holding down payroll costs is knowing when not to use salary as a motivator. As long as pay scales are reasonably competitive, giving workers more money won't increase productivity when:

• A high level of distrust exists between management and labor.

• Performance involves subjective factors that are hard to tie to a given level of compensation.

• The salary increments that the company can afford to pay aren't big enough to be significant to the recipients.

Concentrate instead on building more trust between management and labor. Use psychological rewards for recognition.

Source: *Compensation Review,* AMACOM, Saranac Lake, N.Y.

When merit pay systems are likely to fail

Merit pay systems often fail to motivate employees because workers do not see a direct relationship between pay and performance. This is likely to occur when:

• Performance ratings and raises are based on managers' judgments rather than job-related criteria. Most workers view this type of appraisal as invalid and unfair.

• High and low levels for salaries and merit raises are not known. This means that workers cannot evaluate the relative size of their own raises.

• Everyone receives a regular raise to keep up with inflation at the same time that management insists raises are based heavily on merit.

• Past merit payments are treated as part of the worker's base salary. As a result, the worker continues to receive merit compensation even if performance slips.

• Managers do not recommend widely varying raises for subordinates when wide performance differences exist because they fear having to explain the low raises to those receiving them.

Source: Edward E. Lawler, University of Southern California, *Management Review*, New York.

BONUS SYSTEMS

Choosing a bonus system

Bonus systems have become recognized as an important part of a total compensation package. The best approaches combine features of formula-based systems, self-set incentive systems, and discretionary judgment.

Formula-based systems are the most objective, but often are not commensurate with output or effort. Fine tuning is required. For example: (1) One manager may do well because he inherited a modern plant with good worker morale that competes in a booming market. (2) Another may do poorly because he is operating with obsolete equipment, long-standing labor problems, and a mature market.

Self-set incentive systems (established by manager and his boss) help focus on specific company objectives, have advantage of acceptance through participation. But they, too, sometimes fail because of accidental or external variables (oil embargo, war, currency devaluation, plant fire, recession).

Discretionary bonuses require difficult decisions and consume top management's time, but in principle permit management to take all factors into account in making an award. But they are often perceived as non-objective. They motivate only where there is confidence in the absolute integrity of the management.

Some guidelines for setting up an incentive system:

• Establish a range of bonus levels and standards that employees can easily understand, whether or not they are satisfied with their own awards. Vary for different situations, but avoid complex formulas. Bonus is no substitute for adequate base salary.

• Use bonuses only to reward efforts above the minimum standards set for each job. Do not pay a bonus if the performance standard is not met, even if the manager has worked hard and intelligently. (See general rule below.)

• Put a ceiling on bonus payments to discourage employees from assuming personal financial obligations based upon the most recent bonus. (A ceiling of 50% of base salary is a fair number.)

• Use a discretionary component to take into account special circumstances which would have rendered the formula unfair.

• Base some part of the bonus on overall company performance to encourage team spirit. Also, employees must know that bonuses are not automatic, and that hard times (shortages, inflation, recession) affect all. Small bonuses in a bad year must be offset by higher bonuses in a good year.

As a rule, to motivate, the bonus system must be perceived as fair. The bonus as a sole motivator will fail. It must combine with adequate direction, support, and recognition. Good personal chemistry and opportunity for self-fulfillment are the best performance motivators.

Source: Norman E. Alexander, chairman of the board, Sun Chemical Corporation, New York.

Use bonuses to cut withholding

The withholding tax rate on executive salaries can be cut almost in half by using bonuses and supplemental salary payments.

The individuals take less pay in the form of ordinary salary and receive the difference in the form of one or more lump-sum bonuses. Bonuses and other supplemental wage payments can be subject to withholding rates as low as a flat 20%.

As a result, the individuals' tax bills on April 15 remain the same, but in the meantime, the executives retain use of a larger part of the funds the company pays them. The retained amount can be invested in a money-market fund or an interest-bearing account.

The net effect is that the individuals come out ahead by the amount earned on the retained funds during the course of the year.

Indications of an unsound incentive system

(1) Incentive payments that are greater than 25% of an employee's base pay.

(2) Skilled workers who are seeking downward transfers to increase earnings.

Use caution. Revising out-of-balance programs can trigger strikes. In union shops, propose the changes as a major bargaining issue in contract talks. The best incentive plans allow for continual adjustments. They rely on recognized standard-setting techniques. They are limited to labor-intensive manufacturing.

Surest cure for boredom: money

White-collar "factories," with repetitive production-type clerical jobs, are increasingly finding that financial incentives provide high productivity and job satisfaction.

How incentives work. In bank-owned facilities that process credit-card charges, clericals convert the charge slips into computer data on a typewriterlike device. They're paid on a piecework basis. Top producers can earn up to $20,000 per year. As a result, turnover is low and the quality of work performance is high.

Three reasons it works:

1. Computer checks quickly identify errors, so employees can't sacrifice accuracy for speed.

2. Offer the support staff and the supervisors a percentage of the clerical workers' bonus, which will encourage them to help the employees. That way, they share in the productivity gain.

3. There are constant quantities of almost identical work to process, eliminating hassles about difficulty, fair rates, or "retiming the job."

Source: Dr. Leonard R. Sayles, Columbia University Graduate School of Business.

OVERTIME POLICIES

Rules for sharing overtime

Problems most companies have in giving employees an equal opportunity to share in overtime:
• Mistakes happen, and overtime will be offered to the wrong person.
• Some workers are more willing to accept extra hour assignments than others.
• It's sometimes more convenient to let a worker finish a task he was working on during regular hours, even if he is not next in line for overtime.
Solutions:
• Maintain separate overtime rosters for each group within which overtime is to be shared. Loading-platform workers should not be on the same overtime roster as production workers.
• An overtime offer declined will be counted as an overtime turn worked. Thus, the worker who chooses not to work the hours offered will be "charged" on the roster as if he had worked.
• When it is not convenient to offer overtime to the person next in line, or when, due to a clerical error, management assigns the wrong person, a make-up overtime offer will be made.
• If a make-up assignment cannot be offered within two weeks, remedy with money.
• However, if a worker's record shows that he does not normally accept overtime assignments, the monetary remedy should be prorated. Thus, in the case of a worker who customarily accepts only half the overtime offered him, when management becomes obligated to pay him for four hours of make-up overtime, he should receive pay for only two of those hours (per his usual acceptance rate). Also, he should be "charged" on the overtime roster as if he had either worked, or refused to work, four hours.

Making overtime policies fair

Prime dispute concerns whether employees are obligated to accept a reasonable amount of overtime. When a plant is nonunion, or when union contracts omit this point, the assumption is that employees can avoid overtime only for good cause (just as they might be excused from regular work because of illness, urgent family problems, etc.).

An exception would be in unionized plants, where there's been a history of leniency or where companies have tried unsuccessfully to add compulsory overtime provisions to union contracts.

Distinguish between scheduled overtime and extra hours that suddenly become necessary. If overtime is scheduled a day ahead, employees may have to work unless their excuse is persuasive. On short-notice overtime, lesser excuses (or no excuses at all) may be considered acceptable.

EXECUTIVE COMPENSATION

The corporate owner's salary

The head of a closely held corporation must be careful in setting his own salary.

The problem lies in determining what salary will keep personal and corporate tax liabilities to a minimum.

There are hidden dangers. Salary payments considered unreasonably large by the Internal Revenue Service will be deemed dividends from profits. They will be subject to double taxation, first as corporate income, then as personal income. If too little salary is taken, the corporation may accumulate excessive earnings and face an accumulated earnings tax penalty.

In favor of a low salary:

• The company may be able to afford greater fringe benefits (for example, insurance), which are deductible to the firm and excluded from the individual's income.

• Retention of earnings will increase the value of the firm and maximize the capital gain available if it's sold or liquidated.

You can show a salary is reasonable by comparing it with the salaries of individuals performing similar duties for other firms. The Bureau of Labor Statistics is an excellent source of compensation figures. One way to justify an unusually high salary is to show that the owner took a correspondingly low salary in earlier years to help the firm get established.

How to avoid trouble with the IRS:

• Don't be greedy. A salary that impinges on cash flow will be questioned by the IRS.

• Separate salaries from stock. If salaries are paid in proportion to stockholdings, the IRS may call them dividend distributions instead. It's helpful to have all working shareholders receive raises at the same time other employees do.

• Avoid bonuses. A bonus paid out at the end of a good year might be considered a distribution of profits (taxable to the company and to the recipient).

• Pay dividends regularly. When the IRS doesn't find declared dividends, it looks for hidden ones.

The specific tax effects of various distribution schemes must be worked out on a trial-and-error basis. Consider the different investment opportunities available to corporations and individuals, as well as the differences between the corporate and personal tax rates.

A repayment agreement might prove useful. This calls for the employee to repay the firm any amount of his salary that might later be deemed excessive. The repayment is deductible by the employee. Repayment agreements can be dangerous, and must be carefully considered and drafted by an expert. The repayment of a large amount of salary could result in a firm's having to pay taxes on excessive accumulated earnings.

Compensating key executives

A company learns that one of its key executives has received an offer from a competitor that would boost the executive's salary 30%. The company doesn't want to lose the executive. But it doesn't want to match the outside offer either.

One solution is to offer the executive a deferred compensation program that guarantees him income on top of the ERISA-approved pension plan.

There are advantages for both the executive and the company. A deferred compensation program will provide the executive with retirement income when he needs it and avoid a salary boost that will put him in a higher tax bracket.

A deferred compensation program in lieu of a raise keeps the company from getting caught in a salary war. Properly structured, these programs for key executives are self-financing and not subject to ERISA requirements.

The company takes out dividend-bearing whole life insurance policies on its key executives. Initially, the company pays the premiums on this insurance out of its cash flow. Then it gradually begins paying the premiums with money it borrows against the policies at the standard rate charged by insurers.

Eventually, through the maturing face value of the policies and the benefits that accrue as retired executives die, the company builds up a fund that:

• Finances the extra retirement income promised.

• Covers both the current and start-up costs of running the deferred compensation program. The program can be structured so the company also gets a return on the use of the money it invests in it.

These deferred compensation programs now exist for companies with payrolls ranging from 200 to 15,000 employees, and from 1 to 50 key executives. The benefits offered range from 50% to 90% of the executives' salaries at the time of retirement. The start-up costs vary widely. Each situation requires its own calculations.

Source: Paul A. Fierstein, C.L.U., benefits and compensation consultant, New York.

Effective compensation strategies for foundering companies

Too many managers fall into the trap of thinking that monetary incentives alone are the golden handcuffs to hold on to key executives during troubled times.

But the only effective way is to give a clear sig-

nal that top management recognizes the problems and genuinely intends to turn things around. Money is not the sole answer, as many companies offering exceedingly generous incentive packages have discovered.

Lip service is not enough either. Smart executives know their worth in the marketplace and are constantly testing their value to others. Their perception of where the company is headed vis-à-vis their own personal ambitions is paramount.

The best strategy is to articulate the company's problems honestly and confide in key people. Then, involve these people by giving them a specific role to play in the turnaround. Reinforce their involvement by offering them incentives for achieving the desired performance.

The compensation strategy must also take into account the inherent risks for executives. Some of the dangers for the executive:

• The turnaround may not work.

• Other job opportunities may be lost.

• The turnaround may work but the particular executive no longer has a place in the reorganized company.

• The company may be merged or the top management replaced by someone the executive finds incompatible.

To hold on to executives (or recruit fresh talent from the outside), a troubled company must offer a compensation plan that is realistic about the risk/reward relation. No amount of money will be enough if the performance objectives don't seem believable or achievable. (This is why top management itself often must be changed to create credibility.)

Another indication of sincerity would be getting rid of people who don't measure up. This may be hard both for humane reasons and because it may be difficult to find replacements. But nothing is as demoralizing to a good performer than to be surrounded with peers who aren't giving everything they can to a job. Sooner or later, sharp executives will move to a more challenging environment.

The worst approach is issuing a well-ballyhooed plan or program that sounds good in theory but carries no real top-management commitment to do things differently. All too frequently, entrenched management hopes that business as usual will somehow magically produce results. It won't. And until operations are revamped, fancy new compensation programs, no matter how well planned or rewarding, will not stem the tide.

Source: Robert B. Pursell, vice president, Towers, Perrin, Forster & Crosby, management consultants, New York.

Compensation strategies to encourage planning

Companies often motivate their executives to maximize short-term results, usually at the expense of the company's long-term growth. Some suggestions on how to avoid that trap:

• Understand the factors managers take into consideration (consciously or subconsciously) as they sort their way through short-term and long-term decision-making.

• Examine the managers' time horizons. How long will they be in this job? With this company? If that horizon is close, their outlook will be short-term, too.

• Know how stock ownership and stock options influence managers. They may be effective motivators only when amounts are large and if the potential long-term capital gains seem to outweigh short-term income from bonuses and incentive payments. It's a mistake to assume that ownership of stock or stock options gives managers the same outlook as other shareholders. In fact, managers' salaries, bonuses, and perks often loom larger than stock profits. And the price of company stock does not necessarily reflect the executive's performance.

• Question whether the penalties for not meeting short-term minimum-performance standards outweigh the apparent advantage of aiming for a bigger payoff down the road. (This is often the case.)

To turn things around:

• Extend the performance evaluation period for managers. Build in compensation incentives over several years instead of one year. All incentive plans should encompass some long-range measures. At present, few do.

• Identify the major factors that govern future profitability (market share, productivity, quality control, new product development, personnel). Then, periodically measure each manager's progress toward achieving these goals and incorporate the results in an incentive package. This encourages long-range planning, and gives top management a chance to evaluate middle management's ability to make and implement plans.

• Don't use traditional accounting techniques to measure managers. For example, research and development outlays are normally charged immediately. But to encourage executives to take reasonable business risks, a special management accounting system could capitalize such expenditures over a longer period. Or, profits could be figured before R&D, thus separating development costs from current operations.

Source: Dr. Alfred Rappaport, professor, Kellogg Graduate School of Management, Northwestern University, Evanston, Ill.

The appeal of incentive stock options

Tax-favored stock options offer several benefits to employees:

• They can buy stock at a discount. The discount is not taxable income when the employees buy the stock.

• Employees can translate the discount into a long-term capital gain (maximum tax rate: 20%) by holding the stock at least one year after buying it and two years after receiving the option.

• The rules apply to options granted after May 21, 1976 (the date that tax-favored qualified stock options were phased out). For each employee, up to $50,000 worth of options granted in each pre-1981 year can be converted to tax-favored status. Overall limit: $200,000.

Several criteria must be met. Option prices must be at least 100% of the stock's value when the option is granted (110% for employees who already own 10% or more of the firm's shares). Shareholders must approve the option plan.

Employees must exercise their options while still with the company or within three months after leaving (12 months if the employee is disabled). Options must expire after 10 years (five years for more-than-10% shareholders).

No employee can be granted options on more than $100,000 worth of stock in a year. But an employee who receives less than $100,000 worth of options in a year can carry over one-half the unused portion to any of the next three years.

An employee with more than one option must exercise them in the order in which they were given. And the options may only be transferred to the employee's heirs.

With standard stock options, discounts on employee stock purchases are deductible from the employer's taxable income. Employers that grant tax-favored stock options forgo this deduction.

How cash-poor executives can exercise stock options

Finding the cash to exercise a non statutory stock option is a common problem, even for high-salaried executives. One technique is to exchange stock already owned for the new share options.

An executive wants to purchase 1,000 shares of the company stock. The option price is $20 a share when the market price is $40 a share. The executive already owns company stock bought for $10 a share. The executive exchanges 500 of the old shares at their market value of $40 each ($20,000) for the 1,000 shares (also $20,000).

As a result, the employee must treat the difference between the new shares' option price and their market value ($20,000) as compensation. The maximum tax is 50%, so the executive's net cash outlay is $10,000.

In comparison, an employee who purchases the new stock for cash has the same taxable gain. But $20,000 also has to be paid for the stock. Thus, net cash outlay is $30,000. That's three times the cash needed in a stock exchange.

The Internal Revenue Service has approved option stock exchanges. And the Securities and Exchange Commission has said exchanges may be undertaken by corporate insiders. Special rules apply if you exchange stock already owned for incentive stock options (ISOs).

Source: Francis M. Gaffney, national director of tax services, Main Hurdman & Cranstoun, CPAs, New York.

Paying professional workers

Labor regulations say that employees classified as professionals must be paid their full weekly salary if they do work in a given week, except if they take time off for personal reasons.

Tests of whether the employee is a professional or not:
• Principal work requires advanced knowledge in a field of science or learning.
• The work involves continuous exercise of discretion and judgment.
• Pay is on a salary basis, and is at least $200 per week.

Supervisors' compensation

Inflation hits supervisors hardest. Managers and foremen doubled their salaries over the last 10 years but retained only about 90% or less of their original purchasing power.

In contrast, executives and production workers kept nearly 100% of their purchasing power during that 10-year period.

28 EMPLOYEE BENEFITS

COST OF BENEFITS

How much fringe benefits cost

Computed as a percentage of the total payroll, fringes have climbed an average of more than 10 percentage points over the last decade.

What industries now pay for fringes (% of total payroll):

Food, beverages, tobacco	36.9
Textiles, apparel	29.2
Pulp, paper, furniture	36.1
Printing, publishing	35.0
Chemicals	43.1
Petroleum	44.5
Rubber, leather, plastics	35.0
Primary metals	43.0
Metal products	36.4
Electrical machinery	36.7
Transportation equipment	39.0
Public utilities	40.6
Department stores	31.7
Banks, finance companies	39.4
Insurance	38.3

Source: U.S. Chamber of Commerce, Washington, D.C.

Trimming benefit costs

As benefit costs continue to rise, companies should look harder than ever for ways to cut outlays without reducing services.

Recommended:

• Keep medical, dental, and eye-care plans separate from life insurance. This allows easier price comparisons and more room to negotiate.

• Before renegotiating a benefit plan, figure the cost-benefit ratios offered by prospective carriers. Use the data to win lower prices.

• When a company expands to more than 35 employees, it should renegotiate insurance, since nearly all insurers reduce rates around this level.

Source: Jack O. Remp, benefits consultant, Jack O. Remp Co., Palos Verdes Estates, Calif., quoted in *Business Insurance*.

BENEFIT CHOICES

Fringe-benefit choices

Fringe benefits that are added slowly are better motivators than employers usually realize. Three basic types of fringes:

Necessary fringes:

• Medical, surgical, and major-medical insurance. To save money, exclude routine smaller items from the coverage.

• Group life insurance premiums for the first $50,000 of protection are not included in the executive's taxable income, if the plan does not discriminate. They are deductible for the company.

• Long-term disability insurance. Plans normally provide full salary for 3 to 12 months and partial pay for an additional 6 to 12 months.

• Dues for professional societies and subscriptions.

• Increased vacation time for top-level executives. An added benefit is that it gives the company a chance to evaluate the younger managers who fill in.

Motivational fringes:

• Profit-sharing, pension, and individualized retirement plans.

• Employee stock ownership policies.

• Issuance of shadow stock.

In most cases, the personal fringes listed below are deductible by the corporation only if their value is included in the executive's income. If they produce unreasonable amounts of compensation, deduction may be denied on that basis.

Personal fringes:

• Executive liability insurance.

• Use of the company apartment, plane, dining room.

• Club membership.

• Company car. It's best to set a dollar limit on the car that the executive can purchase.

• Financial consulting.

• Corporate buying. Where feasible, the company acts as a purchasing agent, supplying executives with desirable items at wholesale prices.

• Interest-free loans to executives who are not stockholders. The company must report interest income at 120% of the applicable Federal rate. The executive gets a deduction for the same amount.

• Partnerships that are off the balance sheet. Companies can lease equipment from partnerships formed by employees or their families.

• Office furnishings, flexible working hours, and meetings and conventions in vacation spots.

Source: T. Cohn and R.A. Lindberg, *Compensating Key Executives in the Smaller Company,* AMACOM, New York.

Executive benefits that benefit the company

Fringe benefits, a major form of executive compensation in these days of high personal taxes, have taken on even more importance recently.

While most companies give perquisites to top employees, few of those programs benefit the company as well as the executive. Achieving this requires an understanding of fringe options now available.

Pension plans typically call for benefits to become vested (unforfeitable) over periods of four to 11 years, to encourage employees to stay with the company. But when benefits take a long time to vest, executives are unlikely to value them as compensation. So the company gets little return on its plan contributions.

Instead, arranging full vesting after only three years may cost less than others since employer contributions that fund the plan need not begin until the employee's third year with the company. Other vesting schedules require contributions beginning in the first year. This advantage will be especially valuable to a growing company.

Other pluses:
• Rapid vesting provides employees with a valued benefit.
• The company can budget its pension plan contributions three years in advance, since the maximum number of plan participants three years from now is known today. With other types of plans, the number of participants cannot be predicted more than six months or a year in advance. This makes long-range budgeting more difficult.

Phantom stock plans are a hot area in the field of stock options. A phantom stock plan offers many advantages over a conventional stock options program, particularly when the company is closely held, since executives are treated as though they own company stock.

For example: An executive receives 100 phantom shares. If the company's real stock bears a $1 per share dividend, the executive receives $100 in cash. If at some later date the company's stock rises in value by $5 a share, the executive can trade the phantom shares in for $500.

Advantages to the company:
• Employees are motivated to spur company growth. But they do not acquire company stock. The original owners retain complete control of the company, and no complicated stock repurchase agreements are necessary.
• Dividends paid on real stock are not deductible by the company. But the cash paid under a phantom stock plan is employee compensation and therefore deductible.

Advantages to employees:
• They share in company growth without having to make cash outlays from after-tax dollars or savings to buy stock.
• Value of stock given outright would be taxed to the employee.

Other perk options include: Many companies seek community goodwill by making annual gifts to local charities, colleges, and civic groups. Instead of having the company choose charitable recipients, set up a plan under which the company matches charitable gifts made by employees. The matching can be done on any ratio and may be subject to upper limits.

The program costs the company nothing in the way of extra contributions. But it may prove very valuable to employees who have strong feelings about charitable causes that they are close to.

Another perk is insurance that can be funded through an employee benefits trust. The company pays the insurance premium into the trust a year before it must be paid. The payment then earns high tax-free interest in the trust until it is paid to the insurance company. The company's annual premium cost is reduced by the amount of interest earned in the trust. A deduction for the premium payment earned a year earlier is a bonus.

Many companies have begun making no-interest and low-interest loans to key executives. A drawback is that the company loses the interest it could have earned elsewhere. The tax law requires the corporation to report the interest imputed on the loan at the applicable Federal rate. The executive gets an off-setting interest deduction. As an alternative, allow employees to borrow against their vested retirement plan accounts. Or have the company guarantee an executive's line of credit so he obtains more credit than he would have otherwise. The guarantee should prove valuable to the executive and cost the company nothing.

At conventions, arrange for some official activity for spouses to engage in. This will let an executive legitimately deduct the spouse's costs on the trip.

Source: Edward Mendlowitz, partner, Siegel, Mendlowitz, & Rich, CPAs, New York.

VACATION/HOLIDAY POLICIES

Setting vacation policies

As companies liberalize their vacation policies in response to pressures from unions and the competitive labor market, vacations become a more costly employee benefit.

In 1973, only 26% of several hundred companies polled offered three weeks' vacation to employees after five years of service. By 1980, 43% of the companies surveyed did. Now, 13% of the firms offer six or more weeks maximum vacation, up from 7% in 1973.

The average company vacation policy today:

• Two weeks after one year of service.
• Three weeks after five years of service.
• Four weeks after 15 years of service.
• Five weeks after 25 years of service.
• Six weeks after 26–30 years of service.

To pare vacation cost:

• Get tough about vacation carryovers.
• Get tough about pay in lieu of vacation days. Recommended:
• Be strict about minimum eligibility for vacations. Specifically, no vacation days this summer to employees with less than six months service.
• Stop liberalizing vacation policy by granting longer vacations. Instead, liberalize company policy about pay in lieu of vacation days. Many workers are willing to accept partial pay for days not taken.

Source: Madeline Hellegers, associate, Hay Assoc., management consultants, New York.

Common holiday and vacation policies

A survey of 195 firms shows:
• Most grant 10 paid holidays a year.
• Half require employees to work the day before and after a holiday to be eligible for holiday pay.
• Nearly half allow unused vacation time to be carried over to the next year.
• Some 6% give vacation supplements or bonuses in addition to vacation pay.
• A third let employees take vacation pay instead of time off for part of their vacations.
• Employees who work on holidays get 2½ times their regular pay at 42% of the companies, and double time in 16%.

Source: Survey by the Bureau of National Affairs, Washington, D.C.

Vacation pay for terminated workers

Give terminated workers accumulated vacation pay on their last workday and get them off the payroll. Extending employment to cover the earned vacation time can add to costs. This way, the company avoids:
• Compensating terminated employees for paid holidays falling within the vacation period.
• Paying premiums on their health insurance.

An accident or illness occurring while an employee is on vacation must be covered by the company's benefit plan.

A disadvantage of pay-in-lieu-of-vacation is that workers can apply for unemployment compensation immediately, rather than after the vacation. This may affect the company's experience rating and raise its rates.

What goes into a paid-holiday plan

First, decide what rate will apply if an employee is asked to work on a holiday. Double pay for working is customary.

Restriction to consider: All employees must work their scheduled days before and after the holiday. Allow the stretch of a holiday into a minivacation only if the production schedule can be maintained without paying excessive overtime. If a worker is tardy or absent for part of a day before or after a vacation, the penalty could be no holiday pay rate for the holiday.

One common exception to the surrounding days rule is sick leave or short layoff only. Or management may waive the rule and excuse absence for any other reason acceptable to itself. In this case, disputes may arise as to whether the employer withheld permission unreasonably. The test is would the employee have been excused if holiday pay were not at issue?

For minority religious holidays the safe policy is time off without pay to all who assert religious obligations.

Figuring holiday pay for incentive-rated employees can be tricky. Consider multiplying the number of hours in the work day by the hourly base rate or the average hourly incentive earnings during a recent representative period.

DISABILITY ISSUES

When a worker is injured

Follow these simple guidelines when a worker is injured in the workplace. They will help keep costs down, insure the worker's continued loyalty, and aid in getting him back on the job as soon as he is able.

• Retain a physician familiar with workers' compensation problems.

• Immediately investigate the cause of an injury. Document the activities of the injured worker. File a first report with the insurer the same day.

• Establish contact with the employee to demonstrate concern and to discuss benefits that apply.

• Maintain contact with the doctor, employee, and insurer to speed the employee's return to work.

• Plan a period of readjustment. One possibility is to assign part-time or limited duties.

• Welcome the employee back. Be supportive of the worker's efforts to overcome the disability.

Source: St. Paul Fire & Marine Insurance, St. Paul, Minn.

Disability-plan loophole

Under many disability plans, employees who are unable to return to their jobs are not prohibited from performing other gainful work, even though they are still collecting disability benefits.

Make sure to define disability to include: (1) complete inability, due to illness or accident, to perform any and every duty pertaining to his occupation. (2) Unavailability of other work the employee might be able to do. (3) Absence of gainful employment with any other employer.

In addition, include a clause that says disability payments will be forfeited if the worker refuses to accept appropriate work, when available.

Tax-free disability payments

A corporation's employee benefit plan may call for lump-sum payments to workers under either of two conditions: (1) upon retirement after a stipulated length of service, or (2) upon permanent disability.

In one case, a lump-sum distribution was made to one person disabled prior to normal retirement. He excluded this amount from his income as a tax-free payment for permanent loss of the use of a member of his body. Since the retirement rights were fully vested after ten years of service, claimed the IRS, the person received money that would have been paid even if there hadn't been an injury. According to the IRS, they were taxable retirement benefits. The taxpayer won, however, because the funds were paid out at this time because of a disability, hence they represented a tax-free disability payment.

Masterson vs *United States*, D.C., N.D., Ill., 478 F. Supp. 454.

Limited liability in workers' compensation claims

Employees who become ill at work are not automatically eligible for benefits from workers' compensation funds. In most states, either of two preconditions must be met:

1. The sickness must be occupational in origin. For example, silicosis and other respiratory disorders caused by industrial dust.

2. Bodily injury resulted from the employee's illness. For example, an employee suffering a dizzy spell bumps into a machine and breaks his arm.

But courts frequently decide differently on the basis of the same facts. So it's important to make note of all facts and interview everyone who witnessed the incident. A written record made as soon as possible can be an effective defense against unwarranted workers' compensation claims.

Disability rulings

Disability defined: Courts interpret qualifications for private benefits more liberally than does the Social Security Administration. SSA provides disability payments only after an applicant is judged physically unable to perform any kind of work. In a recent case, a 51-year-old pilot lost his license after a heart attack. The company's insurers balked at paying disability benefits. They claimed he was qualified for and physically able to do both sales and flight-operations work. The court, holding that his job experience in those categories took place too many years before he became a pilot, ordered full disability benefits paid.

Gradual injury, caused by continuous on-the-job strain, is grounds for disability compensation. For example, a registered nurse who had to lift patients from operating tables began suffering back spasms. After a year, disc surgery was required, followed by lengthy recuperation. When the nurse claimed compensation, the hospital's insurer turned her down, claiming she had failed to prove her injury occurred on a specific day. But the court rejected that reasoning. It held that disability can be the cumulative result of continuing occupational stress.

Out-of-office injuries. Employees who are hurt while traveling to or from a business-related function are entitled to compensation. Courts maintain that injuries at social events are job-related if the employees' jobs require their presence there.

286 N.W. 2d 174, 260 N.W. 725.

PENSION PLANS AND PROFIT-SHARING PLANS

Integrated retirement plans

The big mistake management makes with retirement plans is to think about them simply as a way to provide income to retired company officers and employees. The best retirement plans are integrated into company financial and tax planning, and into estate planning for a manager-owner.

A defined-benefit plan provides annual retirement benefits in fixed dollar amounts to retired employees.

For this type of plan, the annual retirement benefit cannot exceed 100% of the average of an employee's compensation in the three highest-paid years, or $90,000 per year, whichever is less. After 1987, the maximum benefit limitation increases each year with the cost of living. But the maximum benefit is 10% less for each year the employee has worked less than 10 years.

A major advantage is that the company can make a deductible contribution of any size that is necessary to fund the benefit. An older owner-manager can reduce the company's taxes while adding significantly to his own retirement income. However, this type of plan is usually less useful for a company with many employees who would have to be covered.

With a defined-contribution plan each year the company contributes to the plan an amount equal to a percentage of the employee's income.

The company's annual contribution to the plan for one employee cannot exceed 25% of the employee's compensation, or $30,000, whichever is less. (After 1987, the dollar limit rises with the cost of living.) The contribution limit applies to each year separately. One year's contribution cannot exceed the limit because a prior year's was under it. There is no limit, however, to the size of the employee's ultimate benefit. The totaled contributions and investment income set the retirement income.

One drawback is that contributions tied to employee compensation can burden a firm in a cyclical business, where profits may be up one year and down the next. Alternatively, the company can adopt a profit-sharing plan that ties contributions to profitability. The same contribution limits apply.

There are special ways to use a retirement plan.

• Reduce excess accumulated earnings to avoid an IRS penalty tax by adopting a defined-benefit plan. The benefits can be funded all at once by removing a large amount from accumulated earnings and placing it in the plan. Accumulated earnings are thereby reduced to an acceptable amount. And the company gets a deduction in the amount of the contribution, further reducing taxes.

• Reduce employee turnover. Benefits under a defined-contribution plan can be made to vest over a period of years. A contribution need not vest for a period of four years, unless the employer wants to be more liberal. If an employee leaves, the unvested benefits are forfeited.

• Provide employee incentives, as in a profit-sharing plan. This ties benefits to profitability, encouraging employees to provide their best efforts.

• Facilitate estate planning. In a small, closely held firm, the top employees are able to direct the plan's investments and arrange its payout procedures so as to reduce their estate taxes. They are not taxed on their retirement plan accounts in the meantime.

Retirement plans are not without problems. For example, the company's contribution to an executive's account in a retirement plan is part of the executive's total compensation. This must be considered if the executive's salary is already large enough to be challenged by the IRS as unreasonable.

Also, a benefit plan cannot discriminate in favor of the company's officers, shareholders or most highly paid executives. But a plan is not discriminatory when benefits are tied to salary, so that the highest-paid executives get the largest benefits. Also, the plan does not have to provide benefits to employees working under a union contract.

It is possible to have more than one plan. But special limitations apply. *Point:* All defined-benefit plans maintained by one employer are considered to be one such plan. And all *defined-contribution* plans are considered to be one defined-contribution plan. If an employer maintains both a defined-benefit plan and a defined-contribution plan, a special computation is necessary.

In such a case, take the actual expected defined benefit as a percentage of the maximum defined benefit allowed under the normal rules. Then take the actual amount of employer contributions to the defined-contribution plan as a percentage of the maximum contributions allowed under the normal rules. The total of these two percentages cannot exceed 100%.

• Top-heavy plans. Special rules apply to plans that provide more than 60% of benefits to key employees, as specially defined. Rules here require much faster vesting for non-key employees, and place other limitations on plan benefits. Closely held corporations should check these rules with their pension experts.

Source: Gerald Reich, partner, Shore & Reich, New York.

Pension plans that guard against inflation

In order to protect retired employees against inflation, many companies feel obliged to boost their monthly pension payments every couple of years. But this has become a heavy financial burden for companies.

As an alternative, design the pension plan so that the payments increase regularly, and employees share the extra cost.

One option is for the worker to accept a reduced pension during the first years of retirement. In exchange, the pension escalates by a fixed percentage each year for life. Typically, within 10 years, the monthly payment is larger than the original fixed amount the worker was entitled to. And it keeps growing.

As an example, a worker with a $100 monthly pension accepts $80, with the amount to grow 3% annually. The monthly payment passes $100 after eight years. At the end of 15 years, it is $125 a month. For the worker with an average life span, this approach yields more than could be made by taking $100 a month from the start and investing a portion of it. If the worker's family or medical history points to an early death, then it would be wise to opt for the full $100 right away.

Another possibility is to have the employee use money from the profit-sharing or thrift plan to buy an annuity from the company with a guaranteed yield that escalates annually. Annuity income is added to the basic monthly pension.

For example, the employee is entitled to collect $35,000 in profit-sharing at retirement. Instead, the employee deposits $4,000 with the company in return for an annuity of $6 a month ($72 a year) that increases by $6 a month each year (to $144 a year by the second year). As a result, after 15 years, the employee collects the basic pension of $100 a month plus $90 a month from the annuity. This $190 payment continues for the rest of the worker's life. Note that there are unresolved tax questions with this approach.

A third option is for workers to put up cash directly from their own capital to buy an escalating annuity. The rationale is that at retirement, many employees have more money than they will ever have again. Frequently, with both this and the other annuity approach, the company matches the employee contribution. That permits the workers to buy a more substantial annuity. Take note that this approach is also under an IRS cloud.

Source: Philip Alden, vice president, Towers, Perrin, Forster & Crosby, management consultants, New York.

Using mutual funds for profit-sharing funds

There are practical advantages to using well-established mutual funds to hold the company's profit-sharing or pension funds. Among them:

• No direct management fees. Mutual-fund performance comparisons reflect the management fees.

• Flexibility in timing. A portfolio manager with good market timing (or access to a timing expert) can liquidate the entire stock portfolio in mutual funds almost instantaneously, moving the capital into short-term debt instruments during periods of serious market decline.

• No start-up costs for commissions, opening accounts, etc.

• A plan invested in a large, well-established mutual fund will almost certainly meet the prudent requirements of the pension law (ERISA).

How do the funds' performances compare? A recent study* indicates that mutual funds, on the average, outperformed bank commingled accounts, investment counselors, or insurance com-

*Financial Analysts Journal, New York.

pany investment programs over a ten-year period.

Advantage: Bank portfolios tend to emphasize the biggest companies on the Standard & Poor's 500 Index. The top-performing mutual funds provide greater diversification and imagination in portfolio selection.

A twist in non-ERISA retirement plans

Most selective, non-ERISA retirement plans (set up to supplement existing pension plans for top executives) work on a rudimentary basis. That is, the company agrees to pay retired top executives so many dollars annually on top of the executive's regular pension. Then, when the executive retires, the company simply deducts those payments from its annual earnings.

A possible alternative is a supplemental, non-ERISA retirement plan for top executives that uses whole life insurance policies as the capital base.

• A company and an executive jointly take out a whole life policy in the executive's name. The executive pays that portion of the annual premium protecting him against sudden death (the term part of the policy). The company pays the part of the premium that builds cash value.

• The company then borrows the money to pay its part of the premium from the insurer at a fixed rate. On current policies that rate is 8%.

• In the first seven years of the policy's life, in order to comply with Section 264 of the Internal Revenue code, the company must pay four of the seven annual premiums out of its own coffers; all others may be borrowed. However, after seven years, the company may borrow additional funds from the insurer to recover those payments.

• When an executive retires, the company uses the tax-free gain in the insurance policy's values to recover the after-tax costs of paying the executive an annual supplemental benefit.

In this example, when the 45-year-old executive retires at 65, he would be able to collect about $12,000 supplementally each year for 15 years. But unlike supplemental pension plans paid out of general company revenues, the annual $12,000 payments do not affect the company's earnings.

The tradeoff is that supplemental pension plans based on a promise to pay top executives out of the company's earnings postpone the burden of deferred compensation bonuses. Supplemental pension plans built on whole life insurance policies require upfront interest payments. But, they cost the company materially less in the long run.

———

Source: Eugene L. Notkin, Capital Associates, Boston.

Simplified employee pensions

Companies that do not want to bother with a group retirement plan can instead set up Individual Retirement Accounts (IRAs) for their employees. There are two ways to do this: Under the Employee Retirement Income Security Act (ERISA), an owner can set up IRA accounts for certain employees, ignoring others, with a maximum annual contribution of $2,000 a year.

Alternatively, the owner can set up a Simplified Employee Pension (SEP). This plan must include all employees who have worked for the company in three of the last five years. The maximum annual contribution is 15% of salary, up to $30,000 a year. Under this type of plan, employees may add their own contribution to the account, up to $2,000 maximum, provided the employer did not contribute that much. The rules applicable to top-heavy plans apply to SEPs.

For both plans costs of administration are minimal and the funds that are deposited into an IRA account vest immediately in the employee.

The disadvantages are that employees may not legally borrow against IRA accounts. (They can legally borrow against other retirement plans.) And money withdrawn from a conventional pension plan is frequently entitled to advantageous tax treatment by the IRS. Money withdrawn from an IRA is always taxed as ordinary income.

———

Source: Marvin P. Lazarus, resident counsel, Martin E. Segal & Co., consultants and actuaries, New York.

Pension plan trap

A deferred-compensation plan for executives may jeopardize the tax-favored status of a company pension plan.

Consider a company's deferred-compensation plan allowing employees to postpone the receipt of part of their salaries until retirement, when it will be taxed at lower rates. The company also has a pension plan that fixes benefits on the basis of employee salaries.

The pension plan includes deferred compensation in the salary base that determines benefits. But top executives are more likely to defer compensation than rank-and-file employees, because executives are in a higher tax bracket. The Internal Revenue Service might argue that the plan illegally discriminates in favor of top executives because they are now accruing pension benefits based on compensation they will receive in future years, while the rank-and-file employees are not. As a result, the plan loses its qualified status and thus the favorable tax treatment that benefits both the company and its employees.

Therefore, carefully consider the consequences of establishing a deferred-compensation plan when a pension plan is already in place. Consult with a specialist to determine how such a plan might be drawn up without an adverse impact.

———

Revenue Ruling 80-359.

How to ease the funding burden temporarily

If business slackens, cash tightens, and profit disappears, it may be time to consider putting a clamp on one big working-capital outflow: the company's annual retirement-plan contribution.

Under the Employee Retirement Income Security Act (ERISA), most plans have a minimum-funding standard. The company is committed, by actuarial formula, to a specified obligation. But it may apply to the Internal Revenue Service for a one-year waiver of that minimum, based on temporary business hardship.

The waiver, if approved, is merely a postponement of payment. The difference between a plan's minimum and reduced contribution, plus assumed income, must be made up incrementally over the following 10-year period, at most.

Waivers can be sought for any five of fifteen consecutive plan years. A new application must be filed each year, giving good reasons.

Source: *Executive Compensation Report*, Boston.

How assets are held

The most common pension fund asset mix: 38% common stocks, 24% bonds, 12% guaranteed investment contracts, 11% cash and equivalents, 5% insured plans, and 5% company stock. Index funds and real estate account for only 1% each.

Plans should vary from this "norm" because of different company objectives and differences in age of work force, etc.

Source: Greenwich Research Associates, Greenwich, Conn.

How to pick a good pension-fund manager

• Ask similar-size companies, local brokers in touch with investment management firms, and the company's lawyers, accountants and board members for candidates.
• Remove the names of banks from the candidate list because bank trust departments invest by committee, and the committees change. Thus, it is impossible to predict future performance based on past performance.
• Remove the names of investment advisers working for brokerage houses, since they often rely heavily on in-house research.
• Don't consider the names of one-person companies. Constant portfolio supervision is critical. One-person companies stop functioning during vacations and illnesses.
• Interview the remaining candidates to determine which have an investment philosophy compatible with the company's pension-fund objectives as well as a superior track record.

To find out about a portfolio manager's track record, ask:
• What has been the performance each quarter for the last 10 years? Eliminate all who fell more than 20% during a bear market.
• What has been the average annual return?
• What has been the compounded rate of return?

The ideal fund manager would be an independent two- to three-person firm composed of individuals who did well working for others and who are now starting out on their own.

These investment managers have proven themselves in the past, yet they will be trying to improve on past records to make their own venture successful.

If they do succeed, they will attract new business. To cope with new business, they may hire untested assistants. If so, monitor personnel shuffles closely; demand a continual better-than-average return on investment; and fire portfolio managers who perform below average four quarters running in a bull market, or allow portfolios to decline more than 20% in a bear market.

Source: Michael Stolper, president, Stolper & Co., San Diego, Calif.

When companies merge

Management is not required to continue the retirement plan of an acquired company. It may be terminated immediately after the merger or purchase.

Each participant in the discontinued pension plan must receive a distribution of benefits that is not less than he would have received if the plan had been terminated before the merger.

OTHER BENEFITS

Corporate dental plans

Dental insurance plans, as well as other medical plans, assume increased importance as employee benefits today as dental costs continue to outpace the general inflation.

When choosing a corporate dental plan it is best to avoid the type of plan that combines dental and medical insurance. Medical plans are designed to *discourage* use, while dental plans are tailored to *encourage* use. In dentistry, early treatment is always cheaper.

Better: A separate plan, based either on a schedule of fees or on reasonable fees prevalent in the region.

Big advantage of the fee schedule system is that costs are predictable, especially during the first three years of the plan. The problem is that it's difficult to adjust fee schedules from region to region in a way that's equitable to employees.

Five items to avoid in any kind of dental plan:
• High coinsurance levels.
• High annual maximums.
• Large deductibles. They tend to discourage use of preventive services.
• Incentive plans. They encourage employees to postpone major services until maximum coverage is available.
• Block benefits. Potential bad experience when blocks are added.

Legal-service plans

Despite the cost, more than 5,000 companies in the U.S. have set up plans that provide employees with legal services. It's done in much the same way that health plans provide medical care.

The chief drawback is that self-insurance is usually necessary because most major insurance companies won't underwrite legal plans, except for some of the Blue Cross affiliates.

The major advantages of a legal plan:
• Lower absenteeism. Employees involved in legal disputes can often avoid court appearances. The company's lawyers can represent the employee in court.
• Higher morale. It's reassuring to know that free counsel is available in the event of a civil or ciminal litigation. Other helpful services include reviewing wills, deeds, and other contracts for employees.
• Tax benefits. Federal tax laws let employees exclude from their gross income both contributions to and benefits from employer-funded legal-service plans. The plan must be approved by the Internal Revenue Service. Remember that plans must be completely nondiscriminatory (nothing special for shareholders and other executives).

Legal-service experts recommend plans that lean heavily on defensive law rather than ones that encourage litigation. Plans shouldn't cover legal action between fellow employees, on-the-job disputes, suits against the company.

Also recommended are closed-panel systems under which the administrators rather than participants choose the attorneys. This permits better quality, lower costs.

Attorneys should be from outside the company. (In-house lawyers may be confronted with conflict of interest.)

Since legal-service plans are relatively new, companies may have difficulty finding experienced administrators. Look for administrators among attorneys who have been associated with union plans. Labor unions were among the first to offer legal-service plans.

Source: Stephen F. Gordon, managing partner, Mirkin, Barre, Saltzstein, Gordon, Hermann and Kreisberg, Great Neck, N.Y., *Personnel Administrator,* Berea, Ohio.

29 UNIONS

KEEPING THE UNION OUT

Is your company ripe for unionization?

Answer the questions on this typical union handout as though you were an employee of your own company. If three or more answers are *yes*, trouble can be avoided by new promotion and personnel policies and improved employee communications. The union asks:
- Are you confused about how your job fits into the company's overall goals?
- Are some people paid more than you are for doing the same job?
- Are your work surroundings unhealthy or unsafe?
- Are promotions based on whom rather than what you know?
- Do supervisors play favorites?
- Can the company change your benefit plans without asking you?
- Are you ignorant of the company's future plans and of its current profits?
- Have fellow workers been fired without good reasons?
- When you put extra effort into the job, are you thanked for it?
- Are your complaints ignored?

- Do supervisors make unexpected changes without asking for employees' opinions?
- If there are layoffs, will favorites be kept and seniority ignored?

Then, using the union questions, modify the questionnaire and ask departing employees to fill it out. Look for patterns in categories but expect some random angry answers.

Source: George F. Truell, Drake Beam Morin, Inc., New York.

Good management can keep a union out

To keep workers from turning to a union:
- Set up a two-way communications program in which workers can tell the company what they want and management can respond openly.
- Eliminate blatant opportunities for supervisor unfairness—for example, work rules that do not spell out penalties for common problems (lateness, not calling in to explain an absence).

These are the steps companies usually take after a union begins organizing. But the company loses credibility by waiting until then.

Basics of a union-free strategy:
• Pay competitive wages and benefits for the area.
• Poll employees twice a year with a written questionnaire asking their views on wages, benefits and grievance-handling procedures.
• Respond fully to employees' comments and complaints. If they request something the company cannot afford, tell them so. A majority of workers will usually be satisfied with this approach.
• Set up a criticism/suggestion box. Encourage use with prizes for good suggestions.
• Make a special effort to be sure first-line supervisors feel part of management, because they are in a key position to influence workers against the company.
• Set up a grievance process to work like one in a union contract. Spell out the steps an employee takes when there is a problem. The usual makeup of a final appeal committee is two managers, two worker representatives, and a fifth person chosen by both sides. (Managers and workers are chosen on a rotating basis.)

Source: Stephen J. Cabot, senior partner, Pechner, Dorfman, Wolffe, Rounick & Cabot, lawyers, Philadelphia.

Tactics used by unions to organize companies

Union organizers commonly try to put a company on the defensive and keep it there, in order to mislead the company into underestimating the union's strength. Some of their methods:
• The union will hold few or no organizing meetings in the early stage of the drive. The real organizing activity is going on behind the scenes. But the company is unaware of this and does not begin its counteroffensive soon enough.
• Organizers challenge the company to respond to each new charge in order to control the pace of the campaign and keep the firm off balance.
• They rely heavily on telephone calls to employees at home, where they are often in a more relaxed, receptive attitude. Counter this by doing the same. It's legal.

• Union organizers get hired as employees. They create unrest, gather information, seek out unfair labor practices and recruit pro-union supporters. This is not considered a legal cause for firing or laying off a worker, even when the organizer is on the union payroll as well as the company's.
• The union will suggest organizing a company union as a compromise. But employees who get a company union become accustomed to collective bargaining, and the employer's position is weakened.
• Organizers hold private parties at workers' homes that appear on the surface to be mainly social. Their real purpose is to get one-on-one opportunities to sign up workers in a congenial atmosphere.
• They make oral and written promises that are not binding and play up minor mishaps or misunderstandings. To defuse situations like these, challenge the union to sign a bond agreement that it will make good on its promises.
• The union might propose a debate with management. It usually has a highly skilled debater on call, while the company usually does not. Management thus provides a forum that would not otherwise be available.

Source: Alfred T. DeMaria, *How Management Wins Union Organizing Campaigns*, Executive Enterprises Publications, New York.

Unionization by definition

One common ploy of unions is to organize one segment of the work force (say, loading workers) and then to seek a National Labor Relations Board "clarification" which would redefine that segment to include other parts of the work force (say, drivers and production workers).

Employers can prevent this union strategy by citing established NLRB policy not to upset a contract's definition of the bargaining unit (e.g., a segment of the work force), or the past practice of the parties, *"even if the agreement was entered into by one of the parties for what it claims to be mistaken reasons. . .* " (Union Electric Co. 69 LRRM 1535).

This precedent is important because the union usually argues that, when it asked for a smaller bargaining unit, it had been misled into believing that the excluded jobs were professional, confidential, or supervisory.

But NLRB policy cuts both ways. Once an employer agrees that certain classes of employees are part of the bargaining unit, the company will not be permitted to carve them out later.

Young workers and the unionizing effort

Union organizers have most success with workers under 30, largely because younger workers are most likely to be dissatisfied with their jobs and company benefits. They are also more apt to compare their company unfavorably with others.

During their first year on the job, focus on convincing young workers that the company has their best interests in mind. Their attitudes are most likely to be favorable during this initial period.

Source: *The Hughes Report,* New York.

How organizers can deceive workers

To create the impression that the National Labor Relations Board is on the union's side in an organizing drive, unions often reproduce official documents (statements of employee rights, notices of elections, etc.) and distribute them with their own propaganda.

The NLRB says such actions are allowed as long as nothing is added to the reproduced document itself. But if the union puts its own message on the government document and wins the elec-

tion, the NLRB may refuse to certify the result because the board's neutrality was compromised.

But do not depend on the NLRB to enforce the rules at its own initiative. File objections if the union makes improper use of board letterheads and notices.

Source: Second Circuit Court of Appeals, 107 LRRM 2039.

What you should find out about the union

Before organizers surface, the union already has learned a great deal about company policies, practices, finances, and history. A common company mistake is not learning at least as much about the union as it has learned about the company.

Your first priority is to know the union officers' backgrounds, especially—have any of them ever been indicted, arrested, or convicted of crimes or violations of labor laws?

Also investigate:

• The union's financial status. Concentrate on officers' salaries, size of strike funds, total amount of dues and assessments collected and initiation fees.

• Details of the bylaws and constitution, including: Provisions for increasing dues, special assessments, charges against members, trials and paying legal fees.

• The history of strikes, including those called by affiliates.

• Benefits negotiated elsewhere by the union. The usual finding: They are less than what the company already granted.

• Instances of elections overturned by the federal government and of unionization attempts rejected by employees.

• Past problems such as illegal strikes, secondary boycotts, and charges of discrimination against minorities, women, and part-time employees.

• Representation of minorities and women among the union's upper echelons. Discrimination is often blatant at this level.

Clipping bureaus and libraries, back issues of union publications, industry associations, the Department of Labor's Bureau of Labor Statistics and the National Labor Relations board can provide information.

One key to success is using facts to show workers if union leaders live high, discriminate, and misuse funds.

Source: Alfred T. DeMaria, *How Management Wins Union Organizing Campaigns,* Executive Enterprises Publications Co., New York.

Fighting a union-organizing campaign

If a company is well run in the first place, management has a very good chance of defeating union organization efforts. But be sure to consult competent legal advisers at each step to avoid losing by some unintentional violation of the labor laws.

What management can say and do:

• Tell employees about experience with unions, including experiences of friends, neighbors, acquaintances. Provide workers with information on the background of union organizers, and poor results of their past promises to other workers.

• Give the union's track record, complete with elections it's lost, companies it's unionized where employees later voted to get rid of it, picket line violence, strikes at other companies, how much striking employees lost in wages, how many years it took them to make up losses. Point out the unavailability of employment insurance for strikers (in most states), meagerness of strike benefits (in most unions). Paint a picture of difficulties workers would have in supporting families if prolonged strike should occur.

• Inform employees about union dues, fees, fines assessments, uses of these funds to pay for professional union employees, organizers at other companies, political campaigns, lobbying, other matters unrelated to workers' direct interests.

• Ask employees to consider who the shop stewards will probably be. These often turn out to be chronic malcontents who are not very popular with workers.

• Point out the shortcomings of the seniority system: It blocks advancement of deserving workers, makes minorities more vulnerable to layoffs.

• Make sure employees realize that the arrival of a union doesn't automatically bring better benefits. The company is not bound to agree to demands and the union's only real recourse is to strike. Stress the company's record on salaries and fringes, if it's a good one. Ask employees to think about how much they really have to gain if the union comes in.

• Describe grievance procedures. They're usually quite lengthy and formal under union set-up. Compare these with the flexibility and speed of the current system, plus management's record of responsiveness in face-to-face talks with individual employees.

• Give employees the facts about authorization cards. Specifically, that they don't have to sign. Even if they do sign, they can still vote against the union in secret ballot.

• Tell employees to report all threats and pressures by union organizers and pro-union workers. Promise immediate protective actions to safeguard freedom to decide without intimidation.

Tactics the employer should use:

• In most companies, pro- and anti-union workers each account for about 20%, with 60% undecided. Don't waste time with the hard-core 20%. Concentrate on the undecideds.

• Outside union organizers can lawfully be barred from company premises.

• Employee-organizers cannot be barred, but their activities can be limited to non-work time (including coffee breaks), non-work areas (including cafeteria, parking lot).

• Employees have a right to wear pro-union buttons. But posters, stickers on walls, and other gear can be barred.

• Any organizing activity that interferes with work or creates safety hazards can be stopped by management. But interference must be bona fide and provable.

Source: *The Supervisor's Handbook on Maintaining Non-Union Status,* Executive Enterprises Publications Co., New York.

How to put down a card-signing campaign

To force an election, union organizers must get 30% of the company's employees to sign authorization cards. The campaign is often low key and conducted off company premises. Alert management is needed to spot the card-signing activity early. To counter it:

• Let workers know that signing a card can lead to union membership, dues, initiation fees, assessments, and support of an organizing strike.

• Obtain a copy of the card and distribute copies with marginal notes that emphasize these liabilities.

• Inform workers they have the right to have signed cards returned to them.

• Use flyers to warn employees that they may be bothered at home, represented by strangers and lose control of their right to communicate with management.

• Use paycheck envelopes for distributing statements of the company's case. It is legal and hits home.

• Stress that names of cardholders are not necessarily kept confidential.

It is essential to get good legal advice before launching an all-out attack. The National Labor Relations Board has approved the use of very strong antiunion language, for example, describing cards as blank checks; warning workers that card signing can be fatal to business.

Source: Alfred T. DeMaria, *How Management Wins Union Organizing Campaigns,* Executive Publications Co., New York.

How to stop union picketing

Unions may not picket for recognition for longer than 30 days without asking for an election.

Unions try to evade the restriction by calling their picket lines "informational" or claiming the purpose is merely to exercise the constitutional right of "free speech."

The 8th Circuit Court of Appeals rejected that tactic in a case where the union tried to get an employer to adopt what it called area-wage standards. The court's reasoning was that picketing involves elements of free speech, but it's not constitutionally protected when the purpose is to achieve an economic goal by "patrolling."

This decision should make it easier for employers to stop picketing by unions that know they are too weak to win elections. However, the law does not give employers the right to ask for elections in all circumstances. But they can petition for NLRB polls after the union officially asks for recognition. (That's why campaigning unions are sometimes careful not to trigger the voting process prematurely.) It pays to petition the NLRB for an election whenever a weak union tries to achieve recognition by means of the picketline route.

NLRB vs *Electrical Workers,* 102 LRRM 2001.

Effective no-access rules

Problem. Employees stay in the plant or office after their shift, or come in early, to hand out union literature or collect membership cards for a union-organizing drive.

Solution: A general no-access rule, which prohibits employees from wandering around work areas except during their duty hours.

To be legal, the rule must apply to all employees. It can't be used only for the union organizers. It's best to include the rule in the employee handbook and post it on the bulletin board.

Note that the rule probably cannot cover nonworking areas such as parking lots.

222 NLRB 1089, 91 LRRM 1323.

Two anti-union propaganda strategies that work

1. A contest with prizes, in which the company asked true-or-false and multiple-choice questions about the union. The (obvious) answers were in letters distributed by management.

Sample questions:

• In a two-year period, this union called at least how many strikes? *10, 25, 75, 1,390.*

• Union dues can be raised whenever the union wants to. *True. False.*

The National Labor Relations Board said the contest didn't interfere with a free choice, particularly since the prizes were small (total: $450).

2. In the last pay envelope before the NLRB election, a message read: "Union dues have not been deducted from your paychecks. It could be different next month if the union wins. Vote NO and protect your paycheck!"

Key was the use of the word *could* rather than *will,* since checkoff of union dues is common but not automatic. The NLRB said the propaganda leaflet did nothing more than state a fact.

L106 LRRM 1127; 253 NLRB 140.

Tell employees that unions mean less freedom

Point out to employees those features of a union's constitution and bylaws that limit freedom of members.

For example, the International Association of Machinists fined two employees several thousand dollars when they quit the union and went back to work in the midst of an eight-month strike. The union's constitution required workers to picket and refrain from working even after they'd quit the union during a strike.

Caution, management's arguments against the union must not sound like threats.

Inform employees about hidden costs of union membership

When a union certification election is near, tell employees about the many union payments they will be making in addition to dues. Often overlooked are: initiation fees; assessments for strike funds; political and charitable contributions; fines for violating union rules or giving inadequate support to strikes; and contributions to international unions or the AFL-CIO.

No time for raises

Think twice before granting a wage hike during a unionizing effort. If it comes too close to the election, the union may charge that the company is trying to buy off employees.

Legal pitfalls in union campaigns

Management shouldn't threaten, promise reprisals, or interrogate employees before a union election. If they do, the election can be set aside and the union recognized even if management wins.

Specific actions supervisors must be told to avoid:

• Threatening to close down, curtail or move the company's operations elsewhere.

• Promising wage increases, promotions, increased benefits or other rewards to workers who vote against the union.

• Attending meetings or taking other actions (such as sending supervisors to gatherings) that give any indication management is spying on employees or trying to determine who is participating in union-organizing activities.

• Making threats to pro-union employees through third parties.

• Asking job applicants about past or future union activities.

• Inquiring about confidential union matters. However, if a worker volunteers this information, it is legal to listen. It is an unfair labor practice to ask for additional information, though.

• Stating that the company will not deal with a union.

• Circulating a petition against the union or encouraging employees to persuade others to oppose the organizing effort.

• Visiting workers' homes to urge them to reject the union.

Source: George F. Truell, *Building and Maintaining Your Nonunion Organization*, Drake Beam Morin, Inc., PEM Div., New York.

No-solicitation rule clarified

If management permits solicitation for charities, political candidates, etc., during working hours, it may be an unfair labor practice to bar a union from distributing leaflets and membership solicitations under similar conditions.

That's true even though a court decision noted that union solicitation and distribution of literature by employees may be done "when both the soliciting and the solicited employee are on personal time, company authorized work breaks, or during nonworking hours, and in a place within the plant but outside normal work areas."

Remember that controlling solicitation of union membership more restrictively than other solicitations is presumptively illegal. The burden is on the employer to prove a business necessity to bar it during work breaks.

NLRB vs *Westinghouse Electric Corp.,* CA Eighth 103 LRRM 2171.

When not to talk to workers

Employers can no longer initiate discussions with workers under any circumstances about their union views. The NLRB reversed an earlier position and now believes that questioning may convey an employer's displeasure and therefore discourage future organizing efforts.

Discussions are legal, however, when workers initiate them by volunteering their views first.

Source: *Monthly Labor Update,* Philadelphia.

When a supervisor can't be fired

Protection provisions of the Taft–Hartley Act do not apply to supervisors (or foremen) since they are members of management. But if a supervisor is fired for reasons the National Labor Relations Board regards as unfair labor practices by the employer, the NLRB may step in.

A company can be held liable for intending to intimidate the rank and file when it discharges a supervisor for:

• Testifying adversely about the company before the NLRB.

• Providing the NLRB with evidence about grievance procedures.

• Refusing a management order to threaten employees with reprisals if they vote for a union.

• Warning employees of company anti-union tactics (for example, that management is building a case against pro-union workers).

• Displaying pro-union sentiment in any other way.

A company beset by union-organizing efforts should make sure all supervisory personnel are on the management team, where they belong. Selection and training of foremen (especially when newly elevated from the ranks) should be aimed at making them true company representatives and discouraging them from committing unfair labor practices. Former NLRB policy regarding small companies was to give them the benefit of the doubt as to whether management actually knew union organizing was under way. No more.

Source: Morris Stone, retired vice president, American Arbitration Assn.

When a manager can be fired

Can a middle-line manager in a company that is about to face a union-organizing drive be fired if he agrees with the union on some issues?

Supervisors who are sympathetic to a union-organizing drive can be fired by a management that is opposing the drive.

A recent NLRB decision. When an employer discharges a supervisor out of a legitimate desire to assure the loyalty of its managerial personnel, the action does not violate the law. The mere fact that employees may feel the same fate will befall them if they engage in similar activity is insufficient to transform otherwise lawful conduct into a violation.

Exception. If the company actively interferes with the right of *rank-and-filers* to organize, the discharge of a pro-union supervisor will be *unlawful* because the coercive effect will be more than incidental.

DRW Corp., 103 LRRM 1506.

The closing anti-union speech

Management's last statement of its case to the workers must be made at least 24 hours before a union election. It's a tactical mistake to provide advance notice, because union organizers gain time to plan questions. Instead, round up employees just before the deadline. Allow enough time to prevent talk from running into the 24-hour prohibition.

Reminder: Monday elections usually favor the union because organizers have all weekend to counter the company's arguments.

NEGOTIATING WORK CONTRACTS

A shift toward management

When faced with an inflationary economy, union leaders find themselves in a defensive position at the bargaining table. Instead of bold, imaginative new programs, union leaders struggle to preserve the status quo and to help insulate workers against inflation.

Management, on the other hand, can show real determination to win back control over work rules and inefficient practices, which may be tolerated when business is booming but not when cost controls and productivity are so crucial.

What to look for:

• More of an effort to determine what employees want and to satisfy those needs before the issues come to the bargaining table.

• Issues of safety in the workplace, equal employment opportunity and just cause for discharge, raised by employees outside of any union structure.

Don't expect greater union participation in management, following the move by United Automobile Workers' leader Douglas Fraser onto the Chrysler board. Because the more labor leaders look like management, the more likely it is that the workers will see them as either suspect or superfluous.

The bottom line for management is to listen to and communicate more sensitively with today's workers. Look for ways to share profits and productivity gains with them. Avoid boss/worker class conflict that is often encouraged by union leadership. Using an ombudsman, for nonunion employees to handle individual worker complaints will generate an atmosphere of fair dealing.

Source: Bert Pogrebin, partner, Rains & Pogrebin, New York.

Where to look for give-backs

One recession strategy is to trade off wage increases for discontinuances of fringe benefits and restrictive work practices that may mean less to employees than money. Specifically:

• Permit key plant personnel to enjoy the benefits of superseniority to the same extent as union stewards.

• Eliminate restrictions on short out-of-classification assignments. It will mean greater productivity when part of the work force is laid off.

• Allow foremen and supervisors to do a limited amount of work in nonemergency situations.

• Dock employees for tools lost through negligence.

• Enforce surrounding-day work requirements for holiday pay, notwithstanding a past practice of negligent enforcement.

• Limit the number of paid sick-leave days. Require a doctor's verification in case of two or more consecutive days of illness.

• Discontinue the practice of automatic pay increases from the bottom to the top of each rate range. A better practice is to establish automatic increases to the midpoint and merit increases after that.

• Limit the number of hours per week stewards will be paid while conducting union business. Many of the steward's legitimate grievance-investigating functions can be conducted during breaks and lunch periods.

These points are also applicable to nonunion shops, which may have gone overboard on fringe benefits to remain competitive with organized plants or to discourage union organization efforts.

Watch the bylaws in a union agreement

A company's agreement with union officers to disregard a contract provision may be worthless if it isn't ratified by the rank and file. The basic question is "Does the union constitution or bylaws require membership ratification of the contract?"

For example, a company and union agreed that, despite a just-cause-for-discharge provision in the contract, drivers could be fired if they became uninsurable. A driver was later dismissed under this sidebar pact, but an arbitrator reinstated him because the new understanding had not been ratified.

The sidebar agreement approach is worth trying, especially if it relieves economic hardship. But be sure safeguards are taken to make the new deal stick. Get them in writing.

Piggly Wiggly Warehouse, 103 LRRM 2646.

Zipper clauses

The final touch in negotiating a union contract should be a completeness of the agreement clause (sometimes called a zipper clause). Typical language:

The parties agree that they have bargained fully with respect to all proper subjects of collective bargaining and have settled such matters as set forth in this agreement.

It's important to have the clause because months after a contract is signed, the union may want to negotiate again over a matter it raised and dropped during contract talks, or over a subject (sub-contracting, for instance) that may not even have come up in discussions. Refusal by the employer to negotiate may lead to an unfair labor charge. But the NLRB has said that a zipper clause is an effective reply to the union's complaint.

The clause does not defend a management effort to change working conditions without the union's consent.

ARBITRATION AND RULINGS

Virtues and drawbacks of nonbinding arbitration

Fast and relatively low-cost settlement of contractual disputes is arbitration's strong suit. When nonbinding, particularly, it also has these lesser-known uses:
- Tests merits of a case prior to litigation.
- Efficient, cheap form of pre-trial discovery.
- Settles disputes without establishing legal precedents.
- Shields internal documents and data from public disclosure.
- Identifies frivolous claims.
- Resolves complex technical, design, liability, or damage claims through the use of expert panels.

The basic drawback of nonbinding arbitration is that if parties don't approach it in good faith, and the matter ends up in court anyway, disclosures made during arbitration can be used against the company.

Source: Frederick C. Kirby, Ph.D., Kirby Research, Inc., Overland Park, Kans.

Arbitration strategy: meeting the surprise attack

All issues should be explored in the grievance procedure before they come to arbitration. But sometimes a union will hold back some evidence for its surprise effect at the arbitration hearing.

Object to the arbitrator's acceptance of material never discussed before. The arbitrator probably will let the union proceed. But the objection will alert him that the evidence had been withheld. He may give the evidence less weight in deciding the case.

If the surprise move puts management at a disadvantage, ask for adjournment of the hearing. Such a request will almost always be granted.

But don't confuse new evidence, which is frowned upon at the arbitration stage, with a different theory of the case. A different theory is to be expected if higher union officials become involved. Management's defense should be careful preparation, to anticipate every possible angle. The next step should be adjournment.

What arbitrators look for in attendance rules

Companies must meet four tests in order to dismiss a union employee for excessive absence, especially when the union contract has an arbitration clause. Most arbitrators want to see attendance rules that are: (1) reasonable, (2) well publicized, (3) applied accurately and consistently, (4) graded for progressive discipline. If these conditions aren't met, in most cases the employee will be reinstated.

One company failed to post its rules and was not allowed to fire a worker absent 33 of the preceding 104 working days.

Company rules concerning attendance must be posted and communicated. In addition, companies must make it clear that they intend to enforce the rules.

Source: Rhoda Rosenthal, "Arbitral Standards for Absentee Discharges," *The Labor Law Journal,* Chicago.

Trap for easygoing managers

If a company lets employees leave work early on slow days, it may find that it has waived its right to keep them on the job until quitting time when it really needs them. Case in point: a worker who asked to leave early because of a snowstorm was denied permission. The worker filed a grievance.

The arbitrator ruled that permission should have been granted, because the company traditionally let workers leave for golf dates and picnics. The arbitrator took pains to note that, if the company hadn't been so permissive, it would have been justified in keeping the employee from leaving.

74 LA 50.

Grounds for protest

Free coffee was provided to employees every day for 10 years. The company then ended the practice to cut costs. The union protested that the company was changing the terms of employment. But the company pointed out that free coffee was not mentioned in the contract.

The arbitrator ruled that the company had to bring back the coffee wagon and pay each worker $25 for the time there was no coffee.

The company had counted the cost of the coffee wagon when it computed the cost of the fringe benefit package it agreed to in the contract. So by cutting out the wagon, it had violated the contract.

Kansas City Board of Public Utilities, FMCS No. 81K/03599.

DEALING WITH UNIONIZED WORKERS

Healing election wounds

Union election wounds should be treated promptly. No matter which side wins, management must move quickly to make the peace. The best technique is to bring opposing sides together informally to discuss the future, not the past. Since organizers warn workers of reprisals, extending friendship to all parties undermines the credibility of the warning.

Never try to get even with employees who make personal attacks on management. Instead, seek them out. Express an understanding of their positions and actions and relationships are restored.

Source: George F. Truell, *Building and Maintaining Your Non-union Organization,* Drake Beam Morin Inc., New York.

Union-management committees

When setting up a joint worker-employer committee, don't put on the agenda only the objectives of management and the union leaders. Instead, survey workers to determine their real complaints.

This protects the committee from jumping right into a popular fad (such as job enrichment)

when the employees actually have a different set of issues they want discussed.

Source: Dr. David Sirota, president, Sirota and Alper Associates, management consultants, New York.

How to defuse workplace problems

Before putting money, hours, and fringe benefits on the bargaining table, listen to and do something about employee complaints. Workers who think management is being fair are less likely to strike.

Set up interviews with employees, hourly workers up through middle managers, in randomly selected and mixed groups. Select an upper-management representative who is not well known to the employees to conduct the sessions. Or choose an outside consultant. Have the office or plant manager sit in to answer questions and respond positively to complaints.

Do not permit any discussion of negotiable items such as pay or benefits. Instead, ask employees about safety, comfort, security, workflow, supervision, and absenteeism. Typical complaints include dirty restrooms, poor ventilation and heating, lack of communication between foremen, work stoppages, inefficient scheduling, not being listened to.

Be aware that strong evidence of us-against-them feelings about supervisors and management means a strike attitude. Appropriate action should be taken to correct deficiencies that are important to workers, even if they seem trivial to management. The cost of rectifying complaints is small compared to a strike.

Source: *Letting the Employee Speak His Mind,* Imberman & DeForest, management consultants, Chicago.

Resolve all the issues in a dispute

Settlements of disputes that could trigger complaints to the National Labor Relations Board don't necessarily work out as planned.

In a recent case, a fired worker claimed he was let go for unlawful reasons. After arbitrators reached a deadlock, management and a union representative (who had gotten the worker's permission to negotiate) worked out a compromise. The employee was given his old job back, but no back pay. The worker then filed an unfair labor-practices charge with the NLRB asking for back pay. . . and won.

The key elements were: (1) the private negotiations did not focus on the central issue of whether the firing was legal, and (2) the employee himself was confused about the terms of the settlement.

Nevertheless, still try to settle grievances privately. But, make sure that every disputed issue is settled. The employee, not just his representative, should agree to the terms.

It's harder to be nice when a union gets in

After signing a union contract, management may no longer make private deals with individ-

uals who need special consideration unless the union consents. This is a point employers might mention during pre-election organizing efforts by a union.

For example, an employee who had recently recovered from a heart attack asked permission to arrive late and leave early. The employer agreed and, as a matter of compassion and good personnel relations, did not reduce the man's pay. The union objected that it had been by-passed. An arbitrator agreed that management had erred.

Obviously, a union wants to be known as the source of all benefits. But management can still get credit for generosity by taking the initiative in approaching the union for exceptions.

Overtime pay when "locked out"

Several workers reported for Saturday overtime, but found the plant gates locked. Their supervisor had overslept. The workers waited 25 minutes and then went home. They expected to be paid for a full day's work, because the union contract stated that all workers who reported properly for overtime would be assured eight hours' pay.

The arbitrator decided the workers had acted unreasonably. They had not waited at the plant for a sufficient length of time. And, they had not tried to contact their supervisor to find out what was wrong. So they were entitled to only 1½ hours' pay.

Neapco Inc. (Pottstown, PA) and USA Local 2479, 286 AAA 6.

Promoting troublemakers

If union rules say that nobody with the authority to hire and fire may belong to the company union, pay special attention to troublemakers who are union members. Do this for a few months, then promote the troublemaker to a hire-and-fire position. That requires the troublemaker to resign from the union.

Frequently, this redirection of energies works well for both the company and the individual. If not, the troublemaker can be fired.

How to meet a union organizer's discrimination claim

Workers in a nonunion shop who are fired for misconduct sometimes run to the appropriate union and claim they were fired for their pro-union activities in violation of the Taft–Hartley Act. But even if management knows the workers are union activists, it can still fire them provided it proves just cause.

An important National Labor Relations Board citation* states: "The mere fact that an employer may desire to terminate an employee because he engages in protected activity [being allowed to try to organize union] does not, of itself, establish the unlawfulness of a subsequent discharge. If an employee provides an employer with sufficient cause for his dismissal by engaging in conduct for which he could have been terminated in any event, and the employer discharges him for that reason, the circumstance that the employer welcomed the opportunity to discharge does not make it discriminatory and therefore unlawful."

The key words are *sufficient cause for his dismissal.* The NLRB isn't likely to look favorably upon a company that discharges a union activist when a lesser form of discipline would be more appropriate.

Fikse Bros. (98 LRRM 1411).

Cutting the cost of discrimination settlements

Companies ordered to pay large sums in settlement of Title VII discrimination lawsuits can sue unions for a share of the costs. Behind the decision was the fact that discriminatory practices were mandated by union contracts.

Lawsuits against unions will probably be futile if the issue was discriminatory hiring, because hiring is usually a management function in which the union has no voice. Exceptions are referrals from union-administered hiring halls.

Northwest Airlines vs *Transport Workers,* 20 EPD Par. 30, 234 U.S. Court of Appeals for District of Columbia.

New hires and the union

Management can tell new employees in right-to-work states that they have the right to join, or not to join, the union. That's what an arbitrator (a law professor) ruled in a case involving a North Carolina company.

The union charged that the company changed the new-employee-orientation lecture to include the information that employees did not have to join the union. Result was a drop-off in union recruitment. The arbitrator ruled that the management's lecture, carefully prepared in advance, was an accurate statement of the law, even though it turned out to be disadvantageous to the union.

Management in this case did not permit supervisors to tell new employees what their legal rights were in their own words. Improvised remarks by supervisors are risky. A better practice would be to follow this successful company's practice of preparing information in advance and reading it to a group of new workers.

Owner's relatives and the union

Relatives of a company's owners start out in a low-level job to learn the business. They are not likely to be pro-union. Should they be allowed in the bargaining unit? It depends on how closely the relatives identify with management, a recent court decision said.

The Court of Appeals told the National Labor Relations Board to look at four factors: (1) How strongly the worker identifies with the owners. (2) Whether he has taken any part in union activities. (3) How often the family gets together. (4) How big a part of the bargaining unit relatives would be.

Linn Gear vs *NLRB,* CA 9th, 11/21/79.

Keep clerical workers out of the bargaining unit

Office and factory clerks can be excluded from union blue-collar bargaining units, if the white-collar workers don't have a "substantial community of interests" with the production work force.

In a recent case, the union tried to absorb two clerical workers on the ground that they already had the same vacations and economic benefits as the regular work force. This was not sufficient, said the court, because the clerical workers had different hours and duties. They also had a different pattern of contact with supervisors. They didn't think of themselves as part of the blue-collar unit.

It's usually wise for management to exclude clericals from bargaining units whenever possible. Even nonsupervisory clerks are often privy to information which employers prefer to keep out of the union's hands.

NLRB vs *Big Three Industries,* 112 LRRM 2135.

Unions may agree to delays in scheduled pay increases

Union dissidents sought to upset an agreement between the company and the union to delay a scheduled increase by arguing that the concession was really an illegal deduction of wages without individual written authorizations. But the court* ruled that deferring a wage increase is not an unauthorized deduction because the union won majority support by showing that more working capital for the company was essential for job security.

A union reluctant to make concessions may argue it cannot do so lawfully. But that is not true, as long as concessions are ratified in the same way the union contract was approved.

Bedecker vs *Food & Commercial Workers,* 8 CA, 24 WH 1239.

Union decertification

Management cannot give undue aid to employees who want to get rid of the union. It cannot encourage workers to circulate a petition against the union, write letters or make speeches.

What management can do is provide information on the decertification process, including the procedures to be followed and sources of assistance in preparing necessary documents.

Source: *The Hughes Report,* New York.

STRIKES

Benefits during a strike

When a company and a union settle a strike, they usually backdate the new contract to the day the old one expired, but the problem of how to handle employee benefits retroactively remains. Should workers be paid for holidays during the strike? Should they be able to collect for disabilities that began while they were out?

In general, labor laws say a strike does not terminate the employer-employee relationship. But companies can attempt to negotiate contract terms that hold down retroactive benefits.

Problem areas:

• Holidays. Companies that commonly give holiday pay to workers on layoff may be vulnerable to pressure for holiday pay during strikes. To avoid this, make holiday pay dependent on working the days before and after the holiday unless excused by management. (This allows workers on layoff to collect, but not strikers.)

• Vacations. Time off is usually based on years of service. Similarly, vacation pay may increase according to yearly incremental schedules. As a result, in a long strike, employees may make significant gains for time spent walking a picket line. To prevent this, base vacation pay on the previous year's work.

• Salary increases. State clearly whether strikes stop the clock for merit and regular salary reviews. The union will usually demand automatic increases. The company should relate raises to time on the job.

• Disability benefits. A worker will expect uninterrupted coverage from a backdated contract unless an exclusion is written into the new contract. An option is to exclude accident and sickness benefits for a disability that begins during the strike.

What a strike costs the company

The net earnings loss during the stoppage is a poor measure. Just the threat of a strike cuts productivity 2%–12% and causes customers to split orders or demand extra production.

Post-strike costs include loss of trained employees, catch-up overtime, customer defections, and reduced sales effectiveness. Average gross losses during a stoppage: $200 (if there are fewer than 100 production workers) to $300 (500–1,000 production workers) per man-day.

Source: Woodruff Imberman, Imberman and DeForest, Chicago.

PART VII

Personal Business

30 YOU AND YOUR FAMILY

THE FAMILY

Family and career: The right mix

Professionally successful men and women are often failures in their personal lives. Just as common are the underachievers in the office who have rewarding family and love lives. Successful executives who can balance their two lives are rare. Some common talents are needed to make each a success, but in general, many traits of successful executives work against them at home.

Business is goal-oriented in the sense that expectations are put on a schedule with emphasis on such end-products as promotion or money. By contrast, love, despite efforts to direct it, basically exists in the present for the sake of pleasure and well-being. Work also demands:

• Efficient use of time. But it is often difficult to quantify the value of time spent watching children play or caressing a lover.

• Organization. Life outside the office, however, usually works best when it is disorderly. For example, in order to grow, teenagers need an environment of change and expansion where they can assemble the pieces of their own personalities. Their development can be scuttled when a parent imposes too much order.

• Aggression and concentration. Love, on the other hand, is protective and spontaneous. In most cases, it just happens. And when it does, barriers are broken, not built.

Many people caught in the conflict between their professional and personal lives resolve it by alienating one or the other. It may take a crisis at home or work (suicide attempt, bankruptcy, etc.) to wake them up to the imbalance.

More observant executives sense over the years that something is fundamentally wrong. Marital satisfaction wanes, promotions are missed, or depression plagues their lives. There are no magic formulas for recognizing the problem, and solving it is even more difficult. The best approaches are to:

• Monitor your motivation. Ask yourself if you need to put in 15 hours a day at the office. Are you doing it to get away from your spouse or because you fear failing as a parent?

• Confront problems head-on. If you are angry at a co-worker or child, do not work off the anger by jogging. Instead, put your energies where they count—into finding a solution.

• Consider professional counseling. Even though you may have just recognized the full impact of the office-versus-home conflict, it is a familiar problem to most counselors.

• See yourself in perspective. There is probably no ideal balance between professional and private lives. But constantly striving for it can be one of the most rewarding aspects of both.

Source: Jay B. Rohrlich, M.D., *Work and Love: The Crucial Balance,* Summit Books, New York.

what each wants from the relationship, is an important step.

Source: Gisele Richardson, president, Richardson Management Associates, Montreal.

Dealing with changes in family relationships

The superbusinessman too seldom has a satisfactory family relationship. He has become a superbusinessman precisely because he has put all his energy and creativity into his work. Unfortunately, wives and children get what's left over and it's rarely enough.

Wives and children usually protest being shut out, by escalating problems to draw attention. This is particularly true of children, who may get into trouble at school, get sick, get pregnant, in order to produce problems so serious that father is forced to turn his attention to them.

Another sign of trouble is a precipitous increase in fighting between husband and wife, or a decrease. An increase means a buildup of resentments, and a decrease can mean that the couple is giving in to despair or boredom.

Problems could be prevented if the superbusinessman's wife has a life of her own, in which she engages in activities that are fulfilling. There would be less need to draw on her husband to provide fulfillment. Equally important is acceptance of the husband's needs for privacy and space. The superbusinessman should be able to come home and say: "I need time for *me* tonight, to do some unwinding. I'm going to sit by myself for an hour. Then I'll be able to relate to everybody from a comfortable space."

To deal with problems that arise, a professional therapist's help is recommended. By the time the husband has become a superbusinessman, the psychological "contract" made between himself and his wife when they were in their twenties is not likely to be valid any longer for either of them. A close examination of their current frame of reference and needs, and help in negotiating

Realities of family life

Even well-educated and informed parents harbor a great many wrong expectations about each other and their relationship with their children. Some of the harsher realities of families:

• There is little, or more likely, no room for personal separateness in a family with several children. People who need extensive space should avoid marriage. And if they marry, they should avoid having children.

• The attempt to build a family relationship solely around love is unreasonable. Families are meant to be a mutually protective society. They work best when members have problems.

• Many delinquent children misbehave just to punish their parents. Parents, in turn, often feel guilty and take their guilt out on the children.

• Problem children often have great difficulty mending their behavior within the family. Often, this is because their parents are the cause of many of their problems.

Source: Dr. Bruno Bettelheim, child psychologist, Stanford University.

Cooling down family fights

Dealing with emotionally violent situations within your family is one of the hardest things you will ever have to do since the peacemaker must be emotionally uninvolved. But when you deal with family members, there are always powerful emotional connections.

In a confrontation between a teenager and parents, one parent must step out of the fight and act as a negotiator. This involves sitting the other two down and listening to both sides. Say nothing while each is talking. Stop your spouse from cutting off the child. Restate what each one tells you, and always give each a chance to add comments. Problem: It will be difficult to convince the teen you are unbiased.

To end the fight, suggest a compromise solution. Phrase it carefully. (Example: Could we do this?) Both the child and the other parent must agree to accept the compromise, a date to start it, and the length of time the compromise solution will be tried.

When intervening in a fight between children, avoid making one right and the other wrong. Involve both. Say instead, "I think it is better if John does not do this, and I think it would help if Jim does not do that."

Source: Peter Martin Commanday, consultant and security expert, New York City school system.

Dividing chores in the two-income family

Family ties are strongest when both husband and wife share household responsibilities as well as contribute to economic needs, according to a survey of married men:
• 32% of the men shop for food.
• 47% cook for the family.
• 80% take care of children under 12.
• The majority of men said they directly influence the decisions about which brands of disposable diapers, pet food, bar soap and toothpaste to buy.

Source: Benton & Bowles, Inc., New York.

When both spouses work, a fair division of household tasks is crucial. One approach is to select the mutually most-hated tasks and hire someone to do as many of them as possible. Negotiate the remaining disliked jobs. Don't alternate jobs. That only leads to arguments about whose turn it is. Schedule quarterly or semiannual review for adjustments and tradeoffs.

Source: Nancy Lee, *Targeting the Top*, Doubleday & Co., New York.

Adoptions

Couples wishing to adopt a child in the face of today's baby shortage may have to wait as long as five years after applying. Waiting lists are so long that some agencies have stopped taking new applications.

In addition, obstetricians, who have traditionally served as intermediaries, are ducking requests for help from childless couples.

Flexibility and persistence improve a couple's chances. There are 100,000 children who, although legally available for adoption, are difficult to place because of age (average age: seven years), race (two out of five are part of a minority group), or disability.

Social agencies are paying more attention to the complexities of placing these unwanted children. Don't stop after an initial rejection. Try several agencies, and ingenuity.

Adoptee's reunion

Adults who were adopted as children now have a much better chance of reunion with their natural parents. A new resource is a computerized data bank, which matches natural parents and their offspring.

The service, Tracer's Reunion Registry, was started by a private investigation agency that had received numerous requests from adoptees looking for their natural parents (and occasional requests from parents who had put children up for adoption).

At the outset, more than 98% of the registrants were adoptees. Currently, there are more than 50,000 names on file, 40% of them natural parents. All registrations are voluntary, and only adoptees 18 or older are listed. Registrants must supply the adoptee's data and place of birth (usually available on birth certificates).

Source: Tracer's Reunion Registry, New York.

Make the family feel the trip is necessary and worthwhile to all concerned. And confront a spouse's jealousies directly. Don't let suspicions fester if there are doubts about the kind of business the trips involve, or the associates on them.

Source: *Business Traveler's Reports,* New York.

What to tell children before a business trip

Children resent business trips and private vacations taken by parents. They feel you would rather travel than be with them.

Explain the nature of your trip. Speculate on the problems they would encounter if they accompanied you.

Leave behind a list of activities for them to do while you are gone. Perhaps lend them the family camera for taking pictures of what they do. Stash little gifts they can open on different days during your absence. Give each child a bonus of spending money.

Another good idea is to tape yourself reading a few favorite stories. The children can play them when they feel lonely.

Source: Kay Kuzma, *Prime-Time Parenting,* Rawson Wade Publishers, New York.

Family morale for business travelers

Frequent business travelers should not keep telling their families how terrible it is to be on the road, because the more the business traveler honestly enjoys trips, the easier it is for a family to feel comfortable sharing priorities with the business. If the traveler really does hate the trips, family egos suffer from feeling that they rank even lower than the detested travel.

Teaching children the value of money

An appropriate timetable:

• Age 5. Start with a weekly or twice-weekly allowance of 50¢. (Regular expenses, such as school lunches or bus fare, would be in addition.)

• Age 10. Increase to $2.50–$3.00 weekly, allowing a small surplus that can be saved for future purchases.

• Age 13. Change to a monthly allowance and encourage the child to prepare a simple budget.

• Age 15. Children are ready to participate in family budget discussions. (But don't burden them with severe financial problems.) Handle their big expenditures (motorbikes, stereos, etc.) with loans. Don't set a schedule of steep payments that leaves the child with virtually no pocket money.

Keep the allowance in line with what other children receive. Too much money can make the child wasteful and guilty. Too little creates resentment.

Basic guidelines:

• Hold fast to the agreed sum. Exceptions should be rare and clearly identified.

• Encourage earnings. They are better than allowances and gifts. Don't pay for routine home chores. But do hire the kids for special work, instead of outside workers, as often as possible.

• Withhold or cut the allowance as a punishment only when the offense is directly related to misusing the money.

• Use money as a reward on a matching basis. For example, an improved report card earns a bonus equal to after-school earnings.

• Give praise when the child does well and keep criticism low-key and constructive. Expect mistakes, anger, and tears. This is a learning-by-doing process.

Source: *Your Money & Your Life,* AMACOM, New York.

The right school for your young child

The morning side of the street is preferred. That's a location on the right-hand side of a thoroughfare, which leads from a residential to a business area. This allows parents to enter and exit easily when they are dropping off their child in the morning. It's advantageous because people are so often late and hurried in the morning. And rush-hour traffic is a problem when trying to get to work on time.

Visit each school you're considering. Be wary of schools that try to sell themselves to you over the phone. The good ones will insist you judge their curriculum firsthand. Talk with the director and the staff members who will be involved with your child.

If possible, make surprise visits to the school at different times of the day after your child has been enrolled. If you're denied admission to areas you wish to see, be suspicious. A school should have nothing to hide from parents.

Ask to see the school's license, insurance contract, and health and fire department inspection forms.

Be sure that only approved persons can pick up your child at the end of the school day. The school should have a strict rule that if someone who is not on the list comes for the child, the parent should be called immediately.

Check cleanliness and hygiene.

Review the school's educational goals. The program should be designed to develop social, emotional, intellectual, and physical skills. See the teacher's lesson plans. Ask how discipline is enforced.

Observe the other children. Will they be compatible with yours?

Finally, ask yourself: "Could I spend a few years of my life here?"

What parents must know about choosing a college

The college entrance picture has changed markedly in the past few years—many good colleges now need students. However, competition for the 15 super-prestige colleges is more intense than before.

For most colleges it's okay to wait until the junior or beginning of the senior year in high school to start planning. But for those who want the top schools, start preparing during sophomore year, right after the Preliminary Scholastic Aptitude Test (PSAT) scores come in. They give a rough idea of how the student will fare in scholarship competition.

Students should write for college catalogs (also usually available in libraries or guidance counselors' office), and then analyze them to get an idea whether a college is right for their particular field of interest. Example, Harvard may not be the best place for would-be engineers.

A student interested in becoming a doctor should look at colleges that are strong in the biological sciences and have good track records for getting graduates into medical schools.

Although most college entrants don't know what they want to study, it's better for students to come to a college with at least some idea of what they want to study. If they're wrong, they can switch later.

Choosing a college is too important to be left entirely to a teenager. Parental assistance can be crucial. Parents can help by collaborating with the student's guidance counselor. Even the best high schools have too many students for guidance departments to service adequately.

Parental perspective is also important in helping choose the right college. Parents have an idea whether their offspring are independent enough to range around in a large state university or whether they'll do better in a smaller, much more personal college. Many students drop out in their first or second year, not because they can't make it academically, but because of discomfort with a particular college—too large, or too confusing, or the religious or social mix is too unfamiliar.

The most common mistakes parents make when helping their high-schoolers plan the future are pressuring children to go to a particular college for prestige reasons alone. Children then feel that the choice serves parents' needs rather than their own; picking a school beyond their child's capacities; and sending children to colleges too far from home before they're ready. Many high school seniors are just not mature enough to be moved far from home and parents.

Source: Max Birnbaum and James Cass, *Comparative Guide to American Colleges,* Harper & Row, New York.

When the kids leave home

After years of living with your children under one roof, their departure ends a phase in your life. Initially, most parents are pleased when children leave home for college or an out-of-town job. But after the pleasure subsides, the new reality needs to be examined.

What makes the problem serious is the parent's failure to realize that the parting is a signal that one chapter of their life is closed. The next chapter depends on how well they handle the transition.

First, say good-bye to the past without fear of grieving or of airing feelings of remorse, guilt and anger. Then, discuss with your spouse where you want to go in life.

To move closer together, couples should congratulate each other on how well they have done with the children; discuss resentments that have built up and start negotiating for changes; set aside time together to share activities and intimate conversation; and recognize that some interests are best pursued individually. Give each other leeway to do so.

Some essential questions to ask: How are you and your spouse really different from the way you were at the beginning of your marriage? What are the implications of those differences? To answer, take inventory of the bonds that connect you and your spouse—activities and interests, degree of intellectual closeness, physical attraction to one another, and the like.

It is especially important to assess the degree to which you have been nurturing or neglecting intimacy. One test of adequate intimacy is to find out how willing partners are to share both good and bad feelings. A common obstacle is willingness to share one or the other, but not both.

Too often, the presence of children masks a hollow marriage that is not worth salvaging. When this situation becomes apparent after children leave home, couples should discuss terminating the relationship.

Seek services of a therapist or counselor. They can provide the necessary objectivity and support that couples need to confront the prospect of separation. Couples should remember that the more valuable a relationship is, the more it is worth saving and the more useful counseling is likely to be.

Source: Gisele Richardson, president, Richardson Management Co., Montreal.

Motives for extramarital affairs

Discovering that one's partner has been unfaithful usually triggers a marital crisis. Often, the affair is a cry for help. Both partners may feel love and devotion for the other, but they are not facing basic problems.

Common hidden motives for having an extramarital affair:

• Unwillingness to confront the possibility of a breakup. Outside excitement takes the partner's mind off the real problem, which may be a lack of intimacy, respect, or sexual satisfaction in the marriage.

• Need for emotional support and courage to break up a weak marriage. Rather than risk being left alone emotionally, the partner looks for a new attachment in the form of an extramarital affair before walking out on the old one.

• Fear of intimacy. Some people find that commitment and intimacy provoke anxiety. The only way they believe they can tolerate marriage bonds is by savoring the feeling of freedom that affairs give them.

• Need to communicate resentment or anger toward the spouse indirectly.

To save the marriage, bring the underlying problem completely out into the open, with the declared objective of making the marriage work. Honestly confronting difficulties can divert the desire for extramarital sex and enable the couple to rework their marriage contract on a new basis. Marriages have been saved, and actually enhanced, by the resolution of an affair.

Source: Dr. Helen Singer Kaplan, psychiatrist, head of the Human Sexuality Teaching Program, New York Hospital-The Cornell University Medical College, New York.

Effect of divorce on careers

A troublesome divorce saps executives of initiative and diminishes their skills. Failing to recognize the emotional trauma of divorce may result in job loss or financial failure.

The roughest period is the first year of the divorce proceedings. Psychologists advise asking for a less demanding job, at least for the time the divorce is being contested. If you own the company, delegate more authority to key employees (which also helps their development).

One-fifth of executives in top echelons of major corporate hierarchies are divorced. Some psychologists predict that five years from now half of the chief executive officers of the 500 largest manufacturing companies will be divorced or separated.

All about "civilized" divorce

With more than 40% of all marriages in the U.S. now ending in divorce, many couples are trying to avoid knock-down drag-out court battles. One alternative is working out the terms of the separation or divorce themselves, with a minimum of outright adversarial conflict.

The motivations behind so-called civilized divorces vary widely but include the desire to reduce both the emotional stress on the couple (and their children) and the substantial cost of a conventional divorce.

Surprisingly, statistics show that most traditional divorce agreements are *not* kept, and most spouse-maintenance and child-support payments are *not* made over the long term.

But even civilized divorces entail tremendous pain and loss of self-esteem by both parties. These emotional problems often impede negotiation of an agreement that both individuals feel is fair and that they can live with.

If there is much hurt and hostility, seek therapy or counseling first, either individually or together. This is not marriage counseling—presumably, the couple is past the point of trying to save their marriage. But a mental-health professional can serve as a neutral third party to help the couple deal with the emotional conflicts and destructive behavior. That helps the couple become constructive, realistic and long-term oriented. Then the individuals can get on with working out their separation.

Mediation (not counseling) is a new approach available from teams combining mental-health experts and lawyers. New York's Postgraduate Center for Mental Health, for example, offers a divorce-mediation program (10–12 sessions long), which helps the divorcing couple deal with both emotional problems and economic matters, such as inventorying the assets accumulated during the marriage, developing information on current and future income, defining custody, visitation rights and responsibilities, and drafting the actual agreement. Mediation does not seek to resolve past conflicts but rather to solve the current problems of divorcing. And there is involvement throughout the process of a lawyer who works with both husband and wife and sees that neither is the "winner" (or "loser") but represents neither in the traditional adversarial sense. (This approach has been approved by the New York City Bar Association). The couple may, if they wish, have the agreement they write checked by other lawyers.

When going the do-it-yourself route, do not try to write the agreement completely on your own. Legal, tax, and accounting advice is necessary even in what looks like a simple divorce.

Establish a climate in which constructive discussions can take place. Keep the lines of communication open. Often, people who are separating do not talk to each other. Instead, they act out their feelings, such as using physical violence, taking the children away and denying the other parent the right to see them. These acts only worsen the situation for everyone concerned.

Recognize that you will always be parents even though you are not going to be husband and wife. Establishing reasonable communication early on will make it easier to keep talking in the future.

Source: Samuel Slipp, M.D., medical director, and Joan Langs, ACSW, director of the divorce mediation program, Postgraduate Center for Mental Health, New York.

Being single. . . again

Being involuntarily single after years of marriage can deal a serious blow to the ego. Essential to cushioning it is to start leading the single life immediately. Force yourself to make a date at least once a week, even if it is only having dinner with someone from work with whom a sexual encounter is a long shot.

But do not expect too much from yourself too soon. Scars of a broken marriage take at least a year, usually two, to heal. You are probably deluding yourself if you believe you are ready for a permanent relationship before that time.

Many brief sexual encounters are normal during this period, and they can be useful in rebuilding the ego. Do not be alarmed if periods of celibacy follow periods of sexual activity. These are also normal and useful in the healing process.

Older people are often surprised to discover that achievement makes them attractive to the opposite sex. But not only is prestige often an aphrodisiac, age itself is frequently attractive. But although younger people often have affairs with those older than themselves, usually they want permanent partners closer to their own age.

The emergence of transitional partners, with whom you form a nurturing though transitory relationship, often occurs during the first year of being single. This type of partner is also part of the healing process. You may feel guilty about breaking off the relationship, but do not. You may well be someone's transitional partner later one.

Your best chance for meeting new partners is in the normal course of business and social events. Also, however difficult it may be at first, ask your friends to introduce you to eligible acquaintances.

Once you have been introduced to a new person, avoid harping on your ex-spouse and introducing your new friend too quickly to your children. But while many dates will ask you to talk about someone other than your former spouse, many will enjoy hearing about children.

Sexual freedom and less formal lifestyles have greatly changed the etiquette of dating over the last few decades. A man should not be surprised if, after a few dates, the woman wants to reciprocate. And after a few dates, a woman should not hesitate to do so. Men should also realize that women make up their minds about sex more quickly today. A woman will not necessarily be thought of as loose if she decides to sleep with a man on the first date.

Much of the traditional courtship still works. Soft music, candlelight, and good food can still melt hearts. So can the grand gesture—an evening at the best spot in town, a spur-of-the-moment trip to Rome.

And although they may remind you of pain you would like to forget, it is essential to continue being a good parent to your children, maybe even a better one. Remember, the divorce or separation may have been harder on the children than on you.

As a result, children may take a keener interest in your new life and be curious to know about your new day-to-day routine. And after meeting some of your new friends, children may even suggest that one of them seems especially marriageable.

Sometimes they are right.

Source: Richard Schickel, *Singled Out,* Viking Press, New York.

DEALING WITH PARENTS

Helping parents with money problems

An executive's parents are faced with inflation and rising home maintenance bills. They refuse to sell their house and are too proud to take outright gifts from their offspring. What can the executive do?

One solution might be to consider a nonamortized bank loan for the parents, using the house as collateral.

How it works:

• The executive negotiates a loan from a bank where a minimum balance equal to the principal of the loan is kept.

• The parents pay interest on the loan and the executive arranges for the principal to be paid back after the parents die and the house is sold.

• With the loan, the executive buys annuities for the parents to supplement their income.

For example, a mother is 65 and has a $120,000 house with no mortgage. She gets a loan from her son's bank for 80% of the house's net value ($96,000), at 15% interest. With the money, she buys a 20-year annuity that pays 15% interest. The annuity covers her interest payments and provides her with $1,000 a month. And by borrowing on the house, rather than selling it, the woman and her family hold onto its appreciation value.

Troubled parent and adult-child relationships

Parent and adult-child relationships that depend too much on rewards and punishments make both sides unhappy. If two or more of the following statements are true about how you think of your parents, problems are brewing.

• I let my parents have their way even though I know this is wrong.

• When I do something that my parents disapprove of, I feel very guilty.

• No matter what I do, I cannot get my parents to see what my problems are.

• I try to anticipate every need that they have.

• I am always fighting with my parents, but I know we love each other.

• I wish they would think about me sometimes instead of only themselves.

• I know they order me around, but that is really very good for me.

Source: Carol Flax and Earl Ubell, *Mother, Father, You: The Adult's Guide for Getting Along Great with Parents and In-laws,* Wyden Books, Ridgefield, Conn.

Coping with visits to elderly parents

Many adult children are reluctant to visit their elderly parents, particularly when the family relationship has been ridden with conflicts. Problem parents are likely to become more so as they age. One who has always been a guilt provoker, excessively demanding, or inclined to play the martyr's role, will likely be more demanding and guilt-provoking when the losses and miseries of old age provide even more reason.

Seeing parents aged and infirm threatens adult children by reminding them of the approach of their own old age and of their own mortality. (Most people with aged parents are usually middle-aged and most susceptible to these fears.)

Also, parents' aging usually reverses the parent-child role. The dependency and frailty of old parents, whether physical or psychological, may make them assume childlike roles. Adult children, in turn, experience a sharp loss because they now are forced to recognize that their parents are not there for them to turn to when they're in need.

To deal with the feelings of reluctance, remember that a mature, parental response on your part is now in order. However enraged or frustrated you are by a parent's behavior, accept that a role reversal has taken place. The parent now is actually dependent and helpless in some way and is not the same old antagonist you remember from early-childhood conflicts.

The key to controlling feelings of rage is:

Compassion. Age brings with it feelings of fright and loneliness.

Visit regularly, so that parents can plan and look forward to the arrival. Remember, though, some parents lead busy, extremely independent lives and may not want too many visits from children.

When going away for an extended period, inform your parents of your return date; when they can expect to hear from you and how often you'll be in touch.

It is important to remember that visiting parents should not be accommodated at the expense of your own adult priorities. Excessive guilt often pushes children into running themselves ragged visiting parents often. And too much indulgence of a parent's wishes, or treating a parent as an infant, can impair the parent's will to go on assuming responsibility for his or her own life. Avoid placating behavior, which is a hangover from the childhood relationship. A realistic and caring attitude is better.

During the visit, listen to a parent's problems, but also try sharing concerns of your own (if they are not overwhelming) with them. Many parents would like to feel themselves still capable of giving advice and of having authority.

Source: Dr. Howard Halpern, *Cutting Loose: An Adult Guide to Coming to Terms with Your Parents,* Simon & Schuster, New York.

Taking care of aging parents

Elderly people suffer emotionally and physically when facing dramatic changes. Ideally, preserve their daily routines and environment as long as possible, even in the face of growing infirmities.

Placement in nursing home should be the last resort. The strain of the move, plus sudden provisions of services which elderly are still capable of providing for themselves, speeds their decline.

The best overall approach is to prolong independent functioning by whatever combination of means necessary.

Steps to take before considering nursing home:
• Hire a cleaning person to come in once a week.
• Arrange with another elderly but healthier neighbor to share meals or visit daily.
• Sign up for *Meals on Wheels* delivery of hot meal daily.
• Register at neighborhood senior citizens center.
• Schedule frequent visits from individual grandchildren.
• Find a smaller apartment with fewer stairs in the same building.
• List local stores that deliver phone orders.
• Familiarize parents with local public transportation routes.
• Purchase a pet as a present that provides company and diversion. The pet should require minimal care.

Set definite limits on your own direct involvement in parents' lives. Adult children who help parents only from a sense of duty pay a price—both in their own resentment for the inconvenience and in their parents' feeling that they are a burden. Instead, assume the role of creative coordinator. Involve a variety of others (neighbors, relatives, social agencies, friends, hired help) who can perform the jobs as well, and perhaps more cheerfully.

Source: Dr. Stephen Z. Cohen and Dr. Bruce Michael Gans, *The Other Generation Gap: The Middle Aged and Their Aging Parents,* Follett Publishing Co., Chicago.

Some alternatives to nursing homes

• Adult day-care centers. They offer one meal a day, transportation to and from medical appointments and various programs to keep people healthy and alert. Get more information from your state's Department of Social Services.

• Congregate homes. Apartment buildings or clusters of detached homes provide low-cost rental housing and essential services for elderly people who need minimal day-to-day help. Eligibility is based on income. For more information contact your local area office of the U.S. Department of Housing and Urban Development.

• Home care. Services include convalescent care, nursing, household maintenance and meals-on-wheels. Most programs are run by the state or the community.

Source: Joseph Michaels, *Prime of Your Life,* Quarto Marketing, New York.

31 YOUR HOME AND AUTOMOBILE

THE HOME

Financing your home

If purchase is contingent on the sale of another property, don't go forward until the commitment on the sale is airtight. With money tight, chances of getting stuck and having to carry two houses are greater than they've been in years.

The best place to look for money—builders or developers who have prior commitments from mortgage lenders. Rates may be more favorable than the current market. Same goes for condominium converters and developers. Most of the big ones have at least standby commitments for financing. But these funds will soon be running out.

The next best bet—the seller. This works in several ways. It is still sometimes possible to assume a mortgage, although many in the past ten years were written with an "acceleration clause," making the outstanding amount due immediately if the house is sold. Even with such a clause, sometimes the loan can be left in the name of the original borrower (who must, of course, consent to remain responsible), and the house can be bought "subject to" that first mortgage held by the seller.

Sellers often can afford to advance some or most of the purchase price themselves. This is called a "purchase loan" or "buying on contract." Each deal is tailor-made. The whole arrangement is totally negotiable. Much depends on the seller's financial condition and eagerness to sell the house.

Generally, purchase loans are short term, one to five years. They give the buyer that much time to make a better long-term mortgage. Typically, monthly payments would be amortized as if they were for a 20- or 25-year payout, with a balloon at the end of the contractual period making the remaining loan due at that time. And some banks are offering similar deals in which the borrower can refinance his mortgage within, say, five years without penalty.

New techniques for buying a home

The long-term, fixed-rate mortgage is still the best deal around for would-be homeowners who can afford it, and can find a lending institution that will offer one.

The problem is how to cope with the current

high interest rates. Alternatives to the traditional fixed-rate mortgage:

• Shared down payment. Among others, Home Partners of America* offers a program in which it puts up 75% of the down payment. In return, the buyer pays the company an 8%–10% return on its capital in monthly installments. In addition, the company gets half the gain in value.

• Investor participation. In the major version of the technique, Ticket Corp.* pairs up investors and prospective home buyers. An investor usually puts down 20% of the purchase price and owns the house jointly as tenants-in-common with the occupant. When the house is sold, the investor and the owner/occupant each get 50% of the gain in value. The occupant pays all carrying costs. If either tenant-in-common dies, the interest goes to their heirs, not the other tenant.

• Land rental. In some cases, separating ownership of the house from the land reduces the price of the former so that less down payment is required.

For example, a $100,000 house might qualify for only an 80% mortgage. But if it's split off from the $20,000 lot, the now $80,000 house may qualify for a 90% mortgage. Under most plans, an investor buys the land and rents it to the homeowner on a long-term lease.

New mortgage plans:

• Graduate payment mortgage (GPM). It's now eligible for Federal Housing Administration insurance. GPMs offer lower payments in the early years when income is low. They increase later when higher income is anticipated.

• Variable-rate mortgage. Interest rates are adjusted every third or fifth year to parallel the national trend. Although there is usually an interest ceiling, as rates soar, so do carrying costs.

• Shared-appreciation mortgage. In return for low interest rates, the lender shares in the gain in value when the house is sold. Example: A lender might cut the interest rates by a third in exchange for a third of the gain in value. This is the least desirable alternative to the standard mortgage. It is potentially the most expensive of all mortgages.

*Home Partners of America is at 520 South Ave W., Westfield, N.J. 07090. Ticket Corp., an equity participation firm, is located at Box 26338, San Jose, Calif. 95159.

Source: Thomas L. O'Dea, O'Dea and Co., Inc., Winston-Salem, N.C.

Kick-out clause keeps home sellers flexible

Selling a house can be a problem when the potential buyer makes the deal contingent on the sale of his own house. After waiting for months, your deal may fall through.

If you include a kick-out clause in the sales agreement, this enables the seller to keep the house on the market until the sale is completed. If another buyer makes an offer, the original buyer has 48 hours to decide whether he wants to buy the house or not.

Family partnership for home purchases

A family partnership may be the best way for many people to buy a home—certainly a lot better than asking relatives for loans.

To make it work, form a partnership in which relatives participate in raising the cash for the purchase price. At some future date, the house is sold or refinanced and the proceeds used to pay off the partners, including a share of any profit.

It differs from a loan in that the partnership, not the resident, owns the house. Each partner has equity participation. Also, profits may be treated as capital gains. Interest earned on a loan would be taxable as ordinary income. An added benefit to the buyer is that no payments are due until the house is sold or refinanced.

Source: *Real Estate Investing Letter,* New York.

The cautious way to buy a condominium

Vacationers will be thinking once again this year about buying condominiums. Condo units are also becoming more attractive to couples moving back to urban centers.

But don't buy on impulse. Experience in buying and selling several single-family homes doesn't alert you to all the things to look for in a good condo deal.

Your lawyer must read the covenant of condominium (also called the master deed or declaration of condominium). Clauses in a covenant are non-negotiable: all participants must have the same wording. There are traps that could make it more desirable to walk away from the whole deal.

• Resale restrictions. The condo association (the governing body of owner representatives that owns and maintains common areas such as hallways, parking lots and swimming pools) may have a 30-, 60-, or 90-day right of first refusal. That delay could cost you a sale. Be advised that Federal Housing Administration, Veterans Administration, and other government-insured mortgages are not available when there are certain resale restrictions. Your resale market could be cut significantly.

• Use restrictions. Does the covenant permit owners to rent their units? If you are buying the condo as an investment, you must be able to rent. If you are planning to live in a unit, you may want this restriction. Other use restrictions may concern children, pets, window decorations, even the type of mailbox you can put up.

• Sweetheart deals. The most common one is when the developer owns the common areas and leases them back to the association. Such leases are usually long term and include escalator clauses and pass-alongs that could cause big jumps in your monthly association fees. In other cases, the developer does not own the common areas, but has a long-term contract to manage them. The best deal for the buyer is when the condo association owns all the common areas. All management agreements with the condo association should strictly control costs and contain termination provisions.

Potential problems that won't show up in the covenant:

• Subsidized fees. Developers of newly built condos often manage common areas for a fee until most of the new units are sold. To speed sales, the developer may keep the management fee below cost. Then, when the condo associa-tion assumes management, the owners' monthly costs soar. It is prudent to check fees charged by similar condo associations in the same area.

• Construction problems. Before you buy, have an engineer inspect the condition of the entire property, if feasible, not just your unit. Reason: If the condo association has to make repairs, you will be assessed for the cost. If you are buying a unit in a converted building, ask the condo salesperson for the engineer's report. Most converted buildings need one to obtain financing.

The best times to buy are when prices are lowest during the pre-construction sale of new units, or early in the conversion of a building. But if you buy too soon, you could end up as one of the few owners. As long as units remain unsold, your investment will not appreciate. Check the price and demand for similar units in the area.

Source: Thomas L. O'Dea, O'Dea and Co., Inc., Winston-Salem, N.C.

Selling your house when credit is tight

As mortgage rates remain high, an increasing number of homeowners are enticing buyers with offers to finance the sale themselves. By offering financing, sellers may make their house so marketable that outside financing will be unnecessary. And the commission saving is substantial.

However, although financing the sale of a house is simple in principle, sellers should have the advice of a lawyer who specializes in real estate.

Four basic methods:

• First mortgage. If you are trying to sell a $100,000 house that has no mortgage (a rarity), and the purchaser can afford only $40,000 cash down, then the purchaser simply gives you a first mortgage for $60,000, which is paid out over an agreed-upon period, at an agreed-upon interest rate. In case of default, you keep the cash and foreclose on the house.

• Second mortgage. If you are trying to sell the same $100,000 house with an existing $50,000 first mortgage, a second mortgage reduces the cash that a buyer would need. The purchaser assumes the first mortgage and gives you a $20,000 down payment. The purchaser then gives you a second mortgage for $30,000. Interest rate and maturity date are negotiable. But many existing first mortgages held by institutional lenders contain a due-on-sale clause, which prohibits the sale of the house without the consent of the lender. Typically, such consent is given only if the interest rate is substantially increased.

• Wrap-around. Similar to second mortgages. Using the same numbers as in the second-mortgage example, you get a $20,000 down payment, but instead of taking back a $30,000 second mortgage, you take back an $80,000 wrap-around mortgage (the amount of the first mortgage plus the remaining $30,000 of the sales price). One advantage is that defaults are quick to catch because the buyer makes all payments directly to you, and you pay the first-mortgage portion to that lender. Another advantage is that the interest rate on the wrap-around is calculated on the entire $80,000, even though the $50,000 first-mortgage portion may be at a lower interest rate. Therefore, you receive the interest average, giving you a higher yield on your $30,000 portion.

• Leasing with purchase option. Lease payments may be applied to the purchase price, an amount ageed on when the deal is made. The best approach is to make the term as short as possible. Should another prospective buyer come along with ready cash, you won't be hindered by a long-term contract. And since you are still the owner, you can depreciate the house as a rental unit.

Source: C. Gray Bethea Jr., vice president and general counsel, CMEI, Inc., Atlanta.

When the new house is a lemon

A buyer may be able to get out of the entire purchase contract if the seller has misrepresented a house with many serious defects.

Normally, when defects show up after the buyers move in, they can sue for damages. Some state courts have ruled that two reasons for suing to void the entire sale are misrepresentation of an important aspect of the house and the presence of many serious defects.

In one case, the builder had assured the buyer there would be no water problem. But the house was flooded soon after the closing. The court said the related damage would be impossible to repair.

Source: *Chastain* vs *Billings,* 570 S.W. 2d 866.

Vacation-home tax traps

Don't be taken in by unreliable reports about writing off all of the expenses of a vacation house as business deductions on next year's federal taxes.

What can be written off on personal returns:
• Interest costs for the mortgage.
• All local property taxes.
• Casualty losses.

To deduct more (such as total utility costs, insurance, maintenance, and depreciation), the homeowner cannot occupy the property for more than 14 days or 10% of the total days available for rental. In addition, the property must be actively marketed for rentals. The IRS won't accept an unsubstantiated claim that the place was offered but no prospective renters came to look at it.

In cases of limited personal use, the business renting the house can show a loss that offsets other income if a profit appears in two of five years.

When personal use is 15 days or more, depreciation and other deductions are prorated between personal and business use. But that's only up to the income actually received from the rentals. Income from other sources cannot be sheltered.

For example, a couple jointly owns a beach-front vacation home. The vacation season for rentals is four months. They occupy the premises for one of these months, and rent it for the other three. Mortgage interest: $3,000 annually. Taxes: $2,000. Rental income: $3,000 per month ($9,000 for the season).

Step one is to deduct interest and taxes ($3,000 plus $2,000) from the gross rent ($9,000), leaving $4,000. That's the maximum amount that can be offset by expenses as follows:

	Personal use ¼	Rental use ¾
Maintenance ($2,000)	$ 500	$1,500
Utilities ($1,600)	400	1,200
Misc. ($2,000)	500	1,500
Depreciation ($5,000)	1,250	3,750
Total	$2,650	$7,950

Result: $3,950 of the cost attributable to the rental use is not deductible.

If, on the other hand, the couple occupies the house for only 12 days (10% of 120 days available for rental) they could deduct the full amount of losses, as long as the venture showed a profit in at least two of five years. Otherwise, the IRS says, the venture is really not a business engaged in for profit, and no losses in excess of income can be deducted.

Supporting documents. Most important are written rental agreements or leases. Also helpful: A journal, restaurant and gasoline receipts, and so on, to record the owner's use of the property.

Use by relatives or employees. Use by family members, even a rarely seen brother-in-law, is considered personal. Either have the relatives use the property at the same time you do, or charge them the full market rent. Also considered as personal use by any member of a partnership or by an S corporation that owns the property.

Combined rental and living spaces. Housing, such as a small hotel with owner's quarters attached, can garner solid deductions, including depreciation, on that portion of the property actually used for rentals. This principal also applies to property that changes status in a given year.

For example, a doctor who had a combined home and office moved to bigger living quarters late in the year. He kept the old office, however, and rented the former living quarters to another family. Full deductions could be taken on the area rented out.

Rarely rented vacation homes. Income from renting a property for less than 15 days does not have to be reported to the IRS. But then deductions for expenses connected with the rental can't be taken.

House-swapping is counted as personal use time for the owner, even if the owner pays rent for the use of the property that the owner gets in exchange.

Example: A city couple swaps houses with country friends. The country home is larger, so the city couple pays rent to equalize the deal. The time the country friends spend in the city counts as personal time against the city folk.

Source: Sideny Kess, partner, Main Hurdman & Cranstoun, New York.

Ways to cut the cost of moving

• Schedule the move between October and May, or around the middle of the month, the moving companies' slack periods. Better and faster service can save as much as 10%-15% of cost.

• Reduce poundage involved in the move by selling or giving away unneeded items. (Give to charity and keep receipts for later tax deductions.)

• Collect refunds due from local utilities before leaving.

• Arrive at the new location before the van does to avoid charge for waiting time.

• Have enough money to pay the exact amount of the estimate plus 10%. That's the maximum customers can be required to pay before goods will be released. Payment must be made in cash, or in certified or traveler's check. A personal check may not be accepted. Get a receipt!

Useful ICC publications include: *Household Guides to Accurate Weights; Arranging for Transportation of Small Shipments; People on the Move;* and *Lost or Damaged Household Goods.*

Source: *How to Move Your Family Successfully,* H.P. Books, Tucson.

Living through a home renovation

Remodeling has become even more important recently because of high purchase prices and mortgage interest rates and the growing trend toward restoring old homes nearer to city centers.

Too many people have an idealized notion of what a renovation entails. To minimize frustration and disappointment, recognize from the start that the project will:

• Cost more than you expect. You may find that you are paying much more than your neighbor paid to remodel just two years ago. Add 20% to the most conservative estimate.

• Take longer than you have been told it will. Assume that everything that can go wrong will.

• Be more disruptive to family members' lives than you can possibly imagine. Renovating, especially if several rooms are involved, is very messy. And there is no way to make it neat.

Once your expectations are realisitic, you can begin to minimize the discomfort. The best defense is to move out (or don't move in) while demolition and other heavy work are going on. If you must live in the middle of a renovation:

• Complete as much work as possible in summer. At that time, you can send children to camp or to visit relatives. Workers can leave bulky supplies and equipment outside. Don't hold off until winter in the expectation that it will cost less because it's off-season. Interior renovation goes on all year long. And prices seem to go only up.

• Use a professional you can communicate with and trust to get the job done in a reasonable period. This could be an architect, architect-builder, builder-designer, or designer-contractor. The most important qualification is rapport with you. The problem with some architects is overoptimism, which can take the form of not leveling with clients about how time-consuming, costly and messy the project will be.

If you have a competent supervisor, stay away from the house as much as possible.

Be realistic in deciding what to have professionals do and what to do yourself. Almost all the jobs required in a remodeling can be done by an intelligent, reasonably handy amateur. Few are exceptionally difficult. But each task can take an enormous amount of time, in some cases months, especially if you hold down a full-time job.

Use experienced workers for heavy work such as demolition, basic carpentry, wiring, plumbing and masonry, floor scraping and refinishing.

If you want to cut costs by doing some things yourself, stick to wall-papering, painting, wood-stripping, sanding, tiling (vinyl, asbestos, ceramic), and laying parquet-wood floor squares (messy, but not hard).

To find the best skilled workers, get names from the previous owner of the house or apartment, neighbors, realtor, bank.

Remember the basics:

Do the remodeling in stages. Get a couple of rooms finished, clean, and livable quickly. The best first choice are children's rooms. Children are very adaptable, but they do best when they know where their clothes and toys are. It helps, too, if they have a place to play that keeps them out from underfoot while the rest of the work goes on. If the renovation is easy on the children, the parents will have it easier, too.

Make sure supplies and workers are ready at the same time. This is especially important when doing the kitchen. If the job is well coordinated, you will be without a functioning kitchen for only two weeks. Remember to order cabinets well ahead. If they are custom-built, plan a six-to-eight-week leadtime. Don't tear out wiring and plumbing until you know the cabinets are on the way.

Keep the place relatively clean. Sweep up every evening, even if the workers are coming back the next day to make a new mess. You will feel better. When bedrooms are being redone, move all your clothes and belongings out. Even if you put your things in drawers, the plaster dust will inifiltrate.

Every week or so, invite friends over. If there is no place to sit, spread a tablecloth on the floor and have a picnic. If there is no kitchen, serve takeout food.

Source: Richard Rosan, president, Real Estate Board of New York.

Dealing with home-improvement contractors

The key to protecting yourself when hiring a contractor for a major alteration is thoughtful contract negotiation. Even contractors with good reputations sometimes get in over their heads. It's especially important now that improving the home has become more attractive than buying a new one.

Consider an attorney when:

• The job is very complicated or expensive.

• Modifications to an existing house will require the structure to be open to the weather for an extended period.

• The nature of the property (swampy, rocky) makes unforeseen difficulties likely.

• A thorough check on the contractor's references is impossible.

Be specific about what work you want done, how, and with what materials.

Don't settle for normal contract language about the project being done in "a workmanlike manner," because homeowners' standards for work they want done is often higher than common trade practice.

To avoid misunderstandings, refer in the contract to architect's drawings, where possible, and actual specifications.

Include a schedule against which to measure work's progress. Use calendar dates, for example, foundation and framing to be completed by March 1; roughing-in by April 1; sheetrock by May 1; woodwork and finish work by June 1.

Push for a penalty clause if the work is completed unreasonably late. For example, all work to be completed by June 1. If, however, work is not completed by June 1, the contractor will pay the homeowner $100 a day thereafter.

Include a payment schedule in the contract. Typically, a contractor gets 10% of the negotiated fee upon signing a contract, then partial payments at completion of each stage of succeeding work.

Your aim should be to withhold any payment until contractor actually begins work on your house. Then hold down succeeding payments as much as possible, so that contractor does not earn his profit until his work is completed.

Make the contractor responsible for abiding by local building codes. If you assume this responsibility, make the contract contingent on your ability to get all necessary building permits. Make sure the final payment is contingent upon approval of the work by municipal inspectors.

Work out procedures to amend the contract. If an unforeseen problem crops up (for example, subsurface boulders obstruct the laying of a new foundation), or if the contractor honestly underestimates his costs, it will be necessary to renegotiate terms. If you try to hold a contractor to unreasonable terms, he will cut corners, stall, or walk off the job.

The contract should have a clause that describes how changes will be made. Typically, all changes above $100 must be agreed to in writing by both parties to the contract.

Contrary to popular myth, an attorney is not necessary to modify a contract. Just write on a separate sheet "Notwithstanding anything else in the contract to the contrary, we agree as follows...(specify the contract modification)." Then, both parties sign the modification.

If the contract submitted by a contractor contains provisions for financing your home-improvement project, cross them out.

Always do your own financing. Terms of lenders working with contractors are usually stiff. Often they give the lender a second mortgage on your house—sometimes without your realizing it. That can leave the homeowner without leverage to force correction of bad workmanship.

Getting out of a contract. It's possible to insert a clause saying what damages you will pay if you cancel a project before work begins. But once work does begin, you should see it through to completion. Courts favor contractors in cases where homeowners want to break off a project halfway through.

Insurance. The contractor should show you the document from his insurance company covering workers' compensation. Standard homeowners' policy does not cover workers (except, in some states, an occasional babysitter). Also fix responsibility for repairing wind, rain, or fire damage as well as possible vandalism at worksite.

Source: Birger M. Sween, attorney, Hackensack, N.J.

How to buy energy savers

Well beyond the most optimistic expectations, Americans have become energy conservers in their homes. The average household has cut energy-use costs by about 16% from pre-energy-crisis levels. Most of the savings to date are from a change in life-style (shortening the heating season, lowering the temperature, shutting off the lights), rather than from new equipment. But new equipment is coming on stream that makes energy conservation even more attractive. Consider new heating systems that are 50% smaller than current ones, with the same heating ability. They are 40% more efficient in reducing the heat lost up the chimney than the old ones. Also available are vastly improved heat pumps, so efficient they eliminate the need for any chimney in the warmer areas of the country where heat pumps are most suitable.

The price range of new equipment is $2,000–$4,000. But now is not the time to start buying the brand-new untested technology. Wait until less reliable products are shaken out of the market by the new developments.

• If improvements must be made soon, consider some cost-effective burners and hot water heaters being imported from Germany and Italy.

• Don't get into the fuel-switching game. Instead invest in add-ons such as hot-water temperature modulators. They raise or lower water temperature according to the weather and can save 10% on fuel costs (leading brands: Enertrol, Mastermind.) Or save up to $100 a year by not heating water overnight. Use a simple switch-timer that turns off heater at night and turns it on to warm up water for early-morning showers.

• Invest in a new heating system if it has a federal label guaranteeing 85% efficiency.

For bigger buildings, don't rush to buy a computerized energy-saving system that's being sold with high promises. Shop around. Get the advice of an expert engineering consultant.

It is usual for the consulting firm to perform an energy audit. Then, if after five years, the customer does not save on energy costs an amount equal to the fee paid for the original consultant, the entire fee is refunded. More and more, firms now provide consultation for a percentage of the saving.

Source: David Hall, Hall & Mackey Marketing, Inc., Portland, Me.

Energy-saving tips

Some simple energy-saving practices can be surprisingly effective in cutting household fuel bills. Examples:

• Turn down the thermostat. For every one degree you set the thermostat back, your fuel saving per heating season will average 3%. Add to that by regularly cleaning the heat and cool-air-return vents.

• Shed more light. Desk and reading lamps are more efficient than room overhead fixtures. Maximize light reflection within each unit. Clean light bulbs as well as fixtures frequently.

• Turn off what needn't be on. Is the coffee machine or percolator running 12 or even 24 hours a day? In the cellar, is the hot-air blower constantly on rather than switching off-on in concert with furnace controls? How about stereos and lights? Consider light-dimmer switches, to enhance the ambience and save up to 10%.

• Use fluorescent light where its harshness can be tempered by incandescent bulbs and daylight. Generally, fluorescent lamps save half the cost of incandescent per light yielded. However, in very high wattages, incandescents are more efficient.

• Planning a new house. The basic idea is to hold in what heat is generated, by means of superinsulation, for example triple-glazed windows; heavy fiberglass layers in floors and ceilings; for all exterior walls, double-wall construction (spaces filled with insulation); air-infiltration barriers attached to framing lumber; and air-to-air heat exchangers. Done correctly, the extra costs can be paid back in fuel savings in as little as 18 months.

Superinsulation can slash fuel bills

Energy-conscious contractors in the United States and Canada are building homes that require little or no gas, oil, or electricity for space heating. Cooling bills, too, are greatly reduced. Superinsulation maintains temperatures by using the heat generated by appliances, lights, water heaters, even human bodies. Modest backup heaters are usually available too.

Cost range: 1%–3% above standard building expenses, including land. The key elements are:

• Solar orientation along the north-south axis. Most solar windows are on the southern wall, where incoming sunlight provides maximum direct heating.

• Triple-glazed windows for heat retention without loss of light or views.

• Heavy insulation in all floors and ceilings.

• Double-wall construction for all exteriors, the large inner cavities filled with insulation.

• Air-infiltration barrier of 6-mil-thick polyethylene sheet fastened to framing lumber during construction. The barrier prevents heat leakage and keeps condensation from reducing effectiveness of insulation.

• Air-to-air exchanger located at the point where stale air is drawn out and fresh air in, it transfers 80% of outgoing heat to the incoming air.

• Entrance hallways at doors to baffle and help contain icy blasts.

Designs of superinsulated homes differ little from conventional houses, except for the concentration of windows on the south wall.

Superinsulated homes in Springfield, Va., average 230 gallons of fuel oil a year for heat, in comparison to 1,200 gallons for neighboring homes. The payback period is approximately 18 months.

Source: *Civil Engineering,* New York.

Energy credits for homeowners

Residential energy tax credits totaling $4,300 are now available to homeowners, tenant stockholders in cooperatives, and members of condominium management associations. Credits are worth more to the taxpayer than an equal amount in deductions because credits reduce the tax bill on a dollar-for-dollar basis. The credits are available only for work that is done on the taxpayer's principal residence.

How the energy credits work:

• Renewable energy credit is available for 40% of the first $10,000 spent on alternative energy systems, such as wind, solar and geothermal power. (Maximum credit: $4,000.) The cost of labor used to install the system is included when computing the credit. Typical qualifying items are solar collectors, heat exchangers, and windmills.

• No credit is available for wood burning systems or for the cost of a conventional furnace that is used to back up a renewable-energy system.

• Passive solar-energy systems are a problem area. These systems use south-facing windows to catch the sun, massive masonry walls to retain heat, awnings and draperies to provide shade. The energy credit is available only for those elements of a passive system that serve no other decorative or structural function. A masonry wall is not eligible for the credit. But glazing on the wall is eligible. Other ineligible items are windows, skylights, greenhouses, awnings, and drapes.

• Conservation credit: 15% of the first $2,000 spent on insulation and other means of energy conservation. (Maximum credit is $300.) Typical qualifying items are storm windows and doors, caulking, weather stripping, automatic furnace ignition systems, and flue-opening controls. The expenditure must be made on a house that was substantially completed before April 20, 1977. No credit is available for any part of the cost of a significant renovation done after that date. That is so even if the purpose of the renovation is to make the house more energy efficient.

Both the energy and the conservation credits

are available retroactively for work done after April 19, 1977.

Burning wood more productively

Heating a home safely and efficiently with wood requires more than a stack of logs and a fireplace. The ground rules: To be cost-effective, one cord of wood should cost no more than 150 gallons of fuel oil. For example, if oil costs you $1.05 a gallon, don't pay more than $157.50 for one cord.

A cord is 128 cubic feet of logs, including air spaces between them. This is the standard commercial measure for wood, but prices vary wildly. Four-foot-long green logs are much cheaper than shorter dry ones. But the latter come ready for the fireplace. (The other must be dried and cut.) So buy green wood in late spring or summer. It will dry in six months, in time for winter use.

There are many types of wood, and harder woods yield more heat. They include oak, ash, and beech. Less efficient are magnolia, cherry, Douglas fir. The least efficient are poplar, spruce, willow.

The most efficient stoves use baffles, long smoke paths, and heat exchangers to extract as much heat as possible. They are more expensive than simpler types. But, in the long run, they save money. A wide variety of wood-burning (and multi-fuel) furnaces is available for central heating systems. Make sure to check local restrictions. Some furnace types are not allowed in certain states.

Except for emergency use, fireplaces are mainly for aesthetic value, since they are essentially poor heaters. Homeowners who want the best of both worlds should consider efficiency-improving modifications or combination fireplace-stove units.

Source: *Heating with Wood,* U.S. Department of Energy, Washington, D.C.

Home fire-detection systems

The best defense against house fire is a combination of smoke-, heat-, and ion-detecting alarms installed throughout the house. They cost from about $200 to as much as $2,000 for sophisticated units that alert police and fire departments.

The three basic detector units sense opaque smoke from a fire, a rise in tempertaure, and electrically charged particles (ions) that are produced in the earliest stages of most house fires, respectively.

The three types are often packaged together. All can be bought to run on house current or on batteries.

What is available:

• Smoke alarm. They often cost less than $10 per unit, including an alkaline 9-volt transistor radio battery. Requires a new battery ($1.50) every six months or so. But they will not detect some types of fires as quickly as an ion detector will. Good for rooms used for entertaining.

• Heat detector. Costing under $25, they are most often hooked up to house current, not operated by a battery. A household unit is normally set to go off at 120°. But a fire may get out of control and give off toxic fumes before the home heat sensor sounds the alarm. Best locations are kitchen, storage areas, furnace room, garage. In remote locations, they can trigger an off-site alarm that will continue ringing even after the sensing element is consumed by fire. (Some battery-powered smoke and ion detectors can be equipped with transmitting devices to do the same thing, but they are not always available.)

• Ion detector. They cost $15–$40 (including the battery). The cheaper versions sometimes use an expensive 11.2-volt silver-zinc battery, which is hard to find. Find a unit that runs on a 9-volt radio battery instead. But it's so sensitive that it can be set off by moderate cigarette smoke, fireplace heat, or even kitchen fumes. Best locations are bedrooms, upstairs hall, furnace room.

Ionization and smoke detectors powered by house current are more expensive and more difficult to install than battery units, especially in older homes. They must be equipped with standby rechargeable batteries; otherwise they won't protect during power outages (a period when fires often start, since candles are being used and power lines get knocked down, sending sparks flying). Nevertheless, most families eventually tire of the battery-changing routine, or they put off changing a dead battery for weeks. Best is a mix of power sources as well as detector types. Use house current in remote locations, like attics; batteries in units that are easy to reach, like

the ceiling of a front hall, within arm's length of stairway to second floor.

Although professionals can sense household air flows and use fewer units to provide adequate protection, do-it-yourselfers should aim for a unit in every room, except bathrooms, and one at both the bottom and the top of every staircase.

Consider buying an extra battery-powered smoke detector that can be carried when traveling, for protection in hotels. The units are lightweight and can be placed atop a hotel-room cabinet, near the ceiling.

YOUR AUTOMOBILE

Driving small cars safely

In a severe crash between a large car and a small one, those in the small car are eight times more likely to be killed. Defense strategies:
• Wear seat belts. A belted occupant of a small car has the same chance of surviving as the unbelted occupant of a big car in a crash between the two.
• Keep your lights on at low beam full time to increase visibility.
• Be aware that light poles and signs along the road may not break away as designed when hit by a lightweight compact car.
• Respect the inability of larger vehicles to maneuver or stop as quickly to escape a collision.

Safe driving— men vs women

Women have much lower accident rates than men, but the reasons have little to do with innate sex differences. Rather, it's because:

• They drive fewer miles and less often at night. This reduces the odds of an accident.
• If a man and woman have both been drinking, he usually drives.
• Women drive less and so are less likely to get overconfident or take risks.
• Women are in fewer fatal car accidents, the prime reason being that they wear seat belts more often than men.

Source: *The Open Road,* Peterson, Howell & Heather, Baltimore.

Accidents with aggressive drivers

Violent and aggressive drivers are dangerous when they get into an accident. If you're in an accident with one, stay calm. Don't escalate any argument. Copy down the other driver's license number immediately. If you are threatened, leave at once. Call the police so that you won't be charged with leaving the scene of an accident . . . but do it from a safe distance. If your car is disabled, lock the doors and wait for the police to arrive.

Car owner's guide to saving money

• Buy bargain tires marked blems. They are perfectly serviceable except for minor cosmetic blemishes on sidewalls.

• Lengthen the life of old windshield-wiper blades by rubbing the edges with a knife or the striking part of a matchbook cover. This exposes the softer material underneath and improves wiping ability.

• Preserve the car's finish by washing it with cold or lukewarm water. But never wash the finish with hot water.

• Run the air-conditioner at least 10 minutes every week. This procedure will maintain coolant pressure and avoid costly air-conditioner breakdowns.

• When you stop for service get out of the car and watch gas-station attendants carefully, particularly if you have an out-of-state license. When the oil is checked, make sure the dipstick is inserted all the way. Some attendants may show you a dipstick that indicates oil is low, then use an empty can and pretend to add a quart of oil.

• Clean corrosion off the battery terminals. Use a wire brush or steel wool to scrape battery posts and cable clamps. Clean the top surface with a mild solution of baking soda and water. Don't let it seep under cell caps.

• Prevent wind resistance, which cuts performance up to five miles per gallon, by keeping the car windows closed while driving.

• Be aware that every five miles per hour over 50 cuts fuel performance by two miles per gallon.

• Use the lightest necessary pressure on the gas and brake pedals.

• Don't downshift to brake a car with a manual transmisson. When accelerating, get into high gear fast; don't worry if the engine sputters.

• Upshift automatic transmissions faster by letting up slightly on the accelerator to encourage a gear change.

• Try to stay near the speed at which your car consumes gas most economically. (If in doubt, ask your dealer. The speed is specified for all new models.) The fuel economy of diesels falls quickly above 55 MPH.

Remember that unnecessary weight in the trunk and on roof racks (used or unused) and underinflated tires increase fuel usage.

Underinflated tires can hurt car performance

• Miles per gallon. Every two pounds of underinflation takes at least 1% off mileage performance. That puts tire inflation on a par with a tune-up in improving a car's fuel economy.

• Tire wear. Tests show that tires underinflated by four pounds have 10% less tread life.

• Safety. Underinflating tires increases the risk of sudden tire failure and accident. It also adversely affects handling properties of cars, reducing the driver's ability to respond sharply and safely in emergency situations.

Check pressure when the tires are cold. It rises three and four pounds per square inch when hot.

Tips on economical driving

• Instead of idling while warming up the engine, start moving at a moderate speed as soon as it begins running smoothly.

When your car needs work

Professional mechanics correctly diagnose mechanical problems only half the time, according to a government survey, and dealer repair shops do a poorer job than independent garages. Diagnostic testing equipment is often inaccurate. Customer complaints are not accurately relayed to the dealer's mechanics.

Use an independent garage that's big enough to afford specialized equipment but small enough to allow customers access to the mechanic making the repairs.

Improving automobile-radio reception

Poor car-radio reception usually means trouble with the antenna.

For FM, adjust the antenna height to exactly 31 inches. For AM, adjust the trimmer. The trimmer is a small adjustment screw found on the back or side of the radio. (In General Motors cars, it's behind one of the knobs.)

To make the adjustment, pick a weak station at the high end of the dial (near 1500). Then turn the trimmer until the reception is the loudest. If poor reception persists, the antenna cable may be corroded or improperly connected to the car fender. Cleaning off the rust and tightening the antenna mounting can sometimes help.

Windshield antennas don't suffer from the same problems, but they have other drawbacks. They're more likely to pick up engine noises, and reception can fade out when the car changes direction.

Source: *Motor,* New York.

The traps in radar traps

Police-operated radar speed traps are here to stay. Unfortunately, inaccurate, even fraudu-

lent, radar readings result in numerous false arrests and penalties.

What can go wrong:
• When mercury-vapor highway lamps light up, they disturb the radar units, causing them to record over-70-MPH speeds on any passing car. The driver has no defense against the evidence.
• Radar signals bounce off the walls of an underpass or high-tension power lines and skew the signal.
• Nearby CB transmitters can throw off the units. The next car that comes within range gets an erroneous reading.
• Malicious mischief. Radar operators can aim the radar antenna at their own control unit and produce readings in the 90-MPH range. Any passing car is nabbed.

A Florida county judge viewed television films of various highway abuses and threw out every radar-trap case pending in his court. That led the Department of Transportation to stop matching federal funds for radar training programs until they meet the new upgraded standards.

Nonetheless, too many ill-equipped squads remain at large, particularly in rural areas where speeding violations still represent an important source of town or county revenue. Driver beware —the scam works if an out-of-town executive, whose time is money, can't spare the time to go to court to challenge a $50 fine.

Foiling car thieves

No car or truck is immune from thievery, but professional thieves tell police that there are ways of making the heist harder.

Recommended:
• Don't rely on factory-installed alarms. Repair manuals that detail how they work are available in libraries.
• Use combinations of systems. For example, an alarm with an ignition cutoff switch hidden under the dashboard or in the glove compartment.
• Replace standard door-lock buttons with tapered ones. They won't stop professional

thieves, but they deter amateurs who are responsible for two-thirds of the country's car thefts.

• Leave only the ignition key when using parking lots. And don't tell the attendant how long the vehicle will be parked. Also note the mileage.

• Learn how to remove and replace the distributor rotor. The car won't run without it. This easy maneuver should be standard when the car is left unattended for more than 24 hours.

32 BEING A SMART CONSUMER

TRAVEL AND VACATION TIPS

How to plan a relaxing vacation

Pick a spot, and don't move too much. Arrangements are what make vacations exhausting.

Plan the vacation so that it's free of all unpalatable tasks. Rent a cottage with a kitchen only if you love to cook. Go hiking or canoeing with an outfitter, unless you love the chores of camping.

Don't vacation with anyone who will make you tense—family you're not getting along with or friends you don't really know well enough to relax with.

Basic wardrobe for a lengthy trip

The goal is to travel with only one carry-on garment bag plus one carry-on underseat case,

with enough room to add new purchases. Here's a list for up to a month away.

• Lightweight black garbardine suit. Works as business suit and for formal wear.

• Blue blazer for business meetings and evening parties (with gray flannel slacks) or for casual occasions (with blue jeans).

• Pair gray worsted flannel trousers.
• Pair blue jeans.
• Two white broadcloth shirts, plain collar.
• White oxford-cloth shirt, button-down collar.
• White cotton-knit polo shirt.
• Black-and-gray-stripped polo shirt.
• Gray cashmere V-neck sweater, long-sleeved.
• Black-white-and-gray-patterned silk tie.
• Solid maroon silk tie.
• Black silk evening bow tie.
• Five pairs black socks (silk, wool, and cotton).
• Five sets of underwear.
• Pair pajamas or one bathrobe.
• Lighweight racing trunks.
• Black plain oxford shoes.
• Black slip-on loafers.
• Tan poplin raincoat with detachable lining (should be worn or carried over arm when boarding plane).

Source: Egon von Furstenberg, *The Power Look,* Holt, Rinehart & Winston, New York.

Passport precaution

Make photocopies of your passport and leave one copy on the bottom of the suitcase and the other copy with a friend, relative, or secretary. Knowing the passport number, date, and place of issue get you a limited passport immediately from an American embassy or consulate if the original is stolen or lost. That will allow you to continue traveling or return to the United States with the least trouble.

Relief from motion sickness

Motion sickness relief is available in a new form. A thin plastic disk about the size of a dime worn behind the ear releases a drug into the bloodstream over three days. The device, "Transderm-V Scopolamine Therapeutic System" was tested on the space shuttle. Prescription required. Cost: about $2.25 each.

For healthier travel overseas

Take along a spare pair of glasses (or contact lenses with plenty of contact-lens fluid).

Have a dental checkup before leaving the U.S. Care is not always readily available in other countries.

Get a list of English-speaking doctors in each country on the itinerary. One source is the International Association for Medical Assistance to Travelers, 350 Fifth Ave., NY 10001.

Sufferers from any unusual illness or allergy should carry a brief note form their own doctor explaining the condition to the doctor who may have to treat it.

People with heart disease, diabetes, epilepsy, or a severe allergy to medication should wear a "Medic Alert" neck emblem or bracelet. That guards against improper medical treatment. For more information contact Medic Alert Foundation, Turlock, Calif.

Source: *14 Ways to Tap Your Success-Power,* Alexander Hamilton Institution, Inc., New York.

Shopping abroad

Overseas travelers should not feel intimidated by the $300 limit on duty-free goods they bring home. Not included in the limit are items over 100 years old, paintings and books by foreign authors. Some others have low import duties, for example, ivory, 6%, cameras, 7.5%, gemstone jewelry, 12%. The best strategy is to use the $300 allowance on items that have the highest duty.

Check the prices at duty-free shops against prices in local stores. The airport and dockside shops generally charge higher, rather than prevailing, prices for their products. In addition, top-of-the-line products are sold, meaning that the prices are high to begin with.

So buy only heavily taxed items in these stores. Liquor, cagarettes, perfume, and some wines may still be bargains.

Source: *Travel Smart,* Dobbs Ferry, N.Y.

Trouble-free sea cruises

The number of cruise ships has grown dramatically, and bargain fares could be widely available this summer and fall if demand is soft, as it was last year.

Before signing on, visit the ships you are interested in while they are in port. If you have never taken a cruise before, make the first one a short one. Choose a cabin near the waterline, in the center of the ship, for minimum motion-sickness problems. Prices are lower than for top-deck staterooms too.

Ask your travel agent what kind of passengers each line attracts. (The longer the cruise, the older the crowd.) Three- and four-day sails out of Miami and Los Angeles are the liveliest.

Get a complete rundown of onboard activities. Gambling is a major at-sea pastime. Some lines operate nothing more than floating casinos.

Christmas, February, and March are the peak periods for the Caribbean, and reservations should be made up to a year in advance. Budget cruises are available at other times.

A small deposit holds an option on a room when you book far in advance for the busiest times. People with flexible vacation schedules can get bargain rates at the last minute when the ship still has a few empty cabins.

A cruise will cost about $1,000 per person for seven days, or $150–$160 a day. And there are even fly-cruise deals that take you from major cities to the port of departure with almost no additional charge for air fare.

Be advised that even no-tip cruises involve some tipping. Other typical extras are bar bills, shore excursions, shopping, port taxes, film, new clothes, and gambling losses.

Don't be a victim of hotel overbooking

It's not always the hotel's fault. Sometimes guests overstay. (Hawaii is the only state that allows hotels to compel guests to leave on time.) But hotels generally accept more reservations than they have rooms, betting that some reservation-holders won't show. Sometimes they bet wrong.

To keep from being a loser:

• Plan trips sufficiently in advance to get written confirmation of reservations. That gives you something extra to argue with should you

need it. If there's no time for a written confirmation, try to get a confirmation number when the reservation is made.

• Get "guaranteed" reservations with a credit card. This does obligate you to pay for the room even if you can't make it. However, it reduces the incentive a hotel clerk has to sell your room to somebody else. American Express has an "assured reservations" program. Under it, the hotel that "walks" you has to pay for first night's lodging in a comparable hotel room nearby, for a long-distance call to inform the office or family where you will be, and for transportation to the substitute hotel. Several chains have a similar policy.

• Arrive early in the afternoon, when last night's guests have checked out, but before the bulk of new arrivals.

• Prepare for a battle of wits. Take your case to a higher-up—probably the assistant manager on duty—since it's unlikely that the desk clerk will find a room after telling you he has none. The assistant manager might be persuaded to "find" one of the rooms that inevitably are set aside by luxury hotels for emergencies such as the arrival of a VIP. Make a loud fuss, some people suggest. This often works, since hotels try to avoid drawing public attention to their overbooking practices.

If neither raving and ranting nor quiet persuasion moves the assistant manager, insist that he call other comparable hotels to get you a room, and at the same or lower price. The better hotels will usually do their best.

Canceling a confirmed reservation

If a confirmed reservation has to be canceled, ask for a cancellation number, the name of the clerk and a written confirmation. Unless canceled sufficiently in advance, confirmed reservations require a guarantee of payment. Without evidence of cancellation, it won't be easy to get out of paying the bill.

Saving on hotel bills

Ask hotels for their corporate rate. All chain motels, and many individual hotels, have them. And business people on personal trips can use the corporate rate, too.

As an example, if the range of rates is $45 to $70, the corporate rate might be $50. That means $50 or less, never more, even if the hotel assigns a deluxe room.

Make arrangements in advance, not at check-in time. To be eligible for corporate rates, a few hotels require a minimum number of visits per year. But many give them to any travelers who write for reservations on their companies' letterheads.

Source: *Business Traveler's Report,* New York.

Quick way to check hotel bills

Adjust the amount of the tips so every item that's added to the bill ends with the same digit. Example: Tip odd amounts to have the bills for all meals end in the numeral six. It takes only a moment to skim the list for items that don't end in six, and thus, don't belong on your bill. The odds of an accidental six occurring on the bill are nine-to-one in favor of the traveler.

Source: *Business Traveler's Report,* New York.

Executive hotel clubs

Hotel chains are beginning to adopt the airlines' idea of a special class of service for executives, which provides concierge service for making restaurant and theater reservations and for arranging use of hotel services. Also, a special class of rooms that feature designer linens, toi-letries, and distinctive stationery. The cost is about $20 a day over regular room charges.

Getting the best food service

The maitre d'hotel is the key to getting the best service and food in a restaurant. When trying a restaurant for the first time, ask for him by name (it's easy to get the name over the phone when making your reservation), and introduce yourself. Ask about the house specialties and listen to his recommendations.

If you have special menu requests, they should be made by midmorning. If the dish is very exotic, allow the chef enough time to order the ingredients.

Tipping: 15% to the waiter, 5% to the captain, $3–$5 to the wine steward, $10 to the maitre d'hotel (on your first visit) and periodically (every 2–3 months) thereafter.

Tips for educated dining

The gourmet avoids repetition in taste, texture, and color. It isn't a good idea to eat sweetbreads, oysters, and chicken at one meal. They all have the same general color and texture.

Other things to avoid are two sauced dishes one after another, or a sauced dish followed by a creamy dish, followed by a custard-like or ice-cream dessert. Dishes should provide taste contrast. Courses should vary from steamed to grilled, or poached, to sauced.

When dining out try to become knowledgeable about all foods—Japanese, German, Indian, Italian. Don't concentrate on French cuisine alone. Seize every opportunity to try a new food. Look for fresh foods and foods of the season—in the spring, baby lamb, and soft-shell crab; in the fall, game.

Trust your own taste in wine. If a wine tastes

bad to the palate it may be a bad wine. Don't try to match wine perfectly to food. There is no absolute rule about which wines go with which foods. In Germany, white wine is drunk with everything.

Eat only what tastes good.

Source: Roger L. Yaseen, president, American chapter "La Chaine des Rotisseurs."

When renting a car

Car-rental competition is hotter than ever, especially among the small intracity and intrastate firms. What to keep tabs on:
• Does the price include fuel? Very few still do. Dry rate means the customer buys the gas. Find out where it's cheapest. Fill up there, too, before dropping the car off.
• Special restrictions or charges for one-way rentals.
• Special weekend or weekly rates.
• When luggage space is important, make sure the reservation spells it out. (A compact or intermediate model may still be suitable.)
• Extra charge if a larger car is substituted. There shouldn't be one if the rental firm does the switching.
• Special corporate discount. Comparison shopping on this could hold surprises.
• Your airline may have a special fly/drive package.
• The policy in case of car trouble.
• In case of accident, does the contract include primary liability coverage? (In California and Florida, only secondary coverage is required.)

Source: *Medical Economics,* Oradell, N.J.

Car-rental myths

• Myth: Small rental companies don't have dealer networks to service users efficiently. Fact: Many smaller companies are building impressive rental networks in major cities.

• Myth: If a rental agency is cheaper in one city, it will be cheaper throughout the country. Fact: Rates vary substantially from city to city.
• Myth: Companies can always save by taking advantage of discount rates. Fact: Discounts are usually offered on the most expensive models, which may easily cost 30% more than smaller vehicles. Corporate discounts may have restrictions.
• Myth: Weekend rates apply only on Saturday and Sunday. Fact: Many agencies stretch out weekend rates to cover several days.

Source: *Travel Smart for Business,* Communications House, Dobbs Ferry, N.Y.

How to save on air travel

• Fly between 9 p.m. and 7 a.m. Get a 20% night-flight discount for most trips over 500 miles.
• Plan business trips so that schedule qualifies the business traveler for vacation excursion fares (discounts up to 50%).
• Fly out-of-the-way carriers looking for new business.
• Make sales or service trips, or tours of branch offices, using the unlimited mileage tickets offered by some airlines.
• Before making flight and car-rental arrangements, find out if a small commuter airline will make the hop to the traveler's final destination.

Source: Harold Seligman, president, Management Alternatives, New York.

Flying with a cold

Take a decongestant before the flight to help clear ears and sinus passages. If the cold is severe, continue taking decongestants, as prescribed on the label, during the flight. Consider postponing the trip. Alcohol and wines can cause nose and throat problems.

Source: American Physical Fitness Research Institute, West Los Angeles.

SOLVING CONSUMER PROBLEMS

Handling some common irritations without a lawyer

If you suffer from noisy neighbors, make the first complaint orally to the noisemaker.

If necessary, follow up, in the case of renters, with the landlord. Write it down. Spell out the specifics of the disturbance. (Include the lease section being violated by the noise.) Send copies to both the noisy neighbor and the landlord.

If still no action follows, complain to the landlord immediately when the disturbance is going on. For example, if the neighbor is playing electric guitar at 2 A.M., phone the landlord then to complain. (It helps, of course, to have other neighbors join in making the complaint.)

Another way is to phone the police. There are laws against noise. Show the police the section of the lease that's applicable.

Or suppose your're crossing the street legally and a driver cuts you off, scaring and endangering but not injuring you. Get the license-plate number and description of the automobile. Then file a complaint with the Motor Vehicle Bureau.

A single complaint won't result in any action as long as there was no physical injury. But the bureau can take action against the driver after a number of complaints.

A common problem with department store billings is being charged for an item that has either been returned or was never received at all. The problem is that most stores work with contract truckers. They're required to get signatures upon delivery, but often leaving a package without doing so in order to collect their fees quickly.

If the package was never received, simply demand to see the trucker's signed receipt. If there isn't one, the trucker is legally responsible for the merchandise.

In cases where an item was returned but never credited, the only real proof is the return receipt. If that's been lost, simply visit or write to the store explaining the entire matter. If you're a good customer and the item is small, chances are the store will take your word for it.

Take the situation where a person with whom you're involved in a business situation is simply impossible to deal with. Unfortunately, you have to deal with him. Put the specifics of his erratic actions into writing. Avoid general allegations such as "he's crazy." Instead, document individual actions (dates, locations, descriptions) that establish his behavior as bizarre. Sign and date the report, and have a witness sign and date it also. Keep a copy as evidence if the dispute goes to litigation.

The second step is to confront him directly with the fact that he is being unreasonable. Warn him that you will not deal with him if he continues to act in that manner. Only then should you go over his head: to his superior, his employer, or his client (in the case of a lawyer) in an effort to get him replaced in dealing with you. But he could sue you for damages unless you exhaust other remedies first.

Do not respond to his bizarre tactics. That will only encourage him. Remain inflexible until he alters his approach or you feel justified in going over his head.

Or you may be taken in by a worthless business seminar. The content of a two-day seminar is only vaguely similar to what was promised and, as such, it is worthless. First, carefully reread the promotional material for disclaimers about the speaker or substitutions that might be allowed.

If you can show that the seminar did not deliver what it advertised, you might get a rebate on part of the course's fee. If you can establish that the lead speaker was the only reason for attending the course, you might get a rebate for the entire course.

The best approach is to write the sponsor requesting your money back. Note: Complain to the members of the sponsor's board of directors. (Before taking it into litigation, it would be helpful if you could find other dissatisfied attendees who will agree to join in the complaint.)

Source: Dan Brecher, Esq., New York.

Legal responsibilities of a lawyer

Lawyers must follow their clients' explicit instructions, even if they think the client is wrong. In a recent case, the client wanted to settle the case, but her lawyer insisted they could get a better deal by going to trial. Instead, the verdict went against them. The client then sued her lawyer for malpractice—and won.

Give written instructions to the lawyer, and keep a copy for yourself.

Source: *Joos et al.* vs *Auto-Owners Insurance Co. et al.,* 288 N.W. 2d 443.

How to complain effectively

Dealing with defective merchandise is greatly simplified by adequate preparation. Basic rule: Save receipts, warranties, and all other papers. After analyzing the defect and deciding on what kind of compensation you want, it's time to take action.

First meet with the salesperson or store manager. Describe the problem. Give him copies of the paperwork. Then ask for a replacement or other compensaton. Be polite but firm. In response to whatever excuse the merchant uses, repeat your demand like a broken record.

Then write to the manager, going over the

points made in the conversation. Include in the letter copies of the sales slips as well as a statement of intention to refer the matter to the Better Business Bureau, a consumer agency, or the manager's superior.

If that fails write directly to the president of the company, not the customer-relations department. Manufacturers of products are listed in the *Thomas Registry.* Names of executives and addresses of companies are in *Standard & Poor's Register of Corporations.*

Recount the facts and the demand for compensation. Include copies of paperwork. Make sure to send a carbon to the store's local manager,

As a last resort, call a consumer agency. They are usually listed in the telephone book. State consumer offices are generally in the attorney-general's office. There are 140 Better Business Bureaus in the country and more than 100 consumer hot lines. Complete listings of hot lines are available from Call for Action, Inc., 575 Lexington Ave., NY 10022.

Withholding credit-card payments

Disgruntled consumers may be able to withhold payments on a credit card they used to purchase goods or services that proved substandard. This is the result of a little-known provision of the Fair Credit Billing Act, which enables the credit-card companies to reclaim disputed amounts from merchants after credit-card slips are signed.

Four conditions must be met for a consumer to be entitled to withhold credit-card payments: the amount of the charge must be more than $50; the charge must be made within the customer's home state, or within 100 miles of the customer's home; the customer must first attempt to settle the dispute with the merchant directly; and the customer must give the bank that issued the card written notice that the attempt to settle has failed.

When the bank receives the customer's notice, it credits the account with the amount of the charge. It then charges this amount back to the bank that serves the merchant. That bank then charges the merchant.

This provision of the law has been little publicized by the banks and credit-card companies. They fear that if too many consumers take advantage of this feature of the law, merchants will begin to refuse credit cards.

Discount-buying club traps

Discount-buying clubs operate on the principle that consumers who band together can purchase brand-name items at reduced prices. Consumers pool their time and money to buy in large quantities at wholesale markets. But most discount-buying clubs, except for food cooperatives, are not good deals.

Problems include:

• Membership fees. If it costs a lot to join, you must spend thousands of dollars to break even. For example, a $500 initiation fee for a club that discounts purchases by 25% means you have to buy $2,000 worth of merchandise before realizing any saving. Many clubs earn most of their income from initiation fees rather than from the sale of merchandise. Result: Little incentive to provide good service.

• Longevity. Many of the clubs do not last long. If the club goes under, the participant has little hope of recovering original fees, down payments, or merchandise ordered. Some states now require clubs to post bonds, which can be used to refund membership fees.

Before joining a discount-buying club, check retail prices. When making purchases, you might do as well on your own, with no risk and no trouble.

Source: U.S. Office of Consumer Affairs.

TVS AND STEREOS

Eliminating television reception problems

If your television reception starts to go bad, do not rush the set to the repair shop right away. The problem may be interference from power lines or nearby electrical apparatus. Usually the interference can be easily screened out. First steps:

• Try another set in the same location. If it has the same symptoms, the problem is probably outside the set.

• Find out if neighbors are experiencing similar poor reception.

Symptoms of interference:

• Twin lines of dots or dashes across the screen. The cause is probably faulty hardware on a nearby power line pole. To test, disconnect the antenna. If the interference stops, notify the power company that it has a problem pole.

• Periodic streaking, flashes across the screen. Usually caused by interference from old

cars and trucks driving past without ignition suppressors. Buy a lead-in interference filter. Or aim the antenna away from the street.

• Occasional herringbone patterns. Lasts 15–30 seconds each time. Caused by police transmitters or CB radios operating nearby. Buy a high-pass filter for the antenna.

To rescue a stereo system

Keep your stereo in top form by using a new, low-cost (average price $70) piece of equipment called an equalizer. It works like a super set of tone controls, modifying the proportion of high, middle, and low frequencies.

Listeners can reshape the sound of a recording to emphasize certain instruments, adjust sound to a room, and reduce tape hiss and other kinds of disturbing noises. It's available from most high-fidelity manufacturers and sound-equipment stores.

33 PERSONAL HEALTH

PSYCHOLOGICAL HEALTH

Creative stress management

Between 50% and 80% of all major diseases —cancer, strokes, heart attacks, even colitis— are stress-related.

Mankind's primitive fight-or-flight mechanism does not work in today's complex society. People encounter problems that can't be solved by either combat or flight. The result is stress, which undermines health and increases susceptibility to disease.

The answer lies in heeding the basics of sound living:

• Keeping fit. Exercise improves the whole neurological process by which the brain gets information from the body and coordinates responses.

• Relaxing. Body and mind as a whole, but also the parts of the body—like the neck and back—where stress impacts. To learn to relax, check the literature on stress management; take a seminar; enroll in an oriental martial arts course that reduces stress by linking mind and body. This will help you find the combination of stress-management techniques that works for you. The payoff will be your ability to refresh yourself from moment to moment.

• Eating regularly. Also, getting plenty of rest and sleep.

• Varying your routine. You can do this by broadening your patterns of mental and physical activity.

Many individuals now manage stress by taking tranquilizers. But this treats symptoms, not causes, and may impair ability to reason over the long term.

Source: Kathryn L. Goldman, Ph.D., head, division of human development at Austin Community College, Austin, Texas.

Executive stress profile

Characteristics of the stress-prone individuals:
• Plans the day unrealistically.
• The first to arrive, and last to leave.
• Always in a hurry.
• Makes no plans for relaxation.
• Feels guilty about doing anything else but work.
• Any unforeseen problem or setback becomes a disaster.
• The stress-prone person is "polyphasic" in thinking. He is involved in one activity when

thinking of several others. He talks fast and interrupts often.

• The need to be recognized is overwhelming. Winning is the end-all. But there's no prize in winning or enjoyment of it. As a result, recognition, money, and possessions are seldom enjoyed. Overextended involvement creates the sense of being fragmented. This leads to significant reduction in work quality.

Test of too much stress:

One who can't answer "yes" to the following questions is probably working under too much stress:

• Do I feel exhilarated after completing an important project?

• Can I "come down" within a few hours after a stressful situation?

• Do I work productively under pressure?

• Can I accept minor work setbacks without developing incapacitating emotional letdowns?

• Do I know how to channel stress into productive work?

How to reduce stress:

• Recognize the aggravating aspects of your job. Stop fighting them.

• Identify your emotional needs, and accept them. Most executives are competitive, need to be liked, need to vent anger. They should have outlets for each of these needs.

• Practice listening. Listening is more relaxing than talking.

• Be sensitive to change. Recognize when it's occurring on the job, and figure out what adjustments are necessary. By consciously recognizing change, you make it manageable.

• Keep alcohol consumption under control. Excessive drinking creates the illusion of dealing with stress, while in fact adding to it.

Source: Rosalind Forbes, *Corporate Stress,* Doubleday, Garden City, NY.

Stress and the middle-aged manager

At least 40 factors contribute to stress-related illnesses. The most important:

• Overload. Putting in too many long hours while taking on too much work. This can lead to job dissatisfaction, tension, lower self-esteem, increased heart rate, higher cholesterol levels.

• Confusion about work role. This ambiguity exists when managers are unclear about job objectives. The result is higher tension, lower job satisfaction, and loss of self-confidence.

• Job conflict. Employees find themselves doing what they don't want to do. And performing work they feel is not part of the job specification. This results in confusion and heightened stress.

The greater the authority of the people sending the conflicting role messages, the more the job dissatisfaction among the managers.

• People pressure. Those who are responsible for people suffer more stress than those in charge of things, such as equipment or budgets. Responsibility for people is significantly related to heavy smoking, raised blood pressure, and higher serum cholesterol. Managers of things have lower incidence of these high-risk factors.

• Boss's attitude. Those who work for a considerate boss feel less pressure than those under the command of managers who pull rank, play favorites, and take advantage of their employees.

• Executive neurosis. This occurs when managers are promoted beyond their abilities and overwork in a desperate attempt to hold on to the top job. This engenders stress both physically and psychologically.

Source: Cary L. Cooper, University of Manchester, Institute of Science and Technology, Manchester, England, "Middle-Aged Men and the Pressures of Work," *Mid-Life,* Brunner/Mazel, Inc., New York.

Work, stress, and your heart

Work may be good medicine. A recent study has confirmed that heart-attack death rates are much higher among men who retire than those who continue working. Apparently feelings of uselessness and idleness are more dangerous to health than work-connected stress.

On the other hand, work can jolt you into a

heart attack. Seventy-five percent of fatal on-the-job heart attacks occur on Mondays. The reasons: the reintroduction to occupational stress, increased activity, pollution exposure after a weekend of rest.

———

Source: *Journal of the American Medical Association,* Chicago.

———

Executives rank sources of stress

What bothers executives most:
• Failure of subordinates to accept or carry out responsibilities: 92% of those responding to a survey listed this as their most serious problem.
  • Inability to get critical information: 78%.
  • Firing someone: 48%.
  • Incompetent co-workers: 47%.
  • Owner or board of directors challenging recommendations: 33%.
  • Subordinates who question decisions: 5%.
  • Conducting performance reviews: 3%.

———

Source: The Atlanta Consulting Group, Atlanta, Ga.

———

Identifying disguised stress

Busy managers are often unaware of the amount of stress they are really under. They deceive themselves into ignoring stress by believing that whatever is bothering them isn't all that bad.

Some stress can be good, for example when it's the basis for motivation, excitement, creativity, and satisfaction. Too much is always harmful.

Signs of stress:
• Irritability, being bothered by little nuisances.
• Increased use of alcohol, as well as caffeine or tobacco.
• Decline in clarity of thought. Reduction of work quality and efficiency.

• Physical discomforts such as headaches, neckaches, backaches, tense muscles and skin irritations.
  • Overeating.
  • Sleep disturbances.
  • Anxiety or timidity.
  • Anger, dissatisfaction, bitterness.
  • Confusion, a sense of being swamped with work.
  • Depression.

———

Source: Herbert W. Greenberg, *Coping with Stress,* Prentice-Hall, Englewood Cliffs, N.J.

———

Avoiding the overload syndrome

Getting overburdened with obligations can lead to serious anxiety and depression. The prime cause of the overload syndrome is outside pressure to accept too many work or volunteer obligations.

Another factor is the initial receptiveness of certain personality types to taking on tasks. Those people are particularly prone to guilt feelings.

Symptoms:
• Fear that the additional responsibilities (which suddenly seem overwhelming) won't be met.
  • Inability to make decisions.
  • Difficulty in communicating with family. The usual excuse is exhaustion.
  • Isolation. The manager begins to discard usual recreational outlets and exercise habits on grounds that there is no time.

How to manage overloading: Ideally, avoid it in the first place. What it takes to say no:
• A clear awareness of priorities. It's easier for a responsible executive to say no if it's clear what's at stake: obligations to family and personal health.
• Accept temporary feelings of guilt. It is embarrassing to say no to a higher executive or a friend who is also overloaded by demands of a volunteer job.
• Get help. A physician can help treat symptoms of overloading. More important, the doc-

tor's advice provides a more acceptable reason to break out of the problem.

Source: *The Psychometabolic Blues,* Woodbridge Press, Santa Barbara, Calif.

Are you a workaholic?

The people who love their work passionately and spend long hours at it are not necessarily work-addicted. True workaholics are men and women who cannot stop working even in non-work situations. They make all other activities and relationships secondary to work. While the reasons differ widely, almost all work addicts share these traits:

• Oriented to activities involving skills and skill development. Averse to activities where skill is not a factor.

• Strongly analytic. Focus on precise definitions, goals, policies, facts, lists, measurements, and strategies.

• Aggressive and unable to leave things alone. An urge to manipulate and control their environment to gain a sense of satisfaction.

• Goal-oriented, product-oriented. Uninterested in the sensations of the present unless they yield products or contribute to their creation.

• Concerned with efficiency and effectiveness. Severely upset by waste and loss. The problem is that many work addicts are usually inefficient because they are perfectionists and refuse to delegate authority, seeing it as a loss of control.

Source: Jay B. Rohrlick, M.D., *Work and Love: The Crucial Balance,* Summit Books, New York.

How to keep from burning out on the job

Burn-out is a clear loss of interest in work. It's a feeling that work no longer has purpose. A treadmill without progress, it is something to dread. Most vulnerable are:

• The workaholic, whose life is consumed by the job.

• The person who quickly tires of routine. He can't maintain enthusiasm without constant challenge.

• The individual trying conscientiously to master a job that runs counter to temperament and talent.

How to rekindle the joys of work:

• Get more rest, since stress plays a big role in a burn-out. Exercise regularly to get into better physical shape.

• Introduce as much variety as possible into the daily routine. One method is to trade some duties with colleagues.

• Extreme solution: Consider changing your job or career. Make the decision to quit during an emotional high, rather than a low, when everything seems hopeless.

Source: *Working Woman,* New York.

Coping with psychological fatigue

Most cases of fatigue are caused by psychological, rather than physical, factors. But the possibility of physical causes has to be checked out first. Get a thorough check-up.

As a rule, if a person has been overworking for some time and then takes three or four days off and sleeps adequately, he should be refreshed.

But often rest is not the answer. People whose tiredness is psychological need stimulation. The more rest such a person gets, the more tired he becomes.

Common causes of psychological fatigue:

• Grieving that hasn't been attended to. Surprising, but typical, examples are getting a new job and moving to a new city can be exhilarating. But the new situation still implies some loss. This holds true for promotions, getting married—all of which mean saying goodbye to certain freedoms, contacts, options. People who don't deal with the negative aspects of even the most positive changes are vulnerable to psychological fatigue. Some of their energies remain bound up in the past, and, through that, in uncompleted grieving.

• Situations of acknowledged loss, i.e., the death of a loved one, or the fact that the children have grown up and left home, or having to face the fact of limited potential (executive's sudden realization that he'll never fulfill career objectives). Unwillingness to face up to resulting emotions leads to fatigue. Normal energies are expended in the effort to repress sadness or anger.

Who's prone to fatigue:

• People who are unwilling to ask for what they want, or who keep waiting for people to guess.

• People who refuse to say what they don't want. Nothing saps energy and produces fatigue as much as unacknowledged resentment.

If chronic tiredness persists and the doctor says there's no physical cause, acknowledge the problem is a psychological one.

Take time to become aware of your feelings. Sit down alone, or with someone who knows how to listen (not someone who imposes his own feelings or ideas). Best choices are a respected friend or preferably a mental health professional. Explore the feelings engendered by work, or by important relationships. Figure out what unmet needs and wants you have in these areas. Then determine which expectations are realistic and which aren't, and how to go about resolving that draining aspect of your life.

Source: Gisele Richardson, Richardson Management Associates, Montreal.

Four revelations of middle age

Psychologists, in recent years, have been shifting their interest from child to adult development. They find that many of the crises and traumas associated with middle age are really simply a dropping away of illusions. Well-adjusted and effective adults are those who can accept the fact that while many of their principles and assumptions were wrong, life can still be enjoyable and productive.

What most people find are no longer reasonable expectations:

1. Rewards for doing worthwhile things will come automatically as long as one does the "right" things.

2. In most situations, rationality prevails.

3. Most people will be committed to what they are doing and will put forth their best effort.

4. There is always one best way to accomplish one's goals or the organization's objectives.

Solving midlife problems

Developing a personal philosophy of life is crucial for meeting crises to be faced day by day. (And those crises can get more complicated as one grows older.) The virtues are:

• Philosophy provides a guideline for living.

• It sounds an alarm when one's behavior is inconsistent with one's beliefs.

• It supports the ability to make a rational explanation of life's events, including the most disruptive or seemingly senseless ones.

What's required in a personal philosophy:

• It must be comprehensive. Ideally it will provide an ability to meet all life's normal crises in a balanced way.

• It requires one's full commitment. Personal philosophy can't be taken on and off like a coat. It has to provide a sense of worth.

Set up a game plan for the rest of your life. Write it down. It should include answers to following questions:

• What things are really important in your life?

• What practical considerations have to be taken into account (earning a living, raising children, lifestyle)?

• What are your greatest personal strengths? Rank them.

• What are your most limiting shortcomings? Rank them, too.

• The activities you most enjoy?

• Most dislike?

With these lists as a guide, make three sets of goals:

1. Long-term—assume normal retirement age plus 20 years.

2. Mid-term—from today until retirement.

3. Short-term—the next one to five years.

Long-term goals tend to be general (they should be), and short-term goals tend to be overly ambitious. A typical long-term goal is "Happiness." A typicaly short-term goal is "To get out of this rat race and open my own business."

Source: *Overcoming Executive Mid-Life Crisis,* John Wiley, New York.

The case for midcareer counseling

A $50,000-a-year manager with 20 years' experience has become uninterested in his job. Consequently, he has become less productive. His boss recalls past achievements, but finds his present work unacceptable. Reluctantly, the boss sees termination as the only way out.

The manager's lessening effectiveness may actually come from not having a clear picture of the boss's expectations. On the other hand, the boss may only *say* his employee's work is unacceptable when the real reason is a personal dislike. The underlying cause may be a breakdown in communications on both sides.

Midcareer counseling, to reconnect the employee's career path with the direction of the company, may be the remedy. The cost is substantial in terms of time required for this type of counseling. But it's slight compared with the $50,000 plus of salary, benefits, and training already invested in a manager with long-term seniority.

Counseling helps the boss gain a better perspective on an employee's strengths as well as weaknesses. And the intervention of an outside counselor spurs the employee to make an effort toward reconciliation because he realizes the alternative is dismissal.

The success rate is about 80%. In terms of dol-

lars, most companies don't find it cost-effective to terminate and replace a long-term employee. For about 10% of an employee's salary, the company can salvage a manager with the potential for renewed productivity.

Source: William Morin, chairman of the board, Drake Beam Morin, New York.

Becoming a more complete person

Many executives submerge their private growth in favor of their corporate career.

The executive's psyche becomes lopsided. While he develops sharp job skills, he has little interest in anything outside the office.

This myopia is more prevalent among specialists than generalists. Specialists are supposed to be single-minded. On the job, they're rewarded for it. However, their total personality suffers from that focus.

Penalties for failing to develop other interests:

• Produces a feeling that life has gone stale.

• Lowers the ability to love or take interest in family and community.

• Leads to despair. You pretend that you don't mind being so job-oriented, but you do.

Rewards of extending your interest:

• You drop some psychological defenses and use that energy to enjoy life more fully.

• You lose the anxiety, confusion, and identity crises of youth. You appreciate the joys that being older brings.

Source: Richard C. Hodgson, *Business Quarterly,* published by the School of Business Administration, University of Western Ontario, London, Ontario.

Turning 50

Life on the 50-year-old plateau is a time of great change for many people. Those who are going to advance to positions of influence in their professions have more or less already done so. Children have grown up; grandchildren may be on the way. Parents are likely to have passed away, creating a sense for the first time among 50-year-olds that they are now the older generation.

The big shifts:

• Reconciliation of dreams with reality. What many individuals fear about their fiftieth birthday is the sense of resignation about limitations and giving up lifelong dreams. The good side is comfort in accepting oneself even without those dreams. Recognizing that now is a a good time to reassess and set new, more appropriate, goals for the last 20 years.

• Greater appreciation of time. It takes most people until 50 to learn that most goals do not become reality as rapidly as expected. The result is a greater sense of leisure and enjoyment of things that exist in the present. The pressure to reach goals eases. An important realization is that it is not so important to achieve goals as it is to use them as standards to structure a life.

• Spiritual awakening. Although there is an initial disappointment in giving up the notions of egotistical immortality cherished since youth, many people begin to see themselves as links in the chain between past and future generations. There is a common energy shift from social and political activities to more spiritual and aesthetic concerns. Even relentless decision making seems less important.

• Renewal of friendships. Acceptance of oneself often generates a recognition of dependency on other human beings. People become more caring about others. This is a time of settling down with one's spouse, of intensifying friendships and appreciating basic human relationships. Some people find opportunities to teach in order to pass on their knowledge to the younger generation.

• Increase in flexibility. Most people bend away from the authoritarian views they held to during their younger years. Parents realize that they cannot force knowledge on their children through discipline, and that the best they can do is set an example and encourage them to learn from experiences.

• Appreciation of the basics of life. Good health becomes something for which one is thankful. Status symbols (the big house, the fancy car, professional awards) lose their importance.

As ambitions fade, many people move to milder climates where the pace of life is slower and life can be enjoyed day by day. But moving to a low-pressure environment can lead to dullness and enervation. Golf all year round is probably more deadly than working all the time.

Also, women tend to have an easier time adjusting to turning 50 then men. In general, there has not been as much pressure on them to achieve. And mothers who suffer pangs of loss when their children become adults usually gain grandchildren within a few years.

Nuptial bonds smooth the way through the 50s. Married people almost always have an easier time adjusting to aging than do singles.

Remember to keep activity appropriate to age and physical condition. It can be extremely dangerous (both from the risk of cardiovascular trouble or such injuries as torn ligaments) to go on an all-out athletic program in the vain hope of recovering one's youth.

Just as some people are unable to come to terms with the stress of reaching 50, some experience symptoms of the midlife crisis most people pass through in their 40s. Examples:

• Extramarital affairs. Turning to outside lovers can sometimes help people over their period of crisis, but it can jeopardize their marriages, too. Few people know how to deal with the extramarital affairs of their spouse, so being open about them is difficult. For those people who have a satisfying enough relationship to be open about an affair, there is probably less need or desire to have one anyway.

• Divorce. Turmoil, dissatisfaction with oneself and emotional depression can all affect the quality of the marriage relationship. In addition, with the children grown, and with women's-liberation consciousness more widespread, there are fewer bonds holding the family together than in the prior decade.

• Managing through the crisis period. A period of turmoil is just that, a period—with an end. Those who have been through crises before and have developed the skills to deal with them will likely have less trouble dealing with turning 50 than others will. Those who have never learned to resolve former crises may experience additional emotional residue from them. Likewise, those who have never had a life crisis may lack the skills needed to resolve their turmoil.

Psychotherapy helps many people ride over the rough spots. Although turmoil may be stressful, it often triggers untapped potential that will enrich one's life later on.

Source: Dr. Ari Kiev, psychiatrist and originator of the Life Strategy Workshops, New York.

Easing the pain of traumatic change

The death of a loved one, the loss of a job, separation, or divorce, all involve change and loss. And all require the same psychological tasks for successful readjustment. A sense of loss accompanies all major changes in life, even when the change is positive, such as a job promotion, marriage or a job transfer.

Stages by which people respond to major loss:
• Shock or denial.
• Fear and paralysis.
• Anger, at others or at oneself.
• Sadness and depression.
• Acceptance and reformulation of goals.

All the stages are important to the process of adaptation, and the omission of any can result in depression or incomplete adjustment because the energy needed to cope with the present remains bound up in the past.

The emotional difference between the terminator and the terminated is that people who are terminated are forced into a position not of their own choosing. They aren't ready for the changes termination brings, even though they may turn out to be blessings in disguise. Terminators, however, are acting out of choice and are ready for the changes that come with terminating.

In terminating either a business or personal relationship, those who initiate the termination have the upper hand. They also have the bulk of the responsibility.

To walk away from the termination with a sense of moral clarity, it is essential to have made a genuine attempt to come to some degree of accommodation with the other party, whether employee or spouse. Terminators should meet with those terminated to share their dissatisfaction when they are still open to finding a solution.

Terminators should answer these questions:
• What do they need from the other party to continue the relationship? What support are they prepared to give?
• What is an acceptable time frame for the changes to be made?
• What don't the terminators want? What aren't they prepared to give?
• How would they describe the consequences if satisfactory changes aren't made?

A reasonable period should be allowed for making changes and adjustments. Announcing requirements for change on Friday, and then deciding on Monday that the relationship won't work, is unfair.

The longer people have to rehearse a new situation and work through feelings about it, the less stress there will be and the less time it will take to adapt. For example, research among widows shows that those whose husbands died after a long illness, such as cancer, had a much less difficult time making the transition to widowhood than those whose husbands died unexpectedly, for example, in a car crash.

People resist making major changes not because they fear what's ahead, but because they are unwilling to give up what they have. The same fear hinders organizational change as well as change in personal life.

Source: Gisele Richardson, president, Richardson Management Co., management consultants, Montreal.

Grappling with depression

Before depression can be treated, the individual must first recognize that he is depressed. But many depressed individuals are unaware of their psychological condition. Indicators of depression:
• A feeling of great misery, not just sadness.
• Incorrigible pessimism.
• Preoccupation with illness, death, even suicide.

• Feelings of guilt.

• Difficulty concentrating, thinking clearly, and remembering.

• Impaired sleep. Depressed people may have no trouble falling asleep, but they may awaken very early. Early morning is the period of maximum incidence of suicide among people who are depressed.

• Infrequent, quiet speech. Sighing.

• A great deal of self-criticism, but little criticism of others.

• Stooped posture, sitting inertly, or agitated pacing.

• Sad, older-looking appearance.

• Eating little and rapid weight loss. (Depressed people who gain weight are usually only mildly depressed.)

• Little or no sexual desire.

• Preoccupation with inner feelings and self-observation.

If you think you may be suffering from depression see your doctor. He will recommend a psychiatrist or antidepressant drugs. Psychiatric therapy works best with individuals who recognize their depression. Drugs can alleviate symptoms, but are not a cure.

Many people experience depression in their fifties and sixties. The reasons may be threefold: (1) disillusionment with work (or principal occupation) and realization that there is little prospect for future improvement; (2) children growing up and leaving home; and (3) friends and contemporaries dying.

Source: Dr. Mortimer Ostow, *The Psychology of Melancholy,* Harper & Row, New York.

Changing destructive habits

Happiness and success are solidly based on feelings of self-worth, usually acquired in childhood. For those lacking self-esteem, however, retraining for a better life is possible. Pinpoint behavior problems, and work to change them.

Signs of problems:

• Name dropping. Frequently mentioning the names of important friends or expensive possessions is an attempt to borrow importance.

• Demeaning others.

• Constantly apologizing. If you think you are wrong most of the time, it may be because of lack of confidence, not efficiency. Playing the loser is part of this pattern. Instead, choose a role model, and imitate that person's successful techniques.

• Denying shortcomings and problems. This is the flip side of blame-taking. It alienates others when you refuse to let them comfort or advise you. Talk over difficulties with friends to get a new perspective.

• Interpreting comments as slights. Few are aimed at you personally. Avoid second-guessing, and accept what people say at face value.

• Compulsively deferring to others. This is the kind of repression that can lead to physical illness. Speak up. Most people prefer it.

Ego-strengthening exercises:

• Work on negative habits, one at a time.

• Cut out activities you do not enjoy. Substitute an ego-bolstering skill. Refuse boring invitations, then spend that time doing something that is important to you, such as improving your tennis game.

• Above all, take action, even if you blunder occasionally. To avoid choice and obligation deepens self-contempt. Pursue goals to achieve a healthy personality.

Self-help groups

If you or a loved one has a problem, chances are there are people around who have lived through the same trouble. They are eager to offer encouragement and other kinds of help to you, in the middle of the night, if necessary, generally without cost.

To help you find the group that you need you might contact the Self-Help Center, 1600 Dodge St., Evanston, IL 60201 or the National Self-Help Clearing House, Graduate Center, City University, 33 W. 42 St., New York 10036.

Specialized self-help groups (check your local

telephone directory for chapters in your area):
- Al-Anon: For families of alcoholics.
- Compassionate Friends: For parents who have lost a child.
- Fortune Society: For ex-offenders.
- Gamblers Anonymous.
- Make Today Count: For those along with their spouses suffering from life-threatening illnesses.
- Mended Hearts: More than 10,000 people and their spouses who have lived with open-heart surgery.
- Overeaters Anonymous.
- Parents Anonymous: For child abusers.
- Reach to Recovery: Formed by the American Cancer Society to help the thousands of women who undergo mastectomies each year.
- Recovery, Inc.: For former patients of mental institutions.

with people who are comfortable and easy to be around.
- When the holidays seem too grim, take a trip or try some totally new experience. Perhaps volunteer work in a hospital, where the emphasis will be on bringing cheer to others.
- Skip those Christmas-shopping crowds by ordering your gifts by mail, and visiting small, local shops or those in out-of-the-way places.
- Keep holiday entertaining simple. If traditions become too much of a burden, try something offbeat (for example, decorating with cut flowers instead of ornate evergreens). Or go out. Above all, don't try to give huge, exhausting affairs.
- Unless you love to receive cards from others, save the bother and expense of sending them yourself.

Fighting holiday blues

Visits to psychiatrists and physicians will jump 25% or more during the holiday season that lasts from Thanksgiving to New Year's. The most common underlying causes of distress: holiday depression, boredom, and burnout. Specifically:
- A longing for happier holidays (real or imagined) in days past.
- Loneliness. This is especially true for those in a new location or those who have recently lost a loved one or gone through a divorce.
- The feeling that holidays should be a happy time, that family life should be perfect, and that presents will bring your heart's desires.
- For those whose health is frail, a primitive fear of not getting through the cold, dark winter.

The best ways to combat these feelings:
- Don't expect too much. Unrealistic anticipation only breeds disappointment. As expectations are reduced, every pleasant surprise becomes a bonus.
- Be selective about the festivities you attend. Enjoy the fellowship more than the alcohol.
- Try not to be alone. But spend your time

Vacations and psychological health

The vacation season is a time of high anxiety for those devoted to their work. The chief sufferers are workaholics and others who derive much of their sense of worth from their jobs. Underlying problems:
- Lack of work denies these people their accustomed emotional feedback and status.
- Many hard workers, especially entrepreneurs, are excitement addicts. Deprived of work, they suffer withdrawal fatigue.
- For some hard-drivers, the fun and relaxation of free time is an unacquired taste. They have been too busy to cultivate the enjoyment of free time.

Left on their own, most of these people would never take vacations. But many are forced to. It's company policy, or they are dragged off by spouses.

Some possible solutions:
- Take a work-vacation around the house. Do chores, paint the porch, landscape the grounds. These are productive work-related activities that are also relaxing.

• Ease into a vacation by using a work-at-home activity as a transition. Work hard around the house for a couple of days. As a sense of accomplishment is fulfilled, start easing off. Go out at night for a dinner or movie. Take an afternoon off to swim or see a ball game. By then, you will feel more ready for a vacation.

• Take an active vacation like canoeing, white-water rafting, hiking, mountain climbing. These activities generate accomplishment and excitement, both vital for the work-obsessed personality.

Avoid passive vacations, such as bus tours or long visits with relatives. Vacations should eliminate anxiety. Boredom only fuels anxiety in work-oriented people.

If family visits are mandated, break them up with periods of strenuous activity. Climb a nearby mountain, or take an overnight hike. Or work around the house of the relative during the visit. It is active and shows a sense of familial commitment.

Finish the vacation a day or two before it is time to return to work. Without transition time, the shocks at either end of the vacation are exhausting.

Some managers never take vacations and resent workers who do. For these people, work is their hobby, their fun, their primary source of social interaction.

These nonvacationing managers take their jolts of excitement and recreation in small doses spread throughout the year—having leisurely lunches and dinners at expensive restaurants, taking clients to racetracks or high-stake poker games.

Most employees have no access to these diversions, at least on company time. A break away from the workplace is essential for them.

Source: Martin G. Groder, M.D., psychiatrist and business consultant, Durham, N.C.

GOOD HEALTH HABITS

Eight rules for staying healthy

Some people work too hard at making themselves healthy. Actually, the human body is an intricate organism with feedback mechanisms to maintain itself in a healthy state. Eight ways to help your body do its best:

• Eat a well-balanced diet. For most people, diet should be high in fiber content.

• Maintain a comfortable weight. Being too thin is not healthier than maintaining your normal weight.

• Do not take vitamin supplements if your diet is proper.

• Learn to cope with stress. The best ways to achieve this is through relaxation exercises, biofeedback courses, psychotherapy.

• Exercise all muscle groups daily without excessive strain.

• Avoid sleep medications. If anxiety or depression causes poor sleep patterns, come to grips with the underlying problems.

• Establish good rapport with a physician you can trust.

• Listen closely to your body. Good health is a combination of using common sense and allowing the body to heal itself. By avoiding all the good things in life, you will not live longer. It will only seem longer.

Source: Dr. Bruce Yaffe, fellow in gastroenterology and liver diseases, Lenox Hill Hospital, New York.

Eating to reduce cholesterol

Do not be misled by reports that some types of cholesterol are beneficial or that there are links between low levels of cholesterol and cancer. The weight of evidence shows that a high level of cholesterol, a fatty alcohol found in the blood, is one of three major risk factors in heart disease. The others are smoking and high blood pressure.

When all three factors are present, your risk of having a heart attack is an awesome 30–40 times greater. Children who inherit a rare high-cholesterol disease from both parents usually die before they are 20. Those who inherit it from one parent seldom reach 50.

Scientists who question the relationship between cholesterol and heart disease point out that, although there may be a link, the medical community has not yet been able to explain how it works. The question is especially tricky because the body itself produces cholesterol, which is essential to its well-being.

Some researchers once thought the body offsets cholesterol eaten in food by decreasing its own production. The fact is, the higher the intake in your diet, the higher your blood cholesterol level. And excessive blood cholesterol promotes arterial disease, which can unquestionably cause serious injury to the heart.

Some doctors have warned patients against lowering blood cholesterol levels because of a connection between these low levels and cancer. However, the National Institutes of Health have reviewed 17 studies of such links and concluded that findings in no way contradict the value of efforts to keep blood cholesterol levels down.

The NIH reasons that there does seem to be a link between male colon cancer and low cholesterol levels. But there is no evidence that reducing high levels to the normal range will cause this or any other type of cancer. And reducing them will cut the odds of having a heart attack.

The right type of diet can reduce blood cholesterol levels by 15%–25%. Sticking to such a diet is usually difficult for Americans, who get an average of 40% of their calories from fat. (In many other countries, the figure is 15%–20%.)

Essential steps to take:
• Eat food with less animal fat.
• Use primarily vegetable fats that are polyunsaturated or monounsaturated. Saturated fats raise the cholesterol levels. Polyunsaturated fats (corn, safflower, soybean oils) lower them. Monounsaturated fats (olive oil) have no effect on cholesterol levels.
• Get regular strenuous exercise.
• Avoid smoking.
• Maintain normal weight.

Apart from other benefits, this regimen promotes high-density lipoproteins (HDLs), which protect against heart disease. Cholesterol travels through the body by attaching itself to a protein. Most is carried by low-density lipoproteins that can deposit it in the cells of the arterial wall. HDLs can remove cholesterol from arterial cells.

Source: Basil Rifkind, M.D., chief, Lipid Metabolism-Atherogenesis Branch of the National Heart, Lung & Blood Institute, National Institutes of Health, Bethesda, Md.

How to beat the disease odds

The leading causes of death for male executives in their forties and fifties are cancer and degenerative diseases of the heart and liver.

A 50-year-old male executive who doesn't get much exercise but who smokes and has mildly high blood pressure has about a 15.5% chance of dying in the next 10 years. (Source: A Life Extension Institute computerized *Health Risk Profile* of a hypothetical executive.)

Causes of death in descending order or probability: heart attack, lung cancer, cirrhosis of the liver, highway accident, stroke, cancer of intestines and/or rectum.

To reduce the odds:
• Not smoking can add 1½ years.
• Exercising can add one year.
• Not drinking can add 8½ months.

- Driving with seat belt can add 6 months.
- Losing weight can add 3½ months.

Source: Dr. Ronald E. Costin, medical director of the Life Extension Institute, New York.

The moderate lifestyle for long life

People with low fat intake, low body weight, and low cholesterol levels die earlier than those who only moderately curtail fat consumption. Death is due to causes other than heart disease (often cancer or respiratory ailments). People with extensive social relationships live longer than those who are socially isolated. Running more than a mile a day decreases risk of heart disease and improves one's psychological state. Cigarette smoking is the most significant risk factor for sudden death due to heart disease.

Source: *Journal of the American Medical Association,* Chicago.

Preventive medicine for cancer

Yes, there are ways to prevent cancer.

Experts believe that the prime causes of the disease relate primarily to remediable traits like smoking, improper diet, inactivity, and depression.

Lung cancer accounts for about one-quarter of all cancer deaths. And cigarettes cause almost 80% of these fatalities, according to the *Journal of the National Cancer Institute.*

Diet has been connected to more than half of all cancers in women and one-third of the cancer cases in men.

Tumors of the digestive organs usually kill more people in a given year than any other type of cancer. Poor diet is the reason: too much food, excessive amounts of fat, not enough fiber or vitamin A.

The two most lethal forms of cancer, those in the digestive and respiratory tracts, are largely caused by factors we can control, diet and smoking.

Source: *Executive Fitness Newsletter,* Emmaus, Pa.

Kicking the cigarette habit

Tactics for giving up cigarettes vary according to the underlying motivation for smoking. Keys to the right strategy:

- Habitual smokers reach for a cigarette in response to such cues as talking on the phone or drinking. First step: Make the cigarettes difficult to reach, or put them in a hard-to-open package.
- Positive-effect smokers actually enjoy smoking. First step: Find an equally enjoyable activity that can't be done while smoking.
- Negative-effect smokers smoke because of nervousness or depression. First step: Professional advice on the basic problem.
- Physically addicted smokers should quit cold turkey. The reactions to quitting are always unpleasant. But the worst of them will be over in a week.

Source: *Executive Fitness Newsletter,* Emmaus, Pa.

EXERCISE

How to regain physical fitness

When people are deprived of physical exercise, they often try to make up for lost time by over-exertion later on, resulting in injury to the body or disenchantment with the whole idea of fitness.

The object is to feel better, so forget about scientifically measurable results at the outset. Army-training statistics show that recruits actually gain weight as they become more physically fit. Training achieves a better sense of well-being and better apportionment of weight.

Listen to your body. It knows what it's doing better than meters on treadmills or stopwatches can tell.

Start out with half an hour of movement at a comfortable pace, four times a week. Then, ask what's comfortable for your body. The point is fitness should be fun. Put yourself in the frame of mind you had as a 12-year-old, when fun and fitness went together.

A brisk walk is the body's most natural and most beneficial activity, and the easiest one to get into after a period of hibernation. Even serious runners don't regard walking as frivolous. They walk for 15 minutes and run for 15, then walk for 15 and run for 30, and so on. Walking can be combined with any activity, from tennis to aerobic dancing. Three miles an hour is the right pace if you are average-size and in average condition. But for someone with short, stubby legs, brisk walking may be at two miles an hour.

Walking has more and better tradition behind it than running. A century ago, there were many six-day races in which competitors walked as far as 500 miles. Diaries and journals tell us that many intellectuals were dedicated walkers. This means that moving our legs is somehow connected with getting our minds in motion.

Timing is all important. Each of us has a peak performance period in the 24-hour day. For most, the peak comes at about 2 P.M. That's the time when exercise is the most beneficial.

People going into a fitness program should acknowledge that if they are putting something new into their lives, they will probably have to leave something out. For many, a normal lunch break may have to be eliminated in order to exercise according to the best schedule.

And there are special problems for women. Because many women today are both career people and homemakers, their family runs the risk of being upset if they take something out of their home life to accommodate a fitness program. Women should let their families know how important their physical fitness is to them as well as others. If necessary, ask a doctor to help counsel the family.

One problem in most fitness programs is that some trainers have convinced people to think in terms of rarified scientific data. A current favorite is maximum oxygen uptake (how much oxygen you take into your system). The measurement can be so discouraging that it is counterproductive. The range of improvement is only 20%, no matter how hard you work at it. After 16 or 18 weeks, if you have improved just 5%, you may wonder what the point is.

The one criterion that comes closest to meaning anything for most people is physical work capacity. Using your muscles in any way that best suits you, especially brisk walking, can improve work capacity by up to 300%.

The prime benefit is reduced fatigue. Physical fitness, because of the increased work capacity of your muscles, means that 5 P.M. is no longer the end of the day. That in itself can be highly rewarding.

Source: Dr. George A. Sheehan, *Running and Being—The Total Experience,* Simon & Schuster, New York.

Simple warm-up exercises

What trainers recommend to prevent injury:
• Toe-touching. Bend forward from the waist, with the knees flexed slightly. Hold the stretch for 30 seconds. Let the arms hang loose, and gradually increase the amount of stretch in the leg and hamstring muscles. Don't force yourself to touch the floor.
• Thigh-muscle stretch. Kneel down. Sit back on your legs. Lean as far back as is comfortable. Then extend one leg in front, and lean back further. The goal: To get your back flat on the floor.
• Seated stretch. Place feet together, with knees apart. Lean forward, and grab the feet, stretching the inner thigh muscles as you do. Hold for 15 seconds. Rest 30 seconds. Repeat. The goal is getting loose enough to touch chin to toes.

Developing flexibility is a slow process. Stop before hitting your pain threshold.

Source: *The Cardiologist's Guide to Fitness and Health Through Exercise,* Simon & Schuster, New York.

Exercise schedule for cardiovascular health

Exercising three times a week to a moderately strenuous degree is plenty to keep the cardiovascular system in good shape. With greater exercise, there are some additional benefits. But the blood fat, blood pressure, and anxiety levels improve very little.

Overexercising is a common problem among physical-fitness advocates from higher socioeconomic levels. A pain in your elbow, calf, wrist, etc., is a signal to stop the workout immediately. Or, if muscles feel generally tired and heavy at the start of a workout, postpone it.

Source: *Executive Fitness Newsletter,* Emmaus, Pa.

Tension-reducing exercises

Basic rules for tense executives:
• Wake up early to avoid hurrying and getting keyed up before leaving the house.
• Take a short walk after lunch. Do it any time that tension is high. (Just say, "I'll be back in five minutes," and go.)
• Have a daily quiet hour. No phone calls or visitors.
• Plan social engagements to allow for a short relaxation period between the end of the business day and the start of the evening's activities.
• Always be aware of those tense moments during the day and, when they come, concentrate on breathing slowly and deeply.

At the beginning of the day:
• Before getting out of bed, slowly stretch arms and legs. (See how a cat does it.)
• Prepare for exercise by laying out a towel, sheet, or exercise mat in a quiet, uncluttered area.
• Kneel down and sit back on your heels (use a cross-legged position if this hurts), keeping the back straight. Place hands on thighs. Face something aesthetically pleasing, and concentrate on breathing for five minutes. Don't hold your breath or inhale too deeply. If you find that your mind wanders, just return your attention to your breath.
• Change to a sitting position with the legs crossed or extended. Bring one foot up onto your opposite thigh and hold it with one hand. With the other hand, take each toe and, with a few circular motions, loosen up the joints. Then do the same with the ankle, rotating on both directions. Next, press and rub all parts of the sole and upper foot. Shake the foot. Repeat on the other foot. Take your time. Show extra kindness to those sensitive spots. Breathe easily. Don't hold your breath.
• Allow a minute or two between exercises.
• Still sitting comfortably, move one arm out in front so that the elbow is bent and the thumb is pointing toward the chest, with palm down. Place your other palm on top of the hand and press downward, gently but firmly, five times. Switch hands.

• Now, place the palms together, fingers pointing toward the chest. Inhale and hold the breath in. Raise the elbows high and hard. This bends the fingers and the wrists backward.

• Apply deep thumb pressure all over the palm of the opposite hand, especially the fleshy shank of the thumb.

• Shake out both hands. Shake the arms overhead, out to sides. Stand up. Shake out the ankles, legs, torso, face. . . .Shake yourself out.

• For spine relaxation, from standing position, bend forward at the neck and let the weight of the head slowly bring your torso down. Let your jaw relax, arms dangle, knees bend slightly. When you have bent over as far as you comfortably can, inhale and exhale slowly and deeply five times. Then, starting at the base of the spine, unbend slowly. Repeat five times.

• This overall relaxer is particularly helpful after work, too. Lie on your back, arms crossed over chest or over your head, legs flexed at the knee, with feet flat on the floor. Slowly breathe in and imagine your whole body being filled with air. Slowly exhale and imagine the air escaping from the lower back and forming a cloud under you. Relax and feel the general floating sensation.

Try to do these exercises at least three times a week. Once a day is optimum. Allow at least three weeks for the calming effects to be felt. If aches result from a particular exercise, try a more comfortable position, do it slower or for a shorter period, or eliminate it for a few days. Check breathing to make sure you're inhaling and exhaling easily, according to the directions.

When time pressures limit your exercise period, sit back in your chair, place the heels and soles of the feet on the floor, let the arms hang loosely, close your eyes, and concentrate on slow breathing for a whole minute.

Eventually more exercises should be added to keep every body part flexible and relaxed.

Source: Leslie Cerier, personal fitness counselor, New York.

Relief from pain-producing jaw tension

Five exercises to ease discomfort:

• Start by opening the mouth wide, then closing it. Do this repeatedly and as rapidly as possible.

• Continue the same motions, but now place the palm of your hand beneath the chin when opening the mouth, and above it when closing. This offers a slight resistance.

• Repeat the same two steps with a sideways motion of the lower jaw, first doing it freely and then doing it against the resistance of the palm of the hand.

• Go through the same steps with a motion that protrudes the jaw.

• Chew a piece of gum alternately on each side of the mouth, then in the center of the mouth. Do each for three to five minutes.

Repeat every exercise five times twice a day during the first week. In each succeeding week, increase the number by five, to a maximum of 25 twice a day.

Source: Patricia Brown, R.N., *American Journal of Nursing,* New York.

Exercise while sitting down

Ways to improve muscle tone and blood circulation during a long trip or meeting:

• Head turning and nodding. Turn head fully in one direction, nod a few times. Then turn the other way and nod. Repeat ten times.

• Apple picking. Stretch one arm, then the other, as if picking fruit from a tree. Be sure shoulders move forward and back.

• Jogging while sitting. Raise right leg as though walking, and at the same time raise left heel. Then left arm and right heel. Continue for at least two minutes.

• Forward bends. Pull stomach in tightly, then drop body trunk while raising soles of feet off the floor. Then relax and sit back up. Repeat 30 times.

• Rising and sitting. Rise slightly from seat without using hands or arms. Sit back down and lift the toes. Repeat 30 times.

Source: *SAS In-the-Chair Exercise Book,* Bantam Books, New York.

Learn to walk more

How to get more exercise from day-to-day activities:

• Park the car farther away from the office or train station and walk.

• Quit taking elevators. Daily climbs of 18 floors or more will increase fitness, studies show.

• Eat lunch in a restaurant at least 10 blocks from the office, and stride briskly both to and from.

• Instead of driving to the shopping center, walk there. If it's too far, ride a bicycle. If there's too much to haul home, make a second trip.

• Carry your own golf clubs. And skip the golf cart, even if you're the lone walker in your foursome.

Source: *The Cardiologists' Guide to Fitness and Health Through Exercise,* Simon & Schuster, New York.

Reducing abdominal bulge

The protruding stomach and abdomen of middle age can be controlled (if not eliminated) by exercises that strengthen abdominal muscles.

They take only a few minutes a day, but should be done every day without fail to be effective:

• Pull stomach and abdomen in as tightly as possible, hold for five to eight seconds. This is a very convenient exercise that can be done many times a day, while waiting for an elevator, sitting at a desk, or in a car.

• Sit on floor with legs stretched out, hands resting lightly in lap. Raise feet four to six inches off floor and hold position as long as possible. (Maybe only a few seconds the first day, but work up to 60 seconds.)

Exercises that can harm you

The most important benefit of exercise is that, properly done, it increases longevity. But exercises that promote a single aspect of the body, such as form, stamina, coordination, speed or strength, generally have a negative impact. Especially dangerous are:

• Muscle-building exercises. They can harm joints and connective tissues. Weight lifters are not known for longevity.

• Skill-producing activities. Ballet, handball, and squash require arduous training and stop-start patterns of play, which are two negatives for long life.

• Marathon sports. Jogging, swimming, cycling, strenuous walking, which can work the body to the point of exhaustion are dangerous because stress and injury occur more easily during body fatigue.

• Speed-oriented activities. Those that require lots of oxygen, such as sprinting or speed swimming, can be fatal, especially for those who have not trained extensively for them.

Source: Dan Georgakas, *The Methuselah Factors: The Secrets of the World's Longest-Lived Peoples,* Simon & Schuster, New York.

FOOD AND DRUGS

Avoid the lure of megavitamins

Another pressure for hard-driving executives to resist is megadoses of vitamins, or of a specific vitamin. The mistaken premise is that they reduce the wear and tear of stress on the body. Professional opposition, based on continuing research in nutrition, is growing in the face of a trend to consume more and more vitamins in ever-larger dosages.

The old advice is still the best—there is no reason to take more than the recommended dietary allowance (RDA) of any vitamin, except for relatively rare individuals who cannot absorb or utilize vitamins adequately.

A megadose is 10 or more times the RDA. This is the level at which toxic effects begin to show up in adults. Even in cases of actual vitamin insufficiency, megadoses are not generally prescribed. Therapeutic doses are generally smaller than 10 times the RDA.

Vitamins are becoming more popular because of a combination of successful merchandising by manufacturers in so-called health magazines, faddism, misinformation, and questionable practices by some professionals.

Most persuasive to hard-nosed executives are enthusiastic testimonials from other executives who have been persuaded by the placebo effect of vitamins that megadoses really do make them feel better.

Some of the medical problems adults may experience as a result of prolonged, excessive intake are:

• Vitamin A. Dry, cracked skin. Severe headaches. Severe loss of appetite. Irritability. Bone and joint pains. Mentrual difficulties. Enlarged liver and spleen.

• Vitamin D. Loss of appetite. Excessive urination. Nausea and weakness. Weight loss. Hypertension. Anemia. Irreversible kidney failure that can lead to death.

• Vitamin E. Research on E's toxic effects is sketchy, but the findings suggest some problems: headaches, nausea, fatigue and giddiness, blurred vision, chapped lips and mouth inflammation, low blood sugar, increased tendency to bleed, reduced sexual function. Ironically, one of the claims of Vitamin E proponents is that it heightens sexual potency.

• The B vitamins. Each B has its own characteristics and problems. Too much B_6 can lead to liver damage. Too much B_1 can destroy B_{12}.

• Vitamin C. Kidney problems and diarrhea. Adverse effects on growing bones. Rebound scurvy (a condition that can occur when a person taking large doses suddenly stops). Symptoms are swollen, bleeding gums, loosening of teeth, roughening of skin, muscle pain.

Vitamin C is the vitamin most often used to excess. Some of the symptoms of toxic effect from Vitamin C megadoses:

• Menstrual bleeding in pregnant women and various problems for their newborn infants.

• Destruction of Vitamin B_{12}, to the point that B_{12} deficiency may become a problem.

• False negative test for blood in stool, which can prevent diagnosis of colon cancer.

• False urine test for sugar, which can spell trouble for diabetics.

• An increase in the uric acid level and the precipitation of gout in individuals predisposed to the ailment.

Better than vitamin pills are:

• Four portions a day of grains (either cereal, bread or pasta).

• Four portions of fruits and vegetables (including at least one fresh fruit or vegetable or fruit juice).

• Two or three portions of milk and milk products.

• Two portions of meat, fish, poultry, eggs, dry beans, peas or nuts.

For people who don't eat properly or want nutrition insurance take a regular multivitamin capsule containing only the RDA of vitamins.

Source: Dr. Victor Herbert, *Nutrition Cultism: Facts and Fictions,* George F. Stickley Co., Philadelphia.

Myths about food

• Myth: Watermelon is not nutritious. Fact: It is rich in vitamins A and C and contains iron.
• Myth: American cheese is more nutritious than skimmed milk. Fact: This cheese contains high levels of saturated fats, which are linked to heart disease, and of sodium, which contributes to high blood pressure.
• Myth: Corn syrup is a harmless sweetener. Fact: It contains no nutritional value other than calories and promotes tooth decay.
• Myth: Apple juice is a very nutritious drink. Fact: It contains only small amounts of vitamin C. Orange, tomato, and vegetable juices are more healthful.

Source: *Nutrition Action,* Washington, D.C.

How to stop food binges

The majority of binge-eaters are women. (Men turn more often to alcohol.) The crisis stages when the binge-eating habit usually starts are in the teens, pregnancy, and over 45 for women, and in adolescence, starting a new career, and 45 or older in men.

Binge-eating is also becoming more of a problem for businesswomen tackling both a career and a family.

Another problem common to both sexes is that executives often begin to binge when their goals are greater than their achievements. Sometimes they are competitive with very successful parents and they see themselves as losing the contest.

Ways to understand your unconscious reasons for losing fat and starting to lose weight:
• Examine your fantasies of what life will be like once you become thin. Many people think they will no longer be shy. Don't count on it. You will be disappointed and put the weight right back on. You have to be realistic about what changes you can expect in your life when you are thin.
• Separate the reason for eating from the act of eating. The two most common unconscious reasons for not losing weight permanently are equating food with love, and fear of intimacy. Many overweight persons were taught by their parents that eating well meant they were good, hence loved. Fear of the opposite sex, particularly being close, also leads to binge-eating (particularly in the 20–30 age group).
• Be honest with yourself about the real reasons for personal failures. Recognize that if you were thin, you still might not have gotten the promotion. Think again about why you were not promoted. Don't use your weight as an excuse.

In planning your diet, allow for eating binges. Work with this tendency to cheat, which all overweight people have. Alternate dieting with small eating binges. The fat person's psychology is best suited to this method of weight loss.

Source: Dr. Joyce Bockar, *The Last Best Diet Book,* Stein & Day, Briarcliff Manor, N.Y.

Hepatitis and seafood

Seafood is often avoided by people who fear they will contract hepatitis from it. While there have been sporadic epidemics of hepatitis from raw seafood, the chance of an individual getting the disease that way is remote.

The virus transmitted is hepatitis A, the mildest form. Usually, it manifests itself subclinically, perhaps appearing as a mild cold. Nearly half of all adults have been exposed to hepatitis A and have antibodies making them resistant to further infection. To be certain, have a blood test to determine your immunity.

Salt talk

How harmful is salt? It depends. A majority of the population (about 80%) can handle large doses. The average daily intake per person is about 4,500 milligrams while the body demands only 200 milligrams. The excess is passed from the body in normal waste.

Salt is a problem in the other 20% of the population when excess salt stays in the blood. One result is high blood pressure (hypertension), which can bring on a heart attack or stroke.

The best bet is to avoid salt. Most people don't know if they are among the susceptible 20%.

Other reasons to avoid salt are: there is already plenty in many foods on most regular diets; it builds up thirst, which means greater consumption of liquids and a higher rate of water retention; and it encourages heavier eating.

Source: *Executive Fitness,* Rodale Press Inc., Emmaus, Pa.

Bran facts

Tasteless and virtually indigestible, bran is touted as a cure-all for ailments, ranging from dental decay to diabetes. Medical evidence, thus far, points to only two conditions where high fiber intake is helpful:

• Routine constipation is greatly improved, without the long-term risks linked to other remedies.

• Diverticular diseases, caused by inflamed sacs on the intestines, can be reduced. However, increased bran intake will cause at least a couple of months of bloating and flatulence.

Other claims for bran, especially in warding off various cancers and bowel diseases, remain unproved. And, in some illnesses where narrowing of the bowels occurs, bran can be hazardous.

Source: *Harvard Medical School Health Letter,* Boulder, Colo.

Mixing food and drugs

Certain foods speed up or slow down a drug's absorption into the bloodstream. And some combinations can be dangerous.

Avoid mixing:

• Tetracycline compounds (antibiotics) with dairy products.

• Monoamine oxidase (MAO) inhibitors (sometimes prescribed for depression and high blood pressure) with aged cheese, Chianti wine, or chicken livers.

• Anticoagulants with excessive amounts of food high in vitamin K, such as liver and leafy green vegetables.

Source: *FDA Consumer,* U.S. Government Printing Office, Washington, D.C.

The dangers of self-medication

Many over-the-counter medications are potent pharmaceutical agents that are safe only when used exactly as directed. They can also interfere with prescription medications given for high blood pressure, stomach disorders, diabetes, glaucoma and heart disease.

Make sure to monitor any elderly person's use of home remedies. Give them a magnifying glass to help them read the fine print on the labels.

The right way to use nonprescription drugs:

• Pay particular attention to the time limitation for use. If the home treatment does not work within the suggested time, see a doctor.

• Use the minimum amount. It is a misconception that stronger aspirin and other products are better. They actually result in more side effects rather than faster relief.

• Know what prescription drugs you are taking, and ask your doctor about reactions with other drugs and alcohol. For example, liquid cold medicines contain as much as 30% alcohol. And alcohol taken with sleeping pills and antidepressant drugs can be fatal.

Source: Nicholas Popovich, pharmacology professor, Purdue University, Lafayette, Ind.

Warning on decongestants

Too much decongestant can be counterproductive. When overused, oral decongestants create nervousness or a narcotic high. Nasal types cause heightened recongestion of breathing passages after membrane-shrinking effect wears off.

Read directions. Use no more frequently than at four-hour intervals. Do not use if serious diseases (designated on label) are present.

Source: Diane Kitt, professor of pharmacy, Purdue University, West Lafayette, Ind.

ILLNESSES AND THEIR TREATMENT

Review a cancer diagnosis

Because cancer is a life-and-death matter, always seek a second opinion on the diagnosis and treatment plan, says Richard Bloch, chairman of the H&R Block tax preparers and a recovered cancer patient.

But how can you be sure of the second opinion?

One solution: Bloch spurred a Kansas City volunteer group to organize Cancer Connection,* which helps cancer patients obtain detailed and thorough reviews of their cases by a variety of top specialists. How it works:

• Counseling. Recovered cancer patients handle a Cancer Connection hot line to talk with patients whose cancer has just been diagnosed. Treatment alternatives are explored.

• Consultation. A panel of five physicians reviews each case privately with the patient for at least a half-hour. (The panel includes a surgeon, radiotherapist, psychiatrist, pathologist, and oncologist.) No examinations are made, but all available medical records are used. A written opinion by the panel goes to both the patient and the patient's personal physician.

There is no charge for the counseling and review.

*For more details contact Adrienne Krashin, H&R Block, 4410 Main St., Kansas City, Mo. 64111.

Ulcers: New light on causes and treatment

The popular image of the typical victim of a peptic ulcer is a hard-driving businessman. Fact: Not so true now, if it ever was. Males between ages 45 and 64 are the most vulnerable group. But when all ages are considered, as many women as men now have ulcers.

Also surprising is that age itself is no barrier. Ulcers are frequent among retired people. But they also afflict teenagers. And the incidence of ulcers is now higher in small towns than in cities.

A hopeful sign is that hospital admissions for peptic ulcers declined 24% from 1970 to 1977. But it's still a big problem. Currently, about 300,000 new cases are diagnosed each year; 350,000 patients are hospitalized; 50,000 have operations; and 6,000 die.

How ulcers occur. Almost everyone suffers now and then from the temporary discomfort of stomach gas or heartburn. It is the normal result of overeating: a buildup of stomach acid.

Not so normal is a painful peptic ulcer that develops in some people, especially those under stress. The gastric secretions wear away the tender lining of the stomach or, more commonly, the even more delicate duodenum, the first segment of the small intestine.

The instant effect is fierce, burning soreness. (An ulcer is, literally, a raw wound.) The condition is not readily relieved by drugstore antacids.

Ulcer terminology is sometimes imprecise, but to doctors:

• Peptic ulcers are, all-inclusively, those ulcers found anywhere in the digestive system.

• Duodenal ulcers are peptic ulcers in the duodenum. They are more than twice as common clinically as gastric ulcers. Soreness is concentrated in the area of the navel.

• Gastric ulcers are peptic ulcers in the stomach.

The worst case is a perforated ulcer where the acid eats through the organ wall, allowing contents to spill out into the body cavity, threatening life. Blood transfusions and an operation are usually necessary. And the incidence is rising among women, though it remains stable among men.

Why ulcers happen. Excessive gastric acid is secreted, especially at night, when the stomach has the least need for it. Usually lacking food to digest, the hypersecreted digestive juices attack the visceral tissue.

Hypersecretion is triggered by a genetic predisposition combined with emotional distress, illness or other trauma, especially in older persons. Chronic causes are the excessive use of alcohol (the leading trigger of ulcerating hypersecretion), aspirin, cigarettes, and coffee.

A developing ulcer is easy to diagnose. And even advanced ulcers respond to a new pharmaceutical, Tagamet®, which represents a new era in ulcer treatment. Tagamet checks gastric-acid secretion for long periods, especially through the night. But it is recommended only for duodenal ulcers.

Source: Dr. Arthur S. Loebel, gastroenterologist and peptic-ulcer consultant, Red Bank Medical Associates in New Jersey; The National Center for Health Statistics, Hyattsville, Md.

Discomforts of hiatal hernia

Hiatal hernia, a condition caused by overeating, obesity, injury to the stomach or a congenital deformity, is fairly common, especially in older people. Symptoms include chronic heartburn or indigestion. It is caused by a weakness in the diaphragm, which allows the stomach to move up into the chest area alongside the esophagus. Stomach acids are not tolerated by the esophagus and some minor, but discomfort-producing, damage may result.

Treatment includes taking antacids, establishing a light diet, avoiding raw fruits and vegetables and juices, and keeping the head elevated at night. Surgical repair is major surgery.

Battling migraines

The best way to deal with recurrent, intense migraine headaches is to try more than one solution. Chronic sufferers (estimated at between 8 million and 12 million Americans) can try one or more of the following:

• Keep a headache diary. Note the times a headache starts and stops and what you were doing, eating and thinking. The records help a doctor evaluate the condition and help patients discover causative factors.

• Avoid aggravating foods and drinks. These include edibles containing tyramine (nuts, chocolate, aged cheese), sodium nitrate (frankfurters), and alcoholic beverages.

• Headache sufferers who are on birth-control

pills should consider switching to another contraceptive method.

• If aspirin doesn't provide relief, ask your doctor about propranolol (marketed by Ayerst Laboratories under the name Inderal®), now considered the safest, most effective antimigraine medicine on the market.

• Get more opinions. Ideally a neurologist should verify that the condition is indeed a migraine.

Colds: what you don't know can hurt you

Doctors cannot cure a cold. But sufferers can help themselves by keeping in mind what is known about the ailment. Essentials:

• Chills don't cause colds, but they encourage existing viruses to multiply.

• Colds spread most effectively by direct contact and are most contagious in their early stages before the symptoms are even noticeable.

• The body's process of curing a cold requires about the same energy as hard physical labor. Keep vigorous exercise to a minimum so your energy goes toward fighting the cold.

• Taking vitamin C may help. Advocates suggest one to three grams a day at the outset of a cold and 500 milligrams daily throughout its duration.

• Avoid stress during a cold. It reduces antibody production in the nose and mouth.

• Don't numb pain by drinking alcohol.

Source: *Executive Fitness Newsletter,* Emmaus, Pa.

How to fight the common cold

Your own body's defenses work better than pills or liquids from the drugstore.

The inflammation that causes a stuffy nose, sore throat, congestion, headache, and general discomfort is a sign that antibodies are fighting the infection. A low-grade fever (below 101 °F) helps to keep cold germs from spreading and multiplying. Treating these symptoms with antibiotics slows down the healing process.

Consume liquids to soothe your throat and prevent the dehydration that comes with a fever. Stay warm by bundling up. Cold viruses can't multiply rapidly when there's a slight fever, so don't attempt to bring one down. Get plenty of rest. The effort your body puts forth to fight a cold is equivalent to hard physical labor. Don't try to work during the worst days of a cold.

Remember, antibiotics kill bacteria, not the viruses that cause colds. Taking them is expensive, useless, and potentially dangerous.

Source: Hal Zina Bennett, *Cold Comfort,* Clarkson N. Potter Publishers, New York.

Backstrain and driving

The probability of spinal disk problems is three times greater for those who spend a big part of their work lives driving. To reduce the strain on your back:

• Keep your head and shoulders erect while driving. Place a 1½-inch-thick pillow, or a wicker back support, at the small of the back. Keep the back pressed against it.

• Change driving position often.

• Take frequent breaks to stretch your legs and do one or two exercises:

1. Grab your wrists, and raise your arms to shoulder height. Try to pull your arms apart for a count of six. Repeat three times.

2. Hold your forehead, then push your head against your hand. Repeat for each side of the head. Do slowly three times.

3. Lace your fingers behind your head and press back against them. Do slowly three times.

Using the car to steady you, do at least four deep-knee bends.

Source: Shirley Linde, *How to Beat a Bad Back,* Rawson, Wade Publishers, New York.

Nearsightedness: two ways to view it

Myopia, or nearsightedness, afflicts more than one-third of the U.S. population. Sufferers usually get advice from either an optometrist (who examines eyes and prescribes remedial devices) or an ophthalmologist (a medical doctor who specializes in eye disorders). Expect the two to have widely differing views about the affliction.

According to optometrist Irwin Suchoff, myopia is becoming more prevalent because of environmental factors such as television watching. Some people develop temporary myopia—accountants at tax time, lawyers preparing briefs, etc.

Preventive measures:
• Schedule a thorough exam once a year.
• Take periodic breaks every half hour when reading. Rest your eyes for at least five minutes by shifting your gaze to other objects.
• Hold reading material at about your forearm's length. Use a lamp with one 100-watt light bulb placed behind you and to the side.

Corrective measures:
• Eyeglasses.
• Exercises. If undertaken early enough, prescribed exercises can help relieve, or even cure, myopia.
• Contact lenses. Hard lenses are usually more effective than soft. But soft lenses require a shorter adjustment and can be worn more casually. New gas-permeable lenses are as comfortable as soft ones, but offer better correction.
• Orthokeratology. The use of hard contact lenses to improve eyesight by changing the cornea's shape. But it is expensive, improvement may be only short term, and it is an unproven therapy.
• Keratotomy. Surgical procedure in which a series of slits are cut into the cornea. It should be considered only as a last resort. It is also quite expensive. Not recommended for progressive myopia.

Ophthalmologist David Knox has a different viewpoint. According to Knox some people are genetically predisposed to myopia. Reading and other environmental factors may aggravate nearsightedness, but do not cause it.

Preventive measures: None. Corrective measures include eyeglasses or contacts. They are safe, proven, and relatively inexpensive.

If you consider contacts, let the ophthalmologist determine which kind is best for you. And gas-permeable lenses do not give as sharp acuity as hard lenses.

Dr. Knox's negative views on alternative cures:
• Exercises. Optometrists believe in visual training, ophthalmologists do not.
• Atropine and other drug therapy. Atropine paralyzes the eye muscle, but it does not improve vision.
• Orthokeratology. A waste of money. Benefits are short term.
• Keratotomy. Not recommended. Induces astigmatism. Risks infection. Gives only minuscule correction and creates glare. Very expensive.

Source: Dr. Irwin Suchoff, professor of optometric sciences at the State University of New York College of Optometry, New York, and Dr. David Knox, associate professor of ophthalmology, Johns Hopkins Hospital, Baltimore.

Taking care of your feet

Basically, the amount of trouble you are likely to have with your feet depends on the shape of the feet you inherit.

Hammertoes are anatomical deformities. The tips of the toes dip toward the ground causing the tips to develop bumps on top. Cure: Shoes with high toe boxes. Ultimate cure: Have the hammertoe corrected and realigned by having microsurgery (a minimal incision), a procedure that can be done in the doctor's office.

Bunions develop when a toe moves in one direction and the bones linking the toe to the foot (the metatarsals) move in another direction. Ambulatory microsurgery can eliminate the bump. The bunion is shaved down. A microincision is made, and a tiny surgical burr is inserted through the incision to reduce the bump. This can be done in the office. Patients can usually return to work the following day. Pain is minimal. Note that pumice stoning the skin off a bunion is ineffective.

Corns result from a lack of fat padding between skin and bone. Artifical pads help. Or, the bone under the corn can be smoothed down so that it does not rub against the shoe. This is also done by microsurgery, and usually allows patients to return to work the same day. Avoid liquid corn removers. They are mild acids, which burn away healthy skin, too.

For a major foot problem, see ambulatory-trained surgical podiatrists familiar with micro-surgery. The cost of treatments varies from $200 to $1,500. They are usually covered by most health insurance plans.

For good-feeling feet wear shoes with high toe boxes and vary the height of shoe heels to keep ankle tendons and muscles from shortening and tightening.

Source: Dr. Louis Shure, podiatrist/foot surgeon, New York.

SURGERY

Operations that are often unnecessary

Major surgery is too often thought of as an easy way to deal with certain ailments. But as medicine becomes more sophisticated, some operations that were once routine have been replaced by less radical treatments or should be performed only when there is clear cause. Examples:

• Tonsillectomy. Now prescribed only for recurring ear infections that cause loss of hearing, after a series of strep throat infections or when enlarged tonsils substantially impair breathing.

• Hysterectomy. To relieve profuse bleeding or back pain ostensibly caused by a large or displaced uterus. Be certain that the uterus is indeed to blame and that the problem cannot be stopped by other means.

• Varicose vein operations for cosmetic purposes. Many patients are disappointed with the results and the ensuing months of discomfort and limited activity. Before the operation, ask the surgeon exactly what results to expect.

• Ruptured disc surgery. Symptoms can often be relieved completely with bed rest, pain-killers, muscle relaxants, and traction. Before an operation, make certain that X-rays prove that the disc is indeed ruptured.

• Exploratory surgery prompted by chronic abdominal pain. Modern X-ray and other diagnostic testing have made this operation virtually obsolete.

Source: George D. LeMaitre, M.D., *How to Choose a Good Doctor,* Andover Publishing, Andover, Mass.

Restorative dentistry: fact and figures

• 50% of the people in the U.S. who are over 65 years old have lost all their teeth.

• 25% of those over 55 years old have lost all their teeth.

• 60% of your adults (ages 20–34) have periodontal (gum) disease.

• 80% of middle-aged adults (35–54) have periodontal disease.

Finances and other personal factors determine how long a restorative dental program takes. A well-planned program can include: replacement of missing teeth; repair of inadequate fillings; and treatment of nonemergency periodontal problems, cosmetic repairs, etc.

Source: Dr. Marvin Mansky, D.D.S., New York.

Getting rid of acne scars

The skin's own healing ability is the key to eliminating or reducing the unsightliness of acne scars. There are three types of scars.

1. Pits: Ranging from tiny dents (sometimes indistinguishable from pores) to deep, ragged craters.

2. Hypertrophic: Fibrous, discolored thicknesses.

3. Atrophic: Thin, slightly depressed patches.

Such scars can be caused by any acne lesion, such as blackheads, pimples, or red, boil-like inflammations. None poses a health threat, but the scars cause some individuals to live with a private, unnecessary anguish about their looks. Treatment is most effective after the acne-prone years, which occur from the mid-teens to the mid-twenties. Usually only a few visits to the dermatologist's office are needed. There are three favored treatments at present.

Dermabrasion. The most widely used technique, it sands the afflicted area down to the level of most scars. Following a consultation and a photographic session (for a before-and-after record), the patient is given a general painkiller (usually Demerol®), and then a local anesthetic (a skin refrigerant). The abrasion is performed with a wire brush or a diamond-dust stone, which is attached to a device resembling a dentist's drill. Scarred tissue and surrounding areas are abraded to ensure uniformity of skin color and tone afterward. Upon healing, the skin will return to its normal texture, minus the scars and some superficial wrinkles.

Once scraped, the face is a raw, draining lymph until the scab forms about two days later. There may be initial pain and itchiness. The scab falls off in about two weeks (plan to take a two-week vacation during the scabbing period), followed by a couple of months when the skin is slightly pink and tender. It's essential to avoid the sun during this period. The healing process goes on, unnoticeably, for about a year.

From dermabrasion, expect elimination of most superficial pits and a 50%–80% improvement of deeper scars. The cost is $500–$1,500. Risks include infection, gouging (during the abrasion), hyperpigmentation (discoloration) if the skin is exposed prematurely to the sun.

Dermabrasion is not recommended for hemophiliacs or individuals allergic to anesthetics or metals. The treatment must be used with extreme caution on dark-skinned people, including blacks, Orientals, and Latins, because of the increased likelihood of hyperpigmentation.

In severe cases, dermabrasion may be repeated, but not more frequently than once a year. Or it may be combined with one of the localized scar-removal methods (such as excision or pit incision).

Excision. This procedure surgically removes the entire scar, including the depression, after which the wound is sewn up along skin lines. The fine stitches are removed five to seven days later. The cost is $50–$250, and the risk minimal.

Pit incision. It removes the base of the acne pit with a tubular surgical instrument. As the wound heals, the pit floor moves upward and into plane with the skin surface. The cost is $50–$250, risk minimal.

Antiscarring treatment is usually confined to the face and is far less effective on other acne-vulnerable areas, such as the neck, back, torso or buttocks. These areas heal less easily than facial tissue, and treatment can lead to additional scarring.

Source: Dr. Rabin M. Sarda, former clinical instructor in dermatology at New York Hospital, Cornell Medical Center, practice in New York.

Eyelid surgery for men

Aware of the unquestionable advantage of maintaining a youthful appearance in today's business world, more and more men are having cosmetic surgery.

The most common kind is eyelid surgery, involving the removal of fatty pockets under the lower lids and the overhanging skin from upper lids, which cause a baggy, aged look around the eyes.

When properly done, this cosmetic surgery will not be obvious. Incisions can't be seen because stitches are hidden in the eyes' natural folds.

Eye surgery (any cosmetic surgery) can be done in an office operating room or a hospital. People using the hospital go in the night before, have surgery the following morning, and then go home. In the office operating room, patient arrives in morning, has surgery the same morning, and goes home by noon.

The operation lasts about two hours. Whether in hospital or office, usually local rather than general anesthesia is used.

After-surgery care: Rest is the primary ingredient. Once home, the patient is directed to lie down and keep ice pack or cold compresses continually applied to eyes. It's important that someone be around the first day, to provide care and aid in the application of cold compresses, which helps limit swelling and bruising around the eyes.

What to expect post-operatively: Very little pain after the first night. Stitches are usually removed two or three days after surgery.

For the first few days, the eyes look bruised and swollen. Patients have been known to return to work three days after surgery, a day after the stitches are taken out, using sunglasses to cover the bruised, swollen eyes. By the first ten days, virtually all swelling and discoloration have disappeared. In 30 days, the patient's surgery is usually not noticeable at all.

The cost of eye surgery ranges from $1,500 to $2,500 (depending on what's done—upper and lower lids or just lower). Most people focus on the bags under the eyes. Just dealing with the lower lids will not provide as satisfactory a result as will treatment of both.

Anyone disturbed by eyes that look aged and baggy, or by a face that appears tired all the time should consider the surgery. The selection of a plastic surgeon is crucial, particularly in regard to his standards for success.

There is no foolproof method to finding a good surgeon, but there are precautions patients can take to guide their choice.

Ask the surgeon for pre- and post-operative photographs of other patients he has operated on. Make sure more than a few photographs are shown, so that the surgeon is showing typical rather than exceptional results. See some former patients of his in person.

• Make sure he is a trained, fully accredited plastic surgeon.

• Draw him out on his standards for successful surgery. In combination with examining photos of former patients, discussion may help prevent selecting a surgeon who will produce the unnaturally taut look too many overambitious cosmetic surgeons inflict.

Source: Dr. Henry Zackin, plastic surgeon, New York.

34 PERSONAL MONEY MATTERS

MANAGING PERSONAL FINANCES

Family money management

Executives who are perfectly capable of managing multibillion-dollar corporations are often inept when it comes to managing their personal finances. The reasons are that they devote too little time to the task, they invest their personal funds too timidly, and they don't think of their families as businesses and, as a result, don't run them like businesses.

The first step in getting organized is to disclose the true state of the family's finances to a spouse. For many executives, this will mean a major change. Many high-salaried executives conceal the true state of their net worth and income from their family members.

Next, actively involve the spouse in managing the family's finances. Set aside a minimum of one day a month to review financial decisions and to agree on guidelines for future decisions. The monthly review should cover the family bud-

get, debt policy, investment strategy, and insurance coverage.

Other steps to take:

• Families with no wills or with wills that were drawn up before the recent changes in inheritance laws should prepare a will now.

• Executives should figure out their net worth to determine their borrowing power.

• Review life-insurance policies. Many were purchased at a time when executives were less financially sophisticated.

• Review the family's investment portfolio to see how effectively it serves as an inflation hedge. Many executives balk at investing in precious metals and collectibles because they feel "it's not me." But most sizable portfolios should probably include 10% of a conventional collectible.

Once a family begins to think of its assets and income in a businesslike way, it will find that disciplining its consumption habits is much easier. Many families overspend because they never identify any alternative use for the cash. Furthermore, families that attempt to operate as businesses should gradually find that they have more money to invest.

Family expenses

Families with incomes of $30,000 and up spend their money on: housing, 22.5% of budget; food, 20.4%; transportation, 8%; clothing, 5.5%; medical care, 3.9%; personal care, 1.9%; all other purchases, 10%; Social Security taxes, 4.7%; personal taxes, 23%.

Source: Bureau of Labor Statistics.

Stopping payment on a check

Give your bank a written request. This is the only way to hold the bank liable if it cashes the check after receiving the stop-payment order. Not all banks honor an oral stop-payment request, and those that do generally honor it for only 14 days.

Source: *The Professional Report,* Scarsdale, N.Y.

How private are your bank records?

When it comes to providing information to nongovernmental sources, each bank establishes its own rules regarding the information it will make available. Ask your bank to explan its policies. Some can provide a written policy statement.

Many banks refuse to disclose any information about you to a private individual, unless there's a court order. But most banks will be very open in supplying information to credit bureaus and other genuine grantors of credit, such as department stores. They certainly will if you list the bank as a credit reference. Generally, the bank will give such information over the telephone if it is familiar with the calling institution. It might, however, ask for a written request if it does not have a standing relationship with the inquirer.

A bank usually discloses:
• Whether your checking account is good or whether there have been overdrafts.
• Whether it has loaned you money, how much, for how long and whether or not you have made your payments on time.
• The size of your savings accounts. Bank officials will talk of "high four figures," or "low five figures," and so on.
• What kinds of loans you have with the bank: mortgage, personal auto.

Banks keep credit agencies up to date about your loan payments and the amount of credit available to you. This information pertains to lines of credit on credit cards as well as other credit lines and actual loans.

If a merchant calls a bank to determine whether a check you are presenting is good, or if a credit card is good for a certain amount, the bank will usually tell a merchant. Department stores' computer terminals often provide the same kind of information, disclosing whether the amount involved can be covered by the account. But the computers usually do not give the exact amount in the customer's account.

Can you prevent a bank from giving out this information? At this time, it is impossible to prevent disclosure of this information unless you do business with a small bank that knows you well. Problem: Most banks have this information on computers and the technology, at least technology at a reasonable price, has not been developed to isolate individual accounts to block the dissemination of such information. Many people want their banks to supply information to credit grantors because this enables them, the individuals, to obtain additional credit more easily.

If you choose a small bank, however, especially one that is not automated, it is possible that the bank would agree not to give out information about you to anyone unless ordered to do so by a court.

The Bank of America, the country's largest bank, has a typical policy. "We will respond to a recognized business or a credit-rating bureau," reports one of their vice presidents.

On an installment loan, the Bank of America will disclose the approximate size of the monthly payment and the remainig balance on the loan. On a practical level, it would be impossible for the bank to single individual accounts on which it would not give out any information.

A better way to go bankrupt

Traditionally, when an individual goes bankrupt, he liquidates his assets and pays off his creditors. In doing so, he tries to conceal enough from his creditors to make a fresh start.

But there's another way to go bankrupt. Just as companies can file for reorganization of their debts under Chapter 11 of the Bankruptcy Code, individual wage earners can file for a reorganization of their debts under Chapter 13.

Instead of bailing out and starting all over, the individual submits to a court-supervised negotiating process. He and the creditors decide what portion of his debts he will pay off and on what schedule. Usually, debtors have three years to pay back their debts under Chapter 13.

Under the U.S. Bankruptcy Code, updated in 1978, bankrupt debtors are given more leeway under Chapter 13 to pay back fewer cents on each dollar owed. The updated code also reduces the power of unsecured creditors to veto Chapter 13 debt-reorganization plans, prohibits creditors from asking debtors to change repayment schedules once a court has approved a plan, and removes all mention of the debtor's bankruptcy from credit reports 10 years after debts have been repaid.

Personal bankruptcy used to be a life-wrenching last resort for people so deeply in debt, and so harried by creditors, that no other option seemed viable. The typical profile: low-income, undereducated laborers or clerical workers. Very young or over 65. Rootless non-homeowners.

Today, people with good jobs—quite often, two-income families—and household incomes as high as six figures declaring bankruptcy not from dire necessity but merely to rid themselves of debts that cramp their life-style. The most common filers are recent college graduates, who file bankruptcy to avoid paying back government-guaranteed student loans, and older, keep-up-with-Joneses types. From suburban executives to Park Avenue professionals, they're unwilling to live within their means.

Lawyers are aggressively promoting this new way out of debt, especially in California, Florida, and New York. But there are two things lawyers don't mention in their ads: One is that lawyers always get paid up front, even before filing the papers. The other is that the bankruptcy goes on the client's credit record for up to 10 years.

Safe-deposit boxes are not so safe

Banks renting safe-deposit boxes to customers cannot be held legally responsible if a box's contents are stolen or damaged in a fire or other disaster. An exception is if a customer can prove that the contents of his box were stolen or damaged because of the bank's negligence, and that the missing or damaged contents were in the box, he can collect. Limited legal liability on safe-deposit boxes is of special interest to investors storing collectibles.

Source: Paul Higgins, vice president, corporate insurance, Bankers Trust Company, New York.

His and her safe-deposit boxes

Immediate access to wills, insurance policies, and other important papers is denied in those states that require banks to seal safe-deposit boxes when a person dies. So rent two. Each spouse keeps the papers needed if the other dies. Even better is a corporate safe-deposit box. It's not subject to "death-sealing."

LOANS

Bank's secret formula for determining your creditworthiness

A credit-scoring test helps banks to quickly process the thousands of small loan (up to $5,000) applications they get each year. Factors in credit scoring: Credit record, worthiness, stability. Irony: Assets owned by the applicant are given little weight. And so systemized are these tests that few banks bother to create their own. They are done by outside firms that specialize in the business.

How credit scoring works: The most important element in granting a loan is the applicant's past credit record. If it is negative, chances of obtaining the loan are extremely poor.

Creditworthiness is considered next. This is based not on income but on characteristics that indicate whether or not the applicant is a good or a bad risk.

The tests usually attach great importance to the stability of the applicant. Examples: How long the applicant has worked at the same place. Length of time lived at the current residence. Negative element: Having an unlisted phone number. This indicates the applicant might be trying to avoid bill collectors.

Scoring systems vary from region to region to take into account different lifestyles. Example: Not owning a car is an important negative item in most parts of the country. But in New York City, where relatively few people have cars, car ownership is less important.

Once completed, the tests are a screening technique. An applicant who falls into the bottom 30% is usually automatically rejected. One in the top 30% may be granted a loan. Many banks put emphasis on credit scoring to satisfy the government's equal-opportunity drive in the credit area. With a blind test, every applicant is judged objectively, without regard to such factors as race or national origin.

Note: Larger loans, those of $10,000–$25,000, are not subjected to the mass-production techniques of credit scoring. Each of these loans is judged on an individual basis. These loans are seldom secured with property or holdings. Most loans in this category are granted or rejected on the basis of the applicant's assets.

Cosigning loans for friends and family

Three out of four cosigners of finance company loans are eventually asked to pay up. There may also be late charges due to a friend's or relative's delinquency. Sometimes even court costs and legal fees. Besides having to pay off the original loan, cosigners may damage their own credit rating in the bargain.

So never cosign a loan unless you can pay it off if necessary.

Try to get the lender to hold your obligation to the principal of the loan. Never pledge your own property to secure such a loan.

Request notification in writing of any missed payments. That way you are aware of the borrower's delinquency and can either make payment yourself or prod the friend or relative before the loan is called or there are penalties.

One-to-one loans: No matter how friendly a loan, it's a good idea to draw up a note stating terms and conditions. Be businesslike. Include a provision for reasonable interest. Good reason for formalizing the loan: the Internal Revenue Service. With documentation, you should be able to take a tax deduction on any loss.

Borrowers should consider credit insurance

Lenders are prohibited by law from stipulating that credit insurance (which insures loan payments in the event of a borrower's illness or death) be purchased before a loan will be made. But there are times when credit insurance is a good idea—and times when it isn't.

A single person without dependents probably should not insure the debt, since the idea is to protect those left behind against debts.

Since credit insurance always costs the same regardless of the borrower's age, health, or occupation, it can be an excellent buy for older people, people in poor health, or people in hazardous occupations.

People who already have substantial life insurance or a salary continuance program may not need credit insurance.

Borrowers with enough savings to carry the cost of debts in case of short-term disability generally can avoid credit insurance.

Source: *Down Easter's Lemon Guide,* Bureau of Consumer Protection, Augusta, Me.

INSURANCE

Insurance alternatives for life or business partners

Business partners, two-income families, and owners of closely held corporations have usually relied on whole life insurance policies to insure against each other's deaths. Several new types of policies may offer even cheaper alternatives.

Next-death plans. Two or more individuals can be covered with permanent, cash-value life insurance that pays death benefits on the first participant to die and then, sequentially, on the others covered.

Premiums are based on the actuarially weighted average age of the participants. Savings are generally 25%–55% compared to the cost of separate whole life policies covering each person individually. When a participant dies premiums are recalculated and new policies automatically issued.

Multiple life. A term policy covers two or more lives and provides either a fixed amount of protection or a decreasing amount. The first variety, known as level-term coverage, is similar to next-death plans, but it is based on a five-year renewable term policy.

Since participants will be older upon each renewal, premiums increase every five years. If two or more members die in a common disaster, benefits will be paid on both. However, if all the members die, total benefits will be paid as though all but one had died. The premium saving over comparable separate term policies is about 15%, depending on the average age of the participants.

Where less coverage is needed as the years pass, companies offer decreasing-term multiple life. Insurance can be bought for 10- 20- or 30-year periods. The amount of protection decreases annually until 80% of the insured period has elapsed. From then on, the coverage is 20% of the original.

In choosing a policy, consider more than just the premiums themselves. In many cases, the type of partnership arrangement will determine coverage. To back a debt or to protect children's dependent years, a decreasing-term policy may be best. A family, however, would also have lifelong needs. Tax implications and cash-flow objectives may also be deciding factors.

Because these less costly insurance plans mean smaller commissions to the agent, many tend to ignore them. If they're not interested in talking about them, persist.

Source: Sal Nuccio, president, Nuccio Organization, Ltd., Yonkers, N.Y.

Term insurance trap

The new select term life insurance policies that promise to save money for buyers who remain healthy are not recommended by insurance consultants. With these policies, the premium drops periodically, provided the person passes a physical every five years. If the customer fails the exam, however, the premium shoots up, making the policy more expensive than standard term.

Cutting insurance costs by raising the deductible

Homeowners can cut insurance costs and increase protection by taking a higher deductible. The premium on a $60,000 home is $200 and rises to $245 when the insurable value rises to $80,000. However, a $500 deductible, instead of $100, lowers the premium to $196 and gets the homeowner another $20,000 worth of protection. Don't let coverage drop below 80% of the home's value (the minimum percentage required for the full compensation on total loss). In most states, reimbursement for partial loss will be limited to the ratio of the purchased coverage to the total value of the home. For example, if fire guts the $8,000 kitchen of an $80,000 home insured for only $60,000 (75%), the insurer will reimburse the homeowner only $6,000 (75%) for the kitchen.

Taking higher deductibles on automobile insurance is more attractive then ever, thanks to inflation. For example, a 45-year-old man living in Kings County, N.Y., drives a late-model full-size American car for nonbusiness purposes. His comparative costs:

Standard comprehensive policy
$100 deductible	$104 per year
$250 deductible	$ 71 per year

Standard collision policy
$100 deductible	$339 per year
$500 deductible	$222 per year

The savings will be about $150 per year (one-third).

The higher deductible is also desirable because it eliminates having to report the accident to the insurance company.

Source: Marvin Sameth, president, Kurtis Sameth Hill, Inc., New York; Philip Gordis, *How to Stay Ahead Financially*, W.W. Norton & Co., New York.

Insuring home collections

Executive families are well advised to check the limitations on coverage of coin collections, jewelry, and silverware in their homeowner insurance policies. Those written after 1976 usually limit fire and theft to $100 per occurrence for currency and coins, and $500 for jewelry, watches, stamp collections, and furs.

In view of inflation and the rise in crime rates, the safe course is to take out a rider on valuables. Average costs are 20¢ per $100 for silverware to $1–$2 per $100 for jewelry. Appraisal is necessary for items worth more than $2,500. Appraiser directories are available from the American Society of Appraisers, Washington, D.C., and the Appraisers Association of America, New York.

Photographic proof

To speed up an insurance claim in case of fire, flood, or other damage to your home, a photographic record of your possessions is the best means of establishing proof of loss.

Check your policy. Items such as the building itself will probably be compensated for to the extent of replacement cost. However, furnishings (for example, sofas and silverware) are usually covered under the heading of actual cash value (ACV). With a photo, you have documentation that an old and valued chair is worth the

$500 you claim rather than, say, the $5 the insurers may offer.

Guidelines for photographing household possessions:

• Use an instant-copy camera, to get the job done to your satisfaction in a day.

• Photograph everything you own. Open cupboards to show contents. Even objects that appear to be inexpensive and ordinary may be costly to replace.

• Don't forget the boiler, water heater, and pump.

• Mark the backs of the photos with model and serial numbers and other pertinent information.

• Unstack pots and pans and group small appliances when shooting kitchen appliances.

• Put silver and bric-a-brac on black velvet material to make them look as valuable as they are. Shoot them with color film.

• Don't neglect the bicycles, tools, and barbecues in the garage.

• Get exterior shots of shrubbery and other landscaping, which are generally covered by insurance.

• File the pictures, along with receipts and related documents, categorizing them by room.

• Store the file and the insurance policy in a bank safe-deposit box.

Insurance after retirement

Getting life insurance coverage for one's later years can be a problem, since most company group policies end at retirement. Premiums are astronomical if the executive buys an individual policy at age 65 or 70. One solution is for the company to make tax-deductible payments on behalf of executives into a fund held by the insurance company (or a trustee). When the executive retires, the fund buys him a paid-up policy. It's called Retired Lives Reserve. The company may buy coverage for executives only, and not for other employees, without losing the tax-deductible feature. (If the company has ten employees or fewer, it most cover all of them, but it can provide more liberally for officers.)

ESTATE PLANNING

For owners of closely held companies

The immediate goal of nearly every owner of a closely held company is to maximize income for the family. The long-range goal is to do the same for the next generation. The problem is that management is so busy running the business that it fails to follow policies that lead to either goal.

The basic strategies:

Retirement plans can be used to separate the owner's worth from the company's. Then even if the company falls on hard times, the owner can retire with financial security. And company contributions to the plan are a valuable tax deduction. The trap to avoid is requiring fixed annual contributions out of company earnings. Then, if the company suffers a few bad years, it may not be able to afford contributions without damaging liquidity.

Corporate recapitalization allows the owner to exchange common stock for preferred stock that pays regular dividend income. Further growth in company value is reflected in new common stock transferred to key employees or the owner's children. It gives them incentive to work for company growth. A drawback is that although the preferred stock gives the owner generous income now, it can be eroded by inflation.

Key-man insurance paid by the company can be used to pay estate taxes when the owner dies.

That way company stock does not have to be redeemed to pay the tax.

Gifts of stock may also give the children a motive to take interest in company affairs. Side benefits are reduction of taxes as long as children are in a lower bracket, and removal of stock from the owner's taxable estate. On the other hand, it is an error to give stock to very young children whose interest may not coincide with the owner's in 20 or 30 years.

With the help of a lawyer and accountant, the owner must find answers to key questions:

• What would happen if the owner dies prematurely? Will the surviving spouse be able to run the company? Can present management continue the business successfully? Is there enough cash for estate taxes?

• Who should inherit the company? Does a child who is not the owner's favorite show the most management ability? Are key employees so essential to the company that they should be offered minority, or even majority, ownership? Can the stock be fairly distributed if only some children are active in the company? Would it be best to sell the company on the owner's death and distribute the proceeds?

Flexible planning is essential. It can be achieved through techniques that are reversible, such as a will to bequeath control of a company to the child who shows the greatest interest, or a revocable trust or an irrevocable trust that expires at a certain date. If circumstances change, the owner can adjust the plans accordingly.

The greatest danger lies in not facing up to these difficult issues. The likely results when the owner dies will then be confusion within the business, unnecessarily high taxes, and acrimony within the family.

Limits on estate planning

Any will or estate plan must take into account the legal limits that govern the allocation of inherited property. The principal ones:

• Under varying state laws, a widow has the right to a minimum portion of her late husband's estate as dower. A particular state's law may specify, for example, 35%. If the widow is left a smaller amount, she can sue. The comparable right to a surviving husband is called curtesy. In a few states, minor children are allowed specified percentages of a parent's estate.

• If a person dies without a will, his property will be distributed according to the intestacy laws of his estate. These apportion his assets to his next of kin (spouse, children, siblings, etc.), according to definitions that vary from state to state. Even when a person has a will, if it is legally flawed, the laws of intestacy override the stated wishes of the deceased. The most common flaw is that the will lacks the minimum number of witnesses specified by state law.

• An individual may have left property to persons who actually die before he does. Or a beneficiary may refuse to accept a bequest for personal or financial reasons. Unless the decedent makes provisions for contingent or successor beneficiaries, the property will go to the remainderman (the person named to get what is left after all specific bequests have been honored). This could leave the remainderman with far more than had been intended.

• A person's will may intend to leave the bulk of the property to favored beneficiaries and very little to the remainderman. But inflation could raise the value of the person's properties far above his expectations. Specific dollar bequests to favored beneficiaries account for a small part of the estate, and the remainderman becomes the chief beneficiary. To avoid this, make bequests in percentages rather in dollar amounts to self-adjust to inflation.

• The laws of some states place restrictions upon certain bequests. A state may provide, for example, that bequests to tax-exempt organizations, such as hospitals or churches, are void if made within 30 days of death. The laws are intended to discourage "bequests under pressure." But they can prevent a person's intentions from being carried out.

• Joint or mutual wills (usually by husband and wife) can ensure that upon the death of the second spouse, property that had been owned by the first spouse to die will go, under a prearranged plan, to relatives or friends of each spouse. Result: The second spouse to die must leave property according to the terms of the joint or mutual wills. But check with your tax adviser first. There can be heavy tax penalties for restrictions on property left to a surviving spouse.

• Many corporations purchase group insurance for employees in which the policy specifies that proceeds have to go to the surviving spouse (or to the children if there is no surviving spouse, or to the parents if there should be no children, and the like). This limits the ability of the employee to designate who will benefit financially from his death.

• The Internal Revenue Service can make a prior claim against an estate. For example, if the deceased owed back taxes, the IRS can attach the cash-surrender value of any insurance policies on the decedent's life which he owned, or in which he had a significant incident of ownership.

Source: Dr. Robert S. Holzman, author, *Estate Planning: The New Golden Opportunities,* Boardroom Books, Millburn, N.J.

In case you are disabled

• The simplest step is to delegate power of attorney to someone with financial expertise to handle yor business and financial affairs. But there are drawbacks: The power ends in some states if you become legally incompetent. It ends in all states when you die. You are personally liable for any acts the proxy commits in your name. Some third parties may be reluctant to deal with the proxy for fear he may be exceeding his mandate.

• Set up a standby trust triggered by a specific event, like an illness. The trust ends when the disability ceases. This avoids probate.

• Declare yourself trustee of all or part of your property. If you become incapacitated, a substitute trustee automatically steps in. This type of trust also avoids probate. But the trust can be overridden in some cases. If you own shares in a Subchapter S corporation, an improperly drafted trust could end the company's favored tax status.

• Avoid a judicial guardianship. It's complex and expensive because the courts require a periodic accounting from the trustee.

Using a recession to reduce estate taxes

When the owner of a privately held company dies, the Internal Revenue Service calculates the value of the stock he leaves his heirs and the estate tax by looking at, among other factors, the price/earnings ratios of public companies that can be used for comparative purposes. So expect the estate tax liability to increase between now and when the owner dies.

To minimize this tax bite, owners of privately held companies should look into recapitalizing their companies now by:

• Issuing and retaining a new block of preferred stock in the company.

• Forming a limited partnership or holding company with common and preferred stock that owns all or part of the operating company to freeze values.

• Transferring ownership of some of the common stock to the heirs or to trusted employees of the company.

What this accomplishes:

• The tax due on common shares transferred to their heir is minimized, because their value will be calculated on the basis of price/earnings multiples that may be temporarily depressed in a recession.

• When the owner dies, the estate tax on the preferred stock of the company or limited partnership interest will be less than that which would have been payable on the common stock, because preferred shares or limited partnership interests in growing companies do not appreciate as fast as common shares.

Source: Arthur Rosenbloom, senior vice president, Standard Research Consultants, New York.

Dangers of a homemade will

Drafting your own will may seem like a money-saver in the short run. The ultimate cost, though, can be high. There are so many technicalities with which to comply. Even if you do everything right, disappointed heirs will be encouraged to attack the will in court in hopes that a formal defect will be found.

In a recent case, a certified public accountant wrote out his own will, signed it and had two of his employees witness it. When the will was probated, one of his granddaughters attacked it, arguing that the witnesses' signatures might not have been properly obtained. As it turned out, the court ruled that the formalities had been substantially complied with. But the judge went on to observe that the "cost of a probate contest might well have been avoided if the drafting and execution of this will had been done by an attorney. The desire to avoid the use of one attorney resulted in the employment of two.... Self-help, at least within this context, clearly represents 'the triumph of hope over experience.' "

Source: The estate of Nathan Agar, 185 NYLJ, No. 53, page 7.

Cut costs of administering your estate

The major problem for executors and lawyers is making sure all assets and obligations are accounted for after a testator dies. The time spent running down assets and redrafting for omissions can increase the legal fee and lead to an unintended estate distribution if a major item isn't mentioned or an unexpected obligation is discovered.

A solution is to have a list of all major assets and obligations drawn up by the testator before the lawyer starts to work on a will. Update the list at least once a year, and keep it with the will. What to include on your list:

• Real estate. Identification of property, location of deed or other title documents, recent tax receipts, and appraisal or firm offer to buy.

• Stocks and bonds. List of all securities and location of certificates.

• Mortgages, notes, cash and equivalents. List of items and where documents are kept. Name, branch, and number of each bank account (specify if joint or in trust account for tax/estate purposes).

• Insurance. List of all policies, where kept, loans outstanding, and names of insurance agents. Include life insurance of which testator is beneficiary, as well as policies on his own life.

• Jointly owned property. Description, location of documents, and nature of interest.

• Miscellaneous property. Include specific items only if value is high.

• Gifts already made. Should be listed, if reportable, on gift/estate tax returns. Be sure gift tax, if any, has been paid.

• Power of appointment. Spell out any powers testator holds or has granted.

• Annuities. List all money to which testator is entitled and where the documents are kept.

• Major objectives. To specify enough details for executor to discharge testator's intent when estate is liquidated.

What to do in advance:

• Keep inventory in loose-leaf book for easy annual update.

• Keep separate records for property of spouse, acquired prior to marriage or inherited separately, to avoid tax problems when testator dies. One way is to route all transactions for this type of property through individual bank accounts for each spouse.

Source: Paul P. Ashley, *You & Your Will,* McGraw-Hill, New York.

Juggling pensions and estate taxes

A common misconception is that those who survive you will have an automatic tax advantage if you arrange for your qualified pension fund to make a lump-sum payment to your beneficiary. Reason: Payouts from pension funds are becoming so large that they can significantly affect estate taxes.

• Lump-sum payments may still be most advantageous, from an income-tax standpoint. But keep in mind that they must normally be included in the taxable estate. Even if the plan names a beneficiary to be paid at the pensioner's death, the Internal Revenue Service will treat the value of the pension as part of the estate.

• If a lump-sum payment is made to a beneficiary other than the estate, the beneficiary can reduce the income-tax bite by using 10-year forward income averaging or, in some cases, by taking advantage of capital gains treatment for pre-1974 contributions to the plan.

Source: Sidney Kess, partner, Main Hurdman, New York.

Keep life insurance out of widow's estate

One solution is to leave life insurance proceeds in a trust, with the widow to receive the income as long as she lives, but having no control over the assets. If the widow cannot invade principal or make decisions about who gets the assets after she dies, they will not be taxed in her estate.

Another way, illustrated in a recent ruling by the Internal Revenue Service, is to have the husband's will provide that life insurance proceeds be held by the insurance company, with income paid to the widow for life. In the IRS ruling the widow had power to invade principal if needed for support (including education) of children. But she could not take principal for her own use. True, she had powers to direct the use of the money, but only for the benefit of others (the children), not for herself.

In this case the children were adults. The result would have been different if they were minors and the local law obligated the parents to support them. Then, using the money to support the children would be held to benefit the mother, and the fund would then be taxable in her estate.

This ruling should be read in the light of more flexible arrangements now possible under the qualified terminable interest (QTIP) property rules.

Source: Rev. Ruling 79-154, 1979-1 Cumulative Bulletin p. 301.

Keeping the estate out of the corporation

The decedent's will called for his executrix to redeem his shares so that the estate would not be involved in the company. However, if a corporation redeems a shareholder's stock at a time where there are earnings and profits sufficient to pay a dividend, the payment will often be taxed as a dividend.

But the court allowed this redemption without taxing it as a dividend because it was done in the interest of the estate rather than the beneficiaries.

Source: *Rickey, Jr. et al.* vs *U.S.,* 5th Cir., 592 F.2d 1251.

Estate planning briefs

High fees of expert financial advisers should not discourage individuals from obtaining a custom-fitted estate plan. Even though personal expenses are not generally deductible for tax purposes, this fee is different because a major consideration in the devising of an estate plan is taxes (estate, gift and income), so that the part of a plan's cost involving determination of tax liability is deductible.

Be sure to have the financial adviser itemize the portion of his bill affecting tax considerations. It should be separate from charges for drawing up the will, setting up trusts, etc.

Source: *Sidney Merians et al.,* 60 T.C. 187.

A decedent's gross estate will include the proceeds of an insurance policy on his life if he held any significant incident of ownership in the policy, such as the right to designate beneficiaries, at the time of his death. But when a divorce decree legally required one decedent to maintain his children as beneficiaries under his employer's group life insurance plan, this incident of ownership was effectively taken from him. The result was that the insurance proceeds weren't includible in his estate.

Source: *Estate of Theodore E. Beauregard, Jr. vs Comm'r.,* 74 T.C. 603, 6/26/80.

Retiring to one state while holding property in another can open an estate to dual tax claims. Most probate courts also require the appointment of an ancillary administrator to handle the title transfer to heirs, resulting in more legal fees.

The solution is to put out-of-state property into a trust for heirs with yourself as administrator. Or transfer ownership to a child with the understanding that you can occupy the property at certain times.

Source: Stanley Hagendorf, attorney, quoted in *Medical World News,* New York.

Be wary of ready-made trust forms, with only names and amounts to be filled in. One state has permanently barred one from sale. In another case, a kit-purchaser's trust was disregarded for tax purposes and the promoter was penalized for intentional disregard of Internal Revenue Service rules and regulations.

Proceeds from Series EE bonds can be paid to surviving relatives without probate court proceedings. If the bonds are held in the names of co-owners, they become the property of the co-owner who dies last.

TAXES

Saving on personal income taxes

In filing their annual personal tax return, executives commonly overlook one or more of these areas:

Capital-loss carry-overs from losing investments of the mid-1970s. Such carry-overs last indefinitely, until they are used up to offset gains or deducted against ordinary income. Even if individuals have no capital transactions for the current year, they should be sure to claim any carry-over against ordinary income. The maximum deduction is $3,000 on a single or joint return. Short-term loss carry-overs are deductible in full to the maximum. Long-term loss carry-overs are deductible on a $2 for $1 basis.

Income averaging. If income was unusually high relative to earlier years, the excess can be taxed as though it were earned over a four-year period.

Extensions. Individuals are entitled to an automatic four-month extension of the time to file the tax return. Obtain it by filing Form 4868 with the local Internal Revenue Service service center by April 15. A further extension can be obtained if the taxpayer shows a good reason for requesting it. In addition to giving the taxpayer extra time to devise tax strategies, an extension delays the deadline for making a contribution to a Keogh plan.

Distribution from a company retirement plan made in a lump sum may be subject to special income averaging. The taxable portion of the distribution is treated as though it were received over a period of 10 years, and taxed at the lowest rates in the single-person tax scale.

Head-of-household status can result in lower tax rates of unmarried individuals. The taxpayer must provide a home for a child, grandchild, or qualifying dependent. A parent who lives apart from the taxpayer or in a nursing home may qualify as a dependent if the taxpayer pays more than half of the parent's support.

Sales taxes. Using the sales tax tables supplied by the IRS may result in too small a deduction. If big-ticket items (a car, boat, expensive furniture) were purchased during the year, tally the tax indicated on sales receipts.

Bad debts must be deducted in the year they go bad. There must be an identifiable event indicating the debt's worthlessness, such as a declaration of bankruptcy or a failed attempt at collection.

Disaster losses occurring in an officially designated disaster area during the year of filing may be deducted from income in either that year or the year before, whichever produces the greatest tax benefit.

Job-hunting expenses are deductible when the taxpayer looks for a new job in an old line of business. Included are travel expenses and the cost of meals taken with others.

• Hobby losses are generally not deductible. But some hobbies occasionally turn a profit. If a hobby has resulted in a profit during any two of the last five consecutive years, the IRS will accept it as a profit-motivated activity. Expenses related to the hobby are deductible.

Periodical-subscription costs are frequently deductible. If the periodical is related to the taxpayer's business, it is a business expense. If the taxpayer has investment income, stock market letters and investment publications are deductible.

Medical-expense deductions are frequently overlooked. Any payment is deductible if applied toward the diagnosis, mitigation, treatment, or prevention of disease, or if it affects any bodily function or structure. This includes:

• The cost of transportation to and from the doctor's office, hospital, drugstore, etc., including transportation to visit hospitalized dependents.

• Social Security taxes paid on the salary of a private nurse (as well as the nurse's salary).

• Insurance on contact lenses.

• Birth-control pills prescribed by a doctor.

• The extra cost of a special diet.

• An air conditioner used to ease breathing problems.

• An adapter that puts subtitles on a television set for the deaf.

• Elastic stockings for swollen legs.

• A face-lifting.

• Hand controls for the car of a handicapped person.

• Attorney's fees to cause the hospitalization of someone who is mentally ill.

But medical expenses are deductible only to the extent that they exceed 5% of the taxpayer's adjusted gross income.

Source: Florence B. Donohue, tax attorney, New York.

Four common tax traps

1. Selling the wrong stock. An executive planning to sell part of a stock holding that he acquired in several lots should tell his broker which lot he wants to unload. If he does not, the basis for determining gain or loss will be attributed to the first lot purchased, and this may be a tax disadvantage.

2. Making the wrong charitable contribution. Executives often contribute stocks rather than cash to charities. In some cases, they contribute the stocks selling at the most depressed price, thereby losing the tax write-off attributable to the decline in value of the stock. By selling the stock first, then contributing the proceeds to the charity, the donor would get two deductions, for the contribution and the capital loss.

3. Borrowing too heavily to invest. Executives who have investment indebtedness, and pay interest charges of $10,000 more than the net investment income, may be limited in their deduction for interest paid in excess of this amount.

4. Using Individual Retirement Accounts incorrectly. Using the IRA as security for a loan is a mistake. The amount collateralized is a taxable distribution from the IRA account.

Source: Robert S. Corman, managing tax partner, Laventhol & Horwath, New York.

The advantages of wash sales

Taxes can sometimes be reduced by selling and repurchasing the same security, a technique known as a wash sale.

An investor who has short-term gains for the year may also hold securities that have declined in value. He sells the securities to get a capital loss, which offsets the gain, then repurchases the same securities. He has saved on taxes and his investment portfolio remains unchanged.

But the same securities cannot be repurchased within 30 days of their sale, or the loss will be disallowed. They can, however, be repurchased after 30 days, and similar securities can be bought immediately.

Or the investor may have a long-term capital loss for the year, and also own securities that have gone up in value. In this case he sells the securities for a profit, without incurring tax because of the offsetting loss, then immediately repurchases the same securities. (The 30-day rule does not apply to profitable sales.)

Thus, the taxpayer's cost basis in the securities is increased. Future profits that may result from their ultimate disposition will be reduced. And current long-term capital losses have been used dollar for dollar to reduce future capital income.

More breaks in capital gains

The new tax law makes long-term capital gains even more valuable for high-bracket taxpayers. Until the 1981 law was passed, there were two different rate ceilings. For earned income, the maximum rate was 50%. For other income, the maximum was 70%. For all taxpayers, only 40% of a long-term capital gain is usually taxed. But high-bracket taxpayers have had to treat this 40% as "other income." This meant the maximum effective rate on long-term gains was 28% (70% tax rate × 40% taxable portion of gain).

The 50% ceiling now covers long-term capital gains. Thus the maximum tax on long-term capital gains is now 20% (50% rate × 40% taxable portion). The change applies to: gains from property sold after June 9, 1981, and to installment payments received after that date on property that was sold earlier. For corporations the capital gains rate is still 28%.

For assets purchased after June 22, 1984 and before 1988, the long-term capital gains holding period is reduced to six months.

Deducting for home entertainment

The cost of a business party at home is tax deductible even if business isn't conducted directly. But it's important to keep good records. Even though entertaining for good will is allowed, the Internal Revenue Service is suspicious when it's done at home. Records should include receipts for food, drink, flowers, bartender, waiters, and all similar expenses; a complete list of everyone who attended, with their business relationships specified; and a statement of the purpose of the party. Better still, dictate a memo at the office the day after a party, stating what business ideas were generated by the party. File the information in the office and keep it up to date.

Caution: If the IRS isn't satisfied with some of the records, the whole deduction may be disallowed.

Deducting weather-caused property damage

Drought-caused damage to personal property is not deductible as a casualty loss. A deductible loss must result from an identifiable event that is sudden, unexpected, or unusual in nature, such as a storm or flood. The event that causes the damage need not be caused by a single storm, however. Unusual and extreme weather conditions occurring over a relatively short period of time have sometimes been considered a single event:

• A tornado and two thunderstorms occurring over an eight-day period were considered to be a single event causing damage to a taxpayer's home, because the three storms were part of the same storm system.

• Over an 18-day stretch, alternate days of freezing and thawing occurred at twice the normal rate, while precipitation was 35% above normal. Ground pressures resulted in deductible damage to the taxpayer's house.

Even though drought-related damage isn't deductible, damage caused by too much rain might be, as borne out by past records:

• Rainfall in 1954 was 40% below normal for six months in some parts of the country. Then came the wettest July since 1889. As a result, the taxpayer could deduct the cost of a collapsed ceiling.

• Rainfall that was 36% above normal over a four-month period in 1972 resulted in deductible damage to a driveway.

A well-documented record of unusual weather can help win the case for a casualty deduction.

Source: Letter Ruling 8025093; *Ferris* vs *U.S.* 9 AFTR 2d 1414, DC Vt. 1962; *Daniel P. Hesler,* T.C. Memo 1954-176; *O'Connell* vs *U.S.* 29 AFTR 2d 72-596.

Taking every deduction for alimony

Alimony payments made under a divorce decree (or a written separation agreement) are deductible by the party who makes them and are includible in the recipient's income. Child support payments are not deductible.

To qualify as deductible alimony, payments must be in cash under a written separation agreement or a divorce decree. They must cease on the death of the payee spouse.

Payments that qualify as deductible alimony include:

• Medical and dental expenses paid for the ex-spouse.

• Insurance premiums on a policy that has been assigned to the ex-spouse when the ex-spouse is the beneficiary or has the power to name the beneficiary.

• Rent paid on residential property occupied by the ex-spouse.

• Mortgage payments on a residence occupied and owned by the ex-spouse. (If property is jointly owned, half of the payments are deductible.) Also deductible: Real estate taxes, insurance, and utility costs borne by such a residence.

Source: Edward Isaacs & Co., CPAs, New York.

New rules for foreign business conventions

New rules governing the deductibility of costs related to foreign business conventions contain both good news and bad news for traveling taxpayers. Fewer deductions will be available, but the ones that do remain available will be more generous then they were before.

Eliminated were:

• The limit of two deductible conventions per year.

• The rule limiting the deduction for travel expenses to the cost of coach or economy fare.

• The requirement that the taxpayer report how much of each day was spent at convention activities.

New restrictions:

• No deduction will be allowed for any convention held outside of North America unless it is at least as reasonable to hold the convention outside as in North America. North America includes the U.S. and its possessions, as well as trust territories of the Pacific, Canada and Mexico. Certain Caribbean countries may also qualify by treaty with the United States.

• No deduction will be allowed for any convention or meeting held aboard a cruise ship.

But reporting requirements have been liberalized. From now on, rules governing the documentation of normal business expenses will be applied to foreign conventions. Required: A contemporary record of the amount, time, place and business purpose of the expense.

Business deduction for an auto accident

When personal use of an automobile leads to a lawsuit, the cost of settling can sometimes be deducted as a business expense. The rules are illustrated by two recent cases.

In the first case, an employee left work early because he was feeling ill. He drove his own car, taking with him some business reports to review at home. On the way, he injured a pedestrian, who sued him. The employee settled for $20,000. Then he tried to claim the amount not covered by insurance as a business expense. The deduction was denied, since the employee was on his way home at the time of the accident. Commuting is a personal activity, so the accident was not work-related.

In a second case, a company's controlling shareholder allowed his son to use a company car for personal business. The son severely injured another motorist. The victim filed a multimillion-dollar suit against the shareholder, his son and the company. The firm's credit line was frozen and its financial viability threatened. The company quickly settled the suit and deducted the settlement as a business expense. The deduction was allowed. The company had a valid business reason for settling the case.

Source: *Hall* vs *Comm'r.*, T.C. Memo 1980-485; Kopp's Company vs *U.S.*, 46 AFTR 2d 80-6018.

Deductions for political contributions

Making a political contribution is not as simple as it used to be. And the rules vary depending on the office a candidate is seeking.

Half of the first $100 of all political contributions is deductible dollar-for-dollar as a tax credit on the federal income-tax return. Since state income taxes are often calculated on the basis of the federal tax paid, this may reduce the state income tax as well.

The maximum credit on the federal tax return is small, however: only $50 ($100 for joint returns).

Individuals used to be able to inflate their credit a bit by donating appreciated property to a candidate or campaign committee. Now the gift is recognized for tax purposes as if the donor had sold the property and donated the proceeds the same day. The current value cannot be written off without noting and paying any capital-gains tax due.

Federal law limits the maximum donation to any one candidate for federal office to $1,000, and up to $2,000 for all candidates in any one year. State or local campaign laws vary.

The cost of running a voluntary activity, such as a fund raiser, is not considered a contribution subject to federal limits unless the cost is more than $1,000. Campaign materials, such as bumper stickers or advertising, are also exempt, as long as they are given to a political party or independent fund-raising committee. The independent committee can act on behalf of a candidate, but it must be run separately from the candidate's own efforts.

Charitable contributions and the tax law

Future contributions to charity can be deducted through the use of a short-term trust. This is best for individuals who give a regular amount to charity each year and intend to keep doing so. Instead of giving cash to the charity, form a trust with a life of under 10 years. Fund the trust with assets that produce about enough for the annual contribution.

For example, $10,000 worth of corporate bonds bearing 15% interest to produce $1,500. Each year for the next nine years, the trust pays $1,500 to charity. Then the individual gets the bonds back. This will provide a deduction now for the present value of the full $13,500 that the trust will pay out over the next nine years. But the individual must pay income tax on the interest earned on the bonds placed in trust, as the interest accrues. This offsets some of the benefits.

The taxpayer receives a large deduction now, while the later offsetting tax on the trust fund income will be spread over nine years.

Another possibility is funding the trust with tax-exempt municipal bonds. The taxpayer benefits from the same current deduction for the value of the trust's future contributions to charity. But since the trust's income is tax-exempt, there will be no offsetting tax in later years.

Or an individual might wish to retain use of some property while alive but bequeath it to charity. Under the law, taxes imposed on most estates are greatly reduced or eliminated. So the bequest will result in little or no estate tax benefit. One solution is to use a charitable remainder trust to obtain an income tax deduction immediately for the transfer of property that will occur at death.

An individual puts income-producing property in trust. Income from the trust is then paid to the individual and the spouse as long as either of them lives. On their death, the trust assets pass to charity. This way, the individual gets an income tax deduction now for the present value of the property that will pass to the charity when the individual dies. (The value of the deduction is computed on the basis of standard mortality tables.)

Be advised that a charitable gift utilizing a trust must be arranged with great care. Numerous technical requirements must be satisfied. So be sure that the arrangement is reviewed by an expert.

Alternatively, if an individual does not want to go through the trouble and legal expense of establishing a trust, the same tax break can be had by contributing income-producing property to a pooled-income fund. This fund is a trust that is maintained by a public charity. The individual retains the right to receive income from property transferred to the fund. On the donor's death, the charity receives the property.

And remember that charitable gifts do not have to be made in cash. Significant deductions can be obtained for contributions of used property (furniture, appliances, books, clothing, toys). Be sure to request an appraisal and a receipt for what the donated items are worth.

A cash contribution to a public charity should not be made in the same year that a taxpayer intends to take a long-term capital gain. Instead, give securities equal in value to the intended donation directly to the charity. You gain a deduction for the full market value of the appreciated securities. You avoid capital gains tax. If the charity is given cash, and the capital gains are taken separately, the taxpayer will get the same charitable deduction but will still be liable for the capital gains tax.

When securities have declined in value, do not give them to charity. The capital loss deduction will be lost. Instead, sell the securities and give the charity the proceeds. This results in deductions for both the contribution and the capital loss.

Source: David S. Rhine, CPA, tax manager, Seidman & Seidman, New York.

Charity begins with the tax return

Being sophisticated in making gifts to charity can pay off in tax savings and make charity dollars stretch further. There are pitfalls, however.

Tax deductions are permitted for cash or property given to a wide range of organizations. To find whether an organization is considered a bona fide charity, check with your accountant, the IRS, or the National Information Bureau in New York.

Generally, charitable deductions can be taken up to 50% of adjusted gross income in a given year. If gifts exceed that, individuals can carry over the excess to the following five years, subject to the same annual ceilings.

Always get a receipt. For property or securities, the needed detail includes cost basis, date of gift, and method used to arrive at fair market value. New proof rules require expert appraisals of personal property gifts and gifts of closely held stock, for gifts over $5,000 ($10,000 for stock). The appraiser must sign an appraisal summary that accompanies the return.

The taxpayer cannot deduct for the time and effort spent doing charitable work. But out-of-pocket costs such as uniforms, postage, stationery, phone calls, use of a car are all deductible, as are those of holding a charitable luncheon or dinner.

Donation of books, clothing, paintings, antiques, stamps, coins, jewelry, and many other items can result in substantial tax deductions. Everyday items like books, old clothes, and toys can easily be donated to the Salvation Army, a local library, or local charities that are pleased to get such gifts. For income tax purposes, deduct the fair market value of these items at the time of the gift. Your accountant (or the local Internal Revenue Service office) will provide specific guidelines on fair market value.

For substantial gifts like expensive paintings, statues, or antiques, use the *Offical Museum Directory* of the American Association of Museums to find the galleries and museums that may accept important works. Moderate-value items such as stamps, coins, period clothes, or folk art can be given to a state or local historical society. Get names of such organizations from *American Association of State & Local History Directory.*

When making gifts of important, expensive items, an expert appraisal is mandatory. Such gifts often trigger IRS audits. As noted above, the appraiser must sign an appraisal summary that accompanies the return, and must include his tax ID number.

The donor of appreciated securities doesn't have to pay taxes on the capital gain, but gets a deduction equal to the market value of the securities on the date of the gift.

A variation is to make a "bargain sale" of appreciated securities to a charity. Sell the securities to the charity for the original cost. For example, $5,000 worth of stock purchased five years ago is now worth $10,000. Sell the securities to the charity for the original $5,000. The deduction is $5,000. Pay capital gains tax on part of the appreciated value of the stock, cutting the deduction slightly (the amount will vary depending on circumstances).

Charitable gift annuities permit making a gift of cash or appreciated securities to a charity (usually a college or religious organization). In return they provide a substantial tax deduction in the year the gift is made, plus a guaranteed annual income for life. The actual amount of the tax deduction and lifetime income received depends on the guaranteed annuity rate provided by the charitable organizations, donor's age, and size of gift.

Example (from a deferred annuity program offered by a small college): The college guaran-tees a 6.8% annuity rate for a man aged 70. If such a person made a $100,000 gift to the college, he would receive $6,800 (6.8%) a year in income for the rest of his life. He also would be permitted to take a $39,478 charitable deduction (39.48% of the value of the gift) in the year in which the gift was made. Of the $6,800 a year in annuity income, 72.4% is tax-free. These latter percentages are determined by IRS tables.

A gift can be arranged so it provides the donor with an annuity for his lifetime. Then, at his death, his spouse (or someone else he has designated) can also receive an income for life. In this case, the annual annuity the donor receives will be slightly less. In the example above, if the 70-year-old donor had a wife the same age, instead of receiving $6,800 a year until his death, and nothing afterward, his wife would continue to benefit from the annuity for the rest of her life.

The mathematics change, based on the donor's age. For example, a 50-year-old man making a $100,000 gift would get a $15, 257 initial deduction and a $5,200 (5.2%) annuity, 53.9% of it tax-free.

Source: Dr. Robert S. Holzman, author, *Estate Planning: The New Golden Opportunities,* Boardroom Books, Millburn, N.J.

Charity deduction at home

Host families for foreign exchange students in the U.S. cannot claim them as dependents. But up to $50 per month of the cost of maintaining an exchange student is deductible as a charitable contribution.

Deductible expenses include unreimbursed amounts spent for books, clothing, transportation, recreation and medical or dental care.

The student must be enrolled full time in the twelfth or lower grade of a U.S. school. The student must live with the taxpayer under a written agreement with a school, charity or other organization that qualifies under Internal Revenue Service rules to receive charitable contributions. But summer vacations are not periods of full-time school attendance, so expenses incurred during those periods can't be deducted.

Source: Sec. 170(g). Regulation §1.170A-2.

Personal charity eased

Fewer than 30% of all taxpayers have enough deductions to itemize. And only taxpayers who itemized benefited from charitable contribution deductions. Now it will be possible to claim a limited amount of such contributions without itemizing.

Limits: $25 in 1982, $75 in 1984 and 50% of all charitable contributions in 1985. Beyond 1985, all contributions will be deductible without itemizing.

Reducing the risk of an IRS audit

There is no way to guarantee that a personal tax return will not be audited. But it is possible to reduce the chance of an audit.

Ten recommendations:

• Answer all questions on the tax return. The Internal Revenue Service computer will flag the unanswered question and target the return for further examination.

• Report all income that may be reported on information returns by others. Banks report interest paid to depositors. Brokers report the entire amount of capital transactions. Corporations report dividends paid to shareholders. If the amounts reported on information and tax returns do not agree, the IRS will want to find out why. See that what is reported agrees with what payers report.

• Categorize each deduction. Do not list deductions under a heading such as miscellaneous. When a deduction is not categorized, the IRS will assume that it can't be proven.

• Attach all forms that must be filed with the return. For example, a deduction for employee business expenses requires the filing of Form 2106. Also be sure that the amounts listed on different forms agree with each other.

• Don't take the largest possible deduction taken by taxpayers generally. That increases the chances of an audit. And the greater a deduction is relative to national averages, the greater is the audit risk. This is not to say that legitimate deductions should not be taken. But when a deduction is legitimately large to begin with, do not make it even larger.

• Avoid round numbers. A deduction that is rounded off to the nearest hundred or thousand dollars will raise IRS suspicions. It appears that the taxpayer is guessing at the deduction's size, rather than reconstructing it from records. (It is all right, though, to eliminate cents.)

• Check arithmetic, If the IRS finds computational errors, it may reexamine the entire return for accuracy. Careless returns suggest careless records, which can undo the taxpayer.

• Avoid tax shelters. Many tax shelters are perfectly legitimate. But because so many are not, the IRS is suspicious of them all. A person who invests in a tax shelter greatly increases chances of audit.

• Pay the right amount of taxes during the year through withholding and estimated tax payments. An audit may result from either an underpayment of taxes or a refund request. If the correct amount is not paid, it is better to overpay rather than underpay. In fact, statistics indicate that taxpayers who overpay are less likely to be audited than those who underpay.

• Never defend a challenged deduction by stating that it has always been treated that way. The IRS may disallow the deduction for earlier years as well.

Source: Dr. Robert Holzman, author, *Estate Planning: The New Golden Opportunities,* Boardroom Books, Millburn, N.J.

What the IRS looks for in an audit

John Smith received word that his 1981 tax return is being audited. His income was about $40,000 that year. He honestly and accurately reported all of it. What's more, his deductions were within reasonable norms for his income level. But Smith was among the unlucky taxpayers whose returns were chosen for audit completely at random. As a result, expensive time and effort went into preparing old records for IRS examination.

No tax advice could have helped Smith avoid the hassle with the tax man. There are, however, ways to cut the odds of an audit.

• If possible, don't lump the bulk of the deductions in the same category in a given tax year. The IRS employs a computer-screening process to flag returns with what the service considers unusually high medical, travel and entertainment, interest expenses—or higher-than-normal charitable deductions and the like. Many taxpayers are guided by the "average" deductions report as to these categories in previous tax year. While the IRS computer program is a closely guarded secret, it seems that the IRS looks for odd combinations of deductions, even if the deductions are "below average," for example, high interest deductions with average charitable deductions. (Why give to charity when the taxpayer had to borrow heavily?)

• Avoid questionable tax shelters. They make the entire return suspect. IRS investigations often work backward from tax returns of the shelter's partnership, too.

• Don't carry a large amount of cash or negotiable securities on air trips. If the wad is noted during a routine airport security search, the IRS will hear about it automatically.

• Be extra careful with claims for substantial refunds. Such claims will set many tax agents off in search of disallowances to match them—and more, if possible. A refund claim virtually amounts to a request for an audit, according to many tax experts, since large claims are automatically flagged by IRS computers.

• Let your accountant ask for tax rulings, without mentioning your name. If the ruling is unfavorable to the taxpayer, the IRS may check to see if the taxpayer acted in line with the ruling or went against it anyway.

• Answer all the questions on the tax return. Often missed: "Did you deduct expenses for an office in your home?" and "At any time during the tax year, did you have an interest in or a signature or other authority over a bank account, securities account, or other financial account in a foreign country....?"

Other audit triggers:

• Taxpayers who are major stockholders or officers of a corporation being audited may also be selected for examination.

• The IRS may pursue supposedly illegal funds through several transactions and entangle a "clean" taxpayer in an audit.

• An informant may tell the IRS about supposedly unreported income or unsubstantiated expenses.

IRS spot checks

IRS auditors sometimes spot check a personal return for travel and entertainment expenses, medical expenses or contributions. How spot checks work: the auditor selects about five to ten out of a possible hundred items to see if expenses are justifiable business costs and if reimbursements were made by an employer. Red flags are expenses for company-owned cars, boats, planes, lodges, hotel suites, and also for trips to resorts.

Rule of thumb—if the taxpayer provides proof on the sample items, the agent will move on to other areas of the return or end the audit. If no acceptable records are produced, however, another sample will be run and the spot check turned into a detailed investigation.

If the deduction is disallowed, take notes on what the agent says, but confess to nothing. Say something like "I want to check out the regulation on that," or, "I didn't know that."

The IRS has three years to audit a return and make additional assessments. The three years start from the filing date or the date on which the return was due, whichever is later.

But if gross income is understated by 25% or more, the IRS has six years to make an assessment. If a fraudulent return is filed, or if no return is filed at all, there is no statute of limitations.

Source: Vernon K. Jacobs, *The Taxpayer's Audit Manual*, Alexandria House Books, Alexandria, Va.

Deductions and the risk of an audit

The following table shows the average deductions claimed by individual taxpayers at different income levels in a recent year.

The greater a taxpayer's deductions are, relative to the national average, the greater the risk is of an Internal Revenue Service audit. Few taxpayers are expected to be average in all respects, so reasonable deviations from the norm are not suspicious. But a person claiming very large deductions should be ready to prove them.

Adjusted Gross Income (AGI)*	Taxes	Interest	Charitable gifts	Casualties thefts
$ 10,000 to $ 16,000	$ 1,275	$1,920	$ 530	$1,165
16,000 to 20,000	1,590	2,155	540	1,005
20,000 to 25,000	1,875	2,280	570	755
25,000 to 30,000	2,245	2,455	645	600
30,000 to 50,000	3,010	2,880	870	765
50,000 to 100,000	5,310	4,585	1,825	1,425
100,000 to 200,000	10,000	7,935	4,675	1,950

*AGI consists of overall income minus certain deductions. So it may be considerably less than overall income. AGI is indicated on line 31 of Form 1040.

IRS payment traps

Do not send more than one tax payment in the same envelope to the IRS. It can cause mistakes in crediting payments.

In a recent case, a taxpayer owed money for both the current year and a prior year (for which she had obtained a payment extension). She sent a separate check for each debt but enclosed both tax forms and the two checks in the same envelope. The IRS applied both checks to the current year's obligation, and marked the prior year's liability delinquent. Several months later, the taxpayer received a refund for the current year with a notation that she had made an arithmetical mistake. She did not realize the IRS had erred. Later, she was sent a bill for the prior year's unpaid taxes plus interest and a late-payment penalty. While the IRS admitted the error, it maintained it was her responsibility to correct it.

Traps in a consent-to-deficiency agreement

Three out of every four tax audits result in increased assessments. Once the assessment is made, the Internal Revenue Service asks the taxpayer to sign Form 870, the waiver or consent-to-deficiency agreement. By signing, the taxpayer waives the right to appeal to the U.S. Tax Court and consents to pay any additional assessments, penalties, and interest.

If the taxpayer signs, the IRS will request immediate payment of any assessment. Your options are to pay now, or wait for a bill. Interest is charged from the day the return was due to the date the amount is paid.

Signing the consent commits the taxpayer but not the IRS. A supervisor may reject the initial auditor's finding and increase the assessment.

If the taxpayer does not sign Form 870, a 30-day letter is sent by the IRS giving the taxpayer 30 days to appeal or to accept the assessment and pay up. If this notice is ignored, a 90-day letter is sent, setting a final time limit for appeal or payment. And it cannot be extended.

Sign without delay when the examiner discovers the taxpayer overpaid. Signing Form 870 eliminates the need to file an amended return to recover a refund. Or assessment is either minimal or about what was expected.

Source: Vernon K. Jacobs, *The Taxpayer's Audit Survival Manual,* Alexandria House Books, Alexandria, Va.

Advance rulings from IRS

The Internal Revenue Service generally issues advance rulings regarding the tax effects of acts or transactions. But don't count on it in certain areas. Specifically, taxpayers are on their own in:

• Any matter involving applications of estate tax to the property or the estate of a living person.

• Any matter involving the federal tax consequences of proposed legislation at any level.

• Proposed transactions that might subject the taxpayer to a criminal penalty.

Source: Revenue Procedure 80-22.

Negotiating with the IRS

The Internal Revenue Service is willing to compromise a tax liability on either of two grounds: questionable liability or collectability.

The amount acceptable by the IRS when liability is in doubt depends upon the degree of doubt about the facts. When collectability is the issue, an acceptable offer must reflect all that can be collected form a taxpayer's income, present or prospective, after giving effect to all priorities (liens) granted to the government. The agreement requires payments from future income. It also makes the taxpayer relinquish some present or potential tax benefits.

When it pays to take your case to tax court

Most people fear going to court against the IRS. But the fact is that it can pay for you (as well as for a business) to take a case to court, even when it seems that the law is against you. After filing, you may well get a chance to compromise the dispute in a way that was not possible before.

Going to court removes your case from the hands of the local IRS agents who examined your return and records looking for violations of the letter of the law. The case is placed in the hands of attorneys in the IRS's regional-counsel office. And these attorneys are primarily concerned with disposing of cases. A court contest costs the IRS time and money, just as it costs you. So if there is no special reason for the IRS to litigate (for example, to emphasize a stand on a particular issue), the regional counsel may well offer a settlement. Even if that offer is only a small portion of the amount that IRS auditors were ready to disallow, you come out ahead.

A $60 filing fee places the case in Tax Court and brings it to the attention of the regional counsel. But you will probably have to retain a lawyer. And the further your case is pressed, the higher the legal fees.

Disagreements the IRS is most likely to settle are those over facts rather than interpretations of the law; in areas where recent decisions have gone against the IRS; and for which the IRS might have insufficient evidence.

But you and your tax attorney might not learn just how weak the IRS's case is until the pre-trial conference.

Expect to take to court disputes involving interest-free loans and property valuations. IRS agents are very tough on these items, but the courts have been more sympathetic to taxpayers.

The IRS is least likely to settle disputes concerning areas of the law that are still developing. Because even if the disputed amount is small and the cost of litigation is high, the IRS might press the case to set a precedent for other taxpayers.

Try to bring your case to the court that will be most sympathetic to your position. There are four choices:

• U.S. Tax Court. It has great expertise in handling complicated tax matters, but you cannot get a jury trial here. And you do not have to pay the disputed tax until after the case is resolved. Since the court is currently severely jammed, you may be able to postpone payment of the tax for years, even if you lose. However, you will have to pay interest on any amount that the court ultimately rules that you owe. And the current interest rate is 13%. But after you file, you can pay any part of the disputed amount at any time. If you win, the government will then pay you a refund with interest calculated at the same rate.

• Tax Court's small-case division. It hears cases when the disputed amount is under $10,000. Procedures are simplified, and taxpayers do not need a lawyer. But if you lose, you cannot appeal.

• District Court. The only place where you can get a jury trial. And the judge might be more sympathetic since he won't be a tax specialist. However, the disputed tax has to be paid in advance. If you win, you get a refund plus interest.

• Claims Court. Again, you have to pay the tax in advance. This court does not have to follow the same precedents as the Tax Court or District Court. If other courts seem unfavorable, try here.

The geographic location of the court you file in is also important. The United States is divided into 12 judicial circuits. The District Courts and Tax Court within each circuit follow the precedents of that circuit's Court of Appeals. But the Courts of Appeals of different circuits do not always agree with each other. And if a particular Court of Appeals has not ruled on an issue, lower courts within that circuit may disagree among themselves. Do a little research to find out which court might see your case most favorably. The effort could bring big rewards.

Source: Edward Mendlowitz, partner, Siegel & Mendlowitz, New York.

IRS turning accountants against their clients

Accountants are starting to ask clients to verify in writing that the data supplied for preparation of tax returns is accurate because of the growing IRS crackdown on preparers of inaccurate (or fraudulent) returns. Negligence can cost an accountant $100 per improper return and may subject the accountant and his clients to closer IRS scrutiny. Mistakes the IRS judges are "willful," however, can set preparers back $500. Accountants are questioning clients much more closely about their financial activities in an extra effort to head off IRS trouble. More significant is that accountants will not be taking the same strong position in handling clients' tax problems in the absence of appropriate substantiation. IRS is presently attempting to turn accountants into an enforcement arm of the government.

Source: Martin Halpern, Laventhol & Horwath, New York.

Don't pay domestics under the table

It doesn't pay, in the long run. Compensating domestic workers in cash, to avoid taxes and paperwork, is the easy thing to do and indeed, very commonplace today. Many housekeepers and janitors, particularly those who are recent immigrants (possibly illegal aliens), even demand this of employers. But it can lead to trouble. Internal Revenue Service agents are quick to turn up at a household's front door, without notice, if they suspect payroll taxes are being evaded by the employer of household help.

The biggest problem is Social Security (FICA) taxes. They are due from anyone who pays a worker more than $50 in a calendar quarter. There is no effective statute of limitations on the goverment's ability to collect these taxes.

Penalties for nonpayment are steep. The employer's share of the tax due (7.05% of gross wages) plus interest at 1.08⅓% a month. In addition, a fine ranging from .5% on underpayment to as much as 5% per month for late filing.

Take the case of a domestic worker who is paid in cash. Years later, the worker lacks eligibility for Social Security retirement benefits and points a finger at a former employer. The domestic can prove he worked for an employer through letters of recommendation, holiday cards from the children, or any similar evidence he has kept.

In another case, a worker is injured in the employer's home or place of business and finds he has no workers' compensation coverage (which is based on reported wages). The employer can be sued for damages as well as sought out by the IRS and local authorities.

Offer to raise the hourly pay so the worker will pay taxes without cost to himself, or pay the tax yourself. If the employee still refuses to put the income on the record (by not providing his Social Security number), insist on paying the FICA tax anyway. Payments can be made in the employee's name to a local Social Security office.

But upon receipt, the Social Security people will waste little time contacting the employee to get the number, and the employer may be put in the position of losing the employee, if he is an illegal alien, or if, for other reasons, he is determined to evade reporting.

Other precautions: Federal unemployment insurance must be paid for employees earning more than $1,000 a quarter. State unemployment insurance and workers' compensation premiums are also due, at least for full-time employees.

Source: Sidney Kess, tax partner, Main Hurdman, CPAs, New York.

Avoiding state tax

Executives whose offices are located in states with high income taxes, but who work at home, can lower their tax payments by splitting their state tax liability, if their home-state tax rate is lower.

An executive who can prove he does only a percentage of his job in his office (located in a high-tax state) only has to pay income tax to that state on the percentage of his salary he earns in his office.

In one case, a resident of New Jersey worked in New York as the publisher of specialty magazines about firearms, home improvements, dogs, and horses. His job included testing new products, which required access to storage facilities, a firing range, and stables—all of which were at his home. Since New Jersey's taxes are lower than New York's, he allocated his state income tax accordingly.

New York contested this allocation, arguing that the testing facilities "could have been set up somewhere in New York," and were located in New Jersey merely for the publisher's convenience.

The court ruled that publisher's allocation was justified. The argument that the testing facilities could have been set up in New York was irrelevant.

Source: Jerome Foreman, CPA, New York; *Myron Fass* vs *State Tax Commission,* 3/15/79; 17-447.

35 INVESTING YOUR MONEY

INVESTMENT STRATEGIES

How interest rates affect investments

Most likely to benefit if interest rates decline are condominiums and cooperative apartments, private homes, gold, diamonds, housing and banking stocks, antiques and certain collectibles, the stock market in general, bonds, and art.

If interest rates fall but inflation continues high, expect the following investments to show the greatest potential: real estate, gold, diamonds, other inflation hedges, and commodities.

If interest rates fall and the inflation rate drops significantly, expect lesser returns from real estate, collectibles, gold (unless a currency panic occurs), diamonds, and art.

If interest rates fall, avoid money market funds, short-term certificates of deposit, and debt instruments.

In general, the higher the interest rate is, the poorer will be investment performance of vehicles that either require financing for investment or provide no regular income payout (art, coins, diamonds). For an investment to thrive, its historical returns should be higher than the payout from such no-risk debt instruments as Treasury notes.

Playing the market with mimimum risk

Investors who want to maintain market positions with little risk often use a combination of Treasury bills and options. They purchase three- or six-month Treasury instruments, the lowest risk form of debt instruments. Using the interest from these instruments (and the interest proceeds only), they buy either puts or calls, depending on their assessment of the market's direction.

At current interest rates and option premiums, investors will be participating in the movement of nearly as much stock as if they had employed all of their capital in stock purchases. But there will be no risk to the amount of the starting capital. The worst case is if all the options expire worthless, investors will have lost no more money than the interest from the T-bills.

Another protective ploy is to purchase a portfolio of relatively near-term convertible bonds selling at a discount from face value. If the underlying common rises in price, the bonds will probably rise to reflect the increasing conversion value. If the common does not rise in price, the investor will receive the full face value plus interest payments at the bond's maturity. The major risk is corporate insolvency.

There are many occasions when it is possible to buy stock and to purchase protective puts priced at such a level that its time premium is no higher than the amount of dividends paid by the company to an investor during the life of the put.

As an example, XYZ Company is selling at 50 and paying a $1.25 quarterly dividend. An investor can purchase a six-month put, with a strike price of 55, for $6. Dividend payouts will ensure against loss regardless of how low XYZ falls. Should XYZ common rise to above 56, the profit on the common more than offsets loss on the put. And if XYZ rises to 60, there would be a 10-point profit on the common, a 2½-point dividend return, and a six-point loss on the put (a 6½-point net gain at no risk).

A full convertible hedge is generally a bearish strategy, if an investor establishes the position for no risk. Purchase convertible bonds, as close to par value as possible, that sell at a zero premium over conversion value. Then sell short an equivalent amount of common shares. (The short sale requires no additional capital as margin in such positions.)

If the common rises in price, the gain on the bonds, plus the difference between bond interest received and stock dividends paid out (the responsibility of the short seller) will usually produce a modest profit. If the common falls, the odds are that the convertible will decline less than the underlying common. The result is a smaller loss on the convertible than the gain on the short sale. There will therefore be a no-risk short-sale profit during down markets in addition to the differential between bond interest and stock dividend.

How to cash in on financial deregulation

When the rules change for an industry, new investment opportunities open up and long-term investments need to be reassessed. Now is the time to take a look at where the profits will be during deregulation of the banking industry and in the developing trend toward superconglomerates in the financial services.

Widespread interstate banking may well become a reality by the late 1980s. The shift will be made by larger banks acquiring smaller banks rather than expanding directly. Investment prospects are stocks of local and regional banks. The states to focus on are Florida and Texas. Both are fast-growing and have fragmented banking structures with many potential acquisition candidates.

Savings-and-loan stocks will become more attractive as adjustable-rate mortgages are phased in and S&Ls begin to earn enough to cover their cost of funds. The best bets are S&Ls in California. They are the strongest in the industry.

Another way to invest in S&Ls is through the many mutual S&Ls that are converting to stock ownership. The advantage is that fresh capital comes in at very low cost and can now be lent at high rates. The conversion trend is strongest in Florida, Texas, California, and Colorado.

The new financial services industry also offers opportunities. Insurance companies (following Prudential's path in buying Bache Halsey Stuart) and other financial companies want to broaden the distribution network for their products. The key is getting a bigger, trained sales force, which some brokerage firms already have in place. Likely candidates for bids are brokerage houses with at least 1,000 salespeople.

Source: Ronald I. Mandle, first vice-president, Paine Webber Mitchell Hutchins; and Perrin Long, analyst, Lipper Analytical Distributors, Inc., New York.

Investment strategies for recessions

Recessions often provide fine investment opportunities, but only to investors who have ready cash available at the right moment. Favorable recession invesments are high-grade corporate bonds, Treasury issues, short-term debt instruments, high-grade and high-yield stocks. Some speculators have done well by investing in cyclical issues after several months of the recession.

If stocks fail to decline on news of bad earnings reports, that could be an indication that the stock market has fully discounted any anticipated slump in earnings and lows have been reached.

Inflation hedges such as stamps, coins, and antiques have proved dangerous during recessions because collectors put them on the market to raise cash, pushing down prices. Real-estate is an illiquid investment, when liquidity is a valuable asset early in a recession.

Move liquid investments into less liquid investments as signs that the recession has bottomed become clear. Start to hedge against inflation. An ideal turnaround investment is distressed real estate in favorable locations.

Source: Gerald Appel, publisher, *Systems & Forecasts,* Great Neck, N.Y.

Ten laws of venture-capital investments

• The probability that a company will succeed is inversely proportional to the amount of publicity received before it began to manufacture its first product.

• An investor's ability to talk about winners is an order of magnitude greater than the ability to remember the losers.

• If a venture-capital investor does not think he has a problem, he has a big problem.

• Happiness is positive cash flow. Everything else will come later.

• The probability of a small firm's success is inversely proportional to the president's office size.

• Would-be entrepreneurs who pick up the check after luncheon discussions are usually losers.

• The longer the investment proposal, the shorter the odds of success.

• There is no such thing as an overfinanced company.

• Managers who worry a lot about voting control usually have nothing worth controlling.

• There is no limit on what a person can do or where he can go if he does not mind who gets the credit.

Source: Frederick R. Adler, senior partner, Reavis & McGrath, *Entrepreneurial Manager's Newsletter,* Worcester, Mass.

STOCKS

Rules for sensible investing in stocks

• Accept the fact that owning securities means taking an occasional loss at the least. Instead of worrying each time the shares drop, set a limit of acceptable loss at 10%.

• Don't waste energy second-guessing earlier decisions. It's futile to anguish about what you should have done.

• Buy or sell at the market once you've made a decision. Delaying a move in the hope of getting a price a fraction of a point better will lead to lost opportunities.

• Regularly sell off stocks that are performing below expectations.

• Avoid knee-jerk reactions to news events. When mass hysteria grips the market, there's little an individual can do except try to profit from it by moving counter to the crowd.

Source: Sidney B. Lurie, executive vice-president, Josephthal & Co., New York.

Stocks vs inflation

Some investors shy away from common stock because of the misconception that stock prices are outpaced by inflation. But the fact is that common stock has been an excellent hedge against inflation. A study of price and dividend movements over the last 110 years shows that common issues yielded an average of 7.37% a year after inflation. Thus an investment of $10,000 in 1871 would now have grown to $25 million. Since 1968, of course, common stock slightly under-performed inflation. But the change was largely due to effects of the 1973–74 bear market. Since then, though, stock prices and dividends have outpaced inflation, even the recent serious spirals.

Source: *Market Logic,* Fort Lauderdale, Fla.

pute the average NYSE index for the previous 10 weeks, then measure the difference between last week's close and the average. When the gap between the last weekly close and the 10-week average remains at 4.0 or below for two to three weeks, investors can expect an intermediate advance. Market tops are usually near when the last week's index is 4.0 or more above the previous 10-week average.

Only once or twice a year will as many as four of the five indicators signal an intermediate bottom. But when four do, it is highly reliable. The same is true for intermediate tops.

Source: *Barron's,* New York, and *Indicator Digest,* Palisades Park, N.J.

A guide to market indicators

• The speculation index. Divide the weekly trading volume on the American Stock Exchange (in thousands) by the number of issues traded. Calculate the same ratio for New York Stock Exchange trading. Divide the AMEX ratio by the NYSE ratio to calculate the speculation index. Strategists believe the market is bearish when the index is more than .38 (and especially so if it rises to .38 and then falls back). Less than .20 is bullish.

• Member short selling. Divide the number of shares NYSE members sell short each week by total NYSE short selling. The index is bearish when readings of .87 are reached. A reading below .75 is very bullish, particularly if it lasts several weeks.

• New highs—new lows. The market is usually approaching an intermediate bottom when the number of new lows reaches 600. The probable sign of an intermediate top is 600 new highs in one week, followed by a decline in number the next week.

• The NYSE short-interest ratio. The total number of outstanding shares sold short each month divided by the average daily trading volume for that month. A strong rally generally comes after the ratio reaches 1.75.

• The ten-week moving NYSE average. Com-

Use a variety of indexes for a clearer market view

Too many investors rely exclusively on the Dow Jones industrial average for a quick view of what the market is doing. But the Dow reflects only stock price changes of 30 large, mature companies. Their performance does not necessarily reflect the market as a whole. The Dow should be supplemented with these indexes:

The over-the-counter composite index gauges the cumulative performance of over-the-counter issues. It points to a bull market when it outpaces the Dow Jones industrial average and to a bear market when it is weaker.

TRIN, an acronym for the trading index, measures the relative volume of rising and declining issues. The market is bullish when the TRIN falls from a reading of above 1.20 to below .70 during one day of trading. It is bearish when the TRIN goes from below .70 to above 1.20. A reading of 1.00 shows an even relationship between advancing and declining stocks.

The Quotron change, named for the company that developed it, measures the daily percentage change for all issues on the New York Stock Exchange (the QCHA index) and the American Stock Exchange (QACH). It gives an excellent picture of what the market is doing in broad terms. Mutual funds track more closely with the Quotron change than the Dow Jones industrial average.

The Dow Jones transportation average is a generally reliable lead indicator of intermediate trends. The Dow Jones utilities average reflects income- and interest-sensitive stocks. It's a good long-term lead indicator.

In a bull market, the total number of shares traded expands on days when advances outpace declines. The opposite occurs in a bear market. A sign of market reversal is a high-volume day when the market moves in one direction all morning, then turns around.

Knowing when to wait before buying

Investors often think they are buying stock at a bargain price, only to see it fall farther because of an overall market falloff. There are signs that such a falloff is ahead, however.

Just before the decline, the market advance becomes very selective. Gains are recorded in just a few industry groups rather than across the board. Speculative interest runs high in the American Stock Exchange and over-the-counter markets.

During the first phase of the decline, the issue that failed to participate at the end of the previous advance show the most severe declines. The strongest industry groups tend to keep rising on short-term rallies. This pattern traps unwary traders who believe that stocks are at bargain levels.

During the second phase of the decline, most groups participate, but the previously strong groups decline only slightly.

During the final stages, even the once strong industry groups fall sharply, and the odds are that the decline will soon come to an end. Wait for evidence that all segments of the market have declined before stepping in to buy.

As a general rule, groups that were strongest during the previous rally will advance sharply when the market starts to recover, although they may not remain in the forefront throughout the next market cycle. Strong market rallies often take place at quarterly intervals. In many cases,

leaders of one quarter will not maintain leadership in the next cycle.

How to avoid selling too soon

Each week, record the number of issues making new highs for that week on the New York Stock Exchange. These and other key data are recorded in *Barron's*, among other sources.

Maintain a moving four-week total of the number of issues making new highs on the NYSE.

Presume that the intermediate uptrend is intact for as long as the four-week total of issues making new highs continues to expand. Investors can hold long positions in most issues without fear until the four-week total turns down. This method is not fool-proof, but in the last 53 years, there has never been a market decline not foreshadowed by at least one week's notice in this indicator.

Source: *Timing and Tactics,* Ventura, Calif.

How to identify swings and capitalize on them

Investors can't hope to catch every intermediate-term high and low in the stock market. But there is a way that investors can improve their ability to forecast midterm swings and exploit them:

Compute daily the total of new highs on the New York Stock Exchange as a percentage of all issues making highs and lows. For example, if 90 issues make new highs and 10 hit new lows, that day's new-high ratio is 90%. Maintain a 10-day moving average of the new-high percentages.

Consider investing in the market when this 10-day average dips below 35% and then rebounds above it. Investors awaiting more significant declines should hold off until the average falls below 25% and then rises above 30%. Consider selling when the moving average tops 80% and then dips back below that mark. If this indicator again rises above 80%, it's usually safe for the investor to reenter the market for a quick trade. But consider selling again when the indicator falls back below that level.

If an investor makes a purchase when the indicator is below 35%, and it then declines another 5%, sell out, or place very close stop-loss orders on the new positions. These false buy signals occur infrequently and mainly during bear markets.

Source: Gerald Appel, publisher, *Systems & Forecasts,* Great Neck N.Y.

How to read the market gaps

In stock market terms, a gap is a price area where no trading has occurred during the day. For example, if a stock trades one day between 54 and 55, then opens at 56 and never drops on the next day, the space between 55 and 56 is a gap. Gaps are meaningful because they often foretell the direction that stocks will take for the next day or two.

Technical analysts keep posted on gaps by comparing the first New York Stock Exchange Index reading (at 10:30 A.M.) with the previous day's trading range. Gaps occur most often when a stock closes at either its highest or lowest price for the day. If the market continues to move in the direction of the gap past 11 A.M., the stock will probably continue to do so throughout the day. Frequently, it does that well into the following day, too. The technique is less useful when volume is extraordinarily high.

Investors can identify gaps by using the daily charges of major market averages published in *The Wall Street Journal* and many local newspapers.

Source: Gerald Appel, publisher, *Systems & Forecasts,* Great Neck, N.Y.

High/low velocity stocks

Beta is a simple statistical concept that is used to estimate the future action of a stock issue on the basis of its past performance. High beta stocks (higher than 1.0) are supposed to be more volatile than the general market. A stock with a beta of 1.25 has moved up 25% faster in a rising market) and has dropped 25% further in a falling market). Low beta stocks are less volatile than the market. If the beta is 0.80, the stock has been 20% less volatile in the past than an average stock. There is no evidence that this approach to investing is consistently successful.

Watching the tape

Most executives can't spare the time to follow the minute-by-minute action of the stock market as reflected on the tape. But there are times when it pays to follow the tape more closely than usual at the broker's office, or to stay in close touch with a broker over the phone. The time to pay attention is when the shareholder senses that the market is near a turn, or there is news that may affect stocks the shareholder owns.

Use the tape to get a sense of the trend of the market's movement. Is volume going into stocks that are advancing or into ones that are declining? For individual stocks, use the tape to study the stock's movement as it nears a cyclical high or low. The action on the tape will reveal whether the stock is in its old cycle or breaking through to a new one.

If the stock is up but meeting resistance trying to reach a new high, check the volume on the bid side compared to that on the offer side. If the volume predominates on the offer side while the price of the stock is not yet advancing, the stock may reach a new high. If the volume is heavy on the bid side, the stock may revert to the old cycle because of overhanging supply.

Source: Elizabeth Sospenso, vice-president, Thomson McKinnon Securities, New York.

Timing your stock trades

Timing sales and purchases by the hour of the day can give investors an advantage.

If the market has closed strong the previous day, or has made a sharp upward turnaround, expect a strong opening. The highest prices of the morning, and possibly of the entire day, are likely to develop at around 10:30 A.M. Sell around that time. Defer buying until later on.

Some decline is likely to take place after a strong opening. Expect the falloff between 10:30 A.M. and noon. A moderate rally is likely to start at midday, but then prices usually back off once again.

On an up day, the market generally stalls from about 1:30 P.M. to 3:00 P.M. Investors will probably do best to buy at around 2:30 P.M.–3:30 P.M.

Day traders tend to close out about 3:30 P.M.–3:45 P.M. Minor market setbacks often take place then. If the market is strong, prices will rise again during the last few minutes of trading, especially on Fridays. If sales have not been made in the morning or during the late-morning rally, this may be the time to sell. Otherwise, wait until the next morning.

If the market has declined sharply on the previous day, and there are stop-loss orders on certain stocks, do not allow them to be exercised during the first half hour of trading. The lowest prices usually hit at that time as the market follows through on the previous day's decline. Lift the stops and try to sell on an intraday rally, or use the lows of the morning as stop-loss points for the rest of the day.

The market rarely declines by more than 20 points over any two days without at least a minor interim rally. It rarely rallies for more than 20 Dow points over a two-day span without at

least some period of decline or consolidation.

Tick readings of plus or minus 500 are usually climactic. The number represents how many stocks have been traded at higher prices and lower prices over the last several minutes. Tick readings appear at varying intervals over brokers' machines. When this magnitude, they generally signal an upcoming reverse in direction, at least for a short time.

Trade at the best price: give limit orders

Whether buying or selling, a basic rule is to give brokers limit orders rather than market orders. Market orders are instructions to trade at the best available price. Limit orders are instructions to trade at a specific price. The difference can often amount to ½ point per share.

Establishing the best price requires four types of information: (1) the high, the low, and the latest prices of the stock for the day; (2) the current bid and asked prices; (3) the number of bidders and sellers at these prices; and (4) the trading volume.

1. Investors who are neither anxious buyers nor panicky sellers have a good chance of completing a trade within the previous day's range. If there is a gap between today's prices and yesterday's close, the stock will usually fill the gap during the day.

2. The spread between bid and asked prices tells investors about the eagerness of buyers and sellers.

3. The number of bidders is important in determining how many buyers and sellers may be at the front of the line. Like the spread, it also points to the amount of buying and selling interest.

4. The amount of trading volume allows the investors to determine how fluid the market is. The more fluid the market, the more likely that traders will be able to buy and sell at the price of their limit orders.

Sell orders are usually best made at about 10:30 A.M. the day after a strong market close; buy orders, at the same time of day following a strong decline. Investors who want to buy after an up day are usually better off waiting for the market to settle down. The best times are 11 A.M. or 1:30 P.M.

Break the rule about sticking to limit orders when there is a risk of a major upward or downward swing. Then, buy or sell at the best available price.

Source: *Pro-Market Advisor,* Rockford, Ill.

To beat volatility, concentrate on value

Faced with unprecedented volatility in financial markets, investors are increasingly adopting the strategy of buying only undervalued stock during major market declines. The rationale is that by buying something for 50¢ that is worth $1, the investor does not have to worry about predicting major economic trends. Also, stock bought at a bargain-basement price is unlikely to go much lower, even in a severe bear market. To find value in stock, look for:

• A company that has at least a 4.5%–5% after-tax return on sales.

• A stock with a price-earnings ratio under seven.

• A rising trend in earnings apparent over the past five years and a definite rise over the past two.

• A stock that sells for no more than 1.2 times book value per share. To compute book value, subtract intangible assets such as goodwill and unfunded pension liabilities but add back hidden inventory profits.

• A comparison of the net working capital with the stock price. Compute the net working capital per share by subtracting total debt and current liabilities from current assets and dividing the result by the number of outstanding shares. Some stocks sell below net working capital per share.

• A return on shareholders' equity that is at least 15%.

• A return on total assets that is at least 9%, to ensure that the company's assets are being used productively.

• A ratio of current assets to current liabilities is at least two to one.

• Weakness in the debt structure. Determine whether high interest rates pose a heavy burden on the company and its profitability. Debt-to-total-capitalization should be under 30%.

• Management that owns a substantial portion of stock. This is often overlooked. History shows that only when management owns stock does the company have the incentive to boost the price of the stock.

• Assets such as land, minerals, timber, or stock holdings in other companies that are carried on the books for a fraction of actual value.

• A target price for the stock, even if it already appears undervalued. Take the average of the high and low price-earnings ratios over the past five years and average that average with the lowest p/e ratio during the same period. For example, for the last five years, a stock has traded between 6 and 12 times earnings for an average ratio of 9. The average of 9 and 6 is 7.5, the optimum current ratio for the stock.

Techniques for evaluating over-the-counter stocks

Growth potential is the single most important consideration. Earnings increases should average 10% over the past six years when acquisitions and divestitures are factored out. Cash, investments, accounts receivable, materials, and inventories should be twice the size of financial claims due within the next year.

In addition, working capital per share should be greater than the market value of the stock (an $8 stock should be backed by $10 per share in working capital). Long-term debt should be covered by working capital, cash, or one year's income. And the balance sheet should show no deferred operating expenses and no unreceived income.

The criteria for final selections include ownership by at least 10 institutions reported in *Standard & Poor's Stock Guide,* and public ownership of between 500,000 and one million shares, with no more than 10% controlled by a single institution. There should also be continued price increases after a dividend or split, and a strong likelihood of moving up to a major exchange. (A good sign is strong broker and institutional support).

OTC stocks to avoid are those of companies expanding into unrelated fields, where they lack the required management experience and depth, and stocks selling at prices far below recent highs. This sign of loss of investor support can take months to overcome.

Source: C. Colburn Hardy, *Physician's Management,* New York.

How to find the winners

Investors should not allow economic forecasts, stock market predictions, or statements by management to interfere with the selection process. A foremost rule is to buy stocks only in companies where earnings are accelerating upward, revenues are rising, and backlogs of orders are increasing. The market follows earnings, and investors will eventually recognize earnings appreciation and bid the stock up.

By the same token, the moment earnings decelerate, the investor should sell, and stay out of the stock for at least a full market cycle. Watch the figures: earnings deceleration can begin even while earnings are still rising. Indeed, sell decisions are more important than buys. It's wrong to become emotionally involved with any stock purchase. Even if you begin to love it, sell it at the first sign of the slightest earnings deceleration.

To stay out of serious trouble, avoid companies in business less than three years, managements that won't provide figures firsthand, and buying a stock on its dividend record alone.

In a down market, shed stocks with flattened earnings (called chicken eggs). These will be the hardest to sell at a profit later in a downturn. Switch to stocks with earnings that have a good chance to rebound sharply (called tennis balls). Leverage could be a factor that creates sharp rebound potential. And don't get hung up on market timing. Use technical analyses and charts of

market price levels only to cross-check your identification of good issues.

Source: James E. Stowers, president, Twentieth Century Investors, Inc., Kansas City, Mo.

The importance of dividends

Smart money managers focus on the total return: capital appreciation plus dividends. Stressing the dividend—and being sure that it is secure —can enhance the consistency of investment results and limit downside risk. To evaluate dividend safety, make sure the dividend is well covered in terms of the company's cash flow and its projected earnings. Ideally, find a company whose management considers the dividend to be sacred. Dividend income accounts for about half the total return on investments expected over several years.

Source: John Durham, president, Delaware Investment Advisers, Philadelphia.

Picking the right industry at the right time

When inflation fears predominate, the groups likely to show strength are metals, gold, silver, natural-resource stocks, oil and gas, and timber. Utilities, banks, finance companies, and other interest-sensitive groups are weak, and long-term debt instruments are dangerous.

When recession fears predominate, drugs, insurance, and basic food stocks are likely to show strength, while autos, chemicals, steel, auto parts, textiles, appliance manufacturers, and other cyclical industries are weaker.

When a recession is many months old, expect strength from autos, chemicals, and other cyclical industries that usually turn upward in anticipation of an economic turnaround. Weaker performers will be defensive stocks.

At a time of strong economic recovery marked by sharply falling interest rates—the most favorable market climate of all—the most volatile industry groups usually do their best.

The case for utility stocks

Conservative investors who might be tempted to lock in high yields on corporate bonds frequently ignore another investment with high, steady dividends: utility stocks. Beyond their growth prospects, utility stocks usually pay dividends as high as the best bond yields. And although dividends are not as secure as interest payments on bonds, relatively few utility companies have had to cut them.

Utility stock dividends tend to rise as corporate profits increase while interest on bonds is fixed. Also, capital can be preserved more efficiently through utility stocks. The stocks remained fairly stable in price over the last decade, while dividends rose from about 6% to 12%. In the same period, bond prices dropped by around 25%.

It's even possible to write options against many utility issues. However, these stocks should be considered a long-term holding. They are unlikely to appreciate until interest rates stabilize. Regulatory climates of state governments are crucial in selecting utility stocks. Get an opinion from investment advisers.

Source: *Value Line Investment Survey,* New York.

Basics for successful option trading

Most investors who deal in puts and calls have their own pet strategies, but the most successful generally follow these basic rules as well.

• They trade in high-priced active issues. (Stocks in the $40–$100 range are favored by professional traders.)

• They stay in the market only when they feel certain about its direction.

• They trade in stocks that have shown a predictable price pattern.

• They treat options as short-term speculative vehicles. If a trade does not go their way within five days, they usually close it out.

• They place limit orders on buy positions. They don't let enthusiasm overrule reason.

• They watch the underlying stock closely if some good news is released. The best prices are often available the morning after the news is released.

• They never feel so certain about any one situation that 100% of cash and confidence go into it. Instead, they diversify, and evaluate the action of the stock unemotionally.

• If an option has gone up by 100% but is expected to go higher, they sell at least 50% of the position and let the rest ride.

Source: Joseph T. Stewart Jr., *Dynamic Option Trading,* John Wiley & Sons, New York.

Using treasury notes for protection

Investors can reduce capital requirements and increase yields by using Treasury notes as collateral to trade in puts and calls on the same issue.

When the investor expects a stock to rise, he can sell put options and use Treasury notes as collateral to buy calls of the same issue with identical strike prices and expiration dates. If the stock rises in price, the calls appreciate. Meanwhile, the investor collects interest on the high-yield Treasury notes.

Sophisticated investors who believe the stock will fall can sell short by using Treasury notes to buy puts, then sell identical calls.

Liquidity in the options is essential so that both sides can be easily unloaded.

Tools of the trade for option investors

Investors who deal in puts and calls can make use of an increasing number of technical and analytical services. Among the best are:

Value Line Options & Convertibles, 711 Third Ave., New York 10017. Recommends the most favorable puts and calls for purchase and sale, and backs up recommendations with large amounts of statistical data.

Daily Graphs Stock Option Guide, Box 24933, Los Angeles 90024. Charts of about 250 listed stocks on which options are available as well as data on the options themselves.

Datalab, Inc., 3624 Science Center, Philadelphia 19104. Produces program modules that can be used with two Texas Instruments calculators to calculate the optimal values of puts and calls as well as other hedge data.

Texas Instruments Securities Analysis Library, Box 53, Lubbock, TX 79408. Works with the same two calculators, but the module is cheaper.

Making profits on a stock split

When a stock splits, the average profit to an investor is 20%. But the greatest profits are generally made in three to six months before the split is announced. The general pattern is that the price stays high for two days after the split announcement and then declines. To spot a candidate for a split, look for:

• A company that needs to attract more stockholders, diversify, or attract additional financing.

• A takeover candidate (heavy in cash and liquid assets) whose management holds only a small percentage of the outstanding shares. (Companies with concentrated ownership rarely split stock unless there are problems with taxes, acquisitions, or diversification.)

• A stock price above $75. A split moves it into the more attractive $35–$50 range.

• A stock that was split previously and price has climbed steadily since then.

• Earnings prospects so strong that the company will be able to increase dividends after the split.

Likely prospects are over-the-counter companies with current earnings of $2.5 million, at least $2 million annually in preceding years, and less than 1 million shares outstanding (or under 2,000 shareholders). A stock split is necessary if management wants to list on a major exchange.

Source: C. Colburn Hardy, *Dun & Bradstreet's Guide to Investments,* Thomas Y. Crowell Co., New York.

Rules for purchasing dually listed call options

Some stock options are traded on more than one stock exchange. Before placing an order, check *Barron's* to find out which exchange does more trading in the option. The best deals are generally found where the option is traded most actively.

Before confirming an order with a broker, ask for competitive quotations from each exchange where the option trades. Ask, too, for the size of bids and offers. Specify on which exchange the option order should be placed.

Buying convertible stock

Corporations with available investment cash should think about the growing number of convertible preferred stocks. These issues can offer tax-sheltered income, potential for long-term capital gains, and some limitation of risk.

To get the maximum tax benefits from the dividend income, it's best to borrow from the broker half the amount needed to buy the stock.

Reducing the cash reduces the amount of annual dividend subject to corporate income tax, while the interest paid to the broker could be fully deductible. Depending on the amount of interest the broker charges, cash flow after taxes could be highly favorable for the corporation.

Preferred issues also offer good leverage. If the price of common stock drops sharply, the decline of preferred shares would ordinarily be less sharp. But if the price of the common rises sufficiently, the preferred shareholder could see substantial long-term capital gains.

Where options are available, companies that want additional income can also sell options against their holdings. But this route would jeopardize some of the capital-gains potential, A complex related tax law requires clearance with your tax counsel.

Source: Murray Kimmel, Herzfeld & Stern, New York.

Tactics for the new-issue market

Because new public-stock offerings are usually priced by the underwriters below estimated share value (to improve chances of a quick oversubscription), they tend to outperform the market for five years or so. And unless a new issue declines at the start (which can always happen), there is no overhanging supply of stock that is bought at higher levels and waiting to be unloaded, which could depress the price and the market action just by being there.

Let your stockbroker know of your interest in the new-issue market. His firm probably has underwriting participations as part of a selling group, and he will respond to customers who already provide good commission business. Or contact a broker affiliated with the lead underwriter, if you're in a position to promise good subsequent business.

Even if you can't buy in on the original offering, you should be able to pick up shares advantageously in the aftermarket. Many new issues open at a premium over the actual offering price, then decline briefly as scalpers take profits. The first or second day after a new issue opens for trading is usually the optimum time.

If the stock's price remains steady for a week or two after the issue date, the odds increase on its fundamental merit. To maximize those odds from the start, ask the following questions:

• Is the company fundamentally sound, with rising earnings?

• Is it in a growing industry with long-term investor interest?

• Are the proceeds form the offering earmarked mainly for expansion?

• Does the company have, apart from the founders, a well-recognized board of directors?

• Is the lead underwriter an established firm with a good track record. (Did its previous new issues sell above the offering price?)

• Is the underwriter receiving, as partial compensation, warrants to buy the stock and/or large blocks retained in its own account?

• Is the stock market climate favorable?

Beware of new issues during periods of excess speculation, particularly in untested stocks. Often this happens as a fad involving high-technology companies. The best defense is to verify the fundamentals.

Source: *New Issues,* Fort Lauderdale, Fla.

The value of small-company issues

New data makes the case again that companies with low stock market value substantially outperform larger ones on Wall Street. A recent study shows that small-company stock averaged a 17% gain over two-year intervals during a 13-year period. The comparable figure for the largest companies was a loss of 5%–6%.

Small companies are often more flexible than larger ones and can more easily shift gears as the economy changes. As a result, small companies can increase their earnings growth at a faster rate, especially since they start from a lower base.

For investors, this means that small companies provide superior capital-gains opportunities. Dividend payouts are usually lower than with large-company stocks, but capital gains are more favorably taxed.

Most brokers will recommend a list of small-company stocks. Investors are usually advised to diversify holdings since some small companies do not survive. Experienced investors also select stocks that have shown a high compounded growth in earnings. It is essential to use only speculative capital for these investments.

Source: *Market Logic,* Fort Lauderdale, Fla.

Investing in penny stocks

In 1980, 123 companies went public by selling shares for $5 or less. Of those, all but 11 appreciated in value; the average climb being 690%. Activity in the penny stocks, as they are called, remained high in 1981. In the first quarter, 76 companies went public, compared with 31 in the first quarter of 1980. Penny stocks continue to offer varied speculative opportunities, if not the bonanzas realized the first year.

Penny stocks come in four basic types, each of which requires a separate strategy:

• Stocks trading on the New York Stock Exchange and the American Stock Exchange for $5 or less. Look for long-term turnaround candidates, takeover and merger candidates, and stocks trading well below book value.

• Stocks traded over the counter, computer-listed by the National Association of Securities Dealers. Focus on traditional growth stocks.

• Stocks traded over the counter, not NASDAQ-listed, for which individual brokers make markets. Study growth stocks doing 250,000–300,000 shares in trading volume weekly. Get research reports from a variety of penny-stock brokers on such companies, and compare the views on each company.

• Stocks offered by underwriters in initial public offerings. Evaluate the assets and growth potential of the companies going public. Avoid those raising money to refinance existing debt. Read prospectuses carefully.

Be careful to check the track records of the underwriters and brokers handling penny stocks of interest. To hedge your bets, diversify your penny-stock holdings.

Source: Jerome Wenger, publisher, *Penny Stock Newsletter,* Columbia, Md., and John Spears, general partner, Tweedy Browne, Inc., New York.

Warnings on playing the takeover game

Unless an investor is a corporate insider, chances are he will be among the last to hear about a takeover prospect. When one broker promotes the rumor, odds are strong that all his office colleagues are promoting it too.

Never buy shares in a takeover candidate simply on the basis of a tip or rumor. Buy the stock only if it meets investment criteria and goals, even without a takeover. The most likely takeover candidates have tangible assets and/or high cash.

Takeover stocks frequently rise sharply on extraordinarily high volume as insiders and professionals take positions at the first hint of a tender offer. The price then usually drifts down as early traders collect their profits. This could be the best time for an ordinary investor to take a position.

Once a takeover or tender offer is announced, the price of the company's share usually rises to within 10% of the indicated offering price and remains at that level until the deal is clinched. It often pays to sell at that point rather than risk the deal falling through.

Source: Gerald Appel, publisher, *Systems & Forecasts,* Great Neck N.Y.

BROKERS

How to take advantage of negotiated commissions

For many years, investors have been legally able to negotiate commissions that stockbrokers charge. But relatively few private investors ever take full advantage of their new power while large institutional investors negotiate commission discounts of up to 70%.

For most individual investors, the choice seems to narrow down to working with discount brokers (which now offer a wide range of rates and services) and a full-service broker at full commission. But many brokerage firms will give concessions if the investor presses every advantage.

Any single order worth more than $4,000, or a group of orders for $10,000 or more in one day, can generally be negotiated. If your annual transactions total $100,000, you are in a position to ask for discounts for all transactions.

Ability to negotiate commissions depends on your relationship with the account executive at the brokerage firm. It also depends on the relationship between the account executive and the firm's branch manager.

A hungry account executive with low volume, who is eager to make every cent possible, may be less willing to negotiate than a larger producer. Unless a firm has a standard discount policy, the branch manager is usually required to approve all requests for negotiated commissions. If an account executive is a big producer, the branch manager may approve the negotiated rate more readily than if the executive is a mediocre producer.

Realistically, if you are the type of investor who usually gives only simple orders to buy and sell, you are entitled to some form of discount. But many individual investors give orders limited to specific prices or deadlines and often change orders as the day wears on. Handling this type of investor is obviously more costly and time-consuming for the broker.

Some account executives even encourage investors to make complex limit orders in order to avoid the question of discounts.

A simple market order for a liquid stock can be executed in moments if the firm is reasonably efficient. Orders for blue-chip and actively traded stocks can generally be executed without great difficulty and require little work on the part of the broker or floor specialist. These transactions are therefore more easily negotiated.

Private investors should be especially wary when dealing with over-the-counter stocks. In these transactions, the commission is often included in the price of the stock. Many investors believe their account executives when they say there is no commission. The fact is that a commission charge of ¼–½ point (sometimes more) has been calculated into the stock price. It, too, is subject to negotiation just like commissions for stocks traded on an exchange.

Always press for discounts. Investors have nothing to lose.

Source: Hans R. Reinisch, executive vice president, Argus Research, and producer of the New York radio show *Wall Street Focus.*

When to change brokers

Get a new broker if:
• Yours doesn't return calls within a half day.
• Bad news breaks for a stock you own and the broker does not phone.
• You have a trading account with a high volume of daily activity, but the broker fails to phone you often when the market is choppy.

• You have an active account, but the broker has not made a profit for you in six months.
• You have a less active account, and the broker has not made a profit for you in one year.
• You ask a question about a recent economic or political development and the broker cannot relate it to your short- and long-term holdings.

Source: E. Lee Hennessee, assistant vice president, Thomson McKinnon Securities, Inc., New York.

Danger signals from an investment broker

Recognize excessive trading (churning). Divide the total cost of commissions and account costs for the past year by the average monthly equity (stocks and cash) in the account to get the turnover rate. The Securities & Exchange Commission considers a turnover rate of more than four excessive. Six is considered churning—producing commissions by buying, selling, and switching more frequently than justified by sound portfolio strategy.

Also watch for excessive markups (greater than 5% above the market price of an investment vehicle). This can mean the brokerage firm is buying the stock at the market price and reselling it at a higher price to customer accounts.

To protect yourself:
• Don't open a margin account unless you want to take significant risks in playing the market. A margin account is inherently speculative and the easiest target for churning.
• Don't have more than one active account at the same time. Having two or more will probably negate claims that the accounts are being churned or that unsuitable investments are being made.

• Make sure any discretionary account agreement is in writing.
• Consider filing a complaint with the SEC. It can censure the broker and help the investor recoup losses.
• Take the matter to arbitration. All the national exchanges are bound legally to settle broker-customer disputes in this fashion, if the customer chooses.

Avoid actual litigation unless there's big money involved. Legal costs in a securities case can run as much as $200 an hour and amount to $50,000 or more since these cases often run on for years. Make sure that you get any sales agreement with a broker in writing.

Source: *Capital Games,* American Institute for Securities Regulation, New York.

Recourse in disputes with stockbrokers

Keep a diary of all conversations with stockbrokers that involve placing of orders, purchase recommendations, and other important matters. A detailed record adds credibility if the dispute goes to court, arbitration, or the broker's boss.

Note the exact time of conversation, as well as the date. The brokerage firm is liable if it fails to place an order promptly and the customer loses money as a result of the delay.

If necessary, complain to the head of the brokerage firm. That's sure to get attention. Complaint letters are regularly examined by the SEC, too. If none of these work, get a new broker.

Source: Nicholas Kelne, attorney, *American Association of Individual Investors,* Chicago.

BONDS

Bond-buying strategy

When interest rates drop, investors have an opportunity to lock in high yields and get capital gains too by buying bonds. One study calculates that 20-year, AAA-rated industrial bonds rose an average of 15.6% during the last five interest-rate swings. These swings, from peak to trough, usually lasted for one year.

The conservative strategy is to buy AAA-rated corporates or Treasury issues.

A more aggressive approach is to buy lower-rated issues that swing more in price, providing greater capital gain opportunity (and greater risk). However, even speculators avoid bonds rated lower than A when the depth of the recession is not completely clear.

Investors who bought bonds late one year or early the next, anticipating the interest-rate peak too early, may be holding bonds for which they have unrealized short-term capital losses. They should realize the losses in the current year by swapping these bonds for bonds of similar quality (commissions are low for bond trading), and deferring the tax on the expected capital gains until the next year.

The tax law has removed most of the capital gain potential from market discount on bonds issued after July 18, 1984. So watch the issue date if looking to capital gain treatment.

Source: *Value Line Investment Survey*, New York.

Convertibles: a conservative way to invest

Bonds that are convertible into common stock offer investors a conservative way to participate in equities. Buy carefully selected convertibles on the basis of their bond value rather than their value if converted into common stock. The payoff is high return potential with reasonable protection. There's an additional opportunity for gain if the stock appreciates—or the value of the bond increases as interest rates decline.

Ask a broker for a list of convertibles (most are rated BB or BBB). Weed out the companies with poor credit ratings and those that look unattractive for other reasons. Select from the remaining list one or more bonds yielding a minimum of 9%.

The importance of sinking funds

At a time when many bonds and convertible bonds are selling well below par, investors looking over their portfolios should note which bonds have sinking fund provisions. When interest rates start to ease, those issues could stage a recovery before other bonds.

How a sinking fund works: The issuing company must set aside funds to redeem a specified portion of the outstanding issue at a specified price and time. The benefit to the investor is that the bond issue will be redeemed (usually by lottery) at par. Investors whose bonds are redeemed make a potentially large profit before the usual maturity date of the bond.

Investors may also benefit indirectly if the issuer purchases bonds on the open market to meet redemption requirements (the usual action taken by companies with sinking-fund obligations when their bonds are trading below par). In that case, investors may not have their bond redeemed at a price above its current value, but the company's purchases will provide price support to their holdings.

Stockbrokers generally can provide sinking-fund information.

Source: *Value Line Convertibles,* New York.

Moving from longer- to shorter-term bonds

According to technical analysts, when the 10-week moving average of the Dow 20-Bond Average (published weekly in *Barron's*) falls below its average level of the previous 10 weeks, it may be time to switch from long-term debt instruments into shorter-term issues or into money-market mutual funds.

When the Dow 20-Bond Average once again moves above its 10-week moving average, it's time to buy long-term bonds again.

Assessing the yield on tax-exempts

If interested in buying a tax-exempt bond selling at face value, have a broker make a quick comparison of after-tax yields on that bond compared to similar bonds selling at a discount. What to ask for:

• The after-tax yield on the face-value tax-exempt.

• The after-tax yield on a selection of similarly rated, intermediate-term (three-to-five-year) issues, selling at a discount. Compute this yield by combining the tax-sheltered interest and the taxed capital gain (the difference between discounted price and face value, less the gains tax) should the investor sell the bond at maturity.

A frequent finding is that discounted bonds provide higher total returns than par bonds when the total yield to maturity is computed this way. An added bonus is that bonds selling at or above par will probably decline in value should interest rates rise again. Discounted bonds with a life of three to five years can be held to maturity with full payment of the face amount guaranteed.

MUTUAL FUNDS AND OTHER TYPES OF INVESTMENTS

Evaluating mutual funds

Before taking a position in a mutual fund, answer these questions:

• Does the fund suit your needs for capital-appreciation potential? Certain funds are extremely volatile in price action. They suit investors with risk capital better than those who cannot afford to run the risk of a sharp decline in their

capital. To find out, secure a price history, either from the fund or by visiting the public library of a financial publication, and analyze the fund's historical ups and downs.

• Does the fund have a good track record during declining markets? A number of funds have shown strong gains on balance since 1974. How did the fund's management handle recent bear markets, however? Does the management make an attempt to reduce portfolio exposure during down markets or does the fund generally stay fully invested? Ask your stockbroker, or ask the broker to recommend another who follows fund performances. (Don't expect helpful answers to questions like these from a commissioned salesperson for the fund.)

• Has the fund's management altered policies in the past counter to your own investment objectives? Certain funds are steadily increasing redemption charges to discourage trading. Or they're imposing restrictions that may not suit your purposes. Verify the facts in the current prospectus. Inquire if any changes are contemplated.

Switching the funds to spread the risk

Families of mutual funds, which have sprung up in recent years, offer a very sound way for the busy executive to spread investment risk during a volatile market.

One management company runs several mutual funds, usually including an aggressive stock fund, an income fund, a money-market fund, tax-exempts, and sometimes even a specialized fund in energy stocks or gold. Investors can go back and forth among the various funds within one family without having to pay a service charge.

For example, an investor might have all his chips in an aggressive growth stock fund. But if the price of gold started to edge upward, his anxiety about the stock market might increase. With a telephone call, he could move into a money-market fund or partially into a gold stock fund. If gold shares later dropped through their uptrend line, he could switch funds.

At a given time, a personal portfolio might be invested 25% in a money-market fund, 15% in a gold fund (a long-term hedge against inflation), and 60% in a long-term growth fund.

Source: James Schabacker, publisher, *Switch Fund Advisory,* Rockville, Md.

The case for tax-managed funds

A safe, sheltered investment that offers a higher yield than tax-exempt municipal bonds may be a tax-managed fund that invests in stocks, but is structured so participants pay no federal tax until they redeem their shares.

Most regular mutual funds pass through at least 90% of the income they generate. As a result, fund shareholders, not the fund itself, are taxed each year.

Tax-managed funds, in contrast, do not distribute realized income and capital gains to shareholders. The fund, not its participants, pays the Internal Revenue Service at the end of each year, and that tax is minimal.

The buyer of shares in a tax-managed fund can watch his investment appreciate without having to worry about a yearly federal tax burden. Then, when it best suits his tax situation, he can cash in. For the gain to be taxed at favorable long-term capital-gain rates, hold shares for 6 months.

Source: W. Gregory Wright, vice-president, United Management Corp., Indianapolis, *Tax Shelter Digest,* Dallas.

Managed commodity funds: pros and cons

There has been a sharp growth recently in the amount of capital placed by investors into managed-money pooled commodity accounts. These are accounts sponsored by brokers and/or by commodity specialists who create limited partnerships.

The advantages are that investors secure professional management of capital, and smaller investors, by participating in partnerships, achieve a diversification not possible in smaller individual accounts. Many partnerships protect the investor against liability for an amount greater than their initial investment. The partnership may close if 50% of starting capital is lost. In individual accounts, investors receive no such protection.

The disadvantage, however, is a great variation in performance—from manager to manager, and for any one manager on a year-to-year basis. While gains of 60% and up in one year can be achieved, losses close to that amount are also not uncommon.

On balance, managed commodity accounts yield comparably with other forms of investments that fluctuate less. One average of several such managed accounts showed a return of 10.1% over nine months. This was approximately the yield from a typical money-market fund during the same period.

Attraction of Ginnie Maes

Investors searching for conservative, high-yielding alternatives to money-market funds can consider government-backed mortgage securities. The most widely traded mortgage issues are Government National Mortgage Association securities, familiarly known as Ginnie Maes. They are pools of mortgages insured by the Federal Housing Administration and the Veterans Administration that are packaged and resold to investors so the original mortgage lenders can free up funds for more mortgage lending.

The minimum investment is $25,000 (and brokers usually offer a 90%–95% margin). The yield is locked in, for an average of twelve years. The investor receives monthly payments of interest and principal. (Corporate and government bonds pay dividends semiannually.)

Interest is fully taxable by the federal government. State taxes vary. In California, for instance, interest on Ginnie Maes is exempt from state income tax. In New York, however, interest is taxable. The principal is taxed as a capital

gain, but investors can defer that liability by purchasing Ginnie Maes with newer mortgages. The capital gains tax is due only when the mortgages actually mature.

Liquidity is excellent. There is a strong secondary market for these issues, and they usually can be promptly sold by a broker. Prices are listed in the daily financial pages.

Source: Donald Sheldon, president, Donald Sheldon Government Securities Inc., New York.

Joint CD purchases

Even though bankers are forbidden to tell customers they can pool resources to buy $100,000 CDs or even $10,000 T-bills, its perfectly legal.

But be sure to draw up an agreement that specifies how the group will handle the death or premature withdrawal of one of the members, and using the CDs and T-bills for collateral.

Precious stones that are safer investments than diamonds

Diamonds are a bad investment, unless you're in the business. Why: Most of us buy at retail and have to sell at wholesale. What your diamond is worth: About 20% of the appraised value. Also: Diamonds are not really that rare.

In fact, rubies, emeralds and sapphires are a much safer investment that diamonds. When prices of investment-grade diamonds plunged as much as 30%, colored gemstones magically held on to heady price gains. Reason: Scarcity. Only some $200 million in rubies, emeralds, and sapphires were sold in the US in a recent year, a fraction of the amount of diamonds sold.

The areas where the finest stones come from: Cambodia, Thailand, Ceylon, Burma and parts of Africa. Scarcity factor: These areas are politically unstable and, therefore, are not reliable sources.

The best gems to buy are stones over one carat that are free of externally visible flaws. Buy one that will look good mounted in jewelry. That way, if the investment does not gain in value, at least you will have a remarkable piece of jewelry, not just a stone in a glass case.

Expect to keep a colored gem for at least five years, when buying for investment. Then, evaluate what the stone would go for on the dealers' (wholesale) market. Alternative: Put stones up for auction at Sotheby Parke Bernet or Christie's. Although you cannot be sure of a definite sales price, you can put a minimum price on your item.

Source: Benjamin Zuker, dealer in colored gems and author of *How to Buy and Sell Gems*, Times Books, New York.

gold market is difficult because gold is a very emotional investment. He recommends weighing the political stability underpinning gold-mining operations in North America and Australia against the risks but higher profitability of South African mines.

According to a Swiss source, gold prices are generally strong on Fridays and lower on Mondays, because investors are reluctant to carry short positions over weekends, when central banks sometimes make announcements that affect prices.

Prices are also stronger toward the end of the year and weaker in summer months. The supply decreases toward the end of the year because laborers on short-term contracts to South African gold mines return home to harvest crops. Demand decreases in summer, when the European gold-jewelry industry closes.

Source: James Sinclair, James Sinclair & Co., and Kees Schager, Arnold & S. Bleichroeder, New York, and Hardy Bockli, Bank Julius Bar, Zurich.

Listening to the gold bugs

Almost all the advisers who pushed gold several years ago continue to believe every portfolio should contain some gold as a protection against inflation or economic collapse.

According to one expert, unless investors are very well capitalized and extremely expert, they should stay away from the gold futures market. Instead, diversify holdings among gold coins, bullion, and stocks of South African gold mines. Pick the mines with the most marginal, high-cost production. These companies are traded and recognized internationally and their reserves are known. As the price of gold goes up, their production becomes economic and they offer an investor very high yields.

Another expert points out that, as a rule, the price of shares in the gold-producing companies moves with the price of gold, although the swings are more exaggerated. Calling the turn in the

High returns from second mortgages

Investors who want an alternative to bonds for long-term income can consider lending mortgage money to well-secured borrowers. Basic are lending to corporations, not individuals, and securing mortgages with corporate collateral or personal assets of the officers (a good collateral). Borrowers can be found through newspaper ads or brokers. Ads usually run under Business Opportunities or Capital Required. A broker's fee should be between 5% and 8%.

To evaluate a broker, ask these questions: What is the track record for mortgages the broker has negotiated in the past? If the investor wants the principal back earlier than anticipated, will the broker find a buyer or repurchase it? How thoroughly does the broker validate the collateral and credit ratings of the borrowers?

Lenders of second mortgage money can expect interest payments that exceed the prime lending rate at the time the mortgage was negotiated. Corporations that raise money in this way are often less than prime borrowers.

Defaults occur on about 5% of this kind of mortgage. Decrease the risk by avoiding inventory, receivables, and intangibles as security. There will probably be prior claims on the assets of a corporation that defaults.

Odds on prepayment increase once interest rates decline. That can leave an investor with a large amount of capital at a time when interest income opportunites are minimal.

Source: Dr. Harold Gildston, president, North Shore Funding Corp., Great Neck, N.Y.

Going for safety with annuities

Insurance companies have been pushing to make annuities desirable again to attract investors' funds. Advantages of annuities are that the principal invested is safe, comparable to a bank account; interest now is relatively high; and interest earned is tax-deferred. Investors should weigh the comparative advantages of annuities versus municipal bonds. Municipal bonds are tax-exempt, not tax-deferred. But annuities are not subject to investment risk.

On the other hand, investors must pay before a stipulated number of years has passed. Investors pay a 7% penalty for cashing in an annuity in the first year, a 1% penalty for cashing it in the sixth year, and zero thereafter.

There are two ways to fund an annuity: a single, lump-sum payment or systematic, e.g., monthly payments. At maturity, the annuity must be cashed in or annuitized.

The interest rate is pegged each year by the insurer. In general, the yearly rate fluctuates with general interest rates. Some policies, however, will offer the investor a current rate of 11.5% or so and a rock-bottom minimum rate of about 4%, leaving the annuity holder with an option to withdraw his principal without penalty if at any time the interest rate drops below 10%.

The payout after cashing in comes in several forms, lump sum, life annuity, and survivor annuity (which can include guaranteed payment

for a predetermined number of years—10 years, or 15, and so on).

Investors pay tax on the interest earned only as received.

A sample annuity investment. A 48-year-old executive invests $100,000 in an annuity yielding 11.5% annually. Assuming that the interest rate remains the same, the annuity's value after seven years is $214,000. At that point, the investor withdraws his principal, puts it to other uses, and pays taxes upon the $100,000 withdrawal, plus a 5% penalty for early withdrawal. He lets the remaining accrued interest continue to compound.

After another ten years, assuming again an annual interest rate of 11.5%, the annuity is worth $338,000. Upon retirement at 65, the investor elects to receive an annuity for life with ten years guaranteed. He will receive $35,000–$38,000 per year.

The executive could avoid the 5% penalty by waiting until he was 59½ to make the withdrawal of principal. Also, these harsh rules do not apply to contracts entered into before 8-13-82.

Source: Paul E. Fierstein, benefits and compensation consultant, New York.

How to get started investing in art

The art market isn't out of the small investor's price range, even though famous paintings now sell for millions. There are still investment-quality prints going at auction for $250. Some 16th- and 17th-century oils attributed to known artists can be had for around $5,000. Lesser-known American Impressionists' paintings run $1,000–$2,000. Japanese and Chinese 19th-century prints, screens, and scrolls are in large supply.

The secrets of success are to collect what's appealing, and to become an expert on a period, an artist, or a school. How to do it:

• Visit museums, art shows, and galleries. A quick way to find an artist to your taste is to flip through a museum's print collection.

• Ask curators about the artist, which galleries sell the paintings, and their recent selling prices.

• Buy two or three works right away. Plunging in speeds learning. Bargains are the artist's early work, drawings, watercolors, smaller canvases, and, frequently posters announcing an exhibition of the artist's work.

• Develop relationships with galleries. Use business trips to visit major dealers in other cities. Many galleries have work by living artists that's not on display but worthy of attention. Ask to see it.

• Visit auctions and begin to bid. Remember: dealers mark up by 100% the art they buy at auctions. Overbidding a dealer by a few dollars results in a big saving.

Avoid mail-order prints. They may be part of multiple editions with only minor variations, which have little if any real investment potential.

The trouble with art as an investment

• Insurance is costly and sometimes difficult to get, especially for expensive works. Other typical costs are for security, maintenance, and warehousing.

• Prices fluctuate widely as fashions change. English portraits have not recovered to the price levels of 50 years ago, much less kept pace with inflation. And Impressionist paintings recently suffered a drop in price at auctions.

• Most investments require a mimimum period of 5–10 years to appreciate. The market is extremely thin. Many collectors are forced to buy at retail and sell at wholesale.

• The risk of getting inaccurate buying or appraisal advice is high, because the field of art is so highly specialized.

A useful rule of thumb is that an outstanding example of a secondary artist's work is a better investment than a secondary example of a better-known artist.

Source: Stephen H. Lash, vice-president, Christie's, *Pension World,* Atlanta, Ga.

Opportunities in Japanese multicurrency convertibles

New Japanese bonds offer a three-way play to Americans bullish on Japan. Purchasers get a minimum annual yield, and profit if the stock price of the company issuing the bond rises and they convert the bond into common stock. They also gain if the yen appreciates against the dollar.

The bonds are denominated in yen but payable in West German marks, Swiss francs, or U.S. dollars. The typical bond offers a 4% annual yield on face value and can be converted into a stipulated number of common shares at 10% above the current market price of those shares.

In a hypothetical best case, the first year the investor holds the convertible, the yen appreciates 15% against the dollar and the stock price rises 20%. The investment yields 25% (15% currency gain plus 10% capital gain after converting the bond to common stock).

In the hypothetical worst case, the first year the investor holds the convertible, the yen depreciates 15% against the dollar and the stock price falls 20%. The investment loses 11% (15% currency loss less the 4% earned on the bond).

Best buyers: Investors looking to diversify out of the dollar into underlying Japanese shares.

The bonds can be purchased from U.S. brokers active in the Eurobond market. The minimum investment is $2,500.

Source: Morris W. Offit, chief executive officer, Julius Baer Securities, Inc., New York.

High interest rates from foreign deposits

Investors with large amounts of capital can use foreign debt instruments to lock into short-term interest rates that are higher than domestic money-market yields. These include:

• Eurodollars: certificates of deposit issued

by American banks in Europe. Yield: about .5%
above U.S. money markets. Risk: since the capital stays in Europe, it could become tied up in
the event of a freeze on U.S. assets.

• Yankee CDs: certificates of deposit issued
by foreign banks with offices in the U.S. Yield:
approximately 1% above domestic CDs. Risk:
although the capital remains in the United
States, accounts are backed only by the bank
and are not federally insured.

• Early-maturity foreign banker's acceptances:
debt instruments issued for periods up to 180
days. Investors in effect are backing a foreign
bank's collateralized loan to a customer in the

United States. Yield: about 1% over domestic
rates. Risk: the investor's loan is guaranteed only
by the bank.

At least $100,000 is required for banker's ac-
ceptances and at least $1 million for Eurodollars
or Yankee CDs. Investments can be made through
large brokerage houses that handle international transactions. Since lending to foreign
banks carries more risk than lending to American banks, investors should deal only with solid
institutions.

Source: Barry Lefkowitz, E.F. Hutton, Beachwood, Ohio.

TAX SHELTERS

How to look at tax shelters

Look at a tax shelter first as a straight business
investment for after-tax yield and only second as
an opportunity for a tax savings. The decision to
invest in a shelter is no different from other investment decisions. The basic criterion: Is the potential yield commensurate with the risk involved?

To determine profit potential, measure the
potential after-tax cost. This allows comparison
of the cost of the tax-shelter investment with
other alternatives such as stocks and bonds acquired with after-tax dollars. Be sure to take into
account how long it will take to get the yield
from after-tax dollars. A three-to-one return ($3
of cash received for each $1 invested) looks bet-
ter than two-to-one at first, but it's not if it takes
several years longer to realize the full profit.

The cardinal rule the Internal Revenue Service
uses in allowing tax shelters is that there must be
evidence of intent to make a profit. If a shelter is
based on deductions of interest and depreciation, with only a remote possibility of the receipt
of revenues, it stands a greater risk of being disallowed. For example, a shelter that marks up a

$10 product to $100, gets a 10% investment tax
credit to make back the $10 initial contribution,
then takes depreciation on the rest, is unlikely to
be approved.

Choose carefully the lawyer or accountant who
will evaluate the deal. An unfamiliar lawyer or
accountant who brings a deal to an investor's attention at a social gathering may simply be representing the promoters. It also can be unwise to
rely on one's own lawyer or accountant in evaluating a deal. They are prejudiced another way:
If the deal goes bust, they could lose a client, so
they have very little incentive to recommend anything so risky. Other lawyers and accountants
have their own deals. These should generally be
shunned, because the fees are often excessive.

Four basic questions for evaluating a tax-
shelter program are:

Is the program sufficiently diversified to protect the investor against loss of his investment?

What are the sharing arrangements and front-
end fees? A general partner's share of revenues
should be reasonably related to the services he
renders to the program. Fees, commissions, and
other front-end-loaded charges should be
reasonable.

Is there a discussion of the partner's previous
activities in the offering documents? If not, be
suspicious.

Does the program provide for additional assessments? Investors must be told the maximum amount of additional capital that the general partner can assess for unexpected expenses, when the assessment can be made, the tax consequences of meeting the assessment, and the penalty if the investor fails to comply.

Source: Myron Neugenboren, partner, L.F. Rothschild, Unterberg, Towbin, New York

Choosing the right tax shelter

In a stagnant economy, the most sensible investment strategy is defensive, one that holds out the possibility of a return, but in the meantime minimizes taxes on wealth already accumulated. A good tax shelter meets these criteria. But the key to using tax shelters properly is to understand their diverse attributes, then pick the vehicle most suitable for individual needs.

What tax shelters can offer:
• Deferral. In other words, an interest-free loan at the expense of the government.
• Leverage. Many shelters allow taxpayers to use borrowed money to increase their deductions.
• Conversion of gains to lower tax rates. Some shelters convert earned or unearned income (both taxed at a maximum rate of 50%) to long-term capital gains (taxed at a maximum rate of 28%).
• Credits. Some shelters offer taxpayers a credit, taken directly against tax due.
Which shelter attributes are most desirable for an investor depends on:
• Age. Investors close to retirement, and to a lower tax bracket, usually benefit from deferring their tax payments.
• Types of income. An investor generating big income may benefit by converting that income to long-term capital gains.

• Liquidity. An investor worried about stability of income should hesitate to get involved in a limited partnership. It is difficult to get out.

Two typical tax-shelter investors:
• The individual with a steady rate of income and a high degree of liquidity should invest pre-tax dollars in business ventures, such as one's own business, real estate, or oil and gas drilling deals.
• The upwardly mobile individual who, from a liquidity standpoint, is temporarily broke, should borrow to attain a $2–$4 writeoff for every $1 of cash invested up front. Such an investor should beware of a tax-advantaged investment that offers an investor no realistic possibility of a return and puts the person at no realistic risk. The IRS will challenge it.

Source: Roxeanne J. Coady and Joel G. Shapiro, Seidman & Seidman, New York.

Three tax-shelter fallacies

The most common misconceptions about tax shelters, and the facts:
The misconception: Tax shelters save taxes. The fact: Most shelters only defer the time tax is to be paid.
The misconception: Tax shelters are good investments. The fact: Most are not. And there is good reason to be wary of any deal promoted primarily for its tax features. A good shelter is a sound investment, with tax advantages as a bonus.
The misconception: The Internal Revenue Service is trying to stamp out tax shelters. The fact: The IRS is attacking deals that have no economic purpose other than the avoidance of taxes. But the government actually fosters many tax shelters, such as qualified retirement plans, municipal bonds, savings bonds, investment credits, accelerated depreciation, and capital gains.

The misconception: Tax shelters are for just about everyone now. The fact: Most tax shelters don't make sense until a taxpayer reaches the 50% tax bracket. All shelters require careful tax planning and expert advice.

Source: Edward Mendlowitz, partner, Siegel & Mendlowitz, New York.

The facts on drilling shelters

Oil and gas drilling deals have been so attractive to high-bracket taxpayers that limited partnerships were able to raise $50 million in as little as three or four weeks. Investors expected a potentially high return on investment in addition to tax write-offs. Now the government's policy of cutting taxes and eliminating the difference between earned and unearned income makes the tax deduction worth less and the income worth more. Oil and gas drilling deals will have to be chosen more on their investment merits and less on their tax-shelter advantages.

The best candidates for a public deal are investors in the 50% tax bracket, with a relatively liquid net worth of at least $100,000 (excluding home, furnishings and automobiles).

The best candidates for a privately offered deal are investors with a reportable income of at least $150,000 and a relatively liquid net worth of at least $250,000 (excluding home, furnishings and automobiles).

The investor would be well advised to restrict his interest to programs where the general partners have a good drilling record (the minimum acceptable results are a two-to-one gross return on gross investment), use a broker with knowledge in oil and gas tax shelters, and diversify a minimum investment of $20,000 over two or three programs.

Source: Laurence B. Rossbach Jr., vice-president, Drexel Burnham Lambert, Inc., New York.

Testing an oil and gas shelter

• Check the general partner's participation. Unless he has put money up that he can lose, the risk is 100% yours.

• No less than 87% of the funds raised should be going into actual drilling operations. Below that level, the odds lengthen against breaking even.

• At least one-third of the drilling prospects must be generated by the partnership. One half is even better. Otherwise, you're paying 100% of expenses for a 60%–75% share of potential revenues. The minimum worth the risk is 80%–90% of the gross.

Don't plan on keeping your money in an oil and gas shelter for less than three years. Most partnerships have one good year, one bad year, and one that's mediocre. Once those three have averaged out and are past, the chances for real success shoot up.

Avoiding a tax peril in subsidized housing shelters

In recent years, tax shelters in subsidized housing (Section 236) have looked like the sweetest deals around. Now, however, rental incomes in subsidized housing lag behind most operating costs. Many projects are unable to meet their financial obligations and, in some cases, have become cash drains to their investors.

To maximize write-offs, most subsidized housing shelters use accelerated depreciation and accrual accounting, which allows investors to deduct payments even if those payments are in arrears. Therefore, if an investor must bail out of a shelter prematurely, or if state housing authorities foreclose on a troubled project, the investor's tax liability may jump.

The solution for many investors faced by this problem is to find new investors willing to join the old ones. The new partners pump more money into the project to restore it to firm financial and physical footing. In return, they get the tax advantages.

Specifically, the new investors form a new limited partnership. The new limited partnership becomes a single limited partner in the old limited partnership, as the old limited partners sell the new limited partner a percent of their equity. Reconstituting the old limited partnership this way is generally not considered a taxable event.

Source: Michael J. Butler, president, New York State Mortgage Loan Enforcement and Administration Corp., New York.

Tax-shelter registration

Most tax shelters must obtain a tax-shelter registration number. Investors must include that number on their returns. This is a red flag for IRS audit.

How to analyze a real estate tax shelter

Basic components to check in a real estate tax shelter:
- Economic value. Determine what is happening in the marketplace in terms of costs, occupancy levels and general economic trends.
- Syndicator and general partner. The most basic safeguard is the reliability of the syndicator and general partner. They must produce evidence of good track records and enough capital to carry a project through low-cash periods. The company that manages the property should also pass the same reliability test and preferably be located near the property.
- Financial projections. Follow the numbers of costs (utilities, debt service, labor, etc.) and income (rentals) through to the anticipated cash flow that each investor will receive.
- Tax implications. A shelter that is attractive to one investor might not be at all good for another.

Source: Paul D. Lapides, president, Prime-PM, Atlanta, Ga.

Being sensible about movie tax shelters

A tax shelter in a glamorous movie is often irresistible to executives in more mundane businesses. But snares are plentiful.

There are two kinds of deals. In the first kind, a limited partnership buys a finished film and finds a distributor. The distributor is responsible for making prints and arranging play dates and promotion. The return to investors is 20%-30% of ticket sales. In the second kind of deal, under the management of the general partner (and promoter), the limited partners put up the cash and collateral to finance production of a film and may even distribute it.

Buying a finished film from a major studio or established independent producer is safer. But deductions are limited to promotion expenses and accelerated depreciation write-offs. Producing a film from scratch is extremely risky. But investors can write off production as well as promotion costs. They also can claim an investment tax credit of 7%-10% and retain a bigger percentage of profits if the film succeeds.

The prime candidates for these shelters are big-dollar investors able to pay up if creditors call their six-figure recourse notes. For example, Orion Pictures sold Peter Sellers' last film, *The Fiendish Plot of Dr. Fu Manchu,* to 25 investors for $13.8 million in cash and notes. The movie bombed, so the investors probably did not get much more out of the deal than tax write-offs.

Many promoters claim that risks can be minimized by preselling film rights to a variety of new markets (videocassettes, pay television, foreign distributors, etc.). While these rights are becoming more valuable, many presale schemes fall apart.

Movies without a name producer, director, or cast have long odds against them. So do films handled by distribution companies that lack proven track records or that try to scrape by on low advertising and promotion budgets.

Movie deals are particularly speculative because investors put all their eggs in one basket. To meet this objection, promoters are now putting together packages so that investors buy pieces of several films.

Source: Michael Cook, Michael Cook, Inc., New York.

The IRS's prime tax-shelter targets

• Cattle breeding. Inflating cattle's purchase price has been standard practice in cattle-breeding shelters. But inflated prices are now a red flag to the Internal Revenue Service. If it cracks down on a promoter, investors will get deductions based only on IRS-approved fair market value.

• Oil drilling. Intangible exploration and pro-duction costs in an oil or gas venture usually run about 60% of total drilling expenses. Since they are immediately deductible, these costs are generally assigned to the limited partners. Some promoters include too many intangible costs with the aim of inflating the first year's write-off. Since the IRS will allow the deductions only for actual costs, an expert should be used to check out the deal and the cost.

• Real estate. To increase tax losses in a real estate shelter, the promoter often attributes part of the purchase price to compensation for his signed promise not to start up a competing business. The investor is then told he can deduct that cost. But if the promoter could not actually compete anyway, the IRS can invalidate the write-off, and investors will have to pay taxes plus interest on any such deductions they've taken.

Source: Robert Stanger, publisher, *The Stanger Report*, Rumson, N.J.

REAL ESTATE

Finding a good real estate deal

• Avoid areas that are too distant. Ideally, the owner should be able to visit the property in a one-day trip. Proximity allows the owner to go to the property often and keep in touch with the local economic climate.

• Find a good partner. Ask to be invited to a meeting of the local property managers' association, which is usually held once a month. Promising general partners for real estate deals are likely to be there. Take your time in choosing a general partner. First and most important is a good track record. Ask for details. Look for assurance that the general partner will not pay more than a 1.5% sales commission.

The two biggest mistakes in real estate investment are paying too much for a property, regardless of its appeal, and letting the property be mismanaged. Structure the partnership deal so the general partner has plenty of incentive to work for you. Most get a high lump sum at the front end and only about 15% of the profits. Get the general partner to invest 1% in the project, and give him about 25% of the profits. That way, he is likely to work harder to generate profits. Pay the general partner a bonus if he meets all targets within the first 12 months.

The time to sell is after the occupancy rate has been boosted to 100%, or the equivalent; when rents have been raised from under the going market rate to well over it; and when the building has a positive cash flow.

Source: Robert J. Underwood, president, Underwood Financial Planning, Birmingham, Ala.

Troubled real estate can be a bargain

Distressed real estate is creating some attractive deals, because the owners or backers need cash in a hurry.

To locate distressed real estate properties (developers who are overextended, properties with tax troubles or foreclosed mortgages, houses or businesses in rundown areas):

• Check the legal notices in the newspapers for foreclosures, bankruptcies, and tax delinquencies.

• Peruse the records at the municipal clerk's office. The records, which are open to the public to examine, list those properties with legal action pending.

• Watch the real estate section of the newspaper for co-op house-for-sale ads that show up again week after week. If the property isn't moving, the sellers will probably listen to an offer that they may have not even considered previously.

• Be alert for houses placed on the market for quick sale, for example, contractors having trouble with unsold houses; recently divorced couples who are desperate to get rid of the house. Contact real estate agents, lawyers and accountants. They usually have clients who are eager to sell property as quickly as possible.

How sellers of commercial buildings trick buyers

The urge to invest in real estate, which is still strong in most parts of the country, exposes buyers to sharp practices by sellers.

The most common distortion is a claim of high-paying tenants. If the rent roll of a commercial building shows that nine tenants pay $6–$8 per square foot and three pay $12, find out who the high-paying tenants are. One may be the building owner, and the others may be affiliated with the seller.

Any fudging of current and future income can cost an investor tens of thousands of dollars. In a small building, where the seller reports that 10 tenants pay $400 a month ($48,000 a year), if buildings in the area sell for six times gross, the market price would be $288,000. But suppose the owner had prepared to sell the building by raising the rents from $350 to $400 a month. That increase in the rent roll cost the buyer $36,000 (the difference between six times $48,000 in annual rents and six times $42,000).

Even worse would be the impact on future rent increases. If the rents in the building were close to market before the increase, the owner may well have offered tenants a free month's rent or a delayed increase. A delayed increase means that the buyer will not realize as much income as forecast. A free month's rent means that the actual increase in rents was only $17 an apartment, not $50. If the new owner tries to jump rents well above that, tenants may move.

Other seller claims that buyers must investigate:

• Low operating expenses. Sellers may be operating the building themselves to avoid a management fee. If buyers cannot take care of the building personally, this fee must be added to real operating expenses. And if sellers do not factor it in, the bank will when it calculates the maximum supportable mortgage.

• Reasonable property tax. If the building has not been assessed for several years, the buyer may have a substantial tax bite on the next reassessment. Also the seller may have made an addition to the building that has not yet been recorded with the tax assessor. As a precaution, ask the local assessment office for a tax card or listing sheet. It will show the building's assessment and when it was assessed. If it was assessed a year and a half ago and there has been no significant addition to the building, reassessment may not hurt the buyer. But if it has not been assessed for eight years, there could be a significant tax boost.

While checking the tax card or listing sheet, check the owner's property description against the one listed. If the owner says that 20,000 square feet are being sold, but the tax card says 15,000 square feet, there has been some addition to the structure that has not been recorded, and therefore, has not been assessed. Or, there may be an assessment error that, when corrected, will raise costs.

• Low insurance premiums. Is coverage in line with the structure's current value? What does the policy cover? Ask to see the policy. Ask an insurance adviser if coverage is insufficient, how much more will proper coverage cost.

• Energy efficient. Verify the owner's claim with the local utility to determine actual energy costs. Also check with regulatory commissions to see whether utility companies are scheduled to increase their tariffs.

• A real buy. Check the income statement with those of comparable buildings in the area. Consult the annual income and expense analysis by geographical area and building type of the Institute of Real Estate Management (430 N. Michigan Ave., Chicago 60611).

Source: Thomas L. O'Dea, O'Dea & Co., Inc., Winston-Salem, N.C.

When renovation pays off

Rehabilitating and then renting older buildings in areas undergoing a renaissance can lead to quick profits. As a rule of thumb, buy on a block where a third or more of the buildings show some signs of recent renovation or improvement. Don't make the mistake of assuming that one or two efforts, even major ones, indicate a trend.

Signs that an old neighborhood has comeback potential are:

• A low crime rate and a declining ratio of low-income families.

• Below-market rents because of poor property maintenance. Avoid areas where rents are cheap because tenants don't want to live there.

• Nearby parks, lakes, rivers, colleges, shopping, or other amenities.

• More owner-occupants than absentee landlords.

• Neighborhood organizations that actively promote community interests and activities.

• Government concern for clean streets, regular trash collection, and visible police protection.

• A willingness by banks to lend money for purchase and rehabilitation of buildings.

Source: Jerry Davis, Rehabbing for Profit, McGraw-Hill, New York.

Investing in raw land

Buying undeveloped land is risky, since it can drop in value or at best lag well behind the inflation rate. Nor is there any tax advantage, because land can't be depreciated, and there's usually no income. However, a parcel of land that is in the path of urban growth can increase enormously in value. Moreover, buying raw land is uncomplicated, and the investment requires no upkeep.

To find the best sites, determine from local planning and zoning records where roads will be built, and where housing or commercial development are spreading. Avoid physical barriers to growth, such as mountains or a lake, or a large parcel of land held by a single owner. (Owners of large holdings may disguise them by deeding them in small parcels to paper, shell, or dummy owners.) Look for acreage that has a special feature, such as a great view, or is strategically located. Avoid one of many identical tracts, whose availability keeps prices low.

Also desirable is land that can be subdivided (check the zoning code), or a tract that can be leased for some interim use to generate income, such as a trailer park, campsite, tree farm, or parking lot.

Before buying, have a civil engineer check the site for usability. Look out for: land that drains poorly, or is the natural drainage repository for adjacent areas. Also be on the alert for a flooding history, even if only once every century, or acreage that has been used as a dump, even if years ago.

Although there is usually no maintenance cost on a raw-land investment, be prepared for an increase in the tax assessment.

How to raise rents successfully

• Time rent increases to coincide with improvements to the building.

• Explain the need for the increase to tenants. Use pie charts and other visuals. It's not necessary to discuss taxes or other advantages of real estate investment.

• Keep rents up to current market levels by closely monitoring what competitors are receiving. When tenant turnover is almost negligible even though the market is tight, and tenants rarely complain about an increase, the rent hikes may be consistently too low.

• Pay close attention to tenant reactions, especially any that are unexpected. They can be used as guidelines to plan and carry out the next increase more effectively.

To put through a higher-than-average increase, consider granting tenants a one-month rent holiday for the first month of the new lease. This softens the blow for the first year, but puts a more profitable rent structure in place for subsequent leases and accustoms tenants to paying the higher rate.

Source: William S. Finlayson, vice-president, Bleznak Organization, Pennsauken, N.J. *Real Estate Investing Letter,* New York.

Slash taxes on wooded vacation sites

Those wooded acres bought for quiet week-ends or rural retirement some day in the future can be a real tax burden now.

One way to cut down on property taxes is to turn land into tree farms (must be five acres or more). Typically, property assessed at $1,000 per acre has been cut as low as $30. And the trees can be sold as a cash crop.

First contact a licensed forester. He'll prepare a forest management report. It should include a complete tree census by species, size, value, and volume in board-feet. Such a survey will cost approximately $500 for a tract of about 60 acres.

Then send a copy of the report to local tax assessor, informing him of the proposed tax change.

Have forester arrange for a tree sale. He'll solicit bids from professional loggers and arrange sale. The forester typically gets 20% of the proceeds of a timber sale. The forest owner gets the rest. And selling valuable hardwoods (especially walnut, chestnut, and black cherry) can add real cash value.

Have the forester arrange for improvement of remaining tree stand. Cost averages $40 per acre. Up to 50% of this is recoverable from state and federal agricultural departments.

Have the forester set up replanting schedule for seedlings. There's a 50% rebate here, too. After two years of demonstrated management as a tree farm, the property will qualify for the lower assessment. Be prepared to show tax assessor that property has generated agricultural income of at least $500 per year. First sale of timber can be prorated to cover this. (If first sale brings $3,000, it is equivalent to six years of proven farm income.)

For extra income, sell wood-cutting permits to the growing number of wood-stove owners for $25 a season. They'll clean up what the professional loggers leave as worthless.

INDEX